THE
FOOD LOVER'S
GUIDE TO WINE

ALSO BY THE AUTHORS

The Flavor Bible

What to Drink with What You Eat

Becoming a Chef

The New American Chef

Chef's Night Out

Dining Out

Culinary Artistry

THE
FOOD LOVER'S
GUIDE TO WINE

KAREN PAGE WITH ANDREW DORNENBURG

PHOTOGRAPHS BY TOM KIRKMAN

LITTLE, BROWN AND COMPANY
NEW YORK | BOSTON | LONDON

Little, Brown and Company
Hachette Book Group
237 Park Avenue, New York, NY 10017
www.hachettebookgroup.com

First Edition: November 2011

Little, Brown and Company is a division of Hachette Book Group, Inc. The Little, Brown name and logo are trademarks of Hachette Book Group, Inc.

Illustration of Charles Krug residence, vineyard, and cellars (page 6, top) courtesy of Charles Krug Winery; Columbian Exposition photograph (page 7, top) by Frances Benjamin Johnston; Sonoma, California, vineyard photograph (page 7, bottom) by Russell Lee.

The publisher is not responsible for websites (or their content) that are not owned by the publisher.

Library of Congress Cataloging-in-Publication Data
Page, Karen.
    The food lover's guide to wine / Karen Page and Andrew Dornenburg ; photographs by Tom Kirkman.
        p.   cm.
    Includes index.
    ISBN 978-0-316-04513-1
1. Wine and wine making.   I. Dornenburg, Andrew.   II. Title.
    TP548.P25   2011
    641.5—dc23   2011020097

10   9   8   7   6   5   4   3   2   1

RRD-OH

Book design: Jean Wilcox, Wilcox Design

Printed in the United States of America

To Madeleine Kamman,

who nurtured Andrew's (and, fortuitously, Karen's) love of wine and food

at her School for American Chefs at Beringer Vineyards in Napa Valley

To the late Joe Heitz,

who never knew that inviting Karen to lunch at his home and serving her Heitz

Martha's Vineyard and Angelica (to accompany Alice's wonderful food) would

change her life forever

To the late Robert Mondavi,

who graciously supported our books from the very first

And to all the writers—past, present, and future—

whose words illuminate the elusive subject of wine for so many, including us

Chapter 5

WINE: THE PERFECT COMPLEMENT FOR EVERY COURSE

236

Chapter 6

ELEVATING THE EXPERIENCE: ESSENTIALS OF SERVING AND ENJOYING WINE

272

Chapter 7

CONTINUING YOUR WINE EXPLORATION: WHAT'S NEXT?

294

APPENDICES 318

GLOSSARY 321

ABOUT THE EXPERTS 325

ABOUT THE AUTHORS 332

ABOUT THE PHOTOGRAPHER 334

ACKNOWLEDGMENTS 334

PREFACE

I have a hard time having a meal without a glass of wine or having a glass of wine without food. When I have one or the other alone, I feel like something is missing.
—JEFF BAREILLES, MANRESA

*There is now abundant scientific evidence for the health benefits of alcohol to go with a few centuries of traditional belief and anecdotal evidence. . . . **The fact is that people who drink moderately and regularly live longer and suffer considerably less heart disease than teetotalers.** . . . Most experts recommend no more than two drinks a day for men, one for women.*
—MICHAEL POLLAN, *IN DEFENSE OF FOOD* (2008)

Drink wine. With food. Not too much.

If we have a single message for readers of this book, it can be summed up in these seven words, inspired by Michael Pollan, the author of the bestselling book *In Defense of Food*. It seems fitting, given our appreciation of his urging readers to "have a glass of wine with dinner" in the chapter "Not Too Much: How to Eat."

Those who seek to embrace products that are good for the environment can champion wine, because wine grape growers have been leaders in the movements toward sustainable, organic, and biodynamic agriculture. The past three decades have marked a revolution in winemaking, which has reached new heights of quality, with wines tasting cleaner and fresher than ever. There has also been expansion in the breadth of styles of wine being made all around the globe—from white to red, still to sparkling, dry to sweet.

With wine's acknowledged health benefits and the increasing availability of better wines at lower prices, it's a wonder that wine is not yet our national beverage. It's true that as of 2009, Americans drank more wine than the French, and in 2010 the United States became the world's largest wine-consuming country for the first time in history, a significant watershed moment in food and wine culture.

However, according to a recent study, the average American's choice of beverage to accompany dinner is not yet wine (as it is in France, Italy, and other parts of the world) but rather beverages that some studies claim are unhealthful: soft drinks like Coke and Pepsi.

What stands in the way of Americans' incorporating into our lives a more healthful beverage that enhances our appreciation of food? Too often, sadly, people feel intimidated by wine.

A bottle of wine is basically nothing more than two and a half pounds of grapes that have been pressed and fermented. It is 80 to 85 percent water, in fact, along with some alcohol (typically 8 to 16 percent); the rest (about 4 percent) consists of "natural compounds," such as acids, sugars, minerals, vitamins, coloring substances, aromatic substances, and sulfites (preservatives). A five-ounce glass of wine contains just 125 calories.

CALORIE COUNTS OF COMMON BEVERAGES

BEVERAGE (TYPICAL SERVING)	CALORIES	INGREDIENTS
Milk (8-ounce glass)	160	Milk
Beer (12-ounce bottle)	150	Water, grain, malt, yeast
Coke (12-ounce can)	140	Carbonated water, high-fructose corn syrup, caramel color, phosphoric acid, flavoring, caffeine
Orange juice (8-ounce glass)	125	Squeezed oranges
Wine (5-ounce glass)	125	Fermented grapes

In countries such as France and Italy, which have a centuries-old wine culture, wine is simply a way of life. We look forward to seeing that happen in this country. But we have a long way to go in encouraging Americans to trade their Cokes for "starter wines" and then move to "better" wines. There's a lot of confusion. Where to start? And what to try next?

The majority of Americans speak no language other than English. Yet many of the top California wines are priced beyond the reach of many people, so to find deals on wines, we sometimes have to look at labels that contain foreign terminology, which can be intimidating.

This book is aimed at helping food lovers along their journey of discovering wines and expanding their enjoyment of them. Many people look for value wines to drink during the week, and some people who see wine as an affordable luxury will stretch to buy a more expensive bottle for the weekend or for special occasions. In restaurants, many order wines by the half-bottle or by the glass, which reflects an increasing interest in careful food-and-wine pairings. Also, now that more people are enjoying wine at home, they need good advice on what to buy.

The polyphenols in red wine (resveratrol in particular) appear to have unique protective qualities.... The health benefits of alcohol may depend as much on the pattern of drinking as on the amount: **Drinking a little every day is better than drinking a lot on the weekends, and drinking with food is better than drinking without it.** (Food blunts some of the deleterious effects of alcohol by slowing its absorption.)

—MICHAEL POLLAN, *IN DEFENSE OF FOOD* (2008)

WHY US?

Why do we think we're up to taking on the mammoth task of helping food lovers explore and master wine? It's primarily because we're not your typical wine writers: We love food first and wine second. In fact, **what we love most about wine is its ability to make food taste even better.**

While we've long enjoyed drinking wine and have been curious to learn more about it, we were initially put off by the encyclopedic wine tomes that dominate the bookstore shelves. Many of those books ask you to learn a lot of wine terminology as well as technical details of the winemaking process. But we didn't want to *make* wine—we simply wanted to *drink* it! (We should mention that after learning about wines' flavors and becoming curious about how those flavors come to be in the glass, many wine drinkers are eager to learn about winemaking.) We longed for a wine book that would provide information on a "need to know" basis.

We wrote our first book on this topic, *What to Drink with What You Eat*, because that was what *we* wanted to know. The book's critical and popular acceptance led us to believe that others shared our wish to see the topic of wine broken down simply yet intelligently.

This book aims to pick up where *What to Drink* left off, providing readers with more insight into wine from a food lover's perspective, even if they're not yet interested in tackling the intricacies of the 1855 Bordeaux classification or the curse of phylloxera. We hope to share just enough information about wine to help you select a bottle to enjoy over dinner at home and to negotiate the wine list and have a more productive discussion with the sommelier the next time you dine out.

With every step along your wine journey, you'll naturally become interested in other aspects of wine, such as how it's made and how winemakers achieve various effects through the winemaking process. In Chapter 7 we list a number of books that can enlighten you on these topics.

We close here with a little secret. No one—not the two of us or any of the dozens of distinguished sommeliers we've interviewed, not even the World's Best Sommelier, Aldo Sohm—has mastered everything there is to know about wine. There are more than six thousand different wines available for sale in the United States, and because we can't claim to have tasted all of them, we honestly can't tell you which are the best. However, we've tasted quite a few and have interviewed dozens of America's best sommeliers (including Master Sommeliers,* holders of the field's most prestigious accreditation), who have themselves tasted quite a few, so we think that collectively we should be able to point you in the right direction.

Cheers to you as you continue on your wine journey!

KAREN PAGE AND ANDREW DORNENBURG

Spring 2011

*Note: Master Sommeliers are identified by the initials MS after their names, while Masters of Wine are identified by MW.

INTRODUCTION ALDO SOHM

*Wine is all about enjoyment. And few sommeliers capture this notion better than **Aldo Sohm of the four-star restaurant Le Bernardin in New York City**, who was named the World's Best Sommelier in 2008. We talked with Sohm about his passion for wine and for helping others share that passion.*

On my recent trip to Alto Adige [in northern Italy], I had one day off and went hiking with my best friend, Norbert Waldnig, who was the Austrian candidate for World's Best Sommelier. Norbert told me, "When people ask me what I do, I don't say, 'I'm a sommelier.' Instead, I tell them, 'I'm an enjoyment manager.' After all, what we do is give people enjoyment and make them feel comfortable." That is how I see it as well.

There are many good wines out there, and a bottle of wine is ever-changing, just like a human being. In its youth, it might not use its power and force wisely. In old age, it is getting cranky: its yeast is dying, and it is passing away. You have to get wines at the right spot in their life cycle.

At a recent tasting, someone said to me, "You have a great job—you can drink all the wines you like!" I replied that I had to respectfully disagree, that I actually buy a lot of wines I don't really like personally. For example, I love mineral-driven wines. I love wines with acidity. I love wines at all points along the spectrum, from modest to extravagant. The wines I like to drink aren't necessarily big, high in alcohol, or super-expensive.

What I *don't* like is overoaked Chardonnay. I don't like the creaminess or the high alcohol—and I find there is so much "makeup" applied that you can't recognize the "woman" anymore! But I buy a lot of these wines, because I sell a lot of them. I will taste oaked Chardonnay to make sure it is properly made and typical for the style—and if it is good, I buy it.

Does it mean that my guests are right and I am wrong? No. After all, not everyone loves spinach, either. What you have to do as a sommelier is flip a switch in your head: when you taste, you have to disregard your personal preference, which is the most difficult thing to do. If I bought only wines that I liked, I would have a very one-dimensional wine list.

ALDO SOHM

Wine does not have to be expensive. We need to get rid of the picture of a sommelier sitting at home drinking Romanée-Conti and Pétrus! That would be lovely, but it is not reality. Actually, it would not be lovely, because your brain can't digest it. Your palate would get used to it, and your palate would get very one-dimensional.

I have the opportunity to taste $1,000 bottles of wine on my job. At home, I most often drink wines that cost less than $15. Lately I have been drinking Muscadet from Pépière and Yellow Muscat. Nothing is more undervalued than German Riesling. Nothing—it is a joke! In Burgundy a wine of the same quality would cost twice as much. Tesch Riesling is totally dry, and I am a big fan of his wines, which are inexpensive.

As you taste more wines along your journey, remember this: you learn the most from the things you *don't* like. It is easy to talk about what you like—and much harder to discuss the things you don't like and how you would make them better. Keep an open mind. It is important to take the opportunity to see if you might have overlooked something.

WINE IS FOOD: WHEN THE TWO BECOME ONE

Although consumed as a beverage, wine is also like a sauce that accents and enhances flavor in food.

—PAUL BERTOLLI AND ALICE WATERS, *CHEZ PANISSE COOKING* (1988)

Wine and food have been so inextricably linked throughout human history that we have to scratch our heads and wonder: How on earth did wine and food become separated in the United States? How did the majority of Americans learn to have soft drinks with their evening meals? And where did the seemingly all-American notion of wine as a mere aperitif or party quaffer come from?

The 1961 classic *Mastering the Art of French Cooking*, by the American-born Julia Child, which was informed by her years in France, judged wine sufficiently important to devote a six-page section at the beginning of the book to the topic. And at the end of each main-course recipe Child recommended specific wines to accompany the dish. She celebrated the art of wine-and-food pairing: "Great combinations of wine and food are unforgettable: kidneys and one of the great red Burgundies, where each rings reminiscent changes on the characteristics of the other; sole in one of the rich white wine sauces and a fine white Burgundy; *soufflé à la liqueur* and a Château d'Yquem. And then there are the more simple pleasures of a stout red wine and a strong cheese, white wine and oysters, red wine and a beef stew, chilled *rosé* and a platter of cold meats."

French-born Madeleine Kamman's 1971 classic, *The Making of a Cook,* proclaimed wine as one of the four "Good Ingredients for Good Dishes" (along with butter, cream, and seasonings). As Kamman noted, presciently, "There is a false belief among new 'connoisseurs' that American wines are not as good as European ones. . . . Of course wines are produced in other countries besides France. Italy, Spain and Portugal, Germany, Austria and Hungary, Switzerland, Greece, South Africa, Chile—all these countries produce wine, and some of it is splendid."

The 1976 "Judgment of Paris," the famous blind wine tasting in which French critics judged California wines to be better than some of France's most renowned offerings, bore out Kamman's statement that the wines of California were every bit as good as those of France—and indeed, that good wines were being made around the globe. The decades since have reinforced that truth.

As interest in wine soared, more books introducing the curious to this mysterious beverage began to appear in American bookstores. However, with the cookbook boom of the 1980s came an explosion of chef-driven cookbooks that often made no mention of wine, with the notable exceptions of works by Chez Panisse's Alice Waters and some others. In fact, many of the bestselling cookbooks since the 1990s do not address wine to any great extent, even as an ingredient:

- The 1,136-page 1997 edition of *Joy of Cooking* features a single paragraph of tips on pairing wine with cheese and two paragraphs on rice wine and sake.
- In its 944 pages, Mark Bittman's 1998 *How to Cook Everything* makes no mention of wine except in six recipes that call for it as an ingredient.
- The 1,040-page *Gourmet Cookbook*, published in 2004, makes no mention of wine except in four recipes that call for it as an ingredient.
- The index to *Martha Stewart's Cooking School,* a 500-page book published in 2008, lists only two recipes that call for wine.

In some ways, the lack of attention to wine by food journalists is a natural extension of the increasing specialization of the fields of cuisine and wine. Wine writers wrote about wine while food writers stuck to food—and rarely were the two topics written about together.

As journalists "chose sides," so did readers. Wine enthusiasts bought books about wine and became wine-centric, choosing restaurants based on their wine lists and selecting their wine before their menu instead of vice versa. And cooking enthusiasts, including many typical Americans, continued to learn about food, while viewing wine as a mysterious subject for specialists instead of a natural companion to food worth equal investigation.

As noted in the Preface, we are unusual because we specialize in writing about both food and wine. But more writers are needed to help to bridge the two topics and eliminate the chasm between them.

When we are introduced in social situations as wine writers, the most common response we receive is an apology—because too many people invariably feel embarrassed that they don't know more about wine. However, we've never had anyone apologize to us after we've been introduced as *food* writers. Wine is a ridiculously vast subject, and no one should feel bad for not knowing "enough" about it.

We want food lovers to extend their passion for flavor to include wine, and we want to help them enjoy wine more by developing a greater understanding of the subject. And unlike certain esoteric wine writers, we don't believe a Ph.D. in oenology (the study of wine) should be required to understand it.

Luckily for us, wine and food have been coming back into the headlines of articles about the "First Table." Every American president and first lady have helped set the national tone for American culture, and that includes gastronomy. The Kennedys celebrated French cuisine and wines as the epitome of glamour, and the Clintons shone a spotlight on the best American ingredients and cuisine. After eight years of a teetotaling president, it's been exciting for the food-loving media to report on a first lady who plants a White House vegetable garden and a president who takes her on a date to a farm-to-table restaurant where wines can be paired to every course.

"I think that President Obama's choice to dine at Blue Hill [in Manhattan]—a restaurant known for its sustainable and local cuisine—was both edgy and such a statement," said Claire Paparazzo, the sommelier of that restaurant, who served the first couple. "I can't help but laugh when people ask what we served them, as if they expect me to reply 'diamond-crusted sea bass' or something ridiculous. What we served them was Blue Hill food—natural produce! And I'm impressed that they were open to different beverages."

While Paparazzo declined to share more about the Obamas' choices, the *New York Daily News* reported tipsters' accounts that the first lady ordered two martinis, while the president ordered the wine pairings that accompanied the tasting menu, which that night included the 2007 Hirsch Vineyard & Blue Hill Special Cuvée, a light Burgundy-style Pinot Noir served exclusively at the restaurant.

TIMELINE: SOME NOTABLE EVENTS IN AMERICAN WINE HISTORY

Wine is about many things, including history. I had a moment when I realized the French have been making wine for two thousand years while California has only been making it for two hundred.

—JEFF BAREILLES, MANRESA

It's not unusual for connoisseurs to look back with regret at having missed the golden age of their particular interest—the Elizabethan age for poetry, perhaps the seventeenth century for Dutch painting, or the heyday of Bach or Mozart. For oenophiles, *this* is the golden age, and there is every reason to predict that the next millennium will enable this specialized world to shine even more brightly.

—WINE WRITER ALEXIS BESPALOFF (1934–2006)

If Americans—collectively and individually—have any future with wine, it is a function of our past. It's important to appreciate this country's relatively brief wine history, especially compared with that of countries that measure their years of winemaking and wine enjoyment in *thousands* instead of *hundreds*. Yet understanding wine's importance in the founding of the United States helps set the stage for our mission to ensure that it's a celebrated part of our future.

Today wine is America's leading finished agricultural product (as measured by retail value). California, the top wine-producing state, makes 90 percent of all American-made wine and three out of every five bottles purchased in this country. Two out of every three bottles of wine produced in the United States is from California, Oregon, Washington, or New York.

As the United States takes its place as the number-one wine-consuming country in the world, we are taking a historic step in our evolution—so let's stop and see where we are and how we got here.

> Wine makes daily living easier, less hurried, with fewer tensions and more tolerance.
> —BENJAMIN FRANKLIN (1706–1790)

> I dined a large company once or twice a week. [**Thomas**] Jefferson dined a dozen every day.
> —JOHN ADAMS, U.S. PRESIDENT, 1797–1801

> My manner of living is plain—a glass of wine and a bit of mutton are always ready.
> —GEORGE WASHINGTON, U.S. PRESIDENT, 1789–1797

DATE	EVENT
1607	**The first settlers arrive** in Jamestown, Virginia, with a primary aim of establishing a wine industry in the New World so that England would not have to buy its wine from France and Spain.
1619	All male heads of households are commanded by law to plant grapevines. The settlers' efforts produce the first wine made from indigenous grapes.
1622	Every Jamestown household is given a grape-growing and winemaking manual, at the king's command.
1624	Virginia passes an act requiring every household to plant twenty vines for every male in the household over the age of twenty.
1743	**Benjamin Franklin** includes instructions on winemaking in this year's edition of his *Poor Richard's Almanack*.
1774	**Thomas Jefferson** plants his first vineyard at Monticello in Virginia.
1776	The United States of America is founded with the signing of the Declaration of Independence on July 4. In August America's future first president, **George Washington**, orders cases of claret, Muscat, and cordials and a keg of brandy.
1779	The "Father of California Wine," **Father Junipero Serra**, a Franciscan missionary, plants **the first California vineyard** at Mission San Diego.
1780s	**Benjamin Rush**, an American doctor, suggests that wine consumed in moderation with food promotes "cheerfulness, strength and nourishment."

DATE	EVENT
1784	**Thomas Jefferson** arrives in Paris as ambassador to France. Within two weeks he purchases 276 bottles of wine, mostly Bordeaux.
1789	On May 29, **President George Washington** hosts the White House's first state dinner, at which guests are served boiled leg of mutton and a single glass of wine each.
1790	On September 6, newly installed **Secretary of State Thomas Jefferson** places a wine order for "40 dozen of Champagne, 30 doz. Of Sauterne [sic], 20 doz. of Bordeaux de Segur, and 10 doz. of [Muscat de] Frontignan" for President Washington.
1792	During the Constitutional Convention in Philadelphia, **George Washington** leads a delegation on a visit to a nearby promising vineyard.
1801–1809	**President Thomas Jefferson**'s passion for wine leads him to have large wine cellars built in the White House and to purchase more than 20,000 bottles of wine during his tenure in office.
1825	Sixty vineyards with a total of 600 acres of grapes have been planted throughout the United States. Five years later there are two hundred vineyards with a total of 5,000 acres of grapes.
1839	**George Calvert Yount** plants the first vineyards in Napa Valley, in what will become Yountville, California. The same year in Washingtonville, New York, **Brotherhood Winery** makes its first wines.
1845	**President James Polk** and **First Lady Sarah Polk** serve six different wines (including rosé Champagne, Sauternes, and ruby port) in six glasses that "formed a rainbow around each plate" at an extravagant dinner during their first year in the White House.
1851	After tasting **Nicholas Longworth**'s pink sparkling Catawba wine (produced in Ohio via the traditional method used to make Champagne) at the Great Exhibition in London, one admiring reviewer proclaimed, "Cincinnati has become the chief seat of wine manufacture in the United States." Within a few years,

A list of devotees of Madeira from late Colonial days through the Civil War reads like a directory of American history. First in place, of course, was **George Washington**, who took a pint with his dinner every day.

—ROY BRADY, *GOURMET* (DECEMBER 1965)

Good wine is a necessity of life for me.

—THOMAS JEFFERSON (1743–1826)

In 1840, the Whigs presented their candidate, William Henry Harrison, as a simple frontier Indian fighter, living in a log cabin and drinking cider, in sharp contrast to an aristocratic, Champagne-sipping Van Buren.

—WHITE HOUSE HISTORICAL ASSOCIATION

PAGES 6-7: CHARLES KRUG RESIDENCE, VINEYARD, AND CELLARS, CIRCA 1860 (PAGE 6, TOP); SAMPLING PARTY, *HARPER'S WEEKLY,* MAY 11, 1872 (PAGE 6, BOTTOM); EXPOSITION GROUNDS, WORLD'S COLUMBIAN EXPOSITION, CHICAGO, 1893 (PAGE 7, TOP); SONOMA, CALIFORNIA, VINEYARD, 1942-43 (PAGE 7, BOTTOM).

DATE	EVENT
	Longworth was producing nearly 100,000 bottles annually, supported by a national advertising campaign. He is the first American winemaker to prove the existence of a lucrative market for wine. Longworth's wine even inspires Henry Wadsworth Longfellow's 1854 poem "Ode to Catawba Wine."
1857	Hungarian immigrant **Agoston Haraszthy** builds the first commercial vineyard in California, which today is the home of **Buena Vista Winery**. During his lifetime, he introduces three hundred wine grape varieties.
1861	The California governor appoints a commission to direct the development of winemaking in the region. Haraszthy is one of the first three commissioners.
	Charles Krug establishes Napa Valley's first commercial winery.
1862	**Schramsberg Winery**, the Napa Valley sparkling wine producer, is founded.
1870s	California becomes America's top wine-producing state.
1873	At the Vienna World's Fair, a Virginia wine is named "Best Red Wine of All Nations."
1876	**Beringer Winery** is founded in Napa Valley and will become the oldest continually operating winery in the United States.
1879	**Inglenook Winery** is founded. Just ten years later it wins gold medals at the World's Fair of Paris.
1880s–1890s	California wines experience their first "golden age," winning awards and medals at several global exhibitions and fairs (including London in 1887, Paris in 1889, Chicago in 1893, San Francisco in 1894, and Bordeaux in 1895).
1880	**President Rutherford B. Hayes**, influenced by **First Lady Lucy Hayes**, an advocate of the women's temperance movement, bans wine and liquor at the White House.
1889	More than 140 wineries are operating in California.

[Nicholas] Longworth proved that good wine indeed could be made from American grapes. Moreover, he demonstrated that, if the wine was priced fairly, Americans would buy it.
—PAUL LUKACS, *AMERICAN VINTAGE: THE RISE OF AMERICAN WINE* (2005)

In 1873, at the Universal Exhibition in Vienna, a bottle of Norton from Hermann took home a gold medal, ratifying it as one of the best red wines in the world.
—TODD KLIMAN, *THE WILD VINE: A FORGOTTEN GRAPE AND THE UNTOLD STORY OF AMERICAN WINE* (2010)

DATE	EVENT
1890–1915	A rootstock louse called **phylloxera** attacks California wineries, destroying 250,000 acres of vineyards.

1893	California wines made from Barbera, Cabernet Sauvignon, Malbec, Riesling, and Sémillon are exhibited at the Columbian Exposition in Chicago.
1900	Dozens of American wines—representing California, New Jersey, New York, Ohio, and Virginia—win medals at the prestigious Paris Exposition.
1917	Congress passes **the Eighteenth Amendment,** banning the commercial production and sale of alcohol in the United States and marking the beginning of Prohibition.
1918	There are more than 2,500 commercial wineries and 713 bonded wineries in the United States.
1919	**The Volstead Act** is ratified, prohibiting the sale of alcohol in the United States as of 1920. Some loopholes allow physicians to prescribe alcohol to their patients, consumers to drink wine for religious purposes, and heads of households to produce two hundred gallons of wine a year for personal use (acknowledging a common practice among Italian Americans).
1920–1933	In California, grape production drops dramatically, nearly destroying the wine industry.
1933	Congress passes **the Twenty-first Amendment, repealing Prohibition** and assigning authority to individual states to allow or ban the production and sale of alcohol. Only about 150 American wineries still exist. As Americans regain legal access to beer and spirits, consumption of wine falls, and most of the wine consumed is fortified to more than 20 percent alcohol, which is still considered its chief appeal.
	Ernest and Julio Gallo found their eponymous winery in Modesto, California.
1934	**Frank Schoonmaker** and *New York Herald Tribune* columnist **Tom Marvel** write *The Complete Wine Book,* one of America's first general-interest books on wine.

Leon D. Adams, considered by wine aficionados and the wine industry to be the seminal wine historian in the United States in the 20th century[,] . . . was a founder [in 1934] of the Wine Institute, the trade organization that represents California's wine industry.
—HOWARD G. GOLDBERG, *NEW YORK TIMES* (SEPTEMBER 16, 1995)

DATE	EVENT
1934–1950s	The majority of table wines are consumed by immigrant families from Southern and Central Europe. Jug wines become popular.
1941	**Earle R. MacAusland** launches *Gourmet* magazine with the January issue, featuring the first of many regular articles on the subject of wine.
	André Tchelistcheff of Beaulieu Vineyards releases his 1936 Georges de Latour Private Reserve Cabernet Sauvignon, named after the man who founded Beaulieu in 1900. It becomes the country's most celebrated red wine for the next three decades.
1943	**Cesare** and **Rosa Mondavi**, Italian immigrants, purchase the Charles Krug Winery, which they run with the help of their sons **Robert** and **Peter.**
1950s	The American wine market is dominated by dessert and fortified wines such as sherry, port, and Madeira. German brands of sweet wine, including Blue Nun, sell well. By the end of the decade, America's big-five winemakers are **Beaulieu, Beringer, Charles Krug** (the largest), **Inglenook,** and **Larkmead.**
1956	*Bon Appétit* magazine is launched as a liquor-store giveaway.
Early 1960s	Wine retailer **Marvin Stirman** and **Alfio Moriconi** cofound the Washington-based **Les Amis du Vin** (The Friends of Wine), an organization for wine lovers that at its height boasts more than 30,000 members in thirty-five chapters. Les Amis' popular wine tastings and classes attract many people who go on to play leading roles in the world of wine and food, including former *Washington Post* food editor **William Rice** and long-time restaurant critic **Phyllis Richman,** not to mention independent wine critic **Robert M. Parker, Jr.**
1960s	Young, affluent, well-traveled Americans begin to develop a taste for drier table wines, and American wineries improve the quality of their offerings.

DATE	EVENT
1960s	Washington state sees its first commercial-scale plantings of wine grapes. The earliest producers spawn **Columbia Winery** and **Chateau Ste. Michelle.** Oenologist **André Tchelistcheff** helps guide Chateau Ste. Michelle's early efforts and mentors new Washington winemakers.
1961	**First Lady Jacqueline Kennedy** appoints French chef **René Verdon** the first professional White House chef, elevating the cuisine of state dinners to a new level starting in April. Bordeaux is the Kennedys' preferred wine.
	Julia Child's first book, *Mastering the Art of French Cooking,* which includes wine recommendations for many recipes, is published in October.
	Heitz Wine Cellars is founded by **Joe and Alice Heitz** in St. Helena, California. Their Martha's Vineyard Cabernet Sauvignon soon becomes one of the first "cult Cabernets."
1962	**Dr. Konstantin Frank** founds Vinifera Wine Cellars in New York's Finger Lakes region, pioneering premium wine production on the East Coast. The White House later serves one of his first wines, a Trockenbeerenauslese Riesling.
1964	**President Lyndon Johnson** is credited with establishing the tradition of serving exclusively American wines at the White House.
	Ernest Hemingway's book *A Moveable Feast,* which celebrates the author's love of wine developed through his European travels, is published, three years after his death and ten years after he won the Nobel Prize for Literature.
1965	**M. Frank Jones** buys the trademark for *Bon Appétit* and turns it into a glossy bimonthly. He writes a wine column for the magazine and persuades leading wine experts **Alexis Lichine, Frank Schoonmaker,** and **Harry Waugh** to contribute as well.
1966	**Ernest and Julio Gallo**'s California winery becomes America's largest.

In the 1960s, 60 percent of wine was Mad Dog 20/20, port, and sherry, and less than 20 percent was table wine or champagne. Jugs with screw tops were the packaging of choice.
—MICHAEL MONDAVI, SON OF CALIFORNIA WINE PIONEER ROBERT MONDAVI

In Europe, we thought of wine as something healthy and normal as food, and also a great giver of happiness and well-being and delight. Drinking wine was not snobbism nor a sign of sophistication nor a cult; it was as natural as eating and to me as necessary.
—ERNEST HEMINGWAY (1899– 1961), *A MOVEABLE FEAST*

Making good wine is a skill. Fine wine is an art.
—ROBERT MONDAVI (1913–2008)

Wine has been a part of civilized life for some seven thousand years. It is the only beverage that feeds the body, soul and spirit of man and at the same time stimulates the mind.
—ROBERT MONDAVI

DATE	EVENT
	Visionary winemaker **Robert Mondavi** celebrates the first harvest at his eponymous California winery in Oakville, California. It will become the state's most famous winery.
	David Lett and **Chuck Coury** plant the first Pinot Noir grapes in Oregon. Thirteen years later, Lett's **1975 Eyrie Reserve Pinot Noir** takes third place at the Gault-Millau Wine Olympiad in Paris, prompting a wave of interest in Oregon Pinot Noir.
1970	Adult per capita consumption of table wine stands at 1.05 gallons.
Early 1970s	President **Richard M. Nixon** is said to have his favorite French wines (such as Château Margaux) secretly poured for him at state dinners, in spite of the White House policy of serving only American wines.
1970s	The United States sees a sudden surge in wine consumption. Hundreds of new wineries open in California.
1972	On July 7, **Frank Prial** creates the "Wine Talk" column in the *New York Times*.
	The November 27 *Time* cover story entitled "American Wine: There's Gold in Them Thar Grapes" celebrates the wine boom in the United States.
1973	**Eddie Osterland** passes the Court of Master Sommeliers examination, becoming America's first Master Sommelier.
	Domaine Chandon is the first American sparkling winery established by a French Champagne house (Moët & Chandon). Its Blanc de Noirs is served at White House receptions.
1974	**Alex** and **Louisa Hargrave** open Hargrave Vineyard, the first commercial winery on Long Island, New York.
1975	Riunite, a fizzy, semi-sweet Italian wine, becomes the top imported wine in the United States. In 1977 it adopts the popular slogan "Riunite on ice, that's nice," and sales boom, peaking seven years later.

DATE	EVENT

Sutter Home Family Vineyards, which has been making a dry white Zinfandel, experiences a "stuck fermentation"—that is, the yeast dies before consuming all the sugar during fermentation of the pink grape juice. When its sweet white Zinfandel is released, sales boom.

1976 The wine merchant **Steven Spurrier** pits California wines against some of France's finest wines in a blind tasting by a Who's Who of nine French judges on May 24. In a watershed event that came to be known as **the Judgment of Paris,** California wines win, bringing their world-class quality to global attention.

Bob Morrisey founds the *Wine Spectator* as a newsprint tabloid.

The Windows on the World Wine School is founded in New York City by **Kevin Zraly.** By 2010 nearly 20,000 students will have graduated.

1977 After four years of offering the Master Sommelier exam, **the Court of Master Sommeliers** is established in London as the examining body for the Master Sommelier diploma. As of 1977 there are 35 Master Sommeliers. By 2010, there are 169 worldwide.

1978 **Ariane** and **Michael Batterberry** found *The International Review of Food and Wine,* later known as *Food & Wine* magazine. Within two years, it has a circulation of 250,000.

A full-time lawyer, **Robert M. Parker, Jr.,** debuts his wine newsletter, *The Wine Advocate,* in August. It eventually has a circulation of more than 50,000 subscribers.

1979 The *Wine Spectator* is purchased by **Marvin Shanken** and transformed into a four-color glossy magazine.

Robert Mondavi and Bordeaux's **Baron Philippe de Rothschild** agree to collaborate on a high-quality Napa Valley Cabernet Sauvignon called **Opus One,** which prompts new global investment interest in the California wine industry.

Riunite made its name . . . with Lambrusco, which was for many years the No. 1 wine import in this country.
—FRANK PRIAL, *NEW YORK TIMES* (MAY 7, 2003)

When the ballots were cast, **the top-scoring red was Stag's Leap Wine Cellars' '72 from the Napa Valley,** followed by Mouton-Rothschild '70, Haut-Brion '70 and Montrose '70. The four winning whites were, in order, **Chateau [Montelena] '73 from Napa,** French Meursault-Charmes '73 and two other Californians, Chalone '74 from Monterey County and Napa's Spring Mountain '73. The U.S. winners are little known to wine lovers, since they are in short supply even in California and rather expensive ($6 plus). Jim Barrett, [Montelena's] general manager and part owner, said: "Not bad for kids from the sticks."
—GEORGE M. TABER, "MODERN LIVING: JUDGMENT OF PARIS," *TIME* (JUNE 7, 1976)

The Court of Master Sommeliers has been the single most influential movement in transforming the place of wine in American culture—not only through the wine itself but through the people involved in educating themselves through the Court. Master Sommeliers working at any level with restaurants have done more to raise the bar in American wine culture than almost anything else. For instance, look where we were with the use of glassware in the 1970s and 1980s, when it was common to use generic one-size-fits-all, mass-produced non-crystal glassware. Now, at the very least, Spiegelau or Riedel crystal glasses are ubiquitous in fine dining. Even in steakhouses and middle-of-the-road white-tablecloth restaurants, quality stemware is the rule, not the exception.

—MICHAEL FLYNN, THE MANSION ON TURTLE CREEK

In the 1980s, my first job, at around age fourteen, was at a small family Italian restaurant in New Jersey. It was the first time I saw **Santa Margherita Pinot Grigio** and the phenomenon that it was. When someone wanted to show off, they would order the Santa Margherita. I thought it must be great. It was the most sophisticated wine choice by far at the time. During college at NYU, I worked at another restaurant, where I learned by listening to people, including wine salesmen, and how they described wine. The salesmen would talk about Tuscans and the **Ruffino Gold Label Ducale Oro**, which was the red-wine equivalent of Santa Margherita.

—ROBERT BOHR, COLICCHIO & SONS

I have been in the business for more than twenty years, and I attribute the dominance of oak in California wine to a couple of things: In the 1980s when the wine boom hit, California looked to Burgundy for a natural place to copy. In Burgundy, they use a lot of French oak. In California, they started with coconut-noted American oak, then switched back to French because it has more vanilla notes. The other thing to bear in mind is that in the 1980s, the dominant style of cooking was mesquite-grilled food. What works best with grilled food? Oaked wines!

—BERNARD SUN, JEAN GEORGES

DATE	EVENT
1980	**Glen Ellen Winery** is founded by **Mike Benziger,** helping the transition from large-scale wine production, prevalent up to this time, to smaller-scale, high-quality wineries. Benziger later becomes one of the first California vintners to embrace sustainable, organic, and biodynamic farming principles. There are 919 wineries in the United States.
1982	*Wine & Spirits* magazine is founded, and four years later **Joshua Greene** takes its helm as editor and publisher. Greene buys the magazine in 1989.
1983	Lawyer-turned-winemaker **Jess Jackson** pioneers a middle-market niche (between $2.49 jug wine and $11 boutique wines) with the $5 **Kendall-Jackson Chardonnay.**
1980s	**President Ronald Reagan** favors serving California wines at state dinners. Sales of Kendall-Jackson Chardonnay soar after **First Lady Nancy Reagan** admits her fondness for it, as reported by the columnist Herb Caen in the *San Francisco Chronicle.*
1984	The first edition of **Kevin Zraly**'s *Windows on the World Complete Wine Course* is published. It becomes an annual guide, with reported cumulative sales of more than three million copies. **Robert M. Parker, Jr.,** resigns his position as a lawyer to devote himself to *The Wine Advocate* full-time.
1985	The *Wine Spectator* implements its 100-point scoring system for wine. Spurred by an influx of capital and mass advertising, U.S. per capita adult wine consumption hits a new high of 2.43 gallons. **Iron Horse Vineyards** creates its Russian Cuvée expressly for the Reagan-Gorbachev summit meetings, which lead to the end of the Cold War.

DATE	EVENT

Head to one of the top restaurants in America, and half the bottles on the tables are Chardonnay. It's the trophy wine of the times: the fourth quarter of **1989.** Few guests are talking with sommeliers. French wines from Bordeaux and Burgundy are the imports of choice.
—JOSHUA GREENE, EDITOR AND PUBLISHER, *WINE & SPIRITS* (APRIL 2009)

The **1990s** were the most transforming ten-year span in the history of fine wine. Everything essential to fine wine—winegrower ambition, a passionate and informed audience, and abundant money—coalesced.
—MATT KRAMER, *MAKING SENSE OF WINE* (2003)

From **1991** to **2005**, sales of red wine in the United States grew by more than 125 percent.
—KEVIN ZRALY, *WINDOWS ON THE WORLD COMPLETE WINE COURSE* (2008)

1986 — **Jack and Dolores Cakebread** of **Cakebread Cellars** in Napa Valley launch the American Harvest Workshop, which brings together leading chefs, artisan food producers, journalists, and other professionals to explore the relationship between wine and food. The annual Workshop celebrates its twenty-fifth anniversary in 2011.

1988 — *Wine Enthusiast* magazine is founded by the husband-and-wife team of **Adam and Sybil Strum** as an outgrowth of their wine accessories catalog.

1989 — **David Rosengarten** and **Joshua Wesson**'s classic book on wine-and-food pairing, *Red Wine with Fish*, is published.

1991 — In **"The French Paradox,"** in November, the popular television program *60 Minutes* examines the paradox that even though the French diet includes a great deal of fat and wine, France's residents have much lower rates of heart disease than those of other countries. In extolling the health benefits of moderate consumption of wine, the program generates new interest in wine among older Americans.

1992 — The chapters of the 1992 edition of Kevin Zraly's *Windows on the World Complete Wine Course* cover the wines of France, California, New York, Germany, Italy, Spain, and Australia, followed by a section on Champagne, sherry, and port. There is no mention of the wines of New Zealand, South Africa, South America, Oregon, or Washington state, among other regions that merit inclusion in later editions.

1993 — **President William Jefferson Clinton** speaks out for wine during American Wine Appreciation Week (February 21–27). He is quoted in *Washington Monthly* as saying, "[I have] reached the age that when all this health data comes out, I want to take another glass of wine," and on MTV as saying, "At least if you use it in moderation, there's no evidence that it causes harm . . . And there's some evidence that wine, for example, is good for your heart if you use it in moderation."

1994 — **First Lady Hillary Rodham Clinton** appoints American-born **chef Walter Scheib** to usher in a new era of American cooking at the White House to accompany the emphasis on American wines.

DATE	EVENT
1995	There are 1,187 wineries in the United States.

The first edition of *Wine for Dummies,* by **Mary Ewing-Mulligan** (who became the first American woman Master of Wine in 1993) and **Ed McCarthy,** is published. Including subsequent editions, it reportedly sells more than a million copies.

The U.S. Departments of Health and Human Services and Agriculture revise their joint **Dietary Guidelines for Americans** to include the recommendation that "drinking in moderation may lower risk for coronary heart disease, mainly among men over age 45 and women over age 55."

1996   **Joshua Wesson** founds **Best Cellars,** which revolutionizes American retail wine selling by categorizing wines by style ("Fizzy, Fresh, Soft, Luscious, Juicy, Smooth, Big, Sweet") instead of by region or varietal.

Per capita wine consumption begins its steady rise over the next decade.

2000   There are 2,188 wineries in the United States.

At the 200th anniversary of the White House on November 1, **Iron Horse sparkling wine** is poured for guests, who include every living president except the ailing Ronald Reagan.

One of America's most celebrated contemporary novelists **Jay McInerney** debuts his monthly wine column "Uncorked" in *House & Garden,* which he will continue to write until the magazine's closing in 2007. His columns are collected in two books, *Bacchus & Me* (2002) and *A Hedonist in the Cellar* (2006). In 2010, he and **Lettie Teague** will be named the *Wall Street Journal*'s wine columnists.

2001   **Karen MacNeil**'s *The Wine Bible* is published. It reportedly goes on to sell more than 500,000 copies.

2002   With this year's addition of North Dakota, wine is now made in commercial wineries in all fifty states.

In the **mid-1990s,** when I was working at Larry Forgione's An American Place in New York City, customers were interested in mostly two things on our all-American wine list: California Cabernet and California Chardonnay, which went really well with dishes like scallops with potatoes and butter. . . . I also got to try everything from Stag's Leap to Sean Thackrey's wines. I still remember my first taste of Jordan Cabernet, which was amazing!

—CLAIRE PAPARAZZO, BLUE HILL

In the **late 1990s,** the top sommeliers in New York were Jean-Luc Le Dû [Daniel], Michel Couvreux [Le Bernardin], and Roger Dagorn [Chanterelle]—they were mostly Frenchmen selling French wine.

—ROBERT BOHR, COLICCHIO & SONS

[Jay McInerney] has become the best wine writer in America.

—MATTHEW DEBORD, *SALON* (NOVEMBER 20, 2000)

DATE	EVENT

At Vong [Jean-Georges Vongerichten's Thai-inspired restaurant], I saw California Pinot Noir and lots of Riesling. I still remember my first introduction to Grüner Veltliner there, which tasted like water rushing over wet slate. . . . While opening 'Cesca [with chef-partner Tom Valenti], I really fell in love with Italian wines. The all-Italian wine list was difficult to read, as it was broken down by region—so you might have no idea of the grapes! I became a huge fan of Salerno winemaker Bruno De Conciliis and others, like Livio Felluga and Ciacci Brunello di Montalcino. On weekends, instead of big California Cabernets, people would order Super Tuscans.

—CLAIRE PAPARAZZO, BLUE HILL

Contrary to wine's male image . . . women buy 77 percent and consume 60 percent of the wine in America.

—*NEW YORK TIMES* (APRIL 27, 2005)

Charles Shaw's $1.99 wines—popularly nicknamed **Two-Buck Chuck**—are introduced at Trader Joe's. After sales soar, other retailers introduce their own $1.99 labels, attracting new price-conscious consumers to wine.

In her *New York Times* article **"The Case for Drinking,"** Abigail Zuger acknowledges that some experts believe that a "drink or two a day of wine . . . is often the single best non-prescription way to prevent heart attacks—better than a low-fat diet or weight loss, better even than vigorous exercise."

2003 Wine blogs start to appear online.

2004 The movie *Sideways* is released, in which Paul Giamatti's character, Niles, disparages Merlot while singing the praises of his beloved Pinot Noir. American sales of Pinot Noir go through the roof as sales of Merlot plummet.

Sommelier and filmmaker **Jonathan Nossiter**'s documentary *Mondovino* is released, bringing new focus to the increasing globalization of the wine industry.

2005 *The Wine Lover's Dessert Cookbook*, by **Mary Cech** and **Jennie Schacht**, spotlights the pairing of desserts with sweet wines. It is part of a year-long wave of new food-and-wine-pairing books.

This year's **Dietary Guidelines for Americans** note, "A daily intake of one to two alcoholic beverages is associated with the lowest all-cause mortality and a low risk of CHD [coronary heart disease] among middle-aged and older adults."

2006 **Gary Vaynerchuk** debuts his passionate—and soon wildly popular—daily video blog on wine, known as "The Thunder Show," on February 21, on **Wine Library TV**. Four years later he is named *Wine Enthusiast* magazine's "Innovator of the Year."

Sommelier **Evan Goldstein** and his mother, chef **Joyce Goldstein**, release their first food-and-wine-pairing book, *Perfect Pairings*.

Our own *What to Drink with What You Eat* is published, winning the Georges Duboeuf Wine Book of the Year Award and the Gourmand World Cookbook Award. In 2007, it wins the International Association of Culinary Professionals' Book of the Year Award.

2007

Adult per capita wine consumption in the U.S. reaches a new high of 2.97 gallons.

The book *Icons of the American Marketplace* names 250 iconic American brands, including three winemakers: **Gallo, Iron Horse,** and **Manischewitz.**

2008

After one of the largest consumer research projects ever conducted by the wine industry, **Constellation Wines U.S.** announces the results of its 18-month study of wine consumption in America, based on 10,000 premium-wine consumers. The single largest segment of consumers (23 percent) identified themselves as "Overwhelmed" by the sheer volume of choices on store shelves.

The movie *Bottle Shock*, dramatizing the events of the 1976 Judgment of Paris, is released. It stars Alan Rickman as wine-tasting organizer Stephen Spurrier and Chris Pine as Chateau Montelena winemaker Bo Barrett.

In a profile in *People* (August 4), the kitchen of the Hyde Park, Chicago, home (said to have a 1,000-bottle wine cellar) of presidential candidate **Barack Obama** is described as having a bottle of Kendall-Jackson Chardonnay on view.

On Election Night, November 4, Michelle and Barack Obama reportedly pop corks on bottles of **Graham Beck Brut NV** sparkling wine from South Africa (which was the celebratory drink at South African president Nelson Mandela's inauguration) to toast his victory.

During the November emergency summit of two dozen world leaders led by **President George W. Bush** to address the global economic crisis, a dinner at the White House pairs an entrée

[Winemaking] parameters are dictated by an international taste and by champions of this taste—including Robert Parker, the *Wine Spectator,* and certain Spanish critics like José Peñín. They are then produced by taste bureaucrats like Michel Rolland and hundreds of indigenous oeonologists like Telmo Rodriguez.

—JONATHAN NOSSITER, *LE GOÛT ET LE POUVOIR (TASTE AND POWER,* 2007)

For the first time, the number of regular wine drinkers in the United States exceeds the number of casual wine drinkers, according to a study issued Friday. "2007 may well be seen as the wine industry's tipping-point year," John Gillespie, president of the Wine Market Council, told a Napa wine conference Friday. **"Wine is literally soaking into the national fabric."** . . . The number of U.S. adults who call themselves wine drinkers has risen 53 percent since 2000, from 49 million to 75 million. . . . Last year, a majority of wine drinkers— 55 percent—consumed wine every week.

—*SANTA ROSA PRESS DEMOCRAT* (JANUARY 19, 2008)

Nationally, wine consumption is up more than 30 percent in a decade, topping 300 million gallons last year for the first time. **The United States** has surpassed Italy as the world's No.-2 wine consumer and **is poised to overtake the front-running French by 2010**, according to the London-based *International Wine and Spirits Record*.

—*USA TODAY* (FEBRUARY 17, 2008)

Although the [Bush] White House said that it paid wholesale, the fact that it opened such an extravagant wine at a gathering intended to avert a global economic meltdown caused widespread indignation.

—MIKE STEINBERGER, *SLATE* (JANUARY 14, 2009)

of thyme-roasted rack of lamb with a 2003 **Shafer Hillside Select Cabernet Sauvignon**, then valued at about $300 a bottle, according to the Associated Press.

Adult per capita consumption of table wine stands at 2.96 gallons.

2009 President Barack Obama's official inauguration lunch at the Capitol features wines by **Duckhorn Vineyards** (2007 Sauvignon Blanc, paired with a seafood stew), **Goldeneye Winery** (2005 Pinot Noir, paired with pheasant and duck), and **Korbel** (sparkling wine, paired with the apple-cinnamon sponge cake served for dessert).

In May **President Obama** and **First Lady Michelle Obama** (whose White House Victory Garden has made headlines) dine at Blue Hill restaurant in New York City. The recommended wine pairings are reportedly among the beverages served.

The U.S. becomes the largest wine market in the world by dollar volume.

At Blue Hill in 2009, our wine list represents the huge shift in American wines over the past fifteen to twenty years. People are still interested in big California Cabernets and wines by Sean Thackrey, but these days he's letting the grapes he buys "connect with the earth" before beginning the winemaking process, which seems to impart a hint of minty or eucalyptus character to all of his wines, so they make you think of the Rhône or southwest France more than California itself. We've seen the influence of other Rhône Rangers, including Edmunds St. John and their brilliant Syrah, and the influx of different grape varieties like Viognier and Roussanne, as well as multivarietal and multivintage wines. . . . There are also more textured offerings from places like Oregon, Washington, and even New York. . . . I am also proud to serve wines by biodynamic and organic winemakers. And my clientele knows me and trusts me to the point where they ask, "Claire, what do you have upstairs that you're not putting on the wine list?"

—CLAIRE PAPARAZZO, BLUE HILL

DATE	EVENT
2010	There are 6,223 wineries in the United States. Ten states boast more than 100 wineries each: California (3,047), Washington (564), Oregon (453), New York (229), Virginia (163), Texas (157), Pennsylvania (141), Ohio (120), Michigan (104), and North Carolina (101).

The **American Medical Association**'s *Archives of Internal Medicine* reports a thirteen-year research study at Brigham and Women's Hospital in Boston of more than 19,000 women over the age of thirty-nine. Results indicate that **wine drinkers are less likely to gain weight than non-drinkers** and that moderate drinkers have a lower risk of obesity. Beer and spirits drinkers had the highest weight gain, while red wine drinkers had the lowest.

The summer wedding-week festivities of **Chelsea Clinton** and **Marc Mezvinsky** put American wines in the spotlight in Rhinebeck, New York. The Virginia winery **Kluge**'s sparkling wines, both its Blanc de Blancs and rosé, are reportedly poured at the rehearsal dinner. Guests are said to take home gift bags containing, among other locally produced items, a bottle of **Clinton Vineyards** (no relation) wine from Clinton Corners, New York.

This year's **Dietary Guidelines for Americans** advise, "Alcohol consumption may have beneficial effects when consumed in moderation. Strong evidence from observational studies has shown that moderate alcohol consumption is associated with a lower risk of cardiovascular disease."

WINNERS OF JAMES BEARD FOUNDATION AWARDS FOR WINE

Outstanding Wine and Spirits Professional
2011: Julian Van Winkle III, Old Rip Van Winkle Distillery
2010: John Shafer and Doug Shafer, Shafer Vineyards
2009: Dale DeGroff, mixologist
2008: Terry Theise, Terry Theise Estate Selections
2007: Paul Draper, Ridge Vineyards
2006: Daniel Johnnes, Dinex Group
2005: Joseph Bastianich, Italian Wine Merchants
2004: Karen MacNeil, Culinary Institute of America
2003: Fritz Maytag, Anchor Brewing Company
2002: Andrea Immer, MS, French Culinary Institute
2001: Gerald Asher, wine editor, *Gourmet*
2000: Kermit Lynch, wine importer
1999: Frank Prial, wine columnist, *New York Times*
1998: Robert Parker, *The Wine Advocate*
1997: Zelma Long, Simi Winery
1996: Jack and Jamie Davies, Schramsberg Vineyards
1995: Marvin Shanken, *Wine Spectator*
1994: Randall Grahm, Bonny Doon Vineyard
1993: Kevin Zraly, Windows on the World
1992: André Tchelistcheff, oenologist
1991: Robert Mondavi, Robert Mondavi Winery

Outstanding Wine Service
2011: Belinda Chang, The Modern (New York City)
2010: Bernard Sun, Jean Georges (New York City)
2009: Aldo Sohm, Le Bernardin (New York City)
2008: John Ragan, Eleven Madison Park (New York City)
2007: Mark Slater, Michel Richard Citronelle (Washington, DC)
2006: William Sherer, Aureole (Las Vegas)
2005: Tim Kopec, Veritas (New York City)
2004: David Lynch, Babbo (New York City)
2003: Jean-Luc Le Dû, Daniel (New York City)
2002: Paul Grieco, Gramercy Tavern (New York City)
2001: Bobby Stuckey and Laura Cunningham, The French Laundry (Yountville, California)
2000: Larry Stone, Rubicon (San Francisco)
1999: Karen King, Union Square Café (New York City)
1998: Reinhardt Lynch, The Inn at Little Washington (Washington, Virginia)
1997: Julian Niccolini and Alex von Bidder, The Four Seasons (New York City)
1996: Roger Dagorn, Chanterelle (New York City)
1995: Daniel Johnnes, Montrachet (New York City)
1994: Piero Selvaggio, Valentino (Los Angeles)
1993: Larry Stone, Charlie Trotter's (Chicago)
1992: Derek Pagan, Bern's Steak House (Tampa)
1991: Peter Granoff and Evan Goldstein, Square One (San Francisco)

YOUR PERSONAL HISTORY WITH WINE

Just as you should have a sense of pride in our nation's collective wine history, you should take pride in your own personal wine history. Our future with wine as individuals is an outgrowth of our past. It's important to have a sense of the key turning points in your relationship with wine.

What has your relationship been with wine over your lifetime? What were your family's attitudes toward wine when you were growing up? Was wine a beverage poured only on special occasions? Did the adults at your table drink wine with dinner every day? Were they teetotalers?

There's no need to be embarrassed by your answers or to fear that they will prevent you from achieving a comfortable mastery of wine. And in case our assurances aren't enough, we'll let you hear it from some of America's best sommeliers, who we believe are in the best position to convince you to be comfortable with your experience of wine and your particular taste and preferences. As experts charged with finding the best possible matches between a chef's cuisine and a winemaker's wine, restaurant sommeliers are uniquely qualified to mediate. And while they are well versed in the language of wine, they are very good at translating technical terminology into plain English.

If the mere idea of encountering America's best sommeliers makes you sit up straighter, relax. While we've run into the occasional haughty sommelier in years past, the very best today distinguish themselves as having one guiding principle: maximizing your pleasure.

Why Sommeliers Are the Perfect People to Teach You About Wine

In the coming decade, sommeliers will emerge as the new rock stars as they help open the alluring world of wine to mere mortals—and they readily admit that they are mere mortals themselves. Like the rest of us, sommeliers love food, they love wine, and they want you to have the even greater pleasure of loving food and wine together!

Their own early experiences with wine may not be so different from yours. We share a few of their stories here so you can appreciate the paths others have taken to enter the world of wine.

Developing a Discerning Palate: Robert Bohr, Colicchio & Sons

When I was growing up, my parents didn't drink wine, but my maternal grandparents did. It was whatever was served in a half-gallon jug—typically Paul Masson Chablis.

I thought I had a reasonable understanding of wine: it was something you drank with dinner and on special occasions. I remember going to my father's parents' house as a kid, and when they asked me what I wanted to drink, I replied, "A glass of Chablis," to which my father's mother responded, *"Over my dead body!"*

ROBERT BOHR

But at age six, I had my own very small wine glass at the holidays, as it was completely natural at my other grandparents' house to have an ounce or two at Easter, Thanksgiving, and Christmas.

Before I drank the wine, my aunt—who was well traveled and the most cultured—would have me look at it and smell it. My earliest memory of "Francophile culture" was receiving as a gift, in first grade, copies of Julia Child and Simone Beck's *Mastering the Art of French Cooking*, volumes I and II.

During college I spent a few weeks in France, where the wine was cheaper than water! So you could buy a case of wine and sit on the steps of the Sacre Coeur and meet all these other kids. With my two friends, I drank a lot of so-so wine, both in Paris and throughout our travels in France. For the first time I came to see wine as a grocery and not a luxury.

A Dry Pink Wine Opens Up the World of Wine:
Inez Ribustello, On The Square

Wine was not at all a part of my life growing up. The only wine served in my parents' house was Franzia White Zinfandel out of a box. I studied in Greece in 1997 and decided to buy some pink wine to bring home for my parents. I assumed it was the same wine they normally drank, and I thought they'd love it.

However, when we opened it, it had wild strawberry flavors and was crisp and clean but not sweet. My parents, who assumed that all pink wine was White Zinfandel–sweet, thought it was horrible. But I thought it was really delicious.

I did some research on the wine and discovered that rosé was a dry wine made from a red grape and that the "blush" wines like White Zinfandel that Americans had fallen in love with were in no way similar to what Europeans were drinking. That was a big revelation.

In the summer of 1998, I went to Peter Kump's culinary school in New York City. I caught the subway right by Best Cellars [the revolutionary wine retailer that first grouped wines by style] and would stop there every day after school. They always had a wine tasting going on, and though I had no business doing it on a student's budget, I would always buy a bottle. On around my tenth visit, one of the assistant managers said, "You know, you could save a lot of money if you just got a job here." I started three days later and loved every minute of it.

When I graduated from cooking school, I realized that I liked to drink wine a lot more than I liked to cook. I kept my job at Best Cellars, and at that time an article came out about Andrea Immer Robinson [then Master Sommelier at Windows on the World]. I cold-called her and left a message that I wanted to make wine my career, and any feedback she could give me would be great. She called me back and told me to keep my job, but months later she called again, telling me she needed a hostess at Wild Blue restaurant, which used to be Cellar in the Sky. I was interested in the job so I could be close to wine.

The day I went in to interview, I found out that an assistant cellarmaster position was open. I was asked if I might be interested in interviewing for that. I think it paid $7.50 an hour, but I got to take Kevin Zraly's [Windows on the World] wine course and classes with Andrew Bell [cofounder of the American Sommelier Association], meaning I could really be immersed in wine.

I learned quickly that "assistant cellarmaster" is a glorified term for box mover! I moved a lot of beer, liquor, and wine boxes, took the classes, and was eventually promoted to beverage director. I fell in love with the work and also with Stephen, now my husband, who was a sommelier. After the September 11 tragedy, I got a job at Blue Fin restaurant in Times Square.

After I left that job, Stephen and I worked the harvest in Burgundy at Domaine Dujac, and from there we went to work in the cellar at Domaine de Triennes in Provence for two months.

Then I got a call from my dad, who said, "I bought you a restaurant"—On The Square, in my home state of North Carolina—"so you can come home and stay home!"

Childhood Memories Found in a Wine Glass:
Hristo Zisovski, Ai Fiori

My dad is from Macedonia and my mom is Greek, and wine is a big part of our family life. My dad made wine in our garage. Every year he and my uncles would buy grapes from the Finger Lakes, make the year's wine, and put it in barrels in the garage.

As a kid, I was allowed to taste wine; it was never forbidden. My dad would say, "I went to college, so I know what goes on — I just want you to stay away from the hard stuff." With that kind of leeway, I never felt rebellious, ever. If I went out, I knew my limit. I was always responsible.

My father owned restaurants, so when I turned twelve there was no more watching Saturday morning cartoons. Instead I was peeling potatoes, helping out the waitresses, and busing tables. At fourteen, I told my dad I wanted to cook next to him — which I did until I went to culinary school at age eighteen.

Wine really didn't come into my life in a major way until I went to the Culinary Institute of America and earned my associate's degree. On the first day of wine class, the instructor had glasses with different things in them — stones, apples, berries, raisins — in a neutral base that exaggerated the aromas.

Later, when it came time to describe what we smelled in glasses of wine, I was the one raising my hand all the time. The wines' aromas would remind me of smells from my childhood. If it was Cabernet Franc, I smelled the roasted peppers from my mom's cooking. If it was Zinfandel, I smelled candy, or Big Red gum, because of the spice. If it was Australian Shiraz, I would smell Big League Chew grape bubble gum.

Those familiar aromas were comforting to me. Smelling the wines opened up all these memory boxes of comfort food from when I was a kid.

A French Perspective: "You Want to Be a *What?*":
Michel Couvreux, Per Se

At first, I thought I was going to be a cook. Then I decided to become a waiter, and in France you go to school to become a waiter. In school you have to study wine, and this was completely new to me. [Michel grew up in Brittany, which is better known for its cider.]

I had no idea about wine and thought it tasted the same everywhere. I was amazed to see different types of wines and to be able to taste the differences right away. I knew this was what I wanted to do. I went back home to my little country village of Pancé and told people I wanted to be a sommelier. They'd ask, "What is a sommelier?" They had never heard of one!

When I studied wine in France, it was all about French wines. We would study Champagne for two or three weeks, followed by two or three weeks on Burgundy, then two or three weeks on Bordeaux, and so on — and about two *hours* studying the rest of the world!

Since I had studied cooking before wine, I had a natural sensibility when it came to food-and-wine pairing. I was more sensitive to the flavors and textures of meat and fish and definitely understood more about the dishes because of all my time in the kitchen. It helped a lot.

After school I had to spend time in the service, and it was the best time of my life! I was in the navy and they were so happy to have a sommelier on board.

HRISTO ZISOVSKI

Dinner was with the captain and his guests, and I handled the wine pairings for them, talked about the wine, provided advice on their own cellars, and was treated like an equal.

I went to work in Paris—at Guy Savoy, among other restaurants—then spent three years at L'Arpège, a Michelin three-star restaurant. The wine list featured only French wine, as is the case in most French restaurants, with few exceptions. At L'Arpège I decided I needed to learn more English and go to New York. The night I gave my resignation, the New York chef-restaurateur David Bouley happened to come in, and he offered me a job.

A Final Word About Your Wine Journey

Wine has a long, storied history in the United States. As our country takes its place as the world's largest consumer of wine, it's time for Americans to overcome any reluctance and to embrace all the sensory pleasure it has to offer.

Best of all, we promise that you can learn about wine in a language that you as a food lover are already comfortable with: that of food and flavor.

2
Chapter

WHAT'S YOUR PLEASURE? THINK OF LEARNING ABOUT WINE AS PLAYTIME

By sampling an assortment of wines you will quickly form preferences and you will discover which wines please you and which don't. Once you have discriminated, there is no reason to be shy in stating your preference for a particular wine or style of wine; it is no more unseemly than saying you prefer salmon over sole, or veal instead of beef.

—PAUL BERTOLLI AND ALICE WATERS, *CHEZ PANISSE COOKING* (1988)

Mark Twain had it right when he wrote, "There are no standards of taste in wine . . . [One's] own taste is the standard, and a majority vote cannot decide for him or in any slightest degree affect the supremacy of his own standard." Twain apparently needs a little help persuading the average American wine drinker of this.

So the first section of this chapter is aimed at convincing you that wine really *is* all about your pleasure. In the second section, we'll help you determine what you find pleasurable in wine, and in the third, we'll help you extend your enjoyment by discovering what other wines you might find pleasurable.

I. IT'S ALL ABOUT YOUR PLEASURE

Is there a wrong way to enjoy wine? That depends. Do you believe there is a wrong way to receive pleasure?

Cat Silirie, No. 9 Park

I have found that everyone—from people in their twenties to those in their seventies—wants to learn about wine. We all have different life experiences, and people at both ends of the age and experience spectrum wonder, "Am I missing something here?" So many people want to learn how to perceive wine. Are they on the right track with their own experiences and perceptions?

When I was teaching a six-week wine course at a Boston adult education center, I opened by comparing our fear of wine to a Woody Allen joke. In *Manhattan,* a woman at a party says, "I finally had an orgasm, and my doctor told me it was the wrong kind."

I would never start a course that way again, because at the beginning everyone was so nervous that they didn't laugh! But I love this example because most people honestly don't know if they are having the "right" experience with wine. Should they be having a more "important" one? "I paid $300 for this wine—should I be having a life-changing experience?" or "I love $10 Pinot Grigio—does that mean I have a lead palate?"

That is really what most people mean when they say they want more knowledge—they want to know if they are having the "right" experience. They also don't like being confronted with that fear, which is why I think they didn't really get my joke—they didn't have the experience to think, "I get what she is saying: *It doesn't matter.* The guy drinking the wine from a box is having a great time!"

In a six-week course, at first the students are like deer caught in the headlights. They are afraid you are going to turn to them and ask, "So, what flavors are *you* getting?" I would never do that. By the fourth or fifth week, I told them what I was up to with that Woody Allen joke, and *then* they all laughed and admitted, "We really didn't know what you were talking about . . ."

A Matter of Taste

Wine is about *your* pleasure. The most important standard of taste is *yours:* "Do I like this wine?" We want to help you find out what *you* like about wine, both in general and specifically. After all, whose taste buds are "right" and whose are "wrong"?

As a Californian, Andrew loves the grassy Sauvignon Blancs with prominent herbal notes typical of many winemakers based there, while Karen, as a Midwesterner, perceives some of those wines as tasting like a mouthful of grass. She typically prefers the stony minerality of a French Sauvignon Blanc or the tropical fruit notes of one from New Zealand. We're not alone among couples who have very different preferences in wines.

Andy Myers, CityZen

Getting to know your partner's palate is fun. My wife hates Riesling, while I think it is the greatest thing in the world. I love this woman, but there are a few things I can't figure out about her—besides her taste in men—including: How can she *not* like Riesling?

As she puts it, she hates "that apple-y thing" and "all that acid." I poured her some super-old Riesling, explaining that it doesn't taste like apples at all. Her response? "It's Riesling—I can tell!" Damn! The upside is that I have an extensive collection of bottles of Riesling that are aging wonderfully because I never get to open them.

We have a good time fighting about wine. She wants nothing to do with learn-ing about it or studying it. She married a sommelier, and she tells me, "You take care of the wine — I'll take care of the bills."

That's why half-bottles are so handy. If there's a half-bottle of Riesling, I will drink it and find a half-bottle of white Rhône that will make her happy. Then the two of us will share a bottle of red wine.

My wife loves white wines from the Rhône [region of France], and she leans toward Grenache [Blanc], Marsanne/Roussanne, and a good Viognier. I personally don't "get" them at all. I admit that I am an "acid head" with wine, so I find white Rhône [which tends to be lower to moderate in acidity] flabby. They just don't move me. But the Mrs. goes nuts for them, so we have an entire shelf in our refrigerator designated for white Rhône.

For reds, we do unite on our love of wines from the Rhône Valley. And if I open a great Burgundy, she will go gaga. If I decant a Brunello for two hours to pull the tannins out of it, she is happy.

Myers and other distinguished sommeliers similarly enjoy the opportunity to get to know their restaurant guests' palates, and they aren't looking to judge them any more than they'd judge their spouses' taste.

Changing Tastes

Remember that what you enjoy today is not necessarily where you'll find your greatest pleasure tomorrow. As you open yourself to tasting different styles of wine from different places, you're bound to discover new ones you're passionate about. Taste is not a constant; it changes with time and experience.

John Ragan, Eleven Madison Park

The progression of a wine drinker's tastes follows a bell curve. When you start drinking wine, you enjoy those that are somewhat sweet. Then there's a point at which you believe, "I am not supposed to drink sweet wine." At the end of the trail, you realize that off-dry or sweet wines can be fantastic with food—and *that* is your most enlightened moment as a wine drinker.

A little sweetness never hurt anybody. When my grandma made tomato sauce, she used to put a little sugar in it. When I first saw her do that, I wondered why, but it turns out you need the sweetness for the flavor balance. For all the people out there drinking California Chardonnay who say they don't like sweet wine, I have a news flash: there is residual sugar in that wine!

Jeff Bareilles, Manresa

I moved to New York from California in 1993, and, coming from an area where Chardonnay and Cabernet were king, I thought I was hot shit because I knew my California wine. I worked at Zoë restaurant [in Manhattan], which had an all-California wine list, and I was familiar with all of them.

Then there were turning points with European wines, starting with Bordeaux. Tasting Bordeaux was astonishing to me because of the earthiness. It is like walking through the woods and getting the aroma of mushroom, leaves, and bark. It was not a big "aha!" moment; it was more that I was drinking wine with friends and realizing that the Bordeaux in my glass was Cabernet-based as well. In the beginning I wasn't sure it was something I liked. But the flavor stuck with me, and I kept tasting it and wanting to understand it.

Later turning points included northern Rhône and, as my palate evolved, eventually it landed in Burgundy. I don't want to apologize for this, but sommeliers tend to have "Burgundy-centric" palates. Burgundies—given the right vintage, producer, and moment—have such an allure; they are fascinating, fantastic wines and can be unusually versatile with a meal.

Wine is a journey, as life is, and it is all-encompassing. There is the wine's location, family, the year, and the winemaker—who is like a chef nurturing an ingredient so it will show its best. Winemakers want their style expressed in the wine; then it is bottled and still alive. When it is opened and consumed, it is alive in us.

The Wine Isn't the Only Thing That Needs to "Open Up"

Experiencing wine is not merely a transaction in which being able to open a fat wallet automatically opens up your perception and judgment. Rather, as Jeff Bareilles suggests above, if you take the time to open to it, you enter a relationship in which the wine offers you its life and life story. However, you need to offer more than mere money in return.

Cat Silirie, No. 9 Park

So many people approach wine in a restaurant by putting their money down and just wanting the wine to "happen" to them. But a great wine experience can't happen that way.

Let's say you plunk your money down for Romanée-Conti—one of the world's most renowned wines—but you don't know anything about it; you just know it's "important." You haven't tasted a lot of Burgundy, but you wait for something to happen because you are drinking "the world's greatest wine." What is the wine supposed to be doing?

This experience is only heightened when you think about the history of the wine, how rare it is, how many centuries it has existed, and you start to imagine how many people have enjoyed it. You imagine the pleasures you hope to have from it. Are you looking for incredible mouthfeel, or perfume, or for it to be perfect with the food you're having or alone by itself? People don't even think that out—they just think, "I have paid the money—now I want it to happen to me!"

Appreciating wine is not just about book learning; you also need to bring some *imagination* to the experience, some sensuality. Before going out to dinner, I say to myself, "What do I feel like eating?" I like licking my chops and imagining what I'm going to eat and what I'll drink with it. That's fun! Then, when I sit down, given all the anticipation, the pleasure is heightened.

The Right Wine for the Right Moment Enhances Pleasure

Is there a right time and place for certain wine experiences? You bet there is.

Justin Leone, Benny's Chop House

I've worked at restaurants where we were charged with putting everything that was poured and eaten into a context that the people at that table would understand. If the guests took a sip of Châteauneuf-du-Pape and had no inclination to like it, I could tell the minute I saw the reactions on their faces. I took the time to tell them a little snippet about the church and how the pope lived in Avignon for a while and—bada-bing!—*voilà*, Châteauneuf-du-Pape. I explained the concept of *garrigue* [a Provençal word for the evocation of pungent, floral Mediterranean herbs such as sage, rosemary, thyme, and lavender and the earth they're grown in], and how the guests can smell the herbs in the wine.

Finally there was recognition on their faces: "I *can* smell that herb!" Now they are part of the experience. Their heads are in their glasses.

At another table, it may be as simple as quoting some lyrics from a Beastie Boys song: "Like a bottle of Châteauneuf-du-Pape, I'm fine like wine when I start to rap." If that brings people in, then that's cool. When you add the human element of providing a snippet of the wine's context and history, enjoyment increases fifty-fold. The wine tastes different because you have a connection to it and understand it. You cannot drink something like wine disconnectedly, because it is a product rooted in the earth itself. If the *chi* ain't flowin', it is not going to reverberate in you to any depth whatsoever.

Chris Miller, Spago

I am a big believer in context for wine. Although wine can be judged objectively, that objective "yes or no" is answered quite early on, and the rest is pretty subjective. You cannot declare a wine simply good or bad, expensive or cheap, because it is all about context. Who is drinking it? What is the time and place? Is a bottle of Ecker Roter Veltliner an amazing wine? Yes, if you are poolside or having it as an aperitif or with a nice light dinner. If you are having dinner at the Michelin three-star restaurant Alain Ducasse, maybe it won't be a great bottle because it may not keep up with the cuisine.

When someone buys a red wine that is too young or a white that is too heavy or too light for the food, there will be a problem. That Roter Veltliner is a better choice for your sashimi than an '82 Margaux. The Veltliner will be the better wine even though it costs a couple of grand less.

Every sommelier grins and bears the "What is your favorite wine?" question. I can give you my top forty to fifty that I just can't live without. How do you compare Jayer to Mascarello? How do I choose between Raveneau and Selosse? They are completely different wines; it depends on who I am drinking them with and where I am. I will probably enjoy a big Rhône red late at night when I'm hanging around with friends rather than the higher-prestige bottle that I might prefer if I were going out for a nice dinner.

TEN SECRETS FOR GETTING MORE PLEASURE FROM WINE

Your active participation can enhance every wine encounter. If you follow these ten steps, you can increase your enjoyment exponentially! (We mention in parentheses the chapters where you can read more on the subject.)

1. **Do your homework.** The more knowledge, context, and interest you bring to a wine experience, the better. Be curious about what you're drinking, who made it, and where. (Chapters 2, 3, 4)

2. **Store it well.** Whether you've purchased a great bottle yourself or been given one as a gift, you'll want to make sure it stays in excellent condition. More than 95 percent of wines are meant to be drunk right away, but if you don't plan to do so, store it in the right conditions—that is, at a consistently cool cellar temperature (about 55 degrees) and on its side, to keep the cork moist so air can't enter. (Chapter 6)

3. **Be age-appropriate.** You're not likely to have a peak experience if you've bottle-aged your Prosecco for a decade—as this is a wine that should be drunk young and fresh—or if you open a just-released fine Brunello and expect it to show its potential immediately. (Chapter 4)

4. **Check the temperature.** While keeping a consistent cellar temperature is the safest way to store any wine, different wines show their best at different serving temperatures. We once dismissed an Italian red as too harsh until we read the back label: the recommended serving temperature was a full 10 degrees lower than it was on our first taste of it. After chilling, it turned around completely—as did our opinion of it! (Chapter 6)

5. **Use good-quality glassware.** You'll read more about this later, but suffice it to say that drinking from a well-made, clean, odor-free, clear, thin-lipped glass really matters when tasting wine. (Chapter 6)

6. **Let it breathe.** So-called big wines (those high in tannin, like Cabernet Sauvignon) can soften a bit (or a lot!) when they are allowed to breathe for anywhere from several minutes to several hours. Give a wine time to show its stuff when necessary. (Chapter 6)

7. **Perceive its character.** If a tree falls in the forest and no one hears, does it make a sound? If a wine is gulped down without taking the time to see and sniff and savor it, does it have a flavor? (Chapter 2)

8. **Pair it with complementary food.** The right food will maximize your pleasure from virtually every wine. If you drink a great Cabernet Sauvignon with raw oysters, whose fault is it if you don't enjoy it? (Chapter 5)

9. **Use your judgment.** Is the wine pleasurable? Which of its characteristics are most striking to you? Take notes (and snap a photo of the label) so you can remember the wine and your impressions. Otherwise, the very nature of tasting wine often leads to foggy memories! (Chapter 2)

10. **Share your experience.** When you find a wine you love, tell your friends about it. Or tell the world: blog it, tweet it. Sharing a peak wine experience with others allows them to enjoy it vicariously and learn from it, and both extends and expands the experience. (Chapter 7)

II. DETERMINING WHAT YOU FIND PLEASURABLE IN WINE

You Already Know What You Like, So Use the
Language You Already Know: Food and Flavor

Don't be afraid to say exactly what you are looking for. Don't be afraid to say, "I don't like wine that tastes like tomatoes." For that person, I would avoid tart-style wines.

—JOHN RAGAN, ELEVEN MADISON PARK

Part of the reason wine can seem intimidating is the language used to describe it—especially if you don't perceive the flavors a so-called wine expert says are supposed to be in there. It is important to know that whatever characteristics *you* perceive and whatever impressions *you* receive are correct, and whatever words you use to describe them are fine.

You've been tasting things all your life, so why not simply turn to the flavors you already know—whether blackberries or black truffles or bubble gum? You don't need to learn any fancy new terms to enjoy wine. Use the language of food and flavor. And use your own favorite flavors to guide you to wines you're likely to love. For example, if you love peaches, you'll want to check out Muscat, Riesling, and Viognier. If you're crazy about cherries, you'll want to give Pinot Noir or one of the other wines listed below a try!

CHOOSING A WINE BY . . . FLAVORS

If You Like . . .	Try . . .
Almonds	fino sherry, wines fermented and/or aged in oak
Apples	Chardonnay (esp. unoaked), ice cider, Pinot Blanc, Riesling, Vouvray
Apricots	Muscat, Riesling, Viognier
Bacon	Côte-Rotie
Blackberries	Cabernet Sauvignon, Petit Verdot, Petite Sirah, Shiraz, Syrah
Black currants, cassis	Cabernet Sauvignon, Syrah
Blueberries	Norton
Butter	Chardonnay (oaked)
Butterscotch	oaked whites
Caramel	oaked whites, tawny port
Cherries	Barbera, Bardolino, Cabernet Sauvignon, Chianti, Grenache, Malbec, Merlot, Mourvèdre, Nebbiolo, Pinot Noir, Primitivo, rosé, Sangiovese, Syrah, Valpolicello, Zweigelt
Chocolate	full-bodied red wines (e.g., Cabernet, Syrah, Zinfandel), PX sherry, tawny port, Uruguayan Alcyone
Cinnamon	Grenache, red wines (oaked), Rhône reds
Cloves	Gewürztraminer (Alsatian), oaked wines (using new oak)
Coconut	American oaked wines, Rioja (made with American oak)
Cream	oaked wines
Dill	Cabernet Sauvignon, California red wines aged in American oak, Rioja

Eucalyptus	Shiraz (Australian)
Figs	Chardonnay
Fruit	New World wines
Grapefruit	Gewürztraminer (Alsatian), Pouilly-Fumé, Riesling, Sancerre, Sauvignon Blanc (New Zealand), Scheurebe (German)
Grapes	Muscat
Grass	Sauvignon Blanc, Sémillon
Green bell peppers	Cabernet Franc, Cabernet Sauvignon (esp. inexpensive), Sauvignon Blanc
Hazelnuts	Sherry, Amontillado
Herbs	Barbera, Pouilly-Fumé, Roussanne, Sauvignon Blanc, Soave, Verdejo, Vermentino
Honey	Chenin Blanc (sweet), Riesling (sweet), Sauternes
Lemon	Muscadet, Pinot Grigio, Sancerre, Sauvignon Blanc, Verdicchio
Lentils	Grüner Veltliner
Lime	Riesling (Australian)
Lychees	Asti, Gewürztraminer
Malt	Topaque
Melon	Chardonnay, Chenin Blanc
Mint	Cabernet Sauvignon, California Shiraz
Mushrooms	bottle-aged wines, Champagne blended with Pinot Meunier, Pinot Noir
Nuts	Champagne (esp. Blanc de Blancs), port, sherry, Verdejo
Olives	Languedoc wines
Orange	Muscat (esp. Orange)
Peaches	Chardonnay (esp. New World), Moscato d'Asti, Muscat, Riesling, Viognier
Pears	Champagne (Blanc de Blancs), Chardonnay, Pinot Blanc, Roussanne
Pepper, black	Petite Sirah, Shiraz/Syrah, Zinfandel, Zweigelt
Pepper, white	Grüner Veltliner
Pineapple	Chardonnay, Chenin Blanc, Semillon
Plums	Lagrein, Malbec, Muscat (black), Pinot Noir, Sangiovese
Quince	Chenin Blanc
Raisins	Muscat (liqueur) or Rutherglen
Raspberries	Beaujolais, Burgundy (red), Grenache, Pinot Noir, rosé, Syrah, Zinfandel
Rose petals	Gewürztraminer, Muscat
Smoke	Chardonnay (oaked), Côte-Rôtie, Fumé Blanc (oaked), Sauvignon Blanc (oaked)
Spices	Gewürztraminer, Grenache, Malbec, Primitivo, Syrah, wines aged in French oak
Strawberries	Beaujolais, Pinot Noir, rosé, Tempranillo
Sweetness	high-alcohol wines (often perceived as sweet), sweet wines
Toast	bottle-aged wines, Champagne (esp. Blanc de Blancs), Chardonnay (esp. oaked)
Tobacco	Barbaresco, Barolo, Tempranillo
Vanilla	oaked wine (esp. Chardonnay), Semillon, Tempranillo
Vegetables	Cabernet Franc, Grüner Veltliner, Sauvignon Blanc
Violets	Barolo, red Bordeaux (esp. Graves, Margaux)

Sommeliers Speak Many Languages (and the Best Speak Yours!)

Few things are more overwhelming in a restaurant than being handed a wine list the size of an encyclopedia, featuring wines from countries around the world. When you're farther along in your wine journey, you may enjoy browsing—but in many cases the best thing, even for an expert, is to have a conversation with the sommelier.

Andy Myers, CityZen

I don't ask guests hard specific questions like "Do you like a tannic wine?" They may be doctors or lawyers or otherwise very well educated, but they may simply not know what tannins are. They may not know squat about wine. That does not make them bad people. Wine can be intimidating, and unfortunately many people think they are "supposed to" know more.

I ask guests, "What do you like? What are you in the mood for?" They may say they are having fish but really love red wine. My response is, "Cool, let's find a red wine for your fish! What kind of red wine do you like? Heavy or light, fruity or earthy?"

Sometimes people don't know how to describe wine. That is why you have a sommelier—I'm here to *help* you describe it. By asking leading questions, I may determine that you like full-bodied wines with lots of fruit to go with your delicate fish.

I keep it simple. I ask very broad questions. Do you want red or white? If they tentatively say, "Red," I think, "Great—you have just eliminated half the wine list." Full-bodied or light? Light? Great, we are down to fifty wines. If we determine you want a light-bodied red wine, with fruit, under $100, we are down to ten to twelve wines. From there, I'll pick three and describe them and see if anything stands out.

I can make any wine sound tasty. I'll joke that I just made it hard for the guests by making all three sound great. If they say that the black-cherry flavor jumped out in the descriptions, I know we are onto the Oregon Pinot Noir, and we are doing wonderfully.

I'll remind people, "If you knew everything about wine, why would you need me?" This is what I do for a living—I'm a trained professional, and I am here to help. At the end of the day, wine is just grape juice. If it didn't give you such a high, no one would care. Let's loosen up! The fact that I know the subregions of Portugal doesn't matter to anyone else. I just needed to know that for a test.

What you as a guest need to know is what makes you happy and what you want to spend—and I will find the right wine for you. If you are out for your anniversary, I want you to have fun and to be able to say, "It may have been a $400 dinner for two, but damn, it was great!"

Encountering a Glass of Wine

Tasting, as much as hearing or seeing, should be a technique akin to awakening; the lesson of gastronomy does not merely concern the primary pleasure that comes from appeasing a need. Science and feeling engender arrays of flavors as complex as arrangements of sounds, volumes, colors, or words. Gastronomy is different, but the emotion can be just as intense and transforming.

—ALAIN SENDERENS, *THE TABLE BECKONS* (1991)

Enjoying a glass of wine is about more than just the physical act of raising a glass to your lips and sipping. It offers an all-too-rare opportunity in this day and age for reflection and contemplation of the moment. A lot goes into a glass of wine, including time, energy, and history. Take a moment to think about the glass and to think beyond it, to engage all your senses.

Meet a glass of wine. Look at it. Smell it. Taste it. What do you notice first? What else do you perceive—a refreshing acidity? A hint of spritz? Flavors of ripe, juicy honeydew melon? What's your gut judgment? That is, would you eagerly take the next sip or would you rather pour the entire glass out? Are you indifferent? Especially with an unfamiliar wine, you might notice how it differs from wines you typically drink. That's when it can pay to give it a chance . . . What *do* you like about it?

If the answer is "Nothing," you might want to make sure it's at the proper temperature and being served with the right food, and then give it a second chance. For example, a wine made from very tannic grapes can be pretty intense, but if you let it open up for a while and serve it with a well-marbled, medium-rare steak (or even a hamburger), it can evoke a whole new pleasure. At that point, if the answer is *still* "Nothing," don't worry—you don't ever have to drink that wine again!

Learning About Wine Should Be Fun

How are wines different from one another? How can you best categorize those differences? Three childhood staples—a **xylophone**, a box of **crayons**, and the game **"Show and Tell"**—can help you organize your thoughts about different wines.

XYLOPHONE

In addition to being one of the highest-point Scrabble words we can think of, "xylophone" can be a useful tool for thinking about wine. When you sit down to taste more than one wine, it can be helpful to arrange them in a manner inspired by the percussion instrument of graduated wooden bars.

Think of wines as falling along a spectrum on any given characteristic, such as color (light to dark), weight (light to full-bodied), or volume (quiet to loud in flavor).

Take **color**. Picture a range of wines from light to dark: from nearly clear to pale yellow to the deepest gold to pink to light red to dark purple. When tasting

multiple wines, you might line them up this way, because increasing depth of color can often suggest a crescendo of flavor intensity.

Or take **weight.** It can be helpful to proceed from light-bodied to full-bodied wines, using the wine's alcohol level (low to high) as an estimate.

By **volume,** we're referring to the "quietness" or "loudness" of the wine's flavor. Very lightly flavored wines such as Pinot Grigio stand in stark contrast to boldly flavored wines such as an oaky Chardonnay or a young Cabernet Sauvignon.

Organizing wines this way makes it easier to generalize about the styles of wine you enjoy most with certain foods. Often people prefer lighter wines with lighter foods, and fuller-bodied and more fully flavored wines with heavier foods.

In addition to color, weight, and volume, wines also vary along other spectra, including aspects of taste, such as **acidity** (from flabby to tart, reflecting its sourness, which induces mouth watering) and **sweetness** (from bone dry to very sweet), and aspects of texture, such as **astringency** (from soft to strong, as a function of its tannin levels, which induce a mouth-puckering sensation).

CRAYONS

When you realize that thousands of different grape varieties are used in the making of wine and that they can vary in a great many ways, it's easy to feel overwhelmed. But little kids don't start out with the big box of sixty-four crayons; they start with a box of eight, including the primary colors—yellow, red, and blue. Likewise, you can get a good start in understanding the world of wine by mastering three primary colors—white, pink, and red—as represented by just eight different types of wine (Riesling, Sauvignon Blanc, Chardonnay, Pinot Noir, Merlot, Cabernet Sauvignon, rosé, and sparkling), plus a bonus—sweet wines!

Six wine grapes are known as noble grapes for their historical role in producing the world's greatest wines. You can think of them as falling along two spectra (or xylophones)—one for white wines and the other for reds (both listed here from light-bodied to full-bodied):

- **White:** Riesling, Sauvignon Blanc, Chardonnay
- **Red:** Pinot Noir, Merlot, Cabernet Sauvignon

Riesling and Pinot Noir are typically lighter-bodied, while Chardonnay and Cabernet Sauvignon are typically fuller-bodied. Sauvignon Blanc and Merlot fall somewhere in the middle.

A wine's body matters just as much as, and often more than, color when pairing it with food. Lighter-bodied wines pair best with lighter dishes, such as sushi, while fuller-bodied wines pair best with heavier dishes, such as steak. We'll explore this subject at greater length in Chapter 5.

Lovers of rosé and/or White Zinfandel will wonder about **pink** wines. Because they have one foot in the world of whites and the other in the world of reds, rosé wines fall somewhere in between the two in terms of the foods they pair with.

Sparkling wines are different because of their mouthfeel—they're filled with bubbles! Whether it's the tiny bubbles that distinguish a finely made Champagne or the bigger bubbles of many Italian Proseccos, the hallmark of all sparkling wines is lots of fizz.

The bonus: Though **sweet** wines are obviously sweet, they, too, cover a spectrum from slightly sweet (also referred to as off-dry) to very sweet. For example, an off-dry Riesling can be paired well with savory dishes that have a hint of sweetness, such as a green salad with apples or pears, or spicy dishes (from Indian to Thai), while a very sweet wine such as Sauternes works best with desserts or rich dishes based on ingredients like foie gras or Roquefort cheese.

"SHOW AND TELL"

Now that you understand the various spectra of wines, it's time to examine the glass of wine in front of you. How can you use all of your senses—including those of sight, smell, taste, touch, and sometimes sound (the enticing fizz of those bubbles in a glass of Champagne)—to understand it?

Wine appreciation is like a grade-school session of "Show and Tell." Just for the fun of it, describe your experience of a wine through all your senses. The better you get at describing wines (especially those you enjoy, of course), the more easily a sommelier or knowledgeable wine-store clerk can help you choose wines you're likely to enjoy.

There's a logical order that will serve you well: Appearance, Aroma, Taste, and Mouthfeel.

Appearance: What a Wine Looks Like

The brighter the wine, the lower the alcohol.

—RULE OF THUMB

The first distinction you make about a wine has more to do with *its* palette than *your* palate. Even from across a room, you can distinguish a wine's color.

White wines range from nearly clear (some Pinot Grigio) to greenish yellow (Sauvignon Blanc) to a brighter lemon yellow (Riesling) to golden yellow (Chardonnay). With aging, white wines tend to darken toward shades of brownish yellow.

Rosé wines range from pale peach (rosé Champagne) to salmon (rosé Syrah) to bright berry pink (White Zinfandel).

Red wines range from garnet (Pinot Noir) to ruby (Cabernet Sauvignon or Merlot) to blackish red (Shiraz). With aging, red wines tend to lighten toward brownish shades of brick red.

Upon closer examination, before even tasting or sniffing the wine, you can gain more clues with just a swirl of your glass. If it swirls the way whole milk or heavy cream does, it's likely to be fuller-bodied and have a higher alcohol content. If it swirls like skim milk, it's probably lighter-bodied, with a lower alcohol content.

Other visual clues to look for include clarity (from brilliant to cloudy), color intensity (from transparent to opaque), liveliness (from flat to vibrant), and bubbles (from none to boldly sparkling).

Roger Dagorn, MS, of Porter House New York, instructs his students at New York City College of Technology to deduce a wine's grape variety and place of origin based on sight clues (and eventually smell) before confirming their predictions through taste.

Here are clues about **white wines:**

- If it is slightly greenish in color, it is likely to be from a cool climate, such as Canada or Germany.
- If it is a more golden yellow, it is likely to be from a warm climate, such as Australia or California.
- If it is cloudy as opposed to clear, it may not be a well-made wine. However, if it is unfiltered or not overly filtered, a cloudy wine may be of high quality.

Clues for **red wine** include the following:

- If it is garnet, it is probably Pinot Noir or Grenache or Tempranillo.
- If it is ruby, it could be Cabernet Sauvignon, Merlot, or Syrah.
- If it has deep purple hues, with little color variation at the rim, it is probably young. If it is brownish, it is probably an older wine.

ROGER DAGORN

Just from looking at a wine, you can learn to make distinctions. If the legs (the vertical lines that run down the inside of the glass after it is swirled) are thick, it is probably higher in alcohol.

CHOOSING A WINE BY . . . COLOR

If you have a strong preference for either white or red wine, shake things up by trying another color. If you typically prefer white wines, try a rosé or a lighter red such as Beaujolais.

If someone only likes red wine, I will have them try these varietals because they are **white wines that taste like red.** The more money you spend on Grüner Veltliner, Savennières, and Chenin Blanc, the bigger the wines will be, because they will be from smaller-yielding vines that have more concentrated flavor. Or try a Marsanne/Roussanne blend, because it is low in acid and high in alcohol with a really thick, oily body. Savennières and Vouvray can have really thick minerality and not enough acid to clean it off the palate—which can be really satisfying for red wine drinkers, because they can feel the wine. These are not flimsy wines.
—HRISTO ZISOVSKI, AI FIORI

Aroma: What a Wine Smells Like
The aroma of a wine describes its spirit or soul.
—PAUL BERTOLLI AND ALICE WATERS, *CHEZ PANISSE COOKING* (1988)

Johannes Leitz [whose family winery in Germany dates back to 1744] says, "The best wines are the wines that smell good." It is so true.
—VANESSA BOYD, PHILIPPE

Aroma in wine is as much a matter of *whether* as *what*. Some wines have a "quiet nose," meaning you have to really search for their very faint scent. On the other end of the spectrum are wines that are wildly aromatic, such as Gewürztraminer: one whiff of its trademark in-your-face lychees-and-rose-petals scent will have even beginning wine tasters calling out its name. As a rule of thumb, red wines have more aromatics than whites, which is the reason they are most often served in bulbous glasses that concentrate their aromas.

The Breakers hotel in Palm Beach, Florida, offers a sixteen-week wine course to all staff members, not just the restaurant workers. When a wine is tasted in class, everyone discusses its nose (or aroma) and its palate (or flavors), plus optimal food pairings.

Virginia Philip, MS, The Breakers

If the men can't describe the floral notes, we tell them they are not buying their wives enough flowers! If the women can't describe the vegetal notes, we say, "Girls, get down to the vegetable aisle—you are not cooking enough!"

The vegetable and fruit aisle is great for wine training. When I was training for the Court of Master Sommeliers exam, I would go to the equivalent of Whole Foods and smell all the different vegetables, fruits, herbs, spices, and other foods. I would take written or mental notes on what each one smelled like. The first time I could smell caramel in a wine, I was jumping up and down! We say to the class, you may not get it the first or second week. It may be eight weeks in, but you will get an "aha" because you finally smell vanilla or cinnamon!

Michaël Engelmann, Gary Danko

The nose of the wine is probably most important, even more than the palate. You confirm on the palate what you suspect from the nose.

Most of us remember the smell of something cooking on the stove at our grandma's home. I remember the smell of my mom making jam—she made fifteen to twenty different ones, like mirabelle [plum], strawberry, and cherry. I could walk in through the garage and, with one sniff, know which fruit was on my mother's stove.

I love smelling everything. My mother makes fun of me because I will smell a dish to conjure its aromas and flavors. When I go to the market, I love smelling peaches and pears. It is normal to smell something at the market before you buy it. But when I go to the woods, I also like to smell the leaves, the dead wood, the grass.

When wine was new for me, like everyone else I took some time to learn the aromas. Aroma is also personal: I may smell raspberry while you may smell cherry.

Jesse Rodriguez, Addison at The Grand Del Mar

I will never forget when Greg Tresner [Master Sommelier at The Phoenician in Arizona] gave me a Viognier and asked me what it smelled like. I knew, but I couldn't describe it. So Greg brought out the individual components: orange rind, honeysuckle blossoms, and Froot Loops—and those were exactly what I was getting!

Greg also taught me the best way to learn aromas, advising me to go to the grocery store on my day off. "If it opens at six AM, get there at six-ten and go to the produce area first. The stuff is freshest then, and you want to smell it right off the bat because it will be very aromatic." If you do this on a weekly basis, your mind starts recalibrating.

When we have a wine tasting, we always talk about the aromatics. I am teaching a class called "Wines That Smell Akin," in which we will taste Austrian Grüner Veltliner, Austrian Riesling, and some richer styles of Sauvignon Blanc. I will also pour some New Zealand Sauvignon Blanc, South African Sauvignon Blanc, and Sancerre. So my class will have to figure out what distinguishes the wines from New Zealand from the South Africans and those from central France.

The students' homework is to buy kaffir lime, jalapeño, and cilantro. I will also have some blue slate and red slate rocks that I brought home from Germany, so they can get used to identifying all those notes. I will also grab some things from our kitchen as well. Here's the full list:

- **Kaffir lime and lime leaf:** This is the classic aroma for Austrian Riesling.
- **Lime zest:** This is good for German Riesling.
- **Jalapeño and cilantro:** These are for New Zealand and South African Sauvignon Blanc.
- **Lentils and peas:** This is a classic smell for Grüner Veltliner. They give a sense of weight, as Grüner Veltliner can be heavier than Riesling.
- **Johnson's Baby Powder:** This is the classic smell of Austrian Grüner Veltliner.
- **Kiwi:** This can be found in German and Austrian Riesling.
- **Rocks, slate:** This is for German Riesling. I have students lift the rock from the water and smell it.
- **Red apple skin:** I want them to smell and taste this for Kabinett Riesling.

Often, when starting out, people confuse sweetness with fruit. You can't smell sweet, but you can smell fruit. When they taste a wine, they will say it's sweet. Then I'll give them some Sauternes and have them taste it alongside the first wine. Then they get it: one is sweet and one is dry and fruity.

CHOOSING A WINE BY . . . SWEETNESS

If You Like Wine That Is . . .	Try . . .
Very dry	Assyrtiko, Bordeaux (white), (Tocai) Friulano, Muscadet, Pinot Grigio, Pinot Gris, Sauvignon Blanc, Viognier
Off-dry	Bugey, Champagne (demi-sec), Chenin Blanc, Gewürztraminer, Riesling (Kabinett or Spätlese), White Zinfandel
Sweet	Asti, Banyuls, Barsac, Brachetto d'Acqui, ice cider, ice wine, Late Harvest wines, Moscato d'Asti, port, Riesling (Auslese, Beerenauslese, or Trockenbeerenauslese), Sauternes, Sherry (PX)

Taste: What a Wine Activates on Your Tongue

While the words "flavor" and "taste" are often used interchangeably, they mean two different things. **Taste** refers to the four basic tastes perceived by the taste buds: sweet, sour, bitter, and salt. The so-called fifth taste, umami, a kind of savory deliciousness, is sometimes perceived in red wines, particularly those that are well aged. **Flavor** refers to the total impact of **taste** in conjunction with **aroma** (discussed above) and **mouthfeel** (which we'll get to next).

- **Sweetness** can range from bone dry (not at all sweet) to very sweet (sometimes described as honeyed).
- Sourness, more commonly referred to as **acidity,** ranges from flabby (very low acid) to aggressive (very high acid).
- **Bitterness** ranges from subtle (barely discernible bitterness) to harsh (very bitter).
- **Saltiness** is typically not found in wine, although certain wines produced in coastal areas (manzanilla sherry, Muscadet) sometimes have faint notes suggestive of a salty sea breeze.

Roger Dagorn, MS, Porter House New York

My students at New York City College of Technology, where I teach an introductory course in wine, love sweet wines the most. They love Sauternes, German Riesling, Muscat de Beaumes-de-Venise, and port.

When I teach the white wines of France, the last wine they taste that day is Sauternes. The other wines they have tasted have all been "too tart," "too acidic," "I don't like this," "I don't like that." Then they taste Sauternes, and they like it! So then I have them tell me why. I want them to understand *why* they like it and why its sweetness works with certain dishes.

Mouthfeel: A Wine's Texture + Temperature + Piquancy + Astringency

I have had guests say that they didn't like it when a wine made their mouth feel "furry," and I realized that they didn't like wine with a lot of tannin—so I knew to pour them Pinot Noir or Burgundy, which are both lower in tannin.

—JOHN RAGAN, ELEVEN MADISON PARK

When you take a sip of wine, how does it feel in your mouth and as it slips across your tongue and down your throat? Is it smoothly silky or more roughly rustic? Flat or bubbly? These are words we use to describe a wine's **texture.**

Your perceptions of a wine will be different depending on its **temperature,** which naturally changes over the course of consuming it, especially in extreme weather. For example, a cool glass of wine will quickly turn into a warm one if you're outside in the hot summer sun. Every wine has its ideal temperature or temperature range. Sparkling wines (such as Champagne) and certain sweet wines require the coldest temperature (about 40 to 45 degrees); full-bodied whites and light-bodied reds are typically best at cellar temperature (about 50 to 55 degrees); and fine full-bodied tannic red wines usually show their best when merely cool (about 60 to 65 degrees).

Piquancy is the word often used to describe the "false heat" perceived from "spicy" ingredients such as chile peppers, which aren't hot in temperature but prompt the illusion of heat. It is common to perceive a high-alcohol wine (one with more than 14 percent alcohol) as being similarly "hot" in the mouth. (As you might imagine, the sensation is exacerbated if you're unwise or unlucky enough to drink such a wine with a chile-laden dish!) The alcohol itself contributes no aroma or taste, but it's an important part of a wine's texture. Most table wines (that is,

---

CHOOSING A WINE BY . . . WEIGHT

If You Like Wine That Is . . .	Try . . .
Light-bodied	Bardolino, Beaujolais, Gamay, Grenache, Muscadet, Pinot Grigio, Pinot Noir (lighter), Riesling, Soave, Vinho Verde
Medium-bodied	Barbera, Bordeaux (white), Chardonnay (unoaked), Chenin Blanc, Chianti, Grenache, Malbec, Merlot, Pinot Blanc (Alsatian), Pouilly-Fumé, Sancerre, Sangiovese, Sauvignon Blanc
Full-bodied	Barbaresco, Barolo, Burgundy (white), Cabernet Franc, Cabernet Sauvignon, Chardonnay (oaked), Gewürztraminer, Meursault, Mourvèdre, Nebbiolo, Pinot Gris (Alsatian), Shiraz, Syrah, Viognier, Zinfandel

dry wines as opposed to dessert wines) range from 12 to 14 percent alcohol, while wines like Moscato d'Asti are a mere 5.5 percent alcohol. High-alcohol wines like Shiraz or Zinfandel can reach 16 percent or more.

Astringency is the mouth-puckering sensation you get when you eat walnuts or sip very strong black tea. You'll also perceive it in wines with a significant amount of tannin. Wines get tannin in two ways: from contact with the skins, seeds, and stems of grapes or from contact with oak barrels. While the sensations produced are similar in both cases, some experienced wine tasters can differentiate between the two sources.

In general, the more tannic the wine, the longer its aging potential. Beaujolais (made from Gamay, a thin-skinned grape) is naturally low in tannin, so you'll want to drink it young—that is, within a year or so after release (or within a few months in the case of Beaujolais Nouveau). Cabernet Sauvignon, a thick-skinned grape, is naturally high in tannin, so many of these wines can age for years, sometimes even for decades.

Strong tannin can be perceived as uncomfortable in the mouth, so remember that there are ways to counteract that quality, such as by decanting the wine (which allows it to "breathe" and can mellow the tannins) or by serving it with an appropriate food, such as a well-marbled rare or medium-rare steak or other red meat. At the School for American Chefs at Beringer Vineyards in Napa Valley, Madeleine Kamman taught Andrew the trick of adding a little butter to the sauce for a steak, which tames a tannic wine's effect on the palate.

A wine's **finish** refers to the length of its flavor—how long you can continue to taste the wine even after you've swallowed. Finish is often considered a defining aspect of a wine's quality. A short finish means the flavor of the wine disappears abruptly, within a few seconds. A wine with a long finish provides sensory enjoyment after you've swallowed, even for as long as a minute or more.

CHOOSING A WINE BY . . . VOLUME

If You Like Wine That Is . . .	Try . . .
Very quiet	Orvieto, Pinot Grigio, Soave, Trebbiano
Quiet	Chardonnay (unoaked), (Tocai) Friulano, Locorotondo, Müller-Thurgau, Muscadet, Pinot Bianco, Prosecco, Silvaner/Sylvaner, Txakoli, Verdicchio
Loud	Cabernet Sauvignon, Châteauneuf-du-Pape, Douro reds, Malbec, Montepulciano, Norton, Priorat, Ribera del Duero, Savennières, Scheurebe, Super Tuscans, Xinomavro
Very loud	Amarone, Bordeaux (red), Cahors, Petite Sirah, Retsina, Tannat

Jesse Rodriguez of Addison at The Grand Del Mar on Tasting Tannin: Wood Tannin vs. Fruit Tannin

People will describe a wine as tannic, but what *kind* of tannin is it? You need to be specific. Jay Fletcher, a Master Sommelier, suggests that when you taste your red wine, swish it between your two front teeth so it hits your gums. This is the most sensitive area in your mouth for fruit tannin. If your mouth feels fuzzy and thick, you're tasting *fruit* tannin—tannin from the skins of the grapes.

Wood tannin you taste on your tongue. Think about your dentist putting a wooden depressor on your tongue—it feels instantly dried out. That is what wood tannin (from oak-barrel aging) is like.

Taste Is Subjective

Judging the quality of a wine can be an objective matter of assessing its **typicity** (is it what you'd expect given the grape, the origin, and the vintage?), **balance** (is it a cohesive whole or do certain characteristics stand out?), and **complexity** (does it fascinate you and hold your interest over time?).

However, the specific flavors *you* taste and whether or not you *enjoy* the overall impression a wine makes are largely subjective matters.

Each of us starts our wine journey from a different place, but what about those who aren't old enough to drink? One sommelier says he teaches his under-age college students to think of everything they consume as if it were a glass of wine—a process worth emulating to make sure you're present to its flavors.

Roger Dagorn, MS, Porter House New York

My goal is to get students to stop and think about whatever they are tasting—whether it is wine, beer, soda, water, or food! I use the Court of Master Sommeliers' wine-tasting chart with my students. The chart provides spaces for the name, producer, appellation, region, grape variety or varieties, vintage, and then their views on sight, smell, and taste. It's important that they take a moment to apply what they know. My students do this for every glass of wine they taste.

A lot of people think they don't have a good sense of smell. We have our motor skills of sight, hearing, and touch, but our senses of smell and taste are genetic. Our descriptions of taste and smell are subjective, but it is still possible to make deductions. I tell my students that they can dislike something as much as the person next to them loves it. That's fine. The terminology used to describe wine is also subjective. It is something I try to instill in them so they can talk the wine jargon with others.

I also tell the story of how one of my instructors once made the point that Chenin Blanc and wines made from Chenin Blanc, such as Vouvray, always smell and taste of quince. At that point I had never tasted quince, but I memorized that "fact." It was ten years before I tasted quince [which has a flavor akin to spiced apples], and when I did I thought, "*This* doesn't taste like Chenin Blanc!" I tell this story so my students won't get tied down to specific verbiage but will use descriptors as tools to associate with wine.

I work with students who have never tasted wine before, and some think they hate it. During the final exam, I give them a glass to taste for extra credit. They have to analyze it by sight, smell, and taste. Then I ask them to deduce the wine's country of origin, grape variety, appellation, and vintage. Out of a class of twenty-eight, two or three will be able to do this, which I think is pretty good. Once a

student from Korea [a country with no wine tradition] who was nineteen and had no clue about wine walked in the door and got it right!

III. DISCOVERING WHAT *ELSE* YOU MIGHT FIND PLEASURABLE IN WINE

It's easy to get into a rut with wine. Let's face it: there are so many classic wine-and-food pairings—Chardonnay and roast chicken, Pinot Noir and salmon, Cabernet Sauvignon and steak—that it's sometimes hard to stray from the comfort of the tried and true. Besides, if you know what grapes or vintners you already like, why change?

But there is so much more pleasure to be had. Now it's easier than ever to branch out and try something new. Many restaurants offer wine not only in bottles, but also by the half-bottle or by the glass—and in some cases even by the half-glass or by the taste! This is a way to try something new at a fraction of the cost of an entire bottle.

Why limit yourself? When dining out, take advantage of the knowledge and experience of the best sommeliers to steer you toward something *else* you're likely to enjoy.

Michael Flynn, The Mansion on Turtle Creek

One of the easiest ways to learn more about wine risk-free is to ask the sommelier, whose job it is to help you choose a wine that will bring you pleasure. Your only responsibility is to communicate what you like and what you wish to spend. The sommelier can translate your preferences into good choices from the wine list.

So many thousands of wines are bottled every year that it is a shame to go back to the same label time and time again. Choosing a wine is not like buying a car; you are not stuck with it! You can try others at very little risk, and in doing so you may discover new wines to enjoy.

Chris Miller, Spago

Do you order steak every time you go to a restaurant? Should you always order the same bottle of wine? Some people do. My best friend will try everything in the world once or twice, but what he really loves is mashed potatoes and ketchup.

I like to support up-and-coming wineries. I believe they will give you either better quality for the same price or the same quality for a lower price. But it is often hard to talk guests into trying different wines. However, when I can persuade a diehard fan of a particular wine to try something new, I often hear, "Oh, my God, *now* I know what love is!"

What will happen if you try something new? You will spend the same amount of money and you will enjoy it, because I have a pretty good idea of the style I am recommending and I know it is similar to what you already like.

The worst-case scenario is that you find you don't like what I've chosen. At the very least, you will feel better about going back to your usual wine, the one you've had a hundred times before. You've learned that there is nothing better for your palate.

Sabato Sagaria of The Little Nell on the Spectrum of Wine Familiarity: Familiar → Gateway → Crossover → Obscure

On one end of the spectrum, you have the familiar wines that everyone knows — such as Pinot Noir, Merlot, and Cabernet Sauvignon. Next, there are "gateway" wines, which are slightly more unusual, and then "crossover" wines, which are even more unusual. At the far end of the spectrum, you have the obscure wine-geek wines. If I try to introduce guests at the familiar end of the spectrum to a wine-geek wine, they won't get it. So, I'll first introduce them to a gateway or crossover wine that has similar characteristics to their familiar choices, so they can keep one foot in their comfort zone while they put one foot out.

For example:

Familiar: German Riesling

Gateway: Eroica Washington State Riesling

Crossover: Grosset Polish Hill Riesling, South Australia

Wine-geek: Pichler Grüner Veltliner Smaragd, Austria, or Robert Weil Spätlese Trocken, Germany

If you like Riesling, you'll like . . . a different style of Riesling. If people are used to German Riesling, I would serve them something different, such as Eroica, which is made in Washington state by Chateau Ste. Michelle in conjunction with the German winemaker Ernst Loosen. I would try a drier-style Riesling from Austria, because Americans still don't know about Austrian Riesling. I would move them away from the sweetness but still give them just a touch. Grüner Veltliner would be a little more wine-geeky. It has structure and more vegetal characteristics. A full-blown wine-geek choice, something really out there, might be a Spätlese Trocken from a producer like Robert Weil, who is doing a bone-dry style. His Trocken is so angular, linear, and precise, it is like shooting a laser through a dark room. Most people don't get it, but if you show it in the right context with food like chilled seafood or crudo, it works well.

Familiar: California Sauvignon Blanc
Gateway: Cloudy Bay Sauvignon Blanc, New Zealand
Crossover: Txomin Etxaniz Txakoli, Spain
Wine-geek: Huet Le Mont, Sec Vouvray, France

If you like Sauvignon Blanc, you'll like . . . unoaked white wines from Italy. I look to the northeast region. Or Movia Sauvignon Blanc from Slovenia. Txakoli is a great crossover, with its grassy characteristics. You can also go to Greece for an unoaked Moschofilero with its tropical characteristics.

Familiar: California Chardonnay
Gateway: Querciabella Batar, Italy
Crossover: Gangloff Condrieu, France
Wine-geek: Beaucastel Blanc, France

If you like Chardonnay, you'll like . . . Viognier, which is a good crossover. It has some of the same texture with a little bit of oak to it. When you go to the wine-geek end of the Chardonnay spectrum, you find Montrachet from Romanée-Conti. If they don't have that [four-figure-priced wine] at your corner bodega, I really like wine from Jermann in Italy, who does really cool blends from local grape varieties. The Vintage Tunina is a fantastic wine. His wines all have stories behind them; Tunina is named for Casanova's poorest lover, who was his housekeeper. He named one wine Where Dreams Have No End. He wanted to make the perfect Chardonnay, and once he got there he changed the name to Dreams. It was inspired by the U2 song "Where the Streets Have No Name." People don't think of Italy for Chardonnay. There is a wine from Tuscany [in the Chianti region] called Batar, which is inspired by the wines of Bâtard-Montrachet. I believe it is a Chardonnay and Pinot Bianco blend made by Querciabella. It is like shooting fish in a barrel for a Chardonnay lover. It is a little too oaky for a wine geek, but if you like California Chardonnay, boom—you are going to love this.

Familiar: California Pinot Noir
Gateway: Groffier Chambolle-Musigny Les Sentiers, France
Crossover: Casanova di Neri, Brunello di Montalcino, Italy
Wine-geek: López de Heredia, Viña Tondonia, Rioja, Spain

If you like Pinot Noir, you'll like . . . Nero d'Avola or Beaujolais from a ripe vintage, which could cross you over to the Old World. For a wine-geek selection, you could go to the Arbois in eastern France. You are dealing with something vegetal in a region most consumers don't know. Jacques Puffeney makes a wonderful one.

Familiar: Merlot
Gateway: Col Solare, Columbia Valley, Washington state
Crossover: Avignonesi Desiderio Merlot, Tuscany, Italy
Wine-geek: Château Musar, Bekaa Valley, Lebanon

If you like Merlot, you'll like . . . a comfort wine. This says to me, "I'm a little insecure about what I order," so my recommendation is going to be restrained. First, instead of hopping continents, I might go to Washington state. Or I will look for a wine that is a blend of Merlot. Sometimes people are looking for a "name," so I mention Sassicaia: "Here's a $300 bottle of Merlot." Merlot is a simple, middle-of-the-road red wine. Italy has some nice examples, like Desiderio from Avignonesi, which has a bull on the label and appeals to the less sophisticated palate as well as the more sophisticated. Here we are changing continents but not grapes. You can go to a Tempranillo from Muga in Spain for a riper, softer, plush wine with not much tannin or dried fruit. Or try Termes from Numanthia. These are crossover wines that toe the line but still have character.

Familiar: California Cabernet Sauvignon
Gateway: Cheval des Andes, Argentina
Crossover: Numanthia-Termes, Toro, Spain
Wine-geek: Niepoort Batuta, Portugal

If you like Cabernet, you'll like . . . Niepoort [from Portugal]. This would be for the wine geek.

Familiar: Zinfandel
Gateway: d'Arenberg Laughing Magpie Shiraz/Viognier, Australia
Crossover: Martinet Bru Priorat, Spain
Wine-geek: Quinterelli Amarone, Italy

If you like Zinfandel, you'll like . . . some of the dry wines from the Douro region of Portugal.

CHOOSING A WINE BY . . . WHAT YOU USUALLY DRINK

If You Like . . .	You Might Also Like . . .
Bordeaux, red	Super Tuscans
Burgundy, red	Barolo
Burgundy, white	Chardonnay (esp. aged), Sylvaner (esp. aged)
Cabernet Sauvignon	Bordeaux (red), Cahors, Carignan, Châteauneuf-du-Pape, Gigondas, Grenache blends, Malbec, Merlot, Portuguese reds (esp. from the Douro), Ribera del Duero, Rioja, Syrah blends, Tannat, Tempranillo (esp. younger and/or from Toro)
Champagne, dry	cava, Crémant, Prosecco, Sekt, sparkling wine
Champagne, sweet	Brachetto d'Acqui, Moscato d'Asti
Chardonnay	Burgundy (white), Chablis (France), Chenin Blanc, Condrieu, Gewürztraminer, Italian white blends featuring Chardonnay, Malagousia, Marsanne, Meursault, Montrachet, Pinot Blanc, Pinot Gris (esp. Alsace), Roussanne, Viognier
Chianti	Barbera, Brunello
Gewürztraminer	Moschofilero, Pinot Gris, Riesling
Merlot	Bordeaux (red), Cabernet Sauvignon (medium-bodied), Malbec (esp. oaked), Nebbiolo, Ribera del Duero, Super Tuscans (Merlot-based), Tempranillo, Zinfandel
Pinot Grigio/Pinot Gris	Albariño, Arneis, Assyrtiko, Fiano, Kerner, Moschofilero, Riesling, Tocai, Tokai (Slovenia), Torrontés, Verdicchio
Pinot Noir	Barbera, Beaujolais (ripe), Brunello di Montalcino, Burgundy (red), Chinon, Ciro (Italy), Garnacha, Grenache, Nero d'Avola, Spätburgunder
Riesling	Albariño, Assyrtiko, Gewürztraminer, Grüner Veltliner, Moschofilero, Pinot Blanc, Pinot Gris, Scheurebe, Txakoli
Sauternes	Bonnezeaux, Monbazillac, Quarts de Chaume
Sauvignon Blanc	Albariño, Assyrtiko, Greco di Tufo, Grüner Veltliner, Moschofilero (unoaked), Pouilly-Fumé, Sancerre, Torrontés, Txakoli, unoaked Italian whites (esp. from northeastern Italy), Verdejo
Sauvignon Blanc, France	Sauvignon Blanc, South Africa
Sauvignon Blanc, New Zealand	Sauvignon Blanc, Chile
Shiraz	Châteauneuf-du-Pape, Nero d'Avola, Priorat, Ribera del Duero, sparkling Shiraz, Syrah, Tinta de Toro, Zinfandel
Zinfandel	Amarone, Châteauneuf-du-Pape, Gigondas, Greek reds, Portuguese reds (esp. from the Douro), Priorat, Shiraz

Sommeliers Sound Off on Branching Out from the Classics

In terms of wine passions, my style has never been obscure wines. I prefer the classics—like **California Chardonnay, New Zealand Sauvignon Blanc, Rioja, Burgundy,** and **Bordeaux.** When I want to try something new, I get excited about classics from other countries—like Portugal or South Africa—that just haven't hit the limelight yet.
—FERNANDO BETETA, MS, NOMI

When I worked at Babbo in New York City, we would sometimes get the "I only drink French wine" people. As we served only Italian wines, I had to translate their French preferences into comparable Italian wines:

• **Red Burgundy:** If they drank mature Burgundy, I would have them try a mature **Barolo.** The acid and tannin levels are different, but the aromatics are so similar that it would stupefy them. They would not believe me until they tried it.

• **White Burgundy:** If they drank Meursault, I would recommend **Trebbiano d'Abruzzo** from Valentini.

• **Red Bordeaux:** Here you have so many options, because you have all the **Super Tuscan** wines that aspire to Bordeaux. You have Sassicaia and other bolder wines that will do well.

It was not just a personal success, as I found I was also educating them out of their shell. I guarantee that the next time someone said to them, "I only drink **Burgundy,**" they would reiterate what I'd said to them verbatim.

It was not just Babbo that was changing the way guests looked at Italian wine, because there was a movement of other Italian restaurants that were changing the perception to "Italian wine is serious." It was fun to be there at that moment.
—ROBERT BOHR, COLICCHIO & SONS

If you like **white Burgundy,** you will like **Chardonnay** with some age. Those from the West Coast, Australia, and New Zealand can be as ripe as one from Burgundy—at one-third the price. Or try an aged **Sylvaner** because it will have some shoulders to it.

If you like **sweet Riesling,** try sweet **Chenin Blanc** from South Africa. Like Chenin Blanc from the Loire Valley, such as Savennières or Vouvray? Try dry Chenin Blanc from South Africa. It will be similar, but with different accents.

If you like **Cabernet Sauvignon**, try a **Grenache** blend or a **Syrah** blend. **Châteauneuf-du-Pape** is the place people love to go. There are appellations next to that like **Gigondas** and others that have depth and richness. Or try a younger-style **Tempranillo** from Spain.

Tell me what you want. How do you feel about white or red wine? Some people are sensitive to low alcohol and high acid or big tannin. I'll ask what they drink at home and then take them to the next level. If you like **Sauvignon Blanc** from **Bordeaux**, why don't we try one from **Napa**? If you like it from the West Coast, let's try **Chile.** Let's take the same grape and travel . . . maybe to **New Zealand**? I may bring them **Sancerre** because it is Sauvignon Blanc. A customer may know a country in general, so then I pinpoint an appellation. I take them to an appellation where I've been and where I know the father and son who have been making wine for generations, where I feel the wines are showing amazingly well and I can tell them why.

—STEPHANE COLLING, SAN YSIDRO RANCH

If you want something different from a California **Chardonnay** and you want to stay in a more opulent style, you can try a Rhône varietal, like **Marsanne** or **Roussanne,** from California or France—something with more weight and fruit that is rounder on the palate, with creamy tones.

If you like **Cabernet Sauvignon**, you'll find there are regions in the world that produce wines in a classic way and a modern way. Spain is definitely one, and **Tempranillo** from Toro is one. The fruit is complex, while the wine is full-bodied. It is a bit of an up-front wine with Old World complexity.

—MICHAËL ENGELMANN, GARY DANKO

I would take **Cabernet Sauvignon** fans to South America because it has a minerality that we don't get in Napa Valley Bordeaux varietals. Then I would introduce them to varietals from the Languedoc, such as **Tannat** and **Cahors,** which have an earthiness and fruitiness that tickle people. These grapes have a grip. From South America, I would recommend **Malbec.** Eventually, I would ease them into **Bordeaux.**

—JEFF BAREILLES, MANRESA

Customers are not going to come up to the bar and order a glass of **Ribera del Duero;** they are going to ask for something they know, like a glass of **Cab, Merlot,** or **Shiraz.** So our staff has to know the "synonyms" for those—that is, wines that taste similar that we have on our list. Customers are not going to ask for a glass of **Rueda,** but they will ask for a glass of **Sauvignon Blanc.** So here we use "synonyms" as an important part of our training.

- When people ask for **Pinot Grigio,** we consider the synonym a **Tokai** from Slovenia. Movia's is super-light, crisp, and gorgeous.

- The synonym for **Sauvignon Blanc** is Angel Rodriguez's wonderful **Verdejo** or a **Grüner Veltliner.**

- The synonym for **Shiraz** we use is a **Syrah** from Côte de Roussillon. Coume del Mas is a great producer whose Syrah and Grenache blend "Schistes" offers Shiraz seekers the same plushness, body, and warmth.

All of our restaurants are primarily Old World focused. Barbara Lynch, our chef-owner, trained first in Italy and then learned French technique before she opened No. 9 Park. We feature wines of France, Italy, Austria, Germany, Spain, and America. We don't try to cover the whole world.

—CAT SILIRIE, NO. 9 PARK

When guests are on the Cabernet page, and I see that there is nothing they are familiar with, I ask, "What do you typically drink? Is there a producer and style you like?" I'm going to say the "R" word here, referring to Rombauer, who is very influential among certain wine drinkers, but I don't think that style goes with our cuisine. It is fascinating that this has become some customers' measure of a wine. It reminds me of Freemark Abbey Cabernet, which was "the" wine in my day. I find that these Rombauer drinkers can be really kind of aggressive. They open the list, don't see it, and they frown. This is a recent phenomenon in the last ten years. A whole group of tasters will look at the list and say, "You don't have Rombauer **Chardonnay**—what do you have that is like that?" I may suggest a L'Angevin Chardonnay Charles Heintz from the Sonoma Coast. It has a little residual sugar, as does Rombauer, and that tends to pacify them. I know that the Rombauer people are not too adventurous. I am not going to get them into a Chenin Blanc from the Loire Valley that is more mineral-driven than fruit-driven. Interestingly enough, they may like a ripe, oaked, **Village-level Burgundy.**

—JEFF BAREILLES, MANRESA

Trust the sommeliers. They don't want to screw you. If people tell me they don't recognize anything on the Chardonnay page, I simply ask what they like. If they tell me they only drink Chateau Montelena, I know not to recommend Kistler, which is a big wine. Instead, I would recommend a Chablis from France. If someone wants something big, rich, and red, I'll ask if they care where it comes from. If they want big, rich, and spicy, I'll bring Priorat or peppery California Syrah.

—MARK MENDOZA, SONA

I try to get guests to try wines from unexpected places by the glass. When they're looking for a California **Cabernet Sauvignon** by the glass, I'll suggest they try the **Carignan**—or the elegant Seven Hills Cabernet from Washington state.

—CLAIRE PAPARAZZO, BLUE HILL

Barolo and Barbaresco are the king and the prince of Italian wines, as many people see it. When people eat Italian they also look for Pinot Grigio and Chianti. So if people ask for **Pinot Grigio**, we ask, "Are you looking for crisp, clean, dry Italian white?" So we will suggest instead a **Tocai** from Friuli or a **Kerner**, all of which make people happy. If guests ask for a **Chianti**, we know they want something with refreshing acid and low tannins that is easy to drink—and that would be **Barbera**. Barbera is so great with food like pasta with tomato sauce or antipasti.

—CAT SILIRIE, NO. 9 PARK

I have a number of **Zinfandel**s on our wine list. Instead of listing them separately, I list them in the "Native and Displaced" section so that people will automatically get a peek at some other things. This way they will see **Malbec**, which is really, really hot these days. They will see **Amarone**, which will also fill the needs of what a guest would hope to get from a Zinfandel. There are very few red wines that are full-bodied and that leave a little residual sugar. You will find it in some Australian Shiraz as well as California Cabernet and Merlot—but Zinfandel and Amarone are true expressions of what it should be. For California guests, Amarone is not the first place they are going to look for a wine. In New York it would be the opposite—for that guest, I would suggest a Zinfandel. A Zinfandel drinker in L.A. I would lead toward an Amarone, as they both have that hint of sweetness, while Amarone has just a little more earthiness.

—DANA FARNER, CUT

CHOOSING A WINE BY . . . STYLE

People who like **crisp white wines** typically don't drink enough **sherry**.
—FERNANDO BETETA, MS, NOMI

If someone wants a Cabernet, I'll ask, "Do you want it on the less fruity or the more fruity side?" **Once people realize that it is all a continuum, and that they are simply here or there, they realize that they are never wrong.** Everyone has a preference and will pick more fruity or less fruity. If they want more fruit they can go to California; for less fruit they can go to Bordeaux.
—VANESSA BOYD, PHILIPPE

If You Like . . .	You Might Also Like . . .
Sparkling wines	cava, Champagne, Crémant, Prosecco, Sekt
Crisp, fresh, light white wines	Albariño, Assyrtiko, Chablis, Chasselas, Chenin Blanc, Frascati, Müller-Thurgau, Muscadet, Orvieto, Pinot Bianco, Pinot Blanc, Pinot Grigio, Rioja (white), Sauvignon Blanc, Savennières, sherry (esp. fino), Soave, Sylvaner, Trebbiano, Verdicchio, Vinho Verde, Viura
Juicy, aromatic, soft white wines	Albariño, Arneis, Chenin Blanc, Falanghina, Fiano, Gewürztraminer, Grüner Veltliner, Moschofilero, Müller-Thurgau, Muscat, Pinot Blanc, Pinot Gris, Riesling, Sancerre, Sauvignon Blanc, Torrontés, Verdejo, Vermentino, Viognier
Full, opulent, rich white wines	Chardonnay (oaked), Chassagne-Montrachet, Fumé Blanc, Gewürztraminer, Greco di Tufo, Marsanne, Meursault, Pouilly-Fuissé, Rioja (white—Reserva, Gran Reserva), Roussanne, Sauvignon Blanc (oaked), Sémillon, Viognier (oaked, e.g., California)
Fruity, lively, juicy, soft red wines	Barbera, Bardolino, Beaujolais, Cabernet Franc, Dolcetto, Gamay, Grenache, Lambrusco, Merlot, Pinot Noir (New World), Pinotage, Sagrantino di Montefalco, Spätburgunder, Valpolicella
Mild, ripe, smooth red wines	Barbera, Carménère, Chianti, Dornfelder, Malbec, Merlot, Nero d'Avola, Pinot Noir, Rioja, Sangiovese, Tempranillo, Vino Nobile de Montepulciano
Dense, powerful, rich red wines	Barbaresco, Barolo, Brunello, Cabernet Sauvignon, Mourvèdre, Nebbiolo, Petite Sirah, Shiraz, Syrah, Zinfandel
Sweet wines	Banyuls, Barsac, ice wine, Madeira, Maury, Muscat, Muscat de Beaumes-de-Venise, port, Riesling (sweet—Auslese, Beerenauslese, Trockenbeerenauslese), Sauternes, sweet sherry, Tokaji, Vin Santo

VANESSA BOYD

A Wine Relationship Is Give-and-Take

Once you're at the table, it's important to be open to and aware of what the wine has to offer to you. A glass of wine is a living, breathing thing, and a great glass of wine can be almost as fascinating a dinner companion as any other.

Andy Myers, CityZen

A great wine meets me halfway. I have something to say to it and it has something to say to me. At that point there is a beautiful connection between man and wine.

It has to do with the style of wine I like, one with a somewhat demure personality. It holds a little something back. A Burgundy is a great example of this. I poured one that was really forward and just great after opening. It expanded over the course of the meal, giving more of itself as time went on. As a person, you give more of yourself to it. If we are both receptive, polite, and in agreement, we both end up a little better at the end of the exchange.

I have been chasing the first wine that I ever loved. It was a Burgundy, and I know now that it probably was not as great as I thought it was at the time. Yet I will always chase that feeling. The harder you try to grab that "I-am-going-to-have-this-experience-with-the-wine," the less likely you are to get it. If you are relaxed and open, if you stop trying to have a moment with the wine, if you let wine happen—it will happen. With great wine there is something that I don't think you can quantify. Even if you could, who would want to? I believe in magic that way.

There is so much happening in a great bottle of wine. From the acidity, to the tannins, to the minerality, to the fruit—there are a thousand little nooks and crannies that your brain can go into just for a second if it needs to.

There are times when a wine makes your attention perk up, and it can happen a hundred times in the same glass. I'll be thinking about how the acid is really pretty, followed by "I'm sorry, honey . . . You were saying?" to my wife over dinner. Then later in the glass, there is a note of apple that's really cool, and this is not happening in some super-geek "I-have-to-analyze-this-wine" way. I don't get that same level of complexity and whimsy from any other spirit.

What's in a Name?

In most of Europe—often referred to in wine circles as the **Old World**—people commonly refer to wines by their **place of origin.** Champagne is a *place* in France that happens to specialize in elegant sparkling wines. Chianti is a *place* in Italy that happens to specialize in tart red wines that pair perfectly with tomato sauce. Rioja is a *place* in Spain that happens to specialize in red wines that pair beautifully with roasted red meats.

In other parts of the world—often referred to in wine circles as the **New World**—we commonly refer to wines by the **type of grape** from which they're made. In the United States, we talk about Chardonnay wine, made from Chardonnay *grapes*, which create a full-bodied white wine. Cabernet Sauvignon is made from Cabernet Sauvignon *grapes*, which create a full-bodied red wine.

In this country, where soft drinks like Coke and Pepsi are still frequently drunk with afternoon and evening meals, people love talking about *brands.* Because of this predisposition, beginning wine enthusiasts invariably ask us to recommend particular winemakers as a shortcut to wines that are worth seeking out. In the chapters that follow, we sometimes suggest specific producers to help you get started. In return, we ask that you gain enough mastery of wine to evolve beyond our (or anyone else's) initial suggestions, so that you don't miss out on wines that are just as delicious—if not much more!

Many sommeliers mention that wine drinkers tend to get too set in their ways regarding what they like to drink, so they miss out on a lot of pleasure. When you are starting out, there is nothing wrong with identifying vintners whose wines you tend to enjoy. Just make sure that doing so doesn't get in the way of the immense pleasure of discovering others.

Raj Vaidya, Daniel

There are a lot of wines that people ask for because they are familiar. They have seen the same bottle everywhere, so it becomes second nature to order it. In a country where Coke, Pepsi, and 7-Up dominate the marketplace, it's not surprising that American consumers are brand-dependent. It provides a sense of comfort. If there is a sommelier "pet peeve," it is that we wish people would be more open to trying something new rather than following the brands they have been told by the media to like.

Chris Miller, Spago

There is something really integral and definitive about comfort wines. They are consistent over the years. Vintage to vintage, you almost always get the same wine. If you could freeze time around bottles of Shafer Cabernet from 1996 to 2005, I am not sure any of them would taste that different. The same goes for other wines as well.

Of course there have been innovations, but Shafer has delivered a consistently good product at a somewhat reasonable price. Customers always had to pay a slight premium for Shafer, but nothing that took it out of their price range. People feel good about the purchase because they are getting a good bottle of wine. Shafer Merlot is $85 on my list, and that is a nice bottle of wine to me, and their Cabernet is in the mid-hundreds and is also a nice bottle of wine.

These wines are going to be great time and again. Guests don't have to think about it, or spend a lot of time with the list. They don't have to worry, "Is the sommelier going to understand me?" or "Am I going to get this wine?" There is also the reaction of guests at the table: "He's going big tonight, he bought the Leonetti . . ." or "It's a special occasion, and Rob is doing well by us tonight . . ." These people could spend twice as much on something they don't know, and they would just not have the same passion.

Cat Silirie, No. 9 Park

I avoid brands across the board. A restaurant can get around using big-name wines by offering really kind, open hospitality, which adds value and discovery. Most guests are not adventurous or experienced, even in big cities. A lot of people are tentative about wine, and they stick to their brands. It is our job as sommeliers to make people feel safe if they do decide to be adventurous.

Instead of trying to find a specific brand of Italian wine, I recommend seeking out a specific DOC [*Denominazione di Origine Controllata*, or quality-designated wine region]. If you love Tuscany and Chianti, that is great; next, try to experience different styles of Chianti. In Italy I feel there is more expression in the *place* than in the *brand*. I love the feeling of place, while another wine buyer may love finding all the cult wines made by a particular man or woman.

We don't have a Chardonnay per se by the glass, but we have always had Chablis [made of Chardonnay grapes in the Chablis region]. We love Chablis. We have had Massachusetts oysters on the menu since the day we opened. One all-time classic pairing with oysters is Chardonnay, but it is certainly an elegant, non-oaked, mineral-style of Chardonnay [like Chablis].

We have a barrel-fermented white from Graves, but people never sit down and say "May I have a half-Sauvignon and half-Sémillon?" They ask for "Chardonnay," meaning they want a full-bodied white. However, that does not mean they have to have that particular grape variety.

It is the same with brands. If someone tells us they drink Kendall-Jackson Chardonnay, we know their wine should have some round mouthfeel and evidence of oak barrel. In this situation, an oaked Graves will work better than an unoaked Chablis.

People end up saying, "I didn't know Chardonnay could be this elegant," or "I didn't know Burgundy was Chardonnay," or "I didn't know Chablis was Chardonnay . . . It is refreshing, elegant, and round"—they have made a discovery.

You have to be extremely nice to people while helping them make the transition. You can't come down from on high! One customer recently told me he loves my wine list because it is as much about what we *don't* have as about what we *do* have. If you have all the big brands, you can't tell people they can't order them. By *not* having the big brands on the list, it gives us a chance to connect.

OLD WORLD VS. NEW WORLD

When wine enthusiasts speak of Old World wines, they're referring to wines from Europe—especially France, Italy, Germany, Spain, Portugal, and Austria—while New World wines are those from the United States, Chile, Argentina, Australia, New Zealand, South Africa, and other non-European wine-producing countries.

Here are a few rules of thumb to help you remember the general differences in flavors and philosophies:

Characteristic	Old World	New World
Roots	Tradition	Technology
Values	Vintage/*Terroir*	Consistency
Climate	Cooler	Warmer
Acidity	Higher	Lower
Alcohol	Lower	Higher
Body	Lighter	Fuller
Flavor	Earthiness	Fruitiness
Aging potential	Longer	Shorter

At No. 9 Park, the food is French and Italian. While there are very, very few California Cabernets, there are many French and Italian wines, because they complement the style of cooking. Very often a group of businessmen will start riffling through the wine list and get a little huffy because they don't recognize many of the big reds on our list. There is no Jordan, no Silver Oak, and they are really thrown for a loop. We don't do this to make people feel uncomfortable or to be contrary. We tell people that ours might not be wines they know but that they will be very comfortable with the wines' styles and flavor profiles—and they may enjoy discovering them.

We had some hockey players come in who had planned on drinking Cabernet, but soon, they were drinking a pretty expensive Dorigo Refosco from Friuli. It is a super-structured, beautifully made red wine. They had so much fun because they were drinking something Italian that they did not expect and had never seen before. This also happened to another regular, and it is now "his" wine.

We never want anyone to feel "wrong" about what they like. We make it very clear that this is our point of view and that we offer some wines that deserve to be discovered. Wine needs to be a discovery.

WHAT SOMMELIERS KNOW: STRATEGIES AND SECRETS FOR MASTERING WINE

It is not necessary to know about wine to appreciate it; what there is to know, beyond the glamour of vintage, producer and varietal, is in the glass in front of your nose.

—PAUL BERTOLLI AND ALICE WATERS, *CHEZ PANISSE COOKING* (1988)

We wholeheartedly agree with Alice Waters and Paul Bertolli that you don't have to know anything about a wine in order to enjoy it. And we'd add a corollary: you can *enhance* your appreciation of a wine with *more* knowledge of it.

Roxane Shafaee-Moghadam of The Breakers in Palm Beach, Florida, recalls, "A few years out of college, I had a friend over for dinner. I offered to cook pork chops, so she offered to bring the wine, a bottle a family friend had given her as a graduation present. It turned out to be a 1983 Château Ducru-Beaucaillou, a second-growth Bordeaux. The 1983 was not a legendary vintage like the 1982, but it was still a good year. Of course we didn't know that. My first impression was simply, 'This is *old!*' I was excited, and I remember thinking to be careful as I took the cork out. I didn't know to decant it, so we drank the dregs, which were enormous—we also didn't know not to do that.

"I was intrigued by it. I had lots of wine books around, but this was the first time I 'researched' a particular wine. I looked up Saint-Julien, where it was from, and I read about the 1983 vintage. I even found the Ducru estate on the map. I thought, 'Wow, this is really good—I'm going to look for more!' Then I found out how naive I was. We did not know that it was pretty rare and expensive. But we discovered all on our own that it was wonderful, and how special it was. The label is very distinctive: It is orange with a gold rim and a drawing of the chateau. Every time I see the label, it humbles me. It is always a touchstone for me, a reminder of how far I've come since the first time I tasted that wine. This is the bottle that began the process of my understanding wine."

STRATEGIES FOR MASTERING FLAVOR

We hear of the conversion of water into wine at the marriage in Cana as of a miracle. But this conversion is, through the goodness of God, made every day before our eyes. Behold the rain which descends from heaven upon our vineyards; there it enters the roots of the vines, to be changed into wine: a constant proof that God loves us, and loves to see us happy.

—BENJAMIN FRANKLIN

Wine is, in essence, simply fermented grape juice. But one of the many wonders to be found in a glass of wine is the countless number of flavors it can contain other than grapes—from lime to cherries to mushrooms to tobacco.

We hope we've begun to whet your appetite for learning more about the winemaking process, which is explored at length in other books on wine (see the recommendations in Chapter 7). Here, we'll provide a simple overview of some of the key factors that influence the way a wine tastes.

As suggested by Waters and Bertolli's reference to "varietal," "vintage," and "producer," there are three primary factors that determine a wine's flavor. Through our conversations with sommeliers, we've come to think of them as the three G's:

1. **Grapes:** The variety (or varieties, in the case of a blend) and quality of the grapes used to make the wine.
2. **God, or Ground, if you prefer:** The goodness of the Creator of the **earth** those grapevines are planted in, along with the **rain** and **wind** (which, when they get out of hand, are called "acts of God") and the surrounding climate during the year the grapes were harvested (which is represented by the date given on the bottle, also known as the vintage).
3. **Guy or Gal:** The winemaker's hand and the decisions he or she makes during the winemaking process (such as the level of ripeness at harvest and whether to use oak barrels or not).

Scott Calvert of The Inn at Little Washington in Virginia ventures a guess that each factor is responsible for roughly a third of any wine's flavor. Expounding on these influences further, he uses a painter's analogy.

"The grape variety gives you the basic 'color palette' of what a wine tastes like," he explains. "Then the winery's climate, site, and soil give you the intensity of those colors. Finally, vineyard practices and winemaking give you the brush strokes.

"You have to know a place to know its wine," he continues. "My formula describes a place in geographical, topographical, climatic, and even cultural terms. When you add up the grape variety + climate + vineyard site + soils + vineyard practices + winemaking, it equals the sum total of what the wine should taste like. Once you research each of these points, you develop a good mental picture of that wine."

While it varies for individual wines, the relative importance of each of the G's to wine in general is a matter of opinion. For years Americans placed much more emphasis on the grape variety and the winemaking process. But over the past five to ten years, the French concept of *terroir* [tair-WAHR, referring to the special characteristics imparted by the soil, climate, and more] has been increasingly embraced in the United States.

"If you talk to people in the Old World, they hardly understand the concept of grape varieties," Calvert explains. "Instead, they think of place. If you ask someone living in the town of Orange, really close to Châteauneuf-du-Pape, 'What are the grapes growing over there?' they don't know. They only know they are the grapes used to make Châteauneuf-du-Pape. They know it is a blend, but they are not certain what types of grapes are in it. They are, however, certain of two things: that the wine came from *this place* and that it was made by *this person*.

"In the United States, when we think of wine, we'll say things like, 'I'm a big Cabernet Sauvignon (grape) fan.' But the Old World is different — it's 'I'm a big Bordeaux (region) fan,' or Châteauneuf-du-Pape (region) fan, or Rhône (region) fan. It is a totally different perspective because they don't think about the grape variety.

"Nowadays, it is nice to bring the two perspectives together, because they both have validity. *Everything* is important to wine and how it is made. If you think the

grape is most important, you have to remember that grapes are the product of *terroir*. Winemaking is important because it can adjust certain flavors, but it is what you get from the place, the soil, and the climate that you are adjusting. So both affect the finished product.

"Until recently, many wineries made as wide a range of wines as they could for economic reasons. Many places in this country planted more kinds of grapes than could ripen rather than finding the best place for each variety. Now that is changing even in California, where you don't see as much Zinfandel and Petite Sirah growing right in Napa; you see it growing up north and closer to the coast.

"The better places for Cabernet are growing that grape more exclusively, and the better places for Pinot aren't doing much else. It's beginning to look like the Old World, where [by law] one place makes one type of wine."

John Ragan of Eleven Madison Park in New York City has witnessed the same phenomenon: "California has now really started to figure out what grows well where. You think of Bordeaux and Burgundy as separate entities in France. It is important to think of Napa Valley and Sonoma as two separate entities as well. You need to think about what grows well where."

- When you think of Chardonnay and Pinot Noir, think Sonoma.
- When you think of Cabernet Sauvignon and Merlot, think Napa.
- When you think of Syrah, think Sonoma Coast.

Ragan continues, "When you break California down to smaller parts, it is more digestible. Learning about wine in Europe can be challenging for people who are used to New World ways—'You mean to tell me they can't [by law] grow any red grapes but Pinot Noir in Burgundy? That seems stupid.' Conversely, understanding California wine can be tough for a European: 'If it says Napa Valley, what grape is it? What do you mean it can be whatever they want it to be? That's not fair—how am I supposed to know?'

"A Californian will say, 'You just know, because Opus One is Cabernet-based.' The Burgundy guy will say, 'You just know that Musigny is Pinot Noir.' It is two different mind-sets. In the not-so-distant future, California may end up being like the Old World. When you say 'Sonoma' and the wine is white, it will be Chardonnay, and if it is red it will be Pinot Noir. In fifty years, Napa may mean Bordeaux-style wine."

GRAPES: THE FRUIT ITSELF

It all starts with the grapes. No grapes, no wine. A grape is simply pulp (mostly water and some sugar), skin, and seeds. Add a bit of yeast, the right land and weather, and some winemaking know-how, and the right grapes can be transformed into a good or even great wine.

In Chapter 2 we covered how particular grapes produce wines of varying color, weight, volume, acidity, astringency, and—cumulatively—*flavors*. Just as you can count on your favorite fruits and flavors to lead you to various wines, you can also do the reverse—that is, you can often, if not always, find certain flavors in wines made from certain wine grapes.

For many people, the first question after deciding whether you're in the mood for white wine or red wine is, Which grape? Are you in the mood for a lighter-bodied, fruitier Pinot Noir or a fuller-bodied and more tannic Cabernet? The type of grape is your first clue to what you're likely to find in the bottle.

Going back to the six Noble Grapes, you can generally turn to the following wines for these signature flavors:

- Riesling — Flowers, lime, minerals, peaches
- Sauvignon Blanc — Grass, grapefruit, herbs, lemon
- Chardonnay — Apples, butter, pears, vanilla
- Pinot Noir — Cherries, raspberries, strawberries, violets
- Merlot — Blackberries, black cherries, plums, vanilla
- Cabernet Sauvignon — Blackberries, black currants, cedar, dark chocolate

While some states have their own even stricter standards, by U.S. law a wine labeled as a particular grape variety (a varietal) must consist of at least 75 percent of that variety. For example, a wine labeled Cabernet Sauvignon must contain at least three-quarters Cabernet Sauvignon grapes, even though many Cabs contain as much as 25 percent of other grapes (often Merlot) to soften the wine's tannins.

Grapes as Part of a Blend

While most wines you'll encounter will be labeled with a single grape, many wines are blended from several different grapes. Blended wines show off multiple grapes in such a way that the whole is greater than the sum of its parts. The world-renowned wine style Châteauneuf-du-Pape from the Rhône region of France is a blend of up to thirteen different grapes. More than one hundred grapes are authorized to be made into port, a single bottle of which can contain as many as forty varieties.

While Parmesan cheese is delicious on its own, when it's blended with basil, pine nuts, and olive oil to make pesto, the synergy of these compatible flavors creates something even more delicious than the individual ingredients. Similarly, think of a blended wine as a "recipe" that shows off the individual characteristics of different grapes, such as the acidity of Barbera, the fruitiness of Cabernet Franc, the aromas and richness of Cabernet Sauvignon, and the deep color and full body of Petite Sirah.

Michael Flynn of The Mansion on Turtle Creek in Dallas observes: "In Texas, people are more oriented to brands—and in wine that means they are a little slavish to the grape variety. They want the big Cabernet or Chardonnay, and they disregard blends in many cases. We decided to prove to people through a wine tasting that they shouldn't ignore them. We poured a Tablas Creek Esprit de Beaucastel rouge from California, which is a southern-Rhône-style red wine blend, along with a Châteauneuf-du-Pape—the real thing. We also poured a Chianti Classico and a Bordeaux.

"People tasted the wines blind. The Bordeaux didn't show very well because it was tannic and had a typical earthy or barnyardy characteristic that was a little hard to get over—even though I had decanted it an hour in advance for that very reason. They liked the others a lot, including the Chianti and the Châteauneuf-du-Pape. Right out of the bottle, the Châteauneuf-du-Pape showed less tannin and more of that pretty wild raspberry fruit and a touch of pepper and leather. To palates used to the softness of ripe California wines, that seemed like an easy stretch. They also liked the California Beaucastel as well, which is a Grenache, Mourvèdre, and Syrah blend.

"The reason for blends has to do with farmers' hedging their bets. There was an economic incentive in some regions to ensure that you had a product that could go to market every year. Even if the house style might change slightly from one year to the next, this or that Bordeaux estate could always rely on one of their *cépages* [principal grape varieties] ripening properly and being the lead player in the blend, while the others might be a little weaker that year and play second fiddle. Ultimately, the varieties were well suited for one another, so you would get a felicitous blend each year."

Some blends are so felicitous that they can be used to wow customers. After she recommended a Gramercy Cellars Tempranillo from Washington state, Dana Farner of CUT recalls: "The guests were so happy and excited that they asked for another bottle of something else that was different. That was great, but a little tough to figure out what other unusual thing to come up with that could match the depth of the Tempranillo. Luckily, I had the Merkin Vineyards Chupacabra from Maynard James Keenan, the lead singer of Tool. It is a wine made in Arizona that is enormous, with crazy ripe fruit and lots of layers of complexity. He does not disclose the blend, so I am not sure what is in it, but the guests just loved it. I really wanted something esoteric that was still full and rich. I was able to give these people a great experience at a reasonable price, since both these wines are under $80, and they were thrilled and blown away."

GOD: EARTH + WIND + RAIN + MORE

The three main neutral grape varieties are Chardonnay, Pinot Gris, and Pinot Blanc. If you don't like Chardonnay from California, don't give up on Chardonnay from Chablis. If you don't like Pinot Gris from Italy, don't be afraid to drink Pinot Gris from Alsace. These are wines that are really camouflaged by the areas they come from. California tastes like California, and Italy tastes like Italy. If you taste Pinot Gris from Alsace, Pinot Grigio from Italy, and Pinot Gris from Oregon, all three will taste very different.

—HRISTO ZISOVSKI, AI FIORI

Why should you care where a wine is made? Are there really differences when grapes of the same type are grown in different places?

When it comes to wine, there is a chicken-and-egg quandary: is it the grapes that celebrate the ground they're grown in, or is it the ground that celebrates the grapes? In truth, the two work in tandem, and the best winemakers find a way to bring out the best in both.

The French have been brilliant at promoting *place* as the primary reason to value a wine. To the French, it is not flavor, not alcohol, not intensity, not color, but

the sense of truth that comes through in a wine because of its sense of place. Once you understand this, you'll find that wines that express their *terroir* can be the most intellectually delicious wines.

Here we want to get you started thinking about how the place where the grapes for your bottle of wine were grown—the ground, the slope of the hill, the weather and more, known collectively as *terroir*—affect its flavor. (For more on this vast topic, see the recommendations for further reading in Chapter 7.) Again, a few of the key components of *terroir* include:

- *Ground:* Everything from the composition of the soil to the presence or absence of pebbles and stones affects the vines, and thus the flavor of the wine.

- *Slope:* The angle of the hill (from 0 degrees to 90 degrees) affects the way the sun hits it, and that affects the growth of the vines, which influences the flavor of the wine.

- *Weather:* The climate of the region where the vines are grown matters, as does the micro-climate of the winery, which can vary even between vineyards right next to each other.

"Climate is huge when it comes to understanding styles of wines," says Sabato Sagaria of The Little Nell in Aspen, Colorado. "I liken growing grapes to growing fruits or tomatoes. The cooler the climate, the more difficult it is to ripen them—so you will have higher acids, and the wines will be brighter, fresher, and crisper. Look at Germany, Austria, and New Zealand, where you get high-acid whites. If you look at a tomato from a warmer climate, it will be juicier and riper—and warmer climates are also where you get fuller-bodied Zinfandels, Shiraz, and Cabernet."

To recap: what does it mean if a region has a cool climate? Look at a green tomato versus a ripe one: the green one had less sunlight and was picked earlier. Burgundy (where French Chardonnay is made) is colder, so the wines have more acid, less alcohol, more crispness, less body and, because they are from the Old World, less fruitiness than New World wines.

It's possible to use the same thinking to contemplate the differences between Chardonnay from France (a cooler region) with Chardonnay from California (a warmer region). California Chardonnay tastes the way it does because it is from a warm-climate region. Warm regions produce grapes with a lot of sugar, and when they are fermented, they produce wines with a lot of alcohol. So a Napa Chardonnay will have a lot of alcohol and will be fuller-bodied. And because oak barrels are often used in the winemaking process, it will often have oak flavors. Lastly, since it is from the New World, it will be fruity. California wines are usually rounder, more buttery, usually higher in alcohol, usually going more to tropical fruit. French Chardonnay (white Burgundy), if it has oak, has more of a roasted-nut quality and more apple and pear fruit.

In France alone, you can taste the difference in climate from north to south. Wines from the north are fragile, delicate, and floral. They are a little drier, since there is less sun, and they have more mineral notes—so these wines work best early in a meal. They also have less oak and more petrol—a petroleum-like note

Dennis Kelly of The French Laundry on Tasting the *Terroir* of Napa Valley Cabernet

Cabernet Sauvignon is so powerful and accepts oak so well that there is less variation in the winemaking techniques in California. However, we had a lot of success [at a tasting with fellow sommeliers] differentiating Cabs made in Howell Mountain versus Spring Mountain versus Oakville.

- **Howell Mountain:** We all expected this wine to be brambly and powerful, and because it is a mountain, we expected great structure, high acidity, and firm tannin. It certainly delivered, and we all knew it was Howell Mountain.

- **Spring Mountain:** It is mountain fruit, so it has good structure. It tends to be slightly less rustic and more polished, with elegance.

- **Oakville:** Oakville is one of my favorite appellations in the valley [it is located primarily on the valley floor]. Some of the most famous wines in the valley come from here, with **Screaming Eagle** [a prized cult Cabernet] being one. These wines are very site-specific, and they tend to be very complex, with dusty earth qualities. If they come from Aiken soil [a rare red soil known to produce berry-scented wines] they tend to have a nice blend of black fruit, which we expect from Cabernet, but they also tend to be very high-toned, with red fruit as well, which lends complexity and elegance to the wine.

Scott Calvert of The Inn at Little Washington on Discovering That Wine Is Not Solely About the Grape

I learned in Burgundy that wines are not solely about the grapes they're made from, which is why I love Burgundy so much. If you spend any time there, as you walk around the vineyards you learn what they are doing, then you eventually go to a winery's tasting room and taste some wine. At some point you can't help but notice the same kinds of smells in your glass as in the mud on your shoes. That could also be said about the next place over, so close I could throw a stone at it, yet it was different. That is how I came up with my approach.

Contrasting Two Wines from Burgundy

Take two places that are almost at opposite ends of the spectrum in Burgundy: **Côte de Nuits** versus **Côte de Beaune.** For Côte de Beaune, the quintessential wine is Pommard, particularly in little places like Grands Épenots, which is one of my favorite spots. Those wines almost always smell and taste like the dirt there, and that dirt has a real mushroomy, gray-clay quality.

For Côte de Nuits, I would go to Chambolle-Musigny. Les Amoureuses is an incredible vineyard, which is Premier Cru [first growth] but should be Grand Cru, the highest classification, above Premier Cru; it is quintessential Chambolle-Musigny. The soil has a little iron in it, so the wines can have a slightly bloody scent. The wines are bigger, rounder, and a lot more forward because of the aspect of the vineyard. This wine has lots of red fruit, as opposed to the darker fruits of Pommard.

These two wines represent opposite ends of the Burgundy spectrum: You have the dirty, earthy, dark, but delicate side of Pommard, and the meaty, rounder, fruity side of Amoureuses Chambolle.

sometimes perceived in wine—on the nose. In the south of France, you have more sun and spice and bold aromatics. The wines are much riper—less floral, but more fruity. Some people believe that the French or the Europeans have a lock on *terroir,* that there is no such thing in New World winemaking.

"However," points out Michael Flynn of The Mansion on Turtle Creek in Dallas, "California does have *terroir;* it is just not the taste of dirt, and it is not usually minerality [as it is in the Old World]. It tastes more of the bright sun and the ripeness of the fruit. That is uniquely Californian in terms of *terroir.* You could argue some of the same points in regard to Australian or South African wines. *Terroir* does not mean just the taste of soil or mineral. It has to do with that, of course, but it also has to do with the particular microclimate, the number of sunny days, the angle of the slope, the drainage of the soil, and also the hand of man, which many people discount altogether. The decisions that generations of winemakers have made, for hundreds of years—these things also figure in the concept of *terroir.*

"At a wine tasting, we talk about minerality in some wines and fruit in others. People can taste the difference between New World and Old World winemaking. You can see the light bulbs go on over their heads. I'm sure most people haven't even thought about that difference. They just like what they like and don't understand why. But the people in our tastings typically have a preference for one or the other, and they can decide in the exercise whether they have an Old World sense of taste or a New World sense of taste."

Michael Flynn suggests this exercise in tasting *terroir*—trying two reds and two whites side by side:

• **Two reds:** Try an inexpensive Spanish Tempranillo-based red from Juan Gil or Vinos Sin-Ley alongside an Argentina Malbec from Pascual Toso, which is a phenomenal value. (His Reserva is around $15 retail, and it's a great example of what Argentine Malbec is all about.) You have two full-bodied red wines with moderate tannin but two completely different personalities. Malbec speaks more of the sun than it does the soil, and quite the opposite is true of the Spanish wine.

- **Two whites:** Sauvignon Blanc is probably the easiest to work through. Take a Château Graville-Lacoste, which is a Graves [from the Bordeaux region]. Stack that up against Murphy-Goode "The Fumé" Sauvignon Blanc [from Sonoma, California]. Both wines have a little touch of wood. The Graville has a touch of Sémillon, but both show a ripe side to their personality and also a nice figgy/melon-y characteristic, too. The Graville will show minerality on the finish, while you will get much less of that with the grapefruit-noted California wine.

The Importance of Vintage

The first wine I fell in love with was a 1995 Chateau Ste. Michelle Chardonnay from Washington state. I was in Charleston with girlfriends, and a sommelier recommended it. I remember thinking it was so different and delicious, and I loved it. When I got back to school, I bought some at a grocery store. The only vintage they had was a 1996, so I bought it anyway and thought it wasn't as good—which is how I learned firsthand about the impact of vintage on wine.

—INEZ RIBUSTELLO, ON THE SQUARE

In the United States, at least 95 percent of the grapes used to make a bottle of wine must be harvested in a single year in order to name that year as a vintage on the label. The vintage distinguishes the same wine by a winemaker from year to year and provides a snapshot of that year.

Roxane Shafaee-Moghadam, The Breakers

When I worked at Tribeca Grill in Manhattan, I once opened a bottle of one of the top selections of Josef Leitz Riesling from the Rosenberg Vineyard in the Rheingau from 2003, which was a very hot year.

I opened it because we had guests who always ordered the 2004 and never the 2003. At the time I thought they were just being a little weird, which shows you how little I knew. I tasted the 2003 and thought, "I really don't like this wine. It is clean, clear, bright fruit, but just not my style."

I thought more about it and decided to open the 2004. That vintage is cooler, more classic, noted for a lot of acidity, especially in Riesling. I tasted it and instantly understood vintage. The wines tasted nothing alike. They looked exactly the same in the glass, smelled similar, and were from the same-sized bottle, but they were completely different.

This is one of the reasons they call Riesling transparent to *terroir* and vintage: there is no way you could taste those wines and not know they were Riesling—and there was no way you could not taste them together and not know how very different the years were.

Drinking Wine at the Right Time

Wine lovers can consult vintage charts for expert opinions of the best vintages from the particular region they're interested in. However, that's only part of the story. An equally important part is when to drink each vintage.

"Who right now [in 2009] would drink a 2005 Latour?" asked Aldo Sohm of Le Bernardin in New York City rhetorically. "It is pointless, because you would get only half the experience.

"Many people rely just on their vintage charts. They come into our restaurant with their little vintage chart and pick the high-rated vintage. This will be a problem, especially with red wine. Take the 2002 vintage, which has great ratings—but they are not showing at their best right now. If you store the 2002 another ten years, *then* they will be great. The guest who orders the 2002 *today* is spending *more* money for a *lesser* experience.

"I will suggest to guests that they try the 2001 instead, because they will pay 20 percent less and get 20 percent more enjoyment over the 2002. The 2004 vintage got terrible reviews upon release, but the wines are showing well now. So you can have a lot of pleasure and save a lot of money. I can be a little obnoxious on the floor trying to make this point. Raveneau is one of the best producers of Chablis, without a doubt. The reviews of the 1997 vintage were terrible, and you would generally never order a 1997 Chablis. Raveneau wine, however, is fantastic! These wines are gorgeous—even from this so-called terrible vintage. I told a customer to try it: 'If you don't like it, I need a wine for my dinner anyway . . . but I guarantee you will love it.' And he did. He saved a lot of money because other people were only paying attention to that stupid vintage chart that said to avoid ordering 1997 Chablis. Some charts, like Hugh Johnson's and Robert Parker's, show the vintage *and* the drinkability. The problem is that people still focus too much on the rating, and not the issue of drinkability."

Although the vintage can indicate which year's wines are likely to have the longest aging potential, a great winemaker typically makes wine you'll want to drink year after year. That's why you want to understand the influence of the winemakers.

GUY/GAL: THE INFLUENCE OF THE WINEMAKER

Get to know the **winemaker**. . . . Is he steadfast, true to his principles, devoted first to wine and next to profit? This was how I found the great wines that you could depend on year in and year out—by finding the great producers.

—SERGIO ESPOSITO, *PASSION ON THE VINE* (2008)

We know, we know—you want to *drink* wine, not *make* wine. Why should you bother learning about winemaking? What effect do the winemakers' decisions have on the flavor of their wines?

Few professionals we can think of, other than chef-restaurateurs, have to master as many skills as winemakers. They must be farmers, chefs, scientists, and entrepreneurs, all rolled into one. Their work necessitates drawing on both sides of their brains, the creative side as well as the analytical.

Many vintners count intuition among the secrets of their winemaking success. "I stop and listen to the fruit," says Chuck Reininger of Reininger Winery in Washington state. "My greatest tools are my palate and my intuition," which he uses to determine how to capture and enhance the best of that fruit in his wines. Reininger's palate registers the flavor, and he uses numbers (such as pH levels) as guidelines, but he ultimately lets his intuitive, artisanal side steer his decisions about when to pick the grapes and how to ferment them to create the balance he's seeking.

Brad McCarthy of Virginia's Blenheim Vineyards credits "100 percent" of his winemaking success to intuition, which he uses to "see" the path his grapes will take from the vineyard to the bottle to the table. "Intuition comes in as you look at

the grapes on the crush pad and ask, 'What are they going to be?' At that moment, I am instantaneously eighteen months down the road pouring a tasting for the wine buyer at Charlie Trotter's [in Chicago] and hearing, 'We'll take it all if you give it more structure and intensity.' " He uses intuition to guide the bets he places on that professional relationship and on his winemaking strategy.

In learning about how wines are made, there's a huge difference between simply stopping at a lot of tasting rooms on a wine-country trip and taking some winery tours and, hopefully, getting to meet the winemaker.

"If you have the chance to speak to the winemaker and be in his cellar, it is a totally different experience," says Michaël Engelmann of Gary Danko in San Francisco. "You want to learn the steps he took to produce the wine. You want to learn why grapes are grown here, why he harvested them when he did, why he chose those specific winemaking techniques, which may alter the taste of the wine. Have him explain the aromas, the best pairings with food. . . . There are a lot of points to learn from the maker.

"Wines are personal opinions: they are what the winemaker likes. I don't believe winemakers make wines for a critic's rating; I believe they make wines they like."

You can also meet winemakers when restaurants host wine dinners, where the winemaker is sometimes in attendance. Roxane Shafaee-Moghadam recalls hosting the American Table Series wine dinners at Per Se, which featured three winemakers, including Wells Guthrie of Copain Vineyards. She recalls, "At these dinners, I felt that I was a translator more than anything. We try to understand what winemakers are saying and translate it for guests.

"Winemakers are artists who don't necessarily know how to represent themselves, because they are speaking a different language. We sommeliers figure out what language needs to be spoken, whether it is emotional, factual, or seasonal. Winemakers often talk too specifically about yields and harvesting practices, as opposed to how these practices manifest themselves in the glass. Most guests care about what they are tasting. Instead of talking about the low yield, they need to talk about the concentration of flavor. Instead of describing the region, they need to discuss ripeness and the kind of fruit you can taste."

Typicity

As winemakers push new boundaries, some of the classic styles of traditional wines are changing, often dramatically. Although typicity is one of the most valued traits in a wine, it is becoming increasingly rare.

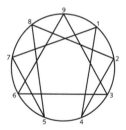

Understanding a Wine's Personality

The 2004 Provenance Vineyards Rutherford Cabernet Sauvignon was awarded an impressive 91 points by a leading wine magazine. We'd rate the 2005 vintage an 8. That is, an 8 on the enneagram, pictured above, a widely used nine-point personality-typing system that has been taught by such varied groups as the FBI, the Jesuits, and Stanford Business School.

Thinking of wines as having personalities can help you make better pairings with food. With that in mind, the powerhouse 2005 Provenance Vineyards Rutherford Cab surely qualifies on this nine-point system as the Challenger, one that must have its own way. It's a full-bodied, intensely flavored red that could obliterate lighter dishes.

In exploring how the enneagram could be applied to wine, we brainstormed with the creativity expert Michael J. Gelb, author of the bestselling book *How to Think Like Leonardo da Vinci* and *Wine Drinking for Inspired Thinking: Uncork Your Creative Juices*. Gelb collects wines, and he says the enneagram is one of the most useful tools for understanding their differences. After all, as he puts it, "the finest wines have their own personality, expressing the unique characteristics of the grape, earth, and season."

We typed various wines, then compared notes with Gelb.

9: The Peacemaker. The heart of a 9 is its agreeable nature, which can mediate any situation. No matter what food is on the table, a 9 wine goes along cheerfully. Rosé is the ultimate 9: its dominant characteristics morph seamlessly from those of a white to those of a red, as needed. Keep an eye out for the exceptionally food-friendly Tapena Rosé from Spain and the Kim Crawford Gisborne Rosé from New Zealand.

8: The Challenger. Like the Provenance Rutherford Cab, these wines dominate. The wine comes first, and the food (almost invariably red meat) must bend to its mighty will. Gelb says, "Barolo, 'the king of wines,' is an 8." We also think of tannic Cab, Malbec, Tannat, and Petite Sirah; one of the best and most restrained type-8 wines we tasted in recent years was the 2004 Neal Family Napa Valley Petite Syrah.

7: The Enthusiast. The ultimate epicure, this type celebrates joie de vivre. Gelb counts himself in this category; when it comes to wine, Champagne, with its lively bubbles, is the quintessential example. Pop a cork, and it's ready to party with anything except red meat—and a sparkling rosé will dance with that, too. With its creamy lemon-curd flavors, whisper of sweetness, and streams of exuberant bub-bles, the J Cuvée 20 Russian River Valley Brut NV will lift your spirits and the flavors of almost all hors d'oeuvres, especially fried or salty ones.

6: The Loyalist. Always there and always reliable, it's your house wine, pairing well with most of the dishes you like to eat at home. Gelb's house wine is the 2004 Muga Reserva Unfiltered Rioja, which he characterizes as "a phenomenal value" for its "remarkable elegance, complexity, and depth." When we're not tasting for our next book, we often opt for one of our favorite Rieslings or, with red-sauced pasta or roast pork, something like the light- to medium-bodied Tortoise Creek Central Coast Merlot.

5: The Investigator. These are "meditation" wines that you can sit with in a corner and examine. With them, food is beside the point. Old Bordeaux is a prime example; Gelb classifies it as "the most intellectual wine." Also worth investigating are wines featuring unusual grape varieties, including charmers such as the Clayhouse Central Coast Adobe White, a Chenin Blanc–dominant blend. It contains 22 percent Princess wine grapes, which have yet to be recognized by the U.S. Alcohol and Tobacco Tax and Trade Bureau, so the grape composition listed on the label totals just 78 percent.

4: The Individualist. When Robert Louis Stevenson wrote that "wine is bottled po-etry," he was surely referring to a Pinot Noir, most likely a red Burgundy. "It's a 4 wine: elusive, artistic, romantic, and difficult to understand," Gelb says.

3: The Achiever. Lots of actors are type 3s, in that they can perform any role. Char-donnay can do the same: from still to sparkling, dry to sweet, steely to oaky. "High-powered California Chardonnay is a 3 that will do anything to entertain and hold your attention," notes Gelb. Matanzas Creek Sonoma Valley Chardonnay boasts balanced oak and a hint of botrytised fruit, and it can star with chicken or pork in a creamy mustard sauce.

2: The Helper. We think of sweet, semi-sparkling Moscato d'Asti and big, fruity Shiraz, with all their food-friendliness, as typical 2 wines. "Australian Shiraz gives ev-erything and just wants to overwhelm you with love," Gelb says. That's certainly the case with Omrah Shiraz from western Australia, whose bright cherry and blackberry fruit and pepper notes cozy up to lamb.

1: The Perfectionist. Sauternes is the ultimate 1 wine. "It transforms noble rot into perfection," Gelb notes. Match it with Roquefort cheese, and you have a Holy Grail pairing.

As a 1 herself, Karen identifies with perfectionists on a quest for ideal matches in every wine-and-food-pairing situation. Luckily, as a 9, Andrew keeps the peace by re-minding her that any agreeable match is worth taking pleasure in.

John Ragan of Eleven Madison Park in New York City notes, "I am passionate about the same things many wine geeks are passionate about—Riesling, Champagne, Burgundy, and Piedmont—and at the end of the day, I am not interested in tasting some crazy wine from some offbeat place so much as a great example of a classic wine. To me, a great textbook example of a Sancerre will beat Sauvignon Blanc from some strange part of the world any day. The more you get into wine, the more focused your palate becomes. You know what you like and you get to know it well.

"With anything you need to search out typicity, which to me is the most valued trait of wine. Typicity is becoming rarer and rarer. I want wine that is typical of what it should be. There is frustration when, for example, you order a Barolo, and you are not thinking too much about it, and you don't know that the producer is using French *barriques* [oak barrels] and rotofermenters. It's a 2003, which is a really ripe vintage, and all of a sudden you have something in your glass that doesn't even taste like Barolo: 'I was in the mood for *Barolo*, but this bottle is not giving it to me!'

"Some Sancerre producers are changing their approach and chasing the New Zealand style because of its popularity. If that is your gripe with Sancerre, look to winemakers that are still traditional, like those in Menetou-Salon. Having said that, I just had a bottle of Channing Daughters Sauvignon Blanc from Long Island, and it was fantastic. So sometimes I eat my words!

"Look to Roero or Gattinara for your Nebbiolo. It is a shade cooler and producers are not charging $150 a bottle, so they are not buying new *barriques*. That is where you will find the grapes and places that still have their true voice. I find those wines really satisfying for myself and the restaurant, because they cost half the price of some super-fancy Barolo and really carry the identity of the grape."

Master Yourself

Know how you learn. You have to understand if you are an auditory learner, visual learner, or kinesthetic learner. Many auditory learners create audio files they can listen to in their cars. Visual learners do very well with flash cards. Kinesthetic learners use multiple sources at the same time and a partially haphazard manner. Understanding what type of learner you are will ease your frustration.

—DREW HENDRICKS, MS, PAPPAS RESTAURANTS

Learning what there is to know about wine is only half the battle. Now that you understand the three things that make wine tick (grapes, God/ground, and the guy/gal who made it), take a look at what makes *you* tick, so you can better understand your favored approach to learning about wine and can organize this information in the way that best serves you.

Sommeliers' Secrets for Taking It to the Next Level

"Some people have this romantic idea that wine tasting is a *Rain Man* sort of thing, where you can do long division in your head," observes John Ragan of Eleven Madison Park in New York City. "I'm sure there are some people like that in wine, but it is not like that in the real world. It is about tasting a lot, paying attention to what you are tasting, and being very systematic. The farther down the road you go with wine tasting, the less it is intuition and the more it becomes mechanics. You have to pay attention to the alcohol, the acidity, the texture, the color. . . . You can't just sniff, taste, and say, 'This is such-and-such.'

"It may seem like that, but these people have been paying attention to all those things along the way. The great thing about blind tasting is that it really, really forces you to pay attention to every aspect of a wine. That is totally different from just drinking wine to enjoy it."

When she teaches wine classes for consumers, Cat Silirie of No. 9 Park in Boston asks them upfront to use their imagination to create a way to handle all the information she'll be sharing. "You have to create a matrix in your mind of how you are going to file all this information," she says. "I believe that learning about wine and tasting wine is a left-brain/right-brain kind of challenge. It is certainly a sensual experience.

"Some people are better with the sensual aspects and might remember scent, flavor, color, and texture, which is certainly more right-brain. Others are more facile at remembering left-brain facts, such as vintage, geography, latitude, and hectoliters per hectare. To be a good taster, you need both.

"Learning how to organize information for themselves really seems to comfort people, because everyone does it a little differently. I will suggest that if you lean toward one way more than the other, let that be how you *lead*—but don't forget to register the sensory or contextual information as well.

"The next technique that works well is a simple matrix of grapes and place. Give each grape variety a personality. It can be very general as long as it gives you a feel for the grape. Sauvignon Blanc is citrusy, grassy, and fresh. Then expand on those characteristics for different places. The Sauvignon Blanc from the Loire Valley also tastes of chalk soil and flintiness. Sauvignon Blanc from New Zealand seems to have less minerality but more of a passion-fruit, bright-fruit aspect. This is a way of personifying the grape.

"For example, if Cabernet is a thick-skinned, broad-shoulder kind of guy, he might be like this from Napa, that from Howell Mountain [an appellation within Napa], and that from Bordeaux."

Does a sommelier have to have a photographic memory to remember every sip of wine? While a lucky few do, most make notes or use an actual photograph for help. Michaël Engelmann of Gary Danko in San Francisco is quick to admit that he can't remember every wine and vintage when he goes to a restaurant. "I have to take notes and write things down," he says. "I will use my phone and take some notes or simply take a picture of the label. At a tasting you don't have to take three pages of notes. It can be a couple of lines or a simple cross next to the one you enjoyed. You have to keep track some way."

What Runs Through Sommeliers' Heads When They Taste Wine?

To remember information during blind tasting, I use B L I C—for Balance, Length, Intensity, and Complexity.

—DREW HENDRICKS, MS, PAPPAS RESTAURANTS

Tasting wine for pleasure is different from tasting it for analysis. While non-professionals are free to drink purely for enjoyment, there is something to be learned from the exercise of tasting the way a professional does: to analyze a wine's structure.

"There are times when I will taste a wine and say, 'Mmmm . . . that is good.' That means I am not working, and you can be sure I am not being overanalytic," says Raj Vaidya of Daniel in New York City. "But as a professional, you need to know what goes into making a wine and how it is made. Those things influence how a wine tastes and indicate how it will age. Knowing the grapes, the regions, and how wine is made is one important part of understanding wine.

"The other part is learning how to taste wine structurally. I don't think everyone needs to know these things, but as wine professionals, we have to start there. When we are tasting, we think about:

- Acid
- Alcohol
- Residual sugar
- Tannin levels

"You recognize all these factors and think about them. More often than not when you taste, you can tell where the wine is from—for example, a cool climate rather than a warm one. More importantly, you know where it is going in terms of aging potential. How much time does it have before it reaches a level that is acceptable or goes too far?

"I tasted a wine recently that is delicious now and that we paid a good bit of money for. I will sell it for a lower price because it is going to be delicious for three to six months. But after that? I am not sure—it is at that point."

Jesse Rodriguez of Addison at The Grand Del Mar
on Making Distinctions in Colors and Flavors

Colorado Master Sommelier Wayne Belding and I were tasting three twenty-plus-year-old Old World red wines—Barolo, Chevrey-Chambertin Grand Cru, and old Rioja—and they all looked alike. The wines you taste for the Master Somme-

TYPICAL WINE-TASTING CHART CATEGORIES

Assessment of Color and Clarity

Assessment of Aromas and Flavors
Red wine
- Fruit: black (e.g., blackberries, black currants, black plums); red (e.g., cherries, raspberries, strawberries); dried (e.g., figs, prunes, raisins)
- Other: earth/mushrooms, flowers, herbs, minerals/stones, oak, spices, other

White wine
- Fruit: tree (e.g., apple, pear); citrus (e.g., grapefruit, lemon, lime, orange); stone (e.g., nectarines, peaches); tropical (e.g., mango, papaya, pineapple)
- Other: earth/mushrooms, flowers, herbs, minerals/stones, oak, spices, other

Assessment of Structure
- Body/alcohol: light-bodied, medium-bodied, full-bodied
- Sweetness: dry, off-dry, sweet, very sweet
- Acidity: low, low/medium, medium, medium/high, high
- Tannin: low, low/medium, medium, medium/high, high
- Oak: none, slight, moderate, strong
- Finish: short, short/medium, medium, medium/long, long

Conclusions
- Climate: cool, moderate, warm
- Style: Old World, New World
- Grape(s)
- Country
- Vintage: more than 10 years ago, 5–10 years ago, less than 5 years ago

lier exam are likely to be relatively young. The reds will be opaque or very bright or dark in color; rarely do you see an orange-brown tinge, which suggests age.

Wayne acknowledged that even though all three looked alike and smelled alike, you could distinguish them by trusting your tongue—for tannin, for acid— and then your sense of smell.

- The first wine was a little more tannic and acidic: Barolo.
- The next one had a mushroom profile: I guessed the Chevrey.
- The last smelled of dill and oak; I thought, "This must be Rioja."

Be a Critical Thinker—and Trust Your Own Palate First (and Last)

Trust your palate first. I trust scores and other people only to a point. Some critics are very talented, and I hope that in my life I can try half the wines they have tried—even a third!

—MICHAËL ENGELMANN, GARY DANKO

Relying on critics—for reviews of movies, books, and, yes, wines—has become a way of life in our busy world, as we look for shortcuts to find the best of the best. However, part of becoming a critical thinker is learning to judge wine *for yourself* rather than relying solely on professional wine critics, whose opinions you may not share. With the wine expertise you're developing by reading this book, you will be in a position to take a critical look at how the wine critics make their evaluations, and what biases they have.

Robert Parker, the publisher of *The Wine Advocate*, has been widely cited as the world's most influential wine critic—indeed, the world's most influential critic of any kind. He has done a great deal for the wine business and is probably the person most responsible for bringing Bordeaux to the serious attention of American wine collectors. In doing so, he has elevated Americans' awareness of wine in terms of dining out, and he has stressed the idea that with great food you need great wine. You may agree or disagree with his palate and ratings, because wine is subjective. However, for helping to bring wine to the forefront of the American gastronomic scene, he should be congratulated.

The criticism one often hears—that wine styles are changing because of the influence of powerful critics such as Parker—is really a criticism of winemakers who focus on wines that will get high scores rather than make the wines they believe to be the best. Many leading critics like highly oaked and/or extracted wines, and producers attuned to these critics' palates may actively change the way they make wine to please them—for example, by using more new oak. The concern is that wines are becoming homogeneous. In years past, it was easier to taste the differences among California, Australia, France, and Italy, but today it is more difficult to do so, as all of these wines seem to be moving toward an "international style" of very high-alcohol, fruit-driven, highly oaked wines.

Sommeliers often sound off on the subject of critics.

Raj Vaidya, Daniel

To be clear, I don't think that wine critics are doing this wrong. People give Robert Parker a hard time about his 100-point system, and they claim Americans appreciate it because they've been schooled here. Well, that is why he came up with it—*he* was schooled here. It's just the way he thinks about wine.

You should taste the wines Robert Parker likes a lot—there are plenty of them—and taste them critically. If you really like them, then drink up! Robert

Parker knows an immense amount about wine. I am thoroughly impressed with his palate every time I am around him. He likes some wines that I don't like as well as some that I do. For example, we both share a passion for Châteauneuf-du-Pape and Burgundy.

Wine writers are people, after all. The most important thing is to learn your own palate, and you have to do that by tasting.

Aldo Sohm, Le Bernardin

When it comes to scoring wines, Robert Parker is a genius for scoring from 0 to 100. I am not a fan of his preferred style of wine—in fact, I am an enemy of it—but the man's genius was to explain wine that way because people can understand it right away. There is a huge difference between 90 points and 95.

The reason I am not a fan of his style is that he likes wine with "animal flavors," like old leather, which are referred to as "brett"—short for *brettanomyces* [breh-TAN-uh-MY-sees], a wild yeast most evident in red wines. Some wine writers are fans of wines with brett character, while others deride it as unsanitary and a fatal flaw. He likes hyperconcentrated wines with 15 to 16 percent alcohol, which I don't like at all.

There is a problem with winemakers changing their wines to suit Parker's palate, which is changing history. He is a great guy, he made wine popular—but with the sun, you also have a shadow. If he scores a wine at 100, the price goes nuts. If there's a wine he doesn't like, I will get more of it because it will be a better buy.

Inez Ribustello, On The Square

People come in thinking they should like Silver Oak and Caymus because they have read so much about them. Unfortunately, some people rely exclusively on others for their opinions. It's the Robert Parker phenomenon. I like Parker, but I don't like the fact that some people think his reviews are the God's given truth. I have tasted wines that he loves that I don't think are that great. I have tasted wines that I love that he didn't think were so great. That is why we carry so many different wines. Just because I don't like oaky Chardonnay doesn't mean you shouldn't love it.

When my husband was in retail in Manhattan, he would get a call about a particular wine. He would say, "I have this vintage but not that one," and then he would hear the person click on his computer to check its scores and say, "No, I can't have that one . . ."

Mastering Wine, One Fact at a Time

A not-insignificant aspect of becoming a Master Sommelier is memorizing seemingly endless streams of wine trivia. Michaël Engelmann of Gary Danko in San Francisco observes, "To be a sommelier you have to know about everything. Learning about the one hundred regions of South Africa is not a lot of fun. People

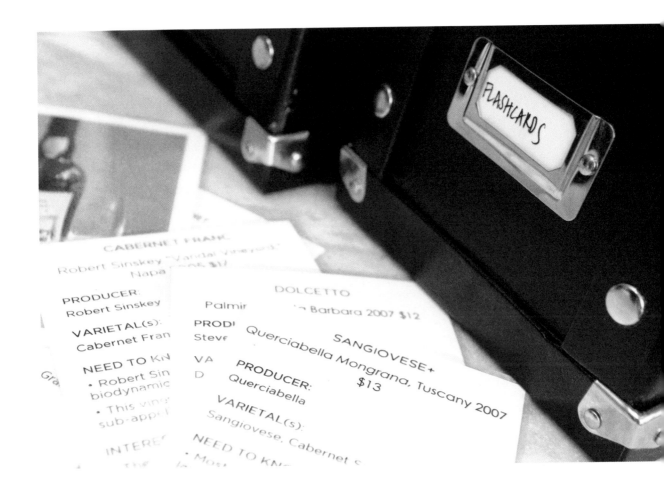

always think I have this fun job. Yes, I get to taste some great wines. What they don't see is the amount of work behind it. I would love to watch a movie or play with PlayStation or hang out and go for a drink after work. Instead, for the last six months, I have been going home after work to study. It takes a lot of dedication to go home after work and open a book."

To help with the task of memorization, sommeliers employ a host of mnemonic devices. Emily Wines, MS, of the Fifth Floor in San Francisco, uses a lot of acronyms. "These were critical to my learning—otherwise, there is just no way to remember it all. I will also use word association, linking an image and a word to each of the items in a list. It is funny to talk to other sommeliers about how *they* learn." She adds, with a laugh, "I learned there are a lot of dirty ones as well!"

You may be starting to feel a little dizzy as you wrap your head around the complexity of the wine world. Fear not—our sommelier friends are a few steps ahead of you and are willing to share some tricks of the trade for memorizing all that wine information. Next, for your amusement, we share a few of their insider secrets:

France: Beaujolais
Drew Hendricks, MS, of Pappas Restaurants, passed on this trick: *"The word Beaujolais has ten letters, which makes it easy to remember that the Beaujolais region has ten crus, or wine-producing regions—in this case, the top villages, for which the wines are named."*

Emily Wines, MS, does it this way: *"One of my favorites is the villages of Beaujolais from north to south: Sometimes Japanese Canadians Marry French Canadians Making Really Beautiful Children."* The villages are Saint-Amour, Julienas, Chanas, Moulin-à-Vent, Fleurie, Chiroubles, Morgon, Regnie, Brouilly, and Côte de Brouilly.

John Ragan of Eleven Madison Park on Tricks for Understanding Guests

Sommeliers also have some tricks for understanding their customers. John Ragan of Eleven Madison Park in New York City used to work in San Francisco, so he has a perspective on how customers in two of the best wine cities differ.

"The difference between the two coasts is striking, and as a sommelier you have to get used to it," he says. "In California, people want to drink California wines. They may have that mission either because they are not from there or because that's what they are familiar with. People will charge you to find something great from California.

"In New York it is different, because you can get your hands on some of the great smaller bottlings in Europe that might not make it to California. People in New York are also more familiar with those wines. I have learned that 'typical wine' is sort of a pejorative term in American culture. In Europe, it is the ultimate compliment: 'This is an absolutely typical Chinon—it is what it *should* taste like.' New Yorkers have that mentality and have a better sense of the nooks and crannies of European wines. Everyone in New York wants to drink Oregon Pinot, whereas in California you could try to roll that rock up the hill every day and it wouldn't stay! They may drink a little of it, but they would rather drink local. In New York there is no home-turf loyalty, and Oregon Pinot is more akin to Burgundy. If you highly recommend something, they will go with you. They will try [the Pinot Noir from Oregon winemakers] Ken Wright, Patricia Green, Tony Soter, or Lynn Penner-Ash. We would sometimes have a little luck converting Californians, but ultimately they like staying local."

France: Rhone
Emily Wines suggests another device for this region: *"For the grapes of Châteauneuf-du-Pape I remember: Girl Scouts Make Rocking Chocolate Chip Cookies But Many Play Pretty Terrible Volleyball."* The grapes are Grenache, Syrah, Mourvèdre, Roussanne, Cinsault, Counoise, Clairette, Bourboulenc, Muscardin, Picpoul, Picardan, Terret Noir, and Vaccarese.

France: Bordeaux/Médoc/Margaux
Michaël Engelmann, of Gary Danko, contributes this: *"I have memorization techniques that are often funny and stupid but seem to work. For the communes of Margaux, I use CLAMS: Cantenac, Labarde, Arsac, Macau, and Soussans."*

France: Burgundy
Mark Mendoza, of Sona, says: *"I like to tell people that they should learn Burgundy first because it is the hardest appellation to learn. I do this because it is based on the single-vineyard concept. Once one understands this idea, the rest of the regions of the world are much easier to tackle."*

Germany
Mark Mendoza learned another trick for German wines: *"I was trying to learn the German levels of quality, and my friend Ken Fredrickson said he used to have a girlfriend named Sabet. He just put a K in front of her name (KSABET), and then he could remember the quality levels*

Kabinett, Spätlese, Auslese, Beerenauslese, Eiswein, Trockenbeerenauslese. I have always remembered this."

Portugal: Vinho Verde

Emily Wines likes this mnemonic sentence: *"The subregions of Vinho Verde are Many Black Bartenders Like Chugging Pisco Sours All Afternoon."* That helps her remember Monção, Balão, Basto, Lima, Cavado, Paiva, Sousa, Amarante, and Ave.

Portugal: Ribatejo

Michaël Engelmann uses this device: *"For the subregions of Ribatejo, I use the word CATS spelled with three C's."* That helps him remember Cartaxo, Chamusca, Coruche, Almeirim, Tomar, and Santarém.

Chapter

4

KNOW YOUR WINES: THE LISTS

Knowledge of wines is a lifetime hobby, and the only way to learn is to start in drinking and enjoying them, comparing types, vintages, and good marriages of certain wines with certain foods.

—JULIA CHILD, *MASTERING THE ART OF FRENCH COOKING* (1961)

Julia's advice is sound: the best way to learn about wines *is* to drink (and enjoy!) them. However, once you've learned the basics regarding the components and characteristics of different wines, you can read about a wine you've never tasted and develop a general idea of its flavor (i.e., aroma + taste + mouthfeel).

The first source for learning about a wine is its bottle—including both the front and the back labels. Beyond that, you can check the listings in this chapter when you want a general profile of a particular wine.

READING A WINE LABEL

On the front and back labels of a bottle of wine you can find clues to the wine's flavor, as discussed in Chapter 3. First, the three G's:

1. **Grapes:** The grape variety that dominates or the blend of grapes.
2. **God/Ground:** The country, region, and/or vineyard of origin, and the weather during the year the grapes were harvested as represented by the vintage date. As a rule of thumb, "The more specific the location, the better the quality." Most table wines are meant to be drunk within a year or two after release, so be wary of inexpensive wines bearing an older vintage date—especially if the bottles have dust on them, which may suggest that the wine is past its prime!
3. **Guy/Gal:** The name of the winery and, in some cases, the actual winemaker.

You'll also want to look for other information on the label:

Alcohol: When grape juice is fermented, the sugar in the grapes is converted into alcohol, expressed as a percentage of the total volume. Less than 12 percent is a lighter-bodied wine; more than 14 percent is a fuller-bodied wine.

Importer: This is sometimes an insider shortcut to quality; if you're unfamiliar with the wine, you can check the name of the importer to see if it's among those best known for choosing high-quality wines. (For more on this, see IMPORTERS on pages 154–155.)

On the back label, you may find some further information:

About the winery: Its history (e.g., how long it's been making wine) and/or winemaking philosophy, such as adherence to sustainable, organic, and/or biodynamic principles.

Winemaker's notes: How the wine is made (e.g., aging and/or oak treatment), a description of the wine's flavors, and other attributes, such as finish. For example:

- "Oak aging: 100% French oak, ten months."
- "Aging: six months in oak casks and six months in the bottle."

Food pairings: Suggestions for foods to accompany the wine.

Residual sugar: The amount of sugar remaining after fermentation can be expressed in grams per liter (or 100 or 1,000 milliliters) or as a straight percentage of the total volume. For example:

- An off-dry Gewürztraminer: 0.21g/100ml
- A Vendange Tardive Gewürztraminer: 95g/1,000ml
- A Late Harvest Chardonnay: 24 percent residual sugar
- Royal Tokaji 5 Puttonyos: 148g/l
- A sparkling ice wine: 180g/l

Brix at harvest: A measure of the grapes' sweetness when they were picked; 1 degree Brix is the equivalent of 1 percent sugar. Most table wines are harvested at 20 to 25 degrees Brix. About 55 percent of the sugar is converted to alcohol during fermentation, resulting in an alcohol level of 12 to 14 percent. This is noted in various ways on labels. A few examples:

- A Late Harvest Chardonnay: 23 Brix at harvest
- A Late Harvest Petite Sirah: 28.0 harvest Brix
- A sparkling ice wine: 37.0 degrees

Other information sometimes found on the back label:

Acid: The total acidity (TA) of a wine by volume, often expressed as a percentage. Most wines have a TA of 0.4 percent (mildly acidic) to 0.8 percent (strongly acidic), with reds averaging 0.65 percent to whites' 0.7 percent.

pH: This is a measure of the wine's acidity on a scale from 0 to 14. Water, which is neutral, has an average pH of 7.0. A pH of 3.0–3.4 is considered desirable for white wines, as is 3.3–3.6 for red wines.

Cases Produced: This number gives a sense of the wine's availability—or rarity! For example: "Cases produced: 785" indicates a much rarer wine than one whose case production numbers in the tens of thousands.

Harvest Date: The vintage date gives the year of harvest, but some labels indicate the month and day. For example: "Harvest date: September 27, 2006."

What Information Is Required on a Wine Label?

By law, certain information must appear on the label of any bottle of wine sold in the United States, including these points:

- The **brand** name.
- The **class or designation of wine** (such as table, sparkling, or dessert wine).
- The **bottling location**.
- The percentage of **alcohol** by volume (ABV).
- The **volume of the container** in milliliters (with the standard wine bottle being 750ml).
- The declaration that the wine **contains sulfites.**
- The **government warning** ("Consumption of alcoholic beverages impairs your ability to drive a car or operate machinery").

READING ABOUT WINES: THE LISTS

You can conquer the world of wine two ways: by **grape** or by **country**. By grape is the most insightful. Say you want to explore Chardonnay. Ask for six under $15 and get the spectrum of California, France, Italy, and Australia. You will see the many faces of Chardonnay. You will see similarities but also draw conclusions. For example, the wine from Australia is more like a California wine. Why is that? It is warmer and riper. It is a good way to learn about and find new treasures. Say you want to learn about Italian reds; that is a little more of a crapshoot. There is not a guide; they are all over the place. It does help you to start understanding the styles of wines made in a specific area as well as the grapes that are grown there.

—SABATO SAGARIA, THE LITTLE NELL

The top varietal wines bought in American stores include Chardonnay, Cabernet Sauvignon, Merlot, and White Zinfandel, accounting for more than 50 percent of sales. So you may find it hard to believe that there are literally *thousands* of different wine grapes in the world! The listings in this chapter will introduce you to hundreds of the more popular wines you may encounter in wine stores and on restaurant wine lists.

Readers of *What to Drink with What You Eat* told us they loved the ease of using the lists in the back of the book: simply look up a beverage to find a wealth

A NOTE ON SERVING TEMPERATURES

Temperature has an enormous effect on the way wine is perceived. For example, the colder the wine, the less accurate your perception of its acidity, alcohol, aroma, and sweetness. The warmer the wine, the less accurate your perception of its tannic astringency.

In fact, since the temperature at which a wine is served is arguably the single most important factor in determining how your palate perceives it, you'll find recommendations listed for every wine in this chapter.

Yet even we will acknowledge that a wine's temperature is a moving target, because wine begins to warm to the temperature of the room starting the minute it's poured (at a rate of about 4 degrees Fahrenheit every 10 minutes).

Ideal temperatures can also vary by season — many prefer their wines served colder in the summer and warmer in the winter. They also vary, of course, by personal preference.

So use these recommendations only as general guidelines — and, of course, only to the extent that they enhance your and your guests' pleasure.

Otherwise, to minimize the hassle of your having to overthink any of this, we'll quote 2005 James Beard Award–winning sommelier Tim Kopec of Veritas restaurant in New York City, who gave us this helpful rule of thumb: "Put your red wine *in* the refrigerator for 15 to 20 minutes before serving — and pull your white wine *out* of the refrigerator 15 to 20 minutes before serving."

TEMPERATURE	DEGREE CHILLED	REFRIGERATE FOR	WINES
<40°F	(At this temperature, your palate won't register much — so only recommended for inexpensive sparkling, sweet, rosé, or white wines.)		
40–45°F	Very cold	65–70 minutes	Sparkling wines; many sweet wines; simpler white wines
45–50°F	Cold	50–60 minutes	Most white wines; lighter rosés
50–55°F	Chilled	40–50 minutes	Fuller-bodied rosés and white wines; light-bodied red wines
55–60°F	Slightly chilled	25–40 minutes	Medium-bodied red wines
60–65°F	Cool	15–25 minutes	Full-bodied and/or tannic red wines
>65°F	(Not recommended; at this temperature, you'll find aromas to be diminished while your palate overregisters alcohol.)		

ICONIC EXAMPLES OF WINES FROM AROUND THE WORLD AT SHERRY-LEHMANN

Notes:

- These guidelines assume a room temperature of 70°F and a refrigerator setting of 37°F: For every ten minutes in the refrigerator, the wine temperature will decrease by about 4°F.

- To expedite chilling, place the wine in the freezer for as long as fifteen to twenty minutes. In addition or instead, place the wine in a reusable plastic sleeve designed for this purpose (such as Nuvo Vino's Rapid Ice Cooler, $5.95).

- Serve less expensive and/or simpler wines even colder.

- Serve more expensive and/or more complex wines a bit warmer.

- Remember that more wines suffer from being served too warm than too cold, so when in doubt, err on the side of cooler/colder.

- If a wine is too cold for your taste, you can warm it by holding the bowl of the wine glass in your hands. To avoid warming a wine too quickly, you'll typically want to hold it by the stem, which is what it's there for.

of foods and flavors to accompany it. Similarly, *The Flavor Bible* allowed readers to grasp the essence of any ingredient through its flavor profile and compatible flavors.

In the same easy-to-access format, we're providing a directory of wines by grape, country of origin, and other key characteristics, along with a full flavor profile of each. Please keep in mind that this section is intended as a series of helpful generalizations for beginning wine enthusiasts (e.g., characterizing Sancerre as white) and *not* as a study guide for professionals (who might otherwise ask about the omission of red Sancerre, which is only a fraction of total Sancerre production and an even smaller fraction of Sancerre exports). While there are obviously exceptions to every rule, we've found these rules of thumb to be enormously useful—and hope you will, too.

KEY TO THE LISTINGS

[The phonetic pronunciation of the name]
Country: The countries where this wine is *primarily* produced
Region: The *primary* regions where this wine is produced
Color: The color of the grapes (and the wine's actual hue)
Grapes: The *primary* grape(s) used to make the wine
Weight: The wine's weight on the palate, from light-bodied to full-bodied
Volume: The intensity of flavor, from quiet to loud
Dry/sweet: The typical level of dryness or sweetness, from dry to sweet
Acidity: The typical acidity, from low to high
Tannin: The typical level of tannins, from low to high
Flavors: The typical aromas and flavors
Texture: The typical mouthfeel characterizations, listed alphabetically
Temperature:* General recommendations for optimal serving temperature
Comparables: Wines that have a somewhat or **very** similar profile
Season: The particular time of year to which the wine is most suited
Pairings: Foods that complement the wine
Tips: Advice for serving, pairing, or otherwise appreciating the wine
Aging: Tips on how long the wine should be aged for optimal pleasure
Producers: Notable producers by location
Iconic example: A well-known example of the wine

Note: In the listings that follow, certain items appear in **bold** or **BOLD CAPS**, to emphasize their relative importance (for example, grapes with a **significant** or **VERY SIGNIFICANT** share of a blend, producers that are **more notable** or **MOST NOTABLE**). Names in CAPS and SMALL CAPS indicate a listing in this chapter.

*Yes, life is too short to worry about whether your wine is at the exact right temperature—but it's also too short not to have a serving temperature at your fingertips when you need one!

ACIDIC WINES

See Beaujolais, Bordeaux—White, Burgundy—Red, Champagne, Chianti, Gamay, Muscadet, Pinot Grigio, Pinot Noir, Riesling, Sancerre, Sangiovese, Sauvignon Blanc, Vinho Verde, Vouvray.

AGED WINES

See Chapter 6.

AGIORGITIKO

[eye-or-YEE-tee-koh]
Country: Greece
Region: Nemea
Color: red
Grapes: Agiorgitiko (aka St. George)
Weight: medium- to full-bodied
Volume: moderate

Dry/sweet: dry
Acidity: low
Tannin: low to medium
Flavors: fruity, with notes of **blackberries**, cassis, cedar, **cherries** (black, dried, and/ or pits), cocoa, currants, earth, game, herbs, **plums**, smoke, **spices**, vanilla
Texture: lush, rich, round, smooth, **soft**, velvety
Temperature: Serve cool, about 60 to 65 degrees.
Comparables: Gamay, Merlot
Pairings: cheese, chicken, meatballs (esp. beef or lamb), oregano, pork or lamb (esp. roasted), salmon, stews, thyme
Aging: Can age as long as five to ten years.

California winemakers have really changed their style since 2004, and it is very encouraging. There has been a lot more influence of the Old World in Napa. They have backed off the oak and ripeness, so the wines are getting more and more elegant, which leads them to be more food-friendly. Stony Hill is a very food-friendly Chardonnay. It has no malolactic fermentation and little to no new oak. Chateau Montelena is one of the classics. Bob Long, of Long Winery, makes incredibly elegant Chardonnay; his wife, Zelma, implemented the style. For our fifteenth anniversary, we decided to serve all 1994 wines. Schramsberg had a 1994 Blanc de Blancs that was showing amazingly. It was fresh, vibrant, and bright. People were a little leery when they heard about a 1994 California sparkling wine. I told them to trust me, and when they tasted it they said, "Wow, that is good." We served Peter Michael Coeur à Coeur and Williams Selyem Pinot Noir. Then we moved into our investors' wines, with Vine Cliff, Long, Araujo, Colgin, Von Strasser, and Frog's Leap, and we were amazed how well 1994 was showing with fifteen years of age. People say California wines can't **age**, but we had fifteen-year-old Chardonnay, Pinot Noir, and Cabernet all showing beautifully.
—DENNIS KELLY, THE FRENCH LAUNDRY

If you need to be convinced how well American wines can **age**, check out Hanzell Vineyards in Sonoma. Try their young Pinot Noir and compare the 2005 to the 2006. Then try the 1974 Pinot Noir to compare to these, which shows how well these wines are aging. You don't have to drink them in two or three years.
—STEPHANE COLLING, SAN YSIDRO RANCH

Producers: Biblia Chora Areti Red, Boutari, **Gaia Estate**, Semeli Mountain Sun, **Skouras**

AGLIANICO

[ah-LYAH-nee-koh]
See also Taurasi.
Country: Italy
Regions: Basilicata (Aglianico del Vulture), Campania (Taurasi)
Color: red
Grapes: Aglianico
Weight: full-bodied (and moderate in alcohol)
Volume: moderate to loud
Dry/sweet: dry
Acidity: medium to high
Tannin: high
Flavors: notes of blackberries, **black cherries**, black currants, black pepper, coffee, **dark chocolate, earth**, herbs, honey (esp. burnt), leather, minerals, plums, roses, smoke, spices, tar, tobacco
Texture: rich; ranges from rough (esp. younger) to smooth (esp. older)
Temperature: Serve cool, about 60 to 65 degrees.
Comparables: Nebbiolo, Taurasi, Touriga Nacional, Zinfandel
Season: autumn
Pairings: beef, cheese, game, game birds, lamb, meatballs, pizza, red meat, sausage
Tip: Aglianico is the primary grape in Taurasi, the famed red wine of Campania.
Aging: Typically serve about five years after the vintage date, although the best can age for a decade or two.
Producers: Bruno De Conciliis, Caggiano, Conserva (certified organic), **D'Angelo**, Feudi di San Gregorio, Mastroberardino,

When pairing to a pasta sauce that's very rich and heavy with meat and tomatoes, I'll recommend **Aglianico**. I love its baked fruit, its notes of tar and earth, and its nice structure without being too, too heavy. People always go for it. My favorite is from Bruno De Conciliis.
—CLAIRE PAPARAZZO, BLUE HILL

I find startling flavor similarities between **Aglianico** and dry Touriga Nacional wine. In both wines I find a lovely burnt-honey characteristic, rose petals, and the unusual and sensual combination of high acidity and high tannin. These are wines for the adventurous wine drinker.
—DANA FARNER, CUT

Feudi di San Gregorio has a red, an **Aglianico** blend called Serpico, that is outstanding. These are flavors that people are unfamiliar with, but they take a sip and you can see a bit of searching on their face, wondering what the reference point is for these flavors. They are just delightful. If you like Grenache, try Serpico.
—MICHAEL FLYNN, THE MANSION ON TURTLE CREEK

Paternoster, Tenuta del Portale, Terra dei Re, Terredora Di Paolo

ALBARIÑO
[ahl-bar-EEN-yoh]
Countries: Spain (Rías Baixas/ Galicia), U.S. (California)
Color: white (with straw hues)
Grapes: Albariño
Weight: light- to medium-bodied
Volume: quiet to moderate
Dry/sweet: dry
Acidity: medium-high to high
Flavors: aromatic and fruity, with notes of almonds, **apples**, apricots, **citrus** (esp. grapefruit, **lemon**, lime), flowers, grass, herbs, kiwi, lychee, **melons**, minerals, nectarines, nuts, orange, **PEACHES**, pears, spices, stones, tropical fruit
Texture: crisp refreshing; sometimes semi-sparkling

Temperature: Serve cold, about 45 to 50 degrees.
Comparables: ALVARINHO (Portugal), PINOT BLANC, (DRY) RIESLING, SAUVIGNON BLANC, VINHO VERDE, VIOGNIER
Season: summer
Pairings: chicken, duck, **fish**, fried foods, salads, **shellfish**, tapas, turkey, vegetable dishes
Aging: Drink young and fresh, within two or three years.
Producers: Spain: Burgans, **Martin Codáx**, Nessa, Nora, Orballo, Pazo de Señorans, Terras Gauda; **U.S.–California:** Bonny Doon (biodynamic), Verdad

ALIGOTÉ
[ahl-EE-goh-TAY]
Countries: Bulgaria, **France (Burgundy/Bouzeron)**, Romania, U.S.

Albariño has the acidity and freshness of Sauvignon Blanc, and the peachy/nectarine-like flavor of Riesling. I love it anytime, but particularly chilled at the beginning of a meal, especially in warm weather—it's like liquid air-conditioning! It's especially good with langoustines or oysters—any shellfish you'd squeeze a lemon on.
—JILL ZIMORSKI, CAFÉ ATLÁNTICO

Color: white
Grapes: Aligoté
Weight: light-bodied
Volume: quiet
Dry/sweet: dry
Acidity: medium-high to high
Flavors: notes of almonds, apples, bread, buttermilk, **citrus**, earth, flowers, grapefruit, honey, lemon, minerals, **nectarines, nuts**, pears, pine nuts, smoke, spices, tangerines, toast, tropical fruits
Texture: crisp, juicy, round
Temperature: Serve cold, about 45 to 50 degrees.
Pairings: charcuterie, cheese (esp. goat and/or young), chicken, fish, potatoes, shellfish, turkey
Tip: Mixing with cassis to make the French cocktail kir.
Aging: Drink young and fresh.
Producers: France: Coche-Dury, Denis Mortet, François Mikulski, Goisot, Guy Roulot, Ramonet, Villaine; **U.S.–California:** Calera

ALSACE WHITES
[AHL-zahss]
See also GEWÜRZTRAMINER, MUSCAT, PINOT BLANC, PINOT GRIS, RIESLING, SYLVANER.
Country: France (Alsace)
Color: white
Grapes: Gewürztraminer, Muscat, Pinot Blanc, Pinot Gris, RIESLING, Sylvaner
Weight: medium- to moderately full-bodied
Volume: moderate
Dry/sweet: dry to off dry
Flavors: highly aromatic, with notes of cinnamon, earth, green apples, lychees, peaches, **spices**
Pairings: boudin blanc, charcuterie, chicken, duck, pork, stews, veal
Tip: Alsace wines tend to be drier and fuller-bodied than

MAKING FINER DISTINCTIONS ABOUT WINES: DURING A VISIT TO ALSACE

On our first visit to Alsace—the region of France close to the German border—a few years ago, we devoted the first day to seeing and tasting Old World Alsace, pairing local wines with specialties like *tarte flambée* (bacon, onion, and cream on a thin crust) and white asparagus. The second day we matched Helfrich's modern wines with Alsatian dishes, such as fish with Italian and Moroccan accents as well as a completely new take on Baeckeoffe (which translates as baker's oven), the region's classic meat-and-potato casserole.

During our visit we sat down with two of the region's most acclaimed chefs to learn about wine from their perspective behind the stove—as opposed to in the vineyard and tasting room (though, believe us, we spent plenty of time there as well). The first was **Michel Husser, chef-owner of Le Cerf (Marlenheim, France):**

The best Alsatian wine to me is Riesling. Riesling from the north is very different than that from the south. The soil and exposure to light, which affect the ripening and flavor of the grapes, is different in each region.

Part of the problem is that even though the villages and the wines are very different, they are all called Riesling. In Burgundy, Chardonnay grapes are made into wines that are completely different from one another, and labeled as anything from Meursault to Puligny-Montrachet to reflect those differences. I am from the north, so naturally I prefer the wine from the north. The best way to put it is that the wines are more "direct." I find northern Riesling to be finer, with more citrus notes. In the south the wine is a little sweeter, with more mineral notes. Many people prefer southern Riesling, with its touch of sweetness. The southern wines are very good for drinking alone and the northern wines are better with food.

If you are cooking lobster with a little cream, you want a Riesling with a little tiny bit of sweetness and minerality, which you will find in the south. On the other hand, if you are grilling the lobster and serving it with fresh herbs, then you want a Riesling from the north, where the wine is finer, with lower alcohol. I do have some favorite pairings, and each varietal has its place.

Crémant [sparkling wine made by the traditional method in Alsace]: I like this best by itself or with tapas and charcuterie. The problem with Crémant is its image compared to Champagne. Most people drink it as an aperitif or even after dinner, but Crémant also goes *with* lunch and dinner. It works fantastically with a simple fish entrée with vegetables if you want to drink something light and refreshing. I also make a langoustine dish with borage ravioli and consommé, which is very light and wonderful with Crémant.

Muscat: This works well as an aperitif or with *tarte flambée.*

Pinot Gris: A very good pairing for summer vegetables is young Pinot Gris. I like to serve it with a vegetable dish with baby zucchini with different textures: both al dente and sautéed in olive oil with some added tomato and basil.

Pinot Noir: Here you have different styles, from classic to rosé. The rosé is perfect with a *tarte flambée* while sitting on the terrace. Pinot also works with the venison dish that I prepare with pears, apples, and quince.

Riesling: Riesling works with so many things because it ranges from dry to sweet. Dry Riesling pairs with many meats. A [sweeter] Vendange Tardive Riesling works with citrus fruits like oranges or with chocolate.

(continued on next page)

(continued from page 101)

Sylvaner: Sylvaner is a simple, pleasant, refreshing wine, and when it is done well, it is excellent. I like it with charcuterie or with *tarte flambée*. I use it a lot for cooking as well because of its acidic structure. If you have a sweet Sylvaner, it will pair with both duck and goose liver.

The benefit and fun of sitting down with a chef who is the son of a winemaker, such as **Hubert Maetz of Hostellini du Rosenmeer,** is to be able to go deeper with food-and-wine pairings because of his experience growing up in the region. He says, "Wine is like a person: when young, they are dynamic. But with age, both become more mature and know who they are."

Aged Gewürztraminer: I like to pair it with small, sweet strawberries. With a little age, it is not so flowery but more spicy and brings out the flavors of the strawberries.

Aged Pinot Gris: An aged Tokay Pinot Gris that is ten to thirty years old and is tasting dry will work with my venison dish with pears, apples, and quince. Older Pinot Gris in general will work with gratin with cream.

Aged Sylvaner: Sylvaner can be simple, but a great one can age like Riesling and work with a lot of different dishes. A ten-year-old Sylvaner will work with pike, baby shrimp, and rouget [a fish]. This wine works really well with shrimp in a gratin. Veal will pair with a Sylvaner from two to fifteen years old. As Sylvaner ages, the aroma changes and the wine gets a little oxidized, which makes it pair well with cheese. I would pair a fifteen-year-old Sylvaner with some goat cheese.

similar wines from Germany. Try a delightful blend of local grapes in Hugel & Fils Gentil, which, in the words of its website, unites "the suave, spicy flavor of Gewürztraminer, the body of Pinot Gris, the finesse of Riesling, the grapiness of Muscat and the refreshing character of Sylvaner."
Producers: Albert Boxler, Barmes Buecher, Beyer, Charles Schleret, Dirler, **Helfrich, Hugel**, Josmeyer, Kreydenweiss, Lucien Albrecht, Marcel Deiss, Ostertag, Paul Blanck, René Muré, Schlumberger, **TRIMBACH**, Weinbach, Willm, **ZIND-HUMBRECHT**
Best value: Trimbach
Iconic example: Zind-Humbrecht

There are some wine regions that tend to be a good bet if you're picking blind off a wine list. I tell people that if you have no idea what to pick and you're looking at the French section of a wine list, you can't go wrong with a wine from **Alsace.**
—JILL ZIMORSKI, CAFÉ ATLÁNTICO

I love **Alsace.** You can drink fragrant Muscat or Sylvaner, which go great with spicy food and are not as high-priced as Gewürztraminer or Riesling. They are both good starter wines for the region. Sylvaner, Pinot Gris, and Muscat from Alsace are not as flamboyant as Gewürztraminer or Riesling but will give you aroma, earth, and a lot of character. They may not be the character you are used to, but it is not a risk to spend $15 on a bottle from a reliable producer like Hugel or Trimbach.
—HRISTO ZISOVSKI, AL FIORI

Alsace is definitely one of my favorite regions, because I like white wine and I love aromatics. Alsatian wines have body to them and even very light tannins that will go with a wide variety of foods: veal, poultry, boudin blanc, charcuterie, pork, stews, duck, and fatty dishes. They are a great value, and they are wines that can age. I like the Grand Cru level of Alsatian wines because they have great expression and depth.
—FERNANDO BETETA, MS, NOMI

There are many approaches to learning about the wines of **Alsace** [Colling is a native of the region]. You can start with Pinot Blanc, then move to Riesling, then to Grand Cru Riesling. That way you can understand the levels and complexity you can get from each wine. Or you can choose a winemaker and try the entry-level Riesling, then the Grand Cru, and eventually the late harvest. Try to understand what winemakers are saying through their labels. This is amazing to do. As an example, try Paul Blanck Riesling. The entry level is called Classique. Then try the next level—Sommerberg or Altenbourg. Then try the Grand Cru Furstentum. You taste from the bottom of the pyramid to the top, tasting increasingly nuanced wines.

—STEPHANE COLLING, SAN YSIDRO RANCH

ALVARINHO

[al-vah-REEN-yoh]
See also ALBARIÑO.
Country: Portugal
Region: Vinho Verde
Color: white
Grapes: Alvarinho
Weight: light- to medium-bodied
Volume: quiet to moderate-plus
Dry/sweet: dry
Acidity: high
Flavors: aromatic and fruity, with notes of apples, apricots, citrus, grapefruit, grapes, herbs, lemon, lime, lychee, nuts, orange peel, peaches, pears
Texture: crisp, semi-sparkling
Temperature: Serve cold, about 45 to 50 degrees.
Comparables: ALBARIÑO, Vinho Verde
Season: summer
Pairings: fish, shellfish, vegetable dishes
Aging: Drink young and fresh.
Producers: Ameal, Aveleda, Louridal, Poema

AMARONE

[ah-mah-ROH-nay]
Country: Italy
Region: Veneto
Color: red
Grapes: CORVINA, Molinara, Rondinella
Weight: full-bodied (and high in alcohol)
Volume: loud to very loud
Dry/sweet: typically dry with an illusion of sweetness
Acidity: medium
Tannin: high (though softens with age)
Flavors: notes of almonds, **bitter chocolate**, blackberries, **cherries,** coffee, currants, dates, dried fruits, earth, figs (dried), flowers, leather, licorice, minerals, mocha, plums, **raisins**, raspberries, smoke, spices, tobacco, vanilla
Texture: rich, syrupy, velvety
Temperature: Serve cool, about 60 to 65 degrees.
Season: winter
Pairings: beef, **cheese** (esp. Parmesan), game, lamb, lasagna, mushrooms, pasta, stews
Aging: Amarone has the structure to be aged for several years, or as long as a decade or two.

Producers: Accordini, Allegrini, Bertani, Bolla, Brigaldara, Brunelli, Bussola, Castellani, Corte Sant' Alda, Dal Forno, Guerrieri-Rizzardi, Le Ragose, Le Salette, **QUINTARELLI,** Roccolo Grassi, Speri, Tedeschi, Tenuta Sant' Antonio, Tommasi, Venturini, Villa Monteleone, Viviani, Zenato
Iconic example: Giuseppe Quintarelli Amarone della Valpolicella

AMERICAN WINES

Top five regions: California (90 percent of U.S. wine production), Oregon, Washington, New York, Virginia

ARGENTINE WINES

Grapes: red: Bonarda, Cabernet Sauvignon, **MALBEC**, Merlot, Syrah; **white:** Chardonnay, **TORRONTÉS**
Tip: Argentina is the world's fifth-largest wine-producing country. Although they're not yet as easy to find as still wines, sparkling wines are coming out of the growing number of Champagne houses (including Moët & Chandon and Mumm) that have established a foothold in Argentina. Don't miss the definitive book *Vino Argentino: An Insider's Guide to the Wines and Wine Country of Argentina,* by Laura Catena (Chronicle Books, 2010).
Producers: Alma Negra, **Alta**

My grandfather, who was born in Italy, always had wine on the dinner table. There was lots of Chianti—sometimes great and sometimes in straw-bottomed bottles if that's all my grandmother could find. He loved old **Amarone**. On my twenty-first birthday, I was given my grandfather's Giacomo Conterno wines. Tasting them—sometimes with nothing more than a great aged Parmesan cheese—opened the door to the world of wine for me.

—JULIA MORETTI, AD HOC

The quality in **Argentina** is rapidly increasing. There is a lot of value in the wines coming out of there.
—DENNIS KELLY, THE FRENCH LAUNDRY

Vista, Bodega Lurton, Canepa, **CATENA**, Chandon Dominio del Plata, **Familia Zuccardi**, La Rural, Luca, Luigi Bosca, **Norton,** O. Fournier, Pascual Toso, **Renacer**, Rutini, Sur de los Andes, Susana Balbo, Terrazas, Tilia, **Trapiche**, Valentin Bianchi, Viña Cobos, Weinert

Iconic example: Catena Zapata

ARIZONA WINES

In 2010, the Scottsdale restaurant FnB, co-owned by general manager Pavle Milic and chef Charleen Badman, hosted a blind wine tasting that pitted Arizona wines against ten well-known wines from around the world (including a 2005 Chateau Lynch-Bages Pauillac Grand Cru and a 2007 Turley "The White Coat"). A panel of judges—chef Chris Bianco, Napa winemaker Tadeo Borchardt, chef Payton Curry, chef Anne Rosenzweig, *Arizona Republic* wine columnist Mark Tarbell, Wine Library's Gary Vaynerchuk, and Laura Williamson, MS—declared two Arizona wines the best of both whites and reds. Arizona wine pioneer Kent Callaghan took first place among the whites with his **2008 Callaghan "Lisa's."** Among reds, placing first was the **2008 Caduceus Cellars Nagual del JUDITH** from the winery owned by musician Maynard James Keenan (of Tool) and produced in collaboration with Eric Glomski. Other Arizona wines that placed in the top ten include **2008 Caduceus Cellars Los Candrones,**

2007 Keeling Schaefer "Three Sisters" Syrah, and **2008 Arizona Stronghold "Nachise."**

ARNEIS

[ahr-NAYSS]

Countries: Australia, **Italy (Piedmont/ROERO)**, U.S. (California, Oregon)

Color: white

Grapes: Arneis

Weight: medium- to full-bodied

Volume: moderate

Dry/sweet: dry

Acidity: low to medium-high

Flavors: aromatic, with notes of **almonds, APPLES,** apricots, flowers, grapefruit, herbs, honey, lemon, licorice, melon, minerals, nuts, orange, peaches, **pears,** vanilla

Texture: smooth, viscous

Temperature: Serve chilled, about 50 to 55 degrees.

Comparables: PINOT BIANCO, PINOT GRIGIO

Season: summer

Pairings: appetizers, chicken, fish, pasta (esp. with light and/or herbed sauces), prosciutto, salads, shellfish, tuna

Aging: Drink young and fresh, within two to three years.

Producers: Italy: Bruno Giacosa, Ceretto, Funtanin, **Vietti;** U.S.– **California:** Seghesio; **Oregon:** Ponzi

AROMATIC WHITES

See GEWÜRZTRAMINER, MUSCAT, RIESLING, VIOGNIER.

ASSYRTIKO

[ah-SEER-tee-koh]

Country: Greece

Region: Santorini

Color: white

Grapes: Assyrtiko

Weight: light- to **medium**-bodied

If you like Sauvignon Blanc or Sancerre, you will find that **Assyrtiko** has some similarities, including a lemony aroma and taste, good acidity, and nice body. I have had ten-year-old oak-aged Assyrtikos that showed very well.
—ROGER DAGORN, MS, PORTER HOUSE NEW YORK

(and relatively low in alcohol)

Volume: moderate to loud

Dry/sweet: typically very dry

Acidity: medium-high to high

Flavors: fruity, with notes of **apples, citrus,** earth, grapefruit, hazelnuts, herbs, **lemon, lime, MINERALS,** orange peel, peaches, pears, smoke, spices, steel, stones

Texture: crisp, fresh, rich

Temperature: Serve cold, about 45 to 50 degrees.

Season: spring–summer

Comparables: PINOT GRIGIO, (dry) RIESLING, SANCERRE, SAUVIGNON BLANC

Pairings: cheese (esp. feta), chicken, fish, pork, salads, shellfish, sour foods (esp. capers, tomatoes, yogurt)

Aging: Has some aging potential, given its high acidity.

Producers: Argyros, Biblia Chora, **Boutari,** Carras, Gaia Estate, Hatzidakis, Koutsoyannopoulos, Markezinis, Sigalas

ASTI (FORMERLY KNOWN AS ASTI SPUMANTE)

[AH-stee]

Country: Italy

Region: Piedmont

Color: white

Grapes: Moscato Bianco

Weight: light-bodied (and low in alcohol)

Volume: quiet to moderate

Dry/sweet: ranges from dry to semi-sweet to sweet
Acidity: medium to high
Flavors: aromatic, fruity, with notes of apples, apricots, cream, flowers, **grapes**, honey, lychees, **peaches**, spices
Texture: semi-sparkling
Temperature: Serve very cold, about 40 to 45 degrees.
Comparables: MOSCATO D'ASTI, which is less sweet and lower in alcohol
Season: summer
Pairings: cake (from angel food to wedding), cookies, desserts, fresh fruit, ice cream, pastries
Aging: Drink young and fresh, within a year or two of release. (Note: Asti is not vintage-dated, so take care to ensure its freshness through a trusted retailer.)
Producers: Bera, Cascina Fonda, Cinzano, Fontanafredda, Gancia, Gianni Voerzio, Giuseppe Contratto, Martini & Rossi, Tosti

AUSTRALIAN STICKIES

Country: Australia (esp. Rutherglen)
Color: white (with a deep golden hue)
Grapes: Gewürztraminer, **Muscadelle, Muscat**, Riesling, Sauvignon Blanc, Semillon
Weight: full-bodied
Volume: loud to very loud
Dry/sweet: sweet dessert wines
Acidity: medium to **high**
Flavors: notes of apricots, brown sugar, caramel, citrus, honey, mango, nectarines, peaches, vanilla
Texture: luscious, rich
Temperature: Serve cold, about 40 to 50 degrees.
Comparables: MUSCAT–LIQUEUR, TOPAQUE–RUTHERGLEN
Pairings: blue or soft cheeses,

In August 2009, a dozen of **Australia**'s most powerful family wineries joined together in an effort to promote their premium and super-premium wines. Members of "Australia's First Families of Wine" include Brown Brothers, Campbells, d'Arenberg, De Bortoli, Henschke, Howard Park, Jim Barry, McWilliam's, Tahbilk, Taylors, Tyrell's, and Yalumba Wines.
—DECANTER (AUGUST 17, 2009)

fruit desserts
Tip: Australia's famed sweet wines are made from either late-harvested grapes (Gewürztraminer, Riesling, Sauvignon Blanc, Semillon) or botrytis-affected grapes (Riesling, Semillon).
Producers: Angove, Campbells, Chambers, d'Arenberg, De Bortoli, Peter Lehmann, Stanton & Killeen
Iconic example: De Bortoli Noble One Botrytis Sémillon

AUSTRALIAN WINES

Grapes: red: Cabernet Sauvignon, Pinot Noir, **SHIRAZ**; white: **Chardonnay**, Riesling, Semillon
Aging: Some consider vintages irrelevant, because the quality is fairly consistent.
Producers: Burge Family, Clarendon Hills, De Bortoli,

Giaconda, Grosset, Hardys, **Henschke** (esp. the distinguished Hill of Grace), Jacob's Creek, Lindeman's, McWilliam's, Mollydooker, Paringa, **PENFOLDS**, Peter Lehmann, Robert Oatley, Rockford Estate, Rosemount, Tahbilk, Yalumba
Iconic example: PENFOLDS GRANGE

AUSTRIAN WHITES
Grapes: GRÜNER VELTLINER, Riesling, Weissburgunder
Dry/sweet: dry
Tip: Austrians will drink Grüner Veltliner with a meal after starting with Riesling.
Producers: ALZINGER, Bründlmayer (Grüner Veltliner), Domäne Wachau, **Emmerich Knoll,** * Franz Hirtzberger,* Franz Prager* (Riesling), F. X. Pichler* (Riesling), Heidi Schröck, Hiedler, Hirsch, Jamek, **Kracher,**

In America, people often think of **Austrian** and German wines as the same, which they are not. There is a cultural difference, and the cuisines are very different. What customers think is that the wine is fruity/sweet. The first thing I tell people is that Austrian wine is always dry, like the Austrian sense of humor, which is also on the drier side, unless you go to dessert wines. There is a freshness that is clean and pure. . . . Start with what an area is known for. If you wanted a white from California, you would start with Chardonnay. Austria made its name with Grüner Veltliner, so start off with Grüner Veltliner, without a doubt.
—ALDO SOHM, LE BERNARDIN

I am a huge fan of **Austrian wines**, especially Alzinger and Prager, because they have less alcohol. They tend to harvest earlier and are very elegant wines.
—DENNIS KELLY, THE FRENCH LAUNDRY

Among **Austrian wines**, I am a big fan of Weissburgunder [Pinot Blanc] and Grüner Veltliner with a bit of age to it. They are a real treat. With Austrian wines, when it comes to pairing, you need to look at the weight of the wine [which ranges from Steinfeder, the lightest/quietest, to Federspiel, which is medium-bodied, to Smaragd, the richest and most full-bodied], because some can be very big. With the rich styles, you need a dish with a bit of heft to it. I would pair them with lighter meats like chicken and duck. I eat a lot of Southeast Asian foods with a bit of spice to them, and I go back and forth between German and Austrian wines for those purposes. They also highlight the flavor and richness of raw seafood. With the bigger styles, I feel trepidation about pairing them with lighter dishes and sweeter dishes because they can taste alcoholic after a while. To spot a bigger style, you want to look at the label; if it says Smaragd, it is going to be a richer style. Also, look at the alcohol level: If it is 13.5 to 14 percent, it is going to be a bigger wine. . . . In Austria, I typically like the cheap, dry, austere, citrusy liter bottles of Grüner Veltliner with a screw cap. That is what I drink at home without thinking too seriously about food. A great Federspiel Weissburgunder, known elsewhere as Pinot Blanc—that is where I would go.

—RAJ VAIDYA, DANIEL

Nigl, R. Pichler, Salomon, Schloss Gobelsburg, Tement

*The Wachau region's "Big Four" producers.

AUTUMN WINES

See AGLIANICO, BARBARESCO, BAROLO, BEAUJOLAIS, BORDEAUX–RED, BURGUNDY–RED, CABERNET SAUVIGNON, CHAMPAGNE, GEWÜRZTRAMINER, HERMITAGE, MADEIRA, MERLOT, PINOT NOIR, RHÔNE WINES (RED), RIOJA, SAUTERNES, SHERRY–PEDRO XIMÉNEZ, VALPOLICELLA (ESP. RIPASSO), VIOGNIER, ZINFANDEL.

BACO NOIR
[BAHK-oh NWAHR]

Autumn is when I start to look for things with nuttier flavors. Nuts and dried-fruit flavors start to show up in our dishes, so the wines will reflect that. For fresher, fruitier wines, I am looking for something with dried-fig or dried-date flavors. Reds that fall into this profile would be reds from southern Italy, like an Aglianico-based wine or Valpolicella Ripasso, or aged California Cabernets. Sherry, Madeira, and Pedro Ximénez sherry all have dried-fig flavors and work with autumn desserts.

—EMILY WINES, MS, FIFTH FLOOR

Countries: Canada, U.S. (Michigan, New York/Hudson Valley)
Color: red
Grapes: Baco Noir
Weight: medium-bodied
Volume: moderate
Dry/sweet: dry
Acidity: high
Tannin: low to medium
Flavors: notes of **blackberries**, black cherries, black currants/cassis, black pepper, **blueberries**, cocoa, earth, leather, **meat**, **plums**, raspberries, **smoke**, spices, tobacco, vanilla
Texture: rich, rustic

Temperature: Serve slightly chilled, about 55 to 60 degrees.
Comparables: CABERNET FRANC, GAMAY, MERLOT
Pairings: cheese, hamburgers, red meat (beef, lamb, venison), ribs, sausages, steaks
Aging: Drink relatively young, within two to five years.
Producers: Canada: Henry of Pelham, Waupoos; **U.S.–Michigan:** Leelanau Cellars

BANDOL
[bahn-DAWL]
Country: France
Region: Provence
Color: red (see below for **rosé** and **white**)
Grapes: Carignan, **Cinsault**, **Grenache**, MOURVÈDRE, Syrah
Weight: full-bodied
Volume: moderate to **loud**
Dry/sweet: dry
Acidity: medium
Tannin: high
Flavors: notes of blackberries, black cherries, chocolate, earth, **herbs (esp. dried)**, jam, leather, licorice, meat, minerals, plums, **spices**, violets
Texture: rich, velvety
Temperature: Serve cool, about 60 to 65 degrees.
Comparable: CHÂTEAUNEUF-DU-PAPE
Pairings: beef, charcuterie, cheese (esp. strong), lamb, sausages
Aging: Can be enjoyed young and fresh (in their first five years); the best can age for a decade or two or possibly longer.

Color: rosé
Grapes: Cinsault, Grenache, Mourvèdre
Weight: medium-bodied
Volume: moderate

Bandol rouge has been the love of my life.

—ALICE WATERS, CHEZ PANISSE

Dry/sweet: dry
Acidity: medium
Flavors: notes of **earth**, herbs, minerals, raspberries, **spices**, strawberries
Texture: Crisp, round
Temperature: Serve cold, about 50 degrees.
Pairings: anchovies, chicken, olives, seafood, tapenade, vegetables
Aging: Drink Bandol rosé young and fresh, though the best have the unusual ability to age well.

Color: white
Grapes: Bourboulenc, CLAIRETTE, Sauvignon Blanc, Ugni Blanc
Weight: light-bodied
Volume: quiet
Dry/sweet: dry
Acidity: medium
Flavors: notes of apples, citrus, earth, **flowers**, minerals, peaches, pears, sea breeze, tropical fruits
Texture: Crisp
Temperature: Serve chilled, about 50 to 55 degrees.
Pairings: bouillabaisse, fish, lobster, tapenade
Aging: Drink young and fresh.
Producers: Château de Pibarnon, Château La Rouvière, Château Pradeaux, **Château Romassan**, Domaine Ott, Domaines Bunan, **DOMAINE TEMPIER**, Mas de la Louvière, Moulin des Costes

BANYULS

[BAHN-yools]
Country: France
Region: Roussillon
Color: red (with dark ruby hues)

I recommend Domaine du Mas Blanc Docteur Parcé **Banyuls**, which is crystalline and clean and all about the Grenache fruit. It is from a legendary producer yet at around $20 for a 500ml bottle, it is definitely within reach.

—BELINDA CHANG, THE MODERN

Grapes: Grenache (primarily)
Weight: full-bodied (and high in alcohol at about 16 to 17 percent)
Volume: moderate to loud
Dry/sweet: sweet
Acidity: medium
Tannin: medium
Flavors: notes of caramel (esp. oaked wines), cherries, chocolate, coffee (esp. oaked wines), nuts, plums, raisins, spices, toast, vanilla
Texture: chewy, luxurious, rich, velvety
Temperature: Serve chilled, about 50 to 55 degrees.
Comparables: MAURY, RIVESALTES, PORT–VINTAGE
Pairings: berries, **CHOCOLATE** (esp. dark), coffee, creamy desserts, dried fruits, fruit desserts
Aging: The best wines have great aging potential.
Producers: Cellier des Templiers, **Chapoutier, Clos de Paulilles**, Domaine de Jau, Domaine de la Casa Blanca, Domaine de la Rectorie, Domaine La Tour Vieille, Ey, La Cave de L'Abbé Rous
Iconic example: Domaine du Mas Blanc

BARBARESCO

[bar-bar-ESS-koh]
Country: Italy
Region: Piedmont
Color: red
Grapes: Nebbiolo

Weight: full-bodied
Volume: moderate (long-aged) to loud (younger)
Dry/sweet: dry
Acidity: high
Tannin: high
Flavors: aromatic, with notes of blackberries, cherries (black and red), earth, flowers, leather, **licorice**, menthol, minerals, **roses**, smoke, spices, **tar, tobacco**, vanilla, violets, white truffles
Texture: chewy, lush, rich, round, soft
Temperature: Serve cool, about 60 to 65 degrees.
Comparable: BAROLO (which is a bit heavier and louder)
Pairings: beef, duck, game, Pecorino cheese, poultry, red-wine sauce, white truffles
Aging: Age for five or ten years (or up to two to four decades, for the very best) before drinking. Best recent vintages: 2008, 2007, 2006, 2004, 2003, 2001, 2000.
Producers: Aldo Conterno, Alfredo Prunotto, **Angelo Gaja, BRUNO GIACOSA**, Bruno Rocca, Ceretto, La Spinetta, Luciano Sandrone, Marchesi di Gresy, Produttori del Barbaresco, Rivetti, Scavino, Vajra, Vietti
Iconic example: Bruno Giacosa

BARBERA

[bar-BEH-rah]
Countries: Argentina, Australia, **ITALY (PIEDMONT, esp. Alba, Asti, Monferrato)**, Mexico, U.S. (California, Virginia)
Color: red (with dark ruby hues)
Grapes: Barbera
Weight: light- to medium-bodied (fuller body and higher in alcohol in warmer regions)
Volume: moderate to loud
Dry/sweet: dry

My [sommelier] wife and I drink a lot of **Barbera** because I eat pizza with abandon. I either drink Giuseppe Mascarello Santo Stefano di Perno or Giacomo Conterno Cascina Francia. Both Barberas are great pizza wines, and they are especially great with a Little Frankie's sausage-and-fennel pizza.

—ROBERT BOHR, COLICCHIO & SONS

Acidity: high
Tannin: low to medium
Flavors: fruity, with notes of **blackberries, BLACK and RED CHERRIES,** black currants/cassis, black pepper, cinnamon, dark chocolate, **earth,** flowers, **HERBS,** meat, **minerals,** mushrooms, **plums** (fresh and dried), raisins, raspberries, smoke, **spices,** toast, vanilla
Texture: lush, rich, silky, smooth, velvety
Temperature: Serve slightly chilled, about 55 degrees.
Comparable: CHIANTI
Pairings: appetizers, beef, chicken, game birds, hamburgers, mushrooms, **pasta, pizza,** red meat, risotto, seafood, **tomato sauce**
Tip: The less expensive the bottle, the cooler it should be served.
Aging: Drink young and fresh, although the best Barberas can age well over time.
Producers: Argentina: Norton; **Italy—d'Alba** (fuller-bodied, lower acidity): Aldo Conterno, Bruno Giacosa, Ceretto, Clerico, Giacomo Conterno, Giuseppe Mascarello, Paolo Scavino, Sandrone, Vietti; **d'Asti** (lighter-bodied, higher acidity): Braida, Icardi, La Spinetta, Maria Borio, Martinetti, Michele Chiarlo, Prunotto, Vietti; **Monferrato/Langhe:** Fontanafredda Briccotondo; **U.S.–California:** Eberle, Palmina, Wilderotter; **Virginia:** Barboursville

BARDOLINO
[bar-doh-LEE-noh]
Country: Italy
Region: Veneto
Color: red
Grapes: Corvina, Molinara, Negrara, Rondinella
Weight: very light-bodied (and low in alcohol)
Volume: quiet to moderate
Dry/sweet: dry
Acidity: medium to high
Tannin: low
Flavors: somewhat bitter yet fruity, with notes of blackberries, **BLACK or RED CHERRIES,** nuts (esp. **almonds**), plums, raspberries, smoke, spices, strawberries
Texture: smooth
Temperature: Serve slightly chilled, about 55 to 60 degrees.
Comparable: lighter-bodied VALPOLICELLA
Season: summer
Pairings: cheese (esp. Asiago or smoked), chicken, lighter meat-and/or tomato-based pasta dishes and stews, meats (esp. grilled), pizza, prosciutto
Tip: Keep an eye out for Bardolino Chiaretto, a lovely value-priced rosé.
Aging: Drink young and fresh, within a few years of release.
Producers: Cavalchina, Guerrieri Rizzardi

BAROLO
[bahr-OHL-oh]
Country: Italy
Region: Piedmont
Color: red (with orange hues)

Grapes: Nebbiolo
Weight: medium- to full-bodied (and high in alcohol)
Volume: moderately loud (long-aged) to loud (younger)
Dry/sweet: dry
Acidity: high
Tannin: high
Flavors: aromatic and bitter, with notes of blackberries, cherries, chocolate, leather, **licorice,** plums, raspberries, **roses,** smoke, **tar, tobacco, VIOLETS, WHITE TRUFFLES**
Texture: creamy, luxurious, rich, satiny, silky, velvety
Temperature: Serve cool, about 60 to 65 degrees.
Comparable: BARBARESCO (which is somewhat lighter)
Pairings: beef, cheese, game, lamb, mushrooms, quail, white truffles
Aging: Age for at least five to ten years (even two or three decades for the very best) before drinking. Best recent vintages: 2008, 2007, 2006, 2004, 2003, 2001, 2000.
Producers: Aldo Conterno, Alfredo Prunotto, **Bartolo Mascarello, Bruno Giacosa,** Cavallotto, Ceretto, Gaja, **GIACOMO CONTERNO, Giuseppe Mascarello,** Giuseppe Rinaldi, Luciano Sandrone, Michele Chiarlo, Paolo Scavino, Pio Cesare, Roberto Voerzio, **Vietti**
Iconic example: Giacomo Conterno

BARSAC
[BAHR-sahk]
Country: France
Region: Bordeaux
Color: white
Grapes: Sémillon (primarily)
Weight: full-bodied (although slightly less than Sauternes)

A big misconception is that people think **Barolo** is a "big" wine. Barolo is an intense wine, but it is never big. A guest will want to start with a California Cabernet and then move into Barolo, but it will never taste right in that order.

—DANA FARNER, CUT

Anyone who loves Burgundy should love Piedmont as well. The wines are similar. They are both aromatic, with the aromatics of **Barolo** being truffles, tar, and pencil lead. With age they have a similar texture and elegance to Burgundy. You also have the cultural aspect, with the food and the wine evolving together, just as in Burgundy. I went to Piedmont with Daniel Humm [chef of Eleven Madison Park] for truffle season. He took me to the restaurants, and I took him to the wineries. We visited traditional producers like Maria Teresa Mascarello and Roberto Conterno and also went to the more modern guys like Gaja and Sondrone, which Daniel loves. But when you talk about Piedmont, you can't simplify it to "traditional" and "modern." If it weren't for the influx of some new ideas, you would still be getting a lot of flawed wines. There would be oxidized wines, wine with too much volatile acidity, so to a small degree the new ideas are a positive change in Piedmont and throughout the world. My favorite Barolo is a Bruno Giacosa 1978 or Giacomo Conterno 1961 Monfortino. They were amazing—with apologies to all others!

—JOHN RAGAN, ELEVEN MADISON PARK

Volume: loud
Dry/sweet: sweet to very sweet
Acidity: medium to high
Flavors: notes of apricots, caramel, cinnamon, citrus, cloves, flowers, ginger, honey, marzipan, nutmeg, nuts, orange zest, passion fruit, peaches, pineapple, tropical fruits, vanilla
Texture: rich, smooth
Temperature: Serve cold to very cold, about 40 to 50 degrees.
Comparable: SAUTERNES
Pairings: biscotti, blue cheese, cookies, desserts (esp. fruit-driven), **foie gras**, fruits (esp. apricots, peaches), ice cream, tarte Tatin
Tip: When pairing Barsac with spicy, savory foods (e.g., Indian or Thai dishes), look for lighter-bodied versions: second-label or lesser-vintage Barsac can work well for this purpose.

Aging: The best Barsacs have aging potential. Best recent vintages: 2007, 2005, 2003, 2001, 1999, 1998, 1997, 1996.
Producers: Château Broustet, Château Caillou, **CHÂTEAU CLIMENS, Château Coutet,** Château de Myrat, Château Doisy-Daene, Château Doisy-Dubroca, Château Doisy-Védrines, Château Nairac, Château Suau
Iconic example: Château Coutet Cuvée Madame

BEAUJOLAIS
[boh-zhoh-LAY]
Country: France (Burgundy/Beaujolais)
Color: red (light in color)
Grapes: Gamay (aka Gamay Noir)
Weight: light- to medium-bodied (and low in alcohol)
Volume: quiet to moderate
Dry/sweet: dry

Acidity: high
Tannin: low
Flavors: aromatic and fruity, with notes of blackberries, **black pepper,** blueberries, **CHERRIES,** cloves, cranberries, earth, **flowers,** minerals, pears, **plums, RASPBERRIES, spices, STRAWBERRIES,** violets
Texture: juicy, soft, velvety (esp. cru Beaujolais)
Temperature: Serve chilled, about 50 (lighter-bodied wines) to 55 degrees (fuller-bodied wines).
Comparables: (light-bodied red) BURGUNDY, DOLCETTO, (light-bodied) PINOT NOIR
Season: spring–summer
Pairings: charcuterie, cheese, chicken, fish, ham, picnics, pork, red meat, salads, salmon, sausages, white meat
Tip: Beaujolais is a red wine that could pass for a white. Beaujolais-Villages represents a step up in quality—and cru Beaujolais represents a step up from that. "Beaujolais" has ten letters to help you remember that there are ten crus (Brouilly, Chénas, Chiroubles, Côte de Brouilly, Fleurie, Juliénas, Morgon, Moulin-à-Vent, Régnié, Saint Amour), which produce richer, medium-bodied Beaujolais.
Aging: Drink most Beaujolais young and fresh (i.e., within a year or two of release), although cru Beaujolais (especially those from Chénas, Juliénas, Morgon, or Moulin-à-Vent) has the potential for somewhat longer aging—and the *very* best cru Beaujolais might last for a decade or longer.
Producers: Château de Pierreux, Château Thivin, **Georges Duboeuf,** Jean-Paul Brun, **Joseph Drouhin, Louis**

What Distinguishes Different Beaujolais Crus?

Brouilly
Flavors: red and dark fruit
Texture: light to hearty
Aging: Drink within a few years of release.

Chénas
Flavors: floral
Texture: silky
Aging: Drink within a decade of release.

Chiroubles
Flavors: floral, fruity
Texture: light
Aging: Drink within a few years of release.

Côte de Brouilly
Flavors: earthy, fruity
Texture: elegant, soft
Aging: Drink within 5 to 7 years of release.

Fleurie
Flavors: floral, fruity
Texture: elegant, silky
Aging: Drink within 5 to 7 years of release.

Juliénas
Flavors: floral, spicy
Texture: structured
Aging: Drink within a decade of release.

Morgon
Flavors: black cherries, earth
Texture: age-worthy, silky
Aging: Drink within a decade of release.

Moulin-à-Vent
Flavors: blackberries, raspberries
Texture: powerful, yet silky with age
Aging: Drink within a decade of release.

Régnié
Flavors: aromatic, raspberries
Texture: light
Aging: Drink within a few years of release.

Saint Amour
Flavors: fruity, spicy
Texture: elegant
Aging: Drink within 5 to 7 years of release.

I like reds that can be served colder in the summer. I like **Beaujolais,** and my favorite is Vissoux. I drink it all the time.
—ROXANE SHAFAEE-MOGHADAM, THE BREAKERS

Vanessa Boyd of Philippe on the Beauty of Beaujolais

Beaujolais works at the beginning of a meal because it doesn't have much tannin. It is great because you can chill it down a bit, and there is such a wide range of expressions.

Morgon has a deep, dark sort of sultry quality to it that you get at the very finish. You order a great Beaujolais for its fruitiness and its playfulness, which you can feel in your heart, and it should finish with crunchy mineral. A **Fleurie** is expressive, outgoing, and drinks younger. **Moulin-à-Vent** has the potential to age. Thinking of Beaujolais as wine to age is a very cutting-edge idea. There is a story about Bernie Sun [the corporate beverage director for Jean-Georges Vongerichten's restaurants]: When he was at Montrachet, he opened a bottle of Beaujolais from the 1920s, and supposedly it was really fresh. The best Beaujolais can age, and that is because of the minerality.

In Beaujolais, it is about the producer. I admire **Marcel Lapierre** for his long-lived wines in Morgon. He bottles half-bottles, which is good because the wine is only good for a couple of days after opening before it starts to lose its acidity. This size is also great for chilling, which helps put a cap on the fruitiness and also helps tame the tannin. A Morgon will have more tannin than a Fleurie. Another great producer is **Jean-Paul Brun,** who has one of the oldest parcels in Beaujolais. His l'Ancien Vieilles Vignes red is dark, a little tannic, and takes two to three years to come around. His older vines just make it naturally tannic. He also makes a Beaujolais Blanc that is varietal-labeled, so it says "Chardonnay" on it.

Jadot, Potel-Aviron, the "Gang of Five" top Morgon producers (Guy Breton, Jean Foillard, Jean-Paul Thévenet, Marcel Lapierre, Yvon Metras)

BEAUJOLAIS NOUVEAU
[boh-zhoh-LAY nooh-VOH]
Country: France
Region: Burgundy
Color: red
Grapes: Gamay

Aside from Nouveau, I love **Beaujolais**. I remember a winemaker telling me years ago that "Beaujolais, as it gets older, turns into Pinot Noir." If you find an inexpensive Beaujolais from a good producer, after a few years, poof—you get all these characteristics of aged Burgundy from the wine. Buy a case and let it age, because it's a lot cheaper than investing in Burgundy! Or here's a good experiment: Scour your parents' wine cooler for some old Beaujolais and check that out with your duck or roast chicken or anything with morel mushroom sauce, and you will have something pretty fantastic. I really like Trenel, and I have also tried some older bottles of Grand Cru from Georges Duboeuf, with great success. They are the more serious producers of Moulin-à-Vent and Saint Amour, which can handle bottle aging and are pretty fantastic.
—BELINDA CHANG, THE MODERN

Under-$20 tip: My favorite **Beaujolais** is Château de Pierreux, which is a Brouilly.
—VIRGINIA PHILIP, MS, THE BREAKERS

Beaujolais is highly underrated. There are incredible cru Beaujolais—Morgon, Côte de Brouilly, and others that are delicious wines at a great price point. Within Beaujolais, the range is wide and diverse, from very light-bodied to fuller in style. You can open a young, lighter wine like a Beaujolais-Villages with classic picnic charcuterie, or one with more body like a Moulin-à-Vent, which can age five years or more, with roasted meat. I always say, "If you go to a bistro or brasserie and there is no Beaujolais on the menu, there is a problem. You may want to run away!"
—MICHAËL ENGELMANN, GARY DANKO

Weight: light-bodied (and low in alcohol)
Volume: quiet to moderate
Dry/sweet: dry
Acidity: medium-high to high
Tannin: low
Flavors: fruity, with notes of bananas, blueberries, **cherries**, flowers, grapes, plums, **raspberries**, spices, **strawberries**
Texture: juicy
Temperature: Serve chilled, about 50 to 55 degrees.
Season: autumn–winter
Pairings: chicken, goat cheese, pork, salmon, Thanksgiving dinner, veal
Aging: Drink extremely young, within six months after release.
Iconic example: Georges

Duboeuf, which put Beaujolais Nouveau on the global map

BEAUJOLAIS-VILLAGES
[boh-zhoh-LAY vee-LAHJ]
Country: France
Region: Burgundy
Color: red
Grapes: Gamay
Weight: light-bodied
Volume: quiet to moderate
Dry/sweet: dry
Flavors: similarly fruity, with a bit more complexity (including notes of pepper and other spices) than regular Beaujolais
Texture: ranges from crisp to soft
Temperature: Serve chilled, about 50 to 55 degrees.
Season: spring

Pairings: cheese (esp. Brie, Cheddar), chicken, salmon, sausages, tuna, turkey
Aging: Drink young and fresh, within a few years of release.
Producers: Georges Duboeuf, Louis Jadot

BEAUMES-DE-VENISE
See MUSCAT DE BEAUMES-DE-VENISE.

BIERZO
[bee-EHR-zoh]
See MENCIA.

BIODYNAMIC GRAPES AND WINES
All of the following producers are either certified or practicing biodynamic wineries and represent a small sample of the growing numbers of such wineries. Biodynamic wines go beyond organic, embracing a more holistic, philosophical, even spiritual approach to winemaking. Demeter lists certified wineries at http://demeter-usa.org/files/Winery.Vineyard%20List.pdf.

Producers: Australia: Heartland; **Austria:** Nikolaihof; **Canada:** Southbrook; **France–Alsace:** Barmes Buecher, Marcel Deiss, Ostertag, Zind-Humbrecht; **Bordeaux:** Château Climens; **Burgundy:** Bize-Leroy, Heritiers du Comte Lafon, Leflaive, Lercy, Pierre Morey, Romanée-Conti; **Champagne:** Jacques Selosse; **Loire:** Clos de la Coulée de Serrant, Huet, Vacheron; **Provence:** Château de Roquefort; **Rhône:** Chapoutier, Clos de Caveau, La Vieille Julienne; **Roussillon:** Ferrer-Ribière; **Germany:** Gysler; **Italy:**

CLAIRE PAPARAZZO

CLAIRE PAPARAZZO OF BLUE HILL ON HER BIODYNAMIC AND ORGANIC WINE PICKS

Domaine Jo Pithon "Les Bergères" Anjou Blanc Chenin Blanc, which pairs with many foods, from eggs to chicken.

Andrea Calek "Babiole" Languedoc, which pairs well with goat.

Movia Pinot Nero Slovenia, which pairs with medium-weight dishes like chicken or pork.

Domaine de Larzac Roussanne-Chardonnay Languedoc, whose nice acidity pairs with a fish like cobia, cooked medium-rare, with zucchini.

Domaine Lignères Carignan Languedoc, for lovers of California Cabernet who are eating a heavier dish, such as braised lamb.

Domaine du Vieux Télégraphe Côtes du Rhône from importer Kermit Lynch, an amazing entry-level wine whose rusticity would pair beautifully with pork or, especially, lamb.

Castello dei Rampolla, COS; **New Zealand:** Felton Road, Milton Estate; **Slovenia:** Movia; **South Africa:** Reyneke, Sadie, Topaz; **Spain:** Alvaro Palacios, Clos Martinet, Pingus, R. Lopez de Heredia; **U.S.–California:** Araujo, Benziger, Bonny Doon, Ceago, Corison, Frey, Grgich Hills, Joseph Phelps, Patianna, Porter Creek, Quintessa, Qupé, Robert Sinskey, Tandem Porter-Bass; **Oregon:** Brick House, Cooper Mountain, Cowhorn, Maysara; **Washington state:** Cayuse, Reeds Lane, Wallula Gap, Wilridge

BLAUBURGUNDER

[blahw-bur-GOON-der]
See PINOT NOIR, for which Blauburgunder is the common name in Austria and Switzerland. In Germany it is also known as SPÄTBURGUNDER.
Countries: Austria, Germany, Italy (Alto Adige), Switzerland

BLAUFRÄNKISCH

[blahw-FRANK-eesh]
Countries: Austria, Czech Republic, Germany, Hungary (native), Slovakia, Slovenia, U.S. (New York, Washington state)
Color: red
Grapes: Blaufränkisch
Weight: medium-bodied
Volume: moderate to moderate-plus
Dry/sweet: dry
Acidity: medium-high to high
Tannin: high
Flavors: fruity, with notes of beets, blackberries, **black cherries,** black currants, **black (or white) pepper,** blueberries, chocolate, earth, game, meat, minerals, plums, raspberries, smoke, **spices,** tobacco

Texture: silky, smooth, soft, velvety
Temperature: Serve slightly chilled, about 55 to 60 degrees.
Comparables: BEAUJOLAIS CRU, **Kekfrankos (Hungary), Lemberger (Germany, U.S.), Limberger (Washington state),** SYRAH, ZINFANDEL
Pairings: duck, game, hamburgers, lamb, venison
Producers: **Austria:** Feiler-Artinger, Gesellmann, Heinrich, Hogue, Kiona, Prieler; **U.S.–New York/Long Island:** Channing Daughters

BLENDED WINES

Wines made from two or more grape varieties are often categorized under their dominant varietal, though the blends are often overlooked altogether. The following wines are examples of blends from various countries:

Argentina: Nicolas Catena Zapata, a blend of Cabernet Sauvignon and Malbec
France: Châteauneuf-du-Pape
Greece: Domaine Gerovassiliou Avaton, a blend of Limnio (said to be the oldest Greek grape variety, mentioned by Aristotle), Mavrondi, and Mavrotragano
Israel: Yatir Forest, a blend of Cabernet Sauvignon and Merlot
Italy: Jermann Vintage Tunina, a blend of Chardonnay, Sauvignon Blanc, and other white varieties, such as Malvasia, Picolit, Pinot Bianco, Ribolla, and Tocai
Portugal: Aveleda Follies, a blend of Chardonnay and Maria Gomes
South Africa: Meerlust Rubicon, a blend of Cabernet Franc, Cabernet Sauvignon, and Merlot

Uruguay: Gewürztraminer-based Viñedo de los Vientos Estival, a white blend
U.S./California: Conundrum, a white blend; Dominus, a red Bordeaux blend produced by Christian Moueix of Château Pétrus; Harlan Estate Proprietary Red Wine; **Insignia,** a red blend produced by Joseph Phelps; Monte Bello, a red blend produced by Ridge; **New Jersey:** Unionville "The Big O" Red Montage, a Bordeaux-style blend; **Virginia:** Barboursville Octagon, a Bordeaux-style blend

BOBAL

[boh-BAHL]
Country: Spain
Regions: **Albacete, Cuenca,** Manchuela, Ribera del Júcar, Utiel-Requena, **Valencia**
Color: red (and rosé)
Grapes: Bobal, often blended with other red grapes such as Cabernet Sauvignon, Garnacha, Merlot, Syrah, and Tempranillo
Weight: medium-bodied
Volume: moderate to loud
Dry/sweet: dry
Acidity: high
Tannin: high
Flavors: fruity, with notes of blackberries, cherries (red), chocolate, earth, herbs (aromas), meat, smoke, spices, strawberries
Texture: crisp, fresh, lively
Temperature: Serve slightly chilled, about 55 degrees.
Pairings: beef, hamburgers, lamb, paprika, pork, venison
Tip: Bobal is the third most widely planted grape in Spain, after Airén and Tempranillo.
Producers: Bodegas Vitivinos (Azua Bobal Roble), Cooperativa UCI–Castelnoble (Realce Bobal Rosado)

BONARDA

[bohn-ARD-uh]
Countries: Argentina (Mendoza), Brazil, Italy (Piedmont)
Color: red
Grapes: Bonarda, sometimes blended with Cabernet Franc or Malbec
Weight: light- to medium-bodied
Volume: moderate
Dry/sweet: dry
Acidity: medium
Tannin: low
Flavors: fruity, with notes of anise, blackberries, black pepper, blueberries, cherries, cinnamon, earth, figs, flowers, herbs, licorice, minerals, **plums**, raisins, raspberries, smoke, **spices**, strawberries, tar, toast, tobacco, vanilla
Texture: elegant, fresh, rich, round, silky, smooth, soft
Temperature: Serve slightly chilled, about 55 to 60 degrees.
Comparables: BEAUJOLAIS, MERLOT
Pairings: barbecue, beef, burritos, charcuterie, cheese, chili, hamburgers, pasta, sausages
Tip: Older, oak-aged Bonarda can be fuller-bodied and louder.
Aging: Drink young and fresh, within a year or two.
Producers: Argentina: Alma Negra, Altos las Hormigas, Bodegas las Hormigas Colonia las Liebres, Catena Zapata Alamos, Crios, Mayol, Nieto Senetiner, Zuccardi; **Italy:** Ca' di Frara

BONNEZEAUX

[bawn-ZOH]
Country: France
Region: Loire/Côteaux du Layon
Color: white
Grapes: Chenin Blanc
Weight: full-bodied
Volume: loud
Dry/sweet: semi-sweet to sweet
Acidity: medium to high
Flavors: notes of almonds, apples, apricots, **candied fruits,** guava, **honey,** melon, **minerals,** pears, **quince,** tropical fruits
Texture: luscious, **rich,** soft, unctuous
Temperature: Serve very cold, about 45 degrees.
Comparable: QUARTS DE CHAUME
Pairings: blue cheese, foie gras, fruit desserts (esp. with apricots, pears, pineapple, rhubarb), ice cream, tarte Tatin
Aging: These wines become richer with aging, so age for at least a decade; the best are said to last indefinitely.
Producers: M. Angeli/ Sansonnière, **Fesles,** René Renou

BORDEAUX—RED

See also CABERNET SAUVIGNON, GRAVES, MÉDOC, POMEROL, SAINT-ÉMILION.
Country: France
Region: Bordeaux
Color: red
Grapes: CABERNET SAUVIGNON and/or **Merlot,** primarily; blends may also feature **Cabernet Franc,** Malbec, Petit Verdot, or others
Weight: medium- to full-bodied (and high in alcohol)
Volume: loud to very loud
Dry/sweet: dry
Acidity: medium
Tannin: high (though softens with age)
Flavors: notes of blackberries, black cherries, **BLACK CURRANTS/CASSIS, cedar** (esp. oaked wines), chocolate, coffee, dark chocolate, earth, herbs, leather (esp. older wines), licorice, **minerals,** mushrooms (esp. older wines), olives, pencil shavings, **plums, smoke,** spices, tobacco, truffles, **vanilla,** violets
Texture: rich, silky, velvety
Temperature: Serve cool, about 60 to 65 degrees.
Comparables: CABERNET SAUVIGNON, MERITAGE, MERLOT
Season: autumn–winter
Pairings: beef, duck, game, lamb, meat, Parmesan cheese, squab, steak, venison
Tips: Bordeaux is divided into the Cabernet Sauvignon–dominated Left Bank (comprising Médoc to the north and Graves to the south) and the Merlot-dominated Right Bank. Bordeaux has seven major appellations: Margaux, Pauillac, Saint-Estèphe, and Saint-Julien in Médoc; Graves; and Pomerol and Saint-Émilion on the Right Bank. Bordeaux wines tend to be blends, while Burgundy wines are single varietals. Bordeaux wines range in price from ten dollars a bottle to thousands of dollars for a prized Château Pétrus.
Aging: Red Bordeaux age better than arguably any other red wine and should be aged five to ten years before drinking. They can age for twenty to twenty-five years or more. Best recent vintages: 2009, 2005, 2000, 1996, 1995, 1990, 1989, 1985, 1982.
Producers: The famed 1855 classification sets forth Bordeaux reds into five tiers, from first growths (highest quality) to fifth growths. Bordeaux's "Big 8" producers include the five first growths—Haut-Brion, Lafite-

Pétrus, aaahhh . . . what a wine! With a billion layers, from the label to the wine itself, it is just beautiful, very elegant. It is one of the few wines that speaks to me. The first time I had Pétrus was at Asiate [at the Mandarin Oriental Hotel in Manhattan, where she worked at the time] at a dinner of collectors, mostly Japanese guests who blind-tasted the wines, and one of them guessed, "A 1964 Pétrus—because nothing else tastes like that." He was right . . . and then he gave me a glass! I honestly cannot forget that silky texture. It is a wine that to me is classy and alive and made me realize that I have an amazing career ahead of me. Pétrus is on every high-end wine list, and in every Bordelais's heart—indeed, in every French person's heart. My dad always promised me a bottle of Pétrus; he gave me plenty of Yquem instead, so I can't complain. The magnum of 1953 I'm holding [in the photo below] came straight from the cellar of Pétrus. It is very authentic; the label is still dusty and a bit damaged by time. I chose it for nostalgic reasons but also because it is the best **Bordeaux** I have ever had—and Bordeaux still today represents wine in the world. Everybody starts with Merlot [on which Pétrus is based]; it is such an underrated grape!

—EMILIE PERRIER, AI FIORI

EMILIE PERRIER

Rothschild, Latour, Margaux, and Mouton Rothschild—plus Ausone, Cheval Blanc, and Pétrus. Château Léoville Las Cases is known as the second growth that deserves to be a first growth. In addition, there are many producers making far more affordable wines, such as Châteaux Doyac, Le Conseiller, and de Reignac.

Iconic example: **Left Bank (Cabernet-based):** Château Latour Pauillac; **Right Bank (Merlot-based):** Château Pétrus Pomerol, often cited as the world's most expensive Bordeaux wine

BORDEAUX—WHITE

Country: France
Region: Bordeaux
Color: white
Grapes: Sauvignon Blanc, Sémillon (primarily)
Weight: medium-bodied
Volume: moderate
Dry/sweet: dry
Acidity: medium-high to high
Flavors: aromatic, with notes of citrus, earth, figs, flowers, green apples, herbs, honey, lemon, melon, minerals, smoke, stones, toast, vanilla
Texture: crisp to creamy (esp. when Sémillon is part of the blend), smooth
Temperature: Serve slightly chilled, about 55 to 60 degrees.
Comparables: GRAVES, SAUVIGNON BLANC
Season: autumn–winter (esp. aged)
Pairings: fish, shellfish
Aging: While most white Bordeaux can be drunk young, the best can be aged for a decade or more. Look for the 2007, **2005**, 2002, and **2000** vintages.

You will spend money on the higher-end **Bordeaux** [from Châteaux] Lafite and Latour. Château Haut-Brion is still the best deal for a first growth, and you still get those great Bordeaux flavors. You can get a third-label Lynch-Bages [Château Haut-Bages] Averous, for under $100—and you can find Château Greysac for $45, so you can drink Bordeaux for under fifty bucks! . . . Bordeaux got famous for its price tags from its classifications in the 1800s. I tell people, "Bordeaux is for the rich, Rhône is for royalty." Rhône was the wine for the pope.

—HRISTO ZISOVSKI, AI FIORI

I participated in a tasting of "Value **Bordeaux**" that was an all-blind tasting over two days, and we tasted more than one hundred wines each day. Bordeaux puts out an image that it is regal and what aristocrats drink, so we forget how much Bordeaux wine is out there. The classified Bordeaux that comes from Médoc or Pauillac is a tiny percentage of Bordeaux. We tasted at all different price points in groups: $8–$15, $15–$20, $20–$30, and $30–$40. It was a great learning experience because each wine had a totally different personality. For the most part the super-inexpensive group was Beaujolais-like in character: fruity, simple, easy to drink, and enjoyable. As you climbed up the ladder, you tasted more concentration, with oak being a bigger player in the wine. Toward the top, even though you are tasting value Bordeaux from great estates making serious wine, you are saying, "Wow, this is great—but I would love to see this in ten to fifteen years!" This reminds you how a great house in a village like Listrac or Moulis can totally outshine someone from Saint-Julien who is not working hard. Then you compare their price tags. . . . You can find complete results at the website for the Bordeaux Wine Bureau [http://www.bordeauxwinebureau.org/top_100.html].

—JOHN RAGAN, ELEVEN MADISON PARK

Iconic examples: Château Carbonnieux, **Château Haut-Brion**, Château Pape-Clément, Domaine de Chevalier, Laville Haut-Brion, Smith Haut Lafitte

BOXED WINES

Tip: After tasting celebrated chef Daniel Boulud's "boxed" dTour wine several years ago at his home in New York City, we became believers in the potential of this packaging. Indeed, the Premium 3-liter box (which holds the equivalent of four bottles) is one of the fastest-growing wine formats. We predict that this environmentally friendly format will continue to gain in popularity

in the years to come: It comes in handy for picnics and other entertaining, keeps well in your refrigerator for weeks, and is still value-priced. Serve it from a decanter if you don't want your guests to be the wiser.

Producers: Argentina: Falling Star Malbec, Maipe Malbec, Yellow + Blue Malbec and Torrontés; **Australia:** Banrock Station Shiraz, Hardys Cabernet Sauvignon, and Shiraz; **Chile:** Quelu Cabernet Sauvignon; **France:** from the Tank Côtes du Rhône and Grenache Blanc; Domaine de L'Estel Vin Du Pays Du Gard Rosé; La Petite Frog Picpoul de Pinet; Le Bord'Eaux Merlot, VRAC Côtes du Rhône; **Hungary:** Pinot Evil Pinot Noir; **New Zealand:** Black Box Sauvignon Blanc, Silver Birch Winery Sauvignon Blanc; **U.S.–California:** Bandit Pinot Grigio, Big House Red, Black Box Cabernet Sauvignon, Chardonnay, and Shiraz; Boho Vineyards Cabernet Sauvignon, Chardonnay, and Merlot; Fish Eye Pinot Grigio; **Washington state:** Washington Hills Riesling

BRACHETTO D'ACQUI

[brah-KAY-to DAH-kwee]
Country: Italy
Region: Piedmont
Color: red
Grapes: Brachetto
Weight: light-bodied
Volume: quiet to moderate
Dry/sweet: sweet
Acidity: medium
Tannin: low to **medium**
Flavors: fruity, with notes of cherries, **raspberries**, roses, **strawberries**, vanilla
Texture: semi-sparkling to sparkling
Temperature: Serve chilled, about 50 to 55 degrees.
Pairings: brunch dishes,

We probably sell more **Brachetto d'Acqui** in California than they do in Italy! Our desserts are playful—things like banana splits and chocolate sundaes that can make you feel like a kid again. They go well with fresh berry flavors. Brachetto has great fruit with a lot of richness and complexity, yet it is light, effervescent, and low in alcohol. It's so much fun with dessert—you can sip it all night long!

—JULIA MORETTI, AD HOC

I love anything that is bubbly and red. I am a fan of Villa Giada **Brachetto d'Acqui**. The winemaker Andrea Faccio is a Brachetto meister. The winery treats its Brachetto with as much respect as its still reds. I went through a big tasting for Rick Tramonto [of Tru restaurant in Chicago] for the breakfast chapter of his book, and I found the best pairing was Brachetto. One of the reasons it works is because the alcohol is only [5 to 7] percent. I also really like it with the Deli Scramble from Carnegie Deli that is made with scrambled eggs and salami.

—BELINDA CHANG, THE MODERN

chocolate desserts, fresh berries, fresh fruit
Producers: Banfi, Braida, Contero, Malvira, Marenco, Vigne Regali, Villa Giada

BRAZILIAN WINES
Country: Brazil
Grapes: red: Cabernet Franc, Cabernet Sauvignon, Merlot, Tannat, Teroldego; **white:** Chardonnay
Tip: Many, if not most, Brazilian wineries produce sparkling wines as well as still wines.
Producers: Aurora, Casa Valduga, Lidio Carraro, Miolo, Salton

BRUNELLO DI MONTALCINO
[broo-NELL-oh dee mon-tal-CHEE-noh]
Country: Italy
Region: Tuscany/Montalcino
Color: red (and dark in hue)
Grapes: Brunello (aka Sangiovese Grosso)
Weight: medium- to full-bodied
Volume: moderately loud (long-aged) to loud (younger)
Dry/sweet: dry
Acidity: high
Tannin: medium to **high**
Flavors: notes of **black and red cherries,** blackberries, black pepper, citrus, coffee, dark chocolate, earth, **flowers,** game, herbs, leather, menthol, minerals, orange peel, plums, smoke, spices, tar, violets
Texture: creamy, rich, silky, smooth, velvety
Temperature: Serve cool, about 60 to 65 degrees.
Comparable: ROSSO DI MONTALCINO (somewhat lighter in weight and quieter in volume, with a fresher characteristic)
Season: winter
Pairings: bistecca alla Fiorentina, cheese (esp. aged and/or Parmesan), game, lamb, pasta with meat sauce, red meat (esp. roasted), steak, stews
Tip: ROSSO DI MONTALCINO is made from the same grape, is slightly lighter in body, is ready to be drunk upon release, and offers terrific value.

Aging: Brunello has such exceptional aging potential that it should not be opened for a decade; the best are known to age for several decades. Best recent vintages: 2004, 2001, 1999.
Producers: Altesino, Angelo Gaja, **Biondi-Santi,** Ca' Marcanda, Case-Basse di Soldera, Castelgiocondo, Castello Banfi, Castello di Romitorio, **Ciacci Piccolomini,** Col d'Orcia, Conti, Costanti, Il Poggione, La Fornace, Le Macioche, Pertimali di Livio Sassetti, Ruffino, Talenti

BUGEY (SPARKLING ROSÉ)
[boo-ZHAY]
Country: France
Region: Bugey
Color: red (with pink hues)
Grapes: GAMAY, Poulsard
Weight: light-bodied (and low in alcohol, about 8 percent)
Volume: quiet to moderate
Dry/sweet: lightly sweet
Acidity: medium to high
Tannin: low
Flavors: notes of **cherries,** cranberries, flowers, minerals, **raspberries,** spices, **strawberries**
Texture: crisp, juicy, sparkling
Temperature: Serve cold, about 45 to 50 degrees.

I love **Bugey**—it is one of my favorite things in the world. It is the one wine I always have in my house, and is the only wine I buy by the case! It is a really good brunch wine. If you try to drink Champagne with pancakes, it is such a sad thing. When you take a sip of Champagne with maple syrup, you are tasting bitter lemon juice with bubbles at $20 or more a bottle. Bugey is perfect because it has sugar to match the sweetness of pancakes. It is also good with eggs. It is a great sitting-outside-in-the-afternoon wine. I love that it is low in alcohol. I love that it has a hint of sweetness without it being overpowering. I love the fruit characteristics—it is like strawberry juice, but it is still wine. I find that sweeter wines tend to taste more like juice, where Bugey still tastes like wine. I am a fan of both Renardat-Fâche and Patrick Bottex's "La Cueille."

—DANA FARNER, CUT

Season: summer
Pairings: aperitif, brunch dishes (from French toast with strawberries to eggs), summer fruit desserts
Aging: Drink young and fresh.
Producers: Patrick Bottex Bugey Cerdon Rosé "La Cueille," Renardat-Fâche Bugey Cerdon

BURGUNDY—RED

See also PINOT NOIR.
Country: France
Region: Burgundy
Color: red
Grapes: Pinot Noir
Weight: light-bodied
Volume: quiet to moderate
Dry/sweet: dry
Acidity: medium to **high**
Tannin: low to medium
Flavors: very aromatic, with notes of **BLACK CHERRIES**, cedar, cranberries, **earth**, flowers, game, meat, **minerals**, **mushrooms**, plums, **raspberries**, smoke, spices, **strawberries**, toast, truffles, vanilla, violets
Texture: delicate, rich, silky, smooth, soft, velvety
Temperature: Serve cool, about 60 degrees.
Comparables: cru BEAUJOLAIS, PINOT NOIR
Season: autumn–winter (esp. older wines)
Pairings: beef bourguignon, duck, game, lamb, mushrooms, rabbit, root vegetables
Tip: Burgundy wines are single varietals, while Bordeaux wines tend to be blends. Look for Burgundies from good vintage years, such as 2005.
Aging: Drink immediately (esp. lesser Pinots) or after five years (better Pinots) and up to two or even three decades (great Pinots). Best recent vintages: 2005, 2003, 2002, 2001, 1999, 1998.
Producers: Bouchard Père et Fils, Comtes Lafon, Domaine Bachelet, Domaine Dujac Morey-St-Denis, Domaine Faiveley, Domaine Leflaive, **Domaine Leroy**, Domaine Perrot-Minot, Domaine Richebourg, **Henri Jayer**, Joseph Drouhin, **Louis Jadot**, Louis Latour, Michel Lafarge, Mugneret-Gibourg, Nicolas Potel, Robert Chevillon, **ROMANÉE-CONTI**, Roulot, Sylvain Cathiard, Tollot-Beaut
Iconic examples: DOMAINE DE LA ROMANÉE-CONTI, **Domaine Leroy**

BURGUNDY—WHITE

See also CHARDONNAY, CHASSAGNE-MONTRACHET, MEURSAULT, POUILLY-FUISSÉ, PULIGNY-MONTRACHET.
Country: France
Region: Burgundy
Color: white
Grapes: Chardonnay
Weight: medium- to full-bodied (and lower in alcohol than California Chardonnay)

As part of our staff wine training, we are planning our first ever voluntary trip during our closing in January. We are flying into Paris, then going to Champagne and the Côte d'Or for about ten days. We are partial to the area because we are all huge **Burgundy** fans. There is something magical about the vineyards of the Côte d'Or. We have all seen pictures of Romanée-Conti with the cross, and La Tâche and Le Montrachet. When you are standing in front of those vineyards, it is so powerful.
—DENNIS KELLY, THE FRENCH LAUNDRY

Pinot Noir is a miracle. If you drink red **Burgundy,** these wines are not self-explanatory. You have to sit down and think about them a little. They are like divas; they all want to be understood, yet they don't care what other people think because they are so eccentric.
—ALDO SOHM, LE BERNARDIN

Burgundy is structured with a quality-classification system that follows price really well. You don't have to spend a fortune to begin to learn about Burgundy and taste some really nice wines. By seeking Village wines and basic Bourgogne from good producers, you get good insight into the world of Burgundy. They give you a very general sense of what Burgundy should taste like. As you learn more, you can step up into Premier Crus—and when you decide to go crazy, you have Grand Cru waiting. Because Burgundy is so geographically transparent, you can experience the place through the wines better than in most places on the planet. It is such a fun way to learn about wines. Once you have a handle on what you like in Burgundy in terms of flavor profile, with the bright cherry, strawberry fruits, that sense of earth with the clay that comes through so many of them on the nose, once you get through that and start to adjust your palate, then you can start exploring more specific appellation wines and the flavors of each place. That is what drives people like me forward to learn more and more.
—SCOTT CALVERT, THE INN AT LITTLE WASHINGTON

Raj Vaidya of Daniel on Burgundy

Burgundy is pretty well accepted to be a great wine, but many people don't know when or how to drink it—or even which ones to drink, because they can be expensive, and people are worried about spending money on something that is inconsistent. What is great about Burgundy is that there is always something to learn, despite it being so old and codified.

Daniel Boulud's cuisine is real artistry; it is delicate. What is special about Burgundy as a pairing wine is that it has the three things you need in order to taste a wine with a number of dishes. I am referring to a bottle here, not just a glass to pair with a course, because you want to see it develop—that is part of the fun.

1. It has good **aromatic** complexity. An aroma that draws you in is important because it has a huge effect on how long it will stay on your palate and how it affects the food you are eating. Just having the structural components in your mouth—acid, alcohol, sugar, and tannin—has plenty of effect, but without the aromatic complexity it can be lost and dulled quite quickly.
2. It has **high acidity.** During the course of a whole meal you want something with good acidity, but you also want something with fruit and alcohol. I tend to avoid very high-acid wines from the Loire Valley for the whole dinner because the wine may have too much acidity.
3. For a red wine, it has a **low amount of tannin.**

If you are experimenting, choose wines with more aromatic structure and less oak that are a little easier to pair, such as basic **Bourgogne Rouge** or a good **Village Chambolle-Musigny.** You should not spend a lot of money on a wine right off the bat, because when you start with Bourgogne and get to really love it, when you put that **Chambolle-Musigny Les Amoureuses** in your glass, you are going to understand why you are impressed, because you have other reference points. God knows I don't drink Amoureuses at home!

We offer pairing menus here, which is a great way for novices to have a fun experience. In reality, you have to pick wines that have higher alcohol, more fruit, and more bang in the glass for those by-the-glass pairings. The reason is that you are getting only one little snapshot of what the wine is. From the moment it is opened to the moment it is drained, only one little snapshot ends up in your glass for a few minutes while you are pairing it with the food. Then you move on to something else. You are not getting a full experience of drinking an entire bottle of that wine. That is why I wouldn't pour an amazing aged Burgundy in a tiny glass and allow someone to have just a little snapshot of it. A great wine is one you want to have a conversation with; you want to have it open up and speak to you. You really experience a wine when you drink it slowly until it is completely opened up, evolved, and expressive. That is never the case for any wine when you just open it. Even if it tastes correct when you first open it. . . . You have to have the full experience.

Volume: moderate
Dry/sweet: dry
Acidity: medium to high
Flavors: aromatic, with notes of apples, butter, butterscotch, chalk, earth, flowers, **hazelnuts**, honey, lemon, licorice, minerals, nuts (esp. roasted), pears, spices, toast, vanilla

Texture: creamy, rich, silky; sometimes crisp
Temperature: Serve chilled, about 50 to 55 degrees.
Comparables: CHABLIS, CHARDONNAY, CHASSAGNE-MONTRACHET, Côte de Beaune, Mâconnais, MEURSAULT, PULIGNY-MONTRACHET

Season: winter
Pairings: butter and cream sauces, chicken, fish, lobster, pasta, scallops, shellfish, shrimp, sole, veal
Under-$15 tip: Open a bottle of Louis Jadot Mâcon-Villages.
Aging: Drink modest wines young and fresh, within three

We recently had Jacques Pépin in for dinner at the restaurant, and one of our regular guests, who was dining with his wife, ordered a 1999 Premier Cru Vosne-Romanée from Méo-Camuzet in **Burgundy.** When he saw Jacques Pépin in the room, he asked me to send him a glass. I am sure Jacques has tasted many great wines in his life, but when he tasted that Vosne-Romanée his face lit up and he was shocked. He said, "What is this wine? You must show me the label!" I brought it over and wrote it down for him. He took it away with him, and I know he was going to try to find some, because it was so shockingly good. That's what great wine tastes like: it's shockingly good. That is why many command the prices they get year in and year out.

—MICHAEL FLYNN, THE MANSION ON TURTLE CREEK

From **Burgundy** I drink Village-level **Chambolle-Musigny.** We have some fancy bottles, but we save those for wine dinners where we need to bring something special.

—ROBERT BOHR, COLICCHIO & SONS

Bordeaux and **Burgundy** are two of the great wine regions of the world, and yet they are at opposite ends of the spectrum. Bordeaux is about business—wine and money—and there is nothing wrong with that. If they are making 20,000 cases, they might ask themselves, "How can we make 22,000?" But Burgundy has always been about artistry. [Its creators] are farmers and winemakers who focus on the art of what they are producing. They will focus on quality, often making 1,000 cases or fewer. For them, their wine is a piece of themselves that they are showing to the world.

—BERNARD SUN, JEAN GEORGES

Burgundy is a good place to learn the importance of the producer. There are fifteen guys making Échézeaux, and a winemaker will have rows of grapes next to another producer who makes crappy wine because they are not treating their grapes right.

—MARK MENDOZA, SONA

After working at Bouley, I went over to Le Bernardin as its sommelier for ten years. I enjoyed working with Eric Ripert a lot, because he was very involved with the wine. Every time he created a new menu, I would taste the food and he would try the wine. He gave me complete freedom with the list. It was good for me because at every other restaurant where I had worked, the majority of the wine sold was red. At Le Bernardin, it was mostly white wine, which I rediscovered. It was a seafood restaurant, so what else are you going to drink? You could drink red wine, but with the finesse of the dishes, **White Burgundy** was magic. Because of that, today I am a big lover of white wine. Some people will say that white wine is not as complex as red wine—but for me, it is the opposite. White wine has so much complexity—especially if you are trying **Meursault** or **Puligny-Montrachet.** It took me years to understand the complexity.

—MICHEL COUVREUX, PER SE

to five years. If you can't wait the recommended full decade, drink Premier Cru after at least three years and Grand Cru after at least five; they may last as long as two decades (Premier Cru) or three (Grand Cru). Best recent vintages: 2009, 2007, 2006, 2005, 2002.
Producers: Coche-Dury, Comtes Lafon, Joseph Drouhin, Faiveley, Louis Jadot, Louis Latour, **Olivier Leflaive,** Ramonet, Raveneau, Roulot

CABERNET FRANC

[KA-ber-nay FRAHNK]
Countries: Argentina, Australia, Canada, **France (Bordeaux, Loire Valley),** Italy (Friuli, Trentino), New Zealand, U.S. (California, New York/Long Island, Washington state)
Color: red (with purple hues)
Grapes: Cabernet Franc, often blended with Cabernet Sauvignon and/or Merlot
Weight: medium-bodied
Volume: moderate to loud
Dry/sweet: dry
Acidity: high
Tannin: medium to high
Flavors: aromatic and fruity, with notes of **black and red currants/** cassis, **blackberries,** black pepper, blueberries, cedar, coffee, earth, grass, **GREEN BELL PEPPERS,** green olives, **herbs,** leather, menthol/mint, minerals, pencil shavings, **plums, RASPBERRIES, red cherries,** spices, stones, strawberries, tobacco, violets
Texture: fine, rich, soft, velvety
Temperature: Serve slightly chilled, about 55 to 60 degrees.
Comparables: Bourgueil, CHINON, POMEROL, SAINT-ÉMILION, Saumur
Season: spring
Pairings: chicken, herbed dishes,

A game I like to play is "If you were a wine grape, which would you be and why?" I'd be **Cabernet Franc**—because when it's made well and it's perfectly ripe, it is this wonderful combination of fruitiness and floral notes, with great acid and structure. It's a grape that's wonderful on its own or in a blend, and its wines are generally a good value. You can find some great examples made [in the Loire]. But if it's not made right and it's not done well, it's terrible!

—JILL ZIMORSKI, CAFÉ ATLÁNTICO

Pillitteri **Cabernet Franc** from Niagara [Canada] has both complexity and restraint—it's like a Bordeaux-meets-California wine that would be perfect with a hanger steak.

—STEVE BECKTA, BECKTA DINING & WINE AND PLAY FOOD & WINE

I tasted the 2008 Hermann J. Wiemer **Cabernet Franc** as a barrel sample—and could already tell it was going to be a blockbuster!

—MICHAEL CIMINO, GLENMERE MANSION

lamb, mushrooms, pork, rabbit, veal, vegetable dishes
Aging: Typically drink young, although the very best can age for decades.
Producers: Canada: Pillitteri; **France–Loire:** Château Yvonne, Clos Rougeard; **U.S.–California:** Jarvis, Oakville Ranch, Signorello; **New York:** Hermann J. Wiemer, Wölffer Estate; **Virginia:** Barboursville; **Washington state:** Columbia
Iconic example: Château Cheval Blanc, a sometimes Cab Franc–dominant blend

---

CABERNET SAUVIGNON

[ka-ber-NAY soh-vee-NYAWN]
See also BORDEAUX–RED.
Countries: Argentina, Australia, Bulgaria, Chile, **France (BORDEAUX–LEFT BANK,** Languedoc-Roussillon), Italy, New Zealand, Romania, South Africa, Spain, **U.S. (CALIFORNIA–NAPA,** Washington state)
Color: red (dark in color, with a purple hue)
Grapes: Cabernet Sauvignon, sometimes blended with

Cabernet Franc, Merlot, Syrah, and/or other red grapes
Weight: full-bodied
Volume: loud
Dry/sweet: dry
Acidity: high
Tannin: high
Flavors: notes of **blackberries**, black cherries, **BLACK CURRANTS AND/OR CASSIS**, black pepper, **cedar** (esp. French oaked wines), **chocolate**, cinnamon, coffee, earth, eucalyptus (esp. California Cabs), green bell peppers, herbs, leather, meat,

minerals, **mint** (esp. Australian or California Cabs), oak, olives, pencil shavings (esp. French oaked wines), plums, raisins, raspberries, smoke, spices, stones, tobacco, tomatoes, vanilla, violets
Flavors: cool climate: black pepper, cedar, green bell peppers, tobacco, violets; **warm climate:** blackberries, blueberries, eucalyptus, herbs, mint
Texture: rough (esp. young); rich, smooth (esp. aged)
Temperature: Serve cool, about 60 to 65 degrees.
Comparables: BORDEAUX–RED, fuller-bodied MERLOT
Pairings: beef, black pepper, cheese (esp. rich), game, hamburgers, lamb, mushrooms, red meats, steak
Season: autumn–winter
Aging: Cabernet Sauvignon has arguably the longest aging potential of all wines, with time softening its rough edges. While it can be enjoyed young, the best California Cabernet can be aged for a decade or two. Best recent vintages (California): 2008, 2007, 2005, 2003, 2002, 2001, 1999.
Producers: Argentina: Catena,

There are so many styles of **Cabernet Sauvignon**. There are producers who make big, brooding, powerful wines with black fruit. Then others produce wines that are incredibly elegant with red fruit, earth, and minerality—and they are right next door to each other! Bryant Family and Colgin are both in the Pritchard Hill area, which is an up-and-coming area for California Cabernet Sauvignon that has all-volcanic soil. They are both exceptional, highly regarded, and amazing. However, they are very different: Bryant Family is more high-toned, with red fruit and more earth. Colgin is incredibly powerful, with more black fruit and smoky minerality. You can see one property from the other. The *terroir* in one is south-facing, the other east-facing. Colgin is in primary rock, whereas Bryant Family is in Aiken soil, which is a highly regarded red volcanic soil. This is the soil you find at other outstanding vineyards like Dalla Valle's Maya and Screaming Eagle.

—DENNIS KELLY, THE FRENCH LAUNDRY

Trapiche; **Australia:** Grant
Burge, Parker Coonawarra
Estate, Penfolds Koonunga Hill,
Tahbilk, Wynns; **Chile:** Carmen
Nativa, Casa Lapostolle, Concha
y Toro, **Cousiño-Macul,** Los
Vascos, Santa Rita; **France:** *see*
BORDEAUX–RED; **Greece:** Katsaros;
Israel: Chillag "Primo"; **Italy:**
Sassicaia; **South Africa** (high
acidity): Kanonkop, Meerlust,
Rust en Vrede, Vergelegen;
U.S.–California: Altamura,
Beringer, Black Box, Cakebread,
Calistoga Estate (value), Caymus,
Chappellet, **Chateau Montelena,**
Chateau Souverain, Chimney
Rock, Clos du Val, Concannon,
Corison, Dominus, Dry Creek,
Eberle, Estancia, Far Niente, Flora
Springs, Freemark Abbey, Geyser
Peak, Hagen Heights, **Harlan
Estate, Heitz Martha's Vineyard,**
Hess Select, Hidden Ridge,
Howell Mountain, **Joseph Phelps,
Laurel Glen,** Murphy-Goode,
Neal Family, Opus One, Ridge,
Robert Mondavi, Sequoia Grove,
Shafer, Silver Oak, Smith &
Hook, **Spottswoode, Stag's Leap,**
Sterling, St. Supery, Trefethen;
New York: Chateau LaFayette
Reynaud; **Washington state:**
Andrew Will, Columbia Crest,
Quilceda Creek

CAHORS
[kah-OR]
Country: France
Region: Southwest
Color: red (and blackish in hue)
Grapes: MALBEC, **Merlot,**
Tannat
Weight: full-bodied
Volume: very loud
Dry/sweet: dry
Acidity: medium
Tannin: high to very high
Flavors: notes of blackberries,

Among **California wines,** I am a big fan of Moraga Vineyards in Los
Angeles [in Bel Air, where Moraga makes a Sauvignon Blanc–based
white wine and a Cabernet-Merlot red blend]. Located on the Russian
River, Soliste makes a wonderful Pinot Noir. Lieff is in Napa and
makes an absolutely phenomenal Cabernet Sauvignon. It is not a big,
fat Cabernet; it is refined and elegant, with soft, generous fruit. I have
tried four vintages and have been very impressed.
—STEPHANE COLLING, SAN YSIDRO RANCH

I give a lot of credit to our younger sommelier, Scott Barber, who has a
keen eye for what is new, hot, and up-and-coming, while I tend to have
a more solid appreciation for those who have been around for a while,
as you might expect. Scott has turned me on to a number of producers
who bear some scrutiny. Peay on the Sonoma Coast of **California** is an
extremely *terroir*-driven winery. Vanessa Wong, the winemaker, used to
be the winemaker for Peter Michael. Peay makes primarily Pinot Noir
and Chardonnay from cool-climate sites on the Sonoma Coast with
very small production.
—MICHAEL FLYNN, THE MANSION ON TURTLE CREEK

People will come to our restaurant to drink **California** and Napa Valley
wine specifically. Being in California, I have had the opportunity to
learn about California wines and about people doing exceptional
things. Stony Hill makes amazing Riesling in the Alsatian style, and
we have vintages back to 1992. We had the sommelier from the Fat
Duck [Michelin three-star restaurant], and he asked for a tasting with
all California wines. We served the Stony Hill Riesling and a Late
Harvest Furmint from the 1990s from Russian River Valley. So it was a
very diverse pairing, all from California.
—DENNIS KELLY, THE FRENCH LAUNDRY

black cherries, chocolate, herbs
(esp. dried), leather, licorice, oak,
PLUMS (FRESH OR DRIED),
raisins, raspberries, smoke,
spices, **tobacco,** violets
Texture: coarse (young); rich,
velvety (older)
Temperature: Serve slightly
chilled, about 55 to 60 degrees.
Comparables: PETITE SIRAH,
TANNAT
Pairings: beef, **cassoulet,** duck
confit, fatty meat dishes, foie gras,
lamb, mushrooms, pork
Tip: Open a bottle of Cahors an
hour or two (or, better yet, several
hours) before serving to let it
breathe.
Aging: Age at least five years

before opening, although the best
will still show well after a decade
or longer.
Producers: Château de Gaudou,
Châteaux du Cedre, Château
Gautoul, Château Lagrezette,
Château les Croisille, Château
Pech de Jammes, Clos de Gamot,
Clos la Coutale, Clos Triguedina,
Croix du Mayne, Domaine
Pineraie, Haute-Serre, Lacapelle
Cabanac, Lamartine, Vigouroux

CALIFORNIA WINES
Red: Cabernet Sauvignon,
Merlot, Pinot Noir, Syrah,
Zinfandel
White: Chardonnay, Riesling,
Sauvignon Blanc

Working at Gramercy Tavern, if you had the tiniest bit of curiosity you had access to everything. This was the first place I tasted 1991 Harlan Estate, because in '96 and '97 it wasn't a big deal yet, but it was still $300 on the list [a bottle now ranges from hundreds of dollars to more than a thousand]. At that moment, I compared it to a Lafite and found the **California** wine could hold its own.

—ROBERT BOHR, COLICCHIO & SONS

Tips: California is the top wine-producing state in the U.S. Its 2,800 wineries produce 90 percent of all American wine. It is the fourth largest wine producer in the world, behind France, Italy, and Spain. California wines represent 62 percent of U.S. consumption and 90–95 percent of U.S. exports. (Source: Wine Institute)

CALIFORNIA CULT WINES

These are wines of very high quality and very limited production—so they are prized by collectors and thus very expensive.
Grapes: Cabernet Sauvignon, typically
Examples: Araujo, Bond, Bryant Family, Caymus, Colgin, Dalla Valle Maya, Dominus, Grace Family, Harlan Estate, Heitz Martha's Vineyard, Pahlmeyer, Peter Michael, Screaming Eagle, Shafer Hillside Select
Iconic example: Grace Family Vineyards

CANADIAN WINES

Red: Cabernet Franc, Gamay Noir, Pinot Noir
White: Chardonnay, Pinot Gris, **Riesling**
Sweet: ice wine (made from Riesling, Vidal grapes)
Flavors: pink grapefruit (in Niagara whites), savory minerality (in Niagara reds)
Tip: Don't miss La Face Cachée de la Pomme's Neige ice cider, which is ice wine made from apples; it's an ideal accompaniment to cheese and paté.
Producers: Blue Mountain, **CAVE SPRINGS, Fielding** (Gewürztraminer, Pinot Gris), Gehringer Brothers, Gray Monk, Hillebrand, **INNISKILLIN** (ice wine), **Jackson-Triggs**, Mission Hill, Nichol Vineyard, **Norman Hardie** (Chardonnay), Quail's Gate, **Southbrook** (rosé, Syrah, white), **STRATUS**, Sumac Ridge, Tinhorn Creek, Waupoos (ice wine)

In my refrigerator I have a lot of **Canadian wine** [after a visit to Canada]. Last night I had a 2007 Cave Springs Vineyard Riesling, which I really like.

—ROXANE SHAFAEE-MOGHADAM, THE BREAKERS

When I moved [from Canada] to become the sommelier at Café Boulud in New York City in 1998, there were virtually no **Canadian wines** on leading restaurant wine lists other than the occasional Inniskillin ice wine. Paul Grieco and I led a group of New York sommeliers to Canada for a weekend, and that was a tipping point that turned several of them on to Canadian wines for the first time. . . . Other than Long Island and the Finger Lakes, there are virtually no wines more local [for New Yorkers] than Canadian wines, which are certainly more local than California wines.

—STEVE BECKTA, BECKTA DINING & WINE AND PLAY FOOD & WINE

CANNONAU

[kah-noh-NOW]
See also GRENACHE.
Country: Italy
Region: Sardinia
Color: red
Grapes: Cannonau (known elsewhere as GRENACHE)
Weight: medium-full to full-bodied (and high in alcohol)
Volume: loud
Dry/sweet: dry
Acidity: low to medium
Tannin: lighter (modern style) to medium (traditional)
Flavors: aromatic, with notes of **blackberries, black cherries**, earth, flowers, **herbs**, leather, meat, **plums**, roses, **spices**, toffee, violets
Texture: rich, round, rustic
Temperature: Serve cool, about 60 to 65 degrees.
Comparables: Garnacha (Spain), GRENACHE (France)
Pairings: cheese, goat, lamb, meats, pasta with meat sauce, pork, tuna
Tip: Cannonau is said to have three times more antioxidants than any other wine grape.
Aging: Drink young (within five years), although the very best can age for a decade or possibly longer.
Producers: Alberto Loi, **Argiolas**, Contini, Santa Maria La Palma, Sella & Mosca

CARIGNAN (AKA CARIGNANE, CARIGNANO)

[kar-in-YON]
Countries: Algeria, Argentina, Chile, **France (Languedoc-**

I carry some **Carignan** from the Languedoc by the producer Mas Jullien, a winemaker who really wanted to express the *terroir* of this area. The Mas Jullien has expressive earthiness with green olive and barnyard characteristics. I often describe this wine as "dirty" because it really expresses what the flavor profile is. It is also a good gauge, because if I describe a wine to a guest as "dirty" and it puts them off, they are not going to like this wine. If I describe this to a guest and they get excited, they are going to like it.

—DANA FARNER, CUT

Roussillon), Israel, **Italy** (**Sardinia**), Mexico, Morocco, Spain (Rioja), Tunisia, Uruguay, U.S. (California)
Color: red
Grapes: Carignan, almost always blended with other grapes
Weight: medium- to **full-bodied** (and high in alcohol)
Volume: moderate to loud
Dry/sweet: dry
Acidity: medium to **high**
Tannin: medium to **high**
Flavors: notes of **black and red cherries**, **blackberries**, black currants/cassis, chocolate, **earth**, flowers, game, green olives, herbs, leather, licorice, meat, **minerals**, nutmeg, **plums**, **raspberries**, smoke, **spices**, strawberries, tobacco, vanilla (esp. oaked), violets, white pepper
Texture: fresh, full, lively, rich, round, smooth, soft, velvety
Temperature: Serve slightly chilled, about 55 to 60 degrees.
Comparables: CARIGNANO (Italy), **Cariñena** (Spain), **Mazuelo** (Spain)
Pairings: barbecue, cheese, game, lamb, pork, red meats (esp. braised, grilled, roasted, or smoked), ribs, stews
Producers: **Chile:** Ordfjell Vineyards; **France–Languedoc:** Mas Jullien; **Israel:** Vitkin; **Italy:** Agricola Punica, Cantini di Santadi; **U.S.–California:** Artezin, Cline, Evangelho, Ridge

CARMENÈRE
[kar-men-AIR]
Countries: Argentina, **CHILE**, France (Bordeaux), Italy, U.S. (California, Washington state)
Color: red (dark in color, with ruby hues)
Grapes: Carmenère, often blended with Cabernet Sauvignon or Merlot
Weight: medium- to full-bodied
Volume: moderate to loud
Dry/sweet: dry
Acidity: low to medium
Tannin: medium to high
Flavors: fruitiness balanced by savoriness, with notes of **blackberries**, **black cherries**, black currants/cassis, black pepper (esp. older wines), **chocolate**, coffee, earth, game, green bell peppers (esp. younger wines), **herbs**, leaves, **meat**, mocha, **plums**, raspberry (esp. older

wines), roses, smoke, soy sauce, **spices**, tar, vanilla, vegetables (esp. younger wines), violets
Texture: rich, silky, smooth, soft
Temperature: Serve cool, about 60 to 65 degrees.
Comparables: CABERNET FRANC, MERLOT
Pairings: barbecue, lamb, pork, ribs, wild boar
Aging: The best have moderate aging potential.
Producers: **Chile:** Almaviva, Concha y Toro, **Montes**, Santa Carolina, Seña, Tamaya, Terra Noble, Viña MontGras

CARMIGNANO
[kar-mee-NYAH-noh]
Country: Italy
Region: Tuscany
Color: red
Grapes: **Sangiovese** (at least 50 percent) and often Canaiolo, Cabernet Franc, and/or Cabernet Sauvignon
Weight: medium-bodied
Volume: moderate
Dry/sweet: dry
Acidity: medium to high
Tannin: medium
Flavors: notes of anise, black cherries, blueberries, chocolate, earth, herbs, leather, licorice,

If people want to step out of Chianti yet stay in familiar territory, they are familiar with Cabernet and Bordeaux. So let's run with that and stretch the boundaries a little. I like to nudge them over to Barco Reale di **Carmignano**, combining the Italian qualities of Tuscany with all its earthiness and herbaceousness. These wines fill in with Cabernet, Cabernet Franc, as well as other Tuscan blending grapes. The wine is like Bordeaux and Tuscany mashed together. The wine is a little more structured, acidic, and familiar on the palate. This is giving people another level of earthiness than straight-up Chianti could afford. It is cool to show them that Tuscany is not synonymous with Chianti and that there are other areas and styles to be observed. Do as they do in Tuscany: have a steak with a little char on it with this, and let the wine do its trick.

—JUSTIN LEONE, BENNY'S CHOP HOUSE

smoke, spices, tobacco, violets
Texture: velvety
Temperature: Serve slightly chilled, about 55 to 60 degrees.
Comparables: BORDEAUX–RED, CABERNET SAUVIGNON, CHIANTI CLASSICO
Pairings: charred steak, cheese (esp. Parmesan), grilled or roasted red or white meats, sausages, veal
Aging: Less expensive versions should be drunk young and fresh, but better wines can age well up to five or six years.
Producers: Capezzana, Fattoria Ambra, Fattoria di Bacchereto, Piaggia

CASETTA
[kah-ZEHT-uh]
Country: Italy
Region: Adige Valley/Vallagarina
Color: red
Grapes: Casetta
Weight: medium- to full-bodied
Volume: moderate
Dry/sweet: dry
Acidity: high to very high
Tannin: low to medium
Flavors: notes of **cherries**, cinnamon, cranberries, herbs, licorice, musk, plums, smoke, **spices**, tobacco, vanilla, violets, white pepper
Texture: silky, soft
Temperature: Serve cool, about 60 to 65 degrees.
Pairings: cheese, lamb, mushrooms, pasta, polenta, prosciutto, red meat, tomato sauce
Aging: Because of its high acidity, Casetta can age for a decade or longer.
Producer: Albino Armani Foja Tonda

CAVA
[KAH-vuh]
Country: Spain
Region: Catalonia (primarily)
Color: white (primarily)
Grapes: Chardonnay, Macabeo, Parellada, **Xarel-lo**
Weight: light- to medium-bodied
Volume: quiet to moderate
Dry/sweet: dry to off-dry
Acidity: **medium** to high
Flavors: aromatic, with notes of almonds, apples, citrus, **earth**, flowers, **lemon**, lime, melon, minerals, pears, toast, yeast
Texture: creamy, crisp, lively, **sparkling**
Temperature: Serve very cold, about 40 to 45 degrees.
Comparables: CHAMPAGNE, SPARKLING WINES
Season: summer
Pairings: almonds, apricots, fish, fried foods, ham (esp. Serrano), nuts, salads, shellfish, sushi, tapas
Tips: Cava is made by the traditional method (of secondary fermentation in bottle) used to make Champagne yet is often available at a fraction of the price. Freixenet [fresh-eh-NET]

produces more than half of the cava made in Spain.
Producers: 1+1=3, Avinyo, Codorníu, Freixenet (esp. Cuvée DS), Jaume Serra Cristalino Brut, Marqués de Gelida, Savia Viva (organic), Segura Viudas (esp. Aria Estate)

CHABLIS
[shab-LEE]
Country: France
Region: Burgundy
Color: white
Grapes: Chardonnay
Weight: light- to **medium**-bodied
Volume: quiet to moderate
Dry/sweet: dry
Acidity: high
Flavors: notes of **chalk**, citrus, flowers, green apples, earth, **flint**, hazelnuts, **lemon**, **minerals**, pears, sea breeze, stones, toast (esp. oaked wines), vanilla (esp. oaked wines)
Texture: crisp
Temperature: Serve cold, about 45 to 50 degrees.
Comparables: BURGUNDY–WHITE, CHARDONNAY
Season: summer
Pairings: cheese (esp. goat),

I like Champagne, which is denser and richer on the palate because of the Chardonnay grapes and suited to special occasions. But the quality-price ratio for **cava** is exceptional, as it is made in the same traditional method used to make Champagne, yet it is lighter in weight and texture, due to the differences in both the grapes used and in the *terroir* in Penedès [where 95 percent of cava is made] versus Èpernay [the capital of Champagne]. Cava is ideally suited to Mediterranean flavors, and it is a sparkling wine you can enjoy every day.
—RON MILLER, SOLERA

Marques De Gelida Ecologico is a super **cava,** and I like it a lot. My roommate brought home a bottle of Freixenet—I loved it in college and found I still liked it. It is correctly made and refreshing.
—BELINDA CHANG, THE MODERN

chicken, fish, oysters, shellfish, shrimp, veal, vegetables
Aging: An average Chablis should be drunk young and fresh. Open better Chablis after two to three years; the best Chablis needs at least five to seven years, although its high acidity allows it to age for even longer.
Producers: Domaine Barat, **Domaine Dauvissat,** J. Moreau et Fils, Joseph Drouhin, Laroche, Louis Michel, Picq, **RAVENEAU,** Verget, William Fevre
Iconic example: Raveneau

I drink a lot of **Chablis** at home with my wife, who is also a sommelier. It sounds so obnoxious, but we drink mostly Raveneau [considered one of the finest and most expensive Chablis produced]. We also drink 2004 Premier Cru Dauvissat, which we bought a lot of.

—ROBERT BOHR, COLICCHIO & SONS

CHAMPAGNE—
IN GENERAL
[sham-PAYN]
Country: France
Region: Champagne
Color: white
Grapes: Chardonnay, Pinot Meunier, Pinot Noir
Weight: light- to full-bodied
Volume: quiet to moderate
Dry/sweet: typically dry (for sweet, see DEMI-SEC AND DOUX)
Acidity: medium to **high**
Flavors: notes of apples, apricots, bread, chalk, citrus, cream, lemon, lime, minerals, nectarines, nuts, orange, pears, quince, smoke, spices, toast, vanilla, yeast
Texture: sparkling; also creamy, rich

CHAMPAGNES BY STYLE

Lighter-bodied: Ayala, Billecart-Salmon, Bruno Paillard, Charbaut et Fils, Jacquesson, Lanson, Laurent Perrier, Nicolas Feuillatte, Perrier-Jouët, Pommery, Ruinart, Taittinger

Medium-bodied: Charles Heidsieck, Cristal, Delamotte, Deutz, Dom Perignon, Henriot, Jacquart, Moët et Chandon, Mumm, Piper-Heidsieck, Pol Roger

Full-bodied: Bollinger, Deutz Prestige Cuvées, Drappier, Egly-Ouriet, Gosset, Jacques Selosse, Krug, Pierre Peters, Pol Roger Sir Winston Churchill, Roederer, Salon, Veuve Clicquot

Temperature: Serve very cold, about 40 to 45 degrees.
Comparables: CAVA, SPARKLING WINES (e.g., from California)
Season: autumn–winter (esp. holidays)
Pairings: caviar, eggs, fried foods, lobster, oysters, popcorn, smoked salmon, sushi
Tips: Only sparkling wine made by the traditional method (with secondary fermentation in the bottle) in the Champagne region of France has the legal right to be called Champagne. Pop the cork on October 28 to celebrate International Champagne Day.
Aging: Drink non-vintage Champagne as young and fresh as possible. Only vintage Champagne may benefit from the aging process, and it can be aged for up to two to three decades, although many prefer it young and fresh as well. Best recent vintages: 2008, 2005, 2004, 2002, 2000, 1999, 1998, 1996.
Producers, in general: Alfred Gratien, Ayala, Billecart-Salmon, Bollinger, Deutz, Dom Perignon, Egly-Ouriet, Gosset, Henriot, Jacquesson, **Krug,** Möet, Perrier-Jouët, Pol Roger, Roederer, Ruinart, Salon Taittinger
Producers, Prestige Cuvée: Bollinger Tradition R.D., Krug Grande Cuvée or Clos du Mesnil, Moët et Chandon, Dom Perignon, Mumm Renée Lalou, Pol Roger

How on earth to remember the names of all those mega-sized Champagne bottles? First, remember this sentence: Moving Jump Ropes Make Small Boys Nervous. The first letter of each word reminds you of these bottle sizes:

M = Magnum (2 bottles)
J = Jeroboam (4 bottles)
R = Rehoboam (6 bottles; this size is no longer made)
M = Methuselah (8 bottles)
S = Salmanazar (12 bottles)
B = Balthazar (16 bottles)
N = Nebuchadnezzar (20 bottles)

Characterizing **Champagne**, Krug is the voluptuous girl, and Taittinger is Audrey Hepburn in a skinny black dress.
—MARK MENDOZA, SONA

I love and adore extremely expensive **Champagne**. Krug is very lush in body. So I always have a few bottles at home, and I don't believe you have to wait for a special occasion to have it—it is a special occasion when you open it!
—ROXANE SHAFAEE-MOGHADAM, THE BREAKERS

Non-vintage Pol Roger **Champagne** is less expensive than Veuve Clicquot and at least twice as good. Entry-level cuvées from Bollinger and Alfred Gratien are also worth seeking out.
—ROBERT BOHR, COLICCHIO & SONS

I am in love with anything by Jacques Selosse, a revolutionary winemaker who is a **Champagne** rebel and rock star. He is making small, artisan-grown solera-style [i.e., multi-vintage] Champagne. He doesn't believe in vintage cuvée—he believes in the art of blending, which, when you think about it, is what Champagne is all about. He's always been cool, but he's now finally getting a lot of recognition. But Salon has always been my favorite Champagne—and it always will be, because its Prestige Cuvée is only released in a declared vintage so you know it will always be amazing quality.
—BELINDA CHANG, THE MODERN

Cuvée Sir Winston Churchill, Roederer Cristal, Taittinger Comtes de Champagne, Veuve Clicquot La Grande Dame
Iconic examples: Krug Grande Cuvée or Clos du Mesnil

CHAMPAGNE—BLANC DE BLANCS
[blahn(k) duh BLAHN(K)]
Country: France
Region: Champagne
Color: white
Grapes: Chardonnay
Weight: lighter- to medium-bodied
Volume: quiet to moderate
Dry/sweet: dry
Acidity: medium to **high**
Flavors: notes of almonds, apples, apricots, brioche, caramel (esp. with age), chalk, citrus, coffee (esp. with age), flowers, ginger, grapefruit, honey, lemon, minerals, nuts (esp. with age), peaches, pears, smoke, spices, toast, vanilla
Texture: creamy, crisp, rich
Temperature: Serve very cold, about 40 to 45 degrees.
Pairings: caviar, fried foods, oysters, smoked fish, white truffles
Producers: Delamotte, Drappier, Gosset, Krug, Pierre Gimonnet, Pierre Peters, Pol Roger, Ruinart, Salon, Taittinger Comtes de Champagne

CHAMPAGNE— BLANC DE NOIRS
[blahn(k) duh NWAHR]
Country: France
Region: Champagne
Color: *Blanc de Noirs* means "white of black," since this white wine is made of red (black) grapes.
Grapes: Pinot Meunier, Pinot Noir
Weight: medium- to full-bodied
Volume: moderate
Dry/sweet: dry
Acidity: medium to **high**
Flavors: notes of apples, cherries, cola, currants, **earth**, ginger, lemon, minerals, raspberries, spices, strawberries, toast, vanilla
Texture: creamy, rich
Temperature: Serve very cold, about 40 to 45 degrees.
Pairings: canapés, egg dishes, salmon, shellfish, smoked fish, sushi (esp. salmon, tuna)
Producers: Bollinger, Egly-Ouriet, Krug, Pol Roger, and Veuve Clicquot all produce a Pinot Noir–dominant Champagne.
Iconic example: Pol Roger Cuvée Sir Winston Churchill

A glass of **Blanc de Blancs Champagne** is an easy way to settle in. You pour something that you can introduce before the food arrives and that can transition into the first bites of food. Everyone will say Champagne is a perfect way to begin, because of its role in that transition. . . . We start our menu with a cold hamachi that has been marinated in cucumber vinegar. Cucumber can play to sweetness or savoriness. With Champagne, you can play all over the board.
—VANESSA BOYD, PHILIPPE

JOHN RAGAN

Most people's experience of **Champagne** is limited to what they are served at a wedding, which may not even be Champagne—it is often cava or Prosecco or a lesser-quality sparkling wine. I brought a bottle of Bollinger to dinner at a friend's home and served it not as an aperitif but as the dinner wine—hence my decision to opt for something richer and fuller like Bollinger. My friend's father looked at me and said, "Oh, my God, I have never tasted Champagne this good in my life!" I said, "This is what good Champagne tastes like—and that is why it is more expensive!" He was blown away. It put him in an entirely different place in regard to his appreciation of Champagne.

—MICHAEL FLYNN, THE MANSION ON TURTLE CREEK

CHAMPAGNE— DEMI-SEC (SEMI-SWEET) AND DOUX (SWEET)

Country: France
Region: Champagne
Color: white
Grapes: Chardonnay, Pinot Meunier, Pinot Noir
Weight: medium- to full-bodied
Volume: moderate
Dry/sweet: off-dry to sweet
Acidity: medium to high
Flavors: notes of almonds, apples, biscuits, citrus, cream, custard, ginger, hazelnuts, honey, minerals, pears, toast, vanilla, yeast
Texture: creamy, crisp, fresh, rich, sparkling
Temperature: Serve very cold, about 40 to 45 degrees.
Pairings: blue cheese, desserts that are less sweet than the Champagne, foie gras, fresh strawberries
Producers: A. Margaine, Ayala, Laurent-Perrier, Moët et Chandon Nectar, Mumm, Piper Heidsieck, Pol Roger, Veuve Clicquot

CHAMPAGNE— GROWER

Country: France
Region: Champagne
Tip: A grower Champagne is produced by the vineyard that grows the grapes, as indicated by the tiny letters "RM" (for Récoltant-Manipulant) on the label (see page 243).
Producers: Diebolt-Vallois, Egly-Ouriet, Guy Charlemagne, Jacques Selosse, Larmandier-Bernier, L. Aubry, Pierre Gimonnet, Pierre Peters, René Geoffroy, Vilmart & Cie

I love **Champagne**, especially the Special Club bottling. They are new to the United States but have been around [in Champagne since 1971]. This is a group of RM growers who submit their wines to a panel. You have to be an RM grower, you have to own all of it, it has to be a lower dosage than your other cuvées, and it has to be a cuvée of the best of what you have to offer. The wines are tasted blind, and often you taste your own wine in the line-up to see if it is good enough to be in the Special Club. What says that a wine is going to be great? Four guys in a room in Midtown [Manhattan] tasting the wine blind? Or is it four guys in overalls at the local pub tasting wine—when that is what they do all the time and they know what goes into it because they are making this wine? The production tends to be small, but you can find them [Oak and Steel in New York City carries Special Club]. They are available through the Terry Theise portfolio; we have Gaston Chiquet and Henri Goutorbe on our list, and they are delicious.

—RAJ VAIDYA, DANIEL

Before my husband and I got married, we would share a glass of Billecart-Salmon **rosé Champagne** once a week at Windows on the World.

—INEZ RIBUSTELLO, ON THE SQUARE

It was not unheard-of in the twenty-seven-course-long menu [at Chicago restaurant Alinea] to serve a **rosé Champagne** as a refresher course. It is like a sorbet, only it uses the bubbles to refresh the palate.

—JUSTIN LEONE, BENNY'S CHOP HOUSE

CHAMPAGNE—ROSÉ

Country: France
Region: Champagne
Color: pink
Grapes: Chardonnay, Pinot Meunier, **Pinot Noir**
Weight: medium-bodied
Volume: quiet to moderate
Dry/sweet: dry
Acidity: medium to **high**
Flavors: notes of apricots, baking spices, black currants, cherries, citrus, coffee, minerals, peaches, pears, raspberries, **strawberries**, watermelon, yeast
Texture: creamy, rich, **sparkling**
Temperature: Serve very cold, about 40 to 45 degrees.
Pairings: berries, bouillabaisse, carpaccio, cherries, lamb (esp. rare), lobster, pork, prosciutto, salmon, tomatoes, tuna

I love [Moët &] Chandon Nectar [Imperial, a **demi-sec Champagne**]—it is really hip and cool in Parisian bars, where people drink it on the rocks or in a cocktail.

—BELINDA CHANG, THE MODERN

People can be surprised when I pair a **sparkler** with dessert. Daniel Humm [the chef] did a play on a malted milkshake made of malt ice cream and a little cream, with a garnish of olive oil. It sounds unusual, but we paired it with a demi-sec from Billecart-Salmon. It was fantastic—but we had to kiss a lot of frogs to find that pairing!

—JOHN RAGAN, ELEVEN MADISON PARK

We introduced people to **grower Champagne** and pointed out the little RM indication on the label, which is a tip-off that you are talking about a grower Champagne. We did the tasting blind and threw in a very popular big-label Champagne, which turned out not to be anyone's favorite. People liked the grower Champagne better, as well they should—and they are also generally less expensive.

—MICHAEL FLYNN, THE MANSION ON TURTLE CREEK

I always have **Champagne** at home. I love it and am a total sucker for it. I like small growers in general, and Pierre Peters is one of my very favorites. I like the Blanc de Blancs; it's a high-toned—that is, bright and vibrant and acid-driven—Chardonnay with a very crisp texture. I also like Champagne from Pierre Gimonnet, who makes a Special Club, a 1999, that is still fresh and vibrant. The small growers René Geoffroy and Vilmart are wonderful; they include Pinot Noir, so they have weight to them, and will age a really long time.

—ROXANE SHAFAEE-MOGHADAM, THE BREAKERS

Producers: Billecart-Salmon, Cristal, Deutz, Dom Perignon, Egly-Ouriet, Gosset, Laurent Perrier, Moët et Chandon, Nicolas Feuillatte, Perrier Jouet, Roederer, Ruinart
Iconic example: Billecart-Salmon

CHARDONNAY— IN GENERAL

[shar-duh-NAY]
See also BURGUNDY–WHITE, CHABLIS.
Countries: Australia, Canada, Chile, France (**Burgundy, Champagne,** Jura, Languedoc), New Zealand, South Africa, **U.S.** (**California,** Oregon, Washington state)

Color: white
Grapes: Chardonnay
Weight: full-bodied (and medium to high in alcohol)
Volume: quiet to loud, often depending on whether it spends time on oak
Dry/sweet: dry
Acidity: medium to medium-high
Flavors: notes of **APPLES,** apricots, banana, **butter,** butterscotch (esp. oaked wines), citrus, coconut (esp. oaked wines), cream (esp. with malolactic fermentation), figs, lemon, lime, mango, melon, minerals, **peaches, pears,** pineapple, smoke (esp. oaked wines), stones, tangerines, toast (esp. oaked wines), tropical fruits, vanilla (esp. oaked wines), yeast (esp. oaked wines)
Flavors: cool climate: apples, lemon, minerals, **pears** (and lighter-bodied); **warm climate:** apricots, **mango,** melon, **pineapple** (and fuller-bodied)
Texture: creamy, silky, smooth, ranging from lean to rich
Temperature: Serve chilled, about 50 to 55 degrees.
Comparables: BURGUNDY–WHITE, CHABLIS, CHASSAGNE-MONTRACHET, **Mâcon,** POUILLY-FUISSÉ, PULIGNY-MONTRACHET (all 100 percent Chardonnay)
Season: autumn–winter (esp. oaked wines)
Pairings: butter, cheese, chicken, cream, fish, pork, scallops, shellfish, veal
Pairings to avoid: chiles, cilantro, dill, oily fish, red meat
Aging: Better oaked Chardonnay can age as long as a decade, but most unoaked Chardonnay should be drunk young and fresh.
Producers: Argentina: Catena, Concha y Toro, Cono Sur, Montes; **Australia:** Giaconda, Leeuwin Estate, Lindemans, Penfolds, Petaluma Tiers Plantagenet, Rosemont; **Canada:** Le Clos Jordanne, Norman Hardie; **Chile:** Concha y Toro, Cousiño-Macul, Santa Rita, Valdivieso, Ventisquero, Veramonte; **France:** *see* BURGUNDY–WHITE; **Greece:** Gerovassiliou, Katsaros; **Italy:** Jermann; **New Zealand:** Babich, Kim Crawford; **South Africa:** Hamilton Russell, Mulderbosch, Thelema; **U.S.–California:** A by Acacia (value), Au Bon Climat, Beringer, Calera, Calistoga Estate (value), **Chalone, Chateau Montelena,** Clos du

Bois, David Ramey, Dehlinger, Dutton-Goldfield, Edna Valley, Far Niente, Flowers, Forest Glen (value), Freestone, **Gallo of Sonoma**, **Grgich Hills**, J. Lohr, Jordan, Kendall-Jackson, **KISTLER**, Kunde, La Crema, Landmark, **Littorai**, Long, **MARCASSIN**, **Matanzas Creek**, Mer Soleil, Merryvale Reserve, Mount Eden, Neely, Nickel & Nickel, Pahlmeyer, Partridge Cellars, Patz & Hall, **Peay**, **Peter Michael**, Ramey, Robert Sinskey, Robert Talbott, Rochioli, Rodney Strong, Rombauer, Saintsbury, Sanford Reserve, Sonoma-Cutrer, **Stony Hill**, Talbott, Talley, Williams-Selyem; **Maryland:** Basignani; **Oregon:** Andelsheim, Argyle, Chehalem, Domaine Drouhin, Domaine Serene, Hamacher Wines, Ponzi Vineyards; **Virginia:** Linden Hardscrabble; **Washington state:** Chateau Ste. Michelle, Columbia Crest, Hogue, L'Ecole

CHARDONNAY—OAKED

Countries: Argentina, Australia, Chile, France (Burgundy), Italy (Alto Adige), New Zealand, South Africa, **U.S. (California)**
Color: white
Grapes: Chardonnay
Weight: full-bodied
Volume: moderate to loud
Dry/sweet: dry
Acidity: medium
Flavors: notes of **apples**, brioche, **BUTTER**, butterscotch, caramel, cinnamon, cloves, coconut, cream, hazelnuts, lemon, nuts, oak, peaches, pineapple, **smoke**, spices, **toast**, **VANILLA**, yeast
Texture: creamy, rich, velvety
Temperature: Serve chilled, about 50 to 55 degrees.

Chardonnay classically tastes like lemon, apple, and pear. There is not much characteristic in the wine. In a warmer climate like California, you will get tropical fruits thrown in. You may get very ripe peach, apricot, and mango also. Chardonnay has the broadest range of variations [of any varietal]. For example, **California** Chardonnay is typically buttery, oaky, rich, fat, tropical fruit, and some baked apple. In **Chablis**, Chardonnay is typically very crisp, stony, green apple, green pear, and chalky. It is refreshing and tart. As for Chardonnay in Burgundy, **Puligny-Montrachet** will have oak, acid, and fruit and be the perfect triangle.
—HRISTO ZISOVSKI, AI FIORI

People love the big California **Chardonnay**. Some people want Peter Michael, which I get in for them. Then there are the wines that are off to the side, which I drink. Neely makes a Chardonnay that has no malolactic, with a minimum aging on lees that just fattens it a little, with crisp acidity and ripe, juicy fruit. It is shocking—you are reminded that Chardonnay is a fruit that tastes really good. It is balanced but has that over-the-top rock-n-roll of a California wine.
—ANDY MYERS, CITYZEN

If you think you don't like California **Chardonnay**, you should try Littorai Chardonnay. It is delicious and has the acid, structure, and purity of fruit that you expect from California, but it is also elegant.
—RAJ VAIDYA, DANIEL

[British wine writer] Jancis Robinson ranked Canadian winemaker Norman Hardie's **Chardonnay** a 17.5 out of 20. At about $35 a bottle, with the restraint and minerality of a top-end Chablis, it's as good as a $100 bottle of white Burgundy.
—STEVE BECKTA, BECKTA DINING & WINE AND PLAY FOOD & WINE

Comparables: other oaked white wines
Season: winter
Pairings: butter and cream sauces, chicken, duck, lobster, pasta, pork, seafood, veal
Producers: Argentina: Catena; **Australia:** Alice White, Jacob's Creek, Lindeman's Bin 65, Penfolds Koonunga Hill, Rosemount, Wolf Blass; **Chile:** Casa Lapostolle, Concha y Toro; **France:** see BURGUNDY–WHITE; **Italy:** Alois Lageder; **U.S.–California:** Au Bon Climat, Babcock, Beringer Napa Valley, Chalone, Chateau Souverain, Chateau St. Jean, Clos du Bois, Edna Valley, Fetzer Barrel Select, Gary Farrell, Kendall-Jackson Vintner's Reserve, Kistler, Qupé, Ridge, Talbott

CHARDONNAY—UNOAKED

Countries: Argentina, Australia, France (Burgundy, esp. Chablis, Mâconnais), U.S.
Color: white
Grapes: Chardonnay
Weight: medium- to full-bodied
Volume: quiet
Dry/sweet: dry
Acidity: low to medium
Flavors: notes of apples, butter, citrus, hazelnuts, lemon, mango,

If a white wine has enough depth and a savory quality to it, you can serve it *after* a red wine. A cru from **Chassagne-Montrachet** often has a "beefy" quality on the nose. The reason this works after our fruity Beaujolais is because it is a white wine acting like a red wine.

—VANESSA BOYD, PHILIPPE

melon, minerals, nectarines, peaches, pears, pineapple, tangerines, tropical fruits
Texture: crisp, lean, velvety
Temperature: Serve chilled, about 50 to 55 degrees.
Comparables: CHABLIS, Mâcon-Villages, POUILLY-FUISSÉ, BURGUNDY–WHITE
Season: spring
Pairings: chicken, curries, eggs, fish, garlic, guacamole, pork, salads, salmon, shellfish, shrimp, trout, turkey
Producers: Argentina: Bodega Septima; **Australia:** Trevor Jones Virgin, Wishing Tree, Yalumba Unwooded, Yellow Tail Tree-Free; **Canada:** Chateau des Charmes Musqué; **France–Burgundy:** Joseph Drouhin, Louis Jadot Mâcon-Villages; *see also* CHABLIS, POUILLY-FUISSÉ; **New Zealand:** Kim Crawford; **U.S.–California:** Fetzer, Four Vines Naked, Iron Horse Unoaked, Mer Soleil Silver Unoaked, St. Supery, Toad Hollow; **Oregon:** Chehalem; **Washington state:** Hogue Genesis

CHASSAGNE-MONTRACHET—WHITE
[shah-SAHN-yuh mawn-rah-SHAY]
Country: France
Region: Burgundy/Côte de Beaune/(southern) Côte d'Or
Color: white
Grapes: Chardonnay
Weight: full-bodied
Volume: moderate to loud
Dry/sweet: dry
Acidity: medium
Flavors: notes of apples, beef,

brioche, butter, butterscotch, flowers, honey, lemon, **minerals**, **nuts**, peaches, pears, smoke, spices, vanilla
Texture: elegant, **rich**, soft
Temperature: Serve chilled, about 55 degrees.
Pairings: chicken, clams, crab, cream sauces, lobster, mushrooms, pumpkin, scallops, veal
Aging: Better wines will age for five years or more, the best for a decade or longer. Best first growths: La Romanée, Les Caillerets.
Producers: Domaine Ramonet, Michel Niellon

CHASSELAS
[SHAHSS-lah]
Countries: France (Alsace, Loire), Germany, **Switzerland**
Color: white
Grapes: Chasselas
Weight: light-bodied
Volume: quiet
Dry/sweet: dry
Acidity: low
Flavors: fruity and aromatic, with notes of apples, citrus, **flowers**, honey, lime, minerals, peaches, pineapple, toast
Texture: crisp, lightly sparkling, soft
Temperature: Serve cold, about 45 to 50 degrees.
Pairings: appetizers, cheese (esp. fondue, raclette), chicken, cream, (white) fish, ham, pork, shellfish, veal
Producers: Switzerland: Dezaley, DuBaril

CHÂTEAUNEUF-DU-PAPE—RED
[shat-toh-NUFF-doo-PAHP]
Country: France
Region: southern Rhône Valley
Color: red (and light in hue)
Grapes: as many as thirteen grapes, including, and most often foremost, **GRENACHE**, but also **Cinsault**, Counoise, **Mourvèdre**, and **Syrah**, along with Bourboulenc, Clairette, Muscardin, Picardan, Picpoul, Roussanne, Terret Noir, and Vaccarese, each producer's blend having its own "recipe"
Weight: full-bodied (and high in alcohol)
Volume: loud
Dry/sweet: dry
Acidity: low to medium
Tannin: medium to **high**
Flavors: notes of blackberries (cooked), black cherries (cooked), black pepper, blueberries, coffee, earth, game, herbs (esp. herbes de Provence), meat, plums, **raspberries** (cooked), smoke, spices
Texture: rich, round
Temperature: Serve cool, about 60 to 65 degrees.
Comparable: ZINFANDEL
Pairings: barbecued meats, beef, cheese, duck, game/game birds, hamburgers, lamb, mushrooms, rabbit, ribs, steak, stews
Tip: If your palate enjoys Châteauneuf-du-Pape more than your wallet does, look to similar yet more gently priced Rhône reds, such as CÔTES DU RHÔNE and GIGONDAS.
Aging: Drink most wines within a few years of the vintage. The best can age for a decade or two (or more), which increases their gaminess and complexity.

BAR BRETON

Châteauneuf-du-Pape is infinitely complex, given the thirteen grapes allowed in the blend. It is a little like Riesling: tasting the wine describes what it is and gives you a sense of place and personality that burns itself on palate and brain. It gives you all the reasons you want to know it and talk about it. This is a good wine to drink in a single sitting. If you open a bottle, in one hour it will change and in two hours it will change again. Beyond that, it doesn't need twenty-five hours in a decanter and twenty-five years of age. It is pleasurable and thought-provoking.

One of the best combinations you could ever have is Châteauneuf-du-Pape with a hamburger and mushrooms. A friend and I will meet for hamburgers with a plate of just one style of sautéed seasonal mushrooms and a bottle of Châteauneuf-du-Pape. At the Tribeca Grill [in New York City] they have over 350 labels, because the wine director, David Gordon, is passionately devoted to this region of the world. The prices go from $35 to $1,600. My favorite is Domaine de la Vieille Julienne 1999. It has a lot of Mourvèdre in the blend, so it has a gamy, dark, black-fruit quality that speaks "darker" than Grenache-based Châteauneuf-du-Pape. I believe in having just a few of the best things together. With this combination, a good bottle of wine and good conversation, I can hang out for a long time.

—ROXANE SHAFAEE-MOGHADAM, THE BREAKERS

Producers: André Brunel, **Chapoutier, Charvin, CHÂTEAU BEAUCASTEL** (a Mourvèdre-dominant wine), **CHÂTEAU RAYAS**, Clos des Papes, **de Marcoux**, Font de Michelle, Grand Veneur, **Henri Bonneau**, La Janasse, Les Bosquet des Papes, Les Cailloux, Mont Olivet, **Pierre Usseglio**, Roger Sabon, Vieille Julienne, Vieux Télégraphe
Iconic examples: Château Beaucastel, Château Rayas

CHÂTEAUNEUF-DU-PAPE—WHITE

Country: France
Region: Rhône Valley
Color: white
Grapes: Bourboulenc (adds acidity), Clairette (adds aroma), Grenache Blanc (adds structure), **ROUSSANNE** (80 to 100 percent)
Weight: full-bodied (and high in alcohol)
Volume: quiet to moderate

Dry/sweet: dry
Acidity: low to medium
Flavors: fruity, with notes of almonds, apricots, citrus, cream, flowers, honey, licorice, melon, minerals, nectarines, nuts, peaches, pears, spices, tangerines, tropical fruits, vanilla
Texture: creamy, crisp, lush, rich
Temperature: Serve slightly chilled, about 55 to 60 degrees.
Pairings: creamy cheeses, fish, mushrooms, pasta, risotto, shellfish, white meats
Aging: Drink most young and fresh, within two or three years of the vintage, although better wines can benefit from five to ten or more years of aging.

The best **Châteauneuf-du-Papes** are among the most natural expressions of grapes, place, and vintage.

—ROBERT M. PARKER, JR., WHO HAS DESCRIBED IT AS HIS FAVORITE RED WINE

Tip: Only 2 percent of Châteauneuf-du-Pape produced is white.
Producers: Beaucastel Hommage à Jacques Perrin, Beaucastel Vieilles Vignes (100 percent Roussanne), Château Rayas, Roger Sabon, Vieux Télégraphe

CHENIN BLANC
[SHEN-inn BLAHN(k)]
See also VOUVRAY.
Countries: Australia, **FRANCE (LOIRE**, Rhône), India, New Zealand, **South Africa**, South America, U.S. (California, Washington state)
Color: white
Grapes: Chenin Blanc
Weight: medium- to full-bodied (with moderate to high alcohol)
Volume: quiet to moderate
Dry/sweet: very dry to off-dry to sweet (in dessert wines such as BONNEZEAUX and QUARTS DE CHAUME)

I'm always excited about **Chenin Blanc**, which may be my favorite grape variety. It's incredibly versatile, and it's fascinating with food, which seems to bring out its minerality and complexity. It pairs with everything from chicken to goat to vegetarian dishes. If you like Sauvignon Blanc, try the Château De Chamboureau Savennières, which is less funky—and less pricey—than others. If you like California Chardonnay, try the 2007 Agnès et René Mosse Anjou Blanc.

—CLAIRE PAPARAZZO, BLUE HILL

I love **Chenin Blanc**. But it is not for everyone. It is like wet wool, which can be a turnoff to some. When you drink it, you feel this thick layer of minerality on your tongue. I happen to like minerality and tannin.

—HRISTO ZISOVSKI, AI FIORI

Under-$15 tip: I love to drink Ken Forrester "Petit" **Chenin Blanc** from South Africa with grilled prawns while sitting out back on my patio.

—TODD THRASHER, RESTAURANT EVE

I can't stop buying **Chenin Blanc** from the Loire, even though I don't sell many. Chenin is cool, weird, and funky. It is a wine that bends and does all sorts of tricks. If there are scallops, I am 90 percent sure I will put Chenin Blanc with it. It works with river fish or any kind of shellfish. It is that "comes from, goes with" style of pairing: Chenin comes out of the Loire Valley, where you have trout, river fish, oysters, and mussels.

—ANDY MYERS, CITYZEN

Acidity: high
Flavors: notes of almonds, **apples** (esp. green), apricots, bananas, brioche, caramel, chamomile, **citrus**, cream, **FLOWERS**, grapes, grass, guava, hay, **HONEY/beeswax**, leaves, **lemon**, **melon**, **minerals** (esp. Loire wines), **peaches**, **pears**, pineapple, **quince**, stones, tropical fruits, vanilla
Texture: from crisp (drier, unoaked) to rich (oaked) to creamy, viscous (sweeter); sometimes sparkling
Temperature: Serve cold, about 45 to 50 degrees.
Comparables: RIESLING, SAVENNIÈRES, **Steen** (South Africa), VOUVRAY
Season: summer
Pairings: dry wines: chicken, fish, pasta, pork, pumpkin, salads, shrimp, squash, turkey; **sweet wines:** blue cheese, foie gras, fruit desserts, spicy Asian or Indian cuisine
Aging: Drink most dry wines young and fresh, although the best have aging potential. Thanks to their acidity, sweet wines can age up to three decades or longer.
Producers: France: Chidaine, Closel, **Huet**, Joy, Laureau, Soulez (*see also* SAVENNIÈRES, VOUVRAY); **Australia:** Plantagenet Off the Rack; **India:** Sula Vineyards; **South Africa** (where Chenin Blanc has notes of chamomile and guava and is known as STEEN): Beaumont, Cederberg, De Trafford, Ken Forrester, **Raats**; **U.S.–California:** **Chappellet**, Dry Creek Vineyard, Ryan;

Washington state: Chateau Ste. Michelle Ice Wine, L'Ecole No. 41
Iconic examples, sweet: the sweet dessert wines BONNEZEAUX, CÔTEAUX DU LAYON, and QUARTS DE CHAUME

CHIANTI
[kee-AHN-tee]
See also SANGIOVESE.
Country: Italy
Region: Tuscany
Color: red
Grapes: Sangiovese, often blended with other grapes
Weight: medium-bodied
Volume: moderate
Dry/sweet: dry
Acidity: high
Tannin: medium to high
Flavors: notes of almonds, blackberries, **BLACK OR RED CHERRIES**, cedar, cinnamon, coffee, **earth**, flowers, herbs, leather, licorice, meat, minerals, plums, smoke, spices, strawberries, tea (black), tobacco, vanilla, violets
Texture: rich, satiny, smooth, soft
Temperature: Serve slightly chilled, about 55 to 60 degrees.
Pairings: beef, cheese (esp. Italian), chicken, grilled steak, lamb, pasta, pizza, pork, **TOMATO SAUCE**
Tip: When looking for the pure flavor of Sangiovese, opt for Chianti Classico (look for the Black Rooster emblem) over more expensive Riservas, since

Isole e Olena **Chianti Classico** [around $20] is a perfect example of what Chianti Classico is supposed to be. It's a light red that will not be overwhelmed by a steak.

—DAVID LYNCH, QUINCE

the latter's flavors are too often obscured by the addition of Cabernet Sauvignon or Merlot.
Aging: Drink most Chianti young and fresh, although the very best can (and should) age for up to a decade.

Producers: Antinori, Baggiolino, Barone Ricasoli, Carpineto, Castellare, Castello di Fonterutoli, Castello di Gabbiano, Dievole, Fabrizio Bianchi, **Fattoria di Felsina, Fontodi,** Fossi, Frescobaldi, **Isole e Olena,** Marchesi Antinori, **Ruffino Chianti Classico Riserva, San Giusto a Rentennano,** Fattoria Sant'Appiano, Fattoria Selvapiana, Volpaia

CHILEAN WINES
Grapes: red: Cabernet Sauvignon, **Carmenère,** Merlot, Pinot Noir; **white:** Chardonnay, Riesling, Sauvignon Blanc
Flavors: notes of grass, meat, smoke

Tip: Chilean wines can offer excellent value for the price.
Producers: Almaviva, Carmen, Casa Marin, **Casa Lapostolle,** Casas del Bosque, **Concha y Toro, Cono Sur, COUSIÑO-MACUL,** Cucao, Dallas Conte,

By the time **Chilean wines** became popular, I had already had them on my list since the 1980s. When I first found them, I thought they were good-quality wines and great values. Chilean wines have a three-tier level: low end, midrange, and high end. Most people didn't realize there was a high-end premium level and that these wines were good. They are still great values. The wines are mostly Bordeaux varietals, so they pair with the same dishes that you would pair with Bordeaux. They are Cabernet, Carmenère, and Merlot, which you'll want to pair with red meat dishes, rack of lamb, filets, sirloins, and dishes with red wine reduction sauces. Even early on, Chile has had excellent Sauvignon Blancs, which work well with appetizers.
—ROGER DAGORN, MS, PORTER HOUSE NEW YORK

DeMartino, **Errazuriz (esp. KAI)**, Gran Araucano, Leyda, **Los Vascos**, Miguel Torres, **Montes, Santa Rita**, Sena, Tabali, Tamaya, Terranoble, Valdivieso, Veramonte, Viña Anita, Viña Calina, Viña MontGras, Viña Ventisquero/Apalta Vineyards
Iconic examples: Concha y Toro Don Melchor, Cousiño-Macul LOTA

CHINON
[shee-NOHN]
Country: France
Region: Loire Valley
Color: red
Grapes: Cabernet Franc
Weight: lighter- to fuller-bodied
Volume: moderate
Dry/sweet: dry
Acidity: medium to high
Tannin: high
Flavors: aromatic, with notes of **blackberries, black cherries**, black pepper, citrus, earth, **green bell peppers**, herbs, meat, minerals, olives (esp. green), pencil shavings, plums, **RASPBERRIES**, smoke, **spices**, strawberries, violets
Texture: smooth, soft, velvety
Temperature: Serve cool, about 65 degrees (for older wines), to slightly chilled, about 55 degrees (for younger wines).
Comparable: CABERNET FRANC
Pairings: mushrooms, pork, red meat (esp. with older, more complex wines), vegetable-based dishes, white meat (esp. with younger, fruitier wines)
Tip: Young Chinon will soften when given air time, and older Chinon will open when decanted.
Aging: Drink most Chinon within two to five years, although the best can age for a decade or two.

Producers: Bernard Baudry, **Breton** (organic), **Charles Joguet**, Couly-Dutheil, Jean-Maurice Raffault, Pierre-Jacques Druet
Iconic example: Charles Joguet

CINSAULT
[san-SOH]
Countries: Algeria, Corsica, France (Languedoc-Roussillon, Rhône), Lebanon, Morocco, South Africa
Color: red or pink/rosé
Grapes: Cinsault, almost always **blended** with other red grapes (e.g., Cabernet Sauvignon, Grenache)
Weight: light-bodied
Volume: quiet
Dry/sweet: dry, with a hint of sweetness
Acidity: high
Tannin: low
Flavors: **aromatic**, with notes of blackberries, black pepper, blueberries, earth, leaves, red meat, smoke, spices, strawberries, tar, vanilla
Texture: soft
Producers: Lebanon's renowned winery Château Musar features Cinsault in its blend.

CIRÒ ROSSO
[chee-ROH ROH-soh]
Country: Italy
Region: Calabria
Color: red (light, with brick or garnet hues)
Grapes: Gaglioppo
Weight: medium-bodied
Volume: moderate to loud
Dry/sweet: dry
Acidity: medium to **high**
Tannin: medium
Flavors: aromatic, with notes of berries, cinnamon, cranberries, dried fruits, earth, herbs,

minerals, plums, **spices**, tar
Texture: rich, round, rustic
Temperature: Serve slightly chilled, about 55 to 60 degrees.
Pairings: beef, cheese, hamburgers, lamb, pork, red meats (esp. roasted), veal, white meats
Aging: Drink young and fresh, although the best can age for as long as ten years or more.
Producers: Fattoria San Francesco, Librandi

CLASSICO WINES
See also CHIANTI, SOAVE, VALPOLICELLA.
Country: Italy
Tip: Italian wines labeled Classico are a step above those without the designation.

COLOMBARD
[KAH-lum-bahrd]
Countries: Australia, France, South Africa, U.S. (California)
Color: white
Grapes: Colombard (aka French Colombard); often used in blends, e.g., with Viognier
Weight: medium-bodied
Volume: quiet
Dry/sweet: dry to off-dry
Acidity: high
Flavors: aromatic and fruity, with notes of apples, **flowers**, grapefruit, **lemon**, nectarines, **peaches**, pears, pineapple, tropical fruits
Texture: crisp
Temperature: Serve chilled, about 50 to 55 degrees.
Pairings: Asian cuisine, fish, goat cheese, oysters, pasta, salads, shellfish
Tip: French Colombard is the second most widely planted white wine grape in California and is used to make bulk (i.e.,

inexpensive) white wine. In France it is used in the making of Armagnac, brandy, and Cognac.
Aging: Drink young and fresh.
Producers: Australia: Banrock Station Colombard/Chardonnay, DeBortoli; **France:** Domaine du Tariquet Vin de Pays

CONDRIEU
[KOHN-dree-uh]
Country: France
Region: Rhône Valley, northern
Color: white
Grapes: Viognier
Weight: full- to very full-bodied (with high alcohol)
Volume: moderate
Dry/sweet: dry
Acidity: relatively low
Flavors: very aromatic, with notes of **apricots, flowers**, melon, nectarines, oranges, pears, roses, spices, vanilla, violets, **white peaches**, white pepper
Texture: rich, round
Temperature: Serve at least slightly chilled, about 50 to 60 degrees.
Pairings: fish (esp. salmon), foie gras, fruit, lobster, pork, seafood (esp. rich dishes)
Tip: Condrieu is to Viognier what Côte de Nuits is to Pinot Noir.
Aging: Drink young and fresh, within five years.
Producers: André Perret, Château du Rozay, Delas, Gangloff, Georges Vernay, **Guigal**, Jaboulet, Mouton, Niero, Pierre Dumazet, **Pierre Gaillard, Vernay**, Villard, **YVES CUILLERON**
Iconic example: Yves Cuilleron Condrieu, which was the house wine at famed Michelin three-star French restaurant La Pyramide under its founder, Fernand Point

Master sommelier Greg Harrington taught me a lot, including the mnemonic "Ski or Swim?" That is, do you go to the region to snow-ski or to swim? If you go somewhere to snow-ski such as Germany, most likely it is a pretty **cool climate.** If it is cool, the grapes don't typically get as ripe, so they don't have as much sugar, so the alcohol is not as high. Since alcohol relates to body, you are talking about lighter-bodied wines here. If you go somewhere to swim, like Australia, it is probably a warm region, so the grapes get riper, the sugar is higher, so the alcohol is higher, and the wine has more weight. Without knowing anything else about the wine, you can say that an Australian Riesling is probably heavier and more full-bodied than a [German] Riesling from the Mosel.
—INEZ RIBUSTELLO, ON THE SQUARE

COOL-CLIMATE WINES
Countries: Austria, Canada, France (Burgundy, Champagne), Germany, New Zealand, U.S. (New York/Finger Lakes, Oregon)
Weight: lighter-bodied (and lower in alcohol)
Volume: moderate to louder
Acidity: higher
Flavors: in general, less fruity; **red wines:** notes of red fruits, such as cherries, cranberries, and pomegranates; **white wines:** notes of green fruits, such as apples, lime, and pear
Texture: generally crisper than warm-climate wines

CO-OP WINES
Countries: France, Germany, Italy
Tip: Those in search of value can check out the wines made by cooperatives in Europe. On the labels, look for the words "Cantina Sociale" (Italy), "Caves Cooperatives" (France), or "Winzergenossenschaft" (Germany).

CORNAS
[kor-NAHSS]
Country: France
Region: Rhône

Color: red (with a ruby hue)
Grapes: Syrah
Weight: full-bodied
Volume: moderate to loud
Dry/sweet: dry
Acidity: medium
Tannin: high to very high
Flavors: fruity, with notes of **bacon**, blackberries, black cherries, **black currants/cassis**, black pepper, black plums, blueberries, earth, green olives, herbs, lavender, leather, licorice, minerals, raspberries, roasted fruit, smoked meat, spices, strawberries, tobacco, violets
Texture: creamy, lush, rich, viscous
Temperature: Serve cool, about 60 to 65 degrees.
Pairings: cassoulet, cheese (esp. strong), duck, lamb, rabbit, squab, venison
Tip: If you love the flavors of Côte-Rôtie and Hermitage but not their price tags, try Cornas.
Aging: Allow five to fifteen years of aging for Cornas's strong tannins to soften.

I am a big fan of **Cornas.** I am also crazy about Jean-Louis Chave and some of the smaller wines from him outside the Hermitage.
—RAJ VAIDYA, DANIEL

Producers: Allemand, Cave des Papes, Chapoutier, Clape, Colombo, Jaboulet, Verset, Voge

CORTESE
[kor-TAY-zay]
See GAVI.

CORVINA
[kor-VEE-nuh]
See AMARONE, BARDOLINO, RECIOTO DELLA VALPOLICELLA, VALPOLICELLA.

CÔTEAUX DU LAYON
[koh-toh doo lay-AWN]
See also BONNEZEAUX, QUARTS DE CHAUME.
Country: France
Region: Loire/Côteaux du Layon
Color: white
Grapes: Chenin Blanc
Weight: full-bodied (and high in alcohol)
Volume: loud
Dry/sweet: off-dry to very sweet
Acidity: medium to high
Flavors: notes of almonds, apples, apricots, **candied fruits** (esp. apricots, pineapple), figs, flowers, golden raisins, **honey**, lemongrass, **quince**, tropical fruits
Texture: creamy, **rich**, round
Temperature: Serve cold, about 45 to 50 degrees.
Pairings: aperitif, blue cheese, desserts (esp. with almonds or plums), foie gras, goat cheese
Tip: For a value-priced sweet wine, versus BONNEZEAUX and QUARTS DE CHAUME, seek out Côteaux du Layon. The best are labeled "Sélection de Grains Nobles."
Aging: Can gain in richness with up to five years of aging,

while the best are said to be able to last as long as a century.
Producers: Baumard (Clos de Sainte Catherine), Cady, de Juchepie, Jolivet, Ogereau, Pierre-Bise, Pithon-Paille

CÔTE DE BEAUNE
[koht deh BOHN]
See BURGUNDY–WHITE.

CÔTE-RÔTIE
[koht roh-TEE]
Country: France
Region: Rhône Valley, north
Color: red
Grapes: SYRAH, Viognier (up to 20 percent)
Weight: medium- to **full-bodied**
Volume: moderate to loud
Dry/sweet: dry
Acidity: low to medium
Tannin: medium to high
Flavors: aromatic, with notes of **bacon**, blackberries, black cherries, black currants, **black pepper**, chocolate, coffee, **earth**, flowers, **GAME**, herbs, leather, plums, **raspberries**, rosemary, **smoke, spices, violets (esp. wines with higher percentage of Viognier)**, white pepper
Texture: rich, silky, smooth
Temperature: Serve cool, about 60 to 65 degrees.
Pairings: beef, cheese (esp. strong), duck, game, lamb, pork, rabbit, venison
Aging: Age five years to (even better) a decade before opening; the very best can age for as long as three decades.
Producers: Chapoutier, Cuilleron, Gerin, **Guigal**, Jasmin, Jayet, Ogier, Rostaing
Iconic examples: Guigal's single-vineyard, i.e., La Landonne (the loudest, most tannic requires the longest aging of the three); La

Mouline (the quietest and most aromatic); and La Turque (the gamiest)

CÔTES DE NUITS
[koht deh noo-EE]
See BURGUNDY–RED.

CÔTES DU RHÔNE
[koht doo ROAN]
Country: France
Region: Rhône Valley, south
Color: red
Grapes: a blend of up to 23 different grapes, often dominated by **Grenache**, plus Carignan, Mourvèdre, and/or Syrah
Weight: medium-bodied (and high in alcohol)
Volume: moderate to loud
Dry/sweet: dry
Acidity: low to medium
Tannin: medium to high
Flavors: fruity, with notes of blackberries, black currants/cassis, **black pepper**, cherries, **earth**, herbs, licorice, meat, plums, **raspberries**, smoke, **spices, strawberries**
Texture: juicy, luscious, smooth
Temperature: Serve slightly chilled, about 55 to 60 degrees.
Comparables: Australian GSM (blend of Grenache, Shiraz, and Mourvèdre), CÔTE-RÔTIE
Pairings: beef, chicken, hamburgers, lamb, Provençal cuisine (esp. with eggplant, herbs, zucchini), roasted meats
Pairing tip: Taste the Paul Jaboulet Aine "Parallèle 45" Côtes du Rhône Rouge (about $13) with cumin-rubbed lamb chops.
Tip: Look for wines designated Côtes du Rhônes-Villages, which are often better.
Aging: Drink most within three to five years.
Producers: Chapoutier, Château

Under-$15 tip: **Côtes du Rhône** is good for both blanc and rouge. I like E. Guigal and Domaine Santa Duc wines.

—VIRGINIA PHILIP, MS, THE BREAKERS

I love **Côtes du Rhône** made from Grenache. Any one of Château Rayas's wines is going to have the white-pepper expression of Grenache. It is lacy, spicy, and light, so you can have two glasses by yourself before dinner, but it also has enough tannin and acidity to stand up to lamb during dinner. A more traditional Côtes du Rhône would be Gramenon, which makes two or three cuvées—some Syrah and some Grenache. For a more modern Côtes du Rhône, I would go with something from Château Beaucastel. They have Coudoulet de Beaucastel, which is very accessible, not too earthy/mineral-y, and a balanced blend of Grenache, Mourvèdre, Syrah, and Cinsault.

—VANESSA BOYD, PHILIPPE

Beaucastel, Château Rayas, Colombo, Gramenon, Guigal, Jaboulet, Mordorée, Perrin et Fils, Santa Duc, Tardieu-Laurent

CRÉMANT
[kray-MAHN]
Country: France
Regions: Alsace (Crémant d'Alsace), Burgundy (Crémant de Bourgogne), Loire (Crémant de Loire)
Color: rosé, white
Grapes: varies—can be blends of white and/or red grapes (e.g., Aligoté, Cabernet Franc, Chardonnay, Chenin Blanc, Gamay, Pinot Meunier, Pinot Noir)
Weight: light- to medium-bodied
Volume: quiet to moderate
Dry/sweet: dry
Acidity: medium to high
Flavors: notes of almonds, flowers, hazelnuts, honey, lemon, licorice, lime, minerals, mint, peaches, pears, stones, vanilla, yeast
Texture: elegant, rich, sparkling
Temperature: Serve very cold, about 40 to 45 degrees.
Pairings: appetizers, fish, shellfish, smoked salmon
Tip: Crémant is sparkling wine made in France outside the region of Champagne by the same traditional method, which by law cannot be called Champagne, so it is typically priced much lower.
Aging: Drink young and fresh, within a year or two.
Producers: Alsace: Lucien Albrecht, René Muré; **Burgundy:** Bailly-Lapierre, Louis Bouillot, Simonnet-Febvre; **Loire:** Baumard, Bouvet-Ladubay, de

Moncontour, **Langlois-Château,** Tessier

CROZES-HERMITAGE— RED

[krohz air-mee-TAHJ]
Country: France
Region: Rhône Valley
Color: red
Grapes: Syrah
Weight: medium- to full-bodied
Volume: moderate to loud
Dry/sweet: dry
Acidity: medium to medium-plus
Tannin: medium to high
Flavors: notes of bacon, black currants, black pepper, blueberries, **cherries,** cocoa, earth, flowers, herbs, licorice, meat, minerals, olives, plums, raspberries, smoke, spices, strawberries, thyme, tobacco, truffles, vanilla, violets
Texture: silky, smooth, velvety
Temperature: Serve cool, about 60 to 65 degrees.
Comparable: a relatively lighter-bodied HERMITAGE–RED
Pairings: beef, braised dishes, duck, game, lamb, pork, stews, venison
Aging: Drink upon release and for the next three to five years, although the very best can age for a decade or even two.
Producers: Alain Graillot, Albert Belle, Chapoutier, Colombier, Delas Frères, Etienne Pochon, Guigal, Jean-Louis Chave, Michel Ferraton, Yann Chave
Iconic example: Paul Jaboulet Thalabert

CZECH WINES

Grapes: Pinot Gris, Ryzlink (Riesling), Welschriesling
Tip: Look for Slámové víno (straw wine)

I love a **dessert wine** to have balanced acidity. I love **Tokaji** and **TBA** [Trockenbeerenauslese] because they have that ripping acidity down the middle. **Sauternes** can be tough to work with because it lacks acidity, and you need to have acidity to cut through the sugar. On the other hand, give me a glass of Sauternes on its own or maybe with some biscotti and I am happy.
—ANDY MYERS, CITYZEN

Producers: Mikrosvin Mikulov (excellent dry Late Harvest Welschriesling), Moravíno Valtice (Late Harvest wines), Vino Marcinèák (straw wine made from Malvasia), Znovin Znojmo (ice wine and straw wine)

DARKER WINES

Tip: As a rule of thumb, the darker the wine, the heavier it is in weight and the louder it is in flavor volume.

DESSERT WINES

See also BANYULS, BRACHETTO D'ACQUI, ICE WINE, LATE HARVEST WINES, MADEIRA, MOSCATO D'ASTI, PORT, RIESLING, SAUTERNES, SHERRY, SWEET RIESLINGS, TOKAJI.
Temperature: Serve very cold, about 40 to 45 degrees.
Tip: Dessert wines are typically served in much smaller portions than table wines, sometimes just an ounce or two.
Producers: France: *see* BANYULS, SAUTERNES; **Israel:** Tzora OR; **Italy:** *see* BRACHETTO D'AQUI, MOSCATO D'ASTI, VIN SANTO; **New Zealand:** Seifried; **U.S.–California:** Bonny Doon, Chateau St. Jean, Dolce, Kendall-Jackson, Navarro, Quady, Topaz

DOLCETTO

[dohl-CHEH-toh]
Countries: Italy (Piedmont/ Alba), U.S. (California)
Color: red (with dark purple hues)
Grapes: Dolcetto
Weight: light- to medium-bodied
Volume: moderate
Dry/sweet: dry
Acidity: medium
Tannin: medium
Flavors: very fruity and aromatic, with notes of **almonds,** BLACK AND RED CHERRIES, blueberries, cherries, chocolate, cranberries, **earth,** grapes, **licorice,** plums, prunes, raspberries, smoke, strawberries, violets
Texture: juicy, luscious, silky, soft
Temperature: Serve cool to slightly chilled, about 55 to 65 degrees. Try serving Dolcetto even colder in the summertime.
Comparables: BARBERA, BEAUJOLAIS
Season: summer
Pairings: antipasto, braised dishes, carpaccio, meat, pasta, *salumi* (Italian cured meats)
Tip: Dolcetto is less acidic than Barbera.
Aging: Drink Dolcetto within one to two years, although the

Vietti is a special producer that makes wines that speak to both Old World and New World palates. Its **Dolcetto** is really approachable right out of the bottle, which is key when you don't have time to let a wine open up. A perfect pairing would be Mario Batali's lamb's tongue salad with ricotta salata.
—JULIA MORETTI, AD HOC

very best can last a bit longer.

Producers: Albino Rocca, Aldo Conterno, Angelo Gaja, Bruno Giacosa, Ceretto, Elio Altare, Fratelli Brovia, Giacomo Conterno, Giuseppe Mascarello, Luciano Sandrone, Marcarini, Pio Cesare, Roagna, Vietti

DOURO REDS

Country: Portugal
Region: Douro
Color: red
Grapes: Often blends; there are more than 100 allowable grapes (often those used in port), including **Touriga Nacional,** Touriga Franca, Tinta Barroca, Tinta Cão, and Tinta Roriz
Weight: medium- to **full-bodied**
Volume: loud
Dry/sweet: dry
Acidity: medium to high
Tannin: medium to high
Flavors: notes of blackberries, black cherries, black currants/cassis, black pepper, cedar, coffee, dark chocolate, earth, figs, flowers, herbs, licorice, meat, **minerals, mint, plums (dried or fresh),** raspberries, smoke, spices, tar, tobacco, vanilla, violets
Texture: rich, round, velvety
Temperature: Serve slightly chilled, about 55 to 60 degrees.
Comparables: SYRAH, ZINFANDEL
Pairings: liver, mushrooms, red meat (beef, lamb, venison—esp. grilled, roasted, or stewed)
Producers: The five so-called Douro Boys are **Quinta de**

Napoles (Niepoort Vinhos), Quinta do Crasto, Quinta do Vale Dona Maria (whose winemaker is the lone female "Douro Boy"), **Quinta do Vale Meao,** and Quinta do Vallado.

ENTRE-DEUX-MERS

[AHN-truh deh MAYR]
See also BORDEAUX–WHITE.
Country: France
Region: Bordeaux
Color: white
Grapes: Muscadelle, **SAUVIGNON BLANC, Sémillon**
Weight: medium-bodied
Volume: loud
Dry/sweet: dry
Acidity: high
Flavors: fruity, with notes of **citrus,** flowers, grapefruit, grass, **lemon,** lime, lychees, peaches, pineapple
Texture: crisp, fresh
Temperature: Serve chilled, about 50 to 55 degrees.
Comparable: SAUVIGNON BLANC
Pairings: fish, fresh goat cheese, oysters, salads, shellfish
Aging: Drink young and fresh, within one to three years.
Producers: Bonnet, de Fontenille, Girolate, Landereau, Marjosse, Nardique la Gravière, Saint-Marie, Tour de Mirambeau, Toutigeac, Turcaud

FALANGHINA

[fah-lahn-GHEE-nah]
Country: Italy
Region: Campagna
Color: white

Grapes: Falanghina, typically blended with other local grapes
Weight: medium-bodied
Volume: moderate
Dry/sweet: dry
Acidity: medium to high
Flavors: aromatic and fruity, with notes of **almonds, apples, citrus,** flowers, herbs, honey, jasmine, lemon, melon, **minerals,** mint, nuts, peaches, pears, pine, pineapple, smoke, tropical fruits
Texture: Ranges from crisp to rich and soft
Temperature: Serve cold, about 45 to 50 degrees.
Comparables: PINOT GRIGIO, SAUVIGNON BLANC
Season: summer
Pairings: anchovies, Caprese salad, fish, olives, pasta, shellfish, shrimp, squid, sushi
Tip: Falanghina often offers an outstanding value; drink young.
Producers: Cantina del Taburno, Feudi di San Gregorio, Mastroberardino, Ocone, Terredora di Paolo

Under-$15 tip: I love Cantina del Taburno **Falanghina** from Italy with grilled squid or shrimp or a nice, simple roasted fish.
—ANDY MYERS, CITYZEN

FIANO

[fee-AH-noh]
Countries: Australia, **Italy (Campagna)**
Color: white
Grapes: Fiano (primarily)
Weight: light- to medium-bodied
Volume: moderate to loud
Dry/sweet: dry
Acidity: medium to high
Flavors: aromatic, with notes of almonds, apples, apricots, earth, **flowers, HAZELNUTS,** herbs, **honey,** minerals, mint, nuts,

The **Douro** region produces fine high-end wines that are fairly full-bodied, with good fruit and tannins. The tannins don't overwhelm the fruit, and the wines still maintain their Old World character. The wines work with beef dishes that have aromatic sauces. The tannins really cut through meats like beef, venison, and lamb without being gamy wines.
—ROGER DAGORN, MS, PORTER HOUSE NEW YORK

peaches, **pears,** smoke, white pepper
Texture: elegant, fresh
Temperature: Serve cold, about 45 to 50 degrees.
Comparable: BURGUNDY– WHITE
Pairings: chicken, fish (esp. white), pork, salads (esp. Caprese), shellfish, white meats
Aging: Generally, drink young and fresh, although the best can age for ten to fifteen years.
Producers: Feudi di San Gregorio, **Mastroberardino,** Terredora di Paolo

FORTIFIED WINES
See also MADEIRA, PORT, SHERRY.
Alcohol: high
Tip: Fortified wines have had alcohol added.

FRAPPATO
[frah-PAH-toh]
Country: Italy
Region: Sicily
Color: red
Grapes: Frappato, sometimes blended with Nero d'Avola
Weight: light- to medium-bodied
Volume: moderate
Dry/sweet: dry
Acidity: medium-high to high
Tannin: low
Flavors: very aromatic and fruity, with notes of blackberries, blueberries, **cherries,** earth, flowers (esp. roses), minerals, raspberries, spices, strawberries
Texture: rich, silky, soft
Temperature: Serve slightly chilled, about 55 to 60 degrees.
Comparable: BEAUJOLAIS
Pairings: cheese (esp. soft, young), chicken, meat, pasta (esp. with tomato sauce), pork, sausages
Producers: Gulfi, Occhipinti,

and Valle Dell'Acate, which has been poured as a house wine at The Little Nell

FRASCATI
[frah-SKAH-tee]
Country: Italy
Region: Lazio
Color: white (with straw hues)
Grapes: a blend containing **Trebbiano** and Malvasia
Weight: light-bodied (and low in alcohol)
Volume: quiet
Dry/sweet: ranges from dry (*secco*) to sweet (*dolce*)
Acidity: medium to high
Flavors: notes of almonds, apricots, citrus, flowers, melon (esp. honeydew), minerals, peaches, pears, stones, tropical fruits
Texture: ranges from still to sparkling (*spumante*); creamy, refreshing
Temperature: Serve cold, about 45 to 50 degrees.
Season: summer
Pairings: calamari, fish (esp. fried and/or spicy), lamb, octopus, pasta, salads, seafood
Tip: Frascati is the signature wine of Rome. Look for fuller-bodied, richer Frascati Superiore.
Aging: Drink young and fresh (within a year or two).
Producers: Fontana Candida, Regillo, Saula, Zandotti

FREISA
[FRAY-zah]
Country: Italy
Region: Piedmont
Color: red (light in color, with a purple hue)
Grapes: Freisa
Weight: light-bodied (and low in alcohol)
Volume: moderate

Dry/sweet: ranges from dry (modern) to off-dry (traditional)
Acidity: high
Tannin: medium to high
Flavors: fruity, with notes of cassis, earth, grapefruit, herbs, pomegranates, raspberries, roses, spices, **strawberries,** violets
Texture: still to semi-sparkling
Temperature: Serve slightly chilled, about 55 to 60 degrees.
Comparables: DOLCETTO, LAMBRUSCO
Season: summer
Pairings: antipasto, charcuterie, chicken, lighter dishes, pork, prosciutto with melon, *salumi* (Italian cured meats)
Producers: **Italy:** Brovia, Cascina Gilli, La Casaccia, Lo Spaventapasseri, Mascarello, Rinaldi, Vajra; **U.S.:** Bonny Doon

FRIULANO (AKA TOCAI FRIULANO)
[free-oo-LAH-noh]
Countries: Italy (Friuli), U.S. (California, New York/Long Island)
Color: white
Grapes: Friulano
Weight: medium- to fuller-bodied
Volume: quiet to moderate
Dry/sweet: dry
Acidity: medium to high
Flavors: aromatic and fruity, with notes of almonds, apples, apricots, **citrus, flowers,** grapefruit, herbs, lemon, melon, **MINERALS,** nuts, ocean breeze, **peaches, pears,** pepper, smoke, spices
Texture: Ranges from crisp and fragrant to creamy and smooth to powerful and viscous
Temperature: Serve chilled, about 50 to 55 degrees.
Comparables: SAUVIGNON

I love to introduce New World palates to Old World grape varieties. Dan Petrovski is one of the most passionate winemakers I've ever met; Massican makes three wines that are inspired by Friuli, and they're all phenomenal. The Annia is made of predominantly Tocai **Friulano**, plus Ribolla Gialla and Chardonnay. I love it with everything from charcuterie to a veal chop.
—JULIA MORETTI, AD HOC

BLANC, **TOCAI FRIULANO** (as it is sometimes still called outside Europe)
Pairings: chicken, cured meats, fish, **pork, prosciutto, risotto,** shellfish, veal, vegetables
Aging: Drink young and fresh.
Producers: Italy: Aldo Polencic, Bastianich, Edi Keber, I Clivi, Jermann, **Livio Felluga,** Marco Felluga, Ronco dei Tassi, Ronco del Gelso, Ronco del Gnemiz, Russiz Superiore, Schiopetto, Scubla, Villa Russiz; **U.S–California:** Massican, Palmina; **New York:** Channing Daughters

FULL-BODIED WINES
Red: Cabernet Sauvignon, Malbec, Petite Sirah, Shiraz, Zinfandel
White: Chardonnay, Gewürztraminer, Marsanne, Roussanne, white Burgundy
Seasons: autumn–winter
Pairings: heavier dishes
Tip: As a rule of thumb, the darker the wine color and the higher its stated alcohol level, the fuller its body.

FUMÉ BLANC
[foo-may BLAHN(K)]
Countries: New Zealand, U.S. (California)
Color: white
Grapes: Sauvignon Blanc
Weight: medium-bodied
Volume: moderate
Dry/sweet: dry
Acidity: low to medium

Flavors: notes of apples, citrus, figs, flowers, grapefruit, grass, guava, herbs, lemongrass, melon, minerals, orange peel, peaches, pears, pineapple, **smoke, toast,** tropical fruits, vanilla
Texture: creamy, crisp, rich
Temperature: Serve chilled, about 50 to 55 degrees.
Pairings: chicken (esp. grilled), pork (esp. grilled), risotto, seafood
Tip: Fumé Blanc often, but not always, refers to Sauvignon Blanc that has been aged on oak.
Producers: Chateau St. Jean, Clos du Bois, **Dry Creek,** Ferrari-Carano, Grgich Hills, Markham, Merryvale, Murphy-Goode, Peter Michael, **Robert Mondavi**
Iconic examples: Dry Creek Vineyard DCV-3 or Robert Mondavi Napa Valley Fumé Blanc

FURMINT
[FOOR-mahn]
Countries: Austria, Hungary (native), U.S. (California)
Color: white
Grapes: Furmint
Weight: medium- to full-bodied (with high alcohol)
Volume: loud
Dry/sweet: ranges from dry

to sweet (as in Hungary's famed TOKAJI dessert wine)
Acidity: high
Flavors: dry wines: notes of **green apples, honey,** lemon, lime, minerals, pears, smoke, spices; **sweet wines:** notes of almonds, **apricots,** butterscotch, caramel, honey, orange
Texture: crisp, rich, viscous
Temperature: Serve chilled, about 50 to 55 degrees.
Pairings: chicken, fish, scallops, seafood, turkey, vegetable dishes
Aging: While most Furmint should be drunk young and fresh, the best has good aging potential.
Producers: Austria: Heidi Schröck, Oremus, Wenzel; **Hungary:** Royal Tokaji Wine Company; **U.S.–California:** Limerick Lane

GALESTRO
[gah-LESS-troh]
Country: Italy
Region: Tuscany
Color: white (with a light straw hue)
Grapes: Trebbiano blended with other Italian white grapes and/or Chardonnay
Weight: light-bodied (and low in alcohol)
Volume: quiet
Dry/sweet: dry
Acidity: medium to high
Flavors: fruity, with notes of apples, flowers, peaches, pears
Texture: crisp, fresh
Temperature: Serve chilled, about 50 to 55 degrees.

Dry wines from Hungary are exciting wines—I call them the Alsace wines of Eastern Europe. They make great sweet wines like Tokaji, but the dry wines like **Furmint** have beautiful acidity with great fruit components. I would pair these wines with foods that have a little more richness to them, but still need the clean acidity to cut the richness.
—MARK MENDOZA, SONA

Season: summer
Pairings: antipasto, cheese, pasta, pizza, prosciutto, risotto, **seafood**, veal, vegetables
Aging: Drink very young and fresh, within a year after release.
Producers: Antinori, Rocca delle Macie, Ruffino

GAMAY (AKA GAMAY NOIR)

[ga-MAY]
See BEAUJOLAIS.
Producer: U.S.–Michigan: Chateau Grand Traverse

GARGANEGA

[gar-GAHN-ah-gah]
See SOAVE.

GARNACHA

[gar-NAH-chah]
See GRENACHE.

GATTINARA

[gaht-ee-NAHR-rah]
See NEBBIOLO.

GAVI

[GAH-vee]
Country: Italy
Region: Piedmont/GAVI
Color: white (light straw hue)
Grapes: Cortese
Weight: **light-** to medium-plus-bodied (and lower in alcohol)
Volume: quiet to moderate
Dry/sweet: dry
Acidity: high
Flavors: aromatic, with notes of anise, apples (esp. green), bananas, **citrus,** flowers, grapefruit, grass, herbs, honey, **lemon, lime, minerals,** nuts, peaches, pears
Texture: crisp, rich; sometimes sparkling
Temperature: Serve well chilled, about 50 degrees.

Season: summer
Pairings: antipasto, chicken, focaccia, pasta, pork, salads, **seafood**
Aging: Typically, drink young and fresh; however, better Gavi can age for a few years.
Producers: Bergaglio, Broglia, Chianlo, La Giustiniana, La Scolca, Villa Sparina

GEORGIA (U.S.) WINES

Producer: Persimmon Creek Vineyards (Seyval Blanc)

GERMAN WINES

See MÜLLER-THURGAU, RIESLING, SILVANER/SYLVANER, SPÄTBURGUNDER.
Regions: Mosel-Saar-Ruwer, Pfalz, Rheingau, Rheinhessen
Grapes: red: Spätburgunder (aka Pinot Noir); **white:** Müller-Thurgau, **RIESLING**
Weight: light- to medium-bodied
Volume: moderate to loud
Dry/sweet: range from dry to very sweet
Acidity: high

When looking at a **German wine** label, you will see two words: one is the name of the town, and the other is the name of the vineyard. Say you have a Piesporter Goldtropfchen. I tell people if you are from Piesport, you are a Piesporter—just as if you are from New York, you are a New Yorker. All they do is add the -er to the end of the town. The vineyard is typically the *other* word. So if you like a wine, try to match one of the two words and you just might find a wine that is similar to the one you like.
—SABATO SAGARIA, THE LITTLE NELL

I've always had a lot of **German wines** on my wine lists because they are such great wines to go with food. There is no oak, super-low alcohol, great acidity, tons of minerality, and tons of fruit. You could not write the script any better for a wine to go with food!
—JOHN RAGAN, ELEVEN MADISON PARK

If you want a **German wine** and want to know the sweetness level, look at the alcohol content. If it is 13.5 percent, it is probably dry. If it is 8 percent, it probably has some sweetness.
—MARK MENDOZA, SONA

What are the great **wines of Germany?** If you ask, a German person will say Pinot Noir. These wines are getting better, and I have had some fantastic young Pinot Noirs. There is a tendency to use a bit of oak.
—RAJ VAIDYA, DANIEL

People will ask about our unusual wines [a section of CUT's list is called Native and Displaced wines]. A **German Pinot Noir** is a tough sell. It is a wine people haven't tried, and they are nervous about it. Becker from the Pfalz in Germany is a producer I have loved ever since I first tasted their Pinot Noir, and when I put it on the wine list I knew it would be a challenge. I had the staff taste it blind, and they universally fell in love with it. We found that a lot of our staff who don't like red wine really loved it. At CUT [a steak restaurant], we have a lot of guests who are not red wine drinkers but feel they must have a red wine because they are having steak. We found out we had a wine for all these white wine guests.
—DANA FARNER, CUT

Believe it or not, I had a Blue Nun [the $6.99 **German wine** made with Müller-Thurgau and Silvaner] recently, and it was quite good. It is a good quaff with takeout Chinese or Thai food!

—BELINDA CHANG, THE MODERN

Tip: Wine bottles from the Rhine are brown; those from the Mosel are green.

Best recent vintages: 2008, 2007, 2005, 2004, 2003

Producers: Bergweiler, Breuer, Burklin-Wolf, **Donnhoff**, Dr. Heger, **Dr. Loosen, Egon Müller, Gunderloch, J. J. PRÜM,** Karthauserhof, Klaus Keller, Kunstler, Leitz, Müller-Catoir, Pfeffingen, **Robert Weil,** Schlossgut Diel, Selbach-Oster, St. Urbans-Hof, Van Volxem, Vollenweider, Zelbach

GEWÜRZTRAMINER (AKA TRAMINER)

[guh-VERTZ-trah-mee-ner]

Countries: Australia, Austria, Chile, **France (Alsace),** Germany, Italy (Alto Adige), New Zealand, U.S. (esp. Oregon, Washington state)

Color: white

Grapes: Gewürztraminer

Weight: medium- to **full**-bodied (with very high alcohol)

Volume: moderate to loud

Dry/sweet: ranges from dry to off-dry to sweet (*see* VENDANGE TARDIVE)

Acidity: low

Flavors: **highly aromatic,** fruity, with notes of **apricots,** bacon, **black pepper,** cashews, cinnamon, citrus, cloves, coconut, cream, **flowers,** ginger, grapefruit, honey, jasmine, **LYCHEES,** mango, melon, minerals, nectarines, nutmeg, papaya, passion fruit, **peaches,** pears, pineapple, **ROSES, spices,** tropical fruits, vanilla

Texture: rich, soft, velvety

Temperature: Serve cold, about 45 to 50 degrees.

Comparables: other Alsatian white wines, e.g., PINOT BLANC, PINOT GRIS, RIESLING

Season: spring–summer

Pairings: cheese (esp. blue or Muenster), curries, duck, foie gras, Kobe beef, paté, pork, smoked salmon, spicy foods (e.g., Chinese, Indian, Thai, Vietnamese, esp. with off-dry Gewürztraminer)

Peak pairing: Gewürztraminer + Muenster cheese + caraway seeds

Aging: Drink most Gewürztraminers relatively young and fresh. Better wines will age well up to five years or even a decade. Grand Cru wines can age even longer.

Producers: Canada: Fielding; **Chile:** Cono Sur; **France– Alsace:** Beyer, Boxler, **Helfrich, Hugel,** Lucien Albrecht, Paul Blanck Altenbourg, Pierre Sparr, Schlumberger, **Trimbach, Weinbach,** Willm, **ZIND-HUMBRECHT; Italy:** Alois Lageder, St. Michael-Eppan; **New Zealand:** Brancott; **U.S.–California:** Chateau St. Jean, Claiborne & Churchill, De Loach, Gundlach Bundschu, Handley, **NAVARRO VINEYARDS** (Anderson Valley), Stony Hill; **New York:** Dr. Konstantin Frank, Hazlitt, Hermann J. Wiemer; **Washington state:** Canoe Ridge, Chateau Ste. Michelle, Columbia Crest, Covey Run, Hogue; **Uruguay:** Stagnari, Viñedo de los Vientos Estival

Iconic examples: Navarro Vineyards (U.S.) or Zind-Humbrecht (France)

GIGONDAS

[jhee-gawn-DAHS]

Country: France

Region: Rhône Valley, south

Color: red

Grapes: GRENACHE, Mourvèdre, Syrah, and other grapes

Weight: medium- to full-bodied (and high in alcohol)

Volume: loud

Dry/sweet: dry

Acidity: low to medium

Tannin: high

Flavors: notes of blackberries, black cherries, black currants/ cassis, black pepper, blueberries, cedar, earth, figs, lavender, licorice, minerals, mushrooms, plums, spices, sweet herbs

Texture: rich, velvety

Temperature: Serve cool, about 60 to 65 degrees.

Comparable: CHÂTEAUNEUF-DU-PAPE

Pairings: beef, cheese, game, red meat, roasts, steak, stews

Aging: Gigondas requires several years of aging for its strong tannins to soften.

Stony Hill, one of the oldest and best wineries in California, makes a totally dry-style **Gewürztraminer** that has traditional lychee characteristics. It's very tropical with great acidity, but still rich and viscous with a little weight on the palate. It goes great with figs, melons, and strawberries, as well as a nice salad. During Indian summer, we have lots of corn, tomatoes, squash, collard greens, and chard, and Stony Hill Gewürztraminer is so fantastic with them. We have a sort of surf-and-turf dish with shrimp and chicken, and it is a fantastic pairing with that, too.

—JULIA MORETTI, AD HOC

Producers: Domaine de la Tourade, Domaine Les Goubert, Domaine Raspail-Ay, Domaine Santa Duc

---

GODELLO
[goh-DAY-oh]
See also VERDELHO.
Country: Spain
Color: white
Grapes: Godello
Weight: medium- to full-bodied
Volume: moderate to loud
Dry/sweet: dry
Acidity: medium to **high**
Flavors: aromatic and fruity, with notes of anise (esp. older wines), **apples (esp. green)**, apricots, **citrus, flowers**, grapefruit, hay, herbs, honey, **lemon, minerals**, peaches, pears, pineapple, quince
Texture: creamy, rich
Temperature: Serve cold, about 45 to 50 degrees.
Comparables: ALBARIÑO (Spain), VERDEJO, **VERDELHO** (Portugal), VIOGNIER (France)
Pairings: cheese (esp. cow's milk), fish (esp. sea bass, swordfish), pasta, risotto, seafood
Aging: Drink young and fresh, within two to three years.
Producers: Ladairo, Pena das Donas Almalarga

I really like **Godello**. It's not planted anywhere else, and it's got some flavors that make it thought-provoking and a little harder to learn to love: notes of hay with kind of a delicate bitter finish, the same way that cava has some bitterness on the finish. Godello is sort of a "Trust me—try this" kind of wine.
—JILL ZIMORSKI, CAFÉ ATLÁNTICO

Go-To Wines: Sommeliers' Picks of Wines That Never Let Them Down

I say that I am not that good at pairing wine and food, but I pick wines with high acidity. The best pairing for everything is **German Riesling** or **Champagne** because it has a little bit of sugar and a lot of acidity!
—RAJ VAIDYA, DANIEL

Attending a dinner party? Don't know what type of food is being served or what to bring? Try bringing wine with elevated acid levels. Examples include **Pinot Noir** from Burgundy, dry **Rieslings**, or **Grüner Veltliner** from Austria. These wines tend to go better with all types of food due to their amplified tones of acidity. . . . Rancho Pinot Grill's Tom Kaufman taught me, "When in doubt, think **red or white Burgundy**—it will always save you." I was having lamb with fava beans that Chrysa Kaufman [Rancho's chef and co-owner] put out, and I ordered a California Cabernet, which was really big at the time and to me just awesome. Tom said, "It's good if you like a lot of tannin," then poured me something basic from Louis Jadot Vosne-Romanée. I thought, "Wow, this is unique. It is mushroomy, has acidity, red fruit, and is not massive. It is rich, subtle, and soft. It allows the food to be expressed because the acidity recalibrates your palate with every bite."
—JESSE RODRIGUEZ, ADDISON AT THE GRAND DEL MAR

A go-to wine I absolutely love for multiple courses is a high-acid-style **white Burgundy**. I am more of a Puligny-Montrachet and Chablis guy. You will enjoy either on its own, especially from a producer like Carillon or Raveneau. It never competes with the food, because it has enough body and fruit to stand up to most things. For red, I love pairing with **Châteauneuf-du-Pape** simply because it is a little fuller-bodied style of wine yet usually does not have substantial tannin. It has red and darker fruits as well, and is one of those incredibly underutilized, really diverse red wines. I have never served a bottle of Châteauneuf-du-Pape to someone and heard, "Oh, that's not for me." Beaucastel [one of the best-known names] is ageworthy and not outrageous in price, but one of my favorite value producers is Clos des Brusquières. Le Vieux Donjon has done some incredible stuff the last couple of vintages. Château Rayas is absolutely amazing and often compared to Burgundy. For a fruitier style that is reasonably priced, Vieux Télégraphe's second label [Vieux Télégramme] can be really good, particularly in the best vintages. Or just downgrade to **Côtes du Rhône** and open Fonsalette—you won't regret it.
—CHRIS MILLER, SPAGO

GRACIANO

[grah-see-AHN-oh]
Countries: Australia, **Spain (Rioja)**, U.S. (California)
Color: red (dark, with a blue hue)
Grapes: Graciano, often blended with others, e.g., Tempranillo
Weight: full-bodied
Volume: loud
Dry/sweet: dry
Acidity: high
Tannin: medium to high
Flavors: aromatic, with notes of blackberries, black cherries, cedar, earth, figs, game, herbs, licorice, meat, mint, smoke, spices, toast, tobacco
Texture: elegant, rich, smooth
Temperature: Serve cool, about 60 to 65 degrees.
Pairings: braised dishes, chorizo, game, lamb, pork, red meat, sausages, stews, tuna
Tip: Try to give the wine an hour or two to breathe before serving.
Aging: Typically, should be drunk within three or four years, while the best can age for a decade or longer.
Producers: Spain: Inspiración Valdemar, Viña Ijalba; **U.S.– California:** Bokisch Vineyards

You seldom see **Graciano** as a single varietal—it's usually part of a blend, where it adds softness, fruitiness, and prettiness to a wine.
—JILL ZIMORSKI, CAFÉ ATLÁNTICO

GRAVES—RED

[grahv]
See also BORDEAUX–RED.
Country: France
Region: Bordeaux, southern part of the Left Bank
Color: red
Grapes: Cabernet Franc,
Cabernet Sauvignon, Merlot
Weight: medium- to full-bodied
Volume: moderate to loud
Dry/sweet: dry
Acidity: medium
Tannin: high
Flavors: notes of blackberries, black cherries, **black currants/ cassis, cedar**, chocolate, cinnamon, coffee, **EARTH**, gravel, leather, meat, **MINERALS**, pepper, plums, **smoke**, spices, strawberries, **tobacco**, vanilla
Texture: rich, soft, velvety
Temperature: Serve the best Graves cool (60 to 65 degrees), although others can be served slightly chilled (about 55 degrees).
Comparables: CABERNET SAUVIGNON, MERLOT
Pairings: cheese, duck, goose, pork, salmon, tuna, veal
Aging: The best should be set aside for nearly a decade before drinking.
Iconic example: Château Haut-Brion

GRAVES—WHITE

[grahv]
See also BORDEAUX–WHITE, SAUVIGNON BLANC.
Country: France
Region: Bordeaux, southern part of the Left Bank
Color: white
Grapes: Muscadelle, **Sauvignon Blanc**, Sémillon
Weight: medium-bodied
Volume: moderate
Dry/sweet: typically **dry** to occasionally sweet
Acidity: medium to high
Flavors: notes of apricots, **citrus**, cream, flowers, grapefruit, herbs, honey/beeswax, minerals, orange, passion fruit, peaches, smoke, toast, tropical fruits
Texture: ranges from crisp and fresh (esp. younger) to creamy and rich (esp. aged)
Temperature: Serve slightly chilled, about 55 degrees.
Comparables: BORDEAUX– WHITE, SAUVIGNON BLANC
Pairings: cheese (esp. Roquefort), chicken, fish, goat and sheep's milk cheeses, lobster, scallops
Tip: Graves produces some of the best white wines in all of Bordeaux.
Aging: Drink young and fresh, although the best versions can age for a decade or even longer.
Iconic example: Château Haut-Brion

GRECHETTO

[greh-KAY-toh]
See ORVIETO.

GRECO DI TUFO

[GREH-koh dee TOO-foh]
Country: Italy
Region: Campania / Tufo
Color: white
Grapes: Greco Bianco (primarily)
Weight: medium- to **full**-bodied
Volume: quiet to moderate
Dry/sweet: dry
Acidity: low to medium-high
Flavors: fruity, with notes of almonds, apples (esp. green), **earth**, flowers, **herbs**, honey, lemon, lime, **minerals, peaches**, pears, slate, spices, stones
Texture: clean, crisp, rich, silky
Temperature: Serve chilled, about 50 to 55 degrees.
Comparables: CHARDONNAY– UNOAKED, SAUVIGNON BLANC
Pairings: appetizers, **chicken**, crab, pasta, pork, risotto, salmon, **seafood, esp. shellfish**
Aging: Drink young and fresh, although the best can age for several years.

When I started consulting with the Greek restaurant Milos on their wine list less than a decade ago, **Greek wines** were largely not available in New York City.... Most Americans were still leery about Greek wines. They had memories of Retsina, with its strong pine-resin flavor, and rustic wines without the polished quality of other regions. But things have changed quite a bit.... Greek wines are accessible in flavor, and with their high acidity and balanced alcohol levels they work especially well with food.... **Assyrtiko** and **Moschofilero** are good value wines from Greece.... Of the Greek wines with the best chance to hit it big in the United States, I'd say **Assyrtiko** among whites and **Xinomavro** among reds. Once the public gets familiar with their pronunciation, the names will start to roll off their tongues.... Anthonopolous is one of the better producers in Greece. Alpha One is made by another great house [Alpha Estate] that employs the latest ultramodern equipment and produces high-quality wines.

—ROGER DAGORN, MS, PORTER HOUSE NEW YORK

Greek wines have a long history, and they are really good wines. People should try the crème de la crème of what is coming from there. I visited the 3,000-year-old vineyards at Sigalas on Santorini, and his wines are a step up compared to others. Greek wines are *terroir*-driven. When I smell Assyrtiko, I smell salt, volcanic [rock], and the Mediterranean. It has a lot of acidity, aromatics, and is especially great with food in the summer. I like it with Mediterranean food like octopus, tomatoes, and goat's or sheep's milk cheeses. It even works with Spanish foods like chorizo, dates, and bacon because it can really stand up to it. Moschofilero will definitely be replacing other aromatic varietals. If you put the reds from the north, like Naoussa and Xinomavro, in a blind tasting, I would be surprised to find they weren't close to Piedmont, as they have the same amber color, aromatics, tannins, and high acid and just scream for warm dishes like truffles, ragout, and other hearty dishes that have been in the oven for three hours. Alpha Estate is wonderful, as is Boutari, which has a Grand Reserve that is approachable at a good price and that will age.

—FERNANDO BETETA, MS, NOMI

Producers: Benito Ferrara, De Conciliis, Feudi di San Gregorio, **Mastroberardino**, Terradora di Paolo

GREEK WINES
Producers: Alpha Estate, Biblia Chora, **Boutari**, Cambas, Costa Lazaridi, Gaia, Gerovassiliou, Karydas, **Kourtakis**, Mercouri, Parparoussis, Porto Carras, **Sigalas**, Skouras, Tselepos

GRENACHE
[gren-AHSH]
See also CANNONAU.
Countries: Australia, France (SOUTH RHÔNE), Spain (where it's known as Garnacha), U.S. (California)
Color: red (relatively light in hue)
Grapes: Grenache, often blended with other grapes (e.g., Mourvèdre, Syrah)
Weight: medium-full- to very

full-bodied (with high alcohol)
Volume: moderate to loud
Dry/sweet: dry (for sweet versions, *see* BANYULS or MAURY)
Acidity: low to medium-plus
Tannin: low to medium
Flavors: very fruity, with notes of blackberries, black currants/ cassis, **black pepper, CHERRIES** (esp. cooked), chocolate, cinnamon, coffee, cranberries, earth, **herbs** (esp. herbes de Provence), jam, lavender, leather, licorice, minerals, nuts, **plums, RASPBERRIES** (esp. cooked), smoke, **SPICES, STRAWBERRIES** (esp. cooked), violets, **white pepper**
Texture: luscious, rich, velvety
Temperature: Serve slightly chilled, about 55 to 60 degrees.
Comparables: BEAUJOLAIS, CANNONAU, CHÂTEAUNEUF-DU-PAPE, CÔTES DU RHÔNE, PINOT NOIR, lighter SYRAH
Pairings: beef, duck (esp. with cherries), game, lamb, red meats, sausages, squab, stews
Tip: Grenache, the key grape used to make CHÂTEAUNEUF-DU-PAPE, is also found in PRIORAT. Pour a glass on September 24 to celebrate International Grenache Day.
Aging: Rhône wines have some of the longest aging potential of all French wines, but most Grenache-based wines are best drunk within the first ten years.
Producers: Australia: Clarendon Hills, Greenock Creek, Hewitson, R Wines Bitch (value), Torbreck; **France:** *see* CHÂTEAUNEUF-DU-PAPE; **Spain:** Bodegas Alto Moncayo, Las Rocas de San Alejandro El Renegado Garnacha, Monte la Sarda; **U.S.–California:** Alban, Beckmen Vineyards, Bucklin, Sine Qua Non

Grenache is pretty fantastic and an overlooked grape. Everyone got so excited about Pinot Noir that it got overhyped. Pinot Noir is an incredibly difficult grape to grow, so good Pinot Noir is never cheap. However, Grenache is easy to grow and inexpensive to buy. What people love about Pinot is the great fruit and acidity, and the nice balance. You can find all these things in Grenache as well. The grape is grown in so many places of the world that offer value. For example, Hewitson from Australia is a great value. In the Southern Rhône, there are plenty of good producers that use a high level of Grenache. You don't have to get Château Rayas. The second level of Vieux Télégraphe makes a wine another level down called Télégramme that is great.

—BELINDA CHANG, THE MODERN

I love **Garnacha!** One of my servers told me, "I love Pinot Noir, but I can't afford to drink it every day—so I drink Garnacha." It's not the same grape or wine, but there are similarities in terms of their fruit-forwardness and their delicious red fruit flavors. It's one of the easiest wines to learn to love.

—JILL ZIMORSKI, CAFÉ ATLÁNTICO

Iconic example: Château Rayas Châteauneuf-du-Pape

GRIGNOLINO

[green-yoh-LEEN-oh in Italian; green-oh-LEEN-oh in English]
Countries: Italy (Piedmont), U.S. (California)
Color: red (and rosé)
Grapes: Grignolino
Weight: light-bodied (and low in alcohol)
Volume: moderate
Dry/sweet: typically dry, but has been made into a sweet wine (see below)
Acidity: high
Tannin: medium to high
Flavors: aromatic and fruity, with notes of **flowers** (esp. roses), herbs (esp. green), lemon, minerals, mint, orange zest, spices, **strawberries**
Texture: crisp, delicate, **frizzante** (semi-sparkling)
Temperature: Serve slightly chilled, about 55 to 60 degrees.
Pairings: antipasto, cheese (esp. Parmesan), fish, lighter meats, pasta (esp. agnolotti), *salumi*

(Italian cured meats)
Tip: Look for Grignolino del Monferrato Casale on the label for a higher-quality example.
Aging: Drink young and fresh, within a year or two of the vintage.
Producers: Italy: Braida, La Casaccia, Michele Chiarlo; **U.S.–California:** Heitz (makes a red, rosé, and a port-style dessert wine)

GRILLO

[GREEL-loh]
Country: Italy
Region: Sicily
Color: white (light golden straw hue)
Grapes: Grillo
Weight: full-bodied
Volume: quiet
Dry/sweet: dry
Acidity: medium
Flavors: aromatic and fruity, with notes of almonds, apples, citrus, **flowers**, green peppers, **lemon**, minerals, peaches, sea breeze, spices, vanilla
Texture: crisp
Temperature: Serve cold, about 45 to 50 degrees.

Pairings: antipasto, cheese (esp. young), chicken, pasta, pork, seafood, vegetables
Aging: Drink young and fresh, within a year or two.
Producers: Contempo, Feudo Arancio

GRÜNER VELTLINER

[GROO-ner VELT-lee-ner]
Countries: AUSTRIA, Czech Republic, Hungary
Color: white
Grapes: Grüner Veltliner
Weight: **medium-** to full-bodied
Volume: quiet to moderate
Dry/sweet: dry
Acidity: medium to **high**
Flavors: aromatic and very fruity, with notes of almonds, apples (esp. green), apricots, baby powder (aroma), celery, **citrus**, cucumber, dill, **flowers**, grapefruit, herbs, honey, **lemon**, **LENTILS**, **lime**, lychees, mango, melon, **minerals**, **peaches**, **pears**, peas, **spices**, stones, vegetables (esp. green), **WHITE PEPPER**
Texture: crisp, refreshing, rich
Temperature: Serve chilled to cold, about 45 to 55 degrees.
Comparables: dry RIESLING, SAUVIGNON BLANC
Season: summer
Pairings: Asian cuisine, chicken, **fish**, green vegetables (e.g., artichokes, arugula, asparagus, broccoli, green beans, peas), herbed dishes and sauces, pork, salads, seafood, veal, Wiener schnitzel
Aging: Drink fresh (within a few years) or age for a decade or longer.
Producers: BRÜNDLMAYER, Domäne Wachau, Emmerich Knoll, Gobelsburg, Hirsch, **Hirtzberger**, Hofer Freiberg,

I love Austrian wines. I call them liquid glass, for being crystalline in structure and for their transparency. They are so clean and so good with food. I love **Grüner Veltliner** because it solves so many problems for me. In a restaurant setting, it is a real go-to varietal with disparate food elements. When you have several people at a table ordering different things, you have to find a common thread in a wine that is going to work with all these dishes. So often it is Grüner Veltliner that is going to work. It goes with all these difficult-to-pair food elements like artichokes, bell pepper, and asparagus. Try pairing anything but Sauvignon Blanc with asparagus, and you have a wine that tastes bitter and acidic. With Grüner, it just sings. It's partly the savory characteristic of the grape, partly the peppery character, the nice citrusy fruit—everything is in balance in these generally dry wines. We have one by Laurenz Moser V that he calls Singing Grüner Veltliner, which is a cross between dry Riesling and Sauvignon Blanc and is really reasonable by the glass. It comes into play a lot with pairings. We have an asparagus risotto with lemon zest that it is just perfect with.

—MICHAEL FLYNN, THE MANSION ON TURTLE CREEK

The quality level of the wine coming from Austria is unbelievable. As much as I hate the faddishness of **Grüner Veltliner**, it is the fad that won't die. I was talking to Dan Phillips [of The Grateful Palate] the other day, and he was saying, "For the last ten years, if you went to any restaurant with a young sommelier and asked them to bring you something to wow you, there was a 99 percent chance they would bring you a Grüner Veltliner and then something from Sine Qua Non. It was the one-two punch forever." I did a tasting of 300 Grüner Veltliners, and the quality was just amazing to me, from the $5 to the $100 bottle. They are remarkable at turning out an amazingly high-quality product at every price level. It is always super-solid. Favorite Grüner? I love anything from the Wachau, but when you are looking for value you don't want Wachau, because that is almost like Grand Cru. You want to look to Kremstal and Burgenland for some of the producers there. Fred Loimer does a great job. Fritz Wieninger has vineyards right at the top of Vienna, which is like having vineyards in Beverly Hills! His wines are really reasonable and really delicious. He is really a nice guy, too.

—BELINDA CHANG, THE MODERN

I love **Grüner Veltliner**, which is great for pairing. It is something to have at home that is cold and really yummy and reasonably priced in liter bottles. Michael Skurnik imports one that is in a green bottle with a soda pop top. It demystifies wine. It is fun, yummy, spicy, bright, refreshing, and a great summer wine to have on hand. It is great with first-course hors d'oeuvres. My wife likes to grill bread to serve with a variety of bruschetta toppings, like red pepper and olive tapenade, and Grüner is perfect with that. It also works with skewers on the grill and light, smoky foods.

—DANA FARNER, CUT

Hogl, Jamek, Kuenhof, **Nigl**, Nikolaihof, **Pichler**, **Prager**, Rainer Weiss, Salomon Undhof, Schloss Gobelsburg

---

HERMITAGE—RED
[ayr-mee-TAHZH]
Country: France
Region: Rhône Valley, north
Color: red (very dark in hue)
Grapes: SYRAH; may contain a small percentage of Marsanne and/or Roussanne
Weight: medium- to **full-bodied**
Volume: moderate (aged) to **loud** (younger)
Dry/sweet: dry
Acidity: low to medium
Tannin: high
Flavors: fruity, with notes of bacon, blackberries, **black currants/cassis**, **black pepper**, chocolate (esp. with age), **earth**, **game**, leather, meat, plums, raspberries, rosemary, smoke, spices, **tar**, tobacco
Texture: rich, silky, viscous
Temperature: Serve cool, about 60 to 65 degrees.
Comparable: CROZES-HERMITAGE
Season: autumn
Pairings: beef, braised dishes, game, lamb, mushrooms, steaks, stews, venison, wild boar
Tip: Hermitage wines are among the best-quality wines in the Rhône. If you have Hermitage taste but not the budget, check out SAINT-JOSEPH.
Aging: Age at least a decade or two before opening.
Producers: Belle, **Chapoutier**, Colombier, Colombo, Delas, **Guigal**, JEAN-LOUIS CHAVE, **Marc Sorrel**, Michel Ferraton, **Paul Jaboulet**
Iconic examples: **Jean-Louis Chave**, Paul Jaboulet's La Chapelle

HERMITAGE—WHITE

Country: France
Region: Rhône Valley, north
Color: white
Grapes: Marsanne
Weight: medium- to full-bodied (and high in alcohol)
Volume: moderate to loud
Dry/sweet: dry
Acidity: low to medium
Flavors: aromatic, with notes of **apricots**, cinnamon, earth, hazelnuts, herbs, honey, melon, **minerals**, nuts, **peaches**, pears, **spices**, vanilla
Texture: oily, rich, round, silky
Temperature: Serve chilled, about 55 degrees.
Comparable: white Crozes-Hermitage
Season: autumn
Pairings: chicken, crab, fish, lobster, pork, shellfish, shrimp, veal

Producers: Chapoutier, Jean-Louis Chave

HIGH-ACID WINES

See also Barbera, Beaujolais, Champagne, Chenin Blanc, Chianti, Gavi, Grüner Veltliner, Pinot Grigio, Pinot Noir, Riesling, Sauvignon Blanc, Trebbiano, Vouvray.

Tip: Generally, the more acidic the wine, the cooler the climate that produced it.

HIGH-ALCOHOL WINES

See Barbaresco, Barolo, California Wines, Madeira, Port, Sherry, Shiraz, Zinfandel.

Countries: warm climates
Alcohol: more than 14 percent
Color: In general, their color is duller than lower-alcohol wines.

HIGH-TANNIN WINES

See Barbaresco, Barolo, Bordeaux–Red, Cabernet Sauvignon, Merlot, Syrah, Zinfandel.

HUNGARIAN WINES

Wines from Hungary are getting better. I have been to Hungary, and the climate is pretty continental but a little warmer. They have excellent foie gras, tomatoes—plus grapes for winemaking. The spelling and the accents are a little harder to master. Not everyone knows to try **Királyleányka**—it is difficult to say! Most people associate Hungary with **Tokaji**—and rightfully so, because it is a great dessert wine. But the rest of the country is producing amazingly fragrant, floral, crisp white wines. **Irsai Oliver** reminds me of Torrontés or Muscat. Hungary's **Blaufränkisch** is also getting better.

—FERNANDO BETETA, MS, NOMI

ICE CIDER

Countries: Canada, U.S. (Massachusetts, New York, Vermont)
Grapes: none—this is made with apples!
Weight: full-bodied (but low in alcohol)
Volume: moderate to loud
Dry/sweet: sweet
Acidity: medium
Flavors: notes of **APPLES**, apricots, caramel, cider, cinnamon, citrus, cloves, flowers, **honey**, marmalade, melon (esp. honeydew), pears, spices, tangerine, vanilla
Texture: fresh, rich, smooth, unctuous, velvety
Temperature: Serve cold, about 45 to 50 degrees.

Not sure what to pair with fresh salads topped with your favorite vinaigrette? Try using wines with **elevated acid levels**, such as a Sauvignon Blanc from Sancerre. This is a classic case of pairing like with like.

—JESSE RODRIGUEZ, ADDISON AT THE GRAND DEL MAR

When you are thinking about **acidity** in wine, you'll find that the farther from the equator, the higher the acid.

—MARK MENDOZA, SONA

Every meal needs some acid. For a wine, **acidity** is its central nervous system. The 1997 vintage in California was a really ripe year. The wine tasted really, really good the first three and four years. Ten years later, the acid had gone away, and the fruit became desiccated and had lost its vibrancy. If you have a Nebbiolo, it will age twenty-plus years because of the acidity. That is why I see acidity as the central nervous system. As a human, if your central nervous system goes out, you die—and the same goes for wine. I have saved every menu from The French Laundry, Per Se, and all the top restaurants I have worked in. I went back and highlighted the wine pairings and noticed "high acid" and "medium-plus acid." There were only a couple of exceptions where I'd gone with the big juiciness of something like a California Zinfandel. For the most finessed pairings, the wines all had high acid, and they always showed exceptionally well. After each bite, your palate was recalibrated and refreshed for the next.

— JESSE RODRIGUEZ, ADDISON AT THE GRAND DEL MAR

Pairings: cheese (esp. Cheddar, fresh goat), cheesecake, desserts (esp. apple and/or cheese), foie gras, game, hors d'oeuvres, **paté**
Aging: Drink young and fresh or age for several years.
Producers: Canada: La Face Cachée de la Pomme Neige, Pinnacle, Winter Gold; **U.S.– Massachusetts: Still River Winery; New York (Finger Lakes):** Eve's Cidery Essence; **Vermont: Eden**

ICE WINE

See also RIESLING–EISWEIN.
Countries: Australia, Austria, Canada, Germany (Eiswein), New Zealand, Slovenia, U.S. (esp. New York's Finger Lakes)
Color: white
Grapes: varies; often Riesling or Vidal
Weight: medium- to full-bodied
Volume: moderate to loud
Dry/sweet: sweet to very sweet
Acidity: high

Flavors: dessert wine, with notes of apples, apricots, cinnamon, flowers, ginger, honey, lemon, lime, melon, peaches, pears, pineapple, tangerine, tropical fruits
Texture: rich, syrupy; sometimes made as a sparkling wine
Temperature: Serve very cold, about 40 to 45 degrees.
Comparables: ICE CIDER, RIESLING–EISWEIN
Pairings: cheese (esp. soft and/ or blue), cookies, custards, foie gras, fruit desserts
Tip: For a delightful alternative, try red ice wine (e.g., Inniskillin) made with Cabernet Franc grapes, whose raspberry and strawberry flavors pair beautifully with chocolate, or ICE CIDER, which we've been crazy about since our first sip of **La Face Cachée de la Pomme Neige Ice Cider.**
Producers: Canada: Cave Spring, **Inniskillin**, Jackson-

Triggs, Waupoos; **Czech Republic:** Znovin Znojmo; **New Zealand:** Seifried; **Slovenia:** Vina Prus Rumeni; **U.S.–California:** Bonny Doon Muscat Vin de Glacière; **New York:** Wagner Vignoles Ice Wine

ICE WINE — SPARKLING

Country: Canada
Color: white
Grapes: Vidal
Weight: medium
Volume: moderate
Dry/sweet: sweet
Acidity: high
Flavors: notes of apples, apricots, grapefruit, honey, lemon, lime, lychees, mango, minerals, nectarines, peaches, spices
Texture: rich, **semi-sparkling**
Temperature: Serve very cold, about 40 to 45 degrees.
Pairings: blue cheese, cakes, custards, foie gras, lighter fruit desserts, soufflés
Tip: This wine is very rare and hard to find, so if you see some, grab it!
Aging: Drink within the first few years after the vintage.
Producer: Inniskillin

Inniskillin put Canadian **ice wines** on the global map in 1991, when its 1989 Vidal Ice Wine won the Grand Prix d'Honneur at Vinexpo in France. Canadian ice wines are generally not as expensive as German eisweins, because we have the weather to produce them every year instead of just every few years.
—STEVE BECKTA, BECKTA DINING & WINE AND PLAY FOOD & WINE

Importers

In learning about a wine, sometimes it pays to start with the *back* label. At a wine store, we're often confronted by interesting-looking but unfamiliar wines. So we flip the bottle over to look at the back label, which gives the name of the importer. This can be a useful shortcut to spotting wines worth trying.

At the Boston restaurant No. 9 Park, sommelier Cat Silirie told us, "My brother, an art director and graphic designer who lives in Atlanta, said to me, 'You will hate me for it, but I go in the store and pick wine by the label. I pick what looks intelligent or has good design, thinking they must be cool people because they hired someone with an aesthetic.'

"The first tip I gave him for getting better wine was to skip the package store and find a specialty shop. I also gave him a list of importers so he could just turn the bottle around and skip the front label. I recommended **Terry Theise, Louis/Dressner, Neil Rosenthal, Eric Solomon, Kermit Lynch,** André Tamers of **De Maison,** who does mostly Spanish wines, **Vin Divino,** and **Winebow.** If you want to go out on a limb, look for specialty importers from your state. Some smaller importers will import for only one or two states, and their stuff will be interesting. The back label will give their name and the state's name.

"The reason you can trust the best importers is because they have a point of view, and most are incredibly eloquent on their particular points of view. In the case of the importers I mentioned, they are all interested in small-production, artisanal wines that are most often expressive wines of place."

Here are some comments from leading sommeliers about their favorite importers:

David Bowler is finding smaller Burgundy producers but is really known for Austrian wines. He has a few American producers as well, like Cobb on the Sonoma Coast.
—ROXANE SHAFAEE-MOGHADAM, THE BREAKERS

Joe Dressner [of Louis/Dressner] is about the code of artisanality and the morality of what is right. That means no chemicals, no pesticides, no fertilizers—and he won't even visit someone who uses mechanical harvesting. That is his code of ethics.
—CAT SILIRIE, NO. 9 PARK

Kermit Lynch. He has done an incredible service for French wine in America. He has a great palate, imports a ton of absolutely great wines that we simply would not know about if not for him. The American French-wine-drinking public owes him one.
—CHRIS MILLER, SPAGO

Kermit Lynch's wines show typicity, regionality, artisanality—plus reading his book *Adventures on the Wine Route* is so much fun!
—CAT SILIRIE, NO. 9 PARK

Kermit Lynch is fantastic, and his wines have an earthy-toned rusticity to them.
—ROXANE SHAFAEE-MOGHADAM, THE BREAKERS

Neal Rosenthal [author of 2008's *Reflections of a Wine Merchant*] is very articulate about sense of place, which is his leading passion. He would not have a Muscadet unless he really believed it was very "Muscadet-y."
—CAT SILIRIE, NO. 9 PARK

Michael Skurnik. He has a great European portfolio, specifically Austria. His Alzinger is awesome. Ecker is one of my favorite value producers, and their Roter Veltliner is insane and killer. It tastes like 85 percent Grüner and 15 percent Sauvignon Blanc, with great acid and herbal notes. Nikolaiof is killer, the producer of some of the best Grüner Veltliners and Rieslings on the planet.
—CHRIS MILLER, SPAGO

Terry Theise [author of 2010's *Reading Between the Vines*]. If I see his name on a label, I know I am safe with just about everything he does. If it is an Austrian wine with his name on the back, there is a pretty good chance it is a good bottle of wine. . . . He has a portfolio within Skurnik and features Bründlmayer, Nigel, Gobelsburg—and all are just incredible wines. He also has a great Australian portfolio. He brings in Ben Glazer's wine, Kastler and Slipstream, which is great on the cheaper side. He also has an insane portfolio for Italy.
—CHRIS MILLER, SPAGO

The most eloquent of all is **Terry Theise** in terms of what drives him, what he is looking for, what he wants from the wine itself, as well as who the people are. The family aspect matters to him greatly. The last point of his five-point manifesto is "Soul is more important than anything, and soul is expressed as a trinity of family, soil, and artisanality." The wine has to have fascinating geology/*terroir*, the people have to work on a small scale with artisanality, and the family—knowing who they are matters.

—CAT SILIRIE, NO. 9 PARK

Importer Terry Theise's Five-Point Manifesto
- Beauty is more important than impact.
- Harmony is more important than intensity.
- The whole of any wine must always be more than the sum of its parts.
- Distinctiveness is more important than conventional prettiness.
- Soul is more important than anything, and soul is expressed as a trinity of family, soil, and artisanality.

I get to see **Terry Theise** a bit, and he is just a god to me in how he perceives and describes wine. He was one of the first people who got me thinking about the concept that the wines I love are going to meet me halfway at the table. The ones I don't like are just going to dominate the conversation and be completely in charge.

—ANDY MYERS, CITYZEN

Terry Theise: He is fantastic, and you can trust pretty much anything with his name on the back as long as you like white wine. Terry Theise is completely the opposite of **Rudi Wiest**. Terry likes white wine with sweetness, likes Champagne, hates anything produced in larger quantities, is antagonistic, an academic, and talks in nebulous and emotional terms. Rudi is very German. He is factual, clear, likes dry wine, talks especially about details. Both are very good at what they do. They both also have strong and long-lasting relationships with the wine growers that they represent because they have known them for twenty-five years plus. They are good friends to their producers. If you see either of their names on the back of bottles, you are guaranteed something good.

—ROXANE SHAFAEE-MOGHADAM, THE BREAKERS

If **Becky Wasserman**'s name is on the back label [of a bottle of Champagne], there is a pretty good chance I am going to like it. She represents small growers, and they are always switching up. She may import 2,000 cases. If I see her name, I know I am safe.

—CHRIS MILLER, SPAGO

We are huge fans of Spain, and we think **Jorge Ordoñez** is one of the great importers for Spanish wines. Protocolo, Borsao, and Sierra Cantabria are all reds from Jorge Ordoñez.

—INEZ RIBUSTELLO, ON THE SQUARE

INDIAN WINES

Region: Nashik Valley (which has been called India's Napa Valley)

Grapes: red: Cabernet Sauvignon, Merlot, **Shiraz,** Zinfandel; **white:** Chenin Blanc, Riesling, **Sauvignon Blanc,** Viognier

Producers: Good Earth Winery, **Sula Vineyards**

INZOLIA (AKA INSOLIA)

[inn-SOHL-yah]
Country: Italy
Regions: Sicily, Tuscany (where it's known as Ansonica)
Color: white
Grapes: Inzolia, sometimes blended with other white grapes such as Chardonnay, Grecanico, or Viognier
Weight: medium- to full-bodied
Volume: quiet to moderate
Acidity: medium to high
Flavors: aromatic, with notes of **almonds,** apples, caramel, **citrus, flowers, grapefruit,** herbs, honey, lemon, lime, melon, minerals, **nuts, orange zest, peaches,** pears, pineapple, sea breeze, tropical fruits, with a bitter finish
Texture: crisp, creamy, rich, round
Temperature: Serve chilled, about 50 degrees.
Comparables: PINOT GRIGIO, SAUVIGNON BLANC
Pairings: antipasto, cheese (esp. goat, Pecorino), fish, legumes, pesto, pork, risotto, shellfish, vegetables
Aging: Drink young and fresh, within a year or two.
Producers: Baglio di Pianetto, Corbera, Cusumano, Feudo Principi di Butera, Martorana

ISRAELI WINES

See also KOSHER WINES.

Grapes: red: Barbera, Cabernet Franc, **Cabernet Sauvignon, Merlot,** Petit Verdot, Pinot Noir, Sangiovese; **white: Chardonnay,** Gewürztraminer, Riesling, **Sauvignon Blanc**

Tip: Not all Israeli wines are kosher, although an estimated 80 percent are.

Producers: Largest: Israel has more than 200 wineries, but in 2010 five large wineries produced 85 percent of the country's wine: Barkan-Segal, Binyamin, **Carmel, Golan Heights** (Gamla, Golan, Yarden), and Teperberg 1870; **Midsized:** Dalton, Galil Mountain, Hevron Heights/ Noah, Recanati, Tabor, Tishbi, and Zion; **Small:** Alexander, Avidan, Bazelet ha Golan, BRAVDO Karmei Yosef, Chillag, Domaine du Castel, Ella Valley, Flam, Gvaot, Margalit, Mony, Pelter, Saslove, Sea Horse, Shiloh, The Cave, Tulip, Tzora, Vitkin, Yaffo, Yatir

ITALIAN WINES

Tip: We have provided phonetic spellings of all the wines listed in this chapter, but if you'd like to hear how to pronounce the Italian names, visit Vino-Italiano .blogspot.com.

Gambero Rosso (gamberorosso .it) publishes *Vini d'Italia,* an influential annual guide to Italian wines. The following have been featured as Winery of the Year over the past decade:

- 2010: Bruno Giacosa
- 2009: Fattoria di Felsina
- 2008: Gaja
- 2007: Benanti
- 2006: Val di Maggio
- 2005: Castello di Ama
- 2004: Masciarelli Wine Estate
- 2003: Ca' del Bosco
- 2002: Barone Ricasoli
- 2001: La Spinetta

JURANÇON SEC

[zhoo-rahn-SAWN seck]
Country: France
Region: Southwest/Jurançon

The red wines of northern **Italy** are highlighted by the **Nebbiolo** grape (Barolo, Barbaresco, and Lombardy's Valtellina), the center is dominated by **Sangiovese** (Chianti, Brunello di Montalcino, Vino Nobile di Montepulciano), and the south is **Aglianico** country (Taurasi, Aglianico del Vulture).

—DAVID LYNCH, QUINCE

Under-$15 tip: Cusumano from Sicily is one of the most solid producers in **Italy.** The wine is made by two brothers, who are super-cute, at a modern winery. They make spot-on Nero d'Avola, Merlot, **Insolia,** and an Insolia-Chardonnay blend. Cusumano has really streamlined, cool labeling, and I noticed the last time I was there that it was in every Italian wine bar. The Italians love it too, so you are still being authentic. It is a really simple label, the wines are cheap [around $10], and they are fantastic.

—BELINDA CHANG, THE MODERN

Cat Silirie of No. 9 Park on Teaching the Wines of Italy Step by Step

Step One: The Three Parts of Italy

When I teach Italian wine to my staff, I don't do it by grapes, because there are more than eight hundred, and that always sends everyone running for the hills! They are certain they are not going to get it because they could never taste or even fathom that much.

I tell them we are going to do some armchair travel. To make it easier, instead of starting with the twenty-one regions and all the grapes, I divide Italy into three parts—north, central, and south—in terms of feeling, climate, and geography. That way you can generalize, by saying "Northern Italian whites are more focused on finesse. With a cooler climate, wine generally has more acidity, and there's a distinct aromatic profile in the far north," and "In the south, it is super-sunny and hot, so the wines are likely to be rich and very flavorful with lower acidity." The central region is simply in between. A lot of people don't realize that Italy is not just one big happy peninsula.

Step Two: The Twenty[-one] Regions

The next thing is learning the regions—where they are and what each one looks like and feels like. There are twenty official regions, but I teach twenty-one because I consider Trentino and Alto Adige as having very distinct *terroirs*, grape varieties, DOC styles, and so on. They learn capital cities, places they want to go, the geography—is it on the ocean or in the mountains? By identifying the zones, which is what Italians call regions, by conjuring a feeling of place, you link the type of wine to the foods you find in that region, which is so Italian. Associating wine with the place and its food—"the taste of place," as we call it—makes it much easier to remember all the different wines.

Especially with the white wines, assigning precise adjectives to the flavors can be tricky. For a lot of tasters, when it comes to the whites, it is hard to describe the fruits, flowers, and flavors of a wine that has such neutrality. Yet when you taste the whites with the food of the zone, you can't believe how well they go together. Pigato, from Liguria, and Verdicchio, from Marche—both coastal regions—are fresh, clean, light, and lemony. If you are tasting them in isolation, it is not like tasting Riesling or Gewürztraminer, which give you a very specific flavor.

We go through the twenty-one zones and identify a classic dish or one you would be likely to eat. In Marche you could be having mountain food or ocean food. In the mountains, you are eating boar stew with pasta, and on the ocean you have delicate seafood with a light touch of olive oil. For one region you want one style of wine; for another you want something else.

Sicily is surrounded by three oceans. You have influences from so many different people—from Moroccan to Arab to Roman. You get the sense that it is not "Italian" at all; it is everything, a polyglot. By contrast, compare Sicily to Alto Adige, which is part of the former Austro-Hungarian Empire, and everyone is wearing *lederhosen*. There is no one Italy. It is more important to paint a picture of a place than to just spew facts. So painting the "taste of place" is a way of talking about *terroir*.

We do a lot of work just by pulling out coffee-table books, photography books, and cookbooks and passing them around.

Step Three: The DOCs (Denominazione di Origine Controllata)

After learning the twenty-one regions, we learn that there are actually 300-plus DOCs. [Like the other European countries, Italy has laws controlling the names, origins, and traits of several of its signature foods and wines, from Parmesan cheese to Chianti.] If you are studying what Piedmont looks and feels like, with its fog and rolling hills, and what people are eating and drinking (truffles, risotto), then you should really know the DOCs.

So now you are identifying grape varieties of a place and identifying the archetypes of what foods and wines to expect in that place.

Step Four: Exceptions to the Rules

As we generalize about regions, it is also important to learn the exceptions within each one. Puglia is a region that is very flat, and the grapes Primitivo and Negroamaro are low in acid and very rich—almost raisinlike. The wines I chose for our list are not like that, because I don't like low-acid wines. However, I found a Perrini Primitivo that is very fresh and aromatic and doesn't smell like stewed figs. Though we look for the typicity of the place, I also want a wine with a little flair. You have the intensity of Puglia with the dried fruit flavor, but you also get a touch of freshness that is unusual. This is an example of being open to surprise. Don't reject a wine because it does not fit your left-brain (i.e., fact-based) expectations!

Color: white
Grapes: Gros Manseng, Petit Manseng, as part of a blend
Weight: medium- to full-bodied
Volume: moderate
Dry/sweet: dry
Acidity: high
Flavors: notes of almonds, apples, apricots, butterscotch, **cinnamon**, citrus, cloves, coconut, **flowers**, herbs, **HONEY, LEMON,** lime, mango, melon, **minerals, orange,** peaches, pineapple, **spices,** toast, tropical fruits, vanilla
Texture: crisp, rich, round
Temperature: Serve chilled, about 50 to 55 degrees.
Pairings: chicken, cured meats, fish, ham (esp. with melon), pork, salmon, shellfish
Aging: Drink dry Jurançon within a few years, although the very best can last a decade or more.
Producers: Bru-Baché, **Cauhapé,** Charles Hours, Clos Lapeyre, Clos Uroulat

JURANÇON—SWEET
[zhoo-rahn-SAWN]
Country: France
Region: Southwest
Color: white
Grapes: Gros Manseng, **Petit Manseng,** as part of a blend
Weight: medium- to full-bodied (and high in alcohol)
Volume: moderate to loud
Dry/sweet: sweet
Acidity: high

A dessert wine that is underrated but so compatible is Domaine Cauhapé **Jurançon.** Gros Manseng and Petite Manseng, the two primary grapes in the wine, are invaluable with dessert pairings because they have juicy orange notes and integrated sugars. This is also the quintessential foie gras wine. The wine just shimmers on your palate.

—JUSTIN LEONE, BENNY'S CHOP HOUSE

Flavors: notes of almonds, apples, apricots, butterscotch, **cinnamon,** citrus, coconut, **flowers,** guava, herbs, **HONEY,** lemon, **LIME,** mango, melon, **minerals, orange,** papaya, peaches, **pineapple, raisins, SPICES,** toast, **tropical fruits,** vanilla
Texture: rich
Temperature: Serve cold, about 45 degrees.
Pairings: cheese (esp. blue or Cheddar), desserts, foie gras, fruit, fruit desserts, paté
Tip: In 1553, at the christening of Henri IV, later to be known as Henry the Great, his lips were rubbed with a clove of garlic and dampened with Jurançon. That was said to be the source of his vigor and ardent spirit.
Aging: Sweet Jurançon can last several years to several decades.
Producers: Bru-Bache, Cauhapé (biodynamic), Charles Hours, Clos Lapeyre, Clos Uroulat

KERNER
[KEHR-nerr]
Countries: Canada, Germany, Italy (Alto Adige), South Africa, U.K., U.S. (Virginia)
Color: white
Grapes: Kerner
Weight: medium-bodied
Volume: loud
Dry/sweet: dry
Acidity: high
Flavors: very aromatic,

With a tomato salad like a Caprese [raw tomatoes and mozzarella], I would pair either a dry Riesling or a **Kerner.**
—CLAIRE PAPARAZZO, BLUE HILL

with notes of **citrus, flowers,** grapefruit, green apples, **herbs,** lemon, lime, mango, **minerals,** peaches, spices
Texture: crisp, lush, rich
Temperature: Serve chilled, about 50 to 55 degrees.
Comparable: RIESLING
Pairings: charcuterie, chicken, fish, pork, veal, tomatoes, tomato salads (e.g., Caprese)
Producers: Italy–Alto Adige: Abbazia di Novacella, Kofererhof, Pacher Hof, Weingut Niklas

KOSHER WINES
See also ISRAELI WINES.
Countries: Argentina, Chile, France, Israel, New Zealand, South Africa, U.S.
Tip: Often a wine bottle's back label will indicate its kosher status:
Kosher: Hebrew for "fit" or "proper." Look for a circled letter, such as U (certified as kosher by the Orthodox Union), K (OK Kosher Certification), or KA (Kosher Australia certification).
Kosher for Passover: Often indicated by a circled letter or letters such as U, K, or KA followed by a P. This means that the wine has passed the even stricter kosher standards for Passover.
Mevushal [meh-VOO-shell]: Mevushal wines have been pasteurized via flash-heating. They can be handled by non-Jews (such as caterers or waiters) and remain kosher.

Pairings for Passover: Gefilte fish with Blanc de Blancs sparkling wine (e.g., Yarden) or New Zealand Sauvignon Blanc (e.g., Goose Bay); **chopped liver** with Gewürztraminer (e.g., Yarden); **roast chicken or turkey** with Chardonnay (e.g., Yarden Odem Organic Vineyard); **beef brisket** with a bigger white wine such as a Chardonnay (e.g., Herzog Special Reserve Edna Valley) or bigger red wine such as a Bordeaux blend (e.g., Barons Edmond Benjamin de Rothschild Haut-Médoc) or Shiraz (e.g., Galil Mountain); **flourless chocolate cake** with a sweet red wine (e.g., Rimon Winery Black Label Pomegranate); and **macaroons** with a Late Harvest Gewürztraminer (e.g., Carmel Winery Shaal Single Vineyard).
Tip: For more producers, visit www.kosherwine.com.
Producers: France: Barons de Rothschild; **Israel:** Bazelet ha Golan, Castel (100 percent Chardonnay "C" Blanc and Cabernet-based Grand Vin), Ella Valley, Galil, Golan, Psagot, Yarden; **New Zealand:** Goose Bay; **Spain:** Capçanes; **U.S.:** Covenant (Cabernet Sauvignon), Herzog Wine Cellars, and its value-priced Baron Herzog line

LAGREIN

[lah-GRINE]
Country: Italy (Alto Adige), U.S. (Oregon)
Color: red (or rosé)
Grapes: Lagrein
Weight: medium- to full-bodied (and moderate in alcohol)
Volume: moderate to loud
Dry/sweet: dry
Acidity: medium to high
Tannin: medium

There is a similarity among **Lagrein**, Taburno, and Blaufränkisch, which are all cooler-climate reds that have a richness to them. There is spice, tarriness, and a high acidity level that is both a blessing and curse to these wines. Acidity in wine is such a necessary ingredient, because it makes the flavors pop through more clearly and makes the wine pair so nicely with food. I will hear guests say they want a wine that is "smooth." What I imagine they mean is that they don't want their mouth drying out from too much tannin or watering too much from acid. If someone is looking for a wine somewhat off the beaten path, Lagrein is a great way to go. The tarriness and acidity make it a great pairing with steak.
—DANA FARNER, CUT

Flavors: fruity, with notes of **blackberries**, black pepper, blueberries, **cherries**, **chocolate (esp. dark)**, coffee, cranberries, earth, grass, **herbs**, **leather**, **meat**, minerals, **PLUMS**, **raspberries**, **smoke**, spices, tar, tobacco, violets
Texture: rich, rustic, silky
Temperature: Serve cool, about 60 to 65 degrees.
Pairings: cheese (esp. aged), game, pork, prosciutto, red meat, speck, steak, stews
Aging: Better wines can age for five years to a decade or longer.
Producers: Italy: Abbazia di Novacella, Alois Lageder, Bottega Vinaia, Franz Gojer/Glogglhof, Josef Niedermayr, La-Vis, Muri-Gries Rosado, San Pietro, St. Maddalena, Terlano, Thurnhof, Tiefenbrunner; **U.S.–Oregon:** Remy

LAMBRUSCO

[lahm-BROO-skoh]
Country: Italy
Region: Emilia-Romagna
Color: red (also rosé and white)
Grapes: Lambrusco
Weight: light- to medium-bodied (and low in alcohol)
Volume: moderate
Dry/sweet: dry to semi-sweet
Acidity: medium to high
Tannin: low to medium
Flavors: fruity, with notes of black cherries, earth, flowers, grapes, plums, **raspberries**, **strawberries**, violets
Texture: semi-sparkling; rich, round, soft
Temperature: Serve cold, about 45 to 50 degrees.
Season: summer
Pairings: berries, cheese (esp. Parmesan), cured meats, hors d'oeuvres, pasta, picnics, pizza,

When people get off the plane in Italy, they all want a certain thing—whether it is coffee, *salumi*, or pasta. I want **Lambrusco**. On my first two trips to Italy, I was with the same person and we went to Emilia-Romagna. We went straight to this deli and the first thing we had was a sampling of all the local Lambrusco. Lambrusco can be variable in quality, but when you get a great one it is like finding a great Burgundy. The combination of Lambrusco with a really nutty Parmesan and great *salumi* is the coolest. It might be better than caviar and Champagne to me. For the price, Terra Calda makes amazing red and white Lambrusco, and it is also readily available.
—BELINDA CHANG, THE MODERN

pork, prosciutto, *salumi* (Italian cured meats), sausages
Aging: Drink young and fresh.
Producers: Cellar Cavicchioli, Francesco Vezzelli, Francis Bellei, Lini, Tenuta Pederzana, Terra Calda, Villa di Carlo, Vittorio Graziano

LANGUEDOC-ROUSSILLON WINES

[lahng-DAWK roo-see-AWN]
Country: France
Grapes: red (and rosé): Cabernet Sauvignon, Carignan, Cinsault, Grenache, Merlot, Mourvèdre, Syrah
Producers: Domaine Clavel Coteaux, Domaine de Coussergues, Mas Julien
Iconic example: Mas de Daumas Gassac

There is a reason you taste olives, herbes de Provence, and Provençal sun when you taste a wine from the **Languedoc**. It is the sense of place. I was a struggling wannabe rock star with no money to my name when I managed to scrape up the money for two bottles of Domaine Clavel Coteaux du Languedoc red. It blew my mind. I could not fully grasp how something made from only grape juice could carry so much information: Nicoise olives, lavender, thyme, brush, and underbrush all in my mouth. I didn't understand, and it inspired me to learn more. That is when I read about and understood *garrigue* and the general qualities of Provençal wine. That is when I fell in love. I thought, "This is such an unbelievable metamorphosis. I need to know more."
—JUSTIN LEONE, BENNY'S CHOP HOUSE

The **Languedoc** is an area of France I am very excited about. Unlike other regions, it is not so strictly regulated, so you have winemakers with more freedom to play. There is an earthiness emerging from this region. There are a lot of wines that are more in the New World style, that really focus on the fruit. Since they are not so regulated, they can use more New World technology in order to make more palate-friendly wines.
—DANA FARNER, CUT

Mas de Daumas Gassac in the **Languedoc** is called the Chateau Latour of the south of France. They are known for really intense reds in the Bordelaise style, and make remarkably age-worthy wines. They also make a sparkling Cabernet Sauvignon that is really good.
—BELINDA CHANG, THE MODERN

LATE HARVEST WINES

Countries: Australia, Austria, Canada, France (Alsace), Germany, South Africa, U.S.
Grapes: varies; the more common white grapes used are Chenin Blanc, Gewürztraminer, Riesling, Sauvignon Blanc, Sémillon; red grapes include Zinfandel
Weight: fuller-bodied (yet lower in alcohol)
Volume: loud
Dry/sweet: sweet to very sweet
Flavors: varies by grape(s); e.g., apricots, cream, orange, peaches (Semillon/Sauvignon Blanc) to cherries, chocolate, raspberries, vanilla (Zinfandel)
Texture: luscious, rich, silky, unctuous

Temperature: Serve cold, about 45 degrees.
Pairings: cheese, desserts, foie gras
Tip: The grapes for these wines are harvested late in the season when very ripe with high levels of sugar. Not all of the sugar is converted to alcohol during the winemaking process, creating sweet dessert wines.
Producers: France–Alsace: *see* VENDANGE TARDIVE WINES; **U.S.– California:** Blacksmith (Syrah), Clayhouse (Petite Sirah), Dashe (Zinfandel), **Dolce** (a Sauvignon Blanc and Semillon blend), Joseph Phelps, Navarro, Ridge (Zinfandel), Rosenblum (Zinfandel), Topaz (Sauvignon Blanc and Semillon), Trefethen (Riesling); **Washington state:** Hogue (Riesling)

LEBANON WINES

Producers: Château Ksara, Château Musar, Kefraya, Massaya
Iconic example: Château Musar

The renowned **Lebanese** producer Château Musar's old vintages are very Bordeaux-like and a great value. A 1982 is fantastic for a couple of hundred dollars, while a comparable Bordeaux would break the bank.
—STEPHANE COLLING, SAN YSIDRO RANCH

LEMBERGER

[LEM-boor-ger]
See BLAUFRÄNKISCH.

LIGHT-BODIED WINES

Red: Beaujolais, Pinot Noir
White: Chenin Blanc, Muscadet, Pinot Grigio, Riesling, Sancerre, Soave, Vinho Verde
Seasons: spring, summer
Pairings: lighter dishes
Tip: As a rule of thumb, the

lighter the wine in color and the lower the stated alcohol level (which is required by law on its label), the lighter the body.

LIGHTER-COLORED WINES

Tip: As a rule of thumb, the lighter the wine in color, the lighter it is in weight and the quieter it is in flavor volume.

LOCOROTONDO

[loh-koh-roh-TOHN-doh]
Country: Italy
Region: Puglia
Color: white
Grapes: Verdeca, blended with other Italian white grapes (e.g., Bianco d'Alessano)
Weight: light- to medium-bodied
Volume: quiet
Dry/sweet: dry
Acidity: high
Flavors: fruity, with notes of almonds, apples (esp. green), citrus, flint, flowers, herbs, honey, lemon, minerals, peaches
Texture: crisp, delicate, fresh; ranges from still to *spumante* (sparkling)
Temperature: Serve chilled, about 50 degrees.
Pairings: antipasto, broccoli rabe, fish, pizza, prosciutto, risotto, shrimp
Aging: Drink young and fresh, within a year or two.
Producer: Cantina del Locorotondo

LOIRE WINES

[lwahr]
See also CHINON, MUSCADET, POUILLY-FUMÉ, SANCERRE, SAVENNIÈRES, VOUVRAY.
Color: white (primarily)
Texture: crisp (primarily)

I hate boring wines. There is a sea of Pinot Grigio out there, including some great ones from Italy, but much of that sea is bad news. We are down to two or three great ones on our list, and everyone else can drink great wine from the **Loire Valley**—which is what I typically recommend anyway.
—RAJ VAIDYA, DANIEL

Sushi with **Loire wines** from the Anjou-Saumur is a wine pairing par excellence. Look for Vouvray, Savennières, and Crémant de la Loire vintage wines of demi-sec sweetness and cushiony ripeness.
—PETER BIRMINGHAM, POURTAL

LOUD WINES—RED

See AMARONE, CABERNET SAUVIGNON, CAHORS, CANNONAU, DOURO REDS, GIGONDAS, MALBEC, PETITE SIRAH, TANNAT, XINOMAVRO.

LOUD WINES—WHITE

See CHARDONNAY–OAKED, GEWÜRZTRAMINER, KERNER, RETSINA, SAUVIGNON BLANC (New Zealand), VOUVRAY.

LOW-ACID WINES

See CHARDONNAY, GEWÜRZTRAMINER, MUSCAT, PINOT BLANC, PINOT GRIS, SÉMILLON, VIOGNIER.

LOW-ALCOHOL WINES

Wines with 12 percent alcohol or less.
See BEAUJOLAIS, BRACHETTO D'ACQUI, BUGEY, FRASCATI, FREISA, GALESTRO, GRIGNOLINO, LAMBRUSCO, **MOSCATO D'ASTI** (5 percent), PINOT GRIGIO, off-dry to sweet **RIESLING** (8 to 9 percent), TXAKOLI, VALPOLICELLA, VINHO VERDE.
Countries: cool climates (Austria, Canada, northern France, Germany)
Color: In general, their color is brighter than that of higher-alcohol wines.

LOW-TANNIN WINES

See BARBERA, BEAUJOLAIS, DOLCETTO, PINOT NOIR, ROSÉ, VALPOLICELLA, white wines.

MÂCON

[mah-KAWN]
See BURGUNDY–WHITE.

MADEIRA—BUAL (AKA BOAL)

[muh-DEER-uh–bwall]
Country: Island of Madeira, southwest of Portugal
Color: white (dark caramel hue)
Grapes: Bual (or Boal)
Weight: full-bodied
Volume: loud
Dry/sweet: sweet (sweeter than Verdelho, but not as sweet as Malmsey)
Acidity: high
Flavors: dessert wine with notes of **caramel**, cinnamon, cloves, **nuts**, praline, prunes, **raisins**, smoke, toffee, vanilla, often with a **walnut** finish
Texture: elegant, **rich**, silky
Temperature: Serve slightly chilled, about 55 to 60 degrees.
Pairings: cheese (esp. blue), dried fruits, foie gras, nut-based desserts (e.g., pecan pie), nuts
Aging: Better Madeira is aged for ten years or longer. A bottle can literally last a lifetime.

At one point in world history, **Madeira** was the most consumed wine. The Rare Wine Company is offering Madeira named after the style traditionally most popular in select American cities. So you'll find New York Malmsey, because this was the style New Yorkers loved. There is Boston Bual, which is the Madeira they loved to the north. There is also Charleston Sercial, which was their favorite to the south. . . . There are so many expressions of Madeira, from dry to semi-sweet. When you are not sure which dessert wine is going to work, go with Madeira. We have a dish that is just like a chocolate sundae, and that is what we pour with it. Madeira is great because it has acidity, which makes it more flexible with dessert. Malmsey is the most flexible because it is the sweetest and has a nuttiness and such an intriguing finish. It has a lot in common with PX sherry, and it is the "ruby port of Madeira." D'Oliveira Bual 1968 is very much like a tawny port with its lightness. It is very versatile and can be served with foie gras at the beginning of the meal as well as with cheese and dessert at the end. Actually 1968 is relatively young for Madeira, because it can really age. I recommend serving Madeira in bowl-shaped glasses as opposed to a fortified-wine glass.

—VANESSA BOYD, PHILIPPE

Producers: Barbeito, **Blandy's,** Cossart Gordon, d'Oliveira, Henriques & Henriques, Rare Wine Co.

MADEIRA—MALMSEY (AKA MALVASIA)

[MAHLM-see]
Country: Island of Madeira, southwest of Portugal
Color: white (dark caramel hue)
Grapes: Malvasia
Weight: full-bodied
Volume: very loud
Dry/sweet: very sweet (the sweetest of the four styles)
Acidity: high
Flavors: dessert wine with notes of **brown sugar, caramel,**

My introduction to **Madeira** came from Joseph DeLissio, sommelier at the River Café [in Brooklyn Heights, New York] when he poured me five Madeiras from the nineteenth century. What shocked me was that at the River Café, the bar backs up to a gigantic window that faces the setting sun. Those Madeiras sat on the top shelf with just a cork sticking in them, and I don't think I finished one bottle in the eight years I was there. Yet in my last year there, they tasted exactly the same. They are incredible—you cannot harm them! You could probably throw them in a 350-degree oven for an hour and they would still taste the same. To me, it was a glimpse of ancient technique and winemaking. I like that . . . the grape varieties grown on Madeira have a distinctiveness associated with each one [of the four styles], and yet are all from the same place.

—SCOTT CALVERT, THE INN AT LITTLE WASHINGTON

chocolate, **coffee,** lemon, maple syrup, **nuts,** orange zest, smoke, toffee, with a walnut finish
Texture: very rich, smooth
Temperature: Serve slightly chilled, about 55 to 60 degrees.
Pairings: cheese, dried fruits, nut-driven desserts (e.g., pecan pie)
Aging: Better Madeira is aged for ten years or longer. A bottle can last a lifetime.
Producers: Barbeito, **Blandy's** **10-Year-Old,** Borges & Borges, Broadbent, Favilla Viera, Henriques & Henriques, Rare Wine Co., Rutherford & Miles

MADEIRA—SERCIAL

[ser-see-AHL]
Country: Island of Madeira, southwest of Portugal
Color: white (light caramel hue)
Grapes: Sercial
Weight: lighter-bodied (lightest of the four styles)
Volume: moderate to loud
Dry/sweet: dry (driest of the

Sercial Madeiras are almost always lower in sugar, brighter, sharper, and never try to approach the level of Verdelho in terms of sweetness and richness.

—SCOTT CALVERT, THE INN AT LITTLE WASHINGTON

four styles)
Acidity: very high
Flavors: notes of almonds, caramel, chestnuts, **citrus,** dried fruits, figs, honey, **nuts,** orange peel, smoke, spices, with a dry walnut finish
Texture: crisp, rich, soft
Temperature: Serve chilled, about 50 to 55 degrees, to taste.
Pairings: traditionally paired with **soup** (e.g., consommé); can also be served with cold meat dishes or as an aperitif or after-dinner drink
Aging: Better Madeira is aged for ten years or longer. A bottle can last a lifetime.
Producers: Barbeito, **Blandy's,** Cossart Gordon, Rare Wine Co.

MADEIRA—VERDELHO

[vehr-DEH-loh]
Country: Island of Madeira, southwest of Portugal
Color: white (caramel hue)
Grapes: Verdelho
Weight: lighter- to medium-bodied (fuller in body than Sercial)
Volume: moderately loud
Dry/sweet: off-dry, with a dry finish (sweeter than Sercial but not as sweet as Bual or Malmsey)
Acidity: medium-high

Flavors: notes of **almonds,** **caramel,** chocolate, citrus, orange peel, peaches, smoke, spices, with a **walnut** finish
Texture: round, silky, soft
Temperature: Serve chilled, about 50 to 55 degrees.
Pairings: aperitif, cheese, cream-based soups, less sweet desserts, nuts
Aging: Better Madeira is aged for ten years or longer. A bottle can last a lifetime.
Producers: Barbeito, **Blandy's,** D'Oliveira, Henriques & Henriques, Rare Wine Co.

MADIRAN

[muh-DEE-ran]
Country: France
Region: Southwest
Color: red
Grapes: a **Tannat**-dominant blend, often with Cabernet Franc and Cabernet Sauvignon
Weight: full-bodied
Volume: loud
Dry/sweet: dry
Acidity: medium
Tannin: high
Flavors: fruity, with notes of **blackberries,** black cherries, black currants, cedar, cinnamon, dark chocolate, **earth,** flowers, jam, licorice, plums, spices, toast
Texture: ranges from rough and rustic (esp. young) to creamy and velvety (esp. aged)
Temperature: Serve cool, about 60 degrees.
Pairings: cassoulet, duck, duck confit, game, goose, lamb, short ribs, steak, stews
Aging: Age for at least five years before drinking; the best can age for a decade or longer.
Producers: Aydie, Bertholmeu, **Bouscassé,** Capmartin, Laffitte-Teston, **Montus**

Malagousia is beautifully balanced and refreshing, with peach, apple, pear, and apricot flavors. It does well with a little oak, and its price is right. It's becoming popular for sommeliers to pour it by the glass in New York City restaurants. . . . Roxane Matsa is a winemaker who is making some very interesting wines that are distributed by Boutari.

—ROGER DAGORN, MS, PORTER HOUSE NEW YORK

MALAGOUSIA

[mah-lah-goo-ZYA]
Country: Greece (Macedonia)
Color: white
Grapes: Malagousia
Weight: very full-bodied
Volume: very quiet to quiet
Dry/sweet: dry
Acidity: medium
Flavors: very aromatic, with notes of apples, apricots, citrus, flowers, grass, green peppers, jasmine, lemon (curd, pith, zest), mango, minerals, mint, **peaches**, pears
Texture: crisp, elegant, silky; either still or with a hint of sparkle
Temperature: Serve cold, about 45 to 50 degrees.
Comparable: CHARDONNAY
Pairings: aperitif, chicken, fish, pasta, salads, shellfish, vegetable dishes
Producers: Gerovassiliou, Matsa Estate

MALBEC

[MAHL-beck]
Countries: ARGENTINA, Australia, Chile, France (Bordeaux, **Cahors**, Loire), South Africa, U.S. (California, New York, Washington state)
Color: red (with garnet hues)
Grapes: Malbec

Under-$20 tip: I recommend **Malbecs** from Zuccardi and Finca Decero.

—VIRGINIA PHILIP, MS, THE BREAKERS

Weight: full- to very full-bodied (and high in alcohol)
Volume: loud
Dry/sweet: dry
Acidity: medium to high
Tannin: generally high, ranging from softer (Argentina) to firmer (France)
Flavors: notes of anise, blackberries, **BLACK CHERRIES**, black currants, blueberries, **dark chocolate**, dried fruits, earth, game, leather, licorice, minerals, **PLUMS**, raspberries, smoke, **SPICES**, tobacco, vanilla, **violets**, white pepper
Texture: rich, round, silky, smooth, soft, velvety
Temperature: Serve cool, about 60 to 65 degrees.
Comparables: Auxerrois, CAHORS (more than 70 percent Malbec), MERLOT/CABERNET SAUVIGNON blends
Pairings: beef, game, lamb, mushrooms, red meat, sausage, short ribs, steak, venison
Producers: Argentina: Alamos, Alma Negra, Altos, Anoro, CATENA, Doña Paula, Elsa, Finca Decero, Las Perdices, Los Siete, Nieto, Norton, **Susana Balbo**, Terra Rosa, **Terrazas, Tikal**, Trapiche, **Zuccardi; France:** *see* CAHORS.

MALVASIA

[mahl-vah-ZEE-uh]
See MADEIRA—MALMSEY.

MARGAUX

[MAHR-goh]
See also BORDEAUX—RED.
Country: France
Region: Bordeaux/Left Bank/ Médoc
Color: red
Grapes: Cabernet Franc, **CABERNET SAUVIGNON, Merlot**, Petit Verdot
Weight: medium- to full-bodied
Volume: moderate to loud
Dry/sweet: dry
Acidity: medium
Tannin: medium to high
Flavors: very aromatic, with notes of blackberries, black currants, cassis, earth, flowers, licorice, vanilla, and **violets**
Texture: delicate, rich, round, **silky**, smooth, soft
Temperature: Serve cool, about 60 to 65 degrees.
Pairings: duck, game, lamb (esp. grilled or roasted), liver, red meat (esp. roasted), steak, stews
Aging: Age for at least a decade before opening. Can age for two to three decades or longer.

MARSALA

[mar-SAHL-ah]
Country: Italy
Region: Sicily
Colors: red: ruby (*rubino*); **white:** amber (*ambra*); golden (*oro*)
Grapes: red: Calabrese, Nerello, Perricone; **white:** Catarratto Bianco, Damaschino, Grillo, Inzolia
Weight: full-bodied (and, as a fortified wine, high in alcohol, around 17 to 20 percent)
Volume: moderate to loud
Dry/sweet: ranges from dry (*secco*) to off-dry (*semi-secco*) to sweet (*dolce*)
Acidity: medium

Flavors: notes of almonds, apples, apricots (esp. dried), **caramel**, cardamom, figs, honey, nutmeg, orange zest, prunes, raisins, **smoke**, spices, **toffee**
Texture: rich, round, soft
Temperature: Serve slightly chilled, about 55 to 60 degrees.
Pairings: dry wines: almonds, anchovies, cheese (esp. goat, Pecorino), consommé, nuts, olives, ricotta, seafood stew, smoked meat; **sweet wines:** biscotti, cake, cheese (esp. Gorgonzola, Parmesan), chocolate (esp. dark), desserts, zabaglione
Tip: Traditionally, Marsala was served between the first and second courses of a meal.
Aging: The best (Vergine/Soleras) can age for five years to a decade or more. Once opened, most Marsala should be drunk within a few months.
Producers: De Bartoli, Donnafugata, Florio, Pellegrino, Rallo
Iconic example: Marco De Bartoli

MARSANNE
[mahr-SAHN]
Countries: Australia, **FRANCE** (Languedoc-Roussillon, **NORTHERN RHÔNE**, southern Rhône), U.S. (California)
Color: white (with yellow hues)
Grapes: Marsanne, often blended with about 15 percent Roussanne and/or Viognier
Weight: full-bodied (and high in alcohol)
Volume: quiet to moderate
Dry/sweet: dry
Acidity: low to medium
Flavors: aromatic, with notes of **almonds**, apples, apricots, **caramel**, citrus, cream, fennel,

FLOWERS, guava, hazelnuts, **herbs, honey, MARZIPAN,** melon, minerals, **NUTS,** orange, **peaches,** pears, **pineapple,** plums, spices, **tropical fruits,** vanilla
Texture: lush, oily, **rich,** smooth, soft, waxy
Temperature: Serve chilled, about 50 to 55 degrees.
Comparables: CHARDONNAY, CHÂTEAUNEUF-DU-PAPE–WHITE, white Crozes-Hermitage, HERMITAGE–WHITE, SAINT-JOSEPH, VIOGNIER
Pairings: chicken, cream sauces, curries, ham, lobster, pork, pumpkin, risotto, salads, seafood
Tip: Drink young and fresh (within one to two years).
Aging: The best Marsanne (e.g., HERMITAGE) typically ages well—up to two decades.
Producers: Australia: D'Arenberg, Mitchelton, Tahbilk, Torbeck; **France:** *see* HERMITAGE; **U.S.–California:** Alban, Beckmen, Cline, **Qupé,** Rosenblum, Tablas Creek; **Michigan:** Domaine Berrien

MARYLAND WINES
Producers: Basignani (esp. Chardonnay), Black Ankle, Boordy, Cygnus, Elk Run, Little Ashby, Saint Michaels, Sugarloaf Mountain

MATARO
See MOURVÈDRE.

MAURY
[moh-REE]
Country: France
Region: Languedoc-Roussillon
Color: red
Grapes: Grenache (primarily)
Weight: medium- to **full**-bodied
Volume: moderate to loud

Dry/sweet: sweet to very sweet
Acidity: low to medium
Tannin: medium (esp. older) to high (esp. younger)
Flavors: aromatic, fruity dessert wine with notes of blackberries, black currants/cassis, black plums, black truffles, cherries, coffee, **dark chocolate,** raisins (esp. older wines), spices
Texture: lush, rich, silky
Temperature: Serve chilled, about 50 to 55 degrees.
Comparables: BANYULS, PORT–VINTAGE
Pairings: berries, blue cheese, cherries, **chocolate** (esp. dark), coffee-flavored desserts, dried fruit, figs, nuts
Tip: For optimal pleasure, once you open a bottle of Maury, finish it. It won't keep well after it's opened.
Aging: Aging allows its strong tannins to soften—and the best can age for decades.
Producers: Coume du Roy, **Mas Amiel**

MÉDOC
[may-DOCK]
See also BORDEAUX–RED.
Country: France
Region: Bordeaux/northern part of Left Bank
Color: red (with blackish-purple hue)
Grapes: Cabernet Franc, **Cabernet Sauvignon,** Malbec, Merlot, Petit Verdot
Weight: medium- to full-bodied
Volume: loud, but quieter than other Bordeaux
Dry/sweet: dry
Acidity: medium
Tannin: high
Flavors: aromatic, with notes of **blackberries,** black cherries, **black currants/cassis,** cedar, chocolate,

earth, **plums** (esp. black), pencil shavings, smoke, spices, tobacco, vanilla
Texture: chewy when young, elegant when mature
Temperature: Serve cool, about 60 to 65 degrees.
Comparables: Haut-Médoc, MARGAUX, PAUILLAC, SAINT-ESTÈPHE, SAINT-JULIEN
Pairings: duck, game, lamb (esp. grilled or roasted), liver (esp. roasted), red meat (esp. roasted), steak, stew
Iconic example: Château Margaux

MELON DE BOURGOGNE

[meh-LONN deh bor-GOHN-yuh]
See also MUSCADET.
Countries: Australia, Canada, France (Burgundy, **LOIRE**), Germany, U.S. (California, Oregon, Washington state)
Color: white
Grapes: Melon de Bourgogne
Weight: light-bodied
Volume: quiet
Dry/sweet: very dry
Acidity: medium to high
Flavors: notes of **apples (esp. green)**, citrus, grass, lemon, lime, grapes, **minerals**, nectarines, **peaches**, pears, sea breeze, tangerines
Texture: crisp
Temperature: Serve cold, about 45 degrees.
Comparable: MUSCADET
Pairings: crab, **mussels**, oysters, seafood (esp. shellfish)
Producers: Canada: Norman Hardie; **France–Burgundy:** Domaine de la Cadette; **Loire:** *see* MUSCADET; **U.S.–Oregon:** Biggio Hamina, De Ponte, Perennial, Roots

When you go to Spain, you can get exciting wines off the beaten path in places like Bierzo, where you are dealing with the **Mencia** grape. It gives you the kind of freshness you get from Beaujolais. I view Mencia as a cross between Pinot Noir and Syrah. It is not as tannic as Cabernet, and it works with lighter red meats, so it makes a good "gateway" to the next wine.
—SABATO SAGARIA, THE LITTLE NELL

MENCIA

[men-SEE-ah]
Country: Spain
Regions: Bierzo, Ribeira Sacra
Color: red
Grapes: Mencia
Weight: medium- to full-bodied
Volume: loud
Dry/sweet: dry
Acidity: high
Tannin: medium to medium-high
Flavors: notes of **blackberries**, black cherries, black pepper, citrus, **earth**, flowers, green olives, **herbs**, leather, meat, minerals, plums, raspberries, **smoke**, **spices**, tar, vanilla, violets
Texture: rich, silky, smooth
Temperature: Serve slightly chilled, about 55 to 60 degrees.
Comparables: Bierzo (Spain), **Jaen** (Portugal), PINOT NOIR, SYRAH
Pairings: cheese (esp. sharp), herb-driven dishes, roasted red meats, stews, vegetable dishes
Tip: Open at least 30 to 60 minutes before serving.
Aging: Should be able to age for several years, possibly longer.
Producers: Alvaro Palacios, Bodega del Abad, Bodegas Peique, Descendentes de José

Palacios, Dominio de Tares, Luna Beberide, Paixar
Iconic example: Palacios Corullon

MERITAGE — RED

[MAIR-eh-tihj]
Countries: Argentina, Australia, Canada, France, Israel, Mexico, U.S. (**California** and more than twenty other states)
Color: red (about 80 percent of Meritage wines are red)
Grapes: a blend of at least two of the traditional red Bordeaux grape varieties (Cabernet Franc, Cabernet Sauvignon, Carmenère, Gros Verdot, Malbec, Merlot, Petit Verdot, St. Macaire), with no single grape making up more than 90 percent of the blend
Weight: full-bodied
Volume: loud
Dry/sweet: dry
Acidity: medium
Tannin: high
Flavors: notes of bacon, **blackberries**, black cherries, black currants/cassis, chocolate (esp. dark), earth, flowers, herbs, leather, licorice, plums (esp. black), vanilla
Texture: rich, smooth
Temperature: Serve cool to

I am very fascinated by the job that the **Meritage Association** [now **Alliance**] did in convincing people that they alone blended Cabernet and Merlot. People often comment that I don't have a Meritage section or a blend section on my wine list. I list wine by the dominant varietal, but the vast majority of my Cabernets are blended with Merlot, and the vast majority of my Merlots are blended with Cabernet.
—DANA FARNER, CUT

slightly chilled, about 55 to 65 degrees.

Pairings: beef, duck, lamb, steak

Producers: Blenheim, Clos LaChance, Cosentino, Davis Bynum, Dominus, Dr. Konstantin Frank, Dry Creek, Flora Springs, Franciscan, Gallo of Sonoma, Kendall-Jackson (Royale), **Opus One,** Quintessa, Robert Mondavi, Rosenblum, Sequoia Grove, St. Francis, St. Supéry, Sterling Vineyards, White Rock (Claret)

MERITAGE—WHITE
[MAIR-eh-tihj]

Countries: Argentina, Australia, Canada, France, Israel, Mexico, U.S. (**California** and more than twenty other states)

Color: white (about 20 percent of Meritage wines)

Grapes: a blend of at least two of the traditional white Bordeaux grape varieties (Muscadelle, Sauvignon Blanc, Sémillon), with no single grape making up more than 90 percent of the blend

Weight: medium-bodied

Volume: moderate

Dry/sweet: dry

Acidity: medium-high to high

Flavors: notes of citrus, figs, grapefruit, grass, honey, lemon, melon (esp. cantaloupe), minerals, nectarines, orange, peaches, pears, smoke, stones, toast, vanilla

Texture: creamy, crisp, juicy, round

Temperature: Serve chilled, about 50 to 55 degrees.

Pairings: appetizers, chicken, crab, fish, lobster, shellfish, turkey

Producers: Clif Family "The Climber," Cosentino "The Novelist," Lion's Ridge, Montgomery Place, Murrieta's Well, St. Supéry "Virtu"

Wölffer on the South Fork does a bang-up job producing a great example of a high-quality Long Island **Merlot.**

—MICHAEL CIMINO, GLENMERE MANSION

MERLOT
[mer-LOH]

Countries: Argentina, Chile, France (**Bordeaux—RIGHT BANK**), Italy (Tuscany), New Zealand, South Africa, **U.S. (California, esp. Napa** and Sonoma; Washington state)

Color: red (with bluish hues)

Grapes: Merlot, often blended with Cabernet Sauvignon

Weight: medium- to full-bodied

Volume: moderate to loud

Dry/sweet: dry

Acidity: lower (e.g., U.S.) to moderately high (e.g., Bordeaux)

Tannin: lower (e.g., U.S.) to medium-plus (e.g., Bordeaux)

Flavors: notes of blackberries, **BLACK CHERRIES, black currants/cassis,** black pepper, blueberries, cedar, cherries, chocolate, cinnamon, cloves, coffee, **dark chocolate,** figs, game, herbs, leather, licorice, meat, mint, mocha, nuts, **PLUMS** (fresh and dried), raspberries, smoke, spices, **strawberries,** tar, toast, tobacco, **vanilla,** violets

Flavors: cool climate: fresh cherries, plums, vanilla; **warm climate:** chocolate, cooked cherries, prunes

Texture: juicy, rich, **smooth, soft,** velvety

Temperature: Serve slightly chilled, about 55 to 60 degrees.
Comparables: lighter CABERNET SAUVIGNON, CARMENÈRE
Pairings: beef, duck, hamburgers, horseradish, lamb, mushrooms, pasta, pizza, pork, sausages, steak, tomato sauce, turkey, veal
Aging: With the exception of fine Bordeaux and the best California or Washington state Merlots (which can age for a decade or longer), drink Merlot relatively young. Best recent vintages (California): 2007, 2003, 2002, 2001, 1997.
Producers: Chile: Casa Lapostolle, Concha y Toro, **Cono Sur,** Dona Javiera, Montes, Veramonte; **Israel:** Chillag "Primo"; **Italy:** Castello di Ama, Livio Felluga, Lodovico Antinori Tenuta dell'Ornellaia Masseto; **New Zealand:** Villa Maria; **U.S.–California:** Beringer, Blackstone, Cakebread, Calistoga Estate, Chappellet, Chateau Souverain, Clos du Bois, **DUCKHORN,** Francis Coppola, Frei Brothers, Gallo of Sonoma, Gundlach Bundschu, Havens, MacRostie, **Matanzas Creek,** Pahlmeyer, Ravenswood, Selene, **SHAFER,** Silverado, Simi, St. Francis, Stags' Leap, Sterling, Wente, William Harrison; **New York: Bedell,** Channing Daughters, Lenz, Wölffer; **Washington state:** Andrew Will, Chateau Ste. Michelle, Columbia Crest, Covey Run, L'Ecole No. 41, **Leonetti Reserve,** Northstar, Snoqualmie
Iconic examples: France: Château Pétrus (Pomerol); **U.S.:** Leonetti Reserve Merlot

The most notorious fictional Merlot defamer, Miles in the 2004 film *Sideways,* lost his heart to a 1961 Cheval Blanc from Bordeaux; ironically, the wine is a Merlot blend. The much-vaunted Bordeaux Château Pétrus, one of the world's most expensive wines (with the 1995 vintage fetching $1,000), also is Merlot-based.

MEURSAULT
[mehr-SOH]
See also BURGUNDY–WHITE.
Country: France
Region: Burgundy/(southern) Côte d'Or/Côte de Beaune
Color: white
Grapes: Chardonnay
Weight: medium- to full-bodied
Volume: moderate
Dry/sweet: dry
Acidity: medium
Flavors: notes of almonds, apples, brioche, **butter, citrus,** earth, **hazelnuts,** herbs, **honey,** lemon, melon, **minerals,** nuts, peaches, **pears,** smoke, spices, stones, toast, **vanilla**
Texture: creamy, fleshy, rich

Temperature: Serve chilled, about 50 to 55 degrees.
Pairings: cheese (esp. Roquefort), crab, fish (esp. cod or turbot), lobster, mushrooms, risotto, shrimp, veal
Aging: Better wines will age for five years or more, the best for a decade or longer. Best Premier Crus: Les Charmes, Les Genevrières, **Les Perrières**
Tip: Meursault has no Grand Cru–designated vineyards.
Producers: Bouchard Père et Fils, **COCHE-DURY, COMTES LAFON,** Matrot, **Roulot,** Vincent Girardin
Iconic example: Domaine des Comtes Lafon

MEXICAN WINES
Producers: Casa de Piedra, Casa Madero, **Château Camou,** L.A. Cetto, Monte Xanic, Pedro Domecq, Santo Tomas

---

MICHIGAN WINES
Producers: Black Star Farms, Bowers Harbor, **Chateau**

At the Masters of Food and Wine event [at the Highlands Inn in Carmel, California], we tasted two different **Meursault** wines by two different winemakers: Dominique Lafon, of Comtes Lafon, and Jean-Marc Roulot, of Domaine Guy Roulot. They are really good friends, and both make great wine with grapes from the same vineyards—but they make very different wines. There is a more linear style to the wine from Jean-Marc Roulot and a fattiness to the Lafon, so you would have the Roulot with your appetizer and the Lafon with your entrée.
—MARK MENDOZA, SONA

The one wine we drink the most from Burgundy is Roulot **Meursault.** This is my favorite white wine producer in the world. I have even worked the harvest there. Meursault has a reputation of being rich, fat, and honeyed, which it can be for sure. Roulot—out of all the producers—makes one with great tension. The wine is taut and springs at you. You have to go to it, but once you do, it will push you back. It has purity, and these wines at the Village level are as good as wines at the Premier Cru level.
—ROBERT BOHR, COLICCHIO & SONS

I grew up in **Michigan**, so while I had tasted some wonderful whites from Traverse City, I knew that many others didn't have fond memories of the reds. When wine importer Dominic Simone wanted to have me taste Chateau Grand Traverse wines, I asked him to only open the whites and not the reds. He opened the Gamay Noir anyway—and I quickly realized this was no Michigan "cherry wine"! I couldn't believe its great, up-front fruit, and a surprising amount of acidity and black pepper notes. I loved it, and added both the Grand Traverse Riesling and the Gamay Noir to our wine list. While the white sold itself, few ordered the red—so I'd open it up for guests and say, "Want to try something cool?" They'd return to order it on their own, since the Gamay went beautifully with chef George Mendes's signature dish of *arroz de pato* [duck rice].

—HEATHER LAISKONIS, ALDEA

HEATHER LAISKONIS

Grand Traverse (esp. Gamay Noir, Riesling), **L. Mawby** (esp. sparkling wines), Left Foot Charley, Peninsula Cellars, Two Lads

MONASTRELL
[mon-uh-STRELL]
See also MOURVÈDRE.
Country: Spain
Color: red
Grapes: Monastrell, often blended with Cabernet Sauvignon, Garnacha, Merlot, Syrah, Tempranillo
Weight: medium- to full-bodied (with very high alcohol)
Volume: loud
Dry/sweet: dry
Acidity: medium
Tannin: high
Flavors: notes of bacon, **blackberries**, black cherries, **black currants/cassis**, chocolate, earth, game, herbs, leather, **licorice**, meat, minerals, pepper, plums (dried and fresh), raspberries, smoke, **spices**, toast, **tobacco**, vanilla
Texture: chewy, fresh, lush
Temperature: Serve slightly chilled, about 55 to 60 degrees.
Comparables: MATARO (Australia, U.S.), MOURVÈDRE (France), Rhône reds
Pairings: beef, cheese (e.g., Manchego), lamb, mushrooms, pork, roasts, steak
Aging: Monastrell's tannic structure allows it to age for two years or more.
Producers: Bleda, Casa Castillo, Casa de la Ermita, Castano, Juan Gil, La Purisma

MONBAZILLAC
[mawn-bah-zee-YAHK]
Country: France

Region: Bergerac
Color: white
Grapes: Muscadelle, Sauvignon Blanc, **Sémillon**
Weight: full-bodied
Volume: moderate to loud
Dry/sweet: semi-sweet to sweet
Acidity: medium to high
Flavors: notes of almonds, **apricots**, citrus, coffee, figs, flowers, ginger, **honey**, lemon, mango, melon, nuts (esp. older wines), orange, passion fruit, pastry, peaches, pears, pineapple, quince, smoke, spices, toffee, vanilla
Texture: creamy, rich, silky
Temperature: Serve very cold, about 40 to 45 degrees.
Comparable: SAUTERNES
Pairings: cheese (e.g., Roquefort), desserts, foie gras, fruit salads or tarts
Aging: Better wines can age from five years to five decades.
Producers: Ancienne Cure, Domaine du Cros Marcillac, La Foncalpre, Theulet, **Tirecul**, Verdots

If people haven't heard of **Monastrell**, they've heard of one of its other names [e.g., Mourvèdre]. Anyone who likes a Rhone-style blend—such as GSM [Grenache, Syrah, Mourvèdre] or Châteauneuf-du-Pape—will like the balance of fruitiness with herbaceous and earthy notes in a Monastrell. These can be even more budget-friendly reds.

—JILL ZIMORSKI, CAFÉ ATLÁNTICO

2006 Juan Gil **Monastrell** (Jumilla): I consider this great wine to be the Silver Oak of Spain.

—GEORGE MILIOTES, MS, CAPITAL GRILLE

MONTEFALCO ROSSO

[mohn-teh-FAHL-koh ROH-soh]

Country: Italy
Region: Umbria
Color: red
Grapes: predominantly **Sangiovese**, blended with Cabernet Sauvignon, Colorino, and/or Merlot
Weight: medium- to full-bodied
Volume: moderate
Dry/sweet: dry
Acidity: medium
Tannin: low to medium
Flavors: notes of blackberries, **black cherries,** cedar, chocolate, cinnamon, cloves, herbs, oak, oregano, plums, sage, spices
Texture: rich, silky, soft
Temperature: Serve cool, about 60 to 65 degrees.
Pairings: beef, braised meat dishes, cheese (esp. aged), pasta, polenta, spaghetti alla carbonara
Aging: Drink young and fresh or, generally, within three to five years.
Producers: Antonelli, **Arnaldo Caprai**, Colpetrone, Romanelli, Tabarrini, Terre de' Trinci, Tiburzi

MONTEPULCIANO

[MOHN-teh-pool-CHAH-noh]

Countries: Australia, **ITALY (ABRUZZI)**, U.S.
Color: red
Grapes: Montepulciano is often blended with Cabernet Franc, Cabernet Sauvignon, Malbec, Merlot, and Petit Verdot
Weight: medium- to **full-bodied**
Volume: loud
Dry/sweet: dry
Acidity: low to **medium**
Tannin: medium
Flavors: aromatic, with notes of **blackberries, black cherries, black pepper,** blueberries (cooked), chocolate/cocoa, **earth,** leather,

For those people looking for something enormous, big, fat, and rich in an Italian wine, that is my opportunity to introduce them to **Montepulciano d'Abruzzo**. It is a fleshy, deep, dark, big, intense, rich wine. If you want big mouthfeel, an inky wine with dominant earth flavors, that is a great place to go. This is not New World wine at all.

—DANA FARNER, CUT

licorice, oak, olives, **plums, spices,** violets
Texture: rich, silky, smooth, soft, velvety
Temperature: Serve cool, about 60 to 65 degrees.
Pairings: cheese, game, grilled meats, lamb, pasta, pork, roasts, *salumi* (Italian cured meats), stewed octopus in tomato sauce
Tip: Montepulciano d'Abruzzo is not related to the Sangiovese-based VINO NOBILE DI MONTEPULCIANO.
Aging: Enjoy Montepulciano young and fresh, within two or three years.
Producers: Italy: Carosso, **Emidio Pepe,** Farnese, **Illuminati,** Masciarelli, Rimbaldi, **Umani Ronchi, Valentini**

MONTRACHET
[mawn-rah-SHAY]
See also BURGUNDY–WHITE, CHASSAGNE-MONTRACHET, PULIGNY-MONTRACHET.
Country: France
Region: Burgundy/Côte de Beaune
Comparables: CHASSAGNE-MONTRACHET, PULIGNY-MONTRACHET

MOSCATO D'ASTI
[mohs-KAHT-oh dah-stee]
Country: Italy
Region: Piedmont (Asti)

Color: white
Grapes: Muscat
Weight: very light to light-bodied (and low in alcohol at 5.5 percent)
Volume: quiet to moderate
Dry/sweet: semi-sweet to sweet
Acidity: medium to medium-high
Flavors: aromatic and very fruity, with notes of almonds, apples, apricots, flowers, grapes, honey, lemon, lychees, melon, mint, **PEACHES,** pears, tangerines, vanilla
Texture: semi-sparkling
Temperature: Serve very cold, about 40 to 45 degrees.
Comparables: ASTI (which is sweeter and higher in alcohol), demi-sec or doux CHAMPAGNE or other sweet SPARKLING WINE
Pairings: berries, brunch dishes, cheesecake, desserts (esp. fruit), melon (esp. cantaloupe)
Tip: Drink young and fresh.
Producers: Albino Rocca, Bera, Braida, Ceretto, Contratto, De Forville, Elio Perrone, La Caudrina, La Morandina, **MICHELE CHIARLO,** Mionetto, Piero Gatti, Prunotto, **LA SPINETTA, Saracco, VIETTI**

Paolo Saracco **Moscato d'Asti** has been the gold standard for great Moscato. Vietti makes a superb Moscato, even though they are better known for their super Barolo. Villa Giada—a tiny winery that has been handed down by generations of the Faccio family—is a sentimental favorite.

—BELINDA CHANG, THE MODERN

For celebrating an event, we keep Albino Rocca **Moscato d'Asti** on hand to pour. By the time we are pouring it, you have had a few drinks already. It is low alcohol, fun, and easy to drink even if you are not a big wine drinker. If you are a serious wine drinker, Moscato d'Asti makes you go, "Oh, my God—I still love wine and this is beautiful!" Honestly, I have not met a Moscato I didn't like. It is light, easy, and cheers everybody up.... If you come to my house I will serve Moscato immediately because I use it as my aperitif wine. I will serve it with cheeses, olives, or cured meat. I like the way its light carbonation and acidity cut the fattiness and refresh my palate for the next bite. I don't like to get too serious, and this is sort of a pop wine—like a three-minute pop song you can't get out of your head for the next twelve days.

—ANDY MYERS, CITYZEN

I love **Moscato d'Asti**! Moscato d'Asti is the cure for anybody who has a problem with sweet wines. It is like Diet Mountain Dew with alcohol. It is the best thing ever! If you grew up drinking Coca-Cola, there is no way you won't like this. Paolo Saracco makes a good one, as does Giorgio Rivetti [La Spinetta]. You can even get it in magnums.

—RAJ VAIDYA, DANIEL

With dessert, it's hard to beat **Moscato d'Asti** or a rosy Brachetto d'Acqui for lighter alcohol, refreshing balance of acidity and sweetness, and price. Pour a little of either over a bowl of fresh berries—add some crème fraîche or whipped cream on top, and you're living large!

—DAVID LYNCH, QUINCE

MOSCHOFILERO

[mohs-koh-FEEL-er-oh]
Country: Greece
Region: Mantinia
Color: white (and rosé)
Grapes: Moschofilero
Weight: light- to medium-bodied (and low in alcohol)
Volume: moderate
Dry/sweet: dry
Acidity: medium to **high**
Flavors: very aromatic, with notes of apples, apricots, citrus, **flowers**, grapefruit, honey, kiwi, lemon, lime, melon, mint, orange zest, passion fruit, peaches, pears, **roses**, **spices**, tropical fruits, violets, white pepper
Texture: crisp
Temperature: Serve chilled, about 50 to 55 degrees.
Comparables: ALBARIÑO, GEWÜRZTRAMINER, VIOGNIER
Season: spring–summer
Pairings: appetizers, artichokes, cheese (esp. feta), chicken, fish (esp. grilled), Greek cuisine, roasted peppers, salads, sardines, shellfish
Aging: Drink young and fresh.
Producers: Boutari, Cambas, Gaia, Nasiakos, Semeli, Sigalas, Skouras, Spiropoulos, Tselepos

MOURVÈDRE (AKA MATARO IN AUSTRALIA AND THE U.S.)

[moor-VEHD-ruh]
See also MONASTRELL.
Countries: Australia, **France (Bandol**, Languedoc, **southern Rhône)**, U.S. (California)
Color: red (with purple-black hues)
Grapes: Mourvèdre, often blended with Grenache and/or Syrah
Weight: medium- to full-bodied (relatively high in alcohol)

Volume: moderate to loud
Dry/sweet: ranges from dry to sweet
Acidity: high
Tannin: high
Flavors: notes of bacon, **BLACK-BERRIES**, black currants/cassis, **black pepper, CHERRIES**, chocolate, cinnamon, cloves, **earth**, flowers, **GAME, herbs, leather** (esp. older wines), licorice, **meat**, minerals, plums, raspberries, smoke (esp. older wines), **SPICES**, thyme, tobacco, vanilla, violets
Texture: chewy, smooth, viscous
Temperature: Serve cool, about 60 to 65 degrees.
Comparables: Mataro (Australia, U.S.), **MONASTRELL** (Spain), SYRAH, ZINFANDEL
Pairings: calf's liver, duck, mushrooms, pork, red meat, sausages, stews, wild boar
Tip: Mourvèdre is the primary grape in Bandol red and rosé wines and also appears in Châteauneuf-du-Pape and Rhône blends.
Aging: Better Mourvèdre benefits from aging as long as ten years.
Producers: Australia: Torbreck; **France:** Domaine Tempier; **U.S.–California:** Cline Cellars, David Girard, Jade Mountain, Ken Volk, Tablas Creek

MTSVANE

[SWAH-nee]
See TSINANDALI.

MÜLLER-THURGAU

[MYEW-lehr TOOR-gau]
Countries: Austria, England, **Germany**, Hungary, Italy (Alto Adige), New Zealand, Switzerland, U.S. (Oregon)
Color: white

Grapes: Müller-Thurgau
Weight: light-bodied
Volume: quiet
Dry/sweet: dry
Acidity: **low** to medium
Flavors: aromatic and fruity, with notes of apples (esp. green), **flowers**, grass, herbs, honey, lemon, lime, lychees, minerals, peaches, raisins, spices, tropical fruits
Texture: crisp, smooth, soft
Temperature: Serve chilled, about 50 to 55 degrees.
Comparables: MUSCAT, RIESLING, SILVANER/SYLVANER
Pairings: asparagus, fish, pork, salads, salty dishes, **seafood**, smoked foods, spicy dishes
Aging: Drink young and fresh, although the best will last a few years.
Producers: Alois Lageder, Kellerei Kaltern, Muri Gries, Terlano

MUSCADET

[moos-kah-DAY]
Country: France
Region: Loire Valley
Color: white
Grapes: Melon de Bourgogne, now known as Muscadet
Weight: very light-bodied
Volume: quiet
Dry/sweet: very dry
Acidity: medium to **high**
Flavors: notes of anise, **apples (esp. green)**, flowers, grapefruit, **LEMON**, lime, melon, **minerals**, peaches, pears, a **hint of salt** (sea breeze), **yeast**
Texture: creamy, **crisp**, refreshing, sometimes with a hint of effervescence
Temperature: Serve cold, about 45 degrees.
Season: spring
Pairings: appetizers, chicken,

clams, fish (esp. grilled), goat cheese, **MUSSELS, oysters,** salads, sardines, **shellfish** (esp. raw)

Tip: Look for Muscadet from the high-quality subregion Muscadet de Sèvre et Maine or those that indicate they have been aged *sur lie* for added flavor complexity and richness.

Aging: Drink young and fresh.

Producers: Château la Noë, Chéreau-Carré, Chóblet, Delhommeau, Domaine de la Louvetrie, **Domaine de la Pépière,** Domaine du Vieux Chai, Domaine les Hautes Noëlles, Foliette Clos de la Fontaine, Guy Bossard, Guy Sagat, Luneau-Papin, Marquis de Goulaine, Sauvion & Fils

MUSCAT—IN GENERAL

[MUHS-kat; moos-KAHT]
See also ASTI, MOSCATO D'ASTI.

Countries: Australia, Austria, France (Alsace), Germany, Italy, U.S. (California)
Color: white
Grapes: Muscat
Weight: medium- to full-bodied
Volume: quiet to moderate
Dry/sweet: ranges from dry to off-dry to sweet
Acidity: low to medium
Flavors: very aromatic, with notes of apples, **flowers,** GRAPES, lemon, melon, **orange, peaches, pears,** pineapple, roses, **spices,** tropical fruits, vanilla, yeast
Texture: still to sparkling; rich
Temperature: Serve very cold, about 40 to 45 degrees.
Pairings: dry wines: charcuterie, cheese, chicken, duck, smoked meats; **sweet wines:** cheese, desserts, foie gras, fruit

Tip: Serve dry Muscat as an aperitif with starters such as prosciutto and melon or speck and white asparagus.

Aging: Drink young and fresh, within a year or two of the vintage.

Producers: Australia: Brown Brothers; **France–Alsace:** Deiss, Dirler, Hugel, Jaboulet, Ostertag, Trimbach, Zind-Humbrecht; **U.S.–California:** Bonny Doon, Navarro, Quady

MUSCAT—BLACK

[MUHS-kat]
Country: U.S.
Region: California
Color: red (with a reddish-pink hue)
Grapes: black Muscat
Weight: full-bodied
Volume: moderate to loud
Dry/sweet: sweet to very sweet
Acidity: low to medium
Flavors: aromatic, with notes of blackberries, cherries, chocolate, lychees, orange, plums, roses, spices
Texture: creamy, luscious, rich
Temperature: Serve cold, about 45 to 55 degrees.
Pairings: berries, cheese (esp. blue), chocolate (esp. dark), desserts (esp. creamy and/or fruit), foie gras, ice cream
Producers: Quady Elysium, Togni

MUSCAT DE BEAUMES-DE-VENISE

[moos-KAHT duh bohm duh vuh-NEES]
Country: France
Region: Rhône Valley, south
Color: white
Grapes: Muscat
Weight: medium- to full-bodied

(and fortified, so high in alcohol, around 15 percent)
Volume: moderate to loud
Dry/sweet: sweet to very sweet
Acidity: low to medium
Flavors: aromatic and fruity, with notes of almonds, **apricots,** citrus, flowers, grapefruit, **grapes, honey,** orange, orange peel (esp. candied), passion fruit, **peaches,** pears, spices, tangerine, tropical fruits, vanilla, white peaches
Texture: moderately rich, round, soft
Temperature: Serve very cold, about 40 to 45 degrees.
Pairings: lighter desserts, esp. those made with fresh berries, caramel, chocolate, or orange
Aging: Drink within three years of release.
Producers: Chapoutier, Domaine Bernardins, Domaine de Beaumalric, Domaine de Coyeux, Domaine de Durban, Jaboulet

MUSCAT—LIQUEUR (AKA RUTHERGLEN MUSCAT)

[MUHS-kat]
Country: Australia
Region: Victoria
Color: white (amber in hue)
Grapes: Muscat (aka Frontignac or Brown Muscat)
Weight: full-bodied (and high in alcohol)
Volume: moderately loud to loud
Dry/sweet: sweet to very sweet
Acidity: low to medium
Flavors: notes of almonds, apricots, blackberries, black cherries, **caramel,** chocolate, coffee, dates, dried fruits, figs, honey, maple syrup, molasses, **nuts,** orange, prunes, **RAISINS,** smoke, spices, toffee
Texture: luscious, rich, silky, smooth, viscous

Temperature: Liqueur Muscat is traditionally served cool (about 60 to 65 degrees) in the winter. During the summer, it is more often enjoyed chilled or over ice.

Comparable: TOPAQUE–RUTHERGLEN

Pairings: bread pudding, cheese, desserts made with bananas, caramel, chocolate, cream, figs, ice cream, mocha, nuts

Aging: It's been aged a long time before release, so you'll want to drink it within a few years.

Producers: Baileys, **Buller**, Campbells, **CHAMBERS**, Morris, Stanton and Killeen

Iconic example: Buller Calliope

MUSCAT—ORANGE

[MUHS-kat]

Country: U.S.

Region: California

Color: white (peachy pink hues)

Grapes: Muscat

Weight: medium- to full-bodied

Volume: moderate to loud

Dry/sweet: sweet to very sweet

Acidity: low to medium

Flavors: aromatic dessert wine with notes of apricots, bananas, butterscotch, **candied orange peel**, citrus, flowers, honey, lychees, melon, minerals, **orange**, papaya,

peaches, spices, tangerines, tropical fruits, vanilla

Texture: creamy, luscious, velvety

Temperature: Serve cold, about 45 to 50 degrees.

Pairings: blue cheese, caramel, cheesecake, chocolate, fresh fruit (esp. berries, melon, peaches), orange desserts

Producers: Quady Electra (semi-sparkling wine with 4 percent alcohol), Quady Essencia (still wine, fortified to 15 percent alcohol), Renwood

MUSCAT—YELLOW

[moos-KAHT; MUHS-kat]

Countries: Austria, Germany, Hungary, Italy, Slovenia, U.S.

Color: white

Grapes: Yellow Muscat (aka Gelber Muskateller or Muscat Blanc à Petits Grains)

Weight: light-bodied (and less than 12 percent alcohol)

Volume: quiet to moderate

Dry/sweet: dry (primarily, although it is also made into sweet wines)

Acidity: medium

Flavors: aromatic and fruity, with notes of apples, apricots, citrus, flint, **flowers**, grapefruit, guava, herbs, lemon, minerals, mint, orange, roses, tropical fruits, yeast

Texture: creamy, crisp, fresh, smooth, sometimes semi-sparkling

Temperature: Serve chilled, about 50 to 55 degrees.

Season: summer

Pairings: appetizers, Asian cuisine, cheeses (esp. fresh), fish, paté, sausages, scallops

Aging: Drink now or age as long as a decade.

Producers: Austria: Heidi Schröck, Neumeister; **Germany:** Stulb; **U.S.–California:** Bonny Doon

NAVARRA REDS

[nah-VAHR-ruh]

Country: Spain

Region: Navarra

Color: red

Grapes: GARNACHA and Tempranillo; increasingly, Cabernet Sauvignon and Merlot

Weight: medium-bodied (and high in alcohol)

Volume: moderate to loud

Dry/sweet: dry

Acidity: medium

Tannin: medium to medium-plus

Flavors: notes of almonds, blackberries, black pepper, cherries, coffee, earth, plums, roses, spices, strawberries, tobacco, vanilla

Texture: elegant, juicy, silky, smooth

Temperature: Serve cool, about 60 to 65 degrees.

Comparables: BORDEAUX–RED, CÔTES DU RHÔNE, RIOJA

Pairings: beef, cheese, ham, lamb, pasta, red meat, roasts, stews

Tip: This up-and-coming region of Spain offers some of the country's best value wines. Don't miss the region's lovely strawberry-noted Garnacha-based rosados.

Yellow Muscat from Austria is bone dry—and people love it. I took Grüner Veltliner off my list by the glass because everyone is pouring it, and I replaced it with this Yellow Muscat. It is fantastic and a huge success. If you wanted to try Yellow Muscat from America, try the Bonny Doon, which is not quite as dry as an Austrian Muscat. I also recommend the Yellow Muscat from Neumeister. On a hot day, you don't need anything more! There are plenty of food pairings for Yellow Muscat—right now I am pairing it with scallops. The wine has a little sweetness in the ripeness, not from the sugar. With a salad with peaches or a vinaigrette with pumpkin-seed oil, it brightens everything up. It is so versatile you could just drink it by itself on the beach.
—ALDO SOHM, LE BERNARDIN

Whereas the red wines from Rioja and Ribera del Duero tend to have a certain earthy or dusty undertone to their flavor—kind of like walking down a hot dirt road in the summertime—**Navarra reds** tend to have more of a straightforward red-fruit profile without that note of dustiness.

—JILL ZIMORSKI, CAFÉ ATLÁNTICO

Producers: Bodegas Guelbenzu, Bodegas Julián Chivite, Bodegas Lezaun, Bodegas Ochoa, Bodegas Y Viñedos Nekeas, Palacios de la Vega

NEBBIOLO

[neb-BYOH-loh]
See also BARBARESCO, BAROLO.
Countries: Australia, **ITALY (PIEDMONT)**, South Africa, U.S. (California)
Color: red
Grapes: Nebbiolo
Weight: medium- to **full-bodied** (and high in alcohol)
Volume: moderate to loud
Dry/sweet: dry
Acidity: very high (though softens with age)
Tannin: very high (though softens with age)
Flavors: aromatic, with notes of anise, **BLACK AND RED CHERRIES**, blackberries, black currants, **chocolate**, coffee/espresso, **earth, flowers**, herbs, leather, **licorice**, menthol, mint, mushrooms, **plums (fresh and dried)**, raspberries, red cherries, **roses**, smoke, spices, strawberries, **TAR**, tobacco, **truffles, violets**
Texture: rich, velvety
Temperature: Serve cool, about 60 to 65 degrees.
Comparables: BARBARESCO, BAROLO
Pairings: cheese, mushrooms, red meats (beef, lamb, venison), *salumi* (Italian cured meats), stews, white truffles
Aging: Age Nebbiolo-based wines for a few to several years before drinking; *see also* aging recommendations for BARBARESCO and BAROLO.
Producers: Italy: **Angelo Gaja**, Luciano Sandrone, Vietti, esp. Perbacco (*see also* BARBARESCO and BAROLO); **U.S.–California:** Palmina; **Virginia:** Barboursville, Breaux
Iconic example: Angelo Gaja

NÉGOCIANT WINES

Wine producers who buy their grapes from others are known as *négociants*.
Tip: Most Burgundy is made by *négociants*.
Producers: Bouchard Père et Fils, Joseph Drouhin, Maison Louis Jadot, Maison Louis Latour

NEGROAMARO

[NEH-groh-uh-MAHR-oh]
Country: Italy
Region: Puglia
Color: red (dark, with ruby hues)
Grapes: Negroamaro
Weight: medium- to full-bodied
Volume: moderately loud to loud
Dry/sweet: dry
Acidity: low to medium
Tannin: high
Flavors: aromatic, with bitter notes of blackberries, black cherries (esp. cooked or dried), black pepper, chocolate (esp. dark), cloves, coffee/espresso, earth, herbs, star anise, tar, tobacco, vanilla, violets, with a hint of sweetness on the finish
Texture: fresh, rich, rustic, smooth, soft
Temperature: Serve cool, about 60 to 65 degrees.
Comparables: Copertino, PRIMITIVO, Salice Salentino
Pairings: aged cheese, game, hamburgers, lamb, liver, pasta, rabbit, **red meat**
Aging: Negroamaro has good aging potential.
Producers: Bacco, Feudo di San Nicola, Guarini, Perrini, Taurino, Tenute Rubino, Tormaresca

NERO D'AVOLA

[NEH-roh DAH-voh-lah]
Country: Italy
Region: Sicily
Color: red
Grapes: Nero d'Avola (often blended with others)
Weight: medium-bodied
Volume: moderate to loud
Dry/sweet: dry
Acidity: medium
Tannin: high

After a long day of wine tasting in California, we'll want to drink something entirely different—and **Nero d'Avola** fills the bill. It's got a great sense of place and is a big tannic wine that you can drink young with anything from spaghetti and meatballs to roast lamb.

—JULIA MORETTI, AD HOC

Sicily is still a bit of an undiscovered region. Terre Nere **Nero d'Avola** fits the profile of "light-plus" to medium-bodied red wine. With a mushroom fricassee that has earthy tones to it, Nero d'Avola would be an alternative to Burgundy or Piedmont reds.

—JESSE RODRIGUEZ, ADDISON AT THE GRAND DEL MAR

Michael Cimino of Glenmere Mansion on Some of His Favorite New York Wineries

In the Finger Lakes, **Dr. [Konstantin] Frank** is very important—it's the winery that put New York winemaking on the map. They produce quality juice year after year. **Hermann J. Wiemer** is arguably the winery that realized the potential of New York Riesling as a world-class wine. We pour **Chateau LaFayette Reneau** Riesling by the glass, and their leaner-styled world-class Owners Reserve Cabernet Sauvignon is the best in the state. In fact, I prefer it to California Cabernet, which I can find too fruit-driven and too high in alcohol. For its quality-to-price ratio, **Wagner** is doing a tremendous job producing the best value-priced wines in the region. We pour its unoaked Chardonnay, which has great apple flavors, by the glass. They also produce three different ice wines, including a lighter-style Riesling and a very rich, pineapple- and apricot-noted Vignoles with great acidity that is ideal with fruit desserts and my all-time-favorite dessert wine. At about $20 a bottle, it's an incredible value.

Having visited many wineries on Long Island, one in particular stands out to me: **One Woman Wines,** whose winemaker Claudia Purita tends her nine acres of vineyards herself. She makes only four wines: two Chardonnays, a rosé, and a Gewürztraminer. The quality is really, really great—you can tell that a lot of love goes into each bottle.

Just fifteen minutes away from Glenmere Mansion you can find **Brotherhood Winery,** which is the oldest (est. 1839) winery in the country. They were previously known for sweet, spiced holiday wines, but ever since the winery was purchased about twenty years ago, the quality has been improving. They produce a Blanc de Blancs sparkling wine from estate-grown Chardonnay grapes from the Hudson Valley that is an incredible value at under $15.

Flavors: fruity, with notes of **blackberries, black cherries,** black pepper, cassis, chocolate, **dried fruits,** earth, flowers, herbs, leather, licorice, mint, **plums,** raisins, **raspberries,** smoke, **spices,** strawberries, tar, toast, tobacco, violets

Texture: fresh, rich, soft

Temperature: Serve cool, about 60 to 65 degrees.

Comparables: BURGUNDY—RED, **Calabrese,** PIEDMONT reds, SHIRAZ, SYRAH

Pairings: arancini, lamb, lasagna, meatballs, Mediterranean cuisine (esp. with capers, herbs, olives), mushrooms, **pizza,** red meat (esp. beef)

Aging: Nero d'Avola has good aging potential.

Producers: Abbazia, Corvo, Cusumano, Donnafugata, Morgante, Regaleali, Terre Nere

NEW JERSEY WINES

Producers: Unionville Vineyards (esp. "The Big O" Red Montage)

NEW WORLD WINES

Examples: Argentina, Australia, Canada, Chile, New Zealand, South Africa, U.S.

Weight: fuller-bodied (and higher in alcohol) than Old World wines

Flavors: notable fruitiness

Texture: smooth

Tip: Look for wines labeled by grape varietal instead of place.

Aging: In general, drink young and fresh.

NEW YORK WINES

Red: Cabernet Franc (Long Island), Merlot (Long Island), Pinot Noir (Finger Lakes)

White: Chardonnay (Long Island), Gewürztraminer (Finger Lakes), Riesling (Finger Lakes), Rkatsiteli (Finger Lakes), Sauvignon Blanc (Long Island)

Tip: Brotherhood Winery (brotherhoodwinery.net) in Washingtonville, claims to be America's oldest winery.

Producers: Finger Lakes: Chateau Frank (sparkling wines), Chateau LaFayette Reneau, Dr. Konstantin Frank, Glenora, Hermann J. Wiemer, Leidenfrost, Wagner (value); **Long Island:** Bedell, Channing Daughters, Lenz, Macari, One Woman, Paumanok, Schneider, Shinn (esp. Rosé), Wölffer (esp. sparkling wines)

I am a fan of **New York wines** from Long Island. They have been developing steadily and striving not to stay where they were ten years ago.

—STEPHANE COLLING, SAN YSIDRO RANCH

I have spent a lot of time at Channing Daughters winery on **New York**'s Long Island. They bottled their Sauvignon Blanc in half-bottles just for us [at Per Se in New York City]. It works great as an aromatic white, and people really enjoy it because the wine is local and the wine is good.

—ROXANE SHAFAEE-MOGHADAM, THE BREAKERS

Under-$20 tip: Momo is great from **New Zealand** and makes a juicy Sauvignon Blanc. Drylands is another great one.

—VIRGINIA PHILIP, MS, THE BREAKERS

Iconic example: Dr. Konstantin Frank Riesling

NEW ZEALAND WINES

Weight: medium to medium-plus
Volume: moderate-plus to loud
Acidity: high
Grapes: red: Cabernet Sauvignon, Merlot, Pinot Noir; white: Chardonnay, SAUVIGNON BLANC, Sémillon
Tip: Brancott produces the majority of New Zealand wine.
Producers: Ata Rangi, **Brancott**, CLOUDY BAY (Sauvignon Blanc), **Craggy Range**, Drylands, Dry River, Felton Road, Goldwater, Kumeu River, Martinborough, Momo, Morton Estate, Neudorf, Sacred Hill, Saint Clair, Te Kairanga, Te Mata (white and red wines), Trinity Hill, **Villa Maria**
Iconic example: Cloudy Bay Sauvignon Blanc

NORTH CAROLINA WINES

Tip: The Biltmore estate, with its mansion built by George Vanderbilt, in Asheville, North Carolina, has been cited as one of the top ten favorite works of architecture in the nation. The estate claims that no U.S. winery can top its 600,000 annual visitors.
Producer: Biltmore Estate (esp. Chardonnay)

NORTON

Country: U.S. (Arkansas, Florida, Illinois, Kentucky, **Missouri,** New Jersey, Tennessee, Texas, **VIRGINIA**)
Color: red (blackish-red, with brick hues)
Grapes: Norton (aka Cynthiana)
Weight: full-bodied
Volume: loud

Dry/sweet: dry
Acidity: medium to high
Tannin: medium
Flavors: aromatic and very fruity, with notes of black pepper, **blueberries** (esp. older wines), cassis, coffee, earth (esp. older wines), elderberries, figs, **grapes,** meat (esp. older wines), mint, plums (fresh and dried), spices, strawberries, sweetness, tea, vanilla
Texture: rich
Temperature: Serve slightly chilled, about 55 degrees.
Comparables: CABERNET SAUVIGNON, ZINFANDEL
Pairings: barbecue, duck, game, lamb, mushrooms, red meat, sausages, venison
Aging: Norton needs five to ten years for its intense fruitiness to subside, giving rise to earthy, meaty, and spicy notes.
Producers: Arkansas: Cowie; Missouri: Adam Puchta, Augusta, Hermannhof, Mount Pleasant, St. James, **Stone Hill;** Virginia: **Chrysalis, Horton,** Rappahannock
Iconic example: Stone Hill

The native grape of America. Good old **Norton.** Born right here in Virginia, in Richmond. . . . It's one hundred percent American, it's ours. And the fact that it makes a phenomenal wine is just icing on the cake.
—JENNI MCCLOUD OF CHRYSALIS IN *THE WILD VINE* (2010)

OAKED WHITES

See also CHARDONNAY, CHENIN BLANC, FUMÉ BLANC, SÉMILLON, VERDELHO.
Flavors: notes of allspice, black pepper, butter, butterscotch, caramel, cinnamon, cloves, coconut (esp. American oaked wines), dill (esp. American),

ginger, nuts (esp. French oaked wines), smoke, spices (esp. French oaked wines), toast (esp. French), toffee, vanilla (esp. French)
Tip: A white wine that has been oaked will be darker in color than the same wine unoaked.

OFF-DRY WINES

See CHENIN BLANC, GEWÜRZTRAMINER, RIESLING– SPÄTLESE, VOUVRAY.

For barbecues or extra-spicy food, serve a wine that's **off-dry,** such as Chenin Blanc from Vouvray or Spätlese Riesling from Germany. If food is really spicy, these wines will tone down the heat.
—JESSE RODRIGUEZ, ADDISON AT THE GRAND DEL MAR

OLD WORLD WINES

Examples: France, Germany, Italy, Portugal, Spain
Weight: lighter-bodied (and lower in alcohol) than New World wines
Flavors: notable earthiness
Texture: rustic
Tip: Look for wines labeled by their place of origin rather than by grape varietal.
Aging: In general, Old World wines are thought to have longer aging potential than New World wines.

Sommeliers tend to be fans of **Old World wines.** We all seem to like Riesling, Grüner Veltliner, and other high-acid whites. We love Burgundy, whether it is white or red, and the northern Rhône Valley, and Italian wines. These are all things we are passionate about.
—DENNIS KELLY, THE FRENCH LAUNDRY

OREGON WINES
Country: U.S.
Grapes: red: Cabernet Sauvignon, Merlot, **PINOT NOIR**; white: Chardonnay, Pinot Blanc, **PINOT GRIS**, Riesling
Tip: Oregon's latitude is approximately the same as Burgundy's.
Producers: Argyle, Beaux Frères, Brick House, **CRISTOM, Domaine Drouhin, Domaine Serene**, Duck Pond, Erath, Eyrie, Fiddlehead, Ken Wright, King Estate, Oak Knoll, Patricia Green, Ponzi, Shea, WillaKenzie

ORGANIC GRAPE AND/ OR WINE PRODUCERS
See also Biodynamic Wines, Sustainable Wines.
A small sampling of winemakers producing organic wines, or wines made from organic grapes, around the world (all practicing or certified):
Argentina: Durigutti; **Australia:** Spring Seed Wine, Woolloo-mooloo; **Austria:** Brundlmayer, Hofer; **Canada:** Frog Pond, Southbrook; **France–Alsace:** Mittnacht, Paul Blanck et Fils; **Bordeaux:** Chateaux Guiraud, Chateau Pontet-Canet; **Champagne:** Vilmart et Cie; **Loire:** Clos Roche Blanche, Clos

Rougeard, Domaine Sauvète, Domaine Vacheron; **Provence:** Mas de Gourgonnier; **Rhône:** Beaucastel, Chapoutier, Vieux Télégraphe; **Germany:** Biffar; **Greece:** Thimiopoulos; **Israel:** Saslove; **Italy:** Le Calcinaie, Le Cinciole, Ocone; **Portugal:** Casa de Mouraz; **U.S.:** Araujo, Benziger, Bonterra, Bucklin, Concannon, Corison, Four Chimneys, Gruet, Ken Wright, King Estate, Neal Family, Pacific Rim, Peay, Porter Creek, Tablas Creek, Turley, Verge

ORVIETO
[or-vee-ETT-oh]
Country: Italy
Region: Umbria
Color: white
Grapes: TREBBIANO, blended with **Grechetto** and/or other grapes
Weight: light- to **medium**-bodied (and low in alcohol)
Volume: very quiet
Dry/sweet: dry (typically, although it is also made as a sweet wine)
Acidity: medium to medium-high
Flavors: fruity, with notes of almonds, apples (esp. green), citrus, earth, figs, flowers, hazelnuts, honey, lime, melon, minerals, nuts, peaches, pears, vanilla

Texture: crisp, rich, smooth
Temperature: Serve chilled, about 50 to 55 degrees.
Comparables: Chardonnay–Unoaked, Pinot Grigio
Pairings: antipasto, bruschetta, cheese, chicken, fish, mushrooms, pasta, salads, shellfish, veal
Tip: Look for Orvieto Classico for a slightly richer wine.
Aging: Typically drink within a year or two, although the best have longer aging potential.
Producers: **Antinori**, Barberani, Bigi, La Carraia, Palazzone, Ruffino

PALOMINO
[pal-uh-MEE-noh]
See Sherry.

PASSOVER WINES
See Israeli Wines, Kosher Wines.

PAUILLAC
[poy-ACK]
See also Bordeaux–Red.
Country: France
Region: Bordeaux/Left Bank/ Médoc
Color: red
Grapes: Cabernet Sauvignon (primarily)
Weight: full-bodied
Volume: loud
Dry/sweet: dry
Acidity: medium
Tannin: high to very high
Flavors: notes of blackberries, black cherries, **BLACK CURRANTS/cassis, CEDAR**, chocolate, earth, leather, minerals, **pencil shavings**, smoke, spices, tobacco
Texture: rich, satiny, velvety
Temperature: Serve cool, about 60 to 65 degrees.
Pairings: beef, cheese, game,

Visiting **Oregon**'s Willamette Valley is like being in nirvana—it is stunning out there. It is a great place, with great people and a great winemaking industry. As with Pinot Noir from other places, you can taste the differences between the soil types. There are two types of soil—volcanic and sedimentary—and the wines that come from them are so distinct. Dundee Hills is from red volcanic soil. They call it the Red Hills of Dundee for a reason. The soil has a high iron content, and the wines actually have that very red-fruit, slightly bloody, meaty scent. In the sedimentary soil, you get wines that are earthier, darker in fruit, and with a little more tannin. WillaKenzie [in the Chehalem Mountains] has that mineral scent on the nose.
—SCOTT CALVERT, THE INN AT LITTLE WASHINGTON

lamb, red meat, mushrooms
Aging: Pauillac can easily age for a decade or two, often longer.
Producers: Lafite-Rothschild, Latour, Mouton-Rothschild

PEDRO XIMÉNEZ (PX)
See SHERRY–PEDRO XIMÉNEZ.

PETIT VERDOT
[peh-TEE vair-DOH]
Countries: Argentina, Australia (South), Canada, Chile, **France (Bordeaux)**, Italy, South Africa, Spain, U.S. (California, New York, Virginia, Washington state)
Color: red (dark in color, with a bluish-black hue)
Grapes: Petit Verdot, often blended with Cabernet Sauvignon and/or Merlot
Weight: medium- to **full**-bodied (and higher in alcohol)
Volume: loud
Dry/sweet: dry
Acidity: medium to high
Tannin: very high
Flavors: aromatic, with notes of allspice, **BLACKBERRIES, black currants, black pepper, blueberries,** cedar, cherries, chocolate, coffee, cloves, earth, green peppers, green tea, leather, licorice, molasses, **plums** (fresh and dried), raspberries, smoke, **spices,** tobacco, vanilla, vegetables, **violets**
Texture: velvety
Temperature: Serve cool, about 60 to 65 degrees.
Pairings: barbecue, beef, chops, duck, game, lamb, mature cheese, red meats, roasts, ribs, steaks, stews
Aging: Can generally age for a few to five years; given tannin levels, the best could be aged for decades.

Producers: Canada: Inniskillin; **U.S.–California:** Geyser Peak, Heitz, Jarvis; **Idaho:** Indian Creek; **New York:** Jamesport, Paumanok; **Virginia:** Barrel Oak, Veritas; **Washington state:** Cadence

PETITE ARVINE
[pet-EET ahr-VEEN]
Countries: Italy, Switzerland
Color: white (pale, with golden hues)
Grapes: Petite Arvine
Weight: medium-bodied
Volume: moderate to loud
Dry/sweet: very dry—although Late Harvest sweet versions are also made
Acidity: medium to **high**
Flavors: fruity, with notes of apples, citrus, flowers, **grapefruit,** honey, lemon, lime, orange marmalade, **minerals,** peaches, pears, rhubarb, with a note of **ocean breeze (salt) on the finish**
Texture: creamy, rich, round
Temperature: Serve very cold, about 40 to 45 degrees.
Pairings: dry: appetizers, asparagus, cheese fondue, chicken, fish, ham, shellfish; **sweet:** almonds, cheese course (esp. blue cheeses), foie gras, walnuts
Producers: Benoit Dorsaz, Chateau Lichten, Domaine de Beudon, **Les Cretes,** Rene Favre & Fils

PETITE SIRAH
[pet-EET see-RAH]
Countries: Australia, Chile, Mexico, **U.S. (California,** Washington state)
Color: red (with blackish-blue hues)
Grapes: Petite Sirah, sometimes blended with Cabernet Sauvignon, Syrah, or Zinfandel

Weight: full-bodied (and high in alcohol)
Volume: very loud
Dry/sweet: dry
Acidity: medium to high
Tannin: very high (though softens with age)
Flavors: intensely fruity, with notes of **BLACKBERRIES,** black cherries, black currants/cassis, **BLACK PEPPER,** blood, **blueberries,** coffee, dark chocolate, **earth,** eucalyptus, flowers, leather, licorice, **meat, plums,** raspberries, smoke, **spices, tar,** violets
Texture: chewy, luscious, rich, velvety
Temperature: Serve cool, about 60 to 65 degrees.
Comparables: SHIRAZ/SYRAH, ZINFANDEL
Pairings: barbecue, beef, black-pepper sauces, game, lamb, ribs, roasts, steaks, stews, veal chops
Aging: While many prefer to enjoy its powerful flavors when young, Petite Sirah can be aged for a decade or even longer.
Producers: U.S.–California: Bogle, Clayhouse Estate, **CONCANNON, David Bruce,** Edmeades, EOS, Epiphany Cellars, Neal Family (organic), Parducci, Ravenswood, **Ridge,** Rosenblum, Sean Thackrey, **STAG'S LEAP, TURLEY,** Villa San-Juliette
Iconic example: Stag's Leap

PICOLIT
[PEE-koh-leet]
Country: Italy
Region: Friuli
Color: white
Grapes: Picolit
Weight: full-bodied
Volume: moderate

Dry/sweet: sweet, with a dry finish
Acidity: medium to medium-high
Flavors: notes of almonds, **apricots, brioche,** butter, chestnuts, citrus, custard, figs, **flowers, honey,** maple syrup, orange peel (esp. candied), peaches, spices, tropical fruits, vanilla
Texture: rich, silky, smooth, viscous
Temperature: Serve slightly chilled, about 55 to 60 degrees.
Comparable: SAUTERNES
Pairings: biscotti, blue cheese, foie gras, fresh berries, fresh fruit, paté
Tip: Picolit is made from dried grapes, which concentrates the flavor and sweetness.
Aging: Picolit can age for up to a decade.
Producers: GIROLAMO DORIGO, **La Roncaia, Livio Felluga, Meroi,** Rocca Bernarda, Ronchi di Cialla, Ronchi di Manzano

PIEDMONT WINES
See also BARBARESCO, BAROLO.
Country: Italy
Region: Piedmont
Grapes: red: Barbera, Dolcetto, Nebbiolo; **white:** Arneis, Gavi di Gavi, Moscato

PIGATO
[pee-GAH-toh]
Country: Italy
Region: Liguria
Color: white (straw yellow with a greenish hue)
Grapes: Pigato
Weight: medium-bodied
Volume: moderate to loud
Dry/sweet: dry
Acidity: high

I love crudo [Italian raw fish] with a wine from Liguria like **Pigato.** The Ligurian olive oil that is put on the crudo is very delicate, but the white wines also seem to have a secret oiliness to them. Another wine that would work is a Cinque Terre Bianco, the local "Five Villages" wine. Marea from Bisson is a blend [of Bosco, Vermentino, and Albarola] that is gorgeous with raw fish. If you have fresh Mediterranean fish with lemon, basil, and the oil of the zone with one of these whites, you just feel like you are there.
—CAT SILIRIE, NO. 9 PARK

Flavors: aromatic and fruity, with notes of **almonds,** citrus, fennel, **flowers, herbs,** honey, lemon, lime, minerals, **peaches,** pears, pepper, **sea breeze**
Texture: crisp and fresh, with hints of "oiliness"
Temperature: Serve slightly chilled, about 55 degrees.
Comparable: VERMENTINO
Pairings: artichokes, calamari, clams, crudo (raw fish), fish, mushrooms, oysters, pasta, **pesto, seafood**
Aging: Drink young and fresh.
Producers: Aschero, Bisson, Bruna

PINK WINES
See ROSÉ, ZINFANDEL–WHITE.

PINOTAGE
[pee-noh-TAHJ]
Countries: New Zealand, **SOUTH AFRICA,** U.S. (California)
Color: red
Grapes: Pinotage (Pinot Noir crossed with Cinsault), often blended with Cabernet Franc,

Cabernet Sauvignon, and/or Merlot
Weight: ranges from lighter- to **fuller-bodied**
Volume: ranges from moderate to loud
Dry/sweet: dry
Acidity: medium to high
Tannin: medium to high
Flavors: fruity, with notes of anise, bananas, **blackberries, black pepper, blueberries,** cherries, chocolate, coffee, **earth, game, herbs,** leather, licorice, marshmallows, **meat,** milk chocolate, **minerals, plums,** raspberries, red currants, **smoke,** spices, tobacco
Texture: chewy, rich, round, smooth, velvety
Temperature: Serve slightly chilled, about 55 to 60 degrees.
Comparables: MERLOT, full-bodied PINOT NOIR, SYRAH
Season: summer
Pairings: barbecue, cheese (esp. Cheddar, goat), game, hamburgers, liver, pizza, **red meat,** steak, stews

Pinotage is a South African grape variety you'll rarely find anywhere else. It's unique—fruit-forward with notes of blackberries and black pepper, plus earthiness, plus a moderate zing of acidity. It's great with steak or anything wild, like venison—especially right off the barbecue. Kanonkop is by far the greatest producer—and at $25 a bottle, it's less expensive here than in South Africa.
—CHRISTOPHER BATES, HOTEL FAUCHÈRE

Aging: Generally ready to drink upon release.
Producers: New Zealand: Te Awa; **South Africa:** Beyerskloof, DeWaal, Fairview, Kaapzicht Estate, **KANONKOP, Neil Ellis, Simonsig,** Spice Route, Stellenzicht; **U.S.–California:** Fort Ross, J Winery
Iconic example: Kanonkop Estate Pinotage

PINOT BIANCO
[PEE-noh bee-YAHN-koh]
See also PINOT BLANC.
Country: Italy
Regions: Alto Adige, Friuli, Veneto
Color: white
Grapes: Pinot Bianco (aka Weissburgunder)
Weight: light- to medium-bodied
Volume: quiet
Dry/sweet: dry
Acidity: medium to medium-high
Flavors: notes of almonds, **apples,** butter, **citrus,** cream (esp. oaked wines), honeysuckle, melon, **minerals, pears,** pineapple, vanilla (esp. oaked wines)
Texture: crisp, refreshing
Temperature: Serve chilled, about 50 to 55 degrees.
Comparables: CHARDONNAY–UNOAKED, **PINOT BLANC, Weissburgunder**
Season: summer
Pairings: almonds, chicken, crab, fish (esp. white), pasta, shellfish, shrimp, sole, squid
Tip: Drink young and fresh, within a few years of release.
Producers: Italy: Alois Lageder, Cantino Andriano, Cantino Terlano, Erste + Neue, Tessere

I love Robert Sinskey **Pinot Blanc** from California. It has the refreshing feel of an elegant white wine. It also has the flavors that some people like in Chardonnay, such as notes of apple, pear, melon, and tropical fruit. It is unoaked and refreshing but unlike other wines you have had before. For people who like California Chardonnay, this is a baby step for them to try something new.
—HRISTO ZISOVSKI, AI FIORI

PINOT BLANC
[PEE-noh BLAHNK]
See also PINOT BIANCO.
Countries: Austria, Canada, Czech Republic, **France (Alsace),** Germany, Italy (Alto Adige), U.S. (California, New York, Oregon)
Color: white
Grapes: Pinot Blanc
Weight: lighter- to fuller-bodied
Volume: quiet (U.S.) to moderate (Alsace)
Dry/sweet: dry
Acidity: low to medium-high
Flavors: notes of almonds, **APPLES (ESP. GREEN),** apricots, butter, **citrus,** cream, **flowers,** grapefruit, **honey,** lemon, melon, **minerals,** nuts, **peaches, PEARS,** pineapple, smoke, spices, tropical fruits, vanilla, yeast
Texture: ranges from crisp and delicate to creamy and rich
Temperature: Serve cold, about 45 to 50 degrees.
Comparables: CHARDONNAY–UNOAKED, **PINOT BIANCO, Weissburgunder** (Austria)
Pairings: Asian cuisine (mildly spicy), bacon, cheese, chicken, fish, ham, quiche, shellfish, turkey, veal
Tip: Often used in CRÉMANT D'ALSACE (sparkling wine).
Aging: Drink young, within two to three years.
Producers: France–Alsace: Albert Mann, Hugel, Josmeyer, Kreydenweiss, Lucien Albrecht, Pierre Sparr, Réné Muré,

Schlumberger, Trimbach, Willm; **Italy:** *see* PINOT BIANCO; **U.S.–California:** Au Bon Climat, Chalone, Robert Sinskey; **Michigan:** Left Foot Charley; **New York/Long Island:** Lieb Family; **Oregon:** Erath

PINOT GRIGIO
[PEE-noh GREE-jyoh]
See also PINOT GRIS.
Countries: Australia, Italy (esp. Friuli), Slovenia, U.S. (California)
Color: white
Grapes: Pinot Grigio (aka PINOT GRIS)
Weight: light- to medium-bodied
Volume: very quiet
Dry/sweet: dry
Acidity: medium to **high**
Flavors: fruity, with notes of **apples** (esp. green), **citrus,** figs, **flowers,** grass, **lemon,** lime, melon, **minerals,** peaches, **pears,** smoke, spices, stones
Texture: crisp, refreshing
Temperature: Serve cold, about 45 to 50 degrees.
Season: summer
Comparable: PINOT GRIS
Pairings: chicken, fish (fresh and cured), pasta, salads, shellfish, vegetables
Aging: In general, drink young and fresh, although the best wines can age for up to five years.
Producers: Italy: Bertani, Bolla, Ecco Domani, Esperto, Eugenio Collavini, Folonari,

Italian **Pinot Grigio** is easy to drink, low in alcohol, refreshing, and often doesn't taste like much. Some are great, but they tend to be light. **Pinot Gris in Alsace** is completely different than in Italy. It is richer and riper, with notes of figs, raisins, and orange. In Alsace it varies from crisp and refreshing to richer and oilier. **Pinot Gris in Oregon** is a balance between the two. You get the refreshingly crisp, not-too-viscous style you get in Italy, but you also get the Alsace flavors of peach and melon.

—HRISTO ZISOVSKI, AI FIORI

There is legitimate **Pinot Grigio**. Scarpetta has flavor and is refreshing. This is the best Pinot Grigio I have had, and I would not feel embarrassed to drink it. It is under $20, versus Santa Margherita [arguably the world's most famous Pinot Grigio], which is around $40. Who does not want a bottle that is twice as good for half the money? I also recommend Pighin Pinot Grigio, which is everywhere and is legitimate, good, inexpensive Pinot Grigio.

—ROBERT BOHR, COLICCHIO & SONS

Jermann, Lagaria, **Lageder, Livio Felluga,** Maso Poli, Mezzacorona, **Pighin,** Santa Margherita, **Scarpetta,** Tiefenbrunner, **Zenato; Slovenia:** Giocato; **U.S.– California:** Forest Glen, Luna, Meridian

---

PINOT GRIS
[PEE-noh GREE]
See also PINOT GRIGIO.
Countries: Argentina, Australia, Austria, **France (Alsace)**, Germany, Italy, New Zealand, **U.S. (Oregon)**
Color: white
Grapes: Pinot Gris
Weight: lighter medium-bodied (Oregon) to medium- to full-bodied (Alsace)
Volume: quiet (Oregon) to moderate (Alsace)
Dry/sweet: dry to sweet (in Late Harvest versions)
Acidity: medium (Oregon) to high (Alsace)
Flavors: aromatic, with notes of almonds, apples (esp. red), **apricots,** bananas, **citrus, flowers,** herbs, **honey,** mango, melon,

minerals, **nuts, peaches, pears,** smoke, **spices,** stones, vanilla, white pepper
Texture: creamy, rich, smooth, soft, sometimes with a hint of spritz
Temperature: Serve cold, about 45 to 50 degrees.
Comparables: CHARDONNAY– UNOAKED (light-bodied), **PINOT GRIGIO,** Rülander (as it's known in Germany)
Season: summer
Pairings: Asian cuisine, bacon, cheese, chicken, fish (esp. salmon), Indian cuisine, pork, quiche, shellfish (esp. oysters), spicy dishes, veal
Aging: Drink most wines young and fresh; better wines can be aged up to two decades.
Producers: Argentina: J & F Lurton; **Canada:** Fielding, Haywire; **France–Alsace** (full-bodied and rich, with notes

Duck Walk Vineyards makes a **Pinot Meunier** varietal wine that blows me away with its quality. It's got a wonderful smoothness with notes of smoke that pair beautifully with duck or pheasant.

—MICHAEL CIMINO, GLENMERE MANSION

Under-$15 tip: Oregon is a good place to look for **Pinot Gris**—like King Estate.

—VIRGINIA PHILIP, MS, THE BREAKERS

of honey, melon, minerals, smoke): Dirler, Domaine Ostertag, **Helfrich,** Hering, Hugel, Kreydenweiss, Lucien Albrecht, Paul Blanck, Pierre Sparr, Schlumberger, **Trimbach,** Weinbach, Willm, **ZIND HUMBRECHT; Italy:** *see* PINOT GRIGIO; **U.S.–California** (fuller-bodied, fruitier, softer): Beringer, Boeger, Clos du Bois, Gallo of Sonoma Reserve, Manzoni, Navarro Vineyards; **Oregon** (fruitier, with notes of pears, softer): Acrobat, Adelsheim, A to Z, Belle Pente, Bethel Heights, Chateau Ste. Michelle, Cooper Mountain, Cristom, Erath, Evesham Wood, **EYRIE, KING ESTATE,** Lemelson, **Ponzi,** Sokol Blosser, St. Innocent, WillaKenzie
Iconic examples: Eyrie Vineyards or King Estate

PINOT MEUNIER
[PEE-noh moon-YAY]
See also CHAMPAGNE.
Countries: Australia, **FRANCE (CHAMPAGNE,** Loire), Germany, U.S. (California)
Color: red
Grapes: Pinot Meunier
Weight: light-bodied
Volume: moderate
Dry/sweet: dry (even bitter)
Acidity: medium-high to high
Tannin: medium
Flavors: aromatic and fruity, with notes of apples, earth,

flowers, raspberries, smoke
Texture: smooth, soft
Temperature: Serve slightly
chilled, about 55 degrees.
Pairings: bacon, barbecue,
duck, mushrooms, pheasant,
smoked meats
Producers: Domaine Chandon
(California), Duck Walk (New
York), Eyrie (Oregon)

PINOT NERO
[PEE-noh NAY-roh]
See PINOT NOIR.

PINOT NOIR
[PEE-noh NWAHR]
Countries: Argentina,
Chile, **France (BURGUNDY,
Champagne)**, Germany, Italy,
New Zealand (Otago), Spain, U.S.
(**California, Oregon**)
Color: red (lighter in hue)
Grapes: Pinot Noir
Weight: lighter- (Old World)
to medium-plus-bodied (New
World)
Volume: quiet to moderate
Dry/sweet: dry
Acidity: medium to high
Tannin: low to medium
Flavors: notes of beets, **BLACK
AND RED CHERRIES** (esp.
younger wines), blackberries,
(dark) chocolate, cinnamon,
cloves, coffee, cola, cranberries,
(red) currants, earth, **flowers**,
game (esp. older wines), herbs,
leather, mushrooms (esp. older
wines), plums, **raspberries**, roses,
smoke, spices, **strawberries**,
tobacco, truffles (esp. older
wines), violets
Flavors: cool climate: earth, sour
cherries; **warm climate:** smoke,
sweet cherries
Texture: rich, silky, smooth, soft,
velvety
Temperature: Serve cool

I can't believe how much American **Pinot Noir** we sell. Everyone wants
it, and it is very food-friendly. I don't order the super-heavy over-the-top
Pinots; I lean harder into Oregon than California. This is a place where
you can offer exactly what most people want: a nice, juicy Pinot Noir at
a good price. Oregon Pinot tends to show a nicer sense of *terroir*. They
are a little dirtier in a nice way, with more earthiness and mushroom
to them. The fruit tends to lean more black than red with a plummy/
black cherry/blackberry note to them. More often than not, to me they
are a little lower in alcohol and more elegant. There is some Pinot
that is coming out closer to Zinfandel than Pinot. California Pinot is
a bigger and richer-style Pinot. It will have nice juicy red fruit with a
more forward style. You will see more vanilla coming from the oak
treatment. The wine in general will be more robust.
—ANDY MYERS, CITYZEN

to slightly chilled, about 50
(younger) to 60 (older) degrees.
Comparables: cru BEAUJOLAIS,
BURGUNDY–RED, SPÄTBURGUNDER
Pairings: bacon, chicken, **duck**,
game birds, **lamb, mushrooms**,
pork, **salmon, tuna**
Tip: With Pinot Noir, be willing
to pay for top quality. If your
budget is limited, look to Chile.
Aging: Without the tannic
structure of Cabernet Sauvignon,
Pinot Noir typically won't age as
long (with the exception of fine
red Burgundies, which can age
for decades). In general, drink
New World Pinot Noir young
(within three to four years). Best
recent vintages (Oregon): 2008,
2006, 2004, 2003, 2002.
Producers: Argentina: Alma
Negra; **Australia:** Coldstream
Hills (Overstreet), Ninth Island;
Austria: Stadlmann; **Canada:** Le
Clos Jordanne; **Chile:** Cono Sur,
Veramonte; **France–Alsace:** Albert
Mann; **Burgundy:** *see* BURGUNDY–
RED; **Italy:** Marchesi Pancrazi
Villa di Bagnolo; **New Zealand:**
Brancott, Craggy Range, Felton
Road, Richardson, Schubert, Te
Mara, Te Muna, Villa Maria, Wild
Rock; **South Africa:** Hamilton
Russell; **U.S.–California:** AU

BON CLIMAT, Belle Glos,
CALERA, Chalone, Clos du Bois,
Copain, Dehlinger, Domaine
Carneros, **Etude**, Gary Farrell,
Fiddlehead, Flowers, Iron Horse,
Kistler, Kosta Browne, La Crema,
Landmark, **Littorai**, MacMurray,
MARCASSIN, Martinelli,
**Merry Edwards, ROCHIOLI,
SAINTSBURY**, Sanford, Sea
Smoke, Taz, Williams-Selyem;
Michigan: Shady Lane Cellars;
Oregon: Andelsheim, Archery
Summit, A to Z, Beaux Frères,
Bethel Heights, Brick House,
Broadleigh, **CRISTOM,
DOMAINE DROUHIN,
Domaine Serene**, Erath, **Eyrie**,
J. Christopher, **KEN WRIGHT**,
King Estate, Peay, **Ponzi**, Shea,
Sokol Blosser, Soter, St. Innocent,
Stoller, Thomas, WillaKenzie,
Willamette Valley Vineyards

POMEROL
[PAWM-uh-rawl]
See also BORDEAUX–RED.
Country: France
Region: Bordeaux/Right Bank
Color: red
Grapes: Cabernet Franc,
Cabernet Sauvignon, **MERLOT**
Weight: medium- to full-bodied
Volume: loud

Dry/sweet: dry
Acidity: medium
Tannin: high (though softens with age)
Flavors: notes of blackberries, black cherries, black currants, blueberries, licorice, minerals, plums, smoke, spices, tobacco, violets
Texture: rich, round, smooth, soft, velvety
Temperature: Serve cool, about 60 to 65 degrees.
Pairings: beef, cheese, game, lamb, oxtails, pheasant, turkey, veal, venison
Aging: Age at least five years; the best vintages by the best producers can last up to five decades.
Iconic example: Château Pétrus

PORT—COLHEITA
[koohl-YAY-tah]
Country: Portugal
Region: Douro
Grapes: a blend of dozens of kinds, but primarily **Touriga Nacional**, along with Tinta Barroca, Tinta Roriz, Tinto Cão, and Touriga Franca
Weight: full-bodied (and high in alcohol, about 20 percent)
Volume: loud
Dry/sweet: semi-sweet to sweet

Acidity: low to medium
Flavors: notes of almonds, black cherries, caramel, chocolate, coffee, cream, dried figs, honey, nuts, plums (fresh and dried), raisins, smoke, spices, toffee, vanilla, walnuts
Texture: rich, silky, smooth
Temperature: Serve cool to slightly chilled, about 55 to 65 degrees.
Comparable: Colheita is the highest-quality **Tawny Port**, the equivalent of a single-vintage.
Season: winter
Pairings: cheese (esp. aged), chocolate (esp. dark), dried fruits, nuts, walnuts

PORTER HOUSE NEW YORK

Aging: Ready to be drunk upon release; enjoy Colheita fresh.
Producers: Feist, Niepoort, Quinta do Noval

PORT—LATE-BOTTLED VINTAGE (LBV)

Country: Portugal
Region: Douro
Color: red (with ruby hues)
Grapes: a blend of dozens of kinds, but primarily **Touriga Nacional**, along with Tinta Barroca, Tinta Roriz, Tinto Cão, and Touriga Franca
Weight: full-bodied (and high in alcohol, about 20 percent)
Volume: moderate to loud
Dry/sweet: sweet
Acidity: medium
Tannin: medium to high
Flavors: fruity, with notes of blackberries, black currants/cassis, cherries, chocolate, figs, flowers, jam, leather, prunes, raisins, raspberries, spices, vanilla, violets, walnuts
Texture: rich, unctuous, viscous
Temperature: Serve cool to slightly chilled, about 55 to 65 degrees.
Season: winter
Pairings: cheese (esp. Cheddar, Roquefort, Stilton), chocolate, desserts, nuts
Tips: LBV port offers some similar characteristics to vintage ports but requires no aging. Given its lower price point, it offers impressive value. In older LBV ports or if sediment is visible, decant before serving. LBV port can keep for a few weeks after opening if refrigerated.
Aging: Ready to be drunk upon release; LBV port should be enjoyed fresh.
Producers: Churchill's, Dow's,

Late-Bottled Vintage port offers an unbelievable value, as it is more affordable but still delivers really high quality. As opposed to $21 for a glass of 2007 Dow vintage port, at Aldea you can have a wonderful glass of 2003 Fonseca Unfiltered LBV port for $11. I love eating almonds with it.
—HEATHER LAISKONIS, ALDEA

Fonseca, Osborne, Quinta do Noval, Sandeman, Smith Woodhouse, Warre's

PORT—RUBY

Country: Portugal
Region: Douro
Color: red (with ruby hues)
Grapes: a blend of dozens of kinds, but primarily **Touriga Nacional**, along with Tinta Barroca, Tinta Roriz, Tinto Cão, and Touriga Franca
Weight: full-bodied (and high in alcohol, about 20 percent)
Volume: moderate to loud
Dry/sweet: semi-sweet to sweet
Acidity: low to medium
Flavors: notes of blackberries, **black cherries**, cassis, dates, figs, licorice, **plums** (fresh and dried), raisins, raspberries, spices
Texture: rich
Temperature: Serve cool to slightly chilled, about 55 to 65 degrees.
Season: winter
Pairings: cheese (esp. blue), dark chocolate, desserts (esp. those made with berries or cherries)
Tips: Ruby port offers a value-priced introduction to port. Reserve versions offer greater richness and complexity. Ruby

port can keep for a few weeks after opening if refrigerated.
Aging: Ready to be drunk upon release; enjoy ruby port young and fresh.
Producers: Churchill's, Cockburn's, Croft, Dow's, Fonseca, Graham's, Niepoort, Quinta do Infantado, Sandeman, Warre's

PORT—TAWNY

Country: Portugal
Region: Douro
Color: red (with tawny hues)
Grapes: a blend of dozens of kinds but primarily **Touriga Nacional**, along with Tinta Barroca, Tinta Roriz, Tinto Cão, and Touriga Franca
Weight: full-bodied (and high in alcohol, about 20 percent)
Volume: loud
Dry/sweet: semi-sweet to sweet
Acidity: low to medium
Flavors: notes of almonds, black cherries, brown sugar, caramel, chocolate, coffee, cream, dried figs, **nuts**, orange, plums, raisins, smoke, spices, toffee, vanilla, walnuts
Texture: rich, smooth
Temperature: Serve cool to chilled, about 50 to 60 degrees.

We offer Fonseca 20-year **tawny port** either with cheese or dessert, or instead of either. It's incredible with Stilton, and we're serving it right now with a Valderone cheese that's a salty blue cheese made of both cow and goat milk that just screams for tawny port.
—HEATHER LAISKONIS, ALDEA

Comparable: MADEIRA

Season: winter

Pairings: apple desserts, cheese (esp. aged and/or blue), chocolate (esp. dark), nut-driven desserts (e.g., pecan pie), pumpkin pie

Tip: Tawny port can keep for a few months after opening if refrigerated.

Aging: Ready to be drunk upon release; enjoy tawny port fresh.

Producers: A. A. Ferreira, Cockburn's 20-Year, Croft, Delaforce, **Dow's**, Ficklin, **Fonseca, Graham's, Niepoort,** Porto Rocha, Quinta do Noval, **Ramos Pinto**, Sandeman, **TAYLOR FLADGATE**, Tesco Finest, Warre's

PORT—VINTAGE

Country: Portugal

Region: Douro

Color: red (with ruby hues)

Grapes: a blend of dozens of kinds, but primarily **Touriga Nacional,** along with Tinta Barroca, Tinta Roriz, Tinto Cão, and Touriga Franca

Weight: very full-bodied (and high in alcohol, about 20 percent)

Volume: loud

Dry/sweet: semi-sweet to sweet

Acidity: low to medium

Tannin: high (though softens with age)

Flavors: notes of blackberries, black cherries, butterscotch, cassis, chocolate, cinnamon, coffee, dates, dried fruits, figs, flowers, licorice, nutmeg, plums, raisins, raspberries, smoke, spices, violets

Texture: rich

Temperature: Serve cool, about 60 to 65 degrees.

Season: winter

Pairings: blue cheese (esp. Stilton), dark chocolate, figs

Comparable: Vintage port is the highest-quality RUBY PORT.

Tip: Decant to remove sediment before serving. As vintage port does not keep well after opening, plan to finish the bottle in one sitting.

Aging: The best vintage port can age for decades (and should age for at least a decade or two before opening), perhaps even a century. Best recent vintages: 2007, 2005, 2004, 2003, 2001, 2000.

Producers: Croft, Delaforce, **Dow's, Fonseca, Graham's, Niepoort, Quinta do Noval**, Quinta do Vesuvio, Smith Woodhouse, **TAYLOR FLADGATE**

Tip: While true port is made only in Portugal, producers in a number of other countries (including Australia, the United States, and South Africa) make port-style wines worth trying. Examples include Australia's Penfolds "Grandfather" Fine Old Liqueur Tawny and California's Benziger, Heitz Ink Grade, Prager, Quady, and V. Sattui's port-like Angelica.

PORT—WHITE

Country: Portugal

Region: Douro

Color: white (with golden, amber, or pink hues)

Grapes: Códega, Esgana Cão, Folgasão, **Malvasia Fina,** Rabigato, Verdelho, Viosinho

Weight: medium- to full-bodied (and high in alcohol, up to 20 percent)

Volume: moderate to loud

Dry/sweet: dry to off-dry to sweet

Acidity: low to medium

Flavors: fruity, with notes of **apricots,** caramel, **citrus,** flowers, green apples, **honey,** melon, **NUTS,** orange, **peaches,** pears, raisins, spices

Texture: rich, smooth

Temperature: Serve chilled, about 50 to 55 degrees.

Season: spring–summer

Pairings: Serve dry white port as an aperitif (either straight up or with club soda or tonic water and a lemon slice over ice), perhaps with shellfish or smoked salmon; sweeter versions can pair with fresh cheeses, fruit desserts (esp. stone fruits), melon (esp. cantaloupe, watermelon), duck with stone fruit (e.g., peaches), white chocolate desserts.

Aging: Drink upon release.

Producers: Churchill's, Dow's, Niepoort, Prager "Aria," Warre's

PORTUGUESE WINES

See also DOURO REDS, PORT, TOURIGA NACIONAL, VINHO VERDE.

Sweet: Madeira, port

White: Alvarinho, Vinho Verde

Red: Touriga Nacional; other traditional port grapes (vinified dry)

Tip: TOURIGA NACIONAL is to Portugal what Malbec is to Argentina and Carmenère is to Chile.

Iconic example: Ferreira Barca Velha, long Portugal's most famous wine

White port is a huge seller for us, because we serve a glass of it with chef George Mendes's tasting menu. It's got a pink hue, so guests who see it across the room want to know what it is and will order it themselves. It tastes like a cross between honeysuckle and sherry. We offer both Rainha Santa white port and Quinta de Santa Ensemia's 10-year white port.
—HEATHER LAISKONIS, ALDEA

With the idea of giving the people what they want, we've been offering even more **Portuguese wines.** When they visit Aldea [one of America's finest Portuguese restaurants], they tend to think, "When in Rome . . ." and look for them on the wine list. Portuguese wines have also been getting more much-deserved great press these days. Our bestselling Portuguese white is called Poema, and it's a delicate, well-balanced wine made of 100 percent Alvarinho by a producer who's been making wine for six generations. It's perfect with our shrimp alhinho, which is flavored with garlic. One of my favorite Portuguese reds is a Herdade de Grous Reserva from the Alentejo region that is a blend of Alicante Bouchet, Syrah, and Touriga Nacional, and beautifully balanced and silky.

—HEATHER LAISKONIS, ALDEA

POUILLY-FUISSÉ
[POO-yee fwee-SAY]
Country: France
Region: Burgundy/Mâconnais
Color: white
Grapes: Chardonnay
Weight: medium- to full-bodied
Volume: moderate
Dry/sweet: dry
Acidity: medium to high
Flavors: fruity, with notes of almonds, apples, cream, earth, grapefruit, lemon, lime, melon, minerals, pears, spices, toast, vanilla
Texture: fresh, round, satiny, soft
Temperature: Serve chilled, about 50 to 55 degrees.
Pairings: chicken, fish (esp. with butter or cream sauce), ham, lobster, shellfish, veal
Tip: Drink within seven to eight years.
Producers: Bouchard Père & Fils, Chalet de Pouilly, Ferret, Georges Duboeuf, Guffens-Heynen, Joseph Drouhin, Laboure-Roi, Louis Jadot, Louis Latour, Merlin, Roger Lassarat

POUILLY-FUMÉ
[POO-yee fyoo-MAY]
Country: France
Region: Loire Valley
Color: white

Grapes: Sauvignon Blanc
Weight: light- to medium-bodied
Volume: moderate
Dry/sweet: very dry
Acidity: medium-high to high
Flavors: aromatic, with notes of apples, **CITRUS,** flowers, **grapefruit, GRASS, gunflint, HERBS,** lime, menthol, minerals, nectarines, pears, **SMOKE,** steel, stones, tangerines
Texture: creamy, **crisp**
Temperature: Serve very cold, about 45 degrees.
Comparables: SANCERRE, SAUVIGNON BLANC
Pairings: cheese (esp. Edam or goat), fish (esp. grilled or roasted), pork, scallops
Aging: Drink young and fresh (within a year or two), although the best can age for as long as five years.
Producers: Blanchet, Bourgeois, Chatelain, **Didier Dagueneau,** Guy Saget, Ladoucette
Iconic example: Didier Dagueneau

PRIMITIVO
[pree-mee-TEE-voh]
Countries: Australia, Chile, **Italy (Puglia),** U.S. (California)
Color: red
Grapes: Primitivo
Weight: medium- to **full**-bodied

(with high alcohol)
Volume: loud
Dry/sweet: dry, with a hint of sweetness
Acidity: low to **medium**
Tannin: low to medium
Flavors: notes of bay leaf, **blackberries,** black pepper, blueberries, **CHERRIES,** chestnuts, cinnamon, dark chocolate, earth, jam, leather, licorice, orange, plums, raisins, **raspberries, SPICES,** stones, strawberries, tobacco
Texture: rich, lush, smooth, velvety
Temperature: Serve cool, about 60 to 65 degrees.
Comparables: Crljenak Kaštelanski (Croatia), ZINFANDEL
Pairings: grilled dishes, pasta (esp. with vegetables), pizza, *salumi* (Italian cured meats)
Producers: Italy: A-Mano, Apollonio, Botromagno, Calatrasi, **Cantele,** Casa Catelli, Fatalone, Felline, Palama, Pervini; **U.S.– California:** Hendry

PRIORAT (AKA PRIORATO)
[pree-oh-RAHT]
Country: Spain
Region: Priorat, southern Catalonia
Color: red
Grapes: Garnacha and/or Cariñena (primarily)
Weight: very full-bodied (and high in alcohol—up to 18 percent)
Volume: loud
Dry/sweet: dry
Acidity: medium to high
Tannin: high to very high
Flavors: notes of **blackberries,** black cherries, black currants/ cassis, black plums, cedar, chocolate, earth, flowers, herbs,

licorice, **minerals,** mushrooms, plums (fresh or dried), smoke, spices, violets
Texture: rich, velvety
Temperature: Serve cool, about 60 to 65 degrees.
Comparables: SYRAH, ZINFANDEL
Pairings: beef, cassoulet, cheese (esp. Manchego), game, lamb, pork (esp. grilled and/or smoked), rabbit, steak, stews, venison
Aging: Priorat can age for five years or, in the case of the very best, much longer. However, many better Spanish wines, including Priorat, are aged extensively before release, so they can be enjoyed immediately.
Producers: ALVARO PALACIOS, Clos de l'Obac, Clos Erasmus, Clos Figueres, Clos Mogador, Finca Dofi, Finca La Planeta, Mas Igneus (organic), Mas Martinet, René Barbier, Vall Llach Embruix, Vinícola del Priorat
Iconic example: Alvaro Palacios "L'Ermita"

Lake County in northern California is primarily known for Sauvignon Blanc. It also is an area good for Syrah. I have known winemaker Cary Tamura for years, and Diogenes makes **private-label** Sauvignon Blanc, Chardonnay, and Syrah for our restaurant that we sell for only $35. The Sauvignon Blanc is listed under "California Aromatic Whites, Sauvignon Blanc, Lake County, Diogenes, Exclusive Bottling for Addison at The Grand Del Mar." However, I call this label Sweat Labor, because I will take my day off and a vacation day to go up to Lake County to work as a cellar rat. That may mean sorting grapes, racking, or bottling wine. Instead of being paid, I ask them to help me out on the price so I can pass the savings on to my customers.
—JESSE RODRIGUEZ, ADDISON AT THE GRAND DEL MAR

I love **Priorat,** which is one of my favorite wine regions. These wines tend to be big and dark and powerful and distinct and unique. I have not yet come across one that I don't like!
—JILL ZIMORSKI, CAFÉ ATLÁNTICO

PRIVATE-LABEL WINES
Don't overlook restaurants' own wines, as you're sure to get one they are proud of, often at a relatively good value. We're fans of Daniel Boulud's Champagne, which is served at all of his restaurants, as well as of La

Caravelle's Blanc de Blancs and rosé Champagnes.

PROSECCO
[proh-SEHK-oh]
Country: Italy
Regions: Friuli, **Veneto**
Color: white
Grapes: Prosecco (aka Glera)
Weight: light-bodied (and light in alcohol)
Volume: quiet
Dry/sweet: dry to off-dry
Acidity: medium to high
Flavors: fruity, with notes of **almonds, apples,** apricots, citrus, cream, custard, flowers, honey, lemon, melon, minerals, orange, peaches, **pears,** toast, tropical fruits, yeast
Texture: still to **semi-sparkling to sparkling;** ranges from crisp and refreshing to creamy and soft
Temperature: Serve very cold, about 40 to 45 degrees.
Comparables: SPARKLING WINES
Season: summer
Pairings: antipasto, asparagus, bread topped with ricotta cheese and eucalyptus honey, eggs, fried foods, prosciutto and melon
Tips: Prosecco is always served in a white wine glass in Italy's Veneto region. A sparkling wine, Prosecco is not made by the

I love **Prosecco** so much that I usually drink whatever a good restaurant is serving. At Cook restaurant in St. Helena, I love their light, effervescent Prosecco, which has notes of lemon curd and minerality that go so well with shellfish, especially mussels and clams. But I couldn't even tell you what it is! [Cook's wine list at the time indicated that it was Ruggeri.]

—JULIA MORETTI, AD HOC

I have always been a fan of Nino Franco **Prosecco**. A more serious bottle within reach is Bisol—their basic non-vintage is fantastic. My new favorite is Prosecco-esque: It is a rosé that's a blend of Merlot and Chardonnay called Le Colture [Prosecco di Valdobbiadene]. It is yeasty with great fruit, and the color is gorgeous.

—BELINDA CHANG, THE MODERN

same method as Champagne. Secondary fermentation takes place in large tanks rather than in the bottle. This lower-cost bulk process is known as the Charmat method. Add peach juice to a glass of chilled Prosecco to create a Bellini cocktail. Substitute a splash of other fruit nectar (melon, blood orange, or pear) for a delicious change of pace.
Aging: Drink Prosecco very young and fresh (ideally, within six to twelve months of release).
Producers: BISOL, Canella, Mionetto (esp. IL), NINO FRANCO (esp. Rustico), Ruggeri, Varaschin, **Zardetto**

PROVENCE WINES
Country: France
Region: Provence
Grapes: Mourvèdre
Producer: Domaine Tempier

PULIGNY-MONTRACHET
[pool-EE-nyee mawn-rah-SHAY]
See also BURGUNDY–WHITE.
Country: France
Region: Burgundy/(southern) Côte d'Or/ Côte de Beaune
Color: white
Grapes: Chardonnay
Weight: full-bodied
Volume: moderate

Dry/sweet: dry
Acidity: medium to high
Flavors: notes of almonds, apples, butterscotch, citrus, cream, flowers, hazelnuts, honey, lemon, **minerals**, nuts, orange, peaches, pears, pineapple, smoke, spices, **steel**, tangerine, vanilla
Texture: elegant, rich
Temperature: Serve chilled, about 50 to 55 degrees.
Pairings: cheese (esp. French), chicken, fish, **lobster**, rabbit, **shrimp**, turkey, veal
Aging: Better wines will age for five years or more, the best for a decade or longer.
Producers: Bzikot, **Drouhin**, Georges Amiot, Latour, **Leflaive**, Louis Jadot, Maison Champy, Matrot, Ramonet

PX
See SHERRY–PEDRO XIMÉNEZ.

QUARTS DE CHAUME
[kahr duh SHOHM]
Country: France
Region: Loire Valley
Color: white
Grapes: Chenin Blanc
Weight: medium- to full-bodied
Volume: loud
Dry/sweet: semi-sweet to sweet
Acidity: medium to high

Flavors: dessert wine with notes of almonds, apples, **candied fruits**, citrus, figs, guava, hazelnuts, **honey**, lemon, melon, **minerals**, orange, peaches, pears, **quince**
Texture: luscious, **rich**, silky, soft, unctuous
Temperature: Serve cold, about 45 degrees.
Comparable: BONNEZEAUX
Pairings: apple desserts (esp. tarte Tatin), banana desserts, foie gras, fruit desserts (esp. with apricots, pears, pineapple, or rhubarb)
Aging: Best aged for a decade, when they develop even greater richness. Chenin Blanc's high acidity can help these wines age for up to several decades or even indefinitely.
Producers: Château de Suronde, Château Pierre-Bise, **Domaine des Baumard**

QUIET WINES—RED
See BEAUJOLAIS, CORVINA.

QUIET WINES—WHITE
See ORVIETO, PINOT GRIGIO, PROSECCO, SOAVE, TREBBIANO.

RECIOTO DELLA VALPOLICELLA
[reh-CHAW-toh deh-lah vahl-poh-lee-CHELL-ah]
Country: Italy
Region: Veneto
Color: red
Grapes: the same grapes used to make Valpolicella—Corvina Veronese, Molinara, Rondinella
Weight: full-bodied
Volume: loud
Dry/sweet: bittersweet to sweet
Acidity: medium
Flavors: made from dried grapes; fruity, with notes of

blackberries, black cherries, chocolate, cinnamon, coffee, licorice, nutmeg, **plums** (fresh and dried), **raisins**, raspberries, spices, star anise
Texture: luscious, rich
Temperature: Serve cool, about 60 to 65 degrees.
Comparable: PORT
Pairings: cheese (esp. blue), chocolate desserts, cookies, nuts and nut desserts, pastries
Producers: Allegrini, Bertani, Quintarella, Tedeschi, Tommaso Bussola, Viviani

REFOSCO
[ray-FOH-skoh]
Countries: Croatia, Greece, **Italy (Friuli)**, Slovenia, U.S. (California)
Color: red (and rosé)
Grapes: Refosco
Weight: ranges from lighter-bodied to fuller-bodied (and moderate in alcohol)
Volume: moderate to loud
Dry/sweet: dry
Acidity: medium to high
Tannin: medium to high
Flavors: fruity, with notes of almonds, anise, **blackberries, black cherries**, black pepper, blueberries, chestnuts, **chocolate**, cloves, coffee, herbs, leather, licorice, minerals, orange peel, **plums**, raspberries, rose petals, spices, **STRAWBERRIES**, tobacco, vanilla, violets
Texture: round, silky, smooth, velvety
Temperature: Serve cool, about 60 to 65 degrees.
Comparables: BEAUJOLAIS,

If you go to a better wine store and ask about southern **Rhône**, if they are smart they are not going to start you with Beaucastel [a top Châteauneuf-du-Pape]. Instead, they will start you with a bottle that is 100 percent Grenache that tastes like raspberries and is really pretty—or they will have you try one that has more Mourvèdre than anything else and is dark and inky.
—MARK MENDOZA, SONA

SHIRAZ/SYRAH, ZINFANDEL
Pairings: aged cheese, antipasto, game, game birds, ham, pasta, pork, *salumi* (Italian cured meats), sausage, smoky dishes
Tip: Open the wine at least thirty minutes before serving to let it breathe.
Producers: Italy: Ca'Bolani, Dorigo, La Tunella, Miani, Scarbolo "Campo del Viotto," Tenuta Luisa, Venica "Bottaz"; **U.S.–California:** Tobin James

RETSINA
[reht-SEE-nuh]
Country: Greece
Color: white
Grapes: Roditis, **Savatiano**
Weight: light- to medium-bodied (and low in alcohol)
Volume: very loud
Dry/sweet: dry
Acidity: low to medium
Flavors: notes of anise, eucalyptus, grapefruit, lemon, mint, **PINE RESIN**, spices, turpentine
Texture: crisp, fresh, oily
Temperature: Serve very cold, about 40 to 45 degrees.
Pairings: cheese (esp. feta), dill, eggplant, fish, garlic, Greek cuisine (esp. appetizers),

hummus, octopus, olives, oregano, salty foods, spinach, taramosalata
Producers: Gaia Estate, Kourtaki, Malamatina

RHODE ISLAND WINES
Producers: Newport Vineyards, Sakonnet Vineyards

RHÔNE WINES
See CHÂTEAUNEUF-DU-PAPE, CONDRIEU, CÔTE-RÔTIE, CÔTES DU RHÔNE, GRENACHE, HERMITAGE, SYRAH, VIOGNIER.
Grapes: red: Grenache (southern Rhône), Syrah (northern Rhône); **white:** Marsanne, Roussanne, Viognier (northern Rhône)

"RHONE RANGER" WINES
The Rhone Rangers is a non-profit organization dedicated to celebrating wines made from Rhône grape varieties in the United States (rhonerangers.org).
Country: U.S.
Region: California (primarily)
Grapes: red: Rhône varieties (Carignane, Cinsault, Counoise, Grenache, Mourvèdre, Petite Sirah, Syrah, etc.); **white:** Rhône varieties (Grenache Blanc, Marsanne, Picpoul Blanc, Roussanne, Viognier, etc.)
Tip: Several of their entry-level Rhône-style wines can be purchased for less than $15.
Producers: Alban, Andrew

Gaia Estate makes an approachable **Retsina** that has only 5 percent added resin as opposed to the usual 20 percent, so there's no turpentine-like aroma. It's bone dry, with notes of oregano, and when served with grilled octopus, I genuinely like it!
—ROGER DAGORN, MS, PORTER HOUSE NEW YORK

Murray, Beckmen Vineyards, Bonny Doon, Cline Cellars, Edmunds St. John, Joseph Phelps, Ojai, Qupé, Sean Thackrey, Sine Qua Non

RIBERA DEL DUERO
[ree-BEHR-uh del-DWAYR-oh]
See also TEMPRANILLO.
Country: Spain
Region: Ribera del Duero
Color: red
Grapes: TEMPRANILLO, sometimes blended with Cabernet Sauvignon, Merlot
Weight: full-bodied
Volume: loud
Dry/sweet: dry
Acidity: low to medium
Tannin: medium to high
Flavors: notes of **blackberries**, **BLACK CHERRIES**, **black currants**, blueberries, cedar, chocolate (esp. dark), coffee, **earth**, herbs, leather, licorice, **meat**, mocha, licorice, plums (fresh and dried), raspberries, **smoke, spices, strawberries**, tea, toast, tobacco, vanilla, **wild game**
Texture: round, silky, soft, velvety
Temperature: Serve cool, about 60 to 65 degrees.
Pairings: beef, cheese (esp. aged), lamb (esp. chops), pork, sausages, steak, stews
Aging: Ribera del Duero will age for five years or more. However, because many better Spanish wines, including these, are aged extensively before release, they can be enjoyed immediately.
Producers: Alejandro Fernandez, **Alion, Arzuaga**, Bodegas Mauro, Bodegas Pingon, Bodegas Reyes, Condado de Haza, Emilio Moro, **LA PESQUERA, PINGUS**, Teofilo

Reyes, **VEGA SICILIA**, Viña Pedrosa
Iconic example: Vega Sicilia "Unico"

RIESLING—IN GENERAL
[REE-sling; REE-zling]
Countries: Australia, Austria, Canada, Chile, **France (Alsace)**, GERMANY, New Zealand, South Africa, U.S. (New York, Washington state)
Color: white
Grapes: Riesling (pale in color, with greenish-gray hues)
Weight: lighter- (U.S.) to medium-bodied (Alsace) (and low in alcohol)
Volume: moderate (U.S.) to loud (Alsace)
Dry/sweet: ranges from very dry to very sweet
Acidity: high to very high
Flavors: **very aromatic**, with notes of **apples (esp. green), apricots, citrus, flowers** (esp. younger wines), grapefruit, grapes, **honey**, lemon, **LIME**, lychees, mango, melon, **MINERALS, nectarines**, papayas, **PEACHES**, pears, petrol (esp. older wines), pineapple, smoke, spices, steel, stones, tangerine, toast, tropical fruits
Texture: crisp
Temperature: Serve cold, about 45 to 50 degrees.
Comparables: ALSACE WHITES
Season: spring–summer
Pairings: Asian cuisine (esp. spicy), charcuterie, chicken, choucroute, ham, Indian cuisine, pork, sausages, seafood, shellfish
Tip: Rieslings from warm climates deliver more lime plus tropical fruit (mango, papaya) notes, while those from cool

Sommeliers all have go-to wines that we are comfortable with. We have the story to tell, and they are reliable for us and for the guest. Stony Hill **Riesling** would be one, in that it is food-friendly, unique, and people are stunned that in Cabernet country you can make a Riesling that is low in alcohol, high in acidity, and mineral-driven.
—DENNIS KELLY, THE FRENCH LAUNDRY

Trimbach makes a **Riesling** Reserve that you can get for $16 to $17, as well as Clos Ste Hune for $300. Why buy the big boys when you can start with something so reasonable? [When you're ready for the next step up from the Reserve, Trimbach Cuvée Frédéric-Émile offers tremendous value for $35.]
—HRISTO ZISOVSKI, AI FIORI

Canadian **Rieslings** are generally dry or off-dry, and of similar depth and complexity as Rieslings from the Pfalz [region of Germany]. . . . If there's a single winery that best represents what we do great in Canada, it's Cave Spring Cellars, which has some of the oldest vines, and is a stalwart for Riesling. Year in and year out, Cave Spring makes the broadest range of Riesling with the greatest consistency. . . . The winery making the very finest wine in Canada today is probably Stratus, whose high-tech, all-green winery is architecturally beautiful and a must-visit if you're in the Niagara area.
—STEVE BECKTA, BECKTA DINING & WINE AND PLAY FOOD & WINE

climates feature notes of lemon plus green apples and minerals.

Aging: Most Rieslings are best enjoyed young and fresh. However, because of their high acidity, better Rieslings have surprising aging potential, up to five or even ten years, and the very best can age for decades, evidencing notes of butter, caramel, or honey.

Producers: Australia (drier, fuller-bodied, with notes of lime and stones): Frankland Estate, Grosset, Jacob's Creek Barossa Valley Reserve, Kilikanoon, Knappstein, Lindeman's, Penfolds, Petaluma, Pewsey Vale, Wolf Blass, Yalumba Y Series; **Austria** (dry, medium-bodied, with notes of kaffir lime and lime leaf, kiwi, peach, and esp. minerals): Bründlmayer, Domäne Wachau, Emmerich Knoll (esp. Schütt), F. X. Pichler, Hiedler, Hirsch, **Hirtzberger**, Loimer, Nigl, **Prager**, Salomon, Schloss Gobelsburg, Wachau; **Canada:** **Cave Spring**, Inniskillin, Jackson-Triggs, **Stratus; Chile:** Cousiño-Macul; **France–Alsace** (drier, earthier, richer, fuller-bodied): Boxler, Deiss, **Helfrich**, Hugel, Lucien Albrecht, Mann, Ostertag, Pierre Sparr, Schlumberger, **Trimbach** (esp. Cuvée Frédéric Émile), Weinbach, **Zind-Humbrecht; Germany** (sweeter, lighter-bodied, with notes of kiwi, lime zest, slate): **Dönnhoff, Dr. L (value), Dr. Loosen, Egon Müller,** Emrich-Schönleber, Franz Kunstler, Gunderloch, Haag Brauneberger, **J. J. Prüm,** Keller, Knebel, Leitz, Müller-Catoir, Robert Weil, Schäfer-Fröhlich, Schlossgut Diel, Selbach-Oster, **St. Urbans-Hof,** Tesch, von Schubert; **New Zealand** (drier, fuller-bodied): Te Kairanga, Villa Maria; **U.S.–California** (fuller-bodied): Chateau St. Jean, Claiborne & Churchill, Loredona, Navarro, Smith-Madrone, Stony Hill, Trefethen; **Michigan:** Black Star Farms, Bowers Harbor, **Chateau Grand Traverse,** Left Foot Charley, Peninsula Cellars, Two Lads; **New York/Finger Lakes** (sweeter): **Dr. Konstantin Frank,** Fox Run, Hazlitt, Hermann J. Wiemer; **Oregon:** Willamette Valley; **Washington state** (sweeter): Chateau Ste. Michelle, Columbia Crest, Covey Run, Eroica, Hogue, Pacific Rim, Snoqualmie

Iconic examples: Alsace: Trimbach Clos Ste Hune, **U.S.: Eroica** (Washington state) or **Dr. Konstantin Frank** (New York)

The Rieslings below are listed in order of ripeness, from least ripe to ripest: Kabinett, Spätlese, Auslese, Beerenauslese, Eiswein, Trockenbeerenauslese.

RIESLING—KABINETT

[KAH-bee-NETT]

Countries: Australia, Austria, **Germany**

Color: white

Grapes: Riesling

Weight: light-bodied (with low alcohol)

Volume: moderate to loud

Dry/sweet: ranges from bone dry to off-dry

Acidity: high

Flavors: notes of apples (red and green), apricots, citrus, flowers, grapefruit, herbs, lemon, lime, minerals, nectarines, orange, peaches, pears, spices, stones, tangerine, vanilla

Texture: crisp, juicy, rich

Temperature: Serve cold, about 45 to 50 degrees.

Season: summer

Pairings: Asian cuisine, chicken, fish, Mexican cuisine, pork, seafood, vegetables

Producers: Germany: Dönnhoff, Dr. Loosen, Egon Müller, Fred Prinz, Fritz Haag, Gunderloch, J. J. Prüm, Künstler, Kurt Darting, Pierre Sparr, Robert Weil, Selbach-Oster

RIESLING—SPÄTLESE

[SHPAYT-lays-uh]

Countries: Australia, Austria, **Germany**

Color: white

Grapes: Riesling

Weight: light- to medium-bodied

Volume: moderate to loud

Dry/sweet: ranges from dry to **off-dry** to sweet

Acidity: high

Flavors: notes of apples, apricots, citrus, flowers, grapefruit, herbs, honey, **lime,** minerals, nectarines, orange, papaya, **peaches,** pears, pineapple, quince, smoke, spices, stones, tangerines, vanilla

Texture: creamy, juicy, rich, velvety

Temperature: Serve cold, about 45 to 50 degrees.

Pairings: cheese, crab, fruit, ham, pork, salads, scallops, spicy dishes, Thai cuisine, veal

Producers: Germany: Dönnhoff, **Dr. Loosen,** Eitelsbacher Karthauserhofberg, Fritz Haag, **Gunderloch, J. J. Prüm,** Leitz, Müller-Catoir, Robert Weil, Schlossgut Diel, Selbach-Oster, St. Urbans-Hof, Weinbach

RIESLING—AUSLESE

[OWZ-lays-uh]
Countries: Australia, Austria, Germany
Color: white
Grapes: Riesling
Weight: light- to medium-bodied
Volume: moderate to loud
Acidity: high
Dry/sweet: ranges from sweet to very sweet
Flavors: notes of apples (baked), apricots, caramel, cinnamon, citrus, flowers, **honey**, lime, melon, minerals, nuts, orange, papaya, passion fruit, peaches, pears, pineapple, spices, tangerine, vanilla
Texture: creamy, rich
Temperature: Serve cold, about 45 to 50 degrees.
Pairings: cheese (esp. rich), desserts, foie gras, fruit, ham, lobster, paté, sweet dishes
Producers: Germany: Dönnhoff, J. J. Prüm, Merkelbach, Selbach-Oster, St. Urbans-Hof

RIESLING—BEERENAUSLESE

[BAY-roon-OWZ-lays-uh]
Countries: Australia, Austria, Germany
Color: white
Grapes: Riesling
Weight: fuller-bodied (and low in alcohol)
Volume: moderate to loud
Dry/sweet: sweet to **very sweet**
Acidity: high
Flavors: notes of apples, apricots, citrus, honey, lime, minerals, papaya, peaches, pineapple, rose petals
Texture: honeyed, unctuous, viscous
Temperature: Serve cold, about 45 to 50 degrees.

Pairings: caramel desserts, cheese (esp. salty), desserts, foie gras, fruit, sweet dishes
Aging: Its sweetness allows it to be aged for as long as two or three decades.
Producers: Dr. Loosen, Kracher

RIESLING—EISWEIN

[ICE-vine]
See also ICE WINE.
Countries: Austria, **Germany**
Color: white
Grapes: Riesling
Weight: medium- to full-bodied (and low in alcohol)
Volume: moderate to loud
Dry/sweet: sweet to **very sweet**
Acidity: high
Flavors: aromatic dessert wine, with notes of apples, apricots, cinnamon, flowers, ginger, **honey**, **lemon**, lime, melon, minerals, papaya, passion fruit, peaches, pears, pineapple, rose petals, tangerines, tropical fruits
Texture: rich, unctuous, viscous

Sabato Sagaria of The Little Nell Compares Rieslings

When I look at Riesling, I look at the texture. In **Alsace** you are talking about a warmer climate, so you get a fatter, rounder wine with some weight. Those are more food-friendly than aperitif wines.

Germany kind of runs the gamut. It has some of the characteristics of Austria, some of Alsace, and even more fruit. It has tropical aromatics that jump out of the glass to you, where the others can be a little more refined. No other country in the world does Riesling like Germany. It is unique and specific to its climate.

If you want a glass of wine to wake up the palate, look to an **Austrian** or **Australian** Riesling; they are bright, zippy, and tend to be on the drier side. People think Riesling equals sweet, but here they get something dry, crisp, and refreshing that wakes up their palate.

Pacific Northwest Rieslings are a drier style—that is, a little of Austria and Australia mixed together.

In **Canada,** the only Riesling I have had is Riesling Ice Wine, and it was some of the best.

Austria is just starting to get expensive, but there are excellent **Rieslings** at half the price of Pichler, like Nigl.
—HRISTO ZISOVSKI, AI FIORI

I am down to only thirty-seven **Rieslings** on our list. I am a fanatic about Riesling. Every sommelier has the same problem. You tell the guests that what they are having would be great with a Riesling, and they reply, "I don't like sweet wine." That's cool, Riesling will be great. "But I don't like sweet wine." I have dry Riesling. "They are always sweet." So I now list Riesling under bone dry, dryish, off-dry, and sweet. It is the only category of wine that people come in with a super-preconceived notion, so I have to tease them: "You don't like sweet things with your food? I guess you have never had Coca-Cola with a hamburger; that would be terrible! I can't imagine why you would want sugar in your beverage!"
—ANDY MYERS, CITYZEN

I hate to say it because it is such a cliché, but my wife [a sommelier] and I drink a lot of **Riesling** at home. We drink Kabinett and taut Spätlese. I wish we had more Egon-Müller, but instead we have J. J. Prüm and Dönnhoff.
—ROBERT BOHR, COLICCHIO & SONS

Belinda Chang of The Modern on Riesling

Probably the reason "wine geeks" gravitate toward Riesling is that it is one of the few grape varieties that expresses very strongly where it has been grown and how it has been treated, whereas you can grow Chardonnay pretty much anywhere around the world and get a pretty similar product if you follow a few steps. Riesling certainly doesn't act that way. That is why everyone gets obsessed with **German** Riesling, learning about the intensity that it has in the Rheingau versus the floral and pretty feminine side it has in the Mosel and everything in between.

Then you find people drawn to **Austrian** Riesling because they do such an amazing ultra-dry style. With the Federspiel and Smaragd regulations in the Wachau, you get to see the really venerable examples of dry styles of Riesling.

It is really cool to see how **Australia, New Zealand,** and even the **U.S.** do it. I wouldn't say it is done super-successfully in California, but definitely in our cooler areas, like Oregon and Washington state, there are some really great examples. The Chateau Ste. Michelle/Dr. Loosen project shows that a serious producer in Germany thinks that Washington state is a great *terroir* for Riesling.

I have seen Riesling everywhere. I have seen it in **Argentina,** and for a long time they thought Torrontés was related [genetically]. I have had Riesling in **Spain,** which is super-weird—I thought, "That's not right." Albariño is better. The last one I discovered was Riesling in **Alsace.**

It is fun to experiment with Rieslings from all over the world. What can't you drink Riesling with? It doesn't fight with anything. We tried it with Cabernet-braised tripe and it worked. We tried it with all the obvious things, like soups, salads, and more delicate vegetable courses, and it filled in everywhere we needed or tried it.

Alsace Riesling can be funky, because it can be sweet or dry, depending on the producer. We know there is one end of the spectrum with **Zind-Humbrecht** and **Weinbach,** who are sort of famous, even notorious, as the latest harvesters in the region. So they are going for a richer, higher-alcohol, higher-sugar style, versus the ultraclassic paradigm in Alsace—**Trimbach** and **Kreydenweiss,** who would never let the slightest hint of sugar be perceived in their Rieslings.

Riesling is just one of those styles of wine that definitely rewards those who study it.

I love German **Riesling** from the Nahe and Mosel, which have been my favorite wines since I knew what fine wine was. When I refer to the Nahe, which is warmer, I am referring to my favorite producer, Dönnhoff. I adore it. I pour it by the glass now. The Nahe has finesse, a bitter edge, and structure in terms of lightness and body. The fruit has a little more breadth with the warmer climate. The Mosel has a more sprightly feel, with a peachy quality to it.

—ROXANE SHAFAEE-MOGHADAM, THE BREAKERS

There was a lot of wine tasting and learning about wine when I was in college. I was working in casual fine dining as a cook and server. My most exciting wine epiphany then was the first time I tasted an old German **Riesling**. As an Indian person, I can say this: every Indian person has a sweet tooth. As much as we like our spice, we like our sweetness. I always enjoyed young German Rieslings without realizing how serious they were. I had occasion to taste a very old wine, and I don't even remember the producer anymore. I remember the vineyard, because one of the peculiarities in the Mosel is that every wine bottle has the same painted label, a picture of a monk with a golden outline. The wine was absolutely mind-blowingly spectacular. It wasn't even a great vintage. It was more austere and drier than anything I had tried before. What really struck me was the minerality and how serious it was. Something sweet can be serious and intense.

—RAJ VAIDYA, DANIEL

A **Riesling** label that says Trockenbeerenauslese scares even me! Yet the wine itself is so delicious and cuddly.

—SABATO SAGARIA, THE LITTLE NELL

Temperature: Serve (very) cold, about 40 to 50 degrees.
Comparable: ICE WINE
Pairings: caramel desserts, cheese (esp. salty), desserts, foie gras, fruit, sweet dishes
Aging: Its sweetness allows it to be aged for as long as two or three decades.
Producers: Dr. Loosen, Schloss Wallhausen

RIESLING— TROCKENBEEREN- AUSLESE (AKA TBA)

[TRAWK-uhn-BAY-roon-OWZ-lays-uh]
Countries: Australia, Austria, Germany
Color: white
Grapes: Riesling

Weight: fuller-bodied (and low in alcohol)
Volume: loud
Dry/sweet: very sweet, with up to 30 percent residual sugar
Acidity: high
Flavors: notes of almonds, apricots, citrus, earth, golden raisins, grapefruit, honey, lemon, lime, lychee, mango, minerals, orange or orange peel, papaya, passion fruit, peaches, pears, pineapple, smoke, spices
Texture: dense, honeyed, syrupy

Temperature: Serve (very) cold, about 40 to 50 degrees.
Pairings: cheese (esp. salty, blue), desserts, foie gras, fruit, fruit desserts
Aging: Its sweetness allows it to be aged for as long as two or three decades.
Producers: Keller, Kracher, Robert Weil

RIOJA—RED

[ree-OH-hah]
See also TEMPRANILLO.
Country: Spain
Region: Rioja
Color: red (with a garnet hue)
Grapes: Tempranillo, often blended with Garnacha and other grapes
Weight: medium-bodied
Volume: moderate (older) to loud (younger)
Dry/sweet: dry
Acidity: low to medium
Tannin: medium to high (though soft)
Flavors: notes of **blackberries/ cassis**, **black cherries**, chocolate, cinnamon, cloves, coconut, coffee, **earth**, herbs, **leather**, lemon, mint, **plums**, raspberries, sage, smoke, **spices**, strawberries, tobacco, **vanilla** (esp. if aged on American oak), violets
Texture: elegant, rich, smooth
Temperature: Serve cool, about 60 to 65 degrees.
Comparable: California CABERNET SAUVIGNON
Season: autumn–winter
Pairings: chorizo, lamb,

The smoky grilled flavors of Peruvian-style grilled chicken work well with oak flavors. And if I get the fried plantains, I have to drink a traditional **Rioja**, such as a 1998 Bodegas Lan Rioja Gran Reserva. Traditional Riojas are typically aged in American oak, which imparts a coconut flavor that is magic with the tropical plantains.

—KATHRYN MORGAN, MS, CITRONELLE

Manchego cheese, pork, roasted red meats, stews, vegetables

Tip: Crianza is the youngest Rioja (released two years after the vintage), while a Reserva has been aged for twelve months on oak and two years in the bottle, and a Gran Reserva has been aged for twenty-four months on oak and three years in the bottle.

Aging: Rioja producers' careful aging before release means the wines are ready to drink upon release, but the best Rioja can continue to age in your cellar for years. Best recent vintages: 2009, 2008, 2007, 2006, 2005, 2004.

Producers: Allende, Artadi, Campo Viejo, Contino, Cune, El Cote de Rioja (value), **Finca**

I think of [oaked] **white Rioja** as a winter white wine, one that has some similarities texture-wise if not flavor-wise with other winter whites such as Gewürztraminer, a Marsanne/Roussanne blend, or an oaked Chardonnay.

—JILL ZIMORSKI, CAFÉ ATLÁNTICO

Allende, Lan, **LÓPEZ DE HEREDIA**, **Marqués de Cáceres**, Marqués de Murrieta, **Marqués de Riscal**, Montecillo, **MUGA**, Palacio Remondo, Remelluri, **Remírez de Ganuza**, Roda, San Vicente, **Sierra Cantabria**, Tobía

RIOJA—WHITE

Country: Spain
Region: Rioja
Color: white
Grapes: Viura (primarily), often blended with Garnacha Blanca

and/or Malvasia

Weight: ranges from lighter (esp. unoaked) to fuller-bodied (esp. oaked)

Volume: ranges from quiet (esp. modern style) to moderate (esp. traditional style)

Dry/sweet: dry

Acidity: low to medium

Flavors: notes of almonds, apples (esp. green), butter, **citrus**, custard, **flowers**, grapefruit, hazelnuts, herbs, honey, **lemon**, melon, minerals, orange, peaches, pears, pineapple, smoke, spices, toast, tropical fruits (esp. with Malvasia in the blend), vanilla

Texture: ranges from creamy and soft (esp. traditional) to crisp (esp. modern)

Temperature: Serve chilled, about 50 to 55 degrees.

Comparable: CHARDONNAY—OAKED

Season: winter

Pairings: chicken, fish, paella, pork, seafood, tapas

Tip: White Rioja is also known as Macabeo in some parts of Spain.

Aging: The best have excellent aging potential, as long as a decade or more.

Producers: Allende, Cune, **López de Heredia**, **Marqués de Murrietta**, Muga

RKATSITELI

[ar-kat-sit-TELL-ee]

Countries: Bulgaria, Georgia, U.S. (New York)

Color: white

Grapes: Rkatsiteli, often

blended with Mtsvane
Weight: light- to medium-bodied
Volume: moderate to moderate-plus
Dry/sweet: dry to off-dry
Acidity: high
Flavors: very aromatic, with notes of apples (esp. green), apricots, chamomile, **citrus**, flowers, grapefruit, herbs, honey, lemon, lime, lychees, mango, melon, minerals, peaches, pears, pineapple, spices, vanilla
Texture: crisp, refreshing, sometimes with a hint of spritz
Temperature: Serve cold, about 45 to 50 degrees.
Comparables: dry GEWÜRZTRAMINER, soft SAUVIGNON BLANC
Pairings: cheese (esp. goat), chicken, fish, oysters, shellfish, veal
Aging: Drink young and fresh.
Producers: Georgia: Tbilvinio Tsinandali; **U.S.–New York/ Finger Lakes:** Dr. Konstantin Frank

RODITIS
[roh-DEE-tees]
Country: Greece
Regions: Attica, Macedonia, Peloponnese (esp. Patras), Thessaly
Color: pink
Grapes: Roditis
Weight: light-bodied
Volume: moderate
Dry/sweet: dry
Acidity: high
Flavors: notes of apples, **citrus**, flowers, grapefruit, jasmine, lemon, lemon zest, melon (esp. cantaloupe), orange, peaches, pears, tropical fruits
Texture: elegant, zesty, sometimes with a hint of spritz
Temperature: Serve chilled, about 50 to 55 degrees.

Beyond Champagne and sparkling wine, **rosé** is probably my favorite style of wine, just for its flexibility. Whereas I tend to think of a Soter Rosé [from Oregon, which she pours by the glass] as more silky, lush, and feminine, **Spanish Rosados** across the board tend to be somewhat bolder in flavor and a little more showy.
—JILL ZIMORSKI, CAFÉ ATLÁNTICO

France's best-kept wine secret, the south-of-France appellation Costières de Nîmes, offers extraordinary value for **rosés** and reds at all price points.
—PETER BIRMINGHAM, POURTAL

Comparable: RETSINA
Pairings: cheese (esp. mild), chicken, fish, lemon, olive oil, salads, **seafood**
Producers: Achaia Clauss, Gaia Estate, Katogi & Strofilia, **Kouros**, Kourtakis

ROLLE
[rohl]
See VERMENTINO.

ROSADO
[roh-ZAH-doh]
Country: Spain
Regions: Navarra, Rioja
Color: rosé
Grapes: Garnacha, often blended with Tempranillo and/ or Viura
Weight: medium-bodied (and moderate in alcohol)
Volume: moderate
Dry/sweet: dry
Acidity: medium
Flavors: aromatic and fruity, with notes of apples (esp. red), cherries (esp. red), currants (esp. red), citrus, flowers, herbs, minerals, nuts, **raspberries**, spices, **strawberries**, tropical fruits
Texture: crisp, luscious
Temperature: Serve well chilled, about 50 degrees.
Season: spring–summer
Pairings: simple cold tapas, such as anchovies, cured meats, olives, sausages, and vegetables;

chicken, fish, lamb, paella, salads
Aging: Drink young and fresh.
Producers: Artazu Artazuri, Borsao (value), Cune, El Coto de Rioja, **Julian Chivite Gran Feudo**, López de Heredia, Marqués de Caceres, Martínez Bujanda, **Monte Toro, Muga**, Ochoa, Vega Sindoa, Viña Tondonia

ROSÉ
[roh-ZAY]
Countries: many, notably France (Loire, Provence, Rhône), Portugal, Spain (Navarra), U.S.
Color: typically red (ranging from pale pink to bright ruby or salmon in hue)
Grapes: varies widely
Weight: light- to medium-bodied
Volume: quiet to moderate
Dry/sweet: ranges from bone dry to off-dry
Acidity: medium to high
Tannin: low
Flavors: notes of apricots, **CHERRIES**, citrus, cranberries, flowers, grapefruit, **herbs**, minerals, peaches, **RASPBERRIES**, spices, **STRAWBERRIES**, tea, tropical fruits, watermelon, white pepper
Texture: ranges from crisp to smooth
Temperature: Serve most rosés well chilled, about 50 degrees.
Season: spring–summer
Pairings: charcuterie, fish, **picnics**, pork, salads, salmon,

Under-$15 tip: Just for sipping on a hot summer afternoon, I turn to Mulderbosch Cabernet Sauvignon **rosé** from South Africa [$13], which tastes like Bing cherries and strawberries in a glass.

—TODD THRASHER, RESTAURANT EVE

In the spring, you want delicate French **rosé** to paint the season. As things heat up, then you move into Italian rosé [known as rosato]. A friend observed that the French make rosé like white wine and the Italians make it like red wine. This is an interesting generalization that is helpful. The French style is delicate, pretty, aromatic, and low in tannin with lively acidity, especially in Provence. An Italian rosé from the south has a touch of bitterness and tannin that is so appetizing with food as well as refreshing.

—CAT SILIRIE, NO. 9 PARK

In general, nothing makes me salivate more than a glass of **rosé** on the table in the sun. Nothing is more of a no-brainer than rosé. You have red berry qualities that can accompany any meat. You also have acidity, freshness, and dry fruit crunch. I am talking about true rosé from Provence, Spain, and some areas of Loire Valley and Tavel in the Rhône. They are able to be sipped and are food-friendly. One of the most extraordinary rosés that is not from Bandol is Château d'Aqueria, a beautiful Tavel. It has the most pure essence of cherry you could imagine. It is brisk, crisp, clean, and loaded with wonderful Rhône herbaceousness. Not only is it inexpensive, acidic, and refreshing, but it is also a wonderful accompaniment to food.

—JUSTIN LEONE, BENNY'S CHOP HOUSE

sausages, shrimp, tuna, vegetable dishes

Tip: If you prefer lighter rosés, try Bandol and Cabernet d'Anjou. For heavier rosés, turn to Tavel and Spanish Rosado.

Aging: Drink young and fresh (within one or two years of the vintage).

Producers: Argentina: Susana Balbo "Crios"; **Canada:** Southbrook Vineyards; **Chile:** Montes "Cherub"; **France:** Château D'Esclans, Château Peyrassol, Domaine Ott (and its value-priced Les Domaniers), Domaine Sorin (esp. value-priced Côtes de Provence), Domaine Tempier, Sauvion, Tavel (Rhône Valley); **Greece:** Gaia Estate, Kir-Yanni; **Italy:** Alois Lageder,

Bardolino Chiaretto; **South Africa:** Mulderbosch; **Spain:** *see* ROSADO; **U.S.–California:** Belle Glos, Bonny Doon "Vin Gris de Cigare," Etude, SoloRosa, Tablas Creek, Uptick; **New York:** Hermann J. Wiemer, Shinn Estate, Wölffer; **Oregon:** Soter, Van Duzer

Iconic example: Tavel Rosé (made of Grenache and Cinsault) from the Rhône Valley

ROSSO DI MONTALCINO

[ROH-soh dee mon-tal-CHEE-noh]

Country: Italy
Region: Tuscany/Montalcino
Grapes: Sangiovese
Color: red
Weight: medium-bodied

Volume: moderate to moderately loud
Dry/sweet: dry
Acidity: medium-high to high
Tannin: medium
Flavors: fruity, with notes of **blackberries**, cedar, **cherries** (black and **red**), chocolate (esp. dark), coffee, **earth**, flowers, herbs, leather, mushrooms, olives, raspberries, red currants, red plums, smoke, spices, strawberries, tar, tobacco, vanilla, **violets**
Texture: fresh, silky, smooth, velvety
Temperature: Serve cool, about 60 to 65 degrees.
Pairings: cheese (esp. Parmesan, Pecorino), hamburgers, pasta with meat sauce, red meat, *salumi* (Italian cured meats)
Tips: Open at least a half-hour before serving. If you love Rosso and want to take it up a step, try an aged BRUNELLO DI MONTALCINO.
Aging: Ready to drink upon release.
Producers: Azienda Agricola Uccelliera, Biondi-Santi, Casanova di Neri, Conti Costanti, Pieri, Poggio di Sotto, Siro Pacenti, Talenti

ROTER VELTLINER

[ROH-ter VELT-lee-ner]

Country: Austria
Regions: Kamptal, Kremstal, Wagram
Color: white (with golden hues)
Grapes: Roter Veltliner
Weight: medium- to full-bodied (and high in alcohol)
Volume: moderate-plus to loud
Dry/sweet: dry
Acidity: high
Flavors: aromatic, with notes of bell peppers, cherries (esp. red),

cinnamon, citrus, earth, flowers, grass, herbs, honey, **lemon**, lime, **minerals**, mint, musk, peaches, raisins, **spices** (esp. white pepper)
Texture: rich
Temperature: Serve chilled, about 50 to 55 degrees.
Comparables: GRÜNER VELTLINER, SAUVIGNON BLANC
Pairings: appetizers, asparagus, chicken, fish, lobster, raw oysters, salads, shellfish, veal
Producers: Ecker, Leth, Setzer, Wimmer-Czerney (biodynamic)

ROUSSANNE

[roo-SAHN]
Countries: Australia; **FRANCE (RHÔNE VALLEY,** Savoie), U.S. (California, Washington state)
Color: white (pale in color, with yellow hues)
Grapes: Roussanne, often blended with Marsanne
Weight: full-bodied (and high in alcohol)
Volume: quiet to moderate
Dry/sweet: dry
Acidity: medium
Flavors: very aromatic, with notes of almonds, apples, **apricots**, chamomile, citrus, figs, **flowers** (esp. when young), **HERBS, honey, lemon, lime, melon, minerals,** nectarines, nuts (esp. with age), orange, **peaches, PEARS,** vanilla
Texture: creamy, crisp, lush, rich, silky
Temperature: Serve chilled, about 50 to 55 degrees.
Comparables: CHARDONNAY, CHÂTEAUNEUF-DU-PAPE–WHITE, white Crozes-Hermitage, HERMITAGE–WHITE, VIOGNIER
Pairings: cheese, chicken, fish, ham, lobster, pork, turkey,

vegetable dishes (esp. rich, e.g., winter squash)
Aging: Can age up to a decade.
Producers: Australia: Aeolia, d'Arenberg; **France–Rhône:** Beaucastel, Jaboulet, Jean-Luc Colombo, Yves Cuilleron; **U.S.–California:** Alban, Austin Hope, Bonny Doon, Copain, DeLille, Eberle, Qupé, Rubicon, Tablas Creek, Turley, Zaca Mesa; **Washington state:** McCrea

RUEDA

[roo-AY-duh]
See also VERDEJO.
Country: Spain
Region: Rueda
Color: white (with straw hues)
Grapes: Verdejo, often blended with Sauvignon Blanc or Viura
Weight: medium- to full-bodied
Volume: moderate
Dry/sweet: dry
Acidity: medium to high
Flavors: aromatic, with notes of almonds, apples (esp. green), apricots, black pepper, citrus, dried herbs, **flowers,** grapefruit, grass (esp. wines with more Sauvignon Blanc), honey, lemon, lime, minerals, nuts, peaches, pears, smoke, spices, toast, vanilla
Texture: crisp, fresh, juicy, smooth
Temperature: Serve cold, about 45 to 50 degrees.
Comparables: PINOT GRIGIO, SAUVIGNON BLANC
Pairings: appetizers, fish, salads, shellfish, vegetables
Aging: Drink young and fresh, within a year or two.
Producers: Basa, Castelo de Medina, Cuevas de Castilla, **Las Brisas,** Martinsancho, **Naia,** Shaya, Valdelapinta, Viñedos de Nieva

SAGRANTINO DI MONTEFALCO

[sah-grahn-TEE-noh dee mohn-tef-AHL-koh]
Country: ITALY
Region: Umbria
Color: red
Grapes: Sagrantino
Weight: full-bodied
Volume: loud
Dry/sweet: ranges from dry to sweet (as in sweet passito-style wines made from dried grapes)
Acidity: medium to high
Tannin: high (and dusty)
Flavors: notes of blackberries, **black cherries,** chocolate, cinnamon, cloves, dark chocolate, nutmeg, plums, **smoke,** tobacco, vanilla, violets
Texture: rich
Temperature: Serve cool, about 65 degrees.
Comparables: PETITE SIRAH, TEMPRANILLO
Pairings: aged cheeses, beef, duck, steak, lamb, pasta, pizza, roasts, *salumi* (Italian cured meats), sausages, stews, truffles (black), wild boar
Producers: Antonelli, Caprai, Colpetrone, Paolo Bea, Terre de' Trinci

SAINT-ÉMILION

[sahn tay-mee-LYAWN]
See also BORDEAUX–RED, CABERNET FRANC, MERLOT.
Country: France
Region: Bordeaux/Right Bank
Color: red
Grapes: Cabernet Franc, **Merlot**
Weight: medium- to full-bodied
Volume: moderate to loud
Dry/sweet: dry
Acidity: medium
Tannin: medium to high
Flavors: notes of blackberries, cedar, cherries (esp. cooked),

If you don't recognize the producer on a bottle of **Saint-Émilion**, which is a big region, don't worry—as long as it is a good vintage. Since 2005 was such a great vintage, a winemaker would have to be terrible to have made a bad wine that year. At $22, go try it!

—HRISTO ZISOVSKI, AI FIORI

chocolate (esp. older wines), coffee (esp. older wines), dried fruit, earth, flowers, leather, smoke, **spices**, strawberries (esp. cooked), truffles, vanilla
Texture: elegant, rich, round, smooth
Temperature: Serve slightly chilled, about 55 to 60 degrees.
Comparables: CABERNET FRANC, MERLOT
Pairings: beef, cheese, chicken, duck, lamb, mushrooms, ribs, salmon, squab
Aging: Serve most wines from a few years to a decade after the vintage. Better bottles should age five to ten years, and the best from fifteen to twenty-five years or longer. Best recent vintages: 2009, 2008, 2006, **2005**, 2000.
Iconic examples: Château Ausone or Château Cheval Blanc

SAINT-ESTÈPHE
[sahn tess-TEFF]
See BORDEAUX–RED.
Country: France
Region: Bordeaux/Left Bank/ Médoc
Iconic example: Cos d'Estournel

SAINT-JOSEPH
[sahn zho-SEFF]
See also SYRAH.
Country: France
Region: Rhône
Grapes: red: Syrah; white:

Marsanne, Roussanne
Tip: If you have HERMITAGE taste but not the budget, seek out Saint-Joseph for a value-priced alternative.
Aging: These good-value wines are typically meant to be drunk within a few years, although the best can age for as long as a decade.
Producers: B. Gripa, Chapoutier, Cuilleron, Dard & Ribo, E. Guigal, Jaboulet, **J. L. Chave**

SAINT-JULIEN
[sahn joo-lee-YENN]
See BORDEAUX–RED.
Country: France
Region: Bordeaux/Left Bank/ Médoc
Grapes: Cabernet Sauvignon (primarily)
Producers: Ducru-Beaucaillou, Léoville-Barton, Léoville–Las Cases

SANCERRE
[sawn-SAYR]
See also SAUVIGNON BLANC.
Country: France
Region: Loire Valley
Color: white
Grapes: Sauvignon Blanc
Weight: light- to medium-bodied
Volume: moderate to loud
Dry/sweet: dry
Acidity: medium-high to high
Flavors: aromatic, with notes of apples (esp. green), **CITRUS,**

I carry the 2007 Bernard Gripa **Saint-Joseph**, which is absolutely delicious. I have it by the half-bottle, which is perfect—but of course it's so good you always end up opening two!

—RAJ VAIDYA, DANIEL

earth, flint, flowers, **grapefruit, GRASS, HERBS,** lemon, melon, menthol, minerals, pears, smoke, steel, stones
Texture: crisp
Temperature: Serve very cold, about 45 degrees.
Comparables: POUILLY-FUMÉ, SAUVIGNON BLANC
Season: summer
Pairings: goat cheese, fish, lemon, oysters, salads, **shellfish,** tomatoes, trout
Aging: Drink young and fresh (within a year or two), although the best can age for five years.
Producers: Alphonse Mellot, Boulay, **Cotat Frères,** Domaine de la Perrière, **Domaine Vacheron,** Edmond Vatan, **François Cotat, Guy Saget, Henri Bourgeois, LUCIEN CROCHET,** Neveu, Pascal Cotat, **Pascal Jolivet,** Vincent Pinard

SANGIOVESE
[SAN-joh-VAY-zay]
See also BRUNELLO DI MONTALCINO, CHIANTI, SUPER TUSCAN WINES
Countries: Argentina, Chile, **ITALY (TUSCANY),** South Africa, U.S. (California, New York, Washington state)
Color: red
Grapes: Sangiovese, sometimes blended with Cabernet Sauvignon
Weight: medium- to full-bodied
Volume: moderate
Dry/sweet: very dry
Acidity: high
Tannin: medium to high
Flavors: notes of **anise,** bay leaf, blackberries, black currants/cassis, blueberries, **CHERRIES** (esp. younger wines), chocolate, coffee, cranberries, dark chocolate, **earth** (esp. older wines), **herbs, leather,** mocha,

mushrooms (esp. older wines), nuts, **PLUMS** (fresh and dried), raspberries, smoke, **spices**, **strawberries**, tea, **tobacco**, tomatoes, vanilla, violets
Texture: rich, smooth
Temperature: Serve cool, about 60 degrees.
Comparables: Brunello di Montalcino, Chianti, Super Tuscan Wines, Vino Nobile di Montepulciano
Season: winter
Pairings: beef, cheese (esp. Parmesan), chicken, herbs and herb-driven dishes, mushrooms, pasta, pizza, sausages, steak, **tomato-sauced dishes**, turkey, veal
Aging: Only the very best examples have a chance of lasting a decade.
Producers: Italy: Antinori Santa Cristina, Barone Ricasoli Castello di Brolio, Castello di Monsanto, Di Majo Norante, Fontodi, La Carraia, Marchesi de Frescobaldi, Ruffino, San Patrignano (*see also* Brunello di Montalcino, Chianti, Vino Nobile di Montepulciano); **U.S.–California:** Bonny Doon, Frey, Pride Mountain, Seghesio, Silverado; **New York:** Adirondack Winery; **Washington state:** Leonetti

SANTA BARBARA WINES
Country: U.S.
Region: California/Central Coast
Tip: After coming into the spotlight in the movie *Sideways,* wines from California's Central Coast have found an even wider following.
Producers: Au Bon Climat, Beckmen, Cambria, Fess Parker, Firestone, Foxen, Hartley-Ostini, Hitching Post, Qupé, Sanford, Silver, Zaca Mesa

SAPERAVI
[sa-per-AV-ee]
Country: Georgia
Color: red
Grapes: Saperavi
Weight: medium- to **full-bodied**
Volume: moderate to **loud**
Dry/sweet: dry to semi-sweet
Acidity: high
Tannin: medium to high
Flavors: notes of **blackberries**, black currants/cassis, blueberries, cedar (esp. oaked wines), chamomile, cherries, coffee, earth, flowers, **pepper**, pomegranate, prunes, smoke, spices, tea (herbal), vanilla (esp. oaked wines)
Texture: rich, rustic
Temperature: Serve cool, about 60 to 65 degrees.

Pairings: braised dishes, cheese, game, lamb, meats (esp. grilled), mushrooms, pork, steak, stews
Aging: Look for Mukuzani, which is aged for three or more years; Kindzmarauli, aged for two years; and Saperavi, aged for one year. The best of these wines can be aged for decades.

SAUTERNES
[soh-TAYRN]
Country: France
Region: Bordeaux
Color: white
Grapes: Sauvignon Blanc, **SÉMILLON**, Muscadelle
Weight: full-bodied
Volume: loud
Dry/sweet: sweet to very sweet
Acidity: medium to high

Flavors: aromatic, with notes of **apricots**, butterscotch, caramel, coconut, cream, dried fruit, **HONEY**, mango, melon, nectarines, nuts (esp. older wines), orange, **peaches**, **pineapple**, spices, toast (esp. older wines), tropical fruits, vanilla

Texture: creamy, luscious, rich

Temperature: Serve cold to very cold, about 40 to 50 degrees.

Comparables: BARSAC, MONBAZILLAC

Season: autumn–winter

Pairings: BLUE CHEESE (ESP. ROQUEFORT), desserts based on custard and/or fruit, foie gras, ham

Tip: When pairing Sauternes with spicy, savory foods (e.g., Indian or Thai dishes), look for lighter-bodied versions—second-label or lesser-vintage Sauternes can work well for this purpose. Look for Sauternes from Château de Fargues, which is made by the owners of Château d'Yquem but sells for a fraction of the price.

Aging: The best can age for decades. Best recent vintages: 2007, **2005**, 2003, **2001**, 1999, 1998, 1997.

Producers: Premiers Crus: **CLIMENS**, Clos Haut-Peyraguey, **Coutet**, de Rayne-Vigneau, Guiraud, Lafaurie-Peyraguey, La Tour Blanche, Rabaud-Promis, Rieussec, Sigalas-Rabaud, Suduiraut; **Other:** de Fargues, Gillette, **Raymond-Lafon**

Iconic example (Premier Cru Supérieur): **CHÂTEAU D'YQUEM**

SAUVIGNON BLANC

[soh-vee-NYAWN blahnk]

See also FUMÉ BLANC.

Countries: Australia, Chile,

France (Bordeaux, Loire Valley), Italy, **NEW ZEALAND**, South Africa, U.S. (California, Washington state)

Color: white (pale in color, with yellow or greenish hues)

Grapes: Sauvignon Blanc, sometimes blended with Sémillon

Weight: light- to **medium-bodied** (from lightest to fullest in body: France → South Africa → New Zealand → California)

Volume: moderate to **loud**

Dry/sweet: dry

Acidity: moderately high to very high

Flavors: aromatic, with notes of asparagus, **citrus**, figs, gooseberries, **grapefruit**, **grass**, green apples, green bell peppers, guava, **herbs**, **LEMON**, **lime**, melon, minerals, nectarines, passion fruit, peaches, pineapple, slate, smoke, steel, stones, tropical fruits

Flavors: cool climate: citrus, grass, lime; **warm climate:** grapefruit, melon, passion fruit

Texture: Ranges from crisp (unoaked) to rounded (oaked); refreshing

Temperature: Serve cold, about 45 to 50 degrees.

Comparables: BORDEAUX–WHITE, FUMÉ BLANC, GRAVES, POUILLY-FUMÉ, SANCERRE

Season: spring–summer

Pairings: cheese (esp. fresh and/or goat), chicken, fish, green vegetables, salads, shellfish, turkey, veal, vegetarian cuisine

Aging: Drink young and fresh, within a few years; better oaked versions may be able to handle limited aging.

Producers: Argentina: Norton; **Australia:** Philip Shaw, Shaw + Smith, The Lane; **Austria:** Tement; **Chile:** Casa Lapostolle, Concha y Toro, Cono Sur, Gran Araucano, Leyda, Los Vascos, Terra Noble, Veramonte, Ventisquero; **France:** *see* BORDEAUX–WHITE; **Greece:** Gerovassiliou; **Italy:** Alois Lageder (Alto Adige), Edi Kante, Venica & Venica; **New Zealand** (notes of cilantro, gooseberries, grapefruit, jalapeño, lime, melon, passion fruit): Astrolabe, **Brancott**, **CLOUDY BAY**, **Craggy Range**, Drylands, Huia, **Kim Crawford**, Kumeu River, Momo, Nobilo, Palliser Estate, Saint Clair, Seresin, The Jibe, Villa Maria,

Styles of **Sauvignon Blanc** vary: **Napa** and **Sonoma** may put a little oak on their wine, which makes it richer. Lieff just released a Sauvignon Blanc that is very impressive and affordable. North of there, in the **Russian River**, you get a cleaner style, as you would find in **Bordeaux**. My favorite vineyard is Moraga in **Los Angeles** [Bel Air], which makes very impressive Sauvignon Blanc with a little age on it. It is very fragrant, very clean and pure. Like Bordeaux, it doesn't have any oak on it. If you tasted them side by side, they would be very close. When you put your nose into a glass of **New Zealand** Sauvignon Blanc, you smell gooseberry, which is very typical of the style.

—STEPHANE COLLING, SAN YSIDRO RANCH

Under-$15 tip: **Sancerre** is famous for **Sauvignon Blanc**, but if you go next door to **Quincy** or **Reuilly** or **Pouilly-Fumé**, it is even less expensive.

—HRISTO ZISOVSKI, AI FIORI

Wairau River, Whitehaven;
South Africa (notes of cilantro,
jalapeño): **Mulderbosch**, Neil
Ellis, Paul Cluver, Springfield,
Steenberg (value), Thelema;
U.S.–California: Beringer, Bogle,
Cakebread, Calistoga Estate,
Chateau Souverain, Diogenese,
Duckhorn, Ferrari-Carano, Fetzer,
Flora Springs, Frog's Leap,
Gainey Vineyard, Geyser Peak,
Hall, Honig, Kunde, Martinelli,
Matanzas Creek, Meridian, **Merry
Edwards**, Moraga, Murphy-
Goode, Rochioli, Scholium
Project, Selene, Spottswoode,
St. Supéry; **Virginia**: Linden,
Pearmund; **Washington state**:
Chateau Ste. Michelle, Columbia
Crest
Iconic example: Cloudy Bay
Sauvignon Blanc

SAUVIGNON GRIS
[soh-vee-NYAWN GREE]
Countries: Chile, France
(Bordeaux), Germany, New
Zealand, Uruguay
Color: white
Grapes: Sauvignon Gris (aka
Sauvignon Rosé)
Weight: medium-bodied
Volume: quiet to moderate
Dry/sweet: dry
Acidity: medium to high
Flavors: aromatic and fruity,
with notes of **citrus, flowers**,
grapefruit, herbs, **lemon**, lime,
mango, **orange**, peaches, pears,
spices, tropical fruits, vanilla
Texture: creamy, crisp, rich,
round
Temperature: Serve cold, about
45 to 50 degrees.
Pairings: appetizers, chicken,
fish, pork, shellfish, sushi
Aging: Drink young and fresh.
Producers: Chile: Casa Silva,
Cousiño-Macul

SAVENNIÈRES
[sah-venn-YAIR]
Country: France
Region: Loire Valley
Color: white
Grapes: Chenin Blanc
Weight: full-bodied
Volume: loud
Dry/sweet: dry (primarily,
although some semi-sweet and
sweet wines are produced)
Acidity: high
Flavors: notes of apples,
beeswax, candied citrus, chalk,
citrus, earth, **flowers**, green
apples, herbs, **honey**, lemon,
melon, **MINERALS**, nuts, **pears**,
pineapple, quince, salt, spices,
white pepper
Texture: lively, rich, viscous
Temperature: Serve chilled,
about 50 to 55 degrees.
Comparables: CHENIN BLANC,
VOUVRAY
Pairings: asparagus, chicken,
cream, fish, goat cheese,
mushrooms, pork, salmon,
scallops, shellfish, turkey, veal,
white meat
Aging: The acidity helps the
ageability of these intense white
wines, which should be aged for
about five years. The very best can
last for decades.
Producers: Chamboureau,
Château d'Epiré, Clos du
Papillon, **Domaine de la
Soucherie**, Domaine des
Baumard, Domaine du Closel,

NICOLAS JOLY'S CLOS DE
LA COULÉE DE SERRANT
(biodynamic)
Iconic example: Nicolas Joly's
Clos de la Coulée de Serrant
(biodynamic)

SCHEUREBE
[SHOY-ray-beh]
Country: Germany
Color: white
Grapes: Scheurebe
Weight: medium- to full-bodied
(with moderate alcohol)
Volume: loud
Dry/sweet: ranges from dry to
off-dry to sweet
Acidity: medium-high to high
Flavors: very aromatic, fruity,
with notes of apricots, **black
currants/cassis, blackberries**,
citrus, flowers, **grapefruit**, herbs,
honey, lime, mango, passion
fruit, peaches, spices, tangerine,
tropical fruits
Texture: rich, ripe
Temperature: Serve chilled,
about 50 to 55 degrees.
Comparables: RIESLING,
SILVANER/SYLVANER
Pairings: rich, spicy, or sweet
dishes featuring butter, fruit,
pork, shellfish, vanilla
Aging: Drink young and fresh.
Producers: Alois Kracher
(dessert Scheurebe), Dürkheimer
Fronhof, Kurt Darting,
Lingenfelder, **Müller-Catoir**,
Schlossgut Diel

I am a big fan of **Scheurebe**. It does very strange things to me; it
is more effective than Champagne! It has an effect on people that
I just can't put my finger on, but it is fantastic and I love it. There
is something fun and exotic in the fruit. I am a fan of Schlossgut
Diel out of the Nahe, which is a great place for the grape because
of the tropical fruit flavors so typical of the region. There are
also some excellent ones coming out of the region of Franken that
are dry.
—RAJ VAIDYA, DANIEL

SECOND-LABEL WINES

A winemaker often sells wines at different price points and under different labels. One dramatic example: a bottle of Château Pétrus can sell for $1,000, but a wine under the label Christian Moueix from the same winery sells for closer to $10 a bottle. Those at the lower price point are often termed "second-label wines," and many of them offer impressive quality for the price. Here are some examples.

PRODUCER (REGION)	LOWER-PRICED LABEL
Alvaro Palacios (Priorat)	Les Terrasses
Bennett Lane (Napa)	Turn 4
Catena (Argentina)	Alamos
Chalone (Napa)	Echelon
Château de Beaucastel (Rhône)	Coudoulet de Beaucastel (outside Châteauneuf-du-Pape)
Château Haut-Brion (Bordeaux)	Château Bahans Haut-Brion, Le Clarence de Haut-Brion
Château Lafite-Rothschild (Bordeaux)	Les Carruades de Lafite
Château Lafleur (Bordeaux)	Les Pensées de Lafleur
Château Latour (Bordeaux)	Les Forts de Latour
Château Margaux (Bordeaux)	Le Pavillon Rouge du Château Margaux
Château Mouton Rothschild (Bordeaux)	Le Petit Mouton de Mouton Rothschild
Château Palmer (Bordeaux)	Alter Ego de Palmer
Château Pétrus (Bordeaux)	Christian Moueix
Château Rayas (Rhône)	Pignan
Cheval Blanc (Bordeaux)	Le Petit Cheval
Copain (California/Anderson Valley)	Tous Ensemble
Cos d'Estournel (St. Estéphe)	Les Pagodes de Cos
Craggy Range (New Zealand)	Wild Rock
Duckhorn (Napa)	Decoy
Etude (California/Napa)	Fortitude
Evharis (Greece)	Ilaros
Fairview (South Africa)	Goats Do Roam
Far Niente (California/Napa)	Nickel & Nickel
Harlan Estate (Napa)	The Maiden
J. Lohr (California/Central Coast)	Cypress
King Estate (Oregon)	Next
Larkmead (California/Santa Barbara)	Meadowlark
Léoville–Las Cases (Bordeaux)	Clos du Marquis
Livio Felluga (Italy)	Esperto
Lynch-Bages (Bordeaux)	Haut-Bages Averous
Mondavi (Napa)	Woodbridge
Movia (Slovenia)	Movia Villa Marija
Opus One (Napa)	Overture
Ornellaia (Italy)	Le Serre Nuove, Le Volte
Ott (Provence)	Les Domaniers
Peay (Sonoma)	Cep
Salon (Champagne)	Delamotte
Sassicaia (Italy)	Guidalberto
Spottswoode (Napa)	Lyndenhurst
Stag's Leap (Napa)	Hawk Crest
Susana Balbo (Argentina)	Crios
Talbott (California/Central Coast)	Kali Hart
Woodward Canyon (Washington state)	Nelms Road

STEPHANE COLLING

If you want to get a value on a Burgundy, go to your wine shop, ask about the big guys, and then ask for their **second or third label**. It's made by the same winemaker who makes the main estate wine, and they put the same effort into this one. If you want a Domaine Leflaive [the most famous estate in] Puligny-Montrachet, you are going to spend $60 to $80 for a bottle. If you look for the Burgundy Blanc or Mâcon Viré-Clessé, you will spend $25 to $30 and have the same quality Domaine Leflaive has because Anne-Claude [Leflaive] pays the same attention as she does to the Puligny. The dedication of the winemakers doesn't change. This is a way to educate yourself: by drinking the second- or third-label wine, you will understand what the winemaker is trying to translate into the wine. When you finally taste the top wine, it will be easy to understand and pinpoint the difference.

—STEPHANE COLLING, SAN YSIDRO RANCH

SEKT

[zaykt]

Countries: Austria, **Germany**, Italy (Alto Adige)
Grapes: Riesling (frequently)
Weight: light-bodied
Volume: quiet to moderate
Dry/sweet: off-dry
Acidity: medium
Flavors: fruity, with notes of apples, citrus, flowers, pears, tropical fruits
Texture: refreshing, **sparkling**
Temperature: Serve very cold, about 40 to 45 degrees.
Pairings: appetizers
Tip: SEKT is the German name for a fruity, sometimes sweet sparkling wine. We've recommended the $3.99 Schloss Biebrich to those looking for an under-$5 bottle.

Aging: Drink young and fresh, within a year or two.
Producers: Arunda (both Brut and Rosé Brut), Schloss Biebrich (value), Szigeti, Wegeler

SÉMILLON OR SEMILLON

[say-mee-YOHN in France, SEM-ill-ahn in Australia]

Countries: **Australia**, Chile, **France** (Bordeaux/Graves), Israel, New Zealand, South Africa, U.S. (California, Washington state)

Color: white (pale with golden hues)
Grapes: Sémillon, sometimes blended with Chardonnay or Sauvignon Blanc
Weight: medium-full- to very full-bodied (and high in alcohol)
Volume: quiet to moderate
Dry/sweet: dry to very sweet
Acidity: low
Flavors: notes of apples, APRICOTS, bananas, beeswax, citrus, custard, **figs**, grass, herbs, HONEY, **lemon**, lime, mango,

Szigeti is a great producer out of Austria. It's run by two brothers who specialize in **sekt** made from totally crazy grape varieties, and it's really cool to see your favorite wine grapes expressed as sparkling wines. They make sparkling wines from Riesling, Grüner Veltliner, Blaufränkisch, and Cabernet Franc, among others, via the *méthode traditionelle*, and they are all totally delicious.

—BELINDA CHANG, THE MODERN

MELON, nectarines, nuts (esp. in older wines), orange, PEACHES, pears, PINEAPPLE, spices, toast (esp. older wines), VANILLA, wax
Texture: creamy, rich, viscous
Temperature: Serve chilled, about 50 to 55 degrees.
Pairings: dry wines: butter-based sauces, chicken, fish, pork, turkey; **sweet wines:** *see* pairings for SAUTERNES.
Tip: The famed Sauternes Château d'Yquem is typically made of 80 percent Sémillon.
Aging: Drink dry wines young and fresh; sweet wines can handle aging of five to ten years or more.
Producers: Australia: De Bortoli, Lindemans, McWilliams, Penfolds, Peter Lehmann, Torbreck, Tyrrell's; **New Zealand:** Millton, Pyramid Valley; **U.S.– California:** Beringer, Clos du Val, St. Supéry; **Washington state:** Chateau Ste. Michelle, L'Ecole No. 41

SHERRY— AMONTILLADO
[ah-mon-tee-YAH-doh]
Country: Spain
Region: Andalucía/Jerez
Color: white (with amber hues)
Grapes: Palomino (primarily)
Weight: light- to medium-bodied (with 16 to 18 percent alcohol)
Volume: moderate
Dry/sweet: dry to off-dry
Acidity: medium
Flavors: notes of apricots, caramel, chestnuts, cream, figs, HAZELNUTS, honey, **nuts**, prunes, raisins, smoke, spices, toast, toffee, vanilla, **walnuts**, yeast
Texture: crisp, rich, smooth
Temperature: Serve chilled, about 50 to 55 degrees.
Pairings: almonds, artichokes,

cheeses (esp. Manchego), chicken, chorizo, ham, **hazelnuts**, olives, smoked fish, soups, tapas
Aging: Amontillado is aged fino sherry. Drink fresh (ideally within two to three years of release) and within a few days after opening.
Producers: Alvear, Antonio Barbadilla, Croft, Delgado Zuleta, Fernando de Castilla Antique, Hidalgo Napoleon, **Lustau Almacenista**, Osborne Solera, Pedro Romero, Sandeman, Savory & James, Valdespino

SHERRY—CREAM
Country: Spain
Region: Andalucía/Jerez
Color: white (with mahogany hues)
Grapes: Palomino (primarily), Pedro Ximénez
Weight: full-bodied
Volume: moderate to loud
Dry/sweet: sweet to very sweet
Acidity: medium
Flavors: notes of candied fruits, chocolate, cinnamon, clove, coffee, figs, nuts, orange, **raisins**, **spices**, toffee
Texture: round, smooth, velvety
Temperature: Serve anywhere from cool to slightly chilled. Can be served over ice with (or without) a slice of orange before a meal.
Pairings: blue and/or firm cheeses, cookies, desserts, foie

gras, fresh fruit, ice cream, nuts
Tip: Cream sherry is a blend of sweet and dry sherries. As a fully oxidized sherry, an unopened bottle will remain drinkable for several years.
Producers: Argueso, Croft, **Lustau**, Osborne, **Sandeman**

SHERRY—FINO
[FEE-noh]
Country: Spain
Region: Andalucía/Jerez or Puerto de Santa Maria
Color: white (with golden or straw hues)
Grapes: Palomino (primarily)
Weight: light-bodied (yet, as a fortified wine, high in alcohol, around 15 to 17 percent)
Volume: moderate
Dry/sweet: very dry to dry
Acidity: medium to high
Flavors: noticeable alcohol, with notes of **almonds**, apples, citrus, lemon, minerals, **nuts**, pears, sea breeze, yeast
Texture: crisp, fresh
Temperature: Serve cold, about 45 to 50 degrees.
Pairings: almonds, anchovies, cheese (e.g., Gruyère, Manchego), fried foods, ham, olives, shellfish (esp. shrimp), tapas, walnuts
Tip: Consider buying sherry in half-bottles, which you're more likely to drink at once.
Aging: Serve very fresh (within a few months of release), and well

Sherry isn't typically as sweet as port, so it offers more food-pairing versatility. We serve chef George Mendes's mussel soup with an Amontillado sherry that is the perfect match for it. His monkfish goes beautifully with a Manzanilla sherry. And at dessert we pair a 1982 PX Reserva sherry with our pear tart. El Maestro Sierra is one of my favorite producers because they bottle their sherry in half-bottles and date them. Freshness is key to sherry, so it helps to make sure they're enjoyed young and fresh.
—HEATHER LAISKONIS, ALDEA

Ron Miller of Solera on Mastering Sherry

Sherry is a versatile wine, and its many expressions pair well with different types of food. It can be an "acquired taste," yet once you are hooked the range of flavors and nuance are seductive. . . . I encourage every one of our guests to try sherry, because it is the perfect wine with tapas.

The following seven sherries (pictured above) are listed from lightest to fullest in body:

1. **Manzanilla** (Hidalgo "La Gitana," Sanlucar de Barrameda). This is one of the lightest and most ethereal sherries. It is nearly clear, like water, but it's clean and fresh-tasting, with hints of yeast and a slightly tangy and even bitter almond flavor. It is aged near the sea, and you can taste briny [sea salt] notes that make it an ideal pairing with seafood.

Pairings: almonds, ham (esp. jamón ibérico), olives, seafood

2. **Fino** (Tío Pepe Muy Fino, González Byass, Jerez). Tío Pepe is one of the most recognizable names in sherry. This fino is typically fuller in body than a manzanilla. It's deeper in color, with more notes of almonds, citrus, and yeast.

Pairings: almonds, ham (esp. jamón ibérico), olives, seafood, simple meat dishes

3. **Amontillado** (Hidalgo Amontillado Napoleon, Sanlucar de Barrameda). This is an aged fino made via the solera system [which blends multiple vintages]. One could think of it as a youthful wine in its adolescent phase. While it has some of the same fino components—including lightness and brininess—the further aging process adds notes of caramel and nuts and perhaps honey, even though it is bone dry and not at all sweet.

Pairings: chicken, ham, sheep's milk cheese, (lighter) stews

4. **Dry Oloroso** (Almacenista Pata de Gallina, González Obregón, Lustau Jerez). A sherry's fermentation is indefinite. This dry oloroso is fortified to an even greater strength. The oxidation makes the flavor even richer, more concentrated and intense. The light caramel color might lead you to think the wine is sweet, but this sherry is bone dry with a rich, round texture and the flavor of walnuts. You'll also find some mushroomlike notes that make it a beautiful pairing with fuller-flavored meat or mushroom dishes or sauces.

Pairings: richer, heartier foods, such as beef, duck, mushrooms, pork, scallops

5. **Sweet Oloroso** (Matusalem Oloroso Dulce Muy Viejo, González Byass, Jerez). This wine has an Oloroso base to which sweet Pedro Ximénez (PX) has been added. Here the PX grapes are "raisined" (dried), pressed, and fermented, which creates a rich, viscous wine with less alcohol but more sugar. You get more flavors of burnt sugar, caramel, and cocoa in this sherry. Sweet oloroso is perfect for rich cheeses, such as Parmesan or aged Mahon or any kind of Manchego, aged or fresh. It's also perfect drizzled over vanilla ice cream.

Pairings: rich cheeses, vanilla ice cream

6. **Lighter PX** (Don PX 2004 Pedro Ximénez, Toro Albala, Córdoba). This sherry is not made in Jerez via the solera system. It is called a Montilla, as the grapes are dried, pressed, and then vinified in Montilla-Moriles. This is an **añada,** or vintage, wine. It's made of 100 percent PX grapes but is a lighter-style wine than the Venerable PX, with lighter flavors of orange blossoms, dates, and figs. It pairs beautifully with many kinds of cheeses, including cow, sheep, and goat's milk cheeses. After dinner in Spain, they serve a combination of nuts and dried fruits—such as almonds, hazelnuts, and prunes—called *musica*, and this PX is fantastic with that.

Pairings: cheese, Crema Catalana, dried fruits and nuts

7. **Venerable PX** ("Venerable" Very Rare Pedro Ximénez, Domecq, Jerez). This is a very dark-colored, very sweet and intense, syrupy sherry with flavors of caramel, dates, prunes, raisins, and nuts. It's definitely one of those wines you might have in place of dessert. If you like something sweet at the end of the night, a *copita* with a 1- to 1½-ounce serving of Venerable is enough!

Pairings: enjoy by itself

chilled. Once the bottle is open, fino sherry is best consumed that day. It can last at most a few days in the refrigerator.

Producers: Croft, Garvey San Patricio, **Lustau**, Osborne, Pedro Domecq La Ina, Savory & James, Tío Pepe, Valdespino Inocente

SHERRY — MANZANILLA

[man-zan-EE-yah]
Country: Spain
Region: Sanlucar de Barrameda
Color: white (almost clear, or with straw hues)
Grapes: Palomino (primarily)
Weight: light-bodied (yet as a fortified wine it is high in alcohol, about 15–16 percent)
Volume: quiet to moderate
Dry/sweet: dry
Acidity: **medium** to high
Flavors: noticeable alcohol and notes of **almonds, apples**, brine, chamomile, green olives, herbs, minerals, **nuts**, olives, **sea breeze, yeast**
Texture: crisp, delicate
Temperature: Serve cold, about 45 to 50 degrees.
Season: spring–summer
Pairings: almonds (esp. Spanish Marcona), anchovies, **fish**, gazpacho, Manchego cheese, olives, sardines, **shellfish (esp. shrimp)**, tapas
Tip: Consider buying sherry in half-bottles, which you're more likely to drink at once.
Aging: Serve very fresh (within a few months of release) and cold. Once the bottle is open, manzanilla sherry is best consumed that day. It can last at most a few days in the refrigerator.

Manzanilla sherry is what I drink regularly.
—RON MILLER, SOLERA

Producers: Hidalgo "La Gitana," La Guita, Lustau, Osborne, Pedro Romero, Sandeman

SHERRY — OLOROSO

[oh-loh-ROH-soh]
Country: Spain
Region: Andalucía/Jerez
Color: white (with amber or mahogany hues)
Grapes: Palomino (primarily)
Weight: medium- to full-bodied (around 18–20 percent alcohol)
Volume: moderate (esp. drier versions) to loud (esp. sweeter versions)
Dry/sweet: ranges from dry to sweet
Acidity: medium
Flavors: aromatic, with notes of almonds, brown or burnt sugar, caramel, chocolate, cocoa, dates, **figs**, maple syrup, molasses, mushrooms, **NUTS**, orange zest, **RAISINS**, smoke, spices, toast, toffee, vanilla, **walnuts**
Texture: rich, round, silky, smooth, soft
Temperature: Opinions vary. Serve anywhere from cool to cold.
Pairings: dry wines: beef, creamy soups, lamb, mushrooms, nuts, olives, venison; **sweet wines:** cheeses (blue, hard, and/or salty), desserts (esp. with dried fruit and/or nuts), flan, foie gras, fresh fruit, nuts
Tip: Because oloroso sherry is fully oxidized, an open bottle will last longer than a fino or manzanilla—as long as a few weeks. An unopened bottle will remain drinkable for several years.
Producers: Barbadillo, Croft, González Byass, Hidalgo Especial, Lustau, Osborne, Sandeman

SHERRY — PALO CORTADO

[PAH-loh kor-TAH-doh]
Country: Spain
Region: Jerez
Color: white (with amber or mahogany hues)
Grapes: **PALOMINO**, Pedro Ximénez
Weight: medium- to full-bodied (with about 19 percent alcohol)
Volume: moderate
Dry/sweet: dry to off-dry
Acidity: **medium** to high
Flavors: notes of almonds, butterscotch, caramel, chocolate, citrus, coffee, dates, earth, hazelnuts, honey, molasses, **NUTS**, orange peel, pine nuts, prunes, raisins, smoke, tea, toffee, walnuts
Texture: rich, round, smooth
Temperature: Serve cool to chilled, about 50 to 60 degrees.
Pairings: almonds, cheeses (esp. Manchego), game birds, meats (fresh and cured), nuts (esp. hazelnuts), olives, seafood, tapas
Tip: This rare style of sherry is difficult to make and hard to come by. Palo Cortado is born a fino but transforms into an amontillado and then matures into a Palo Cortado. Because it is already oxidized, an open bottle will last longer than a fino or manzanilla—as long as a few weeks.
Producers: Antonio Barbadillo, Equipo Navazos La Bota de Palo Cortado, González Byass, Hidalgo Jerez Cortado, **Lustau** (Almacenista or Peninsula)

SHERRY — PEDRO XIMÉNEZ (PX)

[PAY-droh hee-MEN-ess]
Country: Spain

Region: Montilla–Moriles
Color: white (with dark brown or blackish hues)
Grapes: Palomino, Pedro Ximénez
Weight: very full-bodied
Volume: loud to very loud
Dry/sweet: very sweet
Acidity: low to medium
Flavors: notes of black cherries, brown sugar, **caramel**, cherries (cooked), **chocolate (dark)**, cinnamon, coffee, dates, espresso, **figs**, grapes, **molasses**, nuts, plums (fresh and **DRIED**), praline, **RAISINS**, spices, toast, toffee
Texture: rich, round, smooth, syrupy, unctuous, velvety
Temperature: Serve cool to chilled, about 50 to 60 degrees.
Pairings: blue cheese, **chocolate** (esp. dark), **desserts**, figs, ice cream, nuts, orange-flavored desserts, pecan pie
Tip: Serve PX sherry poured over vanilla ice cream.
Aging: As a fully oxidized sherry, an unopened bottle will remain drinkable for several years. Unlike other wines, sherry should be stored upright.
Producers: Croft, **Domecq Venerable**, Gran Barquero, González Byass, **Lustau (San Emilio)**, Osborne, Sandeman, Toro Albala

SHIRAZ

[shih-RAHZ]
See also SYRAH.
Country: AUSTRALIA, South Africa
Color: red (with ruby hues)
Grapes: Syrah, often blended with Grenache and Mourvèdre or with Cabernet Sauvignon
Weight: medium- to very full-bodied (and high in alcohol)

Volume: loud
Dry/sweet: dry to slightly off-dry
Acidity: medium
Tannin: medium
Flavors: fruity, with notes of **BLACKBERRIES** (esp. cooked), black cherries, black currants/cassis, **black pepper**, cedar, cherries, cloves, coffee, cream, **dark chocolate**, earth, eucalyptus, herbs, **jam**, leather, licorice, meat, mocha, **plums**, prunes (esp. older wines), **raspberries, smoke**, SPICES, tar, tobacco, vanilla (esp. oaked versions)
Texture: **rich**, ripe, velvety
Temperature: Serve cool, about 60 to 65 degrees.
Comparable: SYRAH
Pairings: barbecued, roasted, and smoked meats, including beef, game, lamb, pork; cheese
Aging: While its fruitiness can be enjoyed young, the best Shiraz also benefits from aging up to a decade or longer.
Producers: Australia: Banrock Station, Clarendon Hills, **d'Arenberg**, Hardys, Henschke Hill of Grace, Hill of

Content, Jacob's Creek, Margan, McPherson, **PENFOLDS**, Peter Lehmann, Rosemount Estate (Diamond Label), Strong Arms (value), Tim Adams, Wolf Blass, Wynns, Yalumba; **India:** Sula Vineyards; **South Africa:** Boekenhoutskloof, Brampton, Fairview, Solms, Vergelegen
Iconic example: Penfolds Grange (Australia)

SHIRAZ—SPARKLING

Country: Australia
Color: red
Grapes: Syrah
Weight: medium- to full-bodied
Volume: loud
Dry/sweet: dry to semi-sweet
Acidity: low to medium
Tannin: medium to high
Flavors: notes of **blackberries**, black cherries, **black currants/cassis, black pepper**, blueberries, **chocolate (esp. dark)**, earth, licorice, plums, raspberries, spices, strawberries
Texture: sparkling
Temperature: Serve chilled, about 50 to 55 degrees.

It is funny that more people don't realize that **Shiraz** is Syrah. You would have a hard time tasting the Mollydooker [from Australia's McLaren Vale] and the Jaboulet Crozes-Hermitage [in France's Rhône] side by side and believing they are the same grape. As much as I want to demystify the names of grapes, I am almost grateful that Shiraz implies a vastly different wine than Syrah from the northern Rhône.
—DANA FARNER, CUT

Under-$15 tip: One of my favorite things to make at home is pizza, for which I usually keep a few bottles of Hill of Content **Shiraz** on hand.
—TODD THRASHER, RESTAURANT EVE

I like **sparkling Shiraz** in the right context. If you are at a rugby game and don't want to drink beer, it is fun. And I really like sparkling Shiraz with Peking duck—it is brilliant!
—BELINDA CHANG, THE MODERN

Silvaner from [Franken in Germany] is amazing. Silvaner historically was more important than Riesling here, and I can see why. On the best sites, it is more expressive of the mineral character.

—RAJ VAIDYA, DANIEL

Comparable: BRACHETTO D'ACQUI (which is fruitier and sweeter)
Pairings: brunch buffets, Peking or roast duck, roast turkey (including Thanksgiving dinner)
Aging: Drink young and fresh.
Producers: Black Chook, Bleasdale The Red Brute, Burra Creek Princess Royal, Majella, Paringa, Rumball, Trevor Jones, Woop Woop

SILVANER/SYLVANER

[sill-VAH-nerr]
Countries: Austria, France (Alsace), Germany (Franken, Nahe), Italy (Alto Adige), U.S. (California)
Color: white
Grapes: Silvaner (Germany)/ Sylvaner (France)
Weight: light- to medium-bodied
Volume: quiet
Dry/sweet: dry to off-dry
Acidity: medium-high to high
Flavors: fruity, with notes of apples, apricots, earth, grass, lemon, lime, melon, **minerals**, nuts, **peaches**, **pears**, pineapple, smoke, spice
Texture: crisp, refreshing, smooth, soft
Temperature: Serve cold, about 45 to 50 degrees.
Comparable: PINOT GRIS
Pairings: appetizers, charcuterie, chicken, choucroute, fish, oysters, pork, quiche, salads, shellfish, tarte flambé

Tip: Drink young and fresh.
Producers: France–Alsace: Charles Schleret, Domaine Ostertag; **Germany–Franken:** Hans Wirsching; **Nahe:** Hahnmühle; **Italy–Alto Adige:** Abbazia di Novacella, Pacherhof; **U.S.–California:** Rancho Sisquoc

SOAVE

[soh-AH-veh]
Country: Italy
Region: Veneto
Color: white
Grapes: Garganega (primarily), blended with Chardonnay, Pinot Blanc, or Trebbiano
Weight: light- (Soave) to medium-bodied (Soave Classico) (and lower in alcohol)
Volume: very quiet to quiet
Dry/sweet: dry
Acidity: medium to **high**
Flavors: notes of **almonds**, **apples**, citrus, **flowers**, ginger, green apples, **herbs**, honey, **lemon**, **minerals**, nectarines, **nuts**, peaches, **pears**, **spices**, with a gentle lemon finish
Texture: crisp, rich, smooth
Temperature: Serve cold,

about 45 to 50 degrees.
Comparables: CHARDONNAY, PINOT BIANCO
Season: summer
Pairings: basil, chicken, fish, pasta, pesto, polenta with gorgonzola, risotto, shellfish, vegetables
Tip: Soave means "smooth." The best examples come from the Soave Classico region.
Aging: Drink young and fresh.
Producers: Anselmi (for non-traditional Soave), Balestri Valda, Bertani, Bolla (popular), Cantina del Castello, Ca' Rugate, Fratelli Zeni, Gini, Guerrieri Rizzardi, **Inama**, **Masi** (value), Monte Tondo, **PIEROPAN** (esp. Soave Classico), **Pra**, Suavia
Iconic examples: Anselmi, Pieropan

SOUTH AFRICAN WINES

Grapes: red: Cabernet Sauvignon, Merlot, **PINOTAGE**, Pinot Noir, Shiraz/Syrah; **white:** Chardonnay, **CHENIN BLANC** (aka Steen), Colombard, Sauvignon Blanc
Tip: South Africa is the oldest producer of wine in the New World. To learn more, visit www .wosa.co.za or www.sawis.co.za.
Producers: Backsberg, Boekenhoutskloof, Brampton, Buitenverwachting, Cape

There's a little wine store called Enoteca in Calistoga, and I'll ask the owner, Margaux [Singleton], "What's new and under $20?" She always pulls out lovely wines from smaller producers and distributors—including a lovely **Soave** with floral notes and great acidity. It's a little viscous and refreshing on the palate, and an ideal pairing for the charcuterie and cheese we like to have for dinner. I think one of the reasons Soave is making a comeback is because it's so versatile with food—including salads, shellfish, and pasta.

—JULIA MORETTI, AD HOC

Sauvignon Blanc is perhaps the most accessible **South African wine** for beginners. It's not too expensive or complex—just simple deliciousness. Flavor-wise, it's not as overt as New Zealand, nor as reserved as Loire Valley examples—just a juicy, happy-filled glass of wine. You can find great examples from Paul Cluver or Springfield, and don't overlook the brilliant Ashbourne Sandstone, a low-alcohol blend from Hamilton Russell. Two of my favorite reds are the Kanonkop Pinotage and the Meerlust Rubicon, which is a Bordeaux-style blend. The best South African Syrah I've tasted was from the small but impressive producer Mullineux, and just brilliant. I'm also keeping an eye on Adi Badenhorst, who is the ultimate winemaking rebel: After working as a winemaker for some of the biggest names in Stellenbosch, he left for the no-man's-land of Swartland, where he is resurrecting long-forgotten ancient vineyards to make natural wines and also a sherry-styled wine. New releases of South Africa's famed Vin de Constance are pretty delightful sweet wines that go with anything orange and even stand up to chocolate—but I'm still waiting to taste a bottle from the Napoleonic era.

—CHRISTOPHER BATES, HOTEL FAUCHÈRE

In 2002 I was exposed to **South African wines**, especially Mulderbosch Sauvignon Blanc. That wine made me smile on the inside, and I found it very special. The wine had really low alcohol, searingly high acid, and a unique nose. It was distinct from any other Sauvignon Blanc I've ever had and was very precise. I remember exactly where I was and what I was eating at the time: I was at Rancho Pinot Grill in Scottsdale, Arizona, having the squid salad with preserved Meyer lemon, chicory, and Italian parsley. [Co-owner] Tom Kaufman served the Mulderbosch with it, and I went bonkers!

—JESSE RODRIGUEZ, ADDISON AT THE GRAND DEL MAR

South Africa is a really hot zone for innovation and great value. I love the wines of Rustenberg, which have been around for a while. Take their top-of-the-line Bordeaux-style blend called John X. Merriman. It is their flagship wine, made out of Bordeaux varieties aged in new French wood. You can get it retail for $25 a bottle, and it will stand up to Bordeaux two to three times the price. It is the function of the opening of the country to outside investment, the relatively cheap price of land, and the definitely cheap price of labor that makes South Africa one of the most competitive winemaking countries in the world. [Vilafonte winemaker] Zelma Long is making some higher-end reds in South Africa right now that are very, very good. Chenin Blanc is great in South Africa. It was a traditional "bag in the box" varietal for the longest time, but there is both dry and sweet Chenin Blanc coming out that can be profound, rivaling any of the best Loire Valley wines.

—MICHAEL FLYNN, THE MANSION ON TURTLE CREEK

Point, Clos Malverne, Constantia Utsig, Delheim, De Trafford, Fairview, Flagstone, Fleur du Cap, Glen Carlou (Chardonnay), Grangehurst, **HAMILTON RUSSELL**, Haute-Cabriere, Jordan, **KANONKOP** (Pinotage), Klein Constantia Vin de Constance, Meerlust, **MULDERBOSCH**, Neil Ellis, **Paul Cluver** (Sauvignon Blanc), Raats, Rudera, Rupert & Rothschild, Rustenberg, Rust en Vrede, Sadie Family, Sebeka, **Solms**, Spice Route, **Springfield**, Steenberg, Stellenbosch, **THELEMA**, **VERGELEGEN**, Villiera

Iconic example: Vin de Constance from Constantia

SOUTH AMERICAN WINES

See ARGENTINE WINES, BRAZILIAN WINES, CHILEAN WINES, URUGUAYAN WINES.

SPANISH WINES

See also ALBARIÑO, PRIORAT, RIBERA DEL DUERO, RIOJA, SHERRY, TEMPRANILLO, TINTA DE TORO.

Aging: Wines labeled Joven (which are young, light-bodied, and fruity) should be drunk within twelve months. Wines labeled Crianza (indicating that the wine has received at least the minimum aging required by law) should be drunk within a year or two. Wines labeled Reserva (indicating longer aging) can be aged even longer.

Producers: Bodegas Fariña, Conde de Valdemar, Cune, Faustino, Finca Sandoval, Hidalgo, **López de Heredia**, Lustau, Marqués de Cáceres, Marqués de Murrieta, Martin Codax, Muga, Numanthia-Termes, Pedro Romero, Ribas de

Wine drinking in **Spain** is very regional. In the region of Jerez, people drink sherry. In Catalonia or Penedès, they drink cava. In Galicia, they drink Albariño and blended wines like Roera Blanco. In San Sebastián, they drink Txakoli and sparkling cider. In Madrid, they drink both white and red wine. In Barcelona, they drink cava plus red wine with dinner. I tried to order a manzanilla [sherry] in Barcelona once, and they brought me a cup of tea—which is how I learned that *manzanilla* means chamomile in Spanish.

—RON MILLER, SOLERA

Spain has been coming along very well with white wines. I love López de Heredia, which makes beautiful whites. You can find amazing vintages from 1985 or 1989 that are very mature whites and an amazing value for the price.

—STEPHANE COLLING, SAN YSIDRO RANCH

I am excited about the Montsant region in **Spain**. The wines are known in Spain and Europe and fit the profile of a big, rich, chewy red. It is similar to Cabernet Sauvignon or Shiraz and a great [value-priced] alternative to other big red wines.

—JESSE RODRIGUEZ, ADDISON AT THE GRAND DEL MAR

Under-$15 tips: Among **Spanish wines**, there are great values. The farther off the beaten path they are, the more value is there. At home I have my house wines. I also have the house wines for when my dad is here, wines I can drink with him—and not cringe like I do when he fills the glass all the way to the rim with Vega Sicilia [Spain's most expensive wine]. I keep on hand La Ermita, which is a Petit Verdot/ Tempranillo blend. It is $12, and I buy it by the case.

—SABATO SAGARIA, THE LITTLE NELL

Spain is still hot because it is still the source of so many great bargains. I love the wines of Mariano García, who was the winemaker for Vega Sicilia for thirty years before leaving a few years ago to begin projects with his sons Alberto and Eduardo in Ribera del Duero. Among their wines they have the [Bodegas] Mauro, right outside the Ribera del Duero appellation called Sardon del Duero. It's a Tempranillo-based red aged in French barriques [barrels] that is just amazing. It is somewhat polished and very international in style . . . Toro has so much going on at all price levels. We are about to hold a dinner for Numanthia, which is one of Toro's best estates and certainly the most expensive on some levels. They are relatively new, and I am curious how they are able to produce such values there.

—MICHAEL FLYNN, THE MANSION ON TURTLE CREEK

Cabrera, Tondonia, Torres, **Vega Sicilia**, Vega Sindoa, Viña Mayor, Viñedos de Nieva
Iconic example: Vega Sicilia "Unico"

SPARKLING WINES

See also CAVA, CHAMPAGNE, CRÉMANT, PROSECCO, SEKT.
Countries: Virtually all wine-making countries make sparkling wines.
Color: white
Grapes: varies
Weight: light- to full-bodied
Volume: quiet to moderate
Dry/sweet: dry to off-dry
Acidity: medium to high
Flavors: notes of **apples**, caramel, citrus, **lemon**, minerals, **pears**, spices, **toast**, vanilla, yeast
Texture: creamy, effervescent, foamy
Temperature: Serve very cold, about 40 to 45 degrees.
Pairings: Varies by wine; often appetizers, egg dishes, fried and/ or salty foods, sushi
Tip: After being opened, all sparkling wines begin to lose their bubbles, so it's best to drink them as soon as possible. To store an open bottle of bubbly, use a special Champagne stopper. The cap we use at home has a rubber seal, with metal arms that clamp down over the neck of the bottle.
Producers: Australia: Banrock Station, Croser, Domaine Chandon; **England:** Nyetimber; **France:** *see* listings for CHAMPAGNE, CRÉMANT; **Italy:** **Bellavista**, Ca' del Bosco (tip: In Italy's Franciacorta DOC, sparkling wines are made in the traditional method used to make Champagne); **New Zealand:** Cloudy Bay Pelorus, Lindauer;

Sparkling wine is probably the only thing you'll always find in my refrigerator. There may not be mustard or water or juice or milk or bread or Häagen-Dazs ice cream, but there is always sparkling wine. In my refrigerator right now? I have some good bottles. I have a Pierre Peters 1999 and a bottle of Solace rosé that is some pretty delicious stuff. I also have a crazy **Crémant de Loire** that is a blend of Cabernet Franc, Chenin Blanc, and Chardonnay—it's a nutty bottle. The technology is there, so you are seeing great sparkling all over the world. Consider any sparkling **Crémant** from the great producers all over France—whether Blanc de Loire, d'Alsace, or de Jura. I love **cava** from Spain—or **Franciacorta** from Italy, if you want to throw down a few more bucks.... Bruna Giacosa said to her dad [famed Piedmont winemaker Bruno Giacosa] one day, "I don't understand, Father—why don't we make sparkling wine?" So now you can find Giacosa Spumante Extra Brut [made from Pinot Nero grapes], which is really good.... Iron Horse Russian Cuvée has always been an iconic sparkling wine, but it is also a sentimental favorite. I love the story behind the wine [which was created for the Reagan-Gorbachev summit meetings that helped end the Cold War], since the Russians were part of the reason it was made this way, because they like a sweeter style.... Any person from any walk of life can spend any amount you want to and get a solid or even life-changing bottle of sparkling wine.

—BELINDA CHANG, THE MODERN

Try Domaine Carneros for **sparkling wine.** Start with the Carneros Vintage Brut, which is a simpler-style sparkling wine [retailing for $26 a bottle], then move up to the Champagne-style Le Rêve [which retails for $85 a bottle].

—STEPHANE COLLING, SAN YSIDRO RANCH

If Social Services saw the inside of our refrigerator, they would probably take our children away—because it's a million bottles of cava and one bottle of organic milk! We love **sparkling wine.** We especially love pink sparklers, like pink cava. Anime Pink [from Italy] is also very fun, and we even have Iron Horse Wedding Cuvée, which was served at Nixon's daughter's wedding.

—INEZ RIBUSTELLO, ON THE SQUARE

South Africa: Graham Beck; **Spain:** *see* CAVA; **U.S.–California:** Domaine Carneros, **Domaine Chandon**, Gloria Ferrer, **Iron Horse**, J Vineyard, Mumm Napa, Piper Sonoma, **Roederer Estate**, Scharffenberger, **Schramsberg**; **Michigan:** L. Mawby; **New Mexico:** Gruet; **New York:** Dr. Konstantin Frank, Wölffer; **Oregon:** Argyle, Soter Beacon Hill; **Virginia:** Thibaut-Janisson; **Washington state:** Domaine Ste. Michelle

SPARKLING WINES— BLANC DE BLANCS

Grapes: Chardonnay
Producers: France: *see* CHAMPAGNE–BLANC DE BLANCS; **U.S.–California:** Domaine Carneros, Gloria Ferrer, Iron Horse, Schramsberg

SPARKLING WINES— BLANC DE NOIRS

Grapes: Pinot Meunier, **Pinot Noir**
Producers: France: *see* CHAMPAGNE–BLANC DE NOIRS; **U.S.–California:** Domaine Chandon, Gloria Ferrer, Iron Horse Wedding Cuvée, Schramsberg

SPARKLING WINES—ROSÉ

Grapes: varies—often Chardonnay, Pinot Noir
Dry/sweet: dry to off-dry
Flavors: notes of apple, brioche, **cherries**, cinnamon, citrus, figs, flowers, lemon, minerals, orange, peaches, **raspberries**, roses, **strawberries**, vanilla, watermelon
Texture: sparkling; creamy
Temperature: Serve very cold, about 40 to 45 degrees.
Pairings: barbecue, chilies,

I love the way that **spring** changes the wine list. All of a sudden you bring in wine that matches bitter, light, cleaner produce. In the spring, I have a lot of Grüner Veltliner, and the Sauvignon Blanc will be very light and unoaked from New Zealand or France. Torrontés will show up on the wine list in both the spring and summer, because it has both acidity and a really pretty floral element that shows off food well.

—EMILY WINES, MS, FIFTH FLOOR

duck, ham, lobster, mushrooms, salmon, steak, tuna, turkey, venison
Producers: South Africa: Graham Beck; **U.S.–California:** Domaine Carneros, Domaine Chandon, Iron Horse, J, Roederer Estate, Schramsberg; **New Mexico:** Gruet; **New York:** Wölffer

SPARKLING WINES— SWEET

See ASTI, BRACHETTO D'ACQUI, BUGEY, ICE WINE–SPARKLING, MOSCATO D'ASTI.

SPÄTBURGUNDER

[shpat-bur-GOON-der]
See PINOT NOIR.

SPRING WINES

See also BARBERA, BEAUJOLAIS, CABERNET FRANC, CHARDONNAY– UNOAKED, CHENIN BLANC, GEWÜRZTRAMINER, GREEK WINES, GRÜNER VELTLINER, MOSCATO D'ASTI, MUSCADET, RIESLING, ROSÉ, SAUVIGNON BLANC, TORRONTÉS, VOUVRAY.

STEEN

[steen]
See CHENIN BLANC.

SUMMER WINES

See also ALBARIÑO, ARNEIS, BEAUJOLAIS, CAVA, CHABLIS, CHENIN BLANC, DOLCETTO, FALANGHINA, FIANO, GREEK WINES, GRÜNER VELTLINER, LAMBRUSCO, LOIRE WINES, PINOT GRIGIO/PINOT GRIS, PROSECCO, RIESLING, ROSÉ, SANCERRE, SAUVIGNON BLANC, TORRONTÉS, TXAKOLI, VINHO VERDE, VOUVRAY.

SUPER TUSCAN WINES (AKA IGT TOSCANA)

High-quality Tuscan wines that do not adhere to Italy's classic wine laws.
Country: Italy
Region: Tuscany
Color: red
Grapes: often a blend of red grapes, e.g., traditional Sangiovese with non-traditional Cabernet Sauvignon and/or Merlot
Weight: medium- to **full-bodied**
Volume: loud
Dry/sweet: dry
Tannin: medium to high

Flavors: notes of blackberries, black cherries, black currants/ cassis, black pepper, chocolate (esp. dark), coffee, earth, herbs, leather, licorice, mocha, plums, raspberries, **spices, tar, vanilla,** violets
Texture: rich, silky, smooth, velvety
Temperature: Serve cool, about 60 to 65 degrees.
Pairings: cheese (esp. Parmesan or strong), game, pasta with meat sauce, red meats (beef, lamb, venison), stews, wild boar
Tip: Indicazione Geografica Tipica (IGT) signifies a typical regional wine.
Aging: Age for five years to a decade before opening. Best recent vintages: 2008, 2007, 2006, 2004, 2003.
Producers: Antinori (e.g., the 2001 Solaia), Castello Banfi, Fabrizio Bianchi, Fonterutoli, Masseto, Montevertine, **Ornellaia,** Petra, **SASSICAIA,** Tignanello
Iconic example: Sassicaia, a blend of Cabernet Sauvignon and Cabernet Franc

Summer is when you find the sweeter produce like corn and stone fruits. This is when I will bring in oaked Sauvignon Blanc or California Sauvignon Blanc that has lots of melon flavors.

—EMILY WINES, MS, FIFTH FLOOR

When **warm weather** hits, it's time to think about aperitif alternatives. Get white port to replace the old gin and tonic with lemon. Bored with the same old Kir Royal? Try mixing Aperol, Prosecco, and an orange spiral for a Spritz. Red-wine drinking has never been more popular, so try a chilled quality Lambrusco from Medici Ermete or Lini 1910 for authentic taste with artisan *salumi* [Italian cured meats].

—PETER BIRMINGHAM, POURTAL

I don't necessarily go lighter with my reds to pair with grilled steaks in the **summer,** but I definitely go colder—even below cellar temp. Serve reds out of the fridge around 45 degrees, and the heat of the alcohol and tannin are tamped down. The aromatics suffer a bit, but with a big Cabernet, Zin, or Malbec, it's not so much about the aromas.

—DAVID LYNCH, QUINCE

SUSTAINABLE WINE/ GRAPE PRODUCERS

See also BIODYNAMIC WINES, ORGANIC WINES.

Tip: In brief, sustainable winemaking involves limiting a winery's carbon footprint in the vineyard. Requirements for certification vary. For example, Oregon Certified Sustainable Wine (OCSW) indicates that a winery has practiced responsible agriculture and responsible winemaking and has received third-party certification. All producers below are either practicing or certified sustainable, and represent a token sample of the growing number of such producers.

Producers: Austria: Schloss Gobelsburg; **New Zealand:** Catalina Sounds; **South Africa:** Uva Mira; **U.S.–California:** Concannon, Etude; **Oregon:** Chehalem, Cristom, Serene, Sokol Blosser, Soter, WillaKenzie; **Washington state:** Woodward Canyon

Bonus: Yellow + Blue is one of the leading wine importers committed to environmentally responsible production and packaging.

SWEET RIESLINGS

See also RIESLING.

Dry → sweet: RIESLING–KABINETT (some are off-dry); RIESLING–SPÄTLESE (off-dry to sweet); RIESLING–AUSLESE, RIESLING–BEERENAUSLESE, and RIESLING–EISWEIN (sweet to very sweet); RIESLING–TROCKENBEERENAUSLESE (very sweet)

Tip: Not all Rieslings are sweet (esp. RIESLING–KABINETT and some SPÄTLESE)! To help consumers, the International

Riesling Foundation developed its own four-category sweetness scale and participating wineries indicate on the label whether that Riesling is dry, medium-dry, medium-sweet, or sweet.

SWISS WINES

Grapes: red: Blauburgunder (Pinot Noir), Cornalin, Merlot; **white:** Amigne, **CHASSELAS**, Petite Arvine

Importer: Neil Rosenthal

SYLVANER/SILVANER

See SILVANER/SYLVANER.

SYRAH

[see-RAH]
See also SHIRAZ.

Countries: Argentina, **Australia** (*see* SHIRAZ), Chile, **France (SOUTHERN RHÔNE)**, Italy (Piedmont, Sicily), Portugal, South Africa, Spain, **U.S. (California, Washington state)**

Color: red (with dark blue/dark purple hues)

Grapes: Syrah

Weight: full- to very full-bodied (and moderate to **high** in alcohol)

Volume: moderate to loud

Dry/sweet: very dry (esp. Rhône) to dry

Acidity: medium-high

Tannin: medium to high

Flavors: fruity, with notes of bacon, **BLACKBERRIES**, black currants/cassis, **BLACK PEPPER**, blueberries, cedar, cherries, chocolate, earth, floral, game, **herbs**, jam, leather, licorice, **meat**, minerals, mint, olives, plums, **raspberries**, rosemary, **smoke**, **SPICES**, tar, tobacco, violets, white pepper

Flavors: cool climate: bacon, herbs, prunes; **warm climate:** baking spices, eucalyptus, plums

Texture: rich, smooth, soft, velvety

Temperature: Serve cool, about 60 to 65 degrees.

Comparables: fruitier CABERNET SAUVIGNON, CARMENÈRE, CHÂTEAUNEUF-DU-PAPE, CORNAS, CÔTE-RÔTIE, CÔTES DU RHÔNE,

Taste a Sine Qua Non [$150+], one of the most coveted **Syrahs** in California, against a bottle of Vinho Cellars' outstanding Syrah from Santa Barbara [$40]. I would put the latter up against the Sine Qua Non any day of the week. Both wines are great. But it becomes clear that you don't have to chase after the trophy wines to enjoy a nice bottle of wine.

—MARK MENDOZA, SONA

There is such great **Syrah** coming out of California, in many cases at half the price of a comparable California Cabernet, that you would think Syrah would be the next great thing—and for some reason it isn't yet. We have lots of artisanal producers like Pax Cellars, Anthill Farms, Hyde de Villaine, and DuMol, and they are all a hard sell. I don't understand why. You have wines that are lavishly rich in fruit, that can stand up to lots of barrel aging, that have a very definitive flavor profile that ranges from smoked meats to black pepper to black fruits like plum, black currant, black raspberry—you would think the Cabernet drinkers would think this is the greatest thing since sliced bread! I haven't seen it yet. It is a lack of understanding of what Syrah is, because these are world-class wines.

—MICHAEL FLYNN, THE MANSION ON TURTLE CREEK

The grape that I really try to champion is **Syrah**. Because of the smoke, spice, and meat in the wine, it is a great thing to drink with steak, because they enhance each other. What Syrah has over Cabernet and Merlot is a little higher natural acidity. Most people are looking for Shiraz [Syrah made in Australia], so the Rhône [its native region in France] suffers. The northern Rhône has some really beautiful Old World wines, but they are not wildly collected. Robert Parker does give it some attention, but for some reason they don't go for crazy prices at auctions, so the collectors don't get super-excited about them. The people who want a trophy wine on the table typically go for Burgundy and Bordeaux. For the most part, northern Rhône wines fit into the category of "dirtier" wines, so when I describe them I use descriptors of smoke and smoked meat, to the point that I describe it as tasting like salami. Guests are thrilled when they have it! Yet we have two softer Syrahs on the list. The Jasmin Côte-Rôtie is a beautiful, softer, floral northern Rhône wine. It is very drinkable. It is easy to take an adventuresome New World wine drinker to that wine, and they love it. The Cuilleron St.-Joseph "Les Serines" is also soft, juicy, and yummy.
—DANA FARNER, CUT

CROZES-HERMITAGE, HERMITAGE, MALBEC, PINOTAGE, SAINT-JOSEPH, SHIRAZ, ZINFANDEL
Pairings: beef, black-pepper sauces, cheese, game, lamb, pork, venison
Tip: Syrah aged in American oak may smell minty-sweet, while Syrah aged in French oak often has toasty notes.
Aging: Allow a year or two of aging at minimum, while the best can age for a decade or two, or longer.
Producers: Australia: *see* SHIRAZ; **Canada:** Southbrook; **France:** *see* CORNAS, CÔTE-RÔTIE, HERMITAGE; **New Zealand:** Craggy Range; **South Africa:** *see* SHIRAZ; **U.S.–California:** Alban, Anthill Farms, Bonterra, Cline, Clos du Bois, Copain, DuMol, Edmunds St. John, Edna Valley, Fess Parker, Geyser Peak, Hyde de Villaine, Ojai, Qupé, Ridge, Rosenblum, Sine Qua Non, Stags' Leap, Taz, Vinho Cellars, Wind Gap, Zaca Mesa; **Michigan:** Domaine Berrien; **Washington state** (with

flavors of ripe fruit and notes of smoke and spice): Chateau Ste. Michelle, Columbia Crest, Gramercy Cellars, Waters

TANNAT
[tah-NOT]
Countries: Australia, France (Basque), Greece, Uruguay, U.S. (California)
Color: red (and blackish in hue)
Grapes: Tannat, sometimes blended with Cabernet Franc or Cabernet Sauvignon (as in Madiran)
Weight: medium- to full-bodied
Volume: very loud
Dry/sweet: ranges from dry to sweet (as in Alcyone dessert wine)

If a guest typically enjoys Cabernet Sauvignon with steak but says, "Surprise me with a good red I haven't had before," I might suggest a Greek **Tannat** wine. I have a bottle of 2006 Alpha Estate Alpha 1 Tannat on my list for $150.
—ROGER DAGORN, MS, PORTER HOUSE NEW YORK

Acidity: high to very high
Tannin: very high
Flavors: notes of **blackberries**, **black cherries**, black licorice, **black plums**, cassis, chocolate, coffee, earth, herbs, jam, leather, prunes, raspberries, smoke, spices, vanilla
Texture: rich, smooth
Temperature: Serve cool, about 60 degrees.
Comparables: BAROLO, CABERNET SAUVIGNON, ZINFANDEL
Season: winter
Pairings: beef, hard cheeses, lamb, pasta with rich meat sauce, sausages, stews
Tip: Be sure to give dry Tannat plenty of time to breathe before serving—from several hours to several days. Don't miss Alcyone, a bewitching Tannat-based sweet dessert wine from Uruguay that is a perfect pairing for chocolate.
Aging: Time will help to round out the strong tannins in Tannat wines, which can age for years, even a decade or more.
Producers: France (louder): *see* MADIRAN (which is Tannat-based); **Greece:** Alpha One; **Uruguay** (slightly quieter, fruitier): Bouza, Carrau, Castel Pujol, Dante Irurtia, Don Adelio, **Hector Stagnari**; **U.S.–California:** Tablas Creek

TANNIC WINES
Tip: Many health studies point out that red wine is rich in antioxidants such as resveratrol, which is also found in blueberries—especially tannic wines made by prolonged contact with the tannin-rich skins. Some of the most tannic wines are BARBARESCO, BAROLO, BORDEAUX–RED, CABERNET SAUVIGNON, CAHORS, MADIRAN, MALBEC,

MERITAGE, PETITE SIRAH, SHIRAZ, and TANNAT.

Timing: Be sure to give very tannic wines ample time (from hours to days!) to "breathe" before serving, which can mellow them.

TAURASI

[tau-RAH-zee]
Country: Italy
Region: Campania/Taurasi
Color: red
Grapes: primarily Aglianico
Weight: full-bodied
Volume: moderately loud (older) to loud (esp. young)
Dry/sweet: dry
Acidity: medium to high
Tannin: high
Flavors: notes of blackberries, **black cherries**, black pepper, black plums, cloves, coffee, **dark chocolate**, earth, leather, licorice, pine, **spices**, tar, tobacco, violets
Texture: rich
Temperature: Serve cool, about 60 to 65 degrees.
Pairings: aged cheese, chestnuts, game, roasted red meats, tomato sauce
Aging: Nicknamed the Barolo of the South, the best Taurasi has outstanding aging potential—as long as a decade or two or even longer.
Producers: Feudi di San Gregorio, **MASTROBERARDINO**, Salvatore Molettieri, **Terredora di Paolo Taurasi**

TEMPRANILLO

[tem-prah-NEE-yoh]
See also NAVARRA REDS, RIBERA DEL DUERO, RIOJA, TINTA DE TORO.
Countries: Argentina, Chile, **SPAIN** (esp. Navarra, **Ribera del Duero**, **RIOJA**, **Toro**), U.S. (California, Washington)
Color: red

[With a hamburger or grilled steak,] I love the charred edges of Aglianico—the meaty, tarry flavors that are typical of the grape. Go with Aglianico del Vulture from Basilicata or [Aglianico-based] **Taurasi** from Campania.
—DAVID LYNCH, QUINCE

Grapes: Tempranillo, often blended with Cabernet Sauvignon or other Spanish red grapes, such as Carignan, Garnacha
Weight: medium- to full-bodied
Volume: moderate to loud
Dry/sweet: dry

Acidity: low to medium
Tannin: medium to high
Flavors: notes of **blackberries**, **BLACK CHERRIES** (esp. younger wines), black currants/cassis, blueberries, cocoa (esp. older wines), coffee, cream, **EARTH** (esp. older wines), **herbs**, **leather**, licorice, meat, minerals, **plums**, prunes (esp. older wines), **raspberries**, smoke, **spices**, **STRAWBERRIES** (esp. younger wines), **TOBACCO** (esp. older wines), **VANILLA** (esp. American oaked wines), violets
Texture: jammy, lush

I have guests who sit down and say, "Bring me something new and different." I recently was given that challenge, and I brought them a Gramercy Cellars **Tempranillo** [from Washington state]. When I first learned that he [the winemaker, Greg Harrington] was making a Tempranillo, I heard it was very good and had him send me a bottle. I was blown away by it. It is a great expression of New World Tempranillo, with a nod to the Old World. The fruit in the wine has a fresher ripeness than the fruit in a Rioja or Ribera del Duero. The wine does not have that mouth-drying feel that you can get from Ribera, but it still has that leatheriness and deep florality. He chose to use American oak, and I am impressed with the subtlety of it.
—DANA FARNER, CUT

Tempranillo is an underrated varietal when it comes to food and wine pairing. I find it very versatile. There are many examples with substantial acidity that don't have a lot of oak. There are many Tempranillos that you could mistake for Pinot Noir, except they just don't have the same lusciousness. There is a triangle between Tempranillo [from Spain], Sangiovese [from Italy], and Pinot Noir—they are very close to each other in flavor, tannin, and acid. The difference comes in the elegance of the fruit and richness of the grape.
—GREG HARRINGTON, MS, WINEMAKER

Tempranillo is a really good vehicle to get to learn about the different regions of Spain. The first red most people learn about when drinking Spanish wine is Tempranillo from Rioja. But there are three primary regions where it's made, and they're all a little different: While much depends on the producer and how the wines are made, Rioja reds tend to be the softest, with more wood and age. Toro reds tend to be super powerhouses that are bigger, with higher alcohol. And Ribera del Duero reds tend to be somewhere in the middle.
—JILL ZIMORSKI, CAFÉ ATLÁNTICO

Temperature: Serve cool, about 60 degrees.
Comparables: NAVARRA, RIBERA DEL DUERO, RIOJA, **TINTA DE TORO**, **Tinto Fino** (as it's known in Ribera del Duero)
Tip: Tempranillo softens with age, taking on a meatier character.
Pairings: beef, cheese (esp. sheep's milk, e.g., Manchego), chorizo, duck, game, grilled meats, ham, lamb, pork, steak
Aging: While ready to enjoy upon release, Tempranillo-based wines can handle aging exceptionally well.
Producers: Argentina: Zuccardi; **Spain:** Chivite, Dama de Toro, Flaco, Ochoa, Osborne Solaz, Palacio de la Vega, Peromato; **U.S.–California:** Gundlach Bundschu; **Washington state:** Gramercy Cellars
Iconic example: Vega Sicilia (Spain), a blend of Tempranillo, Cabernet, and Merlot

TEROLDEGO
[teh-RAWL-deh-goh]
Country: Italy
Region: Trentino–Alto Adige
Color: red (with garnet hues)
Grapes: Teroldego
Weight: medium- to full-bodied
Volume: moderate to loud
Dry/sweet: dry
Acidity: medium to high
Tannin: low to medium
Flavors: notes of **almonds**, black and red cherries, **BLACKBERRIES**, black currants, black pepper, black truffles, **chocolate (esp. dark)**, **earth**, flowers, herbs, leather, meat (esp. young wines), minerals, **raspberries**, **smoke**, **spices**, strawberries, tar, tobacco, vanilla, violets
Texture: rich, smooth, velvety

Temperature: Serve cool, about 60 to 65 degrees.
Comparables: REFOSCO, SHIRAZ/SYRAH, ZINFANDEL
Pairings: barbecue, cheese, chicken, game, pasta, pizza, pork, red meat, truffles
Aging: In general, drink within three years, although some have longer aging potential.
Producers: Endrizzi, Fedrizzi Cipriano, **FORADORI**

We sell **Teroldego** by the glass, and I will describe it to guests as similar to Merlot — it's dry but fruity, with notes of plum, nice acidity, and a lot of great tannin. Fedrizzi Cipriano is a very old-school producer who doesn't use oak. Foradori is a more modern producer who uses lots of oak that I'll recommend to fans of Napa Cabernet. Teroldego brings out the meatiness of duck or pasta with braised veal sauce.

—EMILIE PERRIER, AI FIORI

THAI WINES
Grapes: red: Sangiovese, Shiraz; **white:** Chenin Blanc, Colombard, Malaga Blanc, Muscat, Viognier
Producer: Siam Winery's Monsoon Valley

TINTA DE TORO
[TEEN-tah deh TOR-oh]
See also TEMPRANILLO.
Country: Spain
Region: Toro
Color: red
Grapes: Tinta de Toro (aka TEMPRANILLO)
Weight: full-bodied
Volume: loud
Dry/sweet: dry
Acidity: low to medium
Tannin: high
Flavors: notes of bitter

chocolate, blackberries, cherries, espresso, game, herbs, hoisin sauce, licorice, meat, **minerals, plums**, smoke, spices, strawberries, tobacco, truffles, vanilla, violets
Texture: silky, smooth
Temperature: Serve cool, about 60 degrees.
Comparables: RIBERA DEL DUERO, RIOJA
Pairings: braised pork ribs, cheeses, red meats
Tip: One of the best wine-and-food pairings we've ever tasted is Bodegas Fariña's Gran Colegiata Crianza, made from 100 percent Tinta de Toro grapes, with a simple yet perfect dish of braised pork ribs with potatoes and smoked paprika, made by the winery's cooks, Merce Temprano and Antonia Rollou.
Producers: Bodegas Fariña, Bodegas Mauro San Roman, Finca Sobreno, Maurodos, **NUMANTHIA-TERMES**, Vega Sauco, Viña Bajos
Iconic example: Bodegas Numanthia-Termes Termanthia

As contrasted with Rioja's characteristic softness and Ribera del Duero's moderation, **Toro reds** [which are often based on the same grape] are bigger and bolder — with a distinctive note of minerality.

—JILL ZIMORSKI, CAFÉ ATLÁNTICO

TOCAI FRIULANO
See FRIULANO.

TOKAJI ASZÚ
[tohk-EYE-ee ah-SOO]
Country: Hungary
Color: white
Grapes: Furmint, blended with Harslevelu, Muscat de Lunel

Tokaji invigorates every fiber of the brain and brings forth an enchanting sparkle of wit and good cheer from the depths of the soul.
—VOLTAIRE

Weight: medium- to full-bodied
Volume: loud
Dry/sweet: sweet to very sweet
Acidity: high
Flavors: highly aromatic dessert wine, with notes of almonds, apples, **apricots**, butter, caramel (esp. older wines), cinnamon, dried fruit, figs, flowers, honey (esp. older wines), marzipan, minerals, nuts, **orange peel**, peaches, raisins, spices, tea, toffee, vanilla, walnuts
Texture: creamy, lush, smooth
Temperature: Serve cold, about 45 to 50 degrees.
Comparables: BARSAC, SAUTERNES
Tip: For much of the past five centuries, Tokaji has been thought to be on a par with Château d'Yquem.
Pairings: blue cheese, desserts (esp. with nuts or rich), foie gras
Tip: Check the label for the sweetness level, which is measured in *puttonyos*, from 3 (least sweet) to 6 (sweetest). Also keep an eye out for the very rare (and very expensive) Essencia, which is even sweeter than 6 *puttonyos*.
Aging: The aging potential of Tokaji is the stuff of legend, and measured in decades.
Producers: Bodegas Oremus, Bodvin, Chateau Megyer, Chateau Messzeláto, Chateau Pajzos, **Disznoko**, Dobogo, **ISTVÁN SZEPSY**, Királyudvar, Pajzos, **ROYAL TOKAJI**
Iconic example: István Szepsy Tokaji Aszú 6 Puttonyos

TOKAY, LIQUEUR
See TOPAQUE–RUTHERGLEN.

TOKAY PINOT GRIS
See PINOT GRIS.
In 2007 the European Union banned this term describing PINOT GRIS from Alsace, to prevent confusion with TOKAJI from Hungary.

TOPAQUE–RUTHERGLEN (FORMERLY KNOWN AS TOKAY)
[toh-PAYK–RUH-thur-glen]
Country: Australia
Region: Rutherglen
Color: white (blackish-brown in hue)
Grapes: Muscadelle (formerly Tokay Muscadelle)
Weight: full-bodied
Volume: loud
Dry/sweet: sweet
Acidity: medium to high
Flavors: sweet dessert wine with notes of apricots, butterscotch, **caramel**, chocolate, flowers, honey, **MALT**, mocha, raisins, spices, **TEA, TOFFEE**
Texture: luscious, rich, silky
Temperature: Topaque is traditionally served cool (about 65 degrees) in the winter. During the summer, it is more often enjoyed chilled or over ice.
Pairings: blue cheese; desserts made with caramel, chocolate, and/or cream
Aging: These wines are aged before release, so enjoy them soon after purchase.
Producers: Campbells, Chambers Rosewood, Morris Liqueur, Pfeiffer

TORO REDS
See TINTA DE TORO.

TORRONTÉS
[toe-rron-TESS, rolling the double r, if possible]
Countries: ARGENTINA, Chile, Spain
Color: white
Grapes: Torrontés
Weight: medium- to **full-bodied** (and higher in alcohol)
Volume: quiet to moderate
Dry/sweet: typically dry
Acidity: medium to high
Flavors: **very aromatic**, fruity, with notes of apples (esp. green), apricots, **citrus, coriander, FLOWERS**, grapes, herbs, honey, jasmine, **lemon**, lime, lychees, mango, melon, **minerals**, nectarines, oranges, oregano, **PEACHES**, pineapple, spices, tangerine, tropical fruits
Texture: crisp, rich, round

Under-$15 tip: I am just in love with **Torrontés.** They offer a great value, are gorgeous food wines, and are perfume-y—but unlike Gewürztraminer, they are very fresh. I especially like Crios from Susana Balbo.
—EMILY WINES, MS, FIFTH FLOOR

Crios de Susana Balbo **Torrontés** from Argentina is floral on the nose, yet dry—like Viognier in some ways, but certainly a lesser-known and therefore less costly varietal. I like it with seafood that has some natural sweetness: crab, lobster, or scallops. It's delicious with a seafood salad or on its own as a patio quaff.
—JILL ZIMORSKI, CAFÉ ATLÁNTICO

Temperature: Serve cold, about 45 to 50 degrees.
Comparables: GEWÜRZTRA-MINER, SAUVIGNON BLANC, VIOGNIER
Pairings: Asian cuisine (esp. Thai, Vietnamese), chicken, fish, Indian cuisine, Mexican cuisine (esp. guacamole), pork, salads, shellfish
Aging: Drink Torrontés young and fresh, ideally within twelve months.
Producers: Argentina: Alamos, Alta Vista, Bodegas Norton, Bodega Tamari, Bodega Tapiz, Crios de Susana Balbo, Mounier, Tilia, Trapiche, Trivento, Zuccardi
Iconic example: Susana Balbo Crios Torrontés

TOURIGA NACIONAL

[too-REE-gah nah-see-yoo-NAHL]
See also DOURO REDS, PORT.
Countries: Australia, PORTUGAL (Dão, Douro), South Africa, U.S. (California, Virginia)
Color: red (with a blackish-red hue)
Grapes: Touriga Nacional
Weight: full-bodied (with moderate to high alcohol)
Volume: loud
Dry/sweet: dry
Acidity: medium to high
Tannin: high
Flavors: aromatic and fruity, with notes of bacon, **blackberries**, black currants, **black pepper,** blueberries, caramel, cedar, **cherries** (esp. red), **chocolate** (esp. dark), coffee, **flowers,** herbs, leather, licorice, maple syrup,

plums (esp. black), prunes, raspberries, smoke, **spices,** strawberries, tea, tobacco, **violets**
Texture: elegant, rich, smooth
Temperature: Serve cool, about 60 to 65 degrees.
Pairings: cheeses (esp. aged), game, goat, lamb, pork, red meat (esp. grilled or roasted), sausages, steak
Tips: Open the wine 30 to 60 minutes before serving. Check out **Ex Aequo,** a joint effort of Portuguese winemaker Bento and Rhône winemaker Michel Chapoutier, made with Touriga Nacional and Syrah.
Aging: Generally drink within five years of the vintage.
Producers: Portugal–Dão (medium-bodied, higher acidity, floral notes): Quinta de Cabriz, Quinta do Roques; **Douro** (fuller-bodied, lower acidity, minty notes): Quinta de Roriz, Quinta do Vallado; **U.S.–California:** York Creek (rosé)

TREBBIANO

[treb-BYAH-noh]
Country: Italy
Regions: Abruzzo, Lugana, Soave (all fuller, louder); Toscano (lighter, quieter)
Color: white
Grapes: Trebbiano, often blended with other grapes
Weight: light-bodied (Toscano) to medium-bodied (Soave)
Volume: very quiet (Toscano) to moderate (Soave)
Dry/sweet: dry
Acidity: high
Flavors: notes of almonds,

apples, chalk, **citrus,** flowers, grass, **herbs,** honey, **lemon,** lime, minerals, **nuts, pears,** spices, stones
Texture: crisp, refreshing
Temperature: Serve cold, about 45 to 50 degrees.
Comparables: FRASCATI, MUSCADET, ORVIETO, PINOT GRIGIO, SOAVE, **Ugni Blanc (France)**
Tip: Trebbiano is also known as Ugni Blanc in France, where it is used in making brandy.
Pairings: antipasto, **fish,** lobster, pasta, prosciutto, risotto, **salads,** seafood soup, shellfish
Aging: Drink young and fresh.
Producers: Antinori, Farnese, Fattoria di Felsina, Isole e Olena, **Valentini**

TRINCADEIRA

[treen-kah-DAY-rah]
Country: Portugal
Color: red
Grapes: Trincadeira
Weight: medium- to full-bodied
Volume: moderate to moderate-plus
Dry/sweet: dry
Acidity: medium to medium-high
Tannin: low to medium-plus
Flavors: aromatic and fruity, with notes of blackberries, blueberries, cherries, cinnamon, earth, **flowers,** herbs, pepper, **plums,** raspberries, **spices,** violets
Texture: elegant, rich, soft
Temperature: Serve cool, about 60 to 65 degrees.
Pairings: cheese, ham, lamb, pork, red meat, stews, swordfish, tuna
Aging: These wines have moderate aging potential, about five to ten years.
Producers: Cortes de Cima, Herdade do Esporão

The two most exciting places on earth at the moment are Portugal and Victoria [Australia]. . . . I think **Touriga Nacional** is as great a grape as Syrah.

—MICHEL CHAPOUTIER, RENOWNED RHÔNE WINEMAKER

TSINANDALI

[tsin-an-DAH-lee]
Country: Georgia
Region: Kakheti
Color: white (with a pale straw hue)
Grapes: **Rkatsiteli**, with Mtsvane
Weight: light- to medium-bodied (and low in alcohol)
Volume: quiet
Dry/sweet: dry
Acidity: high
Flavors: fruity, with notes of **apples**, apricots, citrus, herbs, lemon, lime, melon, minerals, quince, vanilla
Texture: fresh, smooth, soft
Temperature: Serve chilled, about 50 to 55 degrees.
Pairings: appetizers, chicken, fish, mushrooms, pasta (esp. with cream sauces), pork, salads, vegetable dishes, white meats
Aging: Drink young and fresh, within a year or two.
Producers: Alaverdi, Tbilvinio, Teliani Valley, Vinoterra

TURKISH WINES

Producers: Angora Sultana de Denizli, Kavaklidere

TXAKOLI (AKA CHACOLI, TXACOLI, TXAKOLINA)

[CHOC-oh-lee]
Country: Spain
Region: Basque
Color: white (typically)
Grapes: **Hondarribi Zuri** (85 percent) blended with other grapes
Weight: light-bodied (and low in alcohol)
Volume: quiet
Dry/sweet: dry
Acidity: high
Flavors: notes of **apples (esp. green)**, citrus, flowers, grapefruit, grass, green apples, **lemon, lime,**

We pour a **Txakoli** rosé in front of the customer from three feet over the glass, and everyone just flips out. It's a cool show. Txakoli comes from seafood land and works with strong, "fishy" fish. Since this is a rosé, I like to pair it with a cured white salmon with a dried-cherry *gastrique*. The super-tart fruit in the sauce gets right up next to the tart fruit in the wine.

—ANDY MYERS, CITYZEN

melon, **minerals**, peaches, pears, sea breeze, spices, stones, **yeast**
Texture: crisp, semi-sparkling
Temperature: Serve very cold, about 40 to 45 degrees.
Comparables: ALBARIÑO, (dry) RIESLING, VINHO VERDE
Season: summer
Pairings: chicken, crab, fish, oysters, pork, sushi, tapas, Thai cuisine
Tip: Traditionally, one pours Txakoli into the glass while raising the stream of wine to arm's length or higher.
Aging: Drink young and fresh, within a few months after purchase.
Producers: Ameztoi, Arabako, Txomin Etxaniz, Uriondo Bizkaiko

UGNI BLANC
[OON-yee blahnk]
See TREBBIANO.

URUGUAYAN WINES
Grapes: red: Cabernet Franc, Merlot, **TANNAT; white:** Gewürztraminer, Sauvignon Blanc, Viognier
Tip: Don't miss Viñedo de los Vientos's alluring Tannat-based sweet dessert wine Alcyone, which has notes of black cherries, chocolate, marshmallows, and vanilla.
Producers: Alto de la Ballena, Bouza, Carlos Pizzorno, **Carrau**, Casa Filguera, Castillo Viejo, Dante Irurtia, De Lucca, Don Adelio Ariano, H. Stagnari, Juanico, Pisano, Posada del Virrey, **Viñedo de los Vientos**

VALPOLICELLA
[VAHL-pohl-ee-CHEHL-ah]
Country: Italy
Region: Veneto
Color: red (light, with ruby hues)

Grapes: primarily **CORVINA**, Corvinone, Molinara, **Rondinella**
Weight: light- to medium-bodied (and low in alcohol)
Volume: moderate
Dry/sweet: typically very dry to dry (sweet Recioto is made from dried grapes)
Acidity: medium to high
Tannin: low to medium
Flavors: aromatic and fruity, with notes of **almonds. BLACK or RED CHERRIES**, dates, earth, figs, **herbs**, leather, nuts, plums, smoke, spices, strawberries, tar, with a bitter red-cherry finish
Texture: silky, smooth
Temperature: Serve slightly chilled, about 55 degrees.
Comparables: BARDOLINO, CHIANTI, SANGIOVESE
Pairings: antipasto, beef, chicken, lamb, pasta, pizza, risotto (esp. with gorgonzola), sausages
Aging: Drink young and fresh.
Tip: Look for higher-quality wines labeled Classico or Superiore.
Producers: Alighieri, **Allegrini**, Baltieri, Bertani, Brigaldara, Ca' del Monte, Corte Sant' Alda, Dal Forno, Degani, Lamberti, Masi, Nicolis, **Giuseppe Quintarelli**, Tedeschi, Tommasi, Zenato, Zonin

VENDANGE TARDIVE WINES
[vahn-DAHNJ tahr-DEEV]
Country: France
Region: Alsace
Grapes: 100 percent Gewürztraminer, Muscat, Pinot Gris, or Riesling (as it is always a pure varietal wine)
Weight: full-bodied
Volume: loud to very loud
Dry/sweet: dry to sweet

Acidity: medium to high
Flavors: aromatic, with notes of apples (baked), apricots, honey, lychees, minerals, orange marmalade, peaches, pears (poached), pineapple, spices
Texture: creamy, luscious, rich
Temperature: Serve cold, about 45 to 50 degrees.
Comparables: LATE HARVEST WINES
Pairings: cheese, desserts, foie gras, fruit
Tip: Vendange Tardive is a Late Harvest wine; the grapes are harvested later with lots of sugar, which is not fully converted to alcohol during fermentation.
Producers: Albert Boxler, **Hugel**, Josmeyer, Marc Kreydenweiss, Marc Tempe, Pierre Sparr, Schlumberger, Trimbach, Weinbach, Willm, **Zind-Humbrecht**

VERDEJO
[vayr-DAY-hoh]
See also RUEDA.
Country: Spain
Regions: Ribera del Duero, **Rueda**, Toro
Color: white
Grapes: Verdejo, sometimes blended with Sauvignon Blanc
Weight: medium- to full-bodied (and moderate in alcohol)
Volume: moderate to moderately loud
Dry/sweet: dry
Acidity: medium to high
Flavors: aromatic, with notes of almonds, **anise**, apples (esp. green), apricots, cedar, fennel, figs, flowers, grapefruit, grapes, grass, green olives, **HERBS**, honey, **lemon**, lime, lychees, **minerals**, mint, nectarines, **NUTS**, peaches, **pears**, pineapple

Verdejo is Spain's answer to Sauvignon Blanc. If you like Sauvignon Blanc, I promise you'll like Verdejo's similar aromatic and flavor profile. You can find wonderful, inexpensive, acidic, juicy, grassy examples that you're sure to love.

—JILL ZIMORSKI, CAFÉ ATLÁNTICO

and other **tropical fruits**, often with a bitter note to the finish
Texture: **crisp**, elegant, fresh, juicy, rich, smooth
Temperature: Serve cold, about 45 to 50 degrees.
Comparables: CHARDONNAY, SAUVIGNON BLANC
Pairings: appetizers, chicken, **fish**, pork, salads, **shellfish**, veal, vegetable dishes
Aging: Drink young and fresh, within one year.
Producers: Condesa Eylo, **Naia**, Palacio de Bornos, Shaya, Tres Olmos Bodegas Garciarevalo

VERDELHO
[vehr-DEH-loh]
Countries: Australia, Portugal, Spain, U.S.
Color: white
Grapes: Verdelho (aka Gouveio)
Weight: full-bodied
Volume: moderate to loud
Dry/sweet: dry (but sometimes off-dry)
Acidity: medium to **high**
Flavors: aromatic, with notes of apricots, **citrus**, **flowers**, grapefruit, guava, **lemon**, **LIME**, melon, nectarines, **peaches**, pears, pineapple, tangerine, tropical fruits
Texture: clean, crisp, rich
Temperature: Serve cold, about 45 to 50 degrees.
Comparable: GODELLO (Spain)
Pairings: fresh cheese (e.g., chèvre), chicken, fish, pork, salads, shellfish, spicy dishes, veal
Producers: Australia: De

Bortoli, Mollydooker, Woop Woop; **Portugal:** Esporão; **Spain:** Naia; **U.S.–California:** Scholium Project

VERDICCHIO
[vehr-DEEK-yoh]
Country: Italy
Region: Le Marche
Color: white
Grapes: Verdicchio
Weight: light- to medium-bodied
Volume: quiet
Dry/sweet: very dry to dry
Acidity: medium-high to high
Flavors: notes of **almonds**, anise, apples (esp. green), **CITRUS**, earth, **flowers**, **herbs (esp. dried)**, honey, **LEMON**, lime, minerals, nectarines, nuts, peaches, pears, pineapple, plums, vanilla, with a slightly bitter finish
Texture: bright, crisp, fresh, lively
Temperature: Serve cold, about 45 to 50 degrees.
Pairings: antipasto, calamari, cheese (esp. fresh), **fish**, lobster, pasta, *salumi* (Italian cured meats), **shellfish**, white meat
Tip: Look for Verdicchio labeled "Superiore," which indicates the best quality.
Producers: ColleStefano, Fazi Battaglia, Monte Schiavo Pallio di San Floriano, Sartarelli

VERMENTINO
[vair-men-TEE-noh]
Countries: France (Corsica), **Italy** (Liguria, Sardinia, Tuscany), Spain, Uruguay, U.S. (California, North Carolina)
Color: white
Grapes: Vermentino (aka Malvoisie de Corse)
Weight: medium- to full-bodied
Volume: quiet to moderate
Dry/sweet: dry
Acidity: high
Flavors: aromatic and fruity, with notes of almonds, apples (esp. green), citrus, fennel, **flowers**, grapefruit, **HERBS**, leaves, **lemon**, lime, melon, **minerals**, **nuts**, pears, pepper, stones, tropical fruits
Texture: crisp to soft, sometimes with a whisper of spritz
Temperature: Serve chilled, about 50 to 55 degrees.
Pairings: appetizers, **fish**, pasta, **PESTO**, pork, salads, **shellfish**, vegetable dishes
Comparables: GRÜNER VELTLINER, MUSCADET, **PIGATO**, PINOT GRIGIO, **Rolle** (France/Provence), SAUVIGNON BLANC, SOAVE
Aging: Drink young and fresh, within one or two years of the vintage.
Producers: Italy: Argiolas, Santadi, Tenuta Guado al Tasso; **U.S.–California:** Tablas Creek, Uvaggio; **North Carolina:** Raffaldini

Under-$20 tip: My favorite coastal Italian wine is probably **Vermentino**, which is very herbaceous and refreshing—especially Santadi Cala Silente Vermentino di Sardegna, and especially with panzanella [an Italian bread-and-tomato salad accented with red onions, red wine vinegar, and coarse salt].

—DAVID LYNCH, QUINCE

VERNACCIA DI SAN GIMIGNANO

[ver-NAH-chyah dee sahn jee-mee-NYAH-noh]
Country: Italy
Region: Tuscany
Color: white
Grapes: Vernaccia
Weight: medium-bodied
Volume: quiet to moderate
Dry/sweet: dry
Acidity: medium to high
Flavors: aromatic, with notes of apples, citrus peel, earth, flowers, ginger, herbs, honey, leaves, lemon, minerals, **nuts**, passion fruit, peaches, pears, tropical fruits, vanilla, with **a slightly bitter almond finish**
Texture: crisp (unoaked) to soft (oaked)
Temperature: Serve cold, about 45 to 50 degrees.
Comparable: CHARDONNAY
Pairings: appetizers, cheese (esp. soft), chicken, **fish**, pasta, rabbit, risotto, **shellfish**, white meats
Aging: Best drunk young and fresh.
Producers: Cecchi, Falchini, Il Palagetto, La Colonne, Montenidoli, Mormoraia, **San Quirico**, Spalletti, Strozzi, **Terruzzi & Puthod**, Vagnoni

VIN DE PAILLE

[van deh PAH-yuh]
Countries: France (**Hermitage, Jura**), U.S. (California)
Color: white
Grapes: traditionally, Chardonnay blended with Poulsard (red) and Savagnin (white); today, other grapes are being used, from Grenache Blanc to Roussanne
Weight: full-bodied (and high in alcohol, at 14 to 18+ percent)

Volume: loud
Dry/sweet: sweet to very sweet
Acidity: high
Flavors: notes of apples, **apricots**, butterscotch, caramel, coffee, crème brûlee, figs, hazelnuts, **honey**, maple syrup, marmalade, minerals, **peaches**, pears, quince, raisins, spices, white truffles
Texture: chewy, syrupy, unctuous
Temperature: Serve cold, about 45 to 50 degrees.
Pairings: blue cheese; desserts made with caramel, dark chocolate, figs, or walnuts; foie gras
Tip: Vin de Paille translates as "straw wine," because the wines were traditionally made from grapes dried in the sun on straw mats for at least three months.
Aging: Vin de Paille can be enjoyed immediately, but the best are capable of aging for a decade and potentially several decades.
Producers: **France**: Alain Labet, Berthet-Bondet, Chapoutier, Jacques Puffeney; **U.S.–California:** Bonny Doon Angel or Vinferno (certified biodynamic), Sine Qua Non "The Straw Man," Tablas Creek Quintessence

VINHO VERDE

[VEE-nyoh VAIR-deh]
Country: Portugal
Region: Minho
Color: white
Grapes: Alvarinho and up to a half-dozen other grapes, but especially Loureiro, Trajadura
Weight: **light-** to medium-bodied (and low in alcohol)
Volume: quiet to **moderate**
Dry/sweet: very dry to off-dry
Acidity: high
Flavors: fruity, with notes of apples (esp. green), apricots, citrus, grapefruit, lemon, lime, minerals, peaches, pears, smoke, stones
Texture: crisp and fresh, sometimes semi-sparkling
Temperature: Serve very cold, about 40 to 45 degrees.
Season: summer
Comparables: lighter-bodied ALBARIÑO (Spain), lighter-bodied ALVARINHO (Portugal)
Pairings: chicken, **fish**, fried calamari, grilled sardines, mussels, salads, **shellfish**, sushi
Aging: Drink young and fresh, ideally within a year.
Producers: **Aveleda/Casal Garcia**, Casa do Valle, Famega, Fonte, Grinalda, Morgadio da Torre, Opala

Someone sent me an e-mail asking, "Should I feel guilty about loving a $2.99 **Vinho Verde** from Trader Joe's?" No, he should not. No one should feel guilty about loving any wine at all!
—DANA FARNER, CUT

Casal Garcia **Vinho Verde** [which retails for $9 a bottle and has been described by sommelier Daniel Johnnes as "one of the most delicious light white wines I have tasted in a long time"] is excellent. People are excited when they open it because it has a little effervescence, and it's so clean and refreshing, with mineral and fruit flavors.
—INEZ RIBUSTELLO, ON THE SQUARE

I am a white-wine-with-cheese guy. I love the classic pairing of Comte with Château Chalon. Even though you wouldn't consider it a dessert wine, **Vin Jaune** is a crazy character. Comte is a nutty, creamy-textured cheese. With the insanity of the oxidized Jura wine, it is amazing.
—JUSTIN LEONE, BENNY'S CHOP HOUSE

VIN JAUNE
[van ZHOHN]
Country: France
Region: Jura
Color: white
Grapes: Savagnin (Late Harvest)
Weight: medium-bodied
Volume: moderate to loud
Dry/sweet: dry
Acidity: low to medium
Flavors: very aromatic, with notes of almonds, **apples,** apricots, caramel, grapefruit, hazelnuts, lemon, lime, nutmeg, **nuts,** smoke, spices, walnuts
Texture: rich
Temperature: Traditionally served chilled as an aperitif, or cool as a digestif.
Comparable: aged Spanish FINO SHERRY (with similar oxidized flavors)
Pairings: **cheese** (esp. strong, e.g., **Comte,** Reblochon), **chicken,** foie gras, game birds, morel mushrooms, **nuts (esp. walnuts)**
Tip: Allow Vin Jaune to breathe for a few to several hours before serving.
Aging: Vin Jaune has extraordinary aging potential, up to a century or more. It is produced in all four of the Jura AOCs: **Château Chalon** (the most famous), Arbois, Côtes du Jura, and L'Etoile.
Producers: Berthet-Bondet, **Jacques Puffeney,** Montbourgeau

VINO NOBILE DI MONTEPULCIANO
[VEE-noh NOH-bee-lay dee MOHN-teh-pool-CHAH-noh]
Country: Italy
Region: Tuscany
Color: red
Grapes: **Sangiovese,** sometimes blended with other grapes
Weight: medium- to full-bodied
Volume: moderate to loud
Dry/sweet: dry
Acidity: medium
Tannin: medium to medium-high
Flavors: notes of blackberries, **black cherries,** blueberries, cedar, chocolate, earth, flowers, leather, licorice, minerals, mint, plums, smoke, **spice,** tea, tobacco, vanilla, **violets**
Texture: rich, round, velvety
Temperature: Serve cool, about 60 to 65 degrees.
Comparables: BRUNELLO DI MONTALCINO, CHIANTI CLASSICO
Pairings: cheese (esp. aged), chicken, game, game birds, pasta, pizza, roasts, steak, stews, veal, wild boar
Tip: There are good bargains to be found in Vino Nobile di Montepulciano.
Aging: Typically enjoy within a few years of its vintage, although the best will age for five to ten years.
Producers: AVIGNONESI, Bindella, **Boscarelli,** Carpineto, Casanova di Neri, Contucci, Dei, Fassati, Fattoria del Cerro, Federico Carletti, Fognano, La Braccesca, Lodola Nuova, Palazzo Vecchio, **Poliziano,** Romeo, Tenuta Trerose

VIN SANTO
[veen SAHN-toh]
Country: ITALY (Alto Adige, Tuscany, Umbria, Veneto)
Color: white (with amber hues)
Grapes: Varies by region—traditionally, Malvasia, Trebbiano (dried)
Weight: full-bodied (with 14 to 18 percent alcohol)
Volume: moderate to loud
Dry/sweet: off-dry, semi-sweet, or (more typically) sweet, with a dry finish
Acidity: medium to high
Flavors: notes of almonds, apricots (esp. dried), black pepper, **caramel,** cinnamon, coffee, figs, flowers, honey, lemon, licorice, **nuts (esp. toasted),** orange peel (esp. candied), peaches, **raisins,** spices, toffee, vanilla, walnuts, white pepper, with a dry finish
Texture: rich, silky, viscous
Temperature: Serve cool to slightly chilled, to taste.
Pairings: **biscotti** (esp. almond or **hazelnut),** cheese (esp. semi-soft or mascarpone), desserts (esp. nut, orange, or peach), milk chocolate, nuts, pastries, vanilla ice cream
Tip: Try dipping your biscotti in the Vin Santo, as the Italians do. Greece also makes a dessert wine called Vinsanto, which is different in style, with fresh fruit notes along with marked acidity.
Aging: Typically drink young and fresh. However, the very best can age as long as a decade or two.
Producers: Avignonesi, Capezzana, Felsina, Geografico, Isole e Olena, La Sala, Querciabella, Rocca di Montegrossi, Ruffino Serelle, Travignoli, Villa Pillo

VINTAGE-DATED WINES

Tip: Vintage, meaning the year a wine's grapes were harvested, matters especially in regions where the weather is variable, such as Bordeaux and Burgundy. Outstanding vintages often drive both demand and prices up. In regions where the weather is more consistent, such as Australia, vintage matters less. The best producers can produce good wines in less-than-optimal vintage years.

VIOGNIER

[vee-oh-NYAY]

See also CONDRIEU.

Countries: Argentina, Australia, **France** (Languedoc, **Northern Rhône**), U.S. (California)

Color: white (and deep yellow in hue)

Grapes: Viognier

Weight: medium-full to very full-bodied (with high alcohol)

Volume: quiet to moderate

Dry/sweet: dry

Acidity: low

Flavors: **highly aromatic**, fruity, with notes of almonds, apples, **APRICOTS**, **citrus**, cream, **FLOWERS**, ginger, grapefruit, honey, **honeysuckle**, lime, lychees, mango, melon, **minerals**, nutmeg, **orange rind**, **PEACHES**, **pears**, pineapple, spices, tangerine, **tropical fruits**, vanilla

Texture: luscious, rich, round, silky, soft, viscous

Temperature: Serve chilled, about 50 to 55 degrees.

Comparables: CHARDONNAY, **Château-Grillet**, CONDRIEU, GEWÜRZTRAMINER, TORRONTÉS

Season: summer

Pairings: butter and cream sauces, cheese, chicken, crab, curries, fish, ham, lobster, pork, shellfish, Thai and Vietnamese food

Aging: Drink young and fresh before its aroma wanes—within one to two years.

Producers: Argentina: Alma Negra, Zuccardi (sparkling Viognier); **Australia:** Clonakilla, Petaluma, W Wine, **Yalumba; France–Rhône** (*see also* CONDRIEU): Chapoutier, **CUILLERON**, Guigal, Jaboulet, Perret, Vernay, Villard; **Greece:** Gerovassiliou; **U.S.–California:** Alban, Bonterra, **CALERA**, Cline, Cold Heaven, Copain, Edmunds St. John, Fess Parker, **JOSEPH PHELPS**, Kunde, Peay, Qupé, R. H. Phillips, **Stags' Leap**, Zaca Mesa; **North Carolina:** Ray Apple Lassie; **Virginia:** Cooper, **HORTON**, Veritas; **Uruguay:** Posada del Virrey

Iconic examples: Yves Cuilleron Condrieu or Horton Vineyards Viognier

VIRGINIA WINES

Red: Barbera, **Cabernet Franc,** Cabernet Sauvignon, Merlot, Norton, Petit Verdot

White: Chardonnay, **Viognier**

Sweet: Kerner

Tip: Virginia is the fifth-largest wine-producing state.

Producers: Barboursville (esp. its Bordeaux-style Octagon), Boxwood (esp. Topiary), Chester Gap, Chrysalis, Horton, Kluge, Linden, Pearmund (esp. Vin de Sol, a sherry-style aperitif), Three Fox, Veritas, White Hall, Winery at La Grange

VIURA

[vee-OO-rah]

See RIOJA–WHITE.

VOLNAY

[vohl-NAY]

Country: France

Region: Burgundy/Côte de Beaune

Color: red

Grapes: Pinot Noir

Weight: ranges from lighter- to fuller-bodied

Volume: moderate

Dry/sweet: dry

Acidity: medium to high

Tannin: low to medium

Flavors: aromatic and fruity,

I get asked about **Virginia wines** a lot, because I grew up there. I think you have to be very careful about which varietals you choose. I think if you're drinking whites in Virginia, you should explore Viognier, and I think Cabernet Franc and Merlot are the wines to explore if you're drinking reds.

—JILL ZIMORSKI, CAFÉ ATLÁNTICO

Virginia is a region I am keeping an eye on, as I have been impressed by what I've tasted over the last five or six years. I am particularly impressed with Kluge and their 2004 sparkling Blanc de Blancs, which blew me away in a blind tasting. It is very rich and silky and close to or even ahead of the sparkling wines from Napa. I was lucky enough to meet Patricia [Kluge, its founder], and I have visited a few times. It offers amazing value. When I pour it by the glass, people are surprised, asking, *"They make wine in Virginia?"* I find shocking people is a good thing. If a wine is interesting, they will want to learn more.

—STEPHANE COLLING, SAN YSIDRO RANCH

On our list, we carry a few **Virginia** wines from Chrysalis (which makes a lovely Albariño), Horton, and Linden. Virginia is also making some fun dessert wines. Linden is making beautiful Petit Manseng, which is funky with high acid and pairs with our pineapple-and-coconut fallen soufflé. Horton is making a Late Harvest Viognier, and Barboursville makes a wine called Phileo, which is like Moscato d'Asti without its sparkle.

—ANDY MYERS, CITYZEN

I love the direction that **Virginia wines** have been taking. There is lots of movement and, as with the rest of the world, they are learning what varietals grow best where. This is in large part due to Chris Pearmund [of Pearmund Cellars], because he has helped other winemakers and owners find good spots and what to plant, and then he benefits by getting good fruit from them. I would cite Jim Law of Linden Vineyards as a stand-out. Linden has long been, and is still, my favorite vineyard, and the wines get better and better every year. Linden is on a mountainside and on poor soil, which leads to deep root systems. His wines are very site-specific, and I am fondest of the series of wines from Shari Avenius vineyard, including the Chardonnay, Sauvignon Blanc, and the reds. The Winery at La Grange, Three Fox Vineyards, and Chester Gap Cellars also make good wine. If I could look into a crystal ball, I'd expect to see Virginia wines on wine lists across the country. Many in Virginia believe their Cabernet Franc can emerge as an internationally classic style.

—SCOTT CALVERT, THE INN AT LITTLE WASHINGTON

with notes of blackberries, blueberries, cherries, earth, herbs, lilacs, minerals, plums, **raspberries**, roses, spices, strawberries, vanilla, **violets**
Texture: delicate, elegant, satiny, silky, velvety
Temperature: Serve slightly chilled, about 55 to 60 degrees.
Pairings: chicken, Époisses cheese, game birds, red meat
Aging: In general, drink within a few to fifteen years.
Producers: Domaine des Comtes Lafon, Marquis d'Angerville, **Michel Lafarge**

VOUVRAY
[voo-VRAY]
Country: France
Region: Loire Valley
Color: white
Grapes: Chenin Blanc (aka

Pineau de la Loire)
Weight: light- to medium-bodied
Volume: moderate
Dry/sweet: ranges from dry to off-dry to sweet
Acidity: high to very high
Flavors: aromatic, with notes of almonds, **apples**, **apricots**,

chamomile, **flowers**, hay, herbs, **honey**, lemon, melon, **MINERALS**, peaches, pears, quince, tropical fruits
Texture: fresh, rich, soft; sometimes sparkling
Temperature: Serve chilled, about 50 to 55 degrees. Serve sparkling versions even colder.
Comparables: CHENIN BLANC, SAVENNIÈRES
Season: spring–summer
Pairings: dry wines: chicken, fish, fried foods, lobster, rillettes, salmon, scallops, shellfish, trout, white meat (pork, veal), white sauces; **sparkling wines:** appetizers, cheese (esp. blue), desserts (esp. almond, apple, or pear); fish (esp. white), pork (esp. with apples), salmon tartare; **sweet wines:** apple desserts, blue cheese, foie gras
Tip: Try the sparkling version, which represents 60 percent of Vouvray production.
Aging: Vouvray has excellent aging potential, with the best able to age for a decade or longer.
Producers: Aubuisières, Câreme, Champalou, Clos Baudoin, **Clos Naudin**, de la Butte, des Lauriers, Foreau (esp. Vouvray Moelleux), Gaudrelle, **HUET**, Monmousseau, Pichot,

While cava and prosecco are all about freshness, Huet sparkling **Vouvray** is cool because you can drink it with quite a lot of bottle age when it, in fact, improves. Still Chenin Blanc can live a hundred years, and as a sparkling wine it can as well. We are pouring a 2001 and it has that sparkling, rich texture that older Chenin Blanc can take on while still retaining all that minerally, stony character. It is a very serious wine. In terms of food, anything that has apples or pears will work amazingly well with this. If you have a tartare that has an apple or pear component, it will be delicious. It also has enough texture to work with salmon or a poached white fish. It would be really cool with pork loin with apples because those flavors are the flavors you find in the wine. The wine *is* the sauce.

—BELINDA CHANG, THE MODERN

Pinon, Taille aux Loups, Vigneau-Chevreau
Iconic example: Domaine **Huet** Le Haut-Lieu, esp. 1947 (biodynamic)

WARM-CLIMATE WINES
Countries: Australia (Barossa Valley), France (southern), South Africa, South America, U.S. (northern California)
Weight: fuller-bodied (and higher in alcohol)
Acidity: lower
Flavors: in general: fruitier; **red wines:** notes of dried fruits (e.g., figs, prunes, raisins); **white wines:** notes of tropical fruits (e.g., mango, papaya, pineapple)
Texture: more luscious than cool-climate wines

WASHINGTON STATE WINES
Country: U.S.
Grapes: red: Cabernet Sauvignon, Merlot, Syrah; **white:** Chardonnay, Riesling, Sauvignon Blanc, Sémillon
Producers: Abeja, Andrew Will (premium), Arbor Crest, Betz (premium), Cayuse (premium), Charles Smith, **CHATEAU STE. MICHELLE** (Washington's oldest winery), Chinook, **Columbia, Columbia Crest** (value), Covey Run (value), DeLille (premium), **Domaine Ste. Michelle** (sparkling wines), Dunham, **Hogue,** Kiona, L'Ecole No. 41 (value), **LEONETTI** (premium), Matthews Cellar, Quilceda Creek (premium), Snoqualmie (value), Woodward Canyon (premium)

WEISSBURGUNDER
[VICE-boor-gun-der]
See PINOT BLANC.

Chris Miller of Spago on Washington State Wines

Washington Syrah is a special, unique wine—and that is objective. It is special because there are two different styles that predominate. They are best characterized by Walla Walla/Horse Heaven Hills and Red Mountain/Yakima. While you would pair them with the same foods, such as duck, lamb, and lighter fowl choices, they would be different preparations.

Walla Walla/Horse Heaven Hills: This Syrah is less intense on the palate. It is very intense aromatically, with much softer tannin—much like a northern Rhône Syrah. It is like a large-size Pinot with a different fruit profile, as opposed to Cabernet, which Syrah can resemble sometimes. With Walla Walla, you want to go just a touch lighter and work a little spice in as well. You have dark root, earth, and spice with the wine. Grilled food works well, as does lighter braising. You can get down to lighter game like quail and squab with Walla Walla Syrah.

Red Mountain/Yakima: These have a really awesome tannic structure. It is not really huge tannic structure, but it is ever so slightly gritty and rustic in the best kind of way. It is epitomized by **Betz Family La Côte Rousse,** one of my favorite Syrahs outside of France. It has a roasted-olive-tapenade Mediterranean kind of flavor, with great tannins and with all the meatiness of Syrah. It has beautiful red- and blue-fruit profiles. With Yakima, look to more Mediterranean preparations with tomatoes, peppers, and meats that have been grilled or roasted. You can get up to steak with Yakima/Red Mountain.

What the *terroir* has to offer in **Washington state** is great for Syrah. I would characterize their wine to a customer as having the ripe fruit of the New World as well as manifesting the Old World smoke, meat, and spice. You get the best of both worlds with lots of complexity and layers.
—DANA FARNER, CUT

For **Washington state** white wines, Chateau Ste. Michelle and their single-vineyard wines—Cold Creek and Horse Heaven—are fantastic comfort wines. For red wines, the big names, of course, are Andrew Will, Leonetti for a special night, Woodward Canyon, Dunham Cellars, and DeLille Cellars. L'Ecole Merlot was everyone's comfort wine. Then lately two cult wines started popping up—Abeja and Betz Family—and you wondered how people knew as much about them as they did.
—CHRIS MILLER, SPAGO

WINES UNDER $15

See also BOXED WINES.

One of our key missions when writing this book was to help turn America's most common beverage with the evening meal from a soft drink (such as Coke) to wine — any wine. With a can of soda running around $1, a bottle of wine on this list that contains five servings might cost a dollar or two more per serving — but can improve your quality of life immeasurably. **Here's a list of 150-plus delicious value-priced wines we'd be very happy to choose over a can of soda any day (including several that we prefer to other wines twice the price):**

1. 1+1=3 Cava Brut (Spain, $13)
2. A by Acadia Chardonnay (California, $10–13)
3. Acrobat Pinot Gris (Oregon, $12)
4. Adelsheim Pinot Gris (Oregon, $12)
5. Alamos Chardonnay, Malbec, and Torrontés (Argentina, $10)
6. Alta Vista Torrontés (Argentina, $10)
7. Aveleda Alvarinho or Vinho Verde (Portugal, $8–13)
8. Banfi Rosa Regale Brachetto d'Acqui (half-bottle; Italy, $10)
9. Basa Rueda (Spain, $13)
10. Bodegas Fariña Dama de Toro Crianza or Tempranillo (Spain, $10–15)
11. Bogle Chardonnay (California, $9)
12. Bonny Doon Vin Gris de Cigare Rosé (California, $13)
13. Bonterra Cabernet Sauvignon, Merlot, or Syrah (organic; California, $14)
14. Boutari Moschofilero (Greece, $14)
15. Brancott Marlborough Sauvignon Blanc (New Zealand, $13)
16. Brunel Côtes-du-Rhône Rouge (France/Rhone, $10)
17. Burgans Rias Baixas Albariño (Spain, $13)
18. Calistoga Estate Cabernet Sauvignon, Chardonnay, or Merlot (California, $15)
19. Campo Viejo Reserva Rioja (Spain, $13)
20. Capcanes Mas Donis Barrica Rhône Red Blend (Spain, $12)
21. Cartlidge & Browne Pinot Noir (California, $13)
22. Casal Garcia Vinho Verde (Portugal, $9)
23. Casa Silva Reserva Carmenère (Chile, $8)
24. Cave Springs Riesling (Canada, $15)
25. Chambers Rosewood Rutherglen Muscadelle (375ml bottle; Australia, $14–15)
26. Channing Daughters Scuttlehole Chardonnay (New York, $15)
27. Chapoutier Belleruche Côtes-du-Rhône (France, $15)
28. Château Bonnet Entre-Deux-Mers Blanc (France, $13)
29. Chateau St. Jean Chardonnay or Gewürztraminer (California, $10–15)
30. Chateau Ste. Michelle Riesling or Sauvignon Blanc (Washington state, $9–11)
31. Clayhouse Central Coast Adobe White (California, $15)
32. Coastal Vines Pinot Noir (California, $7)
33. Columbia Crest Grand Estates Chardonnay or Merlot or H3 Cabernet Sauvignon (Washington state, $13–14)
34. Concannon Petite Sirah (California, $7–10)
35. Cono Sur Carmenère, Pinot Noir or Sauvignon Blanc (Chile, $6–10)
36. Cousiño-Macul Antiguas Reservas Chardonnay or Sauvignon Gris (Chile, $8–14)
37. Covey Run Chardonnay or Riesling (Washington state, $7–10)
38. Crios Malbec or Torrontés (Argentina, $14–15)
39. Cristalino Brut Cava (Spain, $8)
40. Cune Rioja (Spain, $14)
41. D'Arenberg Grenache, Shiraz, or Shiraz Grenache (Australia, $10–15)
42. De Bortoli db Selection Chardonnay or Pinot Grigio (Australia, $9)
43. Domaine de la Pépière Muscadet de Sèvre et Maine Sur Lie (France, $15)

44. Domaine du Tariquet Chardonnay or Sauvignon Blanc (France, $10–11)
45. Domaine l'Aujardiere Côtes de Grandlieu Sur Lie Muscadet (France, $13)
46. Domaine Ste. Michelle Blanc de Blancs or Brut or Extra Dry (Washington state, $10–12)
47. Don Miguel Gascon Malbec (Argentina, $12)
48. Dr. Konstantin Frank Dry Riesling (New York, $15)
49. Dr. Loosen "Dr. L" Riesling (Germany, $12)
50. Dry Creek Vineyard Dry Chenin Blanc (California, $12)
51. Drylands Sauvignon Blanc (New Zealand, $12–15)
52. Echelon Viognier (California, $11–13)
53. El Coto de Rioja Rosé (Spain, $10)
54. Emiliana Chardonnay (Chile, $9–10)
55. Estancia Pinot Noir (California, $13–15)
56. Fess Parker Frontier Red (California, $11)
57. Fetzer Chardonnay (California, $8)
58. Forest Glen Sauvignon Blanc (California, $9)
59. Four Vines Old Vine Zinfandel (California, $12)
60. Freixenet Cordon Negro (Spain, $10)
61. Gallo Family Sonoma Reserve Pinot Gris (California, $9)
62. Georges Duboeuf Beaujolais-Villages or Beaujolais Cru from Brouilly, Chiroubles, or Julienas (France, $11–15)
63. Geyser Peak Cabernet Sauvignon (California, $14)
64. Gloria Ferrer Sonoma Brut (California, $15)
65. Graham's Six Grapes Reserve Port (half-bottle; Portugal, $14)
66. Gruet Brut Sparkling Wine (New Mexico, $10–14)
67. Guigal Côtes du Rhône (France, $12)
68. Hidalgo Cream Sherry (Spain, $14)
69. Hidalgo La Gitana Manzanilla Sherry (Spain, $15)
70. Hogue Gewürztraminer, Pinot Grigio, or Riesling or dessert wine (Washington state, $9–11)
71. Honig Sauvignon Blanc (California, $14)
72. Hugel & Fils Gentil or Pinot Blanc (France, $11–15)
73. Jaboulet Parallèle 45 Côtes du Rhône or Rosé (France, $13)
74. Jacob's Creek Reserve Shiraz (Australia, $9–12)
75. J. Lohr Syrah (California, $12–15)
76. Joel Gott Riesling, Sauvignon Blanc, or Zinfandel (California, $12–15)
77. Julian Chivite Gran Feudo Rosé (Spain, $10)
78. J. Vidal Fleury Côtes du Rhône (France, $14)
79. J Vineyards & Winery Pinot Gris (California, $15)
80. Kali Hart Chardonnay (California, $14)
81. Kendall-Jackson Vintner's Reserve Chardonnay (California, $13)
82. King Estate Pinot Gris (Oregon, $15)
83. LAN Crianza Rioja (Spain, $12)
84. Las Rocas de San Alejandro Garnacha (Spain, $13)
85. Laurenz Singing Grüner Veltliner (Austria, $13)
86. La Vieille Ferme Côtes du Ventoux or Rouge (France, $9–10)
87. Layer Cake Shiraz (Australia, $15)
88. L'Ecole No. 41 Chenin Blanc (Washington state, $15)
89. Leyda Sauvignon Blanc (Chile, $11)
90. Lindauer Brut (New Zealand, $11)
91. Loimer Grüner Veltliner (Austria, $12)
92. Louis Jadot Beaujolais-Villages or Mâcon-Villages Chardonnay (France, $13)
93. Louis M. Martini Cabernet Sauvignon (California, $15)
94. Lucien Albrecht Crémant d'Alsace or Reserve Pinot Blanc (France, $12–15)
95. Luigi Bosca Malbec (Argentina, $12)
96. Martin Codax Albariño (Spain, $12)
97. Mas Carlot Rosé Vin de Pays d'Oc (France, $10)
98. Mercer Riesling (Washington state, $15)
99. Michael-David Zinfandel (California, $15)

100. Michel Delhommeau Harmonie Muscadet de Sèvre et Maine Sur Lie (France, $13)
101. Michele Chiarlo Le Orme Barbera d'Asti or Moscato d'Asti (Italy, $11–15)
102. Montes Malbec (Chile, $12)
103. Muga Rioja Rosado (Spain, $12–15)
104. Mulderbosch Chenin Blanc (South Africa, $14)
105. Mumm Napa Brut Prestige (California, $14)
106. Murphy-Goode "The Fume" (California, $13)
107. Norton Malbec (Argentina, $11)
108. Osborne Solaz (or Seven, its new boxed wine) (Spain, $9)
109. Pacific Rim Chenin Blanc, Gewürztraminer, Riesling, or Vin de Glacière Riesling (Washington state, $11–15)
110. Penfolds Koonunga Hill Shiraz/Cabernet Sauvignon (Australia, $10)
111. Perrin Côtes du Rhône (France, $13)
112. Pieropan Soave (Italy, $14–15)
113. Pillar Box Red (Australia, $12)
114. Pine Ridge Chenin Blanc Viognier (California, $12)
115. Pollerhof Grüner Veltliner (Austria, $11)
116. Prunotto Barbera d'Asti (Italy, $15)
117. Quady Elysium Black Muscat or Essencia Orange Muscat (half-bottle; California, $13–15)
118. Ramon Bilbao Crianza Rioja (Spain, $13)

119. Ravenswood Vintners Blend Zinfandel (California, $11)
120. Renacer Malbec Reserva (Argentina, $14)
121. Riondo Veneto Prosecco (Italy, $13)
122. Rosenblum Vintner's Cuvée Zinfandel (California, $9)
123. Rudi Wiest Rhein River Riesling (Germany, $11)
124. Sandeman Tawny Port (Portugal, $12)
125. Santa Julia (Organic) Cabernet Sauvignon, Chardonnay, or Tempranillo (Argentina, $9–10)
126. Schloss Biebrich Sekt (Germany, $4)
127. Segura Viudas Aria Brut, Brut Reserva, or Rosé (Spain, $9–12)
128. Shaya Verdejo (Spain, $15)
129. Simonsig Sauvignon Blanc (South Africa, $15)
130. Skouras Moschofilero (Greece, $14)
131. Snoqualmie Gewürztraminer, Riesling, or Sauvignon Blanc (Washington state, $9–13)
132. Sokol Blosser Evolution "Lucky Edition" (Oregon, $15)
133. Steenberg Sauvignon Blanc (South Africa, $10)
134. St. Urbans-Hof Riesling QbA Mosel (Germany, $15)
135. TerraNoble Reserva Carmenère or Sauvignon Blanc (Argentina, $12–15)
136. Terredora Aglianico (Italy, $15)
137. Terre Nero d'Avola (Italy, $9)

138. Tilia Cabernet Sauvignon (Argentina, $9)
139. Tortoise Creek Chardonnay (California, $9)
140. Trapiche Malbec (Argentina, $7–15)
141. Trimbach Pinot Blanc or Pinot Gris (France/Alsace, $15)
142. Ventisquero Reserva Sauvignon Blanc (Chile, $13)
143. Veramonte Cabernet Sauvignon or Sauvignon Blanc (Chile, $9–12)
144. Vesevo Beneventano Falanghina (Italy, $12)
145. Vietti Moscato d'Asti (Italy, $14)
146. Vignerons de Beaumes-de-Venise Muscat de Beaumes-de-Venise (375ml bottle; France, $14)
147. Villa Maria Private Bin Sauvignon Blanc (New Zealand, $13)
148. Vinum Petite Sirah (California, $12)
149. Willm Pinot Blanc (France, $11)
150. Yalumba Museum Reserve Muscat (375ml bottle; Australia, $15)
151. Zardetto Prosecco (Italy, $12)
152. Zuccardi Serie A Malbec (Argentina, $15)

Tip: Buy wines by the case, since retailers often extend a case discount of 10 percent or more.

Note: All suggested retail prices are approximate and often vary by state and by store.

As **winter** dishes become earthier, the wines do as well. I will add bigger, bolder, heartier reds, bringing in big, bold, youthful-style Bordeaux as well as big California Cabernet and Zinfandel. The Pinot Noir in the winter is bigger and richer, versus in the summer, when I want the pretty, elegant, softer style. In the winter I get more into the Central Coast riper-climate wines. In winter, I will go to a big California Chardonnay and Viognier. For Chardonnay, I look to Patz and Hall; it is one I really love because it is a little more restrained.
—EMILY WINES, MS, FIFTH FLOOR

WINTER WINES

See also AMARONE, **BORDEAUX–RED**, **BURGUNDY–RED**, BRUNELLO DI MONTALCINO, CABERNET SAUVIGNON, CAHORS, **CHAMPAGNE**, CHARDONNAY–OAKED, CÔTE-RÔTIE, GRENACHE, GEWÜRZTRAMINER, MADEIRA, MALBEC, MARSANNE/ROUSSANNE, **PORT**, RHÔNE WINES, RIOJA, **SAUTERNES**, SHIRAZ/SYRAH, VIOGNIER, ZINFANDEL.
Weight: full-bodied

XAREL-LO
[char-ELL-oh]
See CAVA.

XINOMAVRO/XYNOMAVRO
[ksee-NOH-mah-vroh]
Country: Greece
Region: Macedonia/Naoussa
Color: red
Grapes: Xinomavro
Weight: lighter-bodied (esp. younger wines) to fuller-bodied (esp. older wines)
Volume: loud
Dry/sweet: dry
Acidity: medium-high to high
Tannin: medium to **high**
Flavors: notes of **black cherries**, black olives, black pepper, dark chocolate, earth (esp. older wines), herbs, leather, lilies, **prunes, raspberries, roses**, smoke, spices, **strawberries**, tobacco (esp. older wines), **tomatoes** (esp. older wines), vanilla, violets

Texture: rich, robust
Temperature: Serve cool, about 60 to 65 degrees.
Comparables: BARBARESCO, BARBERA, BAROLO, BURGUNDY–RED, GRENACHE, PINOT NOIR
Pairings: beef, cheese (esp. aged), Greek cuisine, lamb, mushrooms, pork, salads, tomato sauce, tuna
Aging: Arguably the most age-worthy dry Greek red, Xinomavro becomes more expressive after a decade and can age for decades.
Tip: Decant an hour or two before serving to smooth out the tannins.
Producers: Boutari, Karydas, **Kir-Yianni** (Naoussa and Ramnista), Rapsani, Thimiopoulos, Tsantalis, Vaeni

ZINFANDEL
[ZIN-fan-dell]
Country: U.S.
Region: California
Color: red (and blackish-red in hue)
Grapes: Zinfandel
Weight: medium- to very full-bodied (with high alcohol)
Volume: moderate to very loud

Dry/sweet: dry, with a hint of sweetness
Acidity: medium to medium-plus
Tannin: low-medium to medium-high
Flavors: fruity (berries), with notes of **BLACKBERRIES, black cherries,** black currants/cassis, **black pepper,** blueberries, cedar, cherries, chocolate, **cinnamon,** cloves, coffee, cranberries, cream, dates, flowers, herbs, **JAM,** licorice, mint, nuts, **plums** (fresh and dried), raisins, **raspberries,** roses, smoke, **SPICES,** strawberries, tar, toast, vanilla, violets
Texture: chewy, dense, juicy, rich, ripe, smooth
Temperature: Serve slightly chilled, about 55 degrees (for lighter-bodied wines), to cool, about 65 degrees (for fuller-bodied wines).
Comparables: BONARDA, PRIMITIVO
Pairings: barbecued or grilled foods, beef, hamburgers, lamb, pork, sausage, steak, veal, venison
Aging: In general, drink Zinfandel young to appreciate its fruity freshness, but the best have good aging potential.
Producers: A. RAFANELLI, Biale, Bogle, Cline, Dashe, **Edmeades,** Fife, Four Vines, Frog's Leap, Gary Farrell, Howell Mountain Vineyards, Lolonis, **Martinelli** Jackass Hill, Murphy-Goode, Quivira, Rabbit Ridge,

There's really nothing like **Xinomavro,** with its flavors of raspberries and roses. Some compare it to Grenache or Pinot Noir, whereas it's so ancient that Grenache and Pinot Noir should be compared to Xinomavro. . . . Rapsani makes a Xinomavro-Krassato-Stavroto blend that I first put on my list at Chanterelle.
—ROGER DAGORN, MS, PORTER HOUSE NEW YORK

Rancho Zabaco, **Ravenswood**, Renwood, **RIDGE, Rosenblum**, Roshambo, Seghesio, St. Francis, **TURLEY**
Iconic example: Ridge Zinfandel

ZINFANDEL—WHITE
Country: U.S.
Region: California
Color: red (although the wine is pink!)
Grapes: Zinfandel
Weight: light-bodied (and low in alcohol)
Volume: quiet to moderate
Dry/sweet: semi-sweet
Acidity: medium to medium-plus
Flavors: fruity, with notes of cherries, citrus, cotton candy, melon, orange, peaches, raspberries, strawberries, tropical fruits, watermelon

Texture: crisp, juicy, sometimes with a hint of effervescence
Temperature: Serve very cold, about 40 to 45 degrees.
Season: summer
Pairings: barbecue, charcuterie, chicken, fruit, ham, picnics, spicy cuisine, turkey
Aging: Drink young and fresh (within six months).
Producers: Beringer, Gallo, Mondavi, Sutter Home
Iconic example: Sutter Home

ZWEIGELT
[TSVY-gelt]
Country: Austria
Region: Burgenland
Color: red
Grapes: Zweigelt
Weight: medium- to full-bodied
Volume: moderate to loud
Dry/sweet: dry
Acidity: medium to medium-plus

Tannin: medium-plus
Flavors: fruity, with notes of anise, blackberries, black currants/cassis, **BLACK PEPPER**, blueberries, **CHERRIES, cinnamon**, cocoa, cola, earth, flowers, grapes, **plums, spices**, strawberries, tobacco, violets
Texture: rich, round, smooth, soft
Temperature: Serve cool, about 60 to 65 degrees.
Comparable: BLAUFRÄNKISCH
Pairings: barbecue, goulash, grilled meats, ham, hamburgers, lamb, pork, ribs
Producers: Blauer, Glatzer, Leo Hillinger, Pittnauer, Steininger, Weingut Hofer

If you think you don't like American wines and have a super-European palate, try an older vintage of anything from Ridge Montebello. Even if you don't like **Zinfandel**, you'll like this. I don't typically like Zinfandel, but Ridge's are spectacular.
—RAJ VAIDYA, DANIEL

With barbecue, if you pour a fruit-driven red with body such as **Zinfandel**, try serving it a little chilled. The alcohol does not become so evident, and the fruit has a perceived brightness to it—bringing out the sweet and savory spicy tones in things like barbecue sauce.
—JESSE RODRIGUEZ, ADDISON AT THE GRAND DEL MAR

For years, other sommeliers and I have been converting a lot of **white Zinfandel** drinkers over to Moscato d'Asti. We have them drinking Paolo Saracco Moscato d'Asti all the way through their meal. I have no problem with that because it is a good style of wine and delicious.
—BELINDA CHANG, THE MODERN

We don't offer **white Zinfandel**, but sometimes guests will ask for it. I'll gently suggest an alternative, Jorge Ordóñez Botani Moscatel Seco, which has a lot of tropical fruit [including lime and melon] flavor but finishes dry. This happened just the other night, and the guest really liked it!
—CLAIRE PAPARAZZO, BLUE HILL

WINE: THE PERFECT COMPLEMENT FOR EVERY COURSE

A robust wine overpowers the taste of a delicate dish, while a highly spiced dish will kill the flavor of a light wine. A dry wine tastes sour if drunk with a sweet dessert, and a red wine often takes on a fishy taste if served with fish.

—JULIA CHILD, *MASTERING THE ART OF FRENCH COOKING* (1961)

Selection of a wine begins with the food itself—what is its character and quality and how was it cooked? Is the food delicate, spicy, complex, or simple in flavor, rich or lean, was it grilled or sautéed, braised or roasted? With these questions answered, it then becomes possible to begin to choose a wine. The wine should neither overpower nor be a weak partner to the food; generally speaking, it should be of a similar pitch or tone value.

—PAUL BERTOLLI AND ALICE WATERS, *CHEZ PANISSE COOKING* (1988)

All wines and foods when authentic and true, no matter where they come from, what they are, or how much they cost, merit our respect and our attention in matching them judiciously. It is from the harmonious blending of the moment, the dish, and the wine that genuine culinary emotion is born, due as much to the immediate pleasure as to the future joy of recollection.

—ALAIN SENDERENS, *THE TABLE BECKONS* (1993)

In Chapter 4, you were introduced to the wine-world equivalent of at least one whole sixty-four-count box of crayons. What can you do with all these different "colors" of wine?

As you saw under "Pairings" for the wines listed in Chapter 4, each wine has a suggested range of compatible foods. And, as we'll detail in this chapter, the reverse is true, too—each course of a meal suggests a different style of wine.

Our book *What to Drink with What You Eat* was devoted to food-and-drink pairing, and we don't intend to duplicate that here. Instead, we'll take you through a multicourse meal—picture a xylophone of courses from canapés to white meat to red meat to cheese to fruit to chocolate—and show you how to think about its best wine matches. That way, whether you're planning a much simpler meal or one that's even more elaborate, you'll understand some of the principles of pairing. In no time, you'll be pairing like a pro.

Michael Flynn of The Mansion on Turtle Creek in Dallas put it best: "The whole notion of food-and-wine pairing is that perfectly lovely food paired with the wrong wine just doesn't taste good. Our rule is to make our chefs look the best they possibly can. When guests order the wrong matches with the food, it makes the chef look less good than he otherwise would.

"I wish people would open their minds to the fact that food-and-wine pairing is not some arcane exercise for the initiated. It is almost a social responsibility, because I think the world is a better place for it!"

By the way, while the recommendations in this chapter have food as their driving force, you should also take other important factors into consideration.

Of course you should drink what you like. But if you're anything like us, that may vary from day to day and situation to situation. "Food, mood, and weather is how I go about choosing wine," says Cat Silirie of No. 9 Park in Boston. She explains it this way:

- **Food:** What do you feel like eating? What would be great to drink with it? There is more than one choice.

- **Mood:** What kind of mood are you in? Do you feel like meditating intellectually on an important bottle of wine, or do you feel like slugging back something cold? They're very different moods.

- **Weather:** Is it boiling hot, with high humidity? Then it is probably *not* a time for Barolo. We will chill down some Beaujolais instead.

THE ROLE OF WINE IN A MEAL

When you have food and wine together, they must take each other to a different level. The food has to give back and close the circle. That is the perfect pairing that everyone talks about, but it is extremely hard to achieve it.

—ALDO SOHM, LE BERNARDIN

Wine can play different roles in a meal, depending on the guests. As sommelier Jeff Bareilles of Manresa (Los Gatos, California) has observed, there are three very distinct types of guests: "There are guests who make **wine the primary focus,** other guests who see the **wine as a frame for the food,** and still others who come in with **nothing in mind.** Those in the third camp are my opportunity to pour some tastes and see their eyes light up when the right food lines up with the right wine."

Bareilles finds that the majority of Manresa's guests have what he describes as a "California-centric" palate. "However, I have only about 10 percent California wines on the list here. Our wine list is driven by the cuisine [of chef David Kinch]. There are great California wines out there that I enjoy, but when the alcohol gets a little too high and the oak gets too aggressive, it tends to conflict with the subtle nuances of the dishes. When that happens, the guest is missing something."

When guests come in with nothing in mind and aren't open to a sommelier's suggestions, disasters can easily occur. "If you order linguini with clams, mussels, white wine, chili flakes, and parsley, can you think of anything worse than accompanying it with a California Cabernet?" asks Inez Ribustello of On The Square (North Carolina). "I have had people order that dish and return the wine saying, 'Something is wrong with this wine.' No, no, no, nothing is wrong with the wine—it's the *combination!*"

To come up with the kind of wine-and-food pairings that "close the circle," Eleven Madison Park's sommelier John Ragan and chef Daniel Humm taste together. Ragan describes their collaborative process: "I started working with Daniel [at Campton Place in San Francisco] a few months after he arrived in the United States. It was the first time I had worked with a classically trained chef from Europe. Daniel's food has gotten more pure, restrained, and, in a beautiful way, simpler. He knows what needs to be on the plate, and nothing is extraneous, so finding New World wines to match is always going to be a challenge.

"In San Francisco there are so many excellent small vintners who are doing great things. The wines we chose were a little more elegant in style, a little more restrained, and not over the top. We were able to find great wines for the dishes.

"We worked with Stony Hill a lot. They make Riesling, but they are really known for their Chardonnay. It is unlike any other Chardonnay you have had from Napa. It is grown high up on the hillside, which gives it great minerality. In their youth, they are crisp, taut, and almost tart/citrusy. They also age incredibly well—so at ten to fifteen years, they start to drink even better. If you were drinking a great vintage of Stony Hill you might guess it to be Chablis.

"For reds we had Skewis and Copain, who both make great Pinot Noir. For Cabernet Sauvignon, we had Mayacamas. In a sense, these are all winemakers who make Old World wines in the New World.

"We taste our food-and-wine pairings together, and we are pretty similar, usually standing on the same ground. We will get to the point where we agree on a wine, then one of us will say, 'Yeah, but I think there is something even better out there!'"

COMPOSING A MENU

Wine's principal role is to give pleasure, and that role is best played at table in the context of a menu; when the two are carefully chosen, the wine and the food enhance each other, each subtly altering the other.

—RICHARD OLNEY, *THE FRENCH MENU COOKBOOK* (1970)

We want to provide you with ideas for pairing wines to every course you might serve during a meal. While an elaborate multiple-course dinner at a restaurant might feature an *amuse-bouche* (a light hors d'oeuvre or canapé) followed by soup, fish, white meat, red meat, cheese, fruit dessert, and chocolates, a more typical meal at home might be as simple as a one-pot dish followed by dessert. You can pick and choose the courses and tips that apply from the options laid out below.

Certain rules of thumb apply, although they can be successfully broken in the right instances. For example, wines should generally be served in the order of dry before sweet, quiet before loud, and white before red.

The first principle of creating a menu is moving from light to heavy, in terms of both food and wine. Doing otherwise can lead to premature palate fatigue or a prematurely full stomach! Use the principle of the xylophone to guide you:

CONSIDERING WEIGHT/VOLUME WHEN PAIRING BY COURSE

FOODS/WINES	LIGHTER/QUIETER	MODERATE	HEAVIER/LOUDER
Savory courses	Canapés	Appetizers	Entrées
Savory ingredients	Vegetables	Pork	Beef
	Fish	Poultry	Game
	Shellfish	Veal	Lamb
Techniques	Boiling	Baking	Braising
	Poaching	Roasting	Grilling
	Steaming	Sautéeing	Stewing
Sauces	Citrus/lemon	Butter/cream	Demi-glace
	Vinaigrette	Olive oil	Meat stock
Wines	Pinot Grigio/Gris	Chardonnay	Cabernet Sauvignon
	Riesling	Merlot	Shiraz/Syrah
	Sauvignon Blanc	Pinot Noir	Zinfandel
Sweet courses	Sorbet	Fruit desserts	Chocolate desserts
Sweet wines	Moscato d'Asti	Late Harvest wines	Port/PX sherry

The secret of creating successful menus is practice, practice, practice. In this regard, few restaurants can match the experience of The French Laundry in Yountville, California, which creates new menus for lunch and dinner every single day. You'll get an idea of the potential for a menu to flow from course to course below.

Dennis Kelly on the Progression of a Menu at The French Laundry

We don't create a set list of wines for our menu because we want to get our guests' input to create the right pairing for them. The right pairing for you might not be the right pairing for someone else.

Let's take Riesling as an example. If someone wants an Old World wine, we might pour Karthäuserhofberg Trocken Riesling from Germany. If another guest wants something local, I will pour Stony Hill Riesling.

If we serve a dish with apricots and almonds, Sauternes may be the perfect accompaniment to that. If the guest wants something local, we will pour Topaz from California, which is 65 percent Sauvignon Blanc and 35 percent Sémillon and is modeled after Sauternes. People are amazed at the complexity and elegance they get from this California wine.

Our menu is rewritten for every single service [each lunch and dinner]. Our progression is to start with light, delicate dishes and build to the meat course, progressing down to the dessert course. We approach the wine similarly to how the kitchen approaches each course.

Canapés. We start with canapés, often seafood. We also serve *gougères* [cheese puffs], as we have done for years, as well as the salmon cornets, the first recipe in *The French Laundry Cookbook* [by Thomas Keller].
Wine pairing: Champagne.

Main canapé. Oysters and Pearls or a caviar course.
Wine pairing: More Champagne.

Salad, pasta, or foie gras
Wine pairing: With salad, I'll pair a wine with lower alcohol and higher acid like Riesling or Grüner Veltliner.

Two seafood courses. One fish course, then one shellfish course of lobster or scallops.

Wine pairing: We move to something richer with the seafood courses, like white Burgundy, domestic Chardonnay, or Rhône grape varieties, either Roussanne or Viognier.

First meat course. The first will be delicate, like squab, quail, or duck.

Wine pairing: We are starting to build in power. Now it is on to red. We start with a more delicate red like Pinot Noir or red Burgundy.

Second meat course. This is the peak of the menu, so it will be Kobe beef, Elysian lamb, or veal.

Wine pairing: We'll serve a powerful red like domestic Cabernet Sauvignon or Bordeaux. Côte-Rôtie and Brunello di Montalcino are also favorites here.

Cheese

Wine pairing: We will bring in a white with a little sweetness; frequently we choose a Vouvray.

Sorbet

Wine pairing: None. We just let the sorbet cleanse your palate.

Dessert

Wine pairing: This is when we move into a full sweet wine. We like something fortified, like Madeira. We are big fans of older Madeira with chocolate. Thomas Jefferson was also a big fan of Madeira. A 1968 Oliveira Bual was bottled in 2008, and it spent forty years in an oak barrel in a sun-baked loft.

We want to turn guests on to new things, but we never try to force a square peg into a round hole. If we can open your eyes up to something new and exciting, we want to do that.

When I go out to dine, I do the same thing. I put myself in John Ragan's hands when I went to Eleven Madison Park. He wanted to know what I wanted, and I wanted whatever he was going to recommend, because otherwise I get stuck in my own little world. I wanted to discover things that maybe I had not thought of.

PAIRING WINES TO EACH COURSE

There is an art to pairing wines to courses, because you not only want each wine to match the dish, you also want to have a progression of flavors throughout the dinner.

"You have to always consider what comes before and after any course—dish plus wine—in a menu, because you want those transitions to be flawless," says Justin Leone of Benny's Chop House in Chicago. "Just as you would if you were

GROWER CHAMPAGNE (NOTE THE "RM")

writing an album, you don't want to be skipping around. On the great albums, the songs make sense the way they roll into one another, which is why you could listen to a great album over and over. In the same way, you want a wine progression to be great from beginning to end."

Keep this in mind as we take you through each course and some suggested wine pairings.

Before the Meal

Before a meal, it's important to keep things light and refreshing. There are several lighter-bodied, higher-acid choices that top sommeliers turn to time and again.

Scott Calvert, The Inn at Little Washington

Champagne is the proper way to begin a meal like ours. There is nothing that works better as an entry to this kind of experience than a great glass of bubbly. I keep a limited but excellent selection to play with, and it is usually the first thing I mention. It is a proposal, if you will: Would you like to start with something? Champagne is the first offer. Most often people will say, "That sounds perfect," because the Inn is a celebratory place.

I usually have grower Champagnes [produced by the estate that grows the grapes and identified by the tiny "RM" on the bottle label; see photo above] flowing by the glass. However, I also feature small house producers, and two that I am pouring now are Domaine Boulachin Chaput and Gonet Rosé.

Virginia Philip, MS, The Breakers

We set the tone by bringing the Champagne cart to the table and offering a glass of Champagne or a cocktail. We offer the guests three different types of Champagne at three different price points, ranging from $16 to $60 a glass.

For **Brut**, we have offered Jacquesson or Taittinger La Française. In Champagne, we have picked most of the major players and powerhouses. Our **cava** is the Gramona Imperial—and people love it as a nice alternative to Champagne, which was reaching a price point where it was becoming expensive.

We offer **rosé** because it is pink and one of the favorites of the team. It is so easy to pair with food and opens up the palate. We have offered Ruinart and Henriot rosés as well as many others. It is also easy to pair with food because it can see you through the first course and even through the entrée.

We offer a **Tête de Cuvée** [Champagne makers' best of the best] by the glass because people may not want to buy an entire bottle, and this is a great way to try one. We have offered Mumm René Lalou, Perrier-Jouët, Krug, and La Grande Dame. We are actually one of the only restaurants in the country that is pouring the Lalou by the glass, and it is really lovely.

People see sherry on the wine list and are kind of taken aback, thinking it is going to be grandma's old sweet, sticky stuff. However, we like to offer a dry manzanilla sherry, usually Emilio Lustau. It is a personal favorite and just a great wine, especially if you are sitting there with olives and a little Manchego cheese. We have also paired it with courses such as shellfish with spiny sea urchins with a lemon verjus and green apple gelée, which was a lovely pairing.

Sabato Sagaria, The Little Nell

What do you think of first? Bubbles. When people are in the mood to celebrate, if you throw pink into the mix it is just that much more festive because people are not expecting it. There are multiple ways to go about this. When I was in Italy, what I loved was the Aperol Spritz, which many people don't know much about, but it is the little brother to Campari. It is a bitter with rhubarb and orange characteristics. The classic cocktail they make in Italy is a wine glass with a little Aperol in the bottom, filled with rocks, with Prosecco over that, topped with soda water and garnished with an orange slice. It is a light, refreshing, and colorful aperitif.

Emily Wines, MS, Fifth Floor

The first thing that comes to mind is something light and refreshing. It can be a citrus-based cocktail or a very high-acid wine like a Grüner Veltliner or dry Australian Riesling. Australian Riesling from the Clare Valley is bracingly dry and crisp and can get your mouth watering. If I wanted to do something on the conservative side, I would pour a Sancerre, which is a crowd pleaser. But for myself, I want something lean, mean, and bright.

Canapé Course

With some food in the picture, there is an opportunity for synergy as you strive to bring out the best of the food with the wine and vice versa. Be sure to keep your wines on the lighter side, like the light bites you're serving.

Emily Wines, MS, Fifth Floor

At the beginning of a long meal, I don't want to be hit with high alcohol; I want something more refreshing and lighter in body. When it comes to matching those first little bites, you also want something with some fruit. Riesling, especially one at the Kabinett level, or Chenin Blanc is a bit more luscious and has a little more "give" to it.

New York and Washington state Rieslings have nice body and ripeness. In New York, I am a fan of Hosmer in the Finger Lakes. They make a Riesling that is really gorgeous and has minerality and acidity along with a bit of fruit. It is not overwhelmed by a little pastry in the first bites. In Washington state, I love the Eroica made by Dr. Loosen and Chateau Ste. Michelle.

Alternatively, you could pour a *sec* [dry] Condrieu [from France's Rhône region], or even a very ripe Albariño [from Spain].

Soup Course

The idea of pairing a beverage with a liquid may seem redundant or odd—but wine can provide an important contrast or complement to soup. It can be used to cut the richness (think of black-bean soup with a splash of dry oloroso sherry) or to enhance it (think of corn chowder with a big, buttery California Chardonnay).

Sabato Sagaria, The Little Nell

Soup is a challenging course because you are dealing with many textures, so a lot has to do with the driving force of the ingredients and the spices that are accenting it.

In white wine, less is more when it comes to oak—meaning the less oak a wine has, the more versatile it is. So I try to go with unoaked whites until I have a dish with a cream sauce, and then I transition [to oaked whites] from there.

One of the flavors that chefs like to use in soups is bacon, whether it is clam chowder with bacon or potato soup with bacon. When you have that smokiness, I like to throw in some sweetness. You can pair like or opposing flavors; I like pairing opposites because it catches people off guard a little more.

So with a soup that has a slight smokiness to it, you could use Alsatian or German Riesling that has just a slight hint of sweetness. You could even pour Gewürztraminer for an off-the-wall choice.

Belinda Chang, The Modern

Our chef [Gabriel Kreuther] made a new soup, a tomato gazpacho that had a lot of texture from pureed almonds. We probably tasted twenty-five different wines with the soup, which had a nutty flavor and a rustic texture, but we kept coming back to a Crémant d'Alsace from Agapé. It added an interesting counterpoint of bubbly texture against the soup's own rustic texture. It was a super-cool pairing, and it pointed out to me that I was not using sparkling wines enough as pairing partners.

Salad, Pasta, or Foie Gras Course

Early in a classic multiple-course tasting menu, you might have a smaller vegetable- or starch-based course—or even a rich one, such as foie gras. Each calls for a different approach to pairing.

Aglianico . . . there are probably twenty grape varieties that are great with a dish with tomato sauce from Italy! So I would *not* drink it with Burgundy or Pinot Noir.

If I am having risotto with autumn truffles from Alba, I would love an old, aromatic Barolo. Yet I also like to eat risotto and truffles with a vintage Champagne with eight to ten years of bottle age. The risotto is lifted on the palate by the bubbles and the acidity. The Champagne has a completely different effect than Barolo, which melds and becomes savory, and where you are refreshed by tannin rather than by bubbles.

FOIE GRAS
Belinda Chang, The Modern

We have successfully served foie gras with a sparkling wine, a white wine, a red wine, and a sweet wine [see photo at right].

When I first got the list of our new foie gras dish's ingredients from the chef, I was thinking, "What am I going to do?" The dish is a sautéed foie gras with Medjool compote, preserved lemon, and a vanilla tuille. For some bizarre reason, it worked with every wine. It was amazing with rosé Champagne, with white Bordeaux, with a red Bordeaux–style blend from California, and with Tokaji. The dish had such an amazing balance that no matter what you poured, as long as the wine was very balanced, there was harmony.

Instead of doing a duet pairing, we are doing a quartet pairing [four different wines with the same course]. We pour a little glass of each, and it is a great exercise to show guests the potential of pairing.

Seafood Course

FISH AND SHELLFISH, FROM RAW TO COOKED

As you pair wine across the spectrum, from raw seafood (such as oysters, crudo, or ceviche) to lightly cooked seafood (such as poached or steamed fish) to dishes with heavier sauces (such as lobster with cream sauce or tuna with a reduced red wine sauce), your choices will range from racy whites to reds.

THE MODERN

Sabato Sagaria, The Little Nell

When it comes to pairing seafood, I look to the places most used to doing that, which are coastal regions. You are looking for light, clean flavors. When you are cooking, you squeeze citrus on a seafood dish to brighten up the flavors. I use wine to do the same thing. So I am looking for a high-acid white wine. It could be a high-acid Sauvignon Blanc from New Zealand or from the Loire Valley [in France], which are both great examples. I love Albariño when I think of the food from the area of Rias Baixas [in Spain]. Another wine from Spain would be Txakoli, which is made in the [Basque] region. For the consumer, it can be a little intimating, because the label is written in Basque and there are so many x's and y's that people get scared when they see the bottle!

RAW SEAFOOD (OYSTERS, CRUDO, CEVICHE)
Sabato Sagaria, The Little Nell

I have served as a judge at the International Wines for Oysters Competition [celebrated every November with the Oyster Riot at Old Ebbitt Grill in Washington, DC], and New Zealand conquers the world when it comes to wine with oysters. And if you are doing something with tropical fruits like papaya, mango, or a dish in a ceviche style with fruit characteristics, this is another time to open up New Zealand Sauvignon Blanc.

Michael Flynn, The Mansion on Turtle Creek

We offered a Riesling class, during which we had our chef send out our seafood ceviche salad, which is flavored with a liberal squeeze of lime juice and fiery chili heat. I wanted people to taste the fruity off-dry Rieslings next to the seafood salad and experience the incredible synergy between the two. One of the Rieslings poured was the Max Ferd. Richter Kabinett, which we refer to as the "Zeppelin label." It is a Mülheimer Sonnenlay, but everyone just calls it the Zeppelin because it's easier. The fruitiness of the Riesling really cooled the palate down after a bite of the seafood salad. The lively dance between the wine and food is amazing. All too often, I see people order ceviche in the restaurant while drinking Cabernet with it, and it's hard to stop myself from saying, "Don't do it, don't do it!"

Belinda Chang, The Modern

After serving something like Chablis, you can work on the next level of richness. For example, you can pull out a cool-climate-viticulture style of Chardonnay from Oregon or Washington state. You can move into varietals that have a lot of texture, like Pinot Gris, Grüner Veltliner, or Gewürztraminer, if the course can stand the notes of lychees and flowers. The Italians have it right with crudo, where they take a piece of great fish and serve it with olive oil, lemon, and sea salt. Let the wine be the complex thing for you instead of having them both compete. With lighter salmon or tuna tartare, you can move into red if you want to.

WINNERS OF THE INTERNATIONAL WINES FOR OYSTERS COMPETITION, OLD EBBITT GRILL, WASHINGTON, DC, 2000–2010

Every November since 1995, a panel of judges has convened for the final round of this competition to determine the best wine to drink with raw oysters. In 2010 the judges were José Andrés, Andrew Dornenburg, Michael Franz, Jacques Haeringer, Paul Lukacs, Tom Meyer, Andy Myers, Bill Plante, Karen Page, Phyllis Richman, Justice Antonin Scalia, Marguerite Thomas, Thomas Yannucci, and Eric Ziebold.

The panel's task is to select the gold medal winners from among twenty finalists. (The remaining wines earn silver medals, and the bronze medal winners are chosen during the semi-final round a week before.) An impressive 268 wines from all over the world were entered in the 2010 competition. Within the United States, 130 wines were submitted from seven states. Wineries from twelve other countries—Argentina, Australia, Austria, Chile, France, Germany, Greece, Italy, New Zealand, Portugal, South Africa, and Spain—entered a total of 138 wines.

The ten gold-medal wines are served with more than twenty types of oysters. In 2010, more than 72,000 oysters were consumed by the 2,800 guests at the Oyster Riot.

2010: 2009 Sileni Estates Sauvignon Blanc (Marlborough, New Zealand)

2009: 2008 Spy Valley Sauvignon Blanc (Marlborough, New Zealand)

2008: 2008 Saint Clair "Vicar's Choice" Sauvignon Blanc (Marlborough, New Zealand)

2007: 2007 Kim Crawford Sauvignon Blanc (Marlborough, New Zealand)

2006: 2006 Cono Sur Sauvignon Blanc (Casablanca Valley, Chile)

2005: 2004 Jackson Estate Sauvignon Blanc (Marlborough, New Zealand)

2004: 2004 Matua Sauvignon Blanc 2004 (Marlborough, New Zealand)

2003: 2002 Hunters Sauvignon Blanc (Marlborough, New Zealand)

2002: 2001 Charles Wiffen Sauvignon Blanc (Marlborough, New Zealand)

2001: 2000 Voss Vineyards Sauvignon Blanc (Napa Valley, California)

2000: 2000 Lawson's Dry Hills Sauvignon Blanc (Marlborough, New Zealand)

Emily Wines, MS, Fifth Floor

We have served a crudo made with lime and jalapeño that was such an obvious choice to serve with New Zealand Sauvignon Blanc, because I always get that jalapeño note in the wine. With this crudo, I have poured Whitehaven.

LIGHTLY COOKED SEAFOOD (FISH, SHELLFISH)

I had my first revelation with minerality from a bottle of Domaine des Chazelles Viré-Clessé, a Mâcon white. At the time it was inexpensive, around $12, and I stopped at Whole Foods to pick up some king crab legs. The gates of heaven were opened to me. I understood what they mean when they say, "This wine grows on chalk and limestone." At school at Indiana University I spent some time floating in quarries surrounded by wet walls of limestone. The olfactory sense is the most poignant and triggering sense for memory. The minute I took a whiff of that wine, it transported me back to that cool water and wet limestone. I got the sense that this creature [king crab] lives in the ocean eating minerals and is encased in a mineral shell. When you feast on this product, which is laden with mineral in every way, and put it with this wine born from Jurassic mineral, it hits every level of your being, from primal satisfaction to a connection to the universe you don't even realize you have. You cannot separate product from its place.

—JUSTIN LEONE, BENNY'S CHOP HOUSE

Sabato Sagaria, The Little Nell

When I go to the Loire Valley, I think of food that's more proper and French. You could have a scallop dish with a touch of cream and a little corn to sweeten it up. So for a more classical dish, I think of wines from the Loire Valley.

Albariño has more texture to it and would work with the shellfish characteristics of crab and lobster, either chilled or simply with drawn butter. Txakoli has more acidity, so you can go with a broader gamut of chilled or cooked dishes. I prefer it with chilled dishes because it is cleaner. If someone gives you lobster by itself, it tastes bland—but if you squeeze lime or lemon on it, it pops. The same happens with your wine, except your lemon or lime is in a bottle.

SEAFOOD WITH HEAVIER SAUCES

When you have a dish with a lot of weight and richness to it, a sparkling wine is a way to cut through that. Champagne can be so nice with delicate fish in a cream sauce.

—JOHN RAGAN, ELEVEN MADISON PARK

Emily Wines, MS, Fifth Floor

Here in San Francisco, Dungeness crab reigns supreme. Anything with shellfish flavors, such as crab or lobster, I like with Viognier. In shellfish you have that briny richness that comes out. The peachiness of a very elegant Viognier is really lovely against that.

We serve a lobster-crab cappuccino that is quite rich, and Viognier matches that in body but lends another range of flavors to the dish. It is one of my favorite combinations. I have two favorite Viogniers for this dish. On the conservative end there are Californian Viogniers that work really well, like Calera, which makes a very elegant style that has restrained oak. However, my favorite pairing is a Condrieu from Gangloff.

RED WINE WITH FISH

I love a quirky red wine, like a Grenache-based Cannonau di Sardegna, with fish. A sommelier I worked with gave the advice, "If you want to find a red wine to pair with fish, go to the islands—they are surrounded by water." This wine is juicy, yummy, fun, and still has dirt on it.

—ANDY MYERS, CITYZEN

I have people coming in and asking for only red wine with their meal. [Le Bernardin, a seafood restaurant, offers lamb, duck, and filet mignon only upon request.] As a sommelier, I find this challenging, and I have to be much more precise. There are a few possibilities with red wine and raw fish. You can go with Spätburgunder from Germany, Schiava wine from the northern part of Italy, Gamay, as well as Bourgogne. It is all about the fact that these wines are delicate, especially at a young age.

—ALDO SOHM, LE BERNARDIN

Belinda Chang, The Modern

Right now Gabriel [Kreuther, the chef] is obsessed with panna cotta. We have had almond, cauliflower with caviar, cucumber with smoked salmon sauce and trout caviar, and the current one is stinging nettles with fried lentils and yuzu. The common thread with these panna cottas is mouthfeel: a rich, velvety texture on your palate. You definitely want the wine to do the same thing. A wine with a bit of texture would be a Rhône variety, like a Marsanne-Roussanne or a Viognier. It could also be an unoaked Chardonnay—or Sémillon with bottle age from Australia would be fun. Even older Rieslings from Germany or Austria work, because as they age, they take on richness and viscosity as well as concentration, and that flows over your palate like the panna cotta.

White Meat Course: Chicken, Pork, Rabbit, Veal

The National Pork Board is looking for new slogans to help wake up the consumer to all the porky possibilities. If I were working for the pork board, I'd tell them to go grab a wine glass. The pork board's website has recipes, a handful of which include wine in the cooking. But there are no wine pairings or wine tips.

—BILL DALEY, CHICAGO TRIBUNE (AUGUST 4, 2010)

The versatility of white meats makes wine pairing an issue of the preparation—such as the sauce or other dominant ingredients—more than of the meat.

Sabato Sagaria, The Little Nell

With white meats, it is fun to cross over and showcase two wines with one course. White meats show well, so you can do the high end of white wine with a fatter style. Then you can also pour a lighter-style red wine. The deciding factor is the sauce, but it is the perfect transitioning course.

If you are serving chicken at home, you could have a puree of herbs, olive oil, and some lemon juice for your chicken right off the grill, and pour a Chardonnay. If you wanted to have a red wine, you might make chicken in a red-wine sauce and serve a Pinot Noir.

White meats are like a blank canvas. Viognier works nicely if you are serving chicken or pork on a ragout of corn and mushrooms. If you are serving pork roasted with some sweet potatoes, root vegetables, or corn with flavors that fall toward the sweeter spices, then I would look to a wine with riper fruit characteristics, such as a Viognier or Alsatian Riesling or Californian Chardonnay. If you want to go in a slightly different direction, look to an American or Australian Chardonnay, because it will have more ripe fruit.

Looking at lighter reds, people often overlook cru Beaujolais because they mistakenly think that Beaujolais is only to be had on the third Thursday in November [when the Beaujolais Nouveau is released] and then forgotten the other 364 days of the year. Cru Beaujolais is an interesting wine. It does not see too much oak or new oak, and as a result, the purity of the fruit comes through. You have granite soil that freshens up the wine, so you are looking at a light, fresh wine that has a bad rap. But a lot of investment is going on there nowadays, so with advances in winemaking, wine growing, and techniques, you are seeing better quality. Especially as Beaujolais gets hotter, you are getting riper wines that work nicely.

I love Spanish Rioja because it can be so versatile. It is extremely food friendly. You can look to Sicily and have Nero d'Avola and Cerasuolo di Vittoria, which is made from Nero d'Avola and Frappato and is a juicy picnic red. If you are serving something grilled, it will turn up the flavor profile. Smokiness works really well with wines with ripe fruit flavors.

Virginia Philip, MS, The Breakers

With **chicken**, it depends on the sauce you are pairing it with:

- *Italian:* If it is chicken Alfredo, you want something big and buttery. If it is piccata, we might use Verdicchio—something really crisp. If we add some Parmesan, we are talking a Chianti, such as Lucente or Allegrini Palazzo Della Torre.

- *French:* With coq au vin, we would pour a really hearty Brouilly from Château de Pierreux. That's a great pairing and not your typical everyday Beaujolais. It has very, very firm tannins, medium-plus body, lots of earth, and structure.

- *Asian:* I'd pair cashew chicken with Chinon.

- *Steakhouse:* Here we serve a roasted chicken, which I would have with a Duckhorn Merlot from California or a Foris Pinot Noir from Oregon.

- *All-American:* At the Top of the Point, we serve an "all-American chicken," and I would pour [a Rhône red] from Jean-Luc Colombo or a Shiraz from Mitolo called The Jester.

Inez Ribustello, On The Square

I have tried pairings I thought would be a no-brainer that just didn't work. I recently tried a **veal** scaloppini with a lemon-caper-white-wine sauce that was really, really tangy, and I thought it would be perfect with cava. That didn't work, and I ended up pairing a New Zealand Sauvignon Blanc instead.

Emily Wines, MS, Fifth Floor

Our chef, Jennie Lorenzo, is serving an herb-crusted **pork** loin with cherries, and I have been pairing it with Château Rayas La Pialade Côtes du Rhône. It is gorgeous, light, and soft, and tastes like strawberries and white pepper. It adds a soft fruit and herbal tone that matches right against the dish.

Pinot Noir is the quick fallback for lighter-style meat dishes, but this is a better alternative because of the range of flavors it lends to pairings. Many Pinot Noirs in California are becoming too full-throttle [with higher alcohol] and either are less food friendly or demand heartier dishes. In Côtes du Rhône, with Grenache, you have a great wild, toasted-herb tone with the fruit. Côtes du Rhône will always be an area of great value. The appellation doesn't have the cachet, but there are some amazing deals. It is one of the places I always send people to look for great value.

Belinda Chang, The Modern

This is the most interesting part of the meal, where you have a dish that can go with either white *or* red wine. We served a tagliatelle with saffron and cider-braised **rabbit.** We loved it with white Burgundy, as the dish made the wine taste really citrusy and brought up all its high tones. Then we tried it with Morey-Saint-Denis, which is a richer, earthier Pinot Noir that made the dish taste even richer and highlighted the mushrooms.

Red Meat Course: Beef, Lamb, Game

When it comes to pairing wine with red meat, you're pretty safely in red wine territory. But *which* red?

While different meats can suggest different wines, Virginia Philip, MS, at The Breakers, keeps a couple of very flexible reds in her back pocket at all times. She explains, "Two wines we find pair well with a variety of different meat dishes are Suri di Mu [a Barbera d'Asti from Italy] and Muga Selección Especial Reserva [a Tempranillo from Spain]. If we get stuck on a dish, we look to these two wines. What makes them work is the mix of the high-acid structure, the grape itself, and the earthiness that gives them a more powerful edge. We use them both in our steakhouse and in our brasserie."

BEEF: THE BIGGER, THE BETTER
Sabato Sagaria, The Little Nell

With **beef**, the bigger the wine, the better. Cabernet Sauvignon is an obvious pairing. However, when I pair, 90 percent of the time I try to stay away from the usual suspects. Anyone can get a steak and buy a Cabernet off the shelf. I want to take people someplace unexpected.

This is a chance to turn an everyday pairing into something different. Steak is the king of meats, and if you look to Italy you have Barolo, the king of Italian wines. It is very tannic, so it cuts through the fat.

I also look to Spain, because it is fun and a good crossover. Spain has reinvented itself and respected its heritage, as opposed to Italy with its Super Tuscans, which took Cabernet and made it a crowd pleaser. The Spanish have stuck with Tempranillo and Garnacha, older varieties that have been with them over the years. Ribera del Duero is definitely a meatier expression of Tempranillo than you will find in Rioja.

If you like big, ripe-style wines, look to [Garnacha-based] Priorat, which is a totally different style of Grenache than you would find in Châteauneuf-du-Pape. With Priorat, you could serve venison, steak, or elk. You can go to the heavier end of meat and serve a berry reduction [sauce] because you have high alcohol and ripe fruit in the wine. Priorat would be the crossover wine for people who like Zinfandel.

Emily Wines, MS, Fifth Floor

If you have a meat dish with a lot of fat, it cries out for a wine with weight like California Cabernet. Alexander Valley is an area I have been enjoying because the wines are not that full-throttle. They can be luscious, but they also have a greenness that is a nice contrast to the fruit. There is a new little upstart winery called Skipstone that blows my mind with unbelievable quality. We have an amazing **beef** entrecôte that is smoked *à la minute* and accompanied by Pommes Paillasson, which are essentially giant Tater Tots fried in duck fat and drizzled with herb oil. This dish is great with a big Bordeaux.

Dennis Kelly, The French Laundry

I do most of the cooking at home. I am a big barbecue fan, and I have a Weber Bullet smoker, which is perfect for a few racks of ribs or some tri-tips, maybe over some apple or cherry wood. With my barbecue, I like a smoky Syrah or sometimes a Zinfandel. I like Failla Estate Syrah, which is very reminiscent of Côte-Rôtie with its smokiness and minerality. It is more red fruit–dominated and less heavily extracted. For Zinfandel, I love the wines from Ridge. They have amazing complexity: they are field blends [wines made from several grapes grown in the same vineyard, which is rare], with lower alcohol and less oak influence. The winemaker, Paul Draper, is great about seasoning his oak so you get less coconut and dill flavor. The wines also age very well because they have great acidity.

GAME: FROM TANNIC REDS TO SWEET WINES
Sabato Sagaria, The Little Nell

Game covers the spectrum from quail [light] to squab to venison [heavy]. Pinot Noir pairs well with quail while Syrah, with its rich black fruit, pairs better with venison. Grenache, with its lighter red-fruit freshness, falls in the middle.

Sangiovese is one of my favorite wines to pair with game because it has tannin and high acid. I am an acid

Tip: On a recent visit to Argentina and Chile, we saw this trick practiced successfully time and again: To counteract the earthy, herbal notes in big South American and other red wines, top the red-meat dishes that accompany them with an herbed sauce, such as chimichurri, salsa verde, or even pesto. Your palate will perceive the herbal notes as coming from the sauce and not the wine, which will bring out the wine's fruit flavors.

(continued on page 260)

Tips on Pairing Wine to Various Cuisines

It can be helpful to know which red wines to avoid with spicy foods: you'll want to stay away from those that are high in tannin (such as big Cabernet Sauvignon and Tannat wines) and alcohol, both of which will "fan the flames."

Opt instead for fruitier reds, such as Beaujolais, Pinot Noir, Shiraz/Syrah, and Zinfandel, which will help take the edge off lots of spice. And don't be afraid to chill reds before serving; that will help tame the heat, too.

Below are some tips for pairing wines to various ethnic cuisines:

Chinese

BOTTLEROCKET

With Peking duck or mu shu of the day, we pour a blend of Mourvèdre, Grenache, and Syrah called The Holy Trinity [from Grant Burge in South Australia's Barossa Valley]. We also pair them with Petite Syrah, Pinot Noir, or Chinon.

Chinon works because it doesn't typically have a lot of oak so it is not overpowering. It is clean and crisp, with just enough tannic structure to go with Peking duck or cashew chicken. It also works with plum or spicy pepper sauces. It is a wine with elegance and just a little earth.

For whites, we have Poet's Leap Riesling from Columbia Valley, Washington; Gunderloch Jean-Baptiste Riesling from Germany; and a Côté Tariquet from Domaine du Tariquet [in southwest France] that is 50 percent Chardonnay and 50 percent Sauvignon Blanc. It is great because it has just enough acid and residual sugar, which makes it easy to sip and allows it to work with a great variety of foods.
—VIRGINIA PHILIP, MS, THE BREAKERS

As a fan of Peking duck rolls and mu shu pork, I've learned that hoisin sauce's earthy-spicy-sweet personality mirrors Pinot Noir extremely well. New Zealand Pinot Noir in particular has the right balance for this pairing because it can be as earthy as a Burgundy but with enough vibrant fruit flavors to match the sweeter elements of the dish. I have recommended the 2005 Seresin "Leah" Pinot Noir from Marlborough in New Zealand.
—KATHRYN MORGAN, MS, CITRONELLE

Indian

With Indian food, I stick with Champagne and German Riesling because the food runs the gamut. It can be greasy, fatty, and have a bit of sweetness. So these wines play it safe.
—RAJ VAIDYA, DANIEL

Japanese

Champagne is my go-to wine with Japanese food. Lighter Austrian wines are something I bring to the table as well—and crisp Loire wines can be fantastic. You can take a richer style, like a very mineral-y Sancerre or a Chenin Blanc with some richness to it, like Savennières.
—RAJ VAIDYA, DANIEL

MATCHING WINE TO COMMON DISHES

The dishes you enjoy most suggest various wines that can bring out their best. For more ideas, use Chapter 4 to look up wines that are comparable to those listed below.

Dish	Wine
Barbecue	Riesling (esp. Spätlese), Shiraz, Zinfandel
Charcuterie	Beaujolais cru
Chili	Zinfandel
Fajitas, beef	Zinfandel
Fajitas, chicken	Chardonnay
Fajitas, peppers	Sauvignon Blanc
Hamburgers	Beaujolais, Cabernet Sauvignon, Shiraz, Syrah, Zinfandel
Lasagna	Chianti Classico
Mac and cheese	unoaked Chardonnay
Meatloaf	Cabernet Sauvignon, Merlot
Omelet	Champagne
Pasta with pesto	unoaked Chardonnay from Italy, Sauvignon Blanc
Pizza	Barbera, Chianti Classico, Sangiovese, Zinfandel
Salad, in general	Beaujolais, rosé, Sauvignon Blanc
Salad, caesar	Arneis, Chardonnay
Soup, gazpacho	Sauvignon Blanc
Soup, minestrone	Chianti, Sangiovese
Soup, onion	Beaujolais, Pinot Blanc, Pinot Gris
Stir-fries	Pinot Grigio, Riesling
Sushi	Champagne, sparkling wine

MATCHING WINE TO COMMON CUISINES

Cuisines are so diverse that it's better to pair to the specific characteristics of individual dishes. However, if you just want a wine that should get you in the ballpark, consider these.

Cuisine	Wines
Asian	Chenin Blanc, Gewürztraminer, Riesling, rosé, sparkling wines
Chinese	Gewürztraminer, Riesling
Greek	Greek wines, Retsina, rosé
Indian	Gewürztraminer, Merlot, New Zealand Sauvignon Blanc
Japanese	Champagne, Chenin Blanc, Merlot, Riesling, sake, Sauvignon Blanc, sparkling wine
Mexican	Riesling, sparkling wine, Zinfandel
Middle Eastern	Beaujolais, Pinot Noir, rosé
Moroccan	rosé, Sauvignon Blanc, Vin Gris
Thai	Gewürztraminer, Riesling, Sauvignon Blanc
Vietnamese	Gewürztraminer, Riesling

freak when it comes to pairing food and wine because it freshens the palate and keeps you invigorated.

Barbera is another favorite. It is often overlooked, though it's one of the most widely planted grapes in Italy. Barbera d'Asti and Barbera d'Alba are juicy red wines that are affordable. Vietti makes a fantastic one, as does Giorgio Rivetti's La Spinetta with the rhinoceros on the label, which is more fruit-driven and expressive. Barbera d'Asti is a little brighter and d'Alba is a little juicier. If the game is grilled, I like the juicier fruit of the d'Alba to go with it. If it's pan-roasted, I'd opt for the d'Asti.

Emily Wines, MS, Fifth Floor

A dish on our menu that was unusual was **squab** crusted in peppercorn accompanied by foie gras with a hearty cocoa-based sauce. I served it with a 1969 Banyuls [a sweet French red wine known as an ideal match for chocolate], which was an unusual combination, but the dish needed sweetness and body, and the pairing was amazing. The Banyuls takes some hunting to find, but it is out there, and the old ones don't break the bank.

FOOD-AND-WINE FLAVOR AFFINITIES

In our book *The Flavor Bible* we explore the flavor compatibility of hundreds of ingredients, from apples to zucchini blossoms. Wine can add a third dimension to those flavor affinities, as seen in these examples.

Wine	Foods
Bual Madeira +	chocolate + almonds
Châteauneuf-du-Pape +	hamburgers + mushrooms
Fino sherry +	almonds + olives
Maury +	blue cheese + fresh figs
Merlot +	beef + horseradish
Pinot Noir +	duck + hoisin sauce *or* tuna + soy sauce
Prosecco +	ricotta + honey
Riesling +	pork belly + ginger
Sauternes +	almonds + peaches
Sauvignon Blanc +	fish + herbs

Cheese Course

Want to serve a nice wine with soft cheeses? Try decanting demi-sec Champagne. The off-dry sweetness accentuates the fruit of the Champagne while adding a layer of depth to the pairing. Decanting the Champagne gives it a mousse tone, which is soft and bubbly versus the normal tone of bracing bubbles.

—JESSE RODRIGUEZ, ADDISON AT THE GRAND DEL MAR

On Serving a Single Wine to See You Through an Entire Meal

Often you won't want to pair different wines to each course, and instead will seek one versatile wine to take you from appetizers through your entrée. At a more elaborate meal, you might consider serving this wine instead of water for sipping between more specific wine-and-food pairings. Either way, the recommendations below will give you ideas on what to choose.

Sabato Sagaria, The Little Nell

Champagne is the most versatile beverage in the world. It makes everything better. If you are working with chilled foods, it runs the gamut. With steak tartare, you can serve rosé Champagne. It refreshes the palate after rich, fried food. It even works with marrow. It is the palate cleanser that wakes everything up, keeps you alert with the dancing bubbles, and makes everyone happy.

Fernando Beteta, MS, NoMI

A "pacer" wine is an alternative to having water at the table during dinner: you use it to cleanse your palate. I don't drink a lot of water—I prefer wine. I find that in a long, elaborate tasting menu, you are getting only one ounce of wine, and then you have to wait five to ten minutes for the next wine to come.

A pacer wine needs to be something versatile without a lot of oak in it. **Riesling** or another unoaked, crisp wine is good because it will go with a lot of dishes. In a tasting menu, often chefs will prepare three to four courses that tend to draw on raw seafood or scallops. Tasting menus I have worked with have started with soup, salad, seared fish, game, duck breast, foie gras, and I am thinking, "This menu is all white wine."

Grüner Veltliner is fresh and bright, and I would absolutely have that. **Albariño**, a high-acid wine that is unoaked, would also work. You could also order **Champagne** for a four-course meal and have the sommelier bring a glass of red for your meat. Champagne, by the way, works very well with cheese.

As **rosés** can straddle the worlds of white wine and red wine, they are useful transition wines—and can even handle an entire menu all on their own.

Virginia Philip, MS, The Breakers

If guests don't want white wine or are having seared ahi tuna or salmon as a first course, **rosé** is a great pairing. We serve a dish with seared ahi tuna, cinnamon, and strawberry compote that would not work with white wine but works with rosé.

You need to keep in mind the progression of your courses—both food and wine. Make sure you are going from light- to medium- to full-bodied wines, so that by the time you get to the entrée, you have not killed the guests' palates.

Rosé serves this purpose because it's light, refreshing, goes with a variety of dishes, and is really good. If you have a table with several different dishes and they want only one bottle of wine, a rosé will work with fish, chicken, pork, lighter beef dishes, pigeon, and squab. Here are some options:

- **Light-bodied:** A lighter-side rosé would be Syrah or Grenache, such as **Château de Valcombe** from France or **Van Duzer** from Oregon.

- **Medium-bodied:** Côte Bleue from Jean-Luc Colombo in Provence is a blend of Counoise, Syrah, and Mourvèdre and would be on the medium side.

- **Full-bodied:** If you have red meat on the table, you want to go with a Cabernet-based rosé—and one that would work is the **Dillon** from Bordeaux.

At one time the conventional wisdom was to have a cheese course after the entrée as a way to finish off the (dry!) red wine at the table. However, today's sommeliers overwhelmingly prefer to pair a cheese course with an off-dry or sweet wine.

Belinda Chang, The Modern

The big lesson for me regarding the cheese course in great restaurants was un-learning a common practice. Guests often had some red wine left, so they'd be brought some cheese to take them through the rest of their red wine. I realize now what a big mistake that was. We were bringing guests super-high-acid **goat cheese** and **blue cheese**, which are *not* at their most delicious with still red wine!

I love the idea that white wine is amazing with cheese. I love super-mineral-y or oak-aged white, which is delicious with ripe, firm, tart cheeses, especially really **stinky unpasteurized cheese** like Époisses and St. Marcellin. The texture and acidity of white wine are great with the cheese course.

I love Petite Arvine from the north of Italy, which is a super-funky varietal. It has so much minerality, creaminess, and citrusy lemon notes. I had a Les Crêtes—which is a great producer—Petite Arvine with a cheese plate recently, and it was just delicious.

With cheese I also love oak-aged Chardonnay from Piedmont. A luxury choice would be Gaia, and another choice would be Rocche dei Manzoni, which makes great Chardonnay. Oak-aged Semillon that you find in Australia and New Zealand is also good with cheese.

Peter Birmingham, Pourtal

American dairies produce some of the tastiest and most original handcrafted cheese offerings. With **fresh, double- or triple-cream, or washed-rind cheeses**, try a crisp, dry Australian Riesling from the Clare Valley, or consider a Kabinett or Spätlese Riesling from the Mosel or a Scheurebe from the Rheinpfalz. You will be rewarded with a mind-blowing cheese-wine combination.

Scott Calvert, The Inn at Little Washington

Working with cheese, I like dessert wines because their profiles are as wide-ranging as any other wine. I just love that you can pair a **goat cheese or a delicate cream cheese** with a really nice, delicate Côteaux du Layon. At the other end, you can give the **funky, earthy cheeses** an aged Madeira that brings out all the tobacco and dirt in those cheeses. Madeira, because of its indestructibility alone, is a remarkable drink. With **blue cheese**, it represents the most incredible combination of flavors—it's a naturally perfect match. Think of a great old Madeira, like a Verdelho or a Bual: they are intensely nutty, with incredible acidity on the palate, and a little residual sugar and caramel. That is exactly what blue cheese tastes like.

Emily Wines, MS, Fifth Floor

People still like to end their meal with cheese and red wine, but I find there are not many red wines that work with cheese. Just as you would have dried fruits and nuts or honeycomb with cheese because they work so well together, I like to find wines that echo those flavors.

My favorite cheese wines are Pommeau de Normandie, which is a very interesting *vin de liqueur* made from apple juice and fortified with a little Calvados. I also love Banyuls, with its raisiny flavors. Tawny port or a Madeira on the sweeter side, such as Sercial, and Pedro Ximénez or Moscatel sherry give you those succulent fig and date flavors that work with **salty cheese.** With the fruit and nut flavors of the wine, you can have your cheese straight with no accompaniments. Other sweet wines, like Sauternes and Jurançon, also work well with **blue cheeses.**

Sabato Sagaria, The Little Nell

I prefer sweet wines with cheese. Starting with **hard cheese,** like pecorino, Parmesan, and such, I look to blonder wines, such as a Vin Santo from Italy. I like those cheeses with a little bit of honey, so I look for that characteristic in my wine, such as you'll find in a Beaumes-de-Venise from France.

People don't know as much about dessert wines, so I tend to be less aggressive with my pairings and more classic with cheeses than with other courses. For **sharper cheeses like Cheddar,** I like ice wine. Once you start with **blue veins in your cheese,** you are looking for the darker side of things—like port, Banyuls, and Ripasso from Italy. Since people already know the pairing of port and blue cheese, I do like to use the Ripasso because of the dried-grape and raisiny characteristics. If you want to stay in California, Bonny Doon Framboise [which tastes of raspberries] is something different that works. Quady Black Muscat Elysium is a little off the beaten path but accomplishes the same thing with blue cheese.

Sorbet

Because a sorbet course is served as a palate cleanser, it is not generally accompanied by a wine. "With sorbet, I will serve Paolo Saracco Moscato d'Asti, which I love because it is light and fresh. I love it with any kind of fresh fruit–based dessert because it is so delicate and clean," says Emily Wines, MS, of the Fifth Floor in San Francisco. "I also love Banfi Brachetto d'Acqui for the same reason, plus you get this little glimpse of fresh fruit that is a snapshot in time."

Dessert Course

FRUIT DESSERTS

I was in Argentina and found a sparkling Torrontés produced like a Moscato d'Asti in Patagonia. It is a slightly sweet, simple style of wine that is delicious. It

is very feminine, and even the guys love it! I will pair this with fruit desserts and parfaits, and it is wonderful with berries.

—ALDO SOHM, LE BERNARDIN

When it comes to fruit desserts, some believe "the sweeter the better" applies to the accompanying dessert wine.

Emily Wines, MS, Fifth Floor

Fruit desserts are tricky—it's challenging to pair them with wine. The wine has to be as sweet as the dessert or sweeter to pair with it. If the dessert is very sweet, however, it can be overwhelming to have a sweeter wine with it.

Auslese Riesling is excellent in that it isn't too heavy and offers great sweetness. Or you could move up to a Beerenauslese. If it is an apricot or peach dessert with dried or roasted flavor, I would turn to Sauternes as a standby. I like Muscat de Beaumes-

Pairing Wines to Berries

Jennie Schacht, coauthor with Mary Cech of *The Wine Lover's Dessert Cookbook*, shared with us her helpful rule of thumb: "The darker the berry, the darker the wine you'll want to pair with it." A few examples:

- **Strawberries:** Demi-sec Champagne, Muscat de Rivesaltes
- **Raspberries:** Sauternes, sparkling wine, sweet Vouvray
- **Blueberries:** Brachetto d'Acqui, Graham's Six Grapes Port
- **Blackberries:** Black Muscat, Brachetto d'Acqui

de-Venise with desserts, but sometimes the amount of alcohol can be challenging, so it depends on the weight of the dessert.

With pineapple, I always love ice wine because it reminds me of candied pineapple. The razor-sharp acidity that you get in ice wine and pineapple are a nice match. I do prefer German eisweins for their acidity and minerality, though there are some very good Canadian ice wines as well.

Sabato Sagaria, The Little Nell

I prefer something clear, light, and not too heavy. I prefer ice wine from Canada or Vin de Glacière [made by Bonny Doon in California] with lighter fruit desserts with apples and pears and a little ginger. German eiswein is fantastic, though it gets a little pricey.

When you get into desserts with a little caramel character, I love Alsace, with its Vendanges Tardives. I tell people that the principle is the same as with German wines: the longer the words, the sweeter the wine!

CHOCOLATE DESSERTS

Chocolate desserts are more intense than fruit desserts, enabling them to take on increasingly intense dessert wines as pairing partners.

Virginia Philip, MS, The Breakers

With chocolate desserts, we pour a lot of Braida or Banfi Brachetto d'Acqui, especially if there is a lot of fruit in the dish.

If you have an all-chocolate dish, Banyuls is amazing. It is 100 percent Grenache grapes, and ours will be vintage, so they have some oak aging to them.

Dark chocolate can be hard to work with because it is so powerful. [Banyuls] is a wine that has not only sweetness but a stickiness that complements the chocolate without overpowering it. You can still taste the chocolate and still taste the wine. It tastes nice by itself, but it works better with food. The Chapoutier is definitely consistent and has a little more fruitiness. The Clos de Paulilles Banyuls is also fruity but has a little more grip from being more tannic.

Belinda Chang, The Modern

I love Banyuls with chocolate desserts. Port and Madeira are super styles of wine, but sometimes they can be a little rich and over the top, especially after a long meal.

I love that Banyuls can give you richness and dark red, residual sugar, but it also tends to have a little less alcohol. It also ages forever. You can buy a bottle of 1929 Banyuls for around $100 and totally impress your friends.

Sabato Sagaria, The Little Nell

I love Madeira, a wine that people don't really understand. I am not much of a chocolate eater, but this was one of the most vivid examples that made the pairing click for me. While I was in college at Cornell, I was a teaching assistant for a wine course; I got paid $5.50 an hour and got to bring home two wines. One day they sent me home with a bottle of Bual Madeira, and my mom had just sent me a care package for exams that had some Hershey Kisses with almonds in them. So I was studying late and popped some Kisses while sipping my Madeira. That pairing is what turned me on to Madeira!

Madeira works better with bitter chocolates, especially when you throw nuts into the mixture, because it has its own nutty character that evolves over time with the oxidation. The combination of chocolate, nuts, and Madeira is a home run for me.

Emily Wines, MS, Fifth Floor

Pedro Ximénez sherry can be great with chocolate. I take a glass and rinse it with an orange bitters that has cardamom in it, then pour in the sherry. You end up with a very aromatic beverage that matches up against the bitter chocolate. With a chocolate-coffee dessert, it is fun.

Aldo Sohm, Le Bernardin

I have port on our list, but with chocolate, I prefer a Trockenbeerenauslese — or a Late Harvest Zinfandel from Dashe in California, with moderate alcohol and moderate extraction.

Scott Calvert, The Inn at Little Washington

There are myriad ways to play with chocolate. A sparkler, like a Giacomo Bologna Braida Brachetto d'Acqui, works well with a delicate chocolate dessert such as a

soufflé. Of course, port works for the richer stuff, like dense, bitter chocolate. Vin Santo is fantastic for milk chocolate because of its rich texture and caramel scent.

Maury from Mas Amiel is incredible. I am pouring the 1980, and it is as chocolatey and rich as it gets. It is so complex and so perfectly suited for chocolate that it gets people twisted! Maury is a region that has not received a lot of attention, but it is essentially the same thing as Banyuls. I think of them in the same breath—Maury and Banyuls are not far from each other and make wine from the same grape.

We serve a chocolate trio, with one delicate, one medium, and one very rich. For this I pour multiple choices, because I like to play. With the soufflé, I pour the Brachetto d'Acqui. With the chocolate bombe with malted center, I pour the Vin Santo. With the dark chocolate cake, I pour a Maury or a Banyuls.

ICE CREAM

Pairing sweet wine with ice cream can be very challenging. "The sauce has to be the driving force," explains Sabato Sagaria of The Little Nell in Aspen. "I wouldn't go too high on the alcohol and would stick with a dessert-style Riesling if there is fruit. I would try a Late Harvest Viognier if there are sautéed peaches on the ice cream. For Bananas Foster, you are dealing with banana and cinnamon, so Vin Santo would work. A Late Harvest Gewürztraminer would also work because it has spice to it. Australia does a great job with its 'stickies,' and you could have Muscat from Rutherglen."

Belinda Chang of The Modern in New York City counts herself a lover of well-made ice cream. "Vanilla ice cream with a seasonal fruit like berries in the

HOLY GRAIL FOOD-AND-WINE PAIRINGS

Some food-and-wine pairings can be so extraordinary that any self-respecting food lover will want to sample them at least once.

Food	Wine
Asparagus +	Sauvignon Blanc
Chocolate +	Banyuls
Corn +	buttery, oaky California Chardonnay
Crab +	Riesling
Lamb +	red Bordeaux
Lobster +	white Burgundy, California Chardonnay
Mushrooms +	Pinot Noir
Mussels +	Muscadet
Oysters +	Chablis, Muscadet
Raw Shellfish +	Muscadet, Sancerre
Salmon +	Pinot Noir
Steak +	California Cabernet Sauvignon
White Truffles +	Barbaresco, Barolo

summer pairs with a Vendange Tardive or a Sélection de Grains Nobles Pinot Gris," she says. "You have the brown, spicy Pinot Gris with the oak aging that comes from the wine. Those are fun flavors and textures to pair with the vanilla and berries.

"I would recommend one from Zind-Humbrecht, which would be a super rock-star wine. When you are talking luscious, decadent, and rich, Alsace sweet wines are no question the winners."

After-Dinner Drinks: Digestifs

After dinner, parting can be bittersweet — literally.

Sabato Sagaria, The Little Nell

Digestifs get a little wackier. Italy does a lovely job with them. I am fond of Amaro, and my favorite is by Nonino. It is an elixir with herbal character and both sweetness and complexity. I like it with two ice cubes, and find it a sophisticated way to end the evening.

Galliano is one of those things that should be dusted off more often. At the end of a dinner party my parents would pull out the special pewter glasses, and we would have little sips of it. Galliano on the rocks is something I really enjoy. It is sort of retro, with a little sweetness, and it's a little more approachable than Scotch.

These drinks are high in alcohol, but since they are served on the rocks, they are lighter. It is like jumping into the pool after being in the Jacuzzi.

Emily Wines, MS, Fifth Floor

I love bitters, and in San Francisco we are kind of crazy for bitters. Fernet Branca is the big standby here, but Amaro Averna is a digestif with a little sweetness to it. Nocino, a walnut bitter that is a little sweet, would be another alternative. I serve them neat in a sherry glass, either at room temperature or a little cool, because the alcohol can be a bit much if it is too warm.

Belinda Chang, The Modern

I am a huge Armagnac lover. I love it more than Cognac because it is more fiery, more textured, more flavorful, and less processed. For a wine lover, it is a great way to finish a meal. There is a great variety of producers and styles. Francis Darroze is called the pope of Armagnac. He makes several different cuvées that are not crazy in price. His 1973 is my favorite. It is an awesome way to put me to bed!

ELEVATING THE EXPERIENCE:
ESSENTIALS OF SERVING AND ENJOYING WINE

Like food, wine has mood and weight, which is reflected in the place, occasion, climate, and manner in which it is served.
—PAUL BERTOLLI AND ALICE WATERS, *CHEZ PANISSE COOKING* (1988)

As we're reminded on the surprisingly frequent occasions that we are served wine in glasses that are obviously expensive but thick-lipped, etched, tinted, or otherwise opaque, the nuts-and-bolts advice in this chapter is still sorely needed by many people.

It's not enough to know how to find a good bottle of wine; you've got to be able to serve it in a way that allows you to really enjoy it! This chapter addresses the best ways to elevate the experience of serving and enjoying wine, both in general and specifically at home or at a restaurant.

IN GENERAL

Wine is a living liquid containing no preservatives. Its life cycle comprises youth, maturity, old age, and death. When not treated with reasonable respect, it will sicken and die.
—JULIA CHILD, *MASTERING THE ART OF FRENCH COOKING* (1961)

In Chapter 2 we outlined "Ten Secrets for Getting More Pleasure from Wine." Four of these secrets are covered in greater depth here, making this chapter perhaps the most important one in the book. Tips like "Store it well," "Check the temperature," "Use quality glassware," and "Let it breathe" deserve to be explained and explored in more detail.

Store It Well

Wine is a living, breathing substance. Even if a bottle leaves the winery in immaculate condition, the road it travels to your glass is fraught with peril along the way.

Wine can be mortally wounded by improper handling. If it spends too much time on a hot delivery truck or on a hot wine-store shelf in the summertime, the wine can "bake" and be destroyed.

There is little you can do to ensure that your wine has been treated properly before it reaches your hands, though you should buy from reputable retailers who keep the temperature in their stores cool enough. One perfectionist in this regard is Moore Brothers, the *Zagat Survey*'s number-one-rated wine retailer based in New York. There and at its other locations in New Jersey and Delaware, Moore Brothers guarantees that every bottle it sells has been kept at a consistent 56 degrees from the moment it leaves the winery in refrigerated trucks to the time of purchase.

Regardless of *where* you buy it, plan to drink your wine very soon — or find a way to keep it in cellar conditions, that is, at a constant temperature of about 55 degrees, with the bottle on its side (so the cork doesn't dry out, allowing air in and spoiling the wine), and protected from bright light.

BEFORE OPENING

Don't bother collecting wine if you don't have a wine cellar or at least a wine refrigerator.

—MICHEL COUVREUX, PER SE

How long can you store wine? That depends on the wine. The vast majority should be consumed within a year or two after purchase, and some even more quickly. (Prosecco should be drunk young and fresh, within a year. Beaujolais Nouveau should be drunk within a few months.) While there are rules of thumb regarding aging (which we touched on in Chapter 4), even under the best conditions, successful aging is never a sure thing. There are no guarantees that a wine will be at its peak—or even drinkable—at the time you decide to open it. It is a matter of trial and error.

Aging tends to result in mellower reds and more caramel- and/or nutty-noted whites. "It is a matter of taste," says Emily Wines, MS, of the Fifth Floor in San Francisco. "Some people love the flavor profile of aged wines—but other people just want to taste the fruit and don't like the taste of an aged wine. The best way to learn about aging is to buy a few bottles and drink one every year or two. You will see how it starts to develop and find out what its lifespan is. Aging is not for everybody, and it's not for every wine, either. On occasion you can find something really bizarre, like an aged Sauvignon Blanc that is very interesting, and with the right kind of dish it can be just perfect."

Buying wines to cellar long-term is not for the faint of heart. Nine out of ten wines are meant to be drunk young and fresh—typically within a year or two after purchase. Less than one wine in a hundred will benefit from being aged for several years. Those with the greatest aging potential tend to be tannic reds, such as Cabernet Sauvignon. Red wines get their tannins from contact with the skins of the grapes during the winemaking process, which imparts color as well as flavor and texture.

To repeat: despite experts' best educated guesses, it's never a sure thing that a wine will in fact be good at the time you decide to open it. To cellar wines, you need a protected space in which you can maintain a constant temperature of about 55 degrees and keep out bright light. Even wines with great aging potential don't stand much chance of achieving their promise if they are improperly stored.

A Word About Vintages

A good producer will make good wine every year, argues Michel Couvreux of Per Se in New York City. "The difference will be that a vintage that is not as good will simply not age as long as a good vintage," he says. "I poured a 1986 Château Rayas that was not considered a great vintage—Robert Parker had given it a lousy score—and it was fantastic. This wine was under $700, as opposed to the $1,500 to $3,000 price commanded by a 'top' vintage of that wine. We tasted this wine in a blind tasting and loved it. Investment wine buyers look only at scores: if a wine is 99 to 100 points, they know it will increase in value. But you have to trust your palate!"

DURING OPENING

A top-of-the-line Château Laguiole sommelier's corkscrew can cost $200 to $300 or more. While some of their designs are admittedly beautiful, these corkscrews have no effect on the flavor of the wine. So save your money and spend it on glassware—or more wine—instead!

"I have friends who have a $99 Rabbit wine opener, and the wines they are drinking are just okay," observes Fernando Beteta, MS, of NoMI in Chicago. "Then they come to my house and see how casually I treat old bottles. I can barely find a wine opener! My wine opener of choice at work

is a Laguiole, but at home I will just use whatever is around. Or if the wine comes with a screw cap, so much the better!

"Wines with screw caps, by the way, are great to take to parties or picnics. In terms of the perception of screw caps, I ask doubters, 'Do you buy any high-end whisky or vodka? *They* come with screw caps.' Consumers then don't find them that big a deal. More and more wineries are offering them, and it is great for wines that are intended to be consumed young. They are fun, and I love them. However, I still think cork is best for wines that need to be aged for twenty or thirty years."

AFTER OPENING

Wine is a perishable product, so it won't last forever. "When customers ask me how long a wine will last after opening, my answer is, 'Why are you saving the wine?' They don't put expiration dates on wine the way they do with juice, but would you want to drink that juice after one year?" asks Fernando Beteta. "If you open a bottle of wine, try to enjoy it in the next day or two.

"For the most part, consumers who are not collectors should buy wine to consume with food and have it soon after purchase—and not worry about collecting it. If you are looking for something with age, go to a restaurant and have the sommelier recommend a good vintage," Beteta recommends.

If you don't usually finish an entire bottle of wine in one sitting, you can extend the life of your leftovers by removing the air from the bottle. We've used our VacuVin system (about $15)—a white plastic pump plus a couple of rubber stoppers—on occasion over more than a decade. It's still best to try to finish a bottle as soon as possible (say, within a night or two) after opening, but we've had pumped bottles remain drinkable as long as a week later.

Because the VacuVin system doesn't work on sparkling wines, you'll want to have a few rubber-lipped Champagne stoppers on hand to extend the life of your bubblies. We use a chrome stopper with two hinged arms that clamp around the neck of the bottle (less than $10) to keep it sealed tight.

We got some firsthand evidence of how effective those stoppers can be when we visited a friend in Southampton one August and found in the back of his refrigerator the same half-drunk magnum of fine California sparkling wine we'd left there the August before. When we removed the stopper, there was a loud "POP!" The sparkling wine still had a remarkable amount of fizz, although its flavor wasn't what it had been the year before.

If you find yourself without any such gear to help you extend a wine's life, consider putting it in an airtight container, such as an empty water bottle. Fill it to the top with wine, and then cap it. Or simply place the cork back in the wine bottle and refrigerate until the next day; the low temperature will slow oxidation.

Check the Temperature

Adour-ation: The foodies were hypercritical at the preview of Adour, **Alain Ducasse**'s new wine-themed restaurant in the St. Regis. Among the discerning palates were Payard Patisserie's **François Payard**, The Modern's **Gabriel Kreuther** and Union Square Cafe's **Michael Romano,** who raved about the scallops and sweetbreads. **Andrew Dornenburg** and **Karen Page,** authors of *What to Drink with What You Eat*, pulled out an infrared wine thermometer to test the temperature of their Champagne—a demo of the nifty gadget they'd brought as a gift for their dinner hosts. Still, the maître d' hovered anxiously nearby until they announced, "43.5 degrees." "Perfect!" he declared.

—RICHARD JOHNSON, "PAGE SIX," *NEW YORK POST* (JANUARY 24, 2008)

A few powerful experiences have convinced us of the utmost importance of not only storage temperature but serving temperature. Even a few degrees can make a huge difference in the way you perceive a wine. Check Chapter 4 for the recommended serving temperature of any wine you plan to serve. Of course you should take into consideration your personal preferences regarding temperature. (We prefer starting our red wines a bit cooler. Andrew has very warm hands, so his wine may warm more quickly than others', especially when we drink from stemless wine glasses.) You'll also want to consider the weather. We generally prefer to serve wines colder in the summertime and not quite so cold in the dead of winter.

If you simply keep your wine in a wine rack in the dining room, your home's thermostat setting becomes your personal cellar temperature—which might be 70 degrees or higher. While that temperature is toasty when you come in from the winter cold, it's lousy for wine storage—and also means your red wines will need to be chilled before you drink them. The appliance maker Whirlpool sets its refrigerators at 37 degrees, which will keep your white milk pleasingly icy but your white wines too cold to show their best.

An easy rule of thumb for most table wines is to cool your reds for fifteen to twenty minutes before serving and to take your whites out of the refrigerator fifteen to twenty minutes before serving.

"One of my pet peeves when I go out is that white wine is served too cold and red wine too warm," admits John Ragan of Eleven Madison Park in New York City. "Red wine shows so much better with a little chill, so don't be afraid. Conversely, leave the white wine out of the ice bucket."

Sparkling wines, including Champagne, should generally be served colder than other whites or rosés. Opinions vary, but the preferred temperatures range from 40 to 52 degrees, with general agreement hovering around 40 to 45 degrees. The Mumm winemaker Didier Mariotti told us at a lunch at Per Se in New York City that his goal had been to create a "gastronomic" Champagne, which became evident the moment we tasted the elegant 1998 Cuvée R. Lalou (priced about $160 on release), an equal blend of Chardonnay and Pinot Noir. However, it was served in two different glasses at two different temperatures, and we found that it tasted like two different wines. Served at 42 degrees, it was crisply acidic and refreshed our palates by cutting through the richer dishes. At 52 degrees, the same wine showed even more creaminess, enveloping the dishes we sampled it with.

We both love the Nuvo Vino infrared wine thermometer ($40; nuvovino .com)—Karen regularly carries hers in her purse. It's a pen-sized thermometer that you simply click one inch away from the surface of the wine (it is *never* submerged!) to get a digital temperature reading. Nuvo Vino's website quotes the Bordeaux oenologist Émile Peynaud (author of the 1996 book *The Taste of Wine*) as saying that the same red wine will taste "hot and thin at 70 degrees F, supple and fluid at 64 degrees F, and full and astringent at 50 degrees F."

We are surprised at how often we're served wine at less-than-optimal temperatures. During opening week at one upscale Manhattan restaurant, we sent back two glasses of white wine that were not cold enough; we then switched to Champagne, which was kept well chilled. And while Madeira may be hardy enough to withstand an entire summer in a non-air-conditioned apartment, that doesn't mean it's pleasant to drink at that temperature: We were once served a glass of Madeira, which we prefer just north of cellar temperature (say, 55 to 60 degrees), at 72 degrees, which killed our taste for it, even if the wine was unharmed.

By the way, if you're not able to enjoy a wine you've ordered at a restaurant because its temperature is significantly off, speak up. The proper serving temperature is sometimes a matter of opinion, but it can be helpful to defuse the situation by not stating, "This Madeira is too warm" but rather "This Madeira is not pleasant to drink at 72 degrees."

Use Good-Quality Glassware
The bigger the wine, the bigger the glass.
—JULIA CHILD, *MASTERING THE ART OF FRENCH COOKING* (1961)

The best investment you can make in your enjoyment of wine is to buy excellent wine glasses and use them every day. Too often in the past, we found ourselves using thick-lipped glasses—harder to break and easier to clean—that simply didn't offer the best experience. No more—not since we discovered Zalto Denk' Art glassware from Austria (zalto.us), whose elegant, eye-catching design first piqued our interest and whose dishwasher-safe performance won us over.

Two of Zalto's Universal glasses have become our daily choice for meals at home. Their $60-per-glass price tag would be a lot harder to swallow if they weren't so extraordinarily sturdy. They are beautiful, with thin lips and long, graceful stems. These glasses allow us to swirl and view appealing whites and inhale the bold aromas of reds. After using them every weekday for a year, we had upgraded every sip of wine we drank for just a few dimes a day—and now that we've had them for a few years, the investment can be measured in mere nickels.

ALDO SOHM OF LE BERNARDIN ON GLASSWARE

Not having the proper glass for a wine is like buying a Ferrari and putting on bad tires. You won't enjoy the car—or you will only to a certain extent. What's the point of buying a Ferrari and going cheap on the tires? So don't do it to your wine.

I prefer a glass that is fine and thin, even if it is fragile. A glass is a work of art. I want it to show clean and bright flavors. It is all about how the wine falls on your palate. There are certain spots on your palate where you taste acidity or sweetness. So I want the rim to hit the tip of my tongue so I catch the sweetness. If the rim is straight, the liquid falls toward the back to catch more of the acidity or saltiness. It is esoteric and there is a lot of science to it, but it is the nice tire on the Ferrari.

I have tested Zalto glasses next to Riedel and other glasses, and Zalto is a very powerful glass—even a person who has no idea about wine can recognize a fault in the wine. These glasses are an investment, but they are very sturdy and don't break easily.

When you taste a wine in different-shaped glasses, you find differences in the wine. Maximilian Riedel is very successful at this. He will give you the same wine out of three different-shaped glasses for you to blind taste so you can experience the difference.

ALDO SOHM

How sturdy are they? We have had more than a dozen Zalto glasses transported by van to and from several wine-related television segments, and we didn't lose a single glass! Even with almost daily use, we've only broken one.

If you're seeking more affordable glassware, you might consider the casual glasses we sometimes use: the attractive Riedel (rhymes with "needle") Vivant glassware, available at Target. At about $10 for each lead-free Tyrol crystal glass, from a company with more than three centuries of glassmaking expertise, they are a bargain.

The first time we saw other wine professionals bring their own Riedel glasses to dinner at an inexpensive BYOB restaurant, it struck us as kind of uptight. However, when we went out for Peking duck at a Chinese restaurant in our neighborhood and brought along a nice Pinot Noir, we wished we had done the same—the wine would have tasted a lot better than it did in their inexpensive, thick-rimmed glasses.

"Most people don't even have the correct glassware," observes Fernando Beteta. "It's sad when you go to someone's house and they serve great wine in $2.99 glasses. For your whites and reds I recommend a Universal glass, which you can put in your dishwasher."

MICHEL COUVREUX

MICHEL COUVREUX OF PER SE ON DECANTING

When you open a bottle of wine, an hour later it will be completely different. That is why we decant wines: it helps the wine to open up faster than it does in the bottle. We decant a wine that is young so it will open up. The wine will give you more flavor and intensity. It has just come from the cellar and is cool. We need to bring it up a few degrees. Most of the wines people drink are young, and at the end of the meal they say it tastes so much better.

If you know what you want to drink, look at the wine list online, call the restaurant, give them your credit card information, and ask them to open the bottle before you arrive.

If you are like me, you don't want to open a bottle of wine and wait twenty minutes to have a sip! So have one or two glasses of another wine and give your wine time to open up.

How much time?

- **Italy:** Italian wines need to be decanted. Barolo and Brunello need at least two hours to open because of the tannin and acidity.

- **Bordeaux:** It depends on the vintage. Bordeaux from the 1980s and 1990s need two hours to open up. Check the vintage: older wines may need only thirty to forty-five minutes, because they are more sensitive to oxidization.

- **Burgundy:** If you have a bottle of 1999 to 2002 Grand Cru Burgundy, you'll want to decant two to three hours beforehand, because the wine is too tight. For older Burgundy, I don't decant. I just open it and leave it in the bottle.

- **Rhône:** For all the big Hermitage, Châteauneuf-du-Pape, and Côte-Rôtie, you'll need at least two to three hours. Syrah and Grenache are powerful wines.

- **White Burgundy:** I decant all my white Burgundy. If you buy a case of Premier Cru from Domaine Leflaive, you also get a paper saying it will be best for drinking in 2012 or 2013 or 2020 because she wants you to wait. But who is going to wait? In a restaurant, it is hard to wait. The best way to appreciate it now is to decant a 2004 an hour beforehand, and it will be perfect. A 1992 or earlier vintage just needs to be opened twenty minutes beforehand and not decanted.

- **California wines:** In general, a wine from California does not have the same earthiness and complexity, so if you decant it too far in advance, the alcohol will show more and you will lose the fruit.

  - **California Cabernet:** The 1997, 1994, 2001, and 2003 Cabernets, which were great vintages, need at least two hours, because they are big wines.
  - **California Merlot:** This is a soft, juicy wine and doesn't need more than an hour.
  - **California Pinot Noir:** They don't really need to be decanted because they are about the fruit.

"Decent glassware—meaning good-quality and larger-sized—is a must," agrees Virginia Philip, MS, of The Breakers in Palm Beach, Florida. "When you have a generous six-ounce pour in an eighteen-ounce glass in a restaurant, those ounces become kind of swallowed up. It is important for guests to realize that the larger the glass, the less it's going to look like you're getting."

Reality comes into play when selecting glassware for home versus a fine restaurant. Michel Couvreux of Per Se in New York City argues, "Home is home. You don't need to have all the glasses that Riedel designs. At Cru we had eight different wine glasses and two different Champagne glasses, but it is a restaurant so it is different.

"At home I have four different glasses: Champagne, small white wine, a [more bulbous] Burgundy glass, and a [straighter] Bordeaux glass. That is it. How much room do *you* have for glasses?

"How many of each do I have? I have a lot actually: a dozen for Champagne and a dozen for white wine. For Burgundy and Bordeaux, I have twenty-four of each! I have lots of friends who come to my house, and I love to entertain and cook. If I have friends over for a barbecue, there will be no plastic cups! The Riedel Sommelier Service glasses are expensive [$119 each] and can break easily. I recommend the Riedel Ouverture glasses, which are around $10."

While you're going to the trouble of buying better glasses, make sure they are cleaned properly. Give your glass a sniff before pouring wine into it, and if there are any "off" smells, have it rewashed. If a glass has been sitting on a shelf unused for a while, it may have picked up some musty notes, and if it wasn't rinsed properly, it may still have hints of soap—neither of which will enhance the wine you're about to pour into it. Before dinner parties in our home, we steam our wine glasses over a tea kettle or cappuccino steamer, then wipe them with a lint-free towel or let them air-dry.

Let It Breathe

Almost all wine drinkers agree that the last glass of wine in the bottle is the best and the end of the vintage tastes the most deliciously developed. So when serving vigorous red wines (Cabernet, Zinfandel, Syrah, Malbec, Nebbiolo, and so on) younger than five years and from an excellent vintage, open the wine early in the morning. Take a one-ounce sip (serving a dual purpose: ensuring that the wine is sound and that you'll have a delightful morning) and leave it loosely corked so the wine can relax, developing the aromas and flavors.

—PETER BIRMINGHAM, POURTAL

The myth about decanting—pouring wine into a decanter to give it a chance to "breathe" and to separate out any sediment—is that it benefits only older wines.

If you've ever seen an old red wine poured by candlelight into a crystal decanter on a special occasion, you'll understand how this ritual can add to the romance and anticipation of the wine. It also demonstrates a sommelier's care and respect for the wine and your enjoyment.

Decanting can benefit all kinds of wines, from red to white. We like how decanting whites helps showcase their aromatics.

The exception tends to be Burgundy, whose sediment is too fine to decant off. "Those wines are relatively delicate anyway, so decanting can sometimes bruise the wines," explains Michael Flynn of The Mansion on Turtle Creek in Dallas. "For younger, robust reds, decanting almost always improves the wines and almost never is to the wines' detriment. I recommend decanting whenever possible for reds and sometimes for whites as well."

If you haven't decanted a red wine in advance and find that it tastes "tight," or closed, Jesse Rodriguez of The Addison at the Grand Del Mar Resort in San Diego has a solution. "Pour it into a decanter and swish back and forth, then pour it into another decanter, continuing the process several times," says Rodriguez. "This process oxygenates the wine and softens it."

AWAY FROM HOME: WORKING WITH A SOMMELIER

As a sommelier, I find it sacred to be at a table during a meal. Every meal—no matter how short or long, the size of the table or the dynamic of why you are eating what you are eating—is incredibly precious and not something to be messed around with.

—ROXANE SHAFAEE-MOGHADAM, THE BREAKERS

Now that you know to think of sommeliers as "enjoyment managers," you can choose to take advantage of their expertise more often. Your responsibility is to communicate to them how they can best make you happy—by letting them know what you'd like to drink and how much and a ballpark idea of what you'd like to spend.

Michael Flynn of The Mansion on Turtle Creek in Dallas believes that diners should use sommeliers more often than they do. "So often people don't want to talk to us because they have this preconceived impression that we are out there to try to 'up-sell' them shamelessly to something they can't afford," he says. "But nothing could be farther from the truth. Of course we love to sell expensive bottles of wine, but we feel they are expensive for a reason: they taste extraordinary. There are many more great wines at reasonable prices. If people will just use us and be forthright in letting us know where they are comfortable, we feel that their whole experience will be transformed.

"That is what we love to do. The reason I am not on the street selling wine is because I like instant gratification. I like to see people's faces light up with smiles. That is what motivates many of us in the business."

Emily Wines, MS, of the Fifth Floor in San Francisco likes to start by finding out how much guests would like to drink. "Would you like two bottles, one bottle, or a couple of glasses? If you are having a wide array of dishes, I can offer to pour the equivalent of one bottle of wine. I can start you with a couple of glasses, then pour a half-bottle, and then let you split a glass of dessert wine. That way you have a full experience and get to try lots of different things. That is a lot better than picking a middle-of-the-road Pinot Noir that isn't outstanding with anything but isn't offensive either.

"That is the travesty of Pinot Noir sometimes. I will have a couple come in, and if the wife is having halibut and the man is having beef, they'll ask, 'What should we drink to go with our dinner?' There is no single wine that will be great with both of those dishes. I recommend a half-bottle of white and a half-bottle of red, so that one drinks more with the fish and the other drinks more with the meat, and they both have a great match. Half-bottles give so much more flexibility for dining.

"People have changed. In the past, people just wanted to drink what they wanted to drink and that was it. Today people are thinking about what they are eating and want it to be a whole experience."

DESCRIBING WHAT YOU LIKE

Don't hesitate to mention what kind of wine you like. "If you like toasty, buttery Chardonnay, say so," urges Emily Wines. "Share what you like to drink at home. If you tell a sommelier that you would like Bordeaux but fail to mention that you have never had Bordeaux before and what you usually drink at home is Zinfandel, the sommelier cannot find you a bottle that will be a nice transition instead of something you might find too funky.

"I wish people would be open to trying new things and excited to learn something new," she laments. "I like to take on all levels of knowledge. In the best situation, guests will come away turned on to something they never would have found on their own."

Michael Flynn of The Mansion on Turtle Creek in Dallas adds that he hopes you'll say what you mean. "Some people may say they like a dry wine, but actually they want a wine that is fruity. We hope they can tell us the style of wines they like and even what brands they typically enjoy on a day-to-day basis.

"If they say they like Kendall-Jackson wine, we know they like a wine with a little residual sweetness. If they like Rombauer Chardonnay, we know they like a wine with a little oak. Those comments are always helpful."

THE DELICATE ISSUE OF WHAT YOU WANT TO SPEND

Dana Farner of CUT in Beverly Hills feels it's a big part of her job to be reassuring. "I am disappointed when I go to a table and say, 'Hi, I'm the sommelier,' and the guest just says, 'I'm fine, I'm fine.' I can't help but think that [another sommelier] made them afraid. So I try to make them feel safe: 'I am not going to hurt you!' If they are thinking about a glass, I will offer them a taste of it.

"I want people to be open about what they are looking for, what they like, and what they want to spend. Ninety percent of their decision is based on price. I try to make sure there is something for everyone on the list. L.A. is a crazy town, because someone will walk in wearing jeans, a baseball cap, and beat-up tennis shoes, and want a $1,700 bottle of vintage Cabernet. Someone else can walk in wearing the best suit and the best watch and not want to spend more than $70.

"If people aren't honest, it is very hard for me to give them a good recommendation. I will ask if they see anything interesting on the list. I will talk to the table host with the wine list open and ask, 'From this section, what were you thinking?' At the same time I will point to the prices, so the other guests will not know what I am asking."

"I believe in translating for customers," says Chris Miller of Spago, also in Beverly Hills. "If they like Pinot Noir but are having a heavy veal dish, I'll say, 'Let's give Grenache a go.' You'll still get bright fruit from it, but it will be more substantial and it will be better with the food."

"I love it when a customer says, 'I want to spend $150 and I want to drink.' (Actually, my favorite is when they say, 'I've got eight grand and I want to drink!') It is wonderful when customers ask for pairings. If a customer grants me license, there is so much more I can do for them. I can pop bottles for them and also for another table, so that everyone ends up getting to taste eight different wines instead of four, and each will be fine-tuned to the dish."

Before visiting a restaurant, take the time to visit its website and see if its wine list is posted. This can give you the opportunity to do a little advance research. We've found some great values on pricey wine lists this way, and being able to zero in on the list's nuggets has earned us the respect of the sommelier, who then went on to turn us on to another well-priced wine as our second bottle. When we're at a restaurant, we want to focus on our guests and not take too much precious time to peruse the wine list.

On The Square in North Carolina has a wine store attached to the restaurant, so guests can either buy the wine to take home or, for $5 more, they can drink it in the restaurant. "That means you can drink Protocolo for $12 or Bond St. Eden for $395," says Inez Ribustello. "My friends in New York City joke that it would be cheaper to book a flight and come down here to buy their wine!

"It is always about building trust with people. If someone comes in and says, 'I don't know much about wine, but someone told me I would enjoy a California Merlot' — which for people in this area is still the grape of choice — I am not going to pour a Paloma Merlot [$50–$100] and expect them to come back again, even though it is delicious.

"When someone says, 'I don't know much about wine . . . ,' I immediately think to recommend one under $20 a bottle. There is so much great wine in that price range. We get more excited about a wonderful wine under $20 than we do about one over $50. If you are not making great wine at $50, that is a crime—

Fernando Beteta, MS, of NoMI on His Five "Desperate House Wines" to Always Have at Home

I've found that most things balance in fives. You have the five Spice Girls, five Backstreet Boys, five New Kids on the Block. Five means you have variety. So I came up with the five "Desperate House Wines" so you can have a little collection at home for mixing and matching.

You need variety because you never know what your mood will be. You also want to have choices for your guests. Here are the five wines to always have on hand:

1. *Champagne or sparkling wine.* I always have a bottle of one or the other in the refrigerator.

2. *A crisp white wine.* This could be a **Sauvignon Blanc.** Or I like **Riesling.** You want to have a bottle to go with your starters.

3. *A bold white wine.* This can be a **Chardonnay** from America or a **white Burgundy** from France. These would be for pairing dishes with cream, brown butter, and sage. Just like everyone else, I like Chardonnay. It works with pasta carbonara or, if I am roasting a chicken with potatoes, I really like a Chardonnay for adding that extra dimension.

4. *A light red wine.* I'd suggest **Pinot Noir** or **Sangiovese.** For grilled salmon, Pinot is great. I like a light red with cheese and salami. We cook at home a lot, and if my wife and I want only one wine, this is what we open most often. It will fit with both our first course and our second course pretty well.

5. *A bold red wine.* I recommend **Cabernet, Malbec,** or **Merlot.** This is for grilling, roasts, and lamb. I will start off with a different wine with higher acidity, then move into this wine.

because at that price, you should be! It is a lot harder to find wine that is typical of the region under $20. We get really excited when we find wine that will retail under $10."

Realizing that the subject can be "tricky and sensitive," Emily Wines, MS, of the Fifth Floor in San Francisco suggests a delicate way to indicate your price range. "People don't always want to say up-front what they want to spend, but it is really easy to point to a price on the list and say you want 'something along these lines.' Instantly, the sommelier knows where to go, and she won't offend you by going too low or high."

LET THE SOMMELIER KNOW YOU'RE HAPPY (OR NOT)

If you just don't like the wine that was recommended to you, you should let the restaurant know as soon as possible. "We are much more interested in getting you something you will enjoy to enhance your experience rather than have you suck it up and drink a bottle you ultimately don't care for," emphasizes Michael Flynn of The Mansion on Turtle Creek in Dallas. "I often say to people, 'Don't worry about it—we will make an opportunity out of it.' We may pour it by the glass or use it for staff training, for example."

Sommeliers who like to push the wine envelope for more adventuresome diners need to know if they've pushed too far. Jeff Bareilles of Manresa in Los Gatos, California, recalls, "I poured a barnyardy, earthy Clos Roche Blanche Cabernet Franc to go with risotto with mushrooms and squash for a guest. The wine is light-bodied, fresh, and smells of barnyard funk, which lines up with the mushrooms and squash but can have a little pungency. Every other day someone will say, 'The wine is fine—I just don't like it.' That indicates to me that I should recalibrate and try something lighter in body, like a Jacques Puffeney Poulsard from the Jura. It is floral and acts like a Cabernet Franc without the barnyard. I have no problem changing the wines. It is *your* show—I am here as your gentle guide."

Your happiness becomes the sommelier's happiness. As Andy Myers of CityZen in Washington, DC, observes, "Being on the floor and in restaurants for so many years, I've witnessed a lot. Last night we had a wedding proposal, a fortieth wedding anniversary, and a couple of birthdays, and I got to be a part of all of them. I am privileged to share a little bit of their night and to feed off all that joy and energy. All because I am, in quotes, 'the expert.' They want me to help them make their night more fun, and that excites me; it's very cool."

Restaurants: BYOB and Corkage

Authors **Andrew Dornenburg** and **Karen Page** weren't being cheap at A Voce when they asked the staff to uncork an $11 bottle of Georges Duboeuf Beaujolais Nouveau for their dinner with LAPD Chief **Bill Bratton** and lawyer/actress **Rikki Klieman**, who has a recurring role as a judge on **James Woods**'s new CBS hit, *Shark*. The modest wine was the apt choice to toast their new book, *What to Drink with What You Eat*, which was just named the 2006 Georges Duboeuf Wine Book of the Year. Their other selections—a bottle of bubbly to start, and a Super Tuscan to finish—cost a lot more.

—RICHARD JOHNSON, "PAGE SIX," *NEW YORK POST* (NOVEMBER 21, 2006)

While some restaurants that invest a lot in their wine list and service do not allow guests to bring their own wine, many restaurants do allow this. However, you should observe a certain protocol, beginning with calling the restaurant in advance to ask about their policy.

The restaurant may have specific rules regarding what can be brought in (such as only wines that do not appear on its own list) and how many bottles (which might be limited to one or two or to the number of bottles you order from the list). The fee for this privilege is known as corkage, which can range from $10 to $75 or more per bottle.

When you BYOB, keep in mind that the restaurant is offering you a courtesy. We typically offer some of the wine to the sommelier and/or staff members serving us so they can taste something new. We also tip as if we had ordered wine with our meal. Even with the corkage fee and the extra tip, you will typically come out ahead in cost.

The type of wine to bring is often suggested by the cuisine of the restaurant you're visiting. (See Chapters 4 and 5, and *What to Drink with What You Eat*.) But sommeliers have some other tips for you to consider. Fernando Beteta, MS, of NoMI in Chicago, has found that Gewürztraminer is almost always excellent with Asian food. "We go out for dim sum once a month, and sommeliers always bring Alsatian varietals like Gewürztraminer and Muscat," he says. "When I go BYOB, I always recommend taking *two* bottles in case one is flawed—because you can't

YANNICK BENJAMIN OF LE DÙ'S WINES

just order a second bottle at a BYOB restaurant. I also recommend bringing bottles with screw caps. With sushi, it is much easier to open a New Zealand Pinot Noir [as those producers favor screw caps]."

Where to Look for Wine Bargains

When we wrote our weekly wine column for the *Washington Post,* many of our readers seemed to have a magic cutoff point of $15 for a bottle of wine. And spending less was definitely better! While we found many wines worth mentioning, two smaller winemakers that became favorites of ours included Calistoga Estates, which was founded by the wine retailer Marvin Stirman and the former White House chef Walter Scheib, and Tortoise Creek, founded by the restaurateur Mel Masters. Both wineries could be trusted for consistently delicious, food-friendly wines at that price point.

We polled top restaurant sommeliers on wine regions to keep an eye out for when seeking bargains.

UNITED STATES

If you're lucky, you can find some wines that offer great quality for the price.

There are a lot of great whites from **Oregon**. Oregon Pinot Gris is a great value. Sémillon from **Washington state** is a great quaff and food wine. If you forget about it in your closet, it will age well—and that's a good thing. It also represents great value.
—BELINDA CHANG, THE MODERN

We are not fans of oak on white wines, so we have completely "forced" our opinion on everyone else. People love unoaked whites here. Our exception to the rule right now is Leese-Fitch, which is a [**California**] brand by Don Sebastiani. They have three labels: Leese-Fitch, White Night, and Plungerhead. Among Leese-Fitch wines I like the Chardonnay, Merlot, and Cabernet, which all retail at $11 a bottle. Plungerhead has three good Zinfandels: Lodi, Dry Creek, and Sierra Foothills.

Coastal Vines from **California** is a great new discovery. We are very fond of their Pinot Noir. It is very light with racy fruit. It is $7 and people love it! People love it and buy a case, which with the discount brings it down to $6.30.
—INEZ RIBUSTELLO, ON THE SQUARE

In **California**, the prices are going up, but Gloria Ferrer sparkling wine probably offers the best value. It is not entirely dry, but I find some people really adore it.

You can look to Quady for their Orange Muscat Essensia ($20 for 750ml). It is very sweet, with orange-blossom flavor, and it is pretty delicious. Another Muscat that is a little higher in price [$29 a bottle] is from Merryvale, called Antigua. It is sort of an Australian Rutherglen-style Muscat that is nutty with layers of flavor.

—EMILY WINES, MS, FIFTH FLOOR

BEYOND

Don't hesitate to look even farther afield for more wine values. Here's an alphabetical listing of some countries that sommeliers recommend you scan for bargains.

ARGENTINA

Malbec from **Argentina** is great.

—MICHEL COUVREUX, PER SE

In **Argentina**, Malbec has found a great place in the market and still offers value. Norton is good and is usually a pretty good value.

—EMILY WINES, MS, FIFTH FLOOR

South America is fantastic for lush reds. I won't say you will find a great bottle of wine for $15, but I will say most bottles from there at that price guarantee you a certain kind of wine. If you are OK with oak and concentration without dense tannin, this is very good. Altos Los Amigos Malbec from Mendoza [**Argentina**] is great for the price point.

—ROXANE SHAFAEE-MOGHADAM, THE BREAKERS

One of my favorite Malbecs is Finca Abril. It is called the 1922, which is when the vineyard was planted. It has rich, concentrated fruit but is not overextracted.

—HRISTO ZISOVSKI, AI FIORI

In **Argentina** you are going to see scary Pinot Noir from Patagonia. They are delicious but not timid. They need a little more age, but you are going to see great wine for the price.

—ALDO SOHM, LE BERNARDIN

AUSTRALIA

We have found great Riesling from **Australia**.

—INEZ RIBUSTELLO, ON THE SQUARE

AUSTRIA

There are great buys in **Austria**. . . . We sell a Hofer Freiberg Grüner Veltliner in 1.5-liter bottles, and people love it. It has sweet tea, lemongrass, and peppery notes.

—INEZ RIBUSTELLO, ON THE SQUARE

CHILE

Look for Sauvignon Blanc from **Chile**, like Veramonte Casablanca.

—MICHEL COUVREUX, PER SE

FRANCE

Despite their reasonable price, Trimbach Pinot Gris and Riesling have an extra level of complexity even when they are just bottled. There is something about the aroma that alludes to the future; you can't put an adjective on it. They can be great with charcuterie. I would drink the Riesling as an aperitif on its own and the Pinot Gris with hors d'oeuvres.

—VANESSA BOYD, PHILIPPE

Everyone is concentrating more on their rosé than they ever have before. There is an ocean of really high-quality rosé. Just look beyond Domaine Ott [an upscale rosé that retails for close to $30] to other labels.

—BELINDA CHANG, THE MODERN

Domaine du Salvard Cheverny is a Sauvignon Blanc that is also 15 percent Chardonnay. It has bright acidity, freshness, and minerality, with the Chardonnay rounding out the blend. It feels like cheating to serve it because it is so versatile. This is great with a vegetable dish or fresh salad with apple and pear.

—JEFF BAREILLES, MANRESA

As for reds, E. Guigal **Côtes du Rhône.**

—MICHEL COUVREUX, PER SE

I recommend Rhône wines a lot. They have an impressively high production, and if you are careful of the producer, you can find your way to the right stuff. I often suggest Guigal, Roger Perrin, and Jaboulet. All are big producers, but all are good. I also suggest wines from the southern Rhône, like **Gigondas, Côtes du Rhône,** or **Vacqueyras.** The wine is spicy and the tannins are soft—and the value is good.

—ROXANE SHAFAEE-MOGHADAM, THE BREAKERS

Parallèle 45 [from Jaboulet] is a wine I recommend all the time. You can find it everywhere. It is exactly what you want a wine from the **Rhône** to taste like. It is crowd-friendly and a good food wine.

—EMILY WINES, MS, FIFTH FLOOR

Côtes du Rhône. I like Éric Texier's wines.

—HRISTO ZISOVSKI, AI FIORI

GREECE

Greece seems to be up and coming. I pour Gaia Thalassitis, from Santorini. It is an Assyrtiko, and it goes extremely well with our hamachi tartare.

—ALDO SOHM, LE BERNARDIN

Greek wines are good and getting better. Semeli Mountain Sun from the Nemea region is so good and so cheap—only $12 or $13. It is made from the Agiorgitiko/St. George grape, and it's fun and tastes like a rustic Italian wine. It is a crossover wine like Pinot—it is not heavy or tannic and would go well with pork, chicken, or salmon. The Greek dessert wines from the island of Samos, which is known for fortified Muscat, are good for someone looking for a Beaumes-de-Venise. It has a raisinated, cooked characteristic that you get from island wine, yet it is grapey and fresh.

—HRISTO ZISOVSKI, AI FIORI

HUNGARY

Hungary has great Pinot Grigio. Monarchia Pinot Grigio from the Etyek-Buda region is fantastic.

—INEZ RIBUSTELLO, ON THE SQUARE

ITALY

Italy has great value, which they can't help because the whole country is a vineyard!

—BELINDA CHANG, THE MODERN

In **Italy**, Mionetto makes 'IL' Prosecco, which is a good value.

—EMILY WINES, MS, FIFTH FLOOR

Some of the **Italian whites** are getting so good these days and don't cost a lot of money—such as Feudi di San Gregorio from Campania. They use ancient grape varieties like Falanghina. They have transformed their winemaking into state-of-the-art twenty-first-century winemaking with stainless steel tanks, temperature-controlled fermentation, and limited use of oak barrels. Their Falanghina has an orange peel, honey, and herb profile while being completely dry and unoaked. It is great for playing around with various types of food.

—MICHAEL FLYNN, THE MANSION ON TURTLE CREEK

I make a mean sausage pizza, which I'll pair with one of two favorite pizza wines. From **Italy**, I like the Di Majo Norante Sangiovese. From **Spain**, I'll open a Casa de la Ermita Castillo de Jumilla Crianza. Both are medium- to full-bodied wines that have a lot of character without aggressive tannins, which makes them approachable on their own or with cheese.

—SABATO SAGARIA, THE LITTLE NELL

For a sweet wine, Moscato d'Asti is pretty easy to find under $15.

—EMILY WINES, MS, FIFTH FLOOR

NEW ZEALAND

Their Sauvignon Blancs have become so popular that the most popular Sauvignon Blanc in the United States is from **New Zealand**. There are so many out there; I recommend Whitehaven.

—EMILY WINES, MS, FIFTH FLOOR

I recommend New World Sauvignon Blanc. Highfield Estate Sauvignon Blanc from **New Zealand** is fantastic—it is grassy with fantastic high acid and fruit.

—ROXANE SHAFAEE-MOGHADAM, THE BREAKERS

SPAIN

Whites: for summer, Albariño is perfect.

—MICHEL COUVREUX, PER SE

I love **Spanish** whites. Bodegas Naia makes a Verdejo-based wine that is around $10. Or you can find the super-Naia called Naiades, which is made from old vines, for under $30. It is super-complex, very concentrated, and aged in oak for a year. White Rioja is a great alternative to white Burgundy, with its earthy flavors. It has all the complex flavors of old varietals. I had an early 1990s Rioja that was a third of the price of drinking a Premier Cru Burgundy of that age.

—HRISTO ZISOVSKI, AI FIORI

Spain has lots of great Tempranillo and Garnacha out there that are perfect for barbecuing.

—BELINDA CHANG, THE MODERN

Victoria Pardina Tempranillo is from Cariñena, **Spain,** just outside Rioja. It has New World ripeness, but it is not overly oaked. It has nice acid and minerality that reminds me of Merlot. It is a nice introduction to Spain for people who have a New World palate. For someone having this at home, I would pair it with braised meat, mushrooms, or a simple roast chicken.

—JEFF BAREILLES, MANRESA

CONTINUING YOUR WINE EXPLORATION: WHAT'S NEXT?

Wine is one of the most civilized things in the world, and one of the most natural things of the world that has been brought to the greatest perfection, and it offers a greater range for enjoyment and appreciation than, possibly, any other purely sensory thing which may be purchased. One can learn about wines and pursue the education of one's palate with great enjoyment all of a lifetime, the palate becoming more educated and capable of appreciation and you having constantly increasing enjoyment.

—ERNEST HEMINGWAY, *DEATH IN THE AFTERNOON* (1932)

Now that you understand something of its history, its flavors, and its pleasures, what's next on the path to mastering wine? The road to this goal takes a lifetime to travel. We hope you'll continue to enjoy your journey every single day and every step of the way.

In this chapter we share some resources, including books, magazines, websites, and organizations, that can help you learn about and explore new areas of wine.

We've purposely tried to make this book accessible rather than encyclopedic and not to overwhelm you with too much technical information. There are other wonderful books you can consult to learn more about wine or to have your knowledge reinforced by reading about a topic covered here from another point of view.

There are also delicious ways to learn beyond the printed page, such as . . .

TRY MORE GRAPE VARIETIES

We never kept count of how many grape varieties we had tasted until we were browsing wine-related sites on the Web and stumbled across the Wine Century Club (winecentury.com). This elite but not at all elitist organization, which as of this writing has 1,023 members, welcomes anyone who has sampled 100 or more different varieties. The club was created in 2005 to encourage wine lovers to explore the diverse array of wines from around the globe. Its online membership application, featuring a checklist of 185 varieties, can be found at delongwine.com/century.html.

If you think it sounds easy to reach 100, note that one Master Sommelier counted the varieties he'd tried and could come up with only 82. The WCC's application has been downloaded tens of thousands of times, but less than 3 percent of those who do so actually complete it. There are no membership dues, but those who qualify can receive an impressive certificate suitable for framing, plus a silver *tastevin* [tah-stih-VAHN], which is a shallow silver cup traditionally used by wine professionals to taste wines. The club was founded by Steve De Long, a London-based architect and wine enthusiast, along with his designer wife, Deborah De Long, after they had tasted 188 varieties. As of this writing, they're at 322.

How many different wine grape varieties have *you* tasted? We'll bet that your list includes Chardonnay and Cabernet Sauvignon, two of the world's most popular wine grapes. It might also include some or all of the other four "noble" grapes, so named for their use in creating the finest wines: Merlot, Pinot Noir, Riesling, and Sauvignon Blanc. But that's a small fraction of the thousands of varieties that exist.

The WCC membership represents an international cross section of wine lovers. In the United States, fifteen members are based in Williamsburg, Virginia, the site of the club's first local chapter, launched in 2007. There are now a dozen chapters across the United States as well as in London and Hong Kong.

When we were completing our WCC applications, we regretted not having kept better notes of all the wines from such places as Slovenia and Lebanon that we had tasted while researching our books. We're pretty sure that each of us had tasted more than a hundred varieties. However, we decided that if we were not absolutely positive we'd tasted a grape, it was best to taste it again. After all, what's the downside in that?

"Most people in the wine business or advanced amateurs can get to fifty to eighty grape varieties fairly quickly, but then the work begins," says Steve De Long. "In this way, membership isn't really free at all. It also helps to explain why the club isn't bigger than it is."

WCC members have some tips for those interested in expediting the process. Heather Hatcher, the general manager of the Wine Seller in Williamsburg and head of the WCC's local chapter, suggests exploring the robust red blends of Portugal's Douro region. "The Portuguese grow an array of different grapes that aren't often used in other areas of the world," says Hatcher, who had tasted 200-plus grape varieties at last count.

Longtime WCC member and Georgetown philosophy professor Henry Richardson (who was on his 258th wine grape when we were last in touch) says that many unusual grapes are cultivated in France, Italy, and Spain, especially outside the best-known areas. "Consider wines from the Loire and Corsica, from Friuli and Sicily, and from Galicia and Basque country," he advises. However, for exotic grapes, he recommends turning to countries such as Greece and its excellent,

well-priced imports. "These range from the Xinomavro reds, which are like Malbecs with slightly brighter fruit, to wonderfully fresh whites like the well-priced Biblia Chora, a blend of half Sauvignon Blanc and half Assyrtiko," he says.

As you inch toward your own 100-grape milestone, don't overlook the interesting varieties being cultivated in the United States. In Virginia, Veritas Vineyard's Kenmar, an award-winning dessert wine, is made from Traminette, a cross between Joannes Seyve and Gewürztraminer. And check out some blends, including Sonoma's Bucklin Mixed Blacks (four grapes, including Alicante Bouschet) and Oregon's Sokol Blosser Evolution (nine grapes).

We hope you'll join us in tasting at least 100 grape varieties — and pushing yourself out of any wine rut you might find yourself in. A few tips for expediting your quest to hit 100:

- Pop for a bottle of Châteauneuf-du-Pape, which may include as many as thirteen grapes, such as the reds Grenache, Syrah, Mourvèdre, Cinsault, Counoise, Muscardin, Vaccarese, and Terret Noir, and the whites Picpoul, Clairette, Bourboulenc, Roussanne, and Picardan.
- Pour a glass of port, which can contain as many as forty varieties. Red port grapes include Tinta Amarela, Tinta Barroca, Tinta Cão, Tinta Roriz, Touriga Franca, and Touriga Nacional. White port grapes include Códega, Esgana Cão, Folgasão, Gouveio, Malvasia Fina, Rabigato, and Viosinho.

Plan to taste more than 100 in case you inadvertently double-count some varieties. For example, the exotic-sounding port grape Gouveio is more widely known as Verdelho, and you can't count them both.

If you've tasted multiples of 100 grapes, you can join the ranks of the WCC's thirty doppel members (200 grapes), seven treble members (300), three quattro members (400), and a single quinta member (500). Membership is on the honor system, but beware: the club's website threatens the Roman wine god Bacchus's curse on cheaters.

SAMPLE WINES FROM DIFFERENT REGIONS

While sampling grape varieties will inevitably take you to different countries, you can also make a point of learning more about the wines of other countries.

Let your passions guide you. Given Karen's **Greek** heritage on her father's side, she's been happy to see Greek wines becoming higher in quality and more popular, although they're scarcely on the map yet. Because they rely on indigenous grapes with unfamiliar names like Moschofilero and Xinomavro, it's a bit of a battle to bring them to attention. But they have extraordinary flavor and refreshing character to recommend them. When we were researching *What to Drink with What You Eat*, sommelier Rajat Parr of the Michael Mina Group said to us, only half-joking, "If there were an easier way to pronounce it, Moschofilero would probably be the most famous grape in America. This incredible white wine is like Viognier on steroids!"

Portugal, still up and coming, is a good source of reasonably priced wines.

Spain has been great for a while, especially for its wines that are rooted in tradition and aren't trying to taste like New World versions of Old World wines.

Austrian wines continue to be discovered. Who would have believed fifteen years ago that American restaurants would make Grüner Veltliner available by the glass—and that wine lovers would order it?

New Zealand has some enjoyable Rieslings and, of course, Sauvignon Blancs.

South America continues to produce some impressive values, especially in Argentina and Chile. You can learn more at Wines of Argentina (winesofargentina .org) and Wines of Chile (winesofchile.org).

India is producing some very interesting Chenin Blanc and Shiraz, which would make memorable pairings at your next Indian food outing.

By the way, don't miss the opportunity to explore wines in your own backyard. As of 2002, wines were being made in every American state, so don't miss exploring wines like Syrah from Arizona, Norton from Missouri, and Riesling from Michigan.

GET TO KNOW WINE RETAILERS

You can't buy a Rolls-Royce at a Kia dealership. If you want a deal on a wine, don't look for cheap wine—look for where there is too much wine. Look for a wine that is undervalued.

—DAVID MOORE, MOORE BROTHERS WINE COMPANY

While you're visiting wine stores in search of new adventures, take the time to enjoy a conversation with the fellow wine lovers who work there. In New York City alone, we've loved learning about store owners' passions—whether for quality wines at all price points (as in the case of Sherry-Lehmann) or under-$15 wines (Best Cellars), food-and-wine pairings (as at BottleRocket and Pour Wines), natural wines (as at Appellation Wine & Spirits and often Le Dû's Wines), Italian wines (as at Italian Wine Merchants and Vino), or Rieslings (as at Nancy's Wines for Food, which boasts an incredible selection).

Once, when we were passing Moore Brothers retail wine store on East Twentieth Street in Manhattan, we saw that its rating of 29 for service in the *Zagat Survey* was being trumpeted, and curiosity got the better of us. We stopped in and were offered samples to try, which naturally led to a conversation about the wines (which we loved), leading to a mini-lecture by co-owner David Moore, who talked about his passion for natural wines and lamented the pitfalls of the wine world. We found our impromptu discussion so fascinating that we returned for a longer, seated conversation with Moore (see box on page 300).

A Conversation with Wine Retailer David Moore

Moore Brothers Wine Company specializes in top-quality estate-bottled wines primarily from France, Italy, and Germany—many retailing for less than $15 a bottle. We spoke to the wine importer and seller **David Moore,** a partner in the company with his brother Gregory, formerly the sommelier at Le Bec-Fin in Philadelphia. We asked David what drove their vision to seek out and celebrate small, often little-known, and mostly "natural" wine producers—and how to find those wines. Here's how he replied:

Make sure you are buying a wine made by a person and a family. To find high-quality wine, here's what to look for on the label. On a bottle of French wine, look for the phrase "Mis en bouteille par X, proprietaire" or "Mis en bouteille au Domaine X." For domestic wine, look for "Estate bottled by X" or "Grown, produced, and bottled by X." On the label, if you see only the brand and not the vineyard [designation], such as Napa Valley or Sonoma Coast, the grapes can be from anywhere. If it doesn't say where the grapes are from, [it's bulk wine].

The Difference Between Bulk and Artisanal Wine

Certain wine consulting companies started out by parsing the adjectives in wine reviews so they could figure out the formula to achieve those flavors. They figured out how to manufacture the kinds of things that would make the wine reviewers go "Wow!"

As a result, wines are tasting more alike and more industrial. The good thing about it for industrial winemakers is it doesn't matter where they farm. One large-volume wine producer said, and I quote, "You can grow this shit in asphalt." He is right, even though his wines may not be any good by the standards of someone who understands what agricultural produce is about.

This is not winemaking; it is food processing. I have nothing against food processing. I have nothing against Ragú tomato sauce. I love Oreos, even though I know they are not good for me. But they shouldn't be discussed the same way [as cookies made from scratch]. And they shouldn't be the subject of anyone's time, writing, or talking.

If you want the real stuff in wine, you have to seek it out. It is no different than going to a farmer's market. People understand the difference between canned beans and beans from the farmer's market. Our business is not about being cantankerous guys who jump up and down and rant. We are simply enthusiastic lovers of the people, the work, the cultures, and the traditions that make *real* wine. And wine drinkers deserve to know the difference.

HOW IS "NATURAL" WINE MADE?

If you're a fan of organic produce, raw-milk cheese, or free-range chicken, you're someone who cares about the way your food is made because you understand that it has an effect on flavor as well as on our health and the environment.

Wine is food, and you'd be wise to be curious about the way it is made, beyond the crushing of grapes and the conversion of sugar into alcohol. While so-called natural winemaking can be thought of as akin to the practices used by artisanal suppliers of fruits and vegetables, cheeses, and such, some commonly used industrial winemaking processes can seem to be the wine-world equivalent of fast food manufacture.

Here's one more reason to continue your exploration of wine beyond this book: to discover how different wines are made, so you can vote with your wallet to support winemakers making wines the way you'd like to see them made in the years to come.

KEEP IT FRESH

It's important to keep finding fresh ways to learn about wine so you can stay motivated, along with those with whom you discuss wine.

Cat Silirie of No. 9 Park in Boston observes, "People who teach wine need to be careful, because we talk about it so much. If you are breaking it down so much, you can get cut off from the experience of enjoying wine. I was talking to a Master of Wine, and he said he didn't really know what he liked anymore.

"I work on other ways to communicate about wine to keep stimulated. Perfume is my new study, and I love reading about it. I am reading *Perfumes: The Guide*, by Luca Turin and Tania Sanchez (2008). It lists hundreds of perfumes with descriptions, like wine-tasting notes. It is the same challenge of taking something very sensual and putting it into words. You describe your own very personal evocation but make it real to someone else.

"It is really fun because describing perfume is very close to describing wine or music. You can sense the smell of the perfume from the way the authors describe it. There is very little wine writing that is that evocative."

The Wine Century Club's founder, Steve De Long, is also the creator of the Wine Grape Varietal Table (delongwine.com), a poster featuring 184 different varieties organized by body and acidity and color-coded for red and white wines. The deluxe version comes with an 88-page book describing them.

We also recommend Joyce Lock's enjoyable Wine Wars: A Trivia Game for Wine Geeks and Wannabes, which is no trivial pursuit if you'd like to have fun while you learn more about wine.

When you're too tired to read yet another book or play a game, pop in a DVD to learn about wine. Beginners might enjoy Ted Allen's *Uncorked: Wine Made Simple* series. You can also make your own flash cards to help you memorize bits of wine knowledge to add to your repertoire.

RECOMMENDED RESOURCES

The process of learning about wine will take you to other books, magazines, the Internet, tastings, and more. Here's what three sommeliers suggest.

In France, it is all about French wine. Working in England exposed me to wine from all over the world. After coming to California, I went **tasting** every week in Napa and Sonoma and at every tasting in town [San Francisco], and I listened to people describe wines. I also learned a lot about wine from **books**. I use the **Internet**, but you have to be careful what you read. Anyone can write a blog or a Wikipedia entry. When you are studying, you may consult three books or three websites and see three different views.

—MICHAËL ENGELMANN, GARY DANKO

A method that is sure to help a novice break into the wine scene is to first **take a wine class**. Many are available through local wine stores and are helpful in learning the basic tasting techniques and varietals. Then **buy a wine reference book**, like *The Wine Bible* by Karen MacNeil or *Sotheby's Wine Encyclopedia*. Finally, go back to the wine shop and **buy a case of wine** [most wine shops will give a 10 percent discount on twelve bottles]. Choose the labels you like—yes, buy the labels that most appeal to you, pictures and all!—and/or regions you are interested in. Then, **every time you open a bottle, taste it and read about that particular wine and region**. By doing this, you can begin to create a mental database of wines and their flavors. In no time, you will know a lot of regions and learn which ones you like and which ones you do not like. From here you will be able to start delving deeper into the areas or regions you most enjoyed.

—JORGE MENDOZA, CIOPPINO AT THE RITZ-CARLTON KEY BISCAYNE

For me, the drive to master wine comes from passion. Armed with some basic knowledge, fledgling wine lovers should **taste and taste and taste** some more, and discover what the soul of wine is for them. Whether your interest in wine leads you to learn every detail of the world's wine appellations and pursue the Master Sommelier title (as my two assistants have done) or to explore the soul of wine by planting grapevines, making wine, and studying constantly (as I do) or to find the wines you enjoy with dinner, the journey to master wine is never-ending and always fun.

—JIM ROLLSTON, CYRUS

Sommeliers' Recommended Wine Books

Drinks, by Vincent Gasnier (DK Publishing, 2005).
—HRISTO ZISOVSKI, Ai Fiori

The New Essential Wine Book, by Oz Clarke (Mitchell Beazley, 2001).
"This book is good for beginners. It is jaunty and well-written. He has great maps and visuals that draw the beginning reader into the subject matter and make it kind of fun to read about."
—MICHAEL FLYNN, The Mansion on Turtle Creek

Exploring Wine: The Culinary Institute of America's Guide to Wines of the World, by Steven Kolpan, Brian H. Smith, and Michael A. Weiss (Wiley, 2010).
"This is very good for taking you the next level up from Windows on the World level."
—VIRGINIA PHILIP, MS, The Breakers

German Wine Atlas and Vineyard Register, translated by Nadia Fowler (Mitchell Beazley, 1996).
"It is not in print anymore, which is one of the reasons I adore the book that much more. It has every great region."
—ROXANE SHAFAEE-MOGHADAM, The Breakers

The New Wine Lover's Companion, by Ron Herbst and Sharon Tyler Herbst (Barron's, 2010).
"This is a very helpful book."
—VIRGINIA PHILIP, MS, The Breakers

On Wine, by Doug Frost, MS/MW (Rizzoli, 2002).
—HRISTO ZISOVSKI, Ai Fiori

Oxford Companion to Wine, by Jancis Robinson (Oxford University Press, 2006).

"This is a good book for reference, but it has no maps."
—HRISTO ZISOVSKI, Ai Fiori

"This is hands-down the best book for a wine professional or someone who wants specifics. It is an encyclopedia but a well-written one."
—ROXANE SHAFAEE-MOGHADAM, The Breakers

Oz Clarke's New Wine Atlas, by Oz Clarke (Houghton Mifflin Harcourt, 2001).
"This was my first book on wine. Even today, I go back to it."
—MICHAËL ENGELMANN, Gary Danko.

Sales and Service for the Wine Professional, by Brian K. Julyan (Cengage Learning, 2008).
"This is a good book if you want to be on the floor."
—ANDY MYERS, CityZen

Sotheby's Wine Encyclopedia, by Tom Stevenson (DK Publishing, 2007).
"This is a classic one and covers wines all over the world."
—MICHAËL ENGELMANN, Gary Danko

"My go-to reference in my own library."
—MICHAEL FLYNN, The Mansion on Turtle Creek

"This is my favorite book to study from. It has each appellation, with all the grape varieties, vinification, the oak, the soil, and producers. It is just a good read."
—MARK MENDOZA, Sona

"This is very good, and he updates it often."
—HRISTO ZISOVSKI, Ai Fiori

Vino Italiano, by Joseph Bastianich and David Lynch (Potter, 2002).
"Our staff trains for a solid hour daily. Sometimes we will taste a classic Sangiovese, while other times we'll read a chapter out of **Vino Italiano** or research what Reserva means in Montalcino."
—CAT SILIRIE, No. 9 Park

What to Drink with What You Eat, by Andrew Dornenburg and Karen Page (Bulfinch Press, 2006).
"The two books I reference most often are **What to Drink with What You Eat** and **The Wine Bible** by Karen MacNeil. No matter where you are in your learning progression about wine, you can reference either book and find a new discovery or refresh your memory or your palate. I was making goat cheese and fig flatbread at home and trying to remember what I drank last year during fig

season, so I opened up **What to Drink** and remembered drinking Zinfandel and loving the pairing."

—JULIA MORETTI, Ad Hoc

Windows on the World Complete Wine Course, by Kevin Zraly (Sterling, 2010).

"This is a good beginner's book."

—ROGER DAGORN, MS, Porter House New York

"It is an easy read, and a great book for beginners."

—MARK MENDOZA, Sona

"This is one of the best books for an introduction to wine. I recommend this to new people at Ad Hoc to make them feel comfortable with wine."

—JULIA MORETTI, Ad Hoc

"This is a good zero-to-sixty book. If you want to know just enough about wine to be dangerous, read this."
—ANDY MYERS, CityZen

"This is a great beginning book."
—VIRGINIA PHILIP, MS, The Breakers

The Wine Avenger, by Willie Gluckstern (Fireside, 1998).
"This was one of my first wine books, and it definitely demystifies Riesling. Willie Gluckstern's writing has a wonderful Gary Vaynerchuk style of enthusiasm!"
—VANESSA BOYD, Philippe

Wine Behind the Label, by Philip Williamson and David Moore (Williamson Moore, 2011).
"It has more than 700 pages and covers producers, and Steven Spurrier considers it the best. It is impossible to try every wine, but this helps cover a bit of everything."
—MICHAËL ENGELMANN, Gary Danko

The Wine Bible, by Karen MacNeil (Workman, 2001).
"I love this book. She has a great style of writing that makes the topic not scary. I go back and read this book often, and every time I get something new."
—JULIA MORETTI, Ad Hoc

"The best way to cultivate a passion for wine is to read a good basic introduction to wine, like *The Wine Bible,* and let it open up the world of wine to your own exploration."
—JIM ROLLSTON, Cyrus

Wine for Dummies series (including *Wine for Dummies, California Wine for Dummies, Champagne for Dummies, French Wine for Dummies, Italian Wine for Dummies, Red Wine for Dummies, White Wine for Dummies, Wine Buying Companion for Dummies*), by Ed McCarthy and Mary Ewing-Mulligan, MW (Wiley).
"Here is a Master of Wine writing for beginners in a very effective way. I would definitely recommend that people check these books out."
—MICHAEL FLYNN, The Mansion on Turtle Creek

The Wines of Burgundy, by Clive Coates, MW (University of California Press, 2008).
"This is a great book on Burgundy."
—MICHAËL ENGELMANN, Gary Danko

The World Atlas of Wine, by Hugh Johnson and Jancis Robinson (Mitchell Beazley, 2001).

"I have this next to my bed. It is very detailed and is very precise."

—STEPHANE COLLING, San Ysidro Ranch

"This is a bit cerebral and a fun read with pretty pictures. It is a bit geeky, goes too in-depth at times, but you get a better understanding of the wines when you see the places and can relate to it."

—CHRIS MILLER, Spago

"He is the king of maps."

—MARK MENDOZA, Sona

"I always encourage folks who are serious and want to spend the money to buy this book plus *Sotheby's Wine Encyclopedia* [DK Publishing, 2007]. They can seem intimidating, but time and again these are the books I go back to."

—ANDY MYERS, CityZen

Our Own Wine Book Recommendations

We love the wide range of wine books that are out there, and we encourage you to explore all that are of interest to you.

Many of you may be familiar with our book *What to Drink with What You Eat.* If you're not, we hope you soon will be. We still use the book—or the iPhone app based on it (iTunes.com, $2.99)—almost every day as we decide, well, what to drink with what *we* eat.

Along with the books recommended above by leading sommeliers, especially the big three—*Windows on the World Complete Wine Course, The Wine Bible,* and *Wine for Dummies*—we recommend the following books to readers from beginning to advanced levels.

Adventures on the Wine Route, by Kermit Lynch (North Point Press, 1990). Our restaurateur friend Steve Beckta gave us a copy of this book by the famed wine importer, which Jay McInerney described as "one of the best books on wine in the English language, with its uncommon combination of poetic insight and skeptical common sense."

A Hedonist in the Cellar (Vintage, 2007) and *Bacchus and Me* (Vintage, 2002), by Jay McInerney. His books are as enjoyable to read as they are educational. His whole-brain perspective is a perfect antidote to all the left-brain wine books out there.

A Year in Wine, by Tyler Colman (Simon Spotlight Entertainment, 2008). The blogger behind "DrVino.com" takes readers through a year of wine choices.

The Complete Idiot's Guide to Wine Basics, by Tara Q. Thomas (Alpha, 2008). This is a thorough and enjoyable introduction to wine.

Educating Peter: How Anybody Can Become an (Almost) Instant Wine Expert, by Lettie Teague (Scribner, 2007). The premise of Teague's entertaining book is that if she can teach wine to a neophyte like the *Rolling Stone* movie critic Peter Travers, she can teach it to anyone.

The Emperor of Wine, by Elin McCoy (Harper Perennial, 2005). A provocative biography chronicling the rise of wine critic Robert M. Parker, Jr.

Living in a Foreign Language, by Michael Tucker (Grove Press, 2008). While his book is not exclusively about wine, the well-known *L.A. Law* actor instills passion for the food, wine, and lifestyle of Italy. This book introduced us to our beloved combination of Prosecco, ricotta, and eucalyptus honey.

Oldman's Brave New World of Wine, by Mark Oldman (W. W. Norton, 2010), and *Oldman's Guide to Outsmarting Wine: 108 Ingenious Shortcuts to Navigate the World of Wine with Confidence and Style,* by Mark Oldman (Penguin Books, 2004). Both winners of the Georges Duboeuf Wine Book of the Year Award, these books by a Stanford Law School graduate are insightful and fun to read.

Passion on the Vine, by Sergio Esposito (Broadway Books, 2008). This lifelong journey through Italy and Italian wine and food is filled with tidbits of wine wisdom such as: "The first known quality winemakers were priests and alchemists, men who believed that nature was central to all understanding. . . . Wine is alive, full of yeasts and ever changing, evolving like a plant or a person, a divine creation."

Perfect Pairings and *Daring Pairings,* by Evan Goldstein, MS, and Joyce Goldstein (both University of California Press, 2006 and 2010), are excellent books on food-and-wine pairings.

Practical Intuition, by Laura Day (Three Rivers Press, 1997), is not a wine book, but it may have inadvertently done more to expand our appreciation and enjoyment of wine than any other. Learning to hone your intuition has much in common with learning to enjoy wine: both processes are too often hampered by participants' fears of making fools of themselves. But intuition can open you to facts hidden in your brain that aren't accessible to your five senses—and those facts can deepen your appreciation of wine.

Reading Between the Wines, by Terry Theise (University of California Press, 2010), doubles as a memoir of the importer's remarkable career and a passionate treatise on why wine matters.

Wine Drinking for Inspired Thinking, by Michael Gelb (Running Press, 2010), author of the international bestseller *How to Think Like Leonardo da Vinci.* This right-brain book can teach you to appreciate wine as a muse.

We subscribe to *Decanter.com*'s daily e-mail alerts and *Santé* and *The Tasting Panel* magazines' occasional ones, and to the hard copies of *Wine & Spirits, Wine Enthusiast,* and *Wine Spectator.*

AWARD-WINNING WINE BOOKS: 1994–2011

In the United States, three major awards recognize the year's best wine books: the Georges Duboeuf Wine Book of the Year Award, the International Association of Culinary Professionals Award for Best Book on Wine, Beer or Spirits, and the James Beard Foundation Award for Best Book: Beverage. The winners from 1994 to 2011 are listed here.

YEAR	GEORGES DUBOEUF	IACP	JAMES BEARD
2011	*Oldman's Brave New World of Wine*, by Mark Oldman	*Asian Palate*, by Jeannie Cho Lee, MW	*Secrets of the Sommeliers*, by Rajat Parr and Jordan Mackay
2010	*Been Doon So Long*, by Randall Grahm	*World Whiskey*, by Charles Maclean	*Been Doon So Long*, by Randall Grahm
2009	No award given because the award was moved from fall to spring.	*Ciderland*, by James Crowden	*WineWise*, by Steven Kolpan, Brian H. Smith, and Michael A. Weiss
2008	*WineWise*, by Steven Kolpan, Brian H. Smith, and Michael A. Weiss	*The World Atlas of Wine*, by Hugh Johnson and Jancis Robinson	*Imbibe!* by David Wondrich
2007	*Hip Tastes*, by Courtney Cochran	*What to Drink with What You Eat*, by Andrew Dornenburg and Karen Page	*Romancing the Vine*, by Alan Tardi
2006	*What to Drink with What You Eat*, by Andrew Dornenburg and Karen Page, and *Keys to the Cellar*, by Peter Meltzer	*A History of Wine in America*, by Thomas Pinney	*Whiskey*, by Michael Jackson
2005	*Wine Style*, by Mary Ewing-Mulligan and Ed McCarthy	*Everyday Dining with Wine*, by Andrea Immer	*Scotch Whisky*, by Charles MacLean
2004	*Oldman's Guide to Outsmarting Wine*, by Mark Oldman	*The Brewmaster's Table*, by Garrett Oliver	*Wines of South America*, by Monty Waldins
2003	*Wine for Women*, by Leslie Sbrocco	*Vino Italiano*, by Joseph Bastianich and David Lynch	*Michael Broadbent's Vintage Wine*, by Michael Broadbent
2002	*Decantations*, by Frank Prial	*Bordeaux*, by Stephen Brook	*Wine*, by André Dominé
2001	*The Wine Bible*, by Karen MacNeil	*American Vintage*, by Paul Lukacs	*American Vintage*, by Paul Lukacs
2000	*The Unofficial Guide to Selecting Wine*, by Felicia Sherbert	*Italian Wines 1998*, ed. by Daniele Cernilli and Carlo Petrini	*Terroir*, by James E. Wilson

YEAR	GEORGES DUBOEUF	IACP	JAMES BEARD
1999	*Champagne for Dummies*, by Ed McCarthy	*A Companion to California Wine*, by Charles L. Sullivan	*1855: A History of the Bordeaux Classification*, by Dewey Markham Jr.
1998	*Taste*, by David Rosengarten	*Aperitif*, by Georgeanne Brennan	*Côte d'Or*, by Clive Coates, MW
1997	*Wine for Dummies*, by Mary Ewing-Mulligan and Ed McCarthy	*A Wine and Food Guide to the Loire*, by Jacqueline Friedrich	*A Wine and Food Guide to the Loire*, by Jacqueline Friedrich
1996	*The Windows on the World Wine Correspondence Course*, by Kevin Zraly	*Oz Clarke's Wine Atlas*, by Oz Clarke	*Wine Spectator's California Wine*, by James Laube
1995	*The Winemaker's Year in Beaujolais*, by Michael Buller	*The Oxford Companion to Wine*, by Jancis Robinson	*The Oxford Companion to Wine*, by Jancis Robinson
1994	*A Village in the Vineyards*, by Thomas and Sara Matthews	*Wine Atlas of California*, By James Halliday	*Wine Atlas of California*, By James Halliday

Sommeliers' Recommended Wine Magazines

My problem with scores from magazines is that there is a big difference between tasting a hundred wines in a room with no windows and tasting wine with your food at dinner. Why do some wines score big? Because they are big and massive, and when your palate is fried and fatigued that is what is going to stand out. Why score wine at all?

—ANDY MYERS, CITYZEN

Decanter (decanter.com)
"This is probably my favorite magazine."
—MICHAËL ENGELMANN, Gary Danko
"This is my favorite to read online. It is geared toward Europe, and you can look up vintage reports that go back ten years."
—MARK MENDOZA, Sona
"I get updates from *Decanter* every day, and once a week there will be something useful."
—ANDY MYERS, CityZen

International Wine Review (i-winereview.com)
"With full disclosure, I have had some professional dealings with this magazine over the years, having been the tasting panel director for several years.

They have done some great work in a very short amount of time on subjects such as Portuguese table reds, Tuscan wines, wines of the Douro, Rioja, and the table wines of northern Greece. Their approach is very education-driven and less score-driven. Each report begins with an extensive overview of the winemaking history of each region, the grapes involved, decisions made in the winery, food-and-wine affinity, and only after that do they go to the individual wines, scores, and tasting notes. They are very comprehensive, so it is the type of thing you keep on your computer for reference because each report runs twenty-five to thirty pages."

—MICHAEL FLYNN, The Mansion on Turtle Creek

La Revue du Vin de France (larvf.com)
"This is a French magazine you can get in the U.S. It is very good."
—MICHAËL ENGELMANN, Gary Danko

Santé (santemagazine.com)
— Recommended by ROGER DAGORN, MS, Porter House New York

Sommelier Journal (sommelierjournal.com)
"Very high-end sommeliers write for it. I find it very complete."
—MICHAËL ENGELMANN, Gary Danko

Wine & Spirits (wineandspiritsmagazine.com)
— Recommended by ROGER DAGORN, MS, Porter House New York

Sommeliers' Recommended Wine Websites

Able Grape (www.ablegrape.com)
Thanks to its founder, Doug Cook, head of Twitter Search, this wine search engine enhances your Web-based wine research of, at last count, more than 41,000 sites and 21 million pages.

Alice Feiring (www.alicefeiring.com)
This site was one of five finalists for *Saveur* magazine's Best Wine Blog Award in 2011.

AppellationAmerica.com
This website celebrates the diversity of wine appellations across North America, including all fifty states, as seen by senior editor Alan Goldfarb, editor at large Dan Berger, and oenologist Clark Smith.

Burghound (www.burghound.com)
"Allen Meadows is the guy you should go to when you are talking about Burgundy. He is almost exclusively Burgundy."
—MICHAEL FLYNN, The Mansion on Turtle Creek

CorkSavvy.com
"Use technology! The amazing resources the Internet brings to the table are perfect tools to discover new varietals, obtain information on a point of interest, or see what professionals are saying about wine on various blogs. I like using my iPhone to take photos of wine labels at dinner or a big professional tasting, and then with the touch of a key I upload the photos to my account at CorkSavvy.com, where I can review the labels at my leisure, research the wines on the Internet or in books, and write any notes I need."
—JIM ROLLSTON, Cyrus

DrVino.com

Tyler Colman wrote his Ph.D. dissertation on the political economy of the wine industry in France and the United States (which led to his book *Wine Politics*) and writes a spirited, award-winning blog.

Enobytes.com

This site was one of five finalists for *Saveur* magazine's First Annual Best Wine Blog Award in 2010.

Fermentation.typepad.com

Tom Wark's daily wine blog links to an impressive number of other "Wine Blogs You Need to Read."

Good Wine Under $20 (Goodwineunder20.blogspot.com)

This blog by the former UC Davis instructor Deb Harkness was one of five finalists for *Saveur* magazine's Annual Best Wine Blog Award in 2010 and again in 2011.

Guild of Sommeliers (www.guildsomm.com)

"I am all over their website because it has a ton of information."
—ANDY MYERS, CityZen

Local Wine Events (www.LocalWineEvents.com)

Eric V. Orange (aka EVO) has been working tirelessly for years to create the world's largest online calendar of food, wine, beer, and spirits events. You can search for events where you live or where you're traveling. Many of these tasting opportunities are free, but in other cases you can buy tickets online.

New York Cork Report (lennthompson.typepad.com)

Long Island wines have their own locally based champion in Lenn Thompson, whose blog was one of five finalists in *Saveur* magazine's First Annual Best Wine Blog Awards in 2010.

RobertParker.com

"We call it 'eBob.' I don't even subscribe to the print version anymore, because the database is so deep that you can go way back in the tasting notes online and get everything you want with a couple of keystrokes."
—MICHAEL FLYNN, The Mansion on Turtle Creek

Steven Tanzer's International Wine Cellar (www.wineaccess.com)

"Steven Tanzer is probably the critic I most identify with in terms of his tasting style and tasting notes. His vocabulary is a little more varied than Robert Parker's (though Parker is not doing all his own writing anymore), but Parker often goes back to the same terms to describe flavors and aromas again and again, whereas Tanzer uses a little more descriptive, flowery, and nuanced language. He is a little tougher in the scoring as well, which I also tend to be. Tanzer values minerality, delicacy, and acidity more as a taster in general—though Parker might give me a hard time about that."
—MICHAEL FLYNN, The Mansion on Turtle Creek

"Stephen Tanzer is a great writer."
—MARK MENDOZA, Sona

Stirring the Lees with James Molesworth (on WineSpectator.com)

"He writes about the Rhône Valley."
—MARK MENDOZA, Sona

Vinography.com

Alder Yarrow's blog was one of five finalists for *Saveur* magazine's Annual Best Wine Blog Award in 2010 and won the award in 2011.

WineCampBlog.com

Craig Camp's blog was one of five finalists for *Saveur* magazine's Annual Best Wine Blog Award in 2010.

Wine Library TV (tv.winelibrary.com)

Wine Library TV's Gary Vaynerchuk has hosted the Web's first wine video blog since 2006. If you haven't watched Gary's passionate rants and raves before, beware: they're addictive.

WineReviewOnline.com

The publisher, Robert Whitley, and the editor, Michael Franz, founded this site in 2005 as an online platform for leading wine journalists such as themselves and Michael Apstein, Gerald D. Boyd, Patrick Comiskey, Mary Ewing-Mulligan (MW), W. Blake Gray, Paul Lukacs, Ed McCarthy, Linda Murphy, Leslie Sbrocco, and Marguerite Thomas.

WinesandVines.com

The self-described "Voice of the Wine Industry" covers the business side of wine, from transactions to trends.

Wine Searcher (wine-searcher.com)

What's the best way to find a particular wine you've read about? Our first stop is invariably this site. You can enter whatever information you have about the wine, such as the name or the vintage, and the country or state where you want to buy it or have it shipped to, and it will list retailers that carry it and the current price. Other similar sites include **wineaccess.com** and **winezap.com**.

"This is great to find wine."

—MARK MENDOZA, Sona

WineSpectator.com

"This is pretty great for finding tasting notes on almost any wine."

—MARK MENDOZA, Sona

Wine Terroirs (www.wineterroirs.com)

This site was one of five finalists for *Saveur* magazine's Best Wine Blog Award in 2011.

Sommeliers' Recommended Wine Organizations

American Sommelier Association (ASA) (americansommelier.com)

Court of Master Sommeliers (mastersommeliers.org)

Karen earned her sommelier certificate from the Court of Master Sommeliers. She greatly appreciates the wine education she received from Doug Frost (MS/MW), Greg Harrington (MS), and Keith Goldston (MS).

"The MS program is fantastic for professionals who want to learn how to taste."

—RAJ VAIDYA, Daniel

Sommelier Society of America (SSA) (sommeliersocietyofamerica.org)

Andrew earned his sommelier certificate from the SSA. He greatly appreciates the wine education he received from then-president Darrin Siegfried and his colleagues.

Wine & Spirits Education Trust (WSET) (www.wset.co.uk)

"I took some classes at **WSET** and was able to home-study because of my work schedule. I have also studied with the **American Sommelier Association** and the **Sommelier Society of America.** They are both great organizations."

—ROXANE SHAFAEE-MOGHADAM, The Breakers

"It is not that important for most wine enthusiasts to think about wine too critically unless you are a sommelier. I have to think that way. The WSET program is helpful. What is necessary is a good budget, a good palate, and interest. I do recommend the WSET program for connoisseurs up to the advanced level. It is not an expensive course, relatively speaking, and it teaches you to think critically about wine. If you are buying wines very young and intending to age them, you need to know what you are doing or you will buy wines that are not going to age very well. The WSET does have a focus on wine as a global business, which is helpful to consumers."

—RAJ VAIDYA, Daniel

ON MASTERING WINE: A DELICIOUS LIFELONG JOURNEY

There are many conventions associated with wine that tend to fix it rigidly, define it, categorize it, assign it status and a place in a menu or in combination with food, in effect, to make it predictable. Wine is a living substance and resists these limitations of its potential.

—PAUL BERTOLLI AND ALICE WATERS, *CHEZ PANISSE COOKING* (1988)

We admire your pursuit of knowledge about wine and your interest in mastering it fully. But we caution you to never let your zeal get in the way of appreciating being in the moment with any glass of wine and the potential life experience in front of you. As Richard Olney writes in *The French Menu Cookbook* (1970), "A great wine partakes of the same mystery and inspires the same awe as a work of art."

Legendary food writer M.F.K. Fisher perhaps put it best when she wrote, "Good wine, well drunk, can lend majesty to the human spirit. The rules are simple and if followed will add pleasure to the simplest palate, the simplest meal, and make it grow."

Like America's leading restaurant sommeliers, you will continue your journey every day.

Andy Myers of CityZen in Washington, DC, finds that he learns from the wines themselves: "I love the concept of biodynamic and organic. They speak of fruit days, leaf days, and root days, and I have heard that this can apply to the wine.

"There are days when wines are simply in a good mood. I will open anywhere from fifteen to fifty wines in a night and taste everything we open. Some nights a wine that I know well or have tasted a hundred times before, I will open up and say, 'Man, you are in a good mood today,' and on other days I'll open it and say, 'You are a little cranky!' Wines have moods and personalities just as we do. They are living, breathing things. I poured a Burgundy that was in a good mood and perfect. The next night I poured the same wine again and it was still good but a little smoky and sulfurous. On Thursday it was not nearly as happy as it was on Wednesday."

Great wines have something to say even decades after they were made. Raj Vaidya of Daniel in New York City recalls, "When I was working at Per Se, I had the opportunity to taste eighty vintages of Romanée-Conti. It was spectacular, and it taught me about the humble beginnings of wine. The collectors had invited

Aubert de Villaine, the proprietor of Domaine de la Romanée-Conti, to the tasting. He brought a couple of bottles, including the 1984, because nobody else had one. It was an amazing and intense retrospective over three days. Needless to say, it was absolutely priceless.

"I tasted the best wines of my life at least a few times over. It was as much a privilege to listen to [de Villaine] say how it was his first occasion to taste many of those wines—and probably would be his last. At the same time, he shared how much he had learned about this vineyard that he owns that is so famous and produces one of the most expensive wines in the world. He had a humility and sincerity in how happy he was to recognize the greatness of the wine over a long period of time—how he saw its individual character coming through, things he learned about lesser vintages, or what people were saying were lesser vintages. He was tasting these wines in their teens and twenties, and he was saying, 'They're pretty good and impressive.' He sat there for three days and learned something about something he already knew so intimately.

"It reminded me of why I am in this business—because there is a floor, but no ceiling. There is a base of knowledge that you have to learn to know anything about wine. However, beyond that, there is truly no end to how much you can learn."

APPENDICES

DECANTER MAGAZINE'S POWER LIST

The ten most influential people in the wine industry, according to *Decanter* magazine's 2011 Power List, are:

1.	Pierre Pringuet	CEO, Pernod Ricard
2.	Eric de Rothschild	President, Domaines Baron de Rothschild
3.	Robert Parker	Publisher, *The Wine Advocate*
4.	Mel Dick	Senior Vice President, Southern Wine & Spirits of America
5.	Robert Sands	President and CEO, Constellation Brands
6.	Annette Alvarez-Peters	Wine Buying Director, Costco
7.	Don St. Pierre, Jr.	CEO, ASC Fine Wines
8.	Wu Fei	Chairman and General Manager, COFCO Wines & Spirits
9.	Eduardo Guilisasti	CEO, Concha y Toro
10.	Jancis Robinson, MW	Author, journalist, broadcaster, and consultant

A notable first appearance on *Decanter*'s complete list of 50 at #16 is the Amateur Wine Blogger, reflecting bloggers' fast-rising influence in recent years.

AMERICAN MASTER SOMMELIERS

As of spring 2011, these are the wine professionals who have earned the title of Master Sommelier from the Court of Master Sommeliers in the U.S. (mastersommeliers.org):

Name, Current Location (Year Earned)

Nunzio Alioto, San Francisco, CA (1987)

Darius Allyn, Henderson, NV (2005)

Serafin Alvarado, Woodridge, IL (2005)

Anthony Anselmi, Los Angeles, CA (2011)

Paolo Barbieri, Las Vegas, NV (2003)

Robert Bath, St. Helena, CA (1993)

Jesse Becker, San Francisco, CA (2008)

Wayne Belding, Boulder, CO (1990)

Randall Bertao, Los Gatos, CA (2005)

Fernando Beteta, Chicago, IL (2009)

Richard Betts, Boulder, CO (2003)

Robert Bigelow, Las Vegas, NV (2002)

Shayn Bjornholm, Seattle, WA (2005)

Chris Blanchard, Napa, CA (2008)

John Blazon, Orlando, FL (2004)

Michael Bonaccorsi, Santa Monica, CA (1992)

Thomas Burke, Las Vegas, NV (2007)

Scott Carney, Brooklyn, NY (1991)

Matthew Citriglia, Columbus, OH (2002)

Brian Cronin, San Francisco, CA (2005)

Roger Dagorn, New York, NY (1990)

Frederick Dame, San Francisco, CA (1984)

Brett Davis, Louisville, KY (2009)

Richard Dean, San Bruno, CA (1975)

Gilles de Chambure, Bolinas, CA (2000)

Laura DePasquale, Miami, FL (2004)

Luis DeSantos, Las Vegas, NV (2002)

Fred Dexheimer, Brooklyn, NY (2007)

Cameron Douglas, New Zealand (2007)

Ron Edwards, Charlevoix, MI (2005)

Eric Entrikin, Mountain View, CA (2010)

Catherine Fallis, San Francisco, CA (1997)

Jay Fletcher, Aspen, CO (1996)

Sara Floyd, San Francisco, CA (2003)

Kenneth Fredrickson, Chicago, IL (2000)

Doug Frost, Prairie Village, KS (1991)

Chuck Furuya, Honolulu, HI (1989)

Tim Gaiser, San Francisco, CA (1992)

Steven Geddes, Las Vegas, NV (1995)

David Glancy, Campbell, CA (2004)

Evan Goldstein, San Francisco, CA (1987)

Keith Goldston, Hollywood, CA (2001)

Juan Gomez, Palm Beach, FL (2007)

Peter Granoff, Napa, CA (1991)

Ira Harmon, Las Vegas, NV (1993)

W. Scott Harper, Louisville, KY (2009)

Greg Harrington, Seattle, WA (1996)

Jason Heller, St. Helena, CA (2011)

Eric Hemer, Miami, FL (2003)

Drew Hendricks, Houston, TX (2008)

Jennifer Huether, Toronto, ON (2011)

Jay James, Las Vegas, NV (1997)

Robert Jones, Richmond, VA (2001)

Michael Jordan, Costa Mesa, CA (2007)

Emmanuel Kemiji, Napa, CA (1989)

Brian Koziol, Winter Garden, FL (2007)

Doug Krenik, Littleton, CO (2006)

Geoff Kruth, Petaluma, CA (2008)

Fran Kysela, Winchester, VA (1989)

Joseph Linder, Seattle, WA (2008)

Laura Maniec, New York, NY (2009)

Brian McClintic, San Francisco, CA (2011)

Andrew McNamara, Miramar, FL (2007)

Michael McNeill, Smyrna, GA (1993)

George Miliotes, Orlando, FL (2007)

Sally Mohr, Boulder, CO (1995)

Melissa Monosoff, Wayne, PA (2010)

Steve Morey, Las Vegas, NV (1992)

Kathryn Morgan, Washington, DC (2010)

Ron Mumford, Las Vegas, NV (1999)

Alan Murray, Oakland, CA (2005)

Reggie Narito, Jr., San Jose, CA (2005)

Peter Neptune, Newport Beach, CA (2005)

Larry O'Brien, North Las Vegas, NV (2001)

David O'Connor, San Francisco, CA (1985)

Damon Ornowski, Carbondale, CO (1996)

Eddie Osterland, La Jolla, CA (1973)

Virginia Philip, Palm Beach, FL (2002)

Joseph Phillips, Las Vegas, NV (2008)

Steven G. Poe, Newport Beach, CA (2008)

Jonathan Pullis, Aspen, CO (2009)

Sean Razee, Edwards, CO (2008)

Nate Ready, Dundee, OR (2006)

Paul Roberts, Oakville, CA (2002)

Andrea Immer Robinson, Rutherford, CA (1996)

William Sherer, Las Vegas, NV (1998)

Alpana Singh, Chicago, IL (2003)

Cameron Sisk, Las Vegas, NV (1998)

Jason Smith, Las Vegas, NV (2005)

Robert Smith, Las Vegas, NV (2004)

Joseph Spellman, Chicago, IL (1996)

Matt Stamp, Napa, CA (2011)

Larry Stone, Napa, CA (1988)

Guy Stout, Houston, TX (2005)

Bobby Stuckey, Boulder, CO (2004)

John Szabo, Toronto, ON (2004)

Angelo Tavernaro, Prosser, WA (1993)

James Tidwell, Irving, TX (2009)

Greg Tresner, Phoenix, AZ (2000)

Madeline Triffon, Bingham Farms, MI (1987;
first American woman MS)

Claudia Tyagi, Roseville, MI (1997)

John Unger, Parma, OH (2000)

Roberto Viernes, Kailua, HI (2005)

Kevin Vogt, Las Vegas, NV (1999)

Randa Warren, Tulsa, OK (2007)

Barbara Werley, Grapevine, TX (1997)

Ronn Wiegand, Napa, CA (1986)

Laura Williamson, Tucson, AZ (2005)

Dustin Wilson, San Francisco, CA (2011)

Emily Wines, San Francisco, CA (2008)

Brett Zimmerman, Boulder, CO (2007)

AMERICAN MASTERS OF WINE

As of spring 2011, these are the wine professionals who have earned the title of Master of Wine from the UK-based Institute of Masters of Wine (mastersofwine.org):

Name (Year Earned)

Robert Betz (1998)

Sandy Block (1992)

Roger Bohmrich (1993)

Joel Butler (1990)

Christopher Cree (1996)

Charles Curtis (2004)

Mark de Vere (1997)

Michael Doodan (1993)

Mary Ewing-Mulligan (1993; first American woman MW)

Patrick Farrell (1998)

D. C. Flynt (1998)

Doug Frost (1993)

Lisa Granik (2006)

Tim Hanni (1990)

Peter Koff (1993)

Geoff Labitzke (2006)

Benjamin Lewin (2008)

Peter Marks (1995)

Tim Marson (2009)

Bill Nesto (1993)

Robert Paulinski (2002)

Jean Reilly (2010)

Sheryl Sauter Morano (2003)

Jennifer Simonetti-Bryan (2008)

Liz Thach (2011)

Jean-Michel Valette (1992)

Ronn Wiegand (1991; first MW/MS)

Jay Youmans (2004)

GLOSSARY

Acidic: Noticeably tart or sour-tasting. Acid is typically less than 1 percent of the wine (0.5–0.7 percent). Most table wines have 0.6 percent (red) to 0.75 percent (white) total acidity. It is sometimes indicated on the label as the pH level, which averages 3.0–3.4 for white wines and 3.3–3.6 for red wines.

Aftertaste: *See* FINISH.

Alcohol: The amount of alcohol in wines averaged 12.5 percent thirty years ago; by the 1980s, it had risen to 14 percent and has been creeping higher ever since (to 14.8 percent in 2001). Most wine contains between 5.5 percent (e.g., Brachetto d'Acqui) and 14 percent alcohol. Table wines are allowed a variance of 1.5 percent above the legal limit of 14 percent alcohol.

Alcoholic: Noticeably tasting of alcohol, such wines are typically described as full-bodied. High alcohol may also be perceived as "hot" or "sweet."

Appellation: The specific area where the grapes used in a wine were grown. Each region has its own minimum requirements to use its appellation. Frequently, a minimum of 85 percent of the grapes used must come from that area.

Aroma: The simple, often fruity smell perceived by the nose in a young wine.

Astringent: In describing mouthfeel, the puckery feeling that results from strong tannins (especially in red wines) or high acidity.

AVA (American Viticultural Area): A specific grape-growing region (e.g., Napa Valley) that has been awarded official status by the U.S. Bureau of Alcohol, Tobacco, and Firearms.

Balance: No noticeable domination of any single factor or factors in a wine's structural components, such as acid, alcohol, fruit, residual sugar, or tannin.

Barrel aging: The storing of (mostly white) wines in wood barrels, where they often turn deeper in color, softer in texture, and sweeter in taste.

Big: Descriptive of wine that is heavy in weight and/or loud in flavor.

Bitter: Descriptive of the taste that can be imparted by grape skins or stems.

Blanc de blancs: French for "white from whites," most commonly used to describe Champagne made from 100 percent white grapes (i.e., Chardonnay).

Blanc de noirs: French for "white from blacks," most commonly used to describe Champagne made from 100 percent "black" (red) grapes (i.e., Pinot Noir and/or Pinot Meunier).

Blind tasting: Evaluating a wine without knowing certain or any key information about it (e.g., grape, producer, vintage).

Body: The weight of the wine on the palate, ranging from light to full. Typically closely correlated with alcohol and sugar levels in the wine.

Bouquet: With bottle aging, a wine's AROMA develops greater complexity, evolving into a bouquet.

Brix: A measurement of the sugar content of grapes when harvested. Most grapes used to make table wines are harvested at 21 to 25 Brix.

Brut: Descriptive of dry-style Champagne or sparkling wine. About 90 percent of all Champagne sold is non-vintage brut.

- **Extra brut:** 0–0.6 percent residual sugar
- **Brut:** less than 1.5 percent sugar
- **Extra dry:** 1.2–2 percent sugar
- **Sec:** 1.7–3.5 percent sugar
- **Demi-sec:** 3.3–5 percent sugar
- **Doux:** more than 5 percent sugar

Buttery: Suggesting the aroma or flavor of butter, often a sign of the use of oak in the winemaking process.

Charmat: The bulk method of secondary fermenting in a vat, used in making less expensive sparkling wines such as Prosecco. Contrast with Méthode Traditionelle.

Complexity: The sum total of a wine's flavor, weight, volume, balance, and finesse. Complexity is the common standard for judging quality in a fine wine.

Cool-climate wines: Grapes from cool climates tend to be lower in sugar and higher in acidity (think of French Chablis, which pairs so well with oysters).

Corked: The term used to describe a flawed wine with evidence of TCA (mustiness or the aroma of wet newspapers).

Crisp: Descriptive of a wine (often white) with medium-high to laser-sharp acidity.

Cuvée: A blend or special lot of wine.

Demi-sec: French for "half-dry," referring to a slightly sweet style of wine (e.g., Champagne, Vouvray).

Dosage: A sugar-wine syrup that is added during the making of sparkling wine (including Champagne).

Doux: French for "sweet," referring to the sweetest style of Champagne.

Dry: Having no perceptible sweetness (which is typically perceived at residual sugar levels higher than 0.5 percent).

Earthy: Descriptive of an aroma or flavor of earth or soil.

Fermentation: The process of turning grape juice into wine by using yeast to convert its sugars into alcohol.

Finish: The lingering flavor of a wine after it has been swallowed. The length and pleasure of a wine's finish suggest a great wine.

Flabby: Descriptive of a wine lacking sufficient acidity.

Floral: Having an aroma of flowers (most often ascribed to white wines).

Fortified: Having alcohol, such as neutral spirits, added.

Frizzante: Lightly sparkling, in Italian. *See also* Spumante; Tranquillo.

Fruity: Having noticeable aromas or flavors of fruit.

Grassy: Having noticeable aromas or flavors of grass. Most often ascribed to California Sauvignon Blanc.

Herbaceous: Having noticeable aromas or flavors of herbs, as in Sauvignon Blanc.

Hot: Descriptive of wines with high, unbalanced alcohol content.

Late Harvest: Descriptive of wines harvested later and riper (and thus sweeter) than usual. Usually refers to wines typically served with cheese, dessert, or foie gras.

Length: The duration of the flavors that linger after swallowing. The longer the finish, the better.

Magnum: A bottle that holds 1.5 liters of wine, twice the size of the usual 750ml bottle.

Malolactic fermentation: A form of secondary fermentation taking place after grape juice has been fermented into wine. In this process malic acid ferments into softer lactic acid and carbon dioxide, thereby reducing the wine's total acidity. Used most often with Chardonnay to lessen the fruitiness and/or create a buttery flavor, but also used to soften reds such as Cabernet Sauvignon and Merlot.

Meaty: Descriptive of a savory quality in red wines.

Méthode Traditionelle: The traditional method used to make Champagne, in which wine undergoes a secondary fermentation in the bottle, creating carbonation. Both time-consuming and expensive, it results in a higher-quality wine. Contrast with CHARMAT.

Minerals: Aromas and/or flavors suggestive of flintiness, rocks, or stones.

Musty: Descriptive of a fault in a wine's flavor (perhaps from moldy grapes or contamination from being "corked").

Negociant: A French winemaker who buys wine grapes or wine, as opposed to growing his or her own.

Nose: What is perceived by the nose; *see also* AROMA.

Nutty: Often descriptive of the flavor of oxidized wines (e.g., sherry, Vin Santo).

Oaky: Descriptive of noticeable oakiness in a wine. As a positive, typically used with adjectives such as vanilla, toasty, or even smoky. As a negative, accompanying descriptors might include burnt or plywood.

- **American oak:** caramel, coconut, dill
- **French oak:** butterscotch, cedar, vanilla

Oenophile [EE-noh-file]: A term you might be called when someone sees you reading this book; it means "wine lover." Sometimes spelled "enophile."

Off-dry: Slightly sweet (with about 0.6 to 1.4 percent residual sugar).

Oxidized: Descriptive of wines that have been exposed to air. Like sliced apples, an oxidized wine begins to turn brown and lose its fresh flavors — but other positive flavors, such as caramel and nuts, can result.

Residual sugar: The unfermented grape sugar that remains in a wine. This is typically 0.1 to 0.2 percent in a dry wine and about 1 to 2 percent in an off-dry wine. Wines thought of as sweet contain anywhere from 3 percent to 25 percent or more residual sugar.

Round: Balanced in texture. Round wines have a smooth mouthfeel.

Smoky: Descriptive of the flavor deriving from oak-barrel aging.

Soft: Descriptive of a wine with minimal acidity and/or tannins.

Sommelier [sum-el-YAY]: The professional who advises upon and/or serves your wine in a restaurant.

Spicy: Descriptive of flavors suggestive of spices such as cinnamon, cloves, black or white pepper.

Spumante: Sparkling, in Italian. *See also* FRIZZANTE; TRANQUILLO.

Structure: Apart from flavor, the sum of a wine's parts (e.g., acidity, alcohol, body, glycerin, tannin). *See also* ACIDIC, ALCOHOL.

Sweet: Descriptive of noticeable residual sugar.

Tannin: The component (derived from grape skins, seeds, and stems as well as oak-barrel aging) that causes the mouth to pucker. Most often found in red wines.

Tart: *See* ACIDIC.

Terroir: The character of a wine that arises from its unique expression of place, including geography, soil, climate, and other factors.

Texture: A component of a wine's mouthfeel, along with temperature.

Toasty: Having a noticeable aroma or flavor of toast. Often a function of barrel aging in toasted oak barrels.

Tranquillo: Still wine, in Italian. *See also* FRIZZANTE; SPUMANTE.

Varietal: Wine featuring a single principal grape on its label, often, by law, containing a minimum of 75 percent (U.S.) to 85 percent (Australia, Europe) of the named grape.

Vegetal: Having a noticeable aroma or flavor of green vegetables or plants.

Vendange Tardive: The French term for Late Harvest.

Vintage: The year that the grapes in a particular wine were harvested. By U.S. law, the wine must contain 95 percent grapes from that calendar year.

Vintner: Winemaker.

Warm-climate wines: Grapes from warmer climates tend to be higher in sugar content (which results in more alcohol) and lower in acidity. Think of California Chardonnay, which pairs so well with creamy dishes.

Weight: *See* BODY.

Wine director: The professional who selects and maintains a restaurant's wine cellar and in some cases may serve as the sommelier.

ABOUT THE EXPERTS

Jeff Bareilles, beverage director and sommelier, Manresa (Los Gatos, California) — Jeff Bareilles is a native of the San Francisco Bay Area and attended Saint Mary's College of California, where he first became interested in wine. After graduation, he earned his MFA from California Institute of the Arts, then entered the prestigious Whitney Museum of American Art Independent Study Program in New York City. Today at the Michelin two-star restaurant Manresa, Bareilles is considered one of the region's most innovative sommeliers, pairing uncommon wines with daring and delicious cuisine.

Christopher Bates, general manager and executive chef, Hotel Fauchère (Milford, Pennsylvania) — Christopher Bates worked in all areas of restaurants before attending Cornell University's School of Hotel Administration. A few years later, he landed in Italy and Germany, making wine. With Bates as its general manager and sommelier, The Inn at Dos Brisas earned Relais & Châteaux status and a Mobil Five-Star rating. In 2010, Bates won the Wines of South Africa Sommelier World Cup, and in 2011, he was second runner-up for the title of Best Sommelier in America. He writes for the *Sommelier Journal.*

Steve Beckta, owner-sommelier, Beckta Dining & Wine and Play Food & Wine (Ottawa, Canada) — Stephen Beckta is proprietor of Beckta Dining & Wine, along with the new, small-plates restaurant Play Food & Wine. After graduating from Algonquin College's sommelier program, Beckta departed Ottawa for New York City and became sommelier at Café Boulud, followed by two years at Eleven Madison Park, then returned to his native city. Beckta Dining & Wine was named "Ottawa's Signature Restaurant" by the *Ottawa Citizen* in 2010

and Play Food & Wine was named Favourite Fine Dining Restaurant at the Ottawa Restaurant Awards in 2010.

Fernando Beteta, MS, former wine director, NoMI (Chicago) — Fernando Beteta passed his Master Sommelier exam in 2009. He has international experience in award-winning restaurants and was recently wine director at the Park Hyatt Chicago, where he oversaw a ten-thousand-bottle wine cellar. He was named one of America's best new sommeliers by *Wine & Spirits* magazine in 2007 and took second place in the Best Sommelier in America competition in 2009. A native of Guatemala, he lives in Chicago and works as education director for Tenzing Wine & Spirits.

Robert Bohr, formerly of Colicchio & Sons (New York City) — Robert Bohr is the founder of Grand Cru Wine Consulting, which builds and manages restaurant and private wine collections. He began his restaurant career working at a small, family-owned restaurant in 1988. After graduating from NYU and receiving an informal wine education at Gramercy Tavern, Bohr held his first sommelier positions at Babbo and then Daniel. He later became a retail wine buyer at Zachys. In 2004, Cru opened with Bohr as the wine director, general manager, and partner. In February 2011, Bohr led a group of investors in purchasing Domaine René Manuel, in Meursault, France. He has been featured in the *Wall Street Journal, Food & Wine,* and *Wine Spectator.*

Vanessa Trevino Boyd, wine director, Philippe Restaurant (Houston) — Vanessa Trevino Boyd is an award-winning sommelier with more than ten years of experience in Chicago, New York City, and Houston. She was previously sommelier at Adour

Alain Ducasse in New York's St. Regis Hotel. Her work has been recognized in *Food Arts, Santé, Wine Spectator*, the *New York Times*, the *Houston Chronicle*, and *Wine & Spirits*. She is a graduate of Northwestern University.

Scott Calvert, former sommelier, The Inn at Little Washington (Washington, Virginia) — While sommelier at The Inn at Little Washington, Scott Calvert won *Wine Spectator's* Grand Award in multiple years (including 2003, 2004, and 2005). He was previously a wine consultant for Ilo, Rick Laakkonen's restaurant in the Bryant Park Hotel, which won three stars from the *New York Times*. Calvert began his sommelier training at the River Café in Brooklyn under wine director Joseph DeLissio and became the restaurant's first sommelier. He also started an educational wine program for staff and created the restaurant's first wine-pairing menus.

Belinda Chang, wine director, The Modern at the MoMA (New York City) — Recognized nationally for her superior wine lists and winner of the 2011 James Beard Foundation Outstanding Wine Service Award, Belinda Chang joined Danny Meyer's restaurant, The Modern, as wine director in November 2007. Previously, she ruled the wine cellars of such top Chicago restaurants as Charlie Trotter's and Rick Tramonto's Osteria Via Stato as well as San Francisco's The Fifth Floor. Chang has authored the wine notes for three cookbooks (*Charlie Trotter's Meat and Game* and Rick Tramonto's *Fantastico!* and *Osteria*) and written for several national publications. She has also appeared on wine segments on CBS and NBC and hosted the Chicago episode of Fine Living Network's *We Live Here.*

Stephane Colling, director of food and beverage, San Ysidro Ranch (Santa Barbara) — Stephane Colling was born in Alsace, France, and began his career in wine at age sixteen working at numerous Michelin three-star restaurants around Europe. In 1999, he moved to New York City to work as wine director for The Castle at Tarrytown. For the past eleven years, Colling has worked with some of the finest chefs in New York, including Alain Ducasse, Gabriel Kreuther at The Modern, Joël Robuchon, and Daniel Boulud, and has won several awards. Colling lives in Santa Barbara with his wife, Elizabeth, and new daughter, Celeste.

Michel Couvreux, head sommelier, Per Se (New York City) — As head sommelier, Michel Couvreux manages the extensive wine program at Per Se, chef Thomas Keller's four-star restaurant in New York City. He joined Per Se in September 2009, bringing twenty years of experience at some of the world's top dining establishments, including the Michelin three-star restaurants L'Arpege and Guy Savoy in France as well as the four-star restaurants Bouley and Le Bernardin in New York. Couvreux has also managed the award-winning wine list at Cru. A Master Sommelier candidate, he has received accolades from *Gourmet, New York, Wine Spectator*, and other publications.

Roger Dagorn, MS, wine director, Porter House New York (New York City) — Winner of the 1996 James Beard Award for Outstanding Wine Service while at Chanterelle restaurant, where he worked for sixteen years, Roger Dagorn is one of only 180 Master Sommeliers worldwide. In 2008, he was named Sake Samurai, a title from the Japan Sake Brewers Association bestowed on only twenty-eight experts in the world (and few outside Japan). Dagorn, who has won wide praise from media including the *New York Press* and *Santé* magazine, is an adjunct assistant professor on wine education at the New York City College of Technology, CUNY.

Michaël Engelmann, former sommelier, Gary Danko (San Francisco) — Michaël Engelmann is currently the head sommelier at Rockpool Bar & Grill in Sydney. He is a native of Alsace-Lorraine, and his experience in Michelin-starred restaurants encompasses France, England, and, before Rockpool, Gary Danko in San Francisco. In 2009, he won the title of American Sommelier Association's Best Sommelier in America and was named one of the five Best New Sommeliers in America by *Wine & Spirits* magazine. The same year he won the Johnston Medal award and was named a Rudd Scholar for achieving the highest score in the Court of Master Sommeliers Advanced Sommelier examination in the U.S.

Dana Farner, beverage director, Wolfgang Puck's CUT Steakhouse (Beverly Hills) — An experienced actor and singer, Dana Farner dove into her love affair with wine the first time she blind tasted while working at Blue Water Grill in Manhattan, where she served as sommelier. In 2006, Farner brought her talents to CUT, where she was instrumental in the restaurant winning *Esquire* magazine's Restaurant of the Year and a coveted star from the *Michelin Guide* to Los Angeles. Dubbed "the indie-rock goddess sommelier" by *LA Weekly*'s Pulitzer Prize–winning critic Jonathan Gold, Farner is passionate about introducing new wines and opening new doors to her devoted followers.

Michael Flynn, wine and beverage director, The Rosewood Mansion on Turtle Creek (Dallas) — Michael Flynn was named wine and beverage director at the Rosewood Mansion on Turtle Creek in September 2007. Formerly, he served as wine director and sommelier for Kinkead's in Washington, DC, since its opening in the fall of 1993. Flynn has written for publications such as *Food & Wine, Santé, Sommelier Journal,* the *Wall Street Journal, Washingtonian,* the *Washington Post,* and *Wine Spectator.* In 1996, after passing the rigorous series of advanced examinations with the Court of Master Sommeliers, he became an active candidate for the Master Sommelier diploma. To date, Flynn has passed two out of the final three papers toward that goal. He has been nominated three times for the James Beard Foundation Outstanding Wine Service Award.

Dennis Kelly, head sommelier, The French Laundry (Yountville, California) — As head sommelier, Dennis Kelly leads the wine program at The French Laundry with an unwavering commitment to quality. Kelly strives to make selections that highlight the restaurant's dynamic cuisine and ensures friendly and responsive wine service that exceeds Michelin three-star expectations. He is a Master Sommelier candidate and passed the Advanced Sommelier examination with the Court of Master Sommeliers in April 2007.

Heather Laiskonis, general manager, Aldea (New York City) — Heather Laiskonis has crafted a thoughtful wine program at Aldea that showcases Old World specialties, particularly from the Iberian peninsula, that complement chef George Mendes's innovative Mediterranean cuisine and helped the restaurant earn a Michelin star and a place on *GQ*'s 2010 list of the country's ten best new restaurants. She previously worked at Tribute in Detroit and at Lassi, Gilt, Spigolo, and Tailor in New York City, where she lives with her husband, Michael, the James Beard Award–winning pastry chef at Le Bernardin.

Justin Leone, sommelier, Tantris (Munich) — Leone's adventures in wine began in the bustling bistros and bottle shops of Chicago and continued in Burgundy, where he worked two harvests under the watchful eye of Nicolas Potel. He returned to Chicago to hone his craft amid the groundbreaking cuisine and magical pairings of chef Grant Achatz and wine director Joe Catterson at Alinea, then departed to create the ambitious steakhouse beverage program at Benny's Chop House. His work in wine (including as a consultant, educator, and writer) led him to London and now Munich, where he is sommelier of Tantris, Germany's revered fine-dining institution.

Mark Mendoza, wine director, Sona (Los Angeles) — A California native, Mark Mendoza has served in wine positions at several Bay Area restaurants, including Redwood Park, which *Food & Wine* named as one of its ten Best New Wine Lists in America in 2002. In early 2003, he was named sommelier at Seeger's in Atlanta, a member of Relais & Châteaux. He later joined Sona, where he built a list that boasts over 2,100 selections. Under Mendoza, Sona has received many honors, including *Wine Spectator* Grand Award in 2006, *Wine Enthusiast* Award of Ultimate Distinction, and Wine Service of the Year by *Angeleno* magazine in 2007.

Chris Miller, beverage director, Spago (Los Angeles) — By night, Chris Miller is the beverage director for Wolfgang Puck's flagship Spago Beverly Hills. By day (and sometimes into the wee hours of the morning), he is the owner of Meliora, a boutique Santa Rita Hills winery. Somewhere in between, the award-winning sommelier (Chaîne des Rôtisseurs Best Young Sommelier in the World, StarChefs' Rising Star, *Wine & Spirits* Best New Sommeliers in America, Trefethen Top 40 Sommeliers list, *Wine Spectator* Grand Award) consults and teaches for hospitality groups throughout southern California.

Ron Miller, manager, Solera (New York City) — Though his first passion was music, Ron Miller started his career at sixteen as a short-order cook and found in the restaurant industry a complement to his entertainment ambitions. In 1981, he moved to New York City and advised a Cantonese restaurant on the development of its wine program. Since 1993, he has been with Solera, New York's leading Spanish restaurant. He has traveled extensively throughout Spain, researching Spanish food and wine, and participated in wine columnist Eric Asimov's tasting panels for the *New York Times.*

Julia Moretti, beverage manager, Ad Hoc (Yountville, California) — Julia Moretti managed an extensive beverage program at chef Thomas Keller's quintessential neighborhood restaurant Ad Hoc. She developed and oversaw a wine list that complements a collection of family meals and everyday staples that both evoke and accentuate their countries' origins. Moretti discovered her passion for food and wine in her hometown of Las Vegas, where she served as sommelier and assistant sommelier in restaurants such as Fiamma Trattoria and Restaurant Guy Savoy. Moretti joined The French Laundry in August 2008 as a food runner before being chosen for the role of beverage manager at Ad Hoc.

Andy Myers, sommelier, CityZen at the Mandarin Oriental (Washington, DC) — Andy Myers lost his heart to wine fourteen years ago while working at The Inn at Little Washington in Virginia. In addition to his day job at CityZen, he is also the drummer in the heavy-metal band Fuchida and an advanced-level sommelier with aspirations of someday being the most heavily tattooed Master Sommelier. Till then, he'll just be a tattooed guy who studies a lot. He's a freak for German Riesling but will drink great Burgundy if you let him.

Claire Paparazzo, wine director, Blue Hill (New York City) — Claire Paparazzo has worked in restaurants in New York City for the past fifteen years — first to support her acting career and now to support her passion. Her love of food and wine inspired her to join the American Sommelier Association. Paparazzo was involved with the opening of Blue Hill at Stone Barns, where the experience of working closely with fresh ingredients inspired her to search for local biodynamic and organic wines in creating Blue Hill's wine list.

Emilie Perrier, sommelier, Ai Fiori (New York City) — Originally from Roanne, France, Emilie Perrier came to New York City in 2003. Since then, she has held positions at Murray's Cheese Shop, Asiate, The Modern, L'Atelier de Joël Robuchon, and SHO Shaun Hergatt, all in New York City, before joining Ai Fiori, which earned three stars from the *New York Times*. After *Food & Wine* named her one of its seven sommeliers of the year, she was tapped as a featured expert on the PBS show *Vine Talk*.

Virginia Philip, MS, sommelier and wine director of The Breakers (Palm Beach) — Virginia Philip became the tenth woman in the world to earn the extraordinary accreditation of Master Sommelier. That achievement was complemented when she competed against thirty men and one woman to earn the title of Best Sommelier of the United States in 2002, awarded by the American Sommelier Association. In 2000, Philip joined The Breakers, where she expanded and presides over a collection numbering 28,000 bottles, from which the resort's eight restaurants and bars obtain their wine. She maintains the 1,600-selection list at L'Escalier, its award-winning signature restaurant.

John Ragan, wine director, Eleven Madison Park (New York City) — While in graduate school for urban planning, John Ragan took a trip to California wine country and realized he could love wine for a living. He relocated to Napa, working at The Restaurant at Domaine Chandon and Martini House as a sommelier. A stunning dinner at Campton Place prompted him to move to San Francisco to work with chef Daniel Humm. In 2006, Ragan moved to New York City to continue his work with Humm as wine director of Eleven Madison Park. Ragan's many honors include a 2008 James Beard Foundation Award for Outstanding Wine Service; participation in the prestigious 2004 Chaîne des Rôtisseurs Jeune Sommelier Competition, Pacific Northwest; and serving on the Wines of Germany Advisory Board.

Inez Ribustello, owner and sommelier, On The Square (Tarboro, North Carolina) — Inez Ribustello moved to New York from North Carolina to attend the Institute of Culinary Education. There she began to learn about wine, which inspired her to take a job at Best Cellars, the groundbreaking midpriced wine store. She went on to work at Windows on the World, first as an assistant cellar master and ultimately as the beverage director. After September 11, 2001, she returned home with her fiancé. Together they decided to open their own restaurant, wine bar, and retail store called On The Square. She and her husband now oversee every aspect of their restaurant as well as raise precious Cynthia and sweet Stephen.

Jesse Rodriguez, wine director, Addison at The Grand Del Mar (San Diego) — Jesse Rodriguez spearheads The Grand Del Mar's wine program, which includes wine events, the creation of proprietary wines, and other related programs that have garnered coveted recognition from *Food & Wine, Santé, Wine*

& Spirits, Wine Spectator, Forbes.com, and Esquire. He was named Best Sommelier: Reader's Choice Best of 2008 in *Ranch & Coast: San Diego's Luxury Lifestyle Magazine.* Before joining the team at The Grand Del Mar, Rodriguez was part of the talented group at Napa Valley's The French Laundry, helping the restaurant become the only dining venue in California to garner a Michelin three-star rating, and a sommelier at The Phoenician in Scottsdale. He is certified as an advanced sommelier by the American Chapter of the Court of Master Sommeliers and credentialed as a Certified Wine Educator by the Society of Wine Educators.

Sabato Sagaria, food and beverage director, The Little Nell (Aspen, Colorado) — Before joining The Little Nell, Sabato Sagaria served as wine director of The Inn at Little Washington and The Greenbrier. He received a bachelor's degree from Cornell University's School of Hotel Administration and is a candidate for the title of Master Sommelier. When he is not sipping and swirling, you can find him on the golf course, snowboarding, and living life in Aspen to the fullest.

Roxane Shafaee-Moghadam, sommelier educator, The Breakers (Palm Beach) — Roxane Shafaee-Moghadam has been a sommelier at several venerable New York City restaurants, including The Tribeca Grill, Montrachet, and Per Se. As head sommelier for chef Thomas Keller, she found kinship in a staff dedicated to service. After four years working at the highest level, she decided to hone her skills as a writer and educator at The Breakers Palm Beach. She will sit for the Master Sommelier accreditation in 2012.

Cat Silirie, wine director, Barbara Lynch Gruppo (Boston) — One of Boston's most respected and beloved wine experts, Cat Silirie brings over two decades of experience to the position of wine director and wine buyer for Barbara Lynch Gruppo, which includes Boston's acclaimed No. 9 Park, B&G Oysters, The Butcher Shop, and Sportello. Silirie and her wine programs have been praised in numerous local and national publications, including *Food & Wine, Food Arts, Details,* the *New York Times,* and the *Boston Globe.* In addition, she was twice named Best Sommelier by *Boston* magazine and has been described by the *New York Times*'s Kay Rentschler as "Boston's pre-eminent sommelier."

Aldo Sohm, wine director, Le Bernardin (New York City) — Aldo Sohm is the wine director of Le Bernardin, New York City's oldest four-star restaurant, where he oversees a wine collection consisting of 15,000 bottles and 900 selections. He received the 2009 James Beard Award for Outstanding Wine Service and in 2008 was the first representative of America to win the highly coveted title Best Sommelier in the World from the World Sommelier Association. In 2007, Sohm was named Best Sommelier in America after having upheld a similar title in his native Austria for four consecutive years starting in 2002, a feat never before or since accomplished.

Raj Vaidya, sommelier, Daniel (New York City) — Raj Vaidya's passion for fine cuisine was cultivated within his family while growing up in Asia. In 2002, he took over the wine program at the Relais & Châteaux property The Ryland Inn in New Jersey. Since then, he has held key positions at Seeger's in Atlanta and at Per Se and Cru in New York City. Vaidya has also worked with Robert Sinskey Vineyards, a biodynamic estate in Napa. He holds degrees in philosophy and political science from Rutgers University, and in 2008, he completed the Wine and Spirits Education Trust's diploma program, making him a candidate for the Master of Wine program in London.

Emily Wines, MS, wine director, Kimpton Hotels & Restaurants, including The Fifth Floor (San Francisco) — Going to France for the first time in 1997 opened Emily Wines's eyes to a new obsession: wine. She developed her passion at top restaurants including Jardiniere and The Fifth Floor. In 2008, she took the Master Sommelier exam and passed all three portions on her first try, earning the prestigious Remi Krug Cup. In addition to running the wine program for The Fifth Floor, she has been the corporate wine director for Kimpton Hotels and Restaurants since October 2008.

Jill Zimorski, beverage director, Think-FoodGroup (Washington, DC) — A graduate of the University of Virginia, Jill Zimorski was previously restaurant manager at Charlie Palmer Steak in Washington, DC. In July 2006, she was named the sommelier at José Andrés's Café Atlántico and minibar. As of January 2010, she was named beverage director of the entire ThinkFoodGroup, which also includes Andrés's Jaleo.

Hristo Zisovski, beverage director, Ai Fiori at the Setai Hotel (New York City) — Hristo Zisovski is an advanced sommelier with the Court of Master Sommeliers. He was raised in his family's Greek diners, where he worked throughout his childhood. Zisovski eventually landed at Jean Georges, where he spent seven years as chef sommelier. Under his tenure, the restaurant received the 2010 James Beard Foundation Award for Outstanding Wine Service. Cited as one of forty top sommeliers by Trefethen, Zisovski was named *Wine & Spirits* magazine's 2007 Best New Sommelier, and in 2009 he was third runner-up for the title of America's Best Sommelier.

ABOUT THE AUTHORS

Karen Page and **Andrew Dornenburg** are the award-winning author team behind some of the world's most influential books on food and drink, which have been described by *The New Yorker* as "the best place to experience the cult of the New American chef." They were cited in Relais & Châteaux's magazine *L'Âme et l'Esprit* as two of a dozen "international culinary luminaries," along with Gael Greene, Patrick O'Connell, Alice Waters, and Tim and Nina Zagat. As "accomplished authors, respected food authorities, and industry leaders," Page and Dornenburg were named Honorary Culinary Ambassadors by the Culinary Institute of America and were featured as among those at the forefront of American dining on the cover of the fiftieth-anniversary issue of *Chef* magazine.

They have made appearances as keynote speakers globally, including at the 92nd Street Y in New York City; the Culinary Institute of America in Hyde Park, New York, and St. Helena, California; the Faulkner Society Words and Music Festival in New Orleans; the Flavor Experience in San Diego; the Flemish Primitives in Bruges, Belgium; Food Educators Network International in New Orleans; Gastronomy by the Seine in Paris; the Harvard Business School in Boston; the International Association of Culinary Professionals in Philadelphia and Portland, Oregon; the Medill School of Journalism at Northwestern University in Evanston; the Pillsbury Bake-Off in Orlando; Relais & Châteaux in Chicago and New York City; the Schlesinger Library at Radcliffe College in Cambridge, Massachusetts; the Smithsonian Institution in Washington, DC; and Women Chefs & Restaurateurs in Louisville, New York, and Washington, DC, along with numerous other cooking schools across America.

The authors have been interviewed by *Today* show host Matt Lauer and *Good Morning America* hosts Juju Chang and Bianna Golodryga and have appeared on *At the Chef's Table* (PBS), *CBS News Weekend* with Dan Raviv, *Chef's Table* (WHYY), CNBC, CNN, *The Diane Rehm Show* (NPR),

Extension 720 with Milt Rosenberg (WGN), the Food Network, *Food Talk* with Mike Colameco (WOR), *Good Food* (KCRW), *The Kojo Nnamdi Show* (WAMU), *The Leonard Lopate Show* (WNYC), Martha Stewart Living Radio, *MasterChef* (BBC), *Morning Edition* (NPR), NY1 News, *The Ronn Owens Show* (KGO), *The Splendid Table* (NPR), *Weekday* with Steve Scher (KUOW), and other leading TV and radio shows.

As former weekly wine columnists for *Washington Post,* which won the 2009 James Beard Award for best newspaper food section during their tenure, Page and Dornenburg had their columns syndicated to dozens of newspapers across the country and around the world. Their column about Queen Elizabeth II's historic visit to Jamestown and Virginia wines was featured in *The Week,* the newsweekly distilling the best of news, opinion, and ideas from the U.S. and international media.

A native of Detroit, **Karen Page** was offered admission to Northwestern University at age sixteen. While there, she conducted research under a grant from the National Endowment for the Humanities and was named one of six honorable mentions in *Glamour* magazine's Top 10 College Women competition. Honored with the National Organization for Women's Susan B. Anthony Award for founding the National Association of Young Professional Women, she later earned her MBA at Harvard, which named her one of five finalists for the Fitzie Foundation Award, recognizing the most outstanding woman student. Page was one of a hundred outstanding alumnae named by Northwestern University's president to the Council of 100, and she was featured in 1994 as one of six outstanding Harvard Business School alumnae in the *HBS Bulletin.* She served a two-year term on the board of directors of Women Chefs & Restaurateurs and was granted the Melitta Bentz Award for Women's Achievement in honor of the billion-dollar German coffee-products company's female founder. She has served on the steering committee for the Citymeals-on-Wheels Annual Power Lunch for Women for the past decade.

San Francisco native **Andrew Dornenburg** is a former restaurant chef who cooked at top restaurants in New York and Boston with Anne Rosenzweig, Chris Schlesinger, and Lydia Shire; catered for leading art galleries and museums; and cooked at the James Beard House. He studied with the legendary Madeleine Kamman at the School for American Chefs at Beringer Vineyards in Napa Valley and earned his sommelier certificate from the Sommelier Society of America. Dornenburg was cited by Regis Philbin on *Regis and Kelly* and in the *New York Post*'s "Page Six" as one of McDonald's most famous former employees (along with Jeff Bezos, Jay Leno, and Shania Twain).

Paired personally as well as professionally, the two have been married since 1990, when they ran the Montreal International Marathon together on their honeymoon. They live in New York City.

Website: www.KarenAndAndrew.com
E-mail: DornenburgPage@gmail.com
Twitter: @KarenAndAndrew
Facebook: www.facebook.com/KarenAndAndrew

ABOUT THE PHOTOGRAPHER

An epiphany-inspiring bottle of Charmes-Chambertin at a tender age sent **Tom Kirkman** on a quest for the wine Grail, leading him to tour wine-producing countries extensively over the years. His photography has appeared in numerous publications, including *Wine Enthusiast, Condé Nast Traveler,* and *Santé.* He has frequently photographed for the James Beard Foundation, with which he has had a rewarding relationship for more than fifteen years.

Website: http://www.flickr.com/photos/tomkirkman
E-mail: tomkirkman@comcast.net

ACKNOWLEDGMENTS

If the only prayer you ever say is "thank you," that would be enough.
—MEISTER ECKHART

We could not be more grateful to all of those who have contributed to bringing this book into being, and we offer them a heartfelt "thank-you":

First and foremost, we must thank all of the leading sommeliers who shared their knowledge and insights with us and were endlessly patient in answering all our follow-up questions, as well as the follow-up questions to our follow-up questions, over the past several years: Jeff Bareilles, Christopher Bates, Steve Beckta, Fernando Beteta, Robert Bohr, Vanessa Trevino Boyd, Scott Calvert, Belinda Chang, Michael Cimino, Stephane Colling, Michel Couvreux, Roger Dagorn, Michaël Engelmann, Dana Farner, Michael Flynn, Dennis Kelly, Heather Laiskonis, Justin Leone, Mark Mendoza, Chris Miller, Ron Miller, David Moore, Julia Moretti, Andy Myers, Claire Paparazzo, Emilie Perrier, Virginia Philip, John Ragan, Inez Ribustello, Jesse Rodriguez, Sabato Sagaria, Roxane Shafaee-Moghadam, Cat Silirie, Aldo Sohm, Raj Vaidya, Emily Wines, Jill Zimorski, and Hristo Zisovski.

We must also thank the other experts we'd interviewed about wine for our book *What to Drink with What You Eat* (contributing substantially to our wine education), many of whom have continued to serve generously as resources for us: Colin Alevras, Mike Anthony, Dan Barber, Joe Bastianich, Daniel Boulud, Richard Breitkreutz, Joe Catterson, Rebecca Charles, George Cossette, Sandy D'Amato, Traci des Jardins, Rocco DiSpirito, Brian Duncan, Philippe Gouze, Paul Grieco, Jill Gubesch, Greg Harrington, Daniel Johnnes, Karen King, Tim Kopec, Lisane Lapointe, Jean-Luc Le Dû, Matt Lirette, Philippe Marchal, Danny Meyer, Alan Murray, Patrick O'Connell, Rajat Parr, Eric Renaud, Paul Roberts, David Rosengarten, Suvir Saran, Arthur Schwartz, Charles Scicolone, Piero Selvaggio, Craig Shelton, Alpana Singh, Joseph Spellman, Larry Stone, Bernie Sun, Don Tillman, Derek Todd, Christopher Tracy, Corinne Trang, Greg Tresner, Madeline Triffon, Scott Tyree, David Waltuck, Joshua Wesson, and Janos Wilder.

Our publisher, Little, Brown, has been our partner since 2005 in creating the most beautiful books of our careers. We can't thank enough: our editor, Michael Sand (especially for ensuring yet another fabulous cover, and for proposing the use of the black-and-white images that add so much to Chapter 1); his editorial assistant, Melissa Caminneci; Peggy Freudenthal; copyeditor Peg Anderson; the upbeat-even-in-the-face-of-mind-numbing-data-overload Deborah Jacobs; proofreaders Katie Blatt and Gail Cohen; publisher Michael Pietsch; marketing director Heather Fain; marketing manager Amanda Tobier; and associate director of publicity Carolyn O'Keefe (for tirelessly ensuring that the world knows our books exist). Special thanks to Hachette Book Group Chairman and CEO David Young for sharing that *What to Drink with What You Eat* is his favorite food and drink book—we hope he has a new one as of November 2011!

Many thanks to our "green-wearing" literary agent, Janis Donnaud, especially for her efforts to ensure that our books are available to readers around the world—including, for the first time in 2011, China.

We thank the *Washington Post's* food editor, Joe Yonan, for giving us the opportunity to write about wine on a weekly basis, and Jane Touzalin and Bonnie Benwick for their assistance. Thanks, too, to all the sommeliers and other experts who shared their expertise with us for our column, including Nadine Brown, Michael Gelb, David Lynch, Kathryn Morgan, and Todd Thrasher, whose insights made it into these pages. Thanks to Alfredo Bartholomaus, Carrie Crespo, Heather Freeman, Lisa Klinck-Shea, Rebecca Rader, Aileen Robbins, and others for their special contributions to our wine education, and to Ron Zimmerman of The Herbfarm for allowing us to earn an "Herbfarm Certificate of Experience: 1795 Madeira" as Certified Drinkers of the Last of the Oldest Wine in the World (a 1795 Barbeito Terrantez Madeira that was the oldest known wine being offered by the glass anywhere in the world).

Wine is such a vast topic that you need never stop discovering more about it. We've learned as much through the generosity of friends who have shared some of their treasures with us as from friends whose mere presence often inspires the opening of a celebratory bottle, including: Rosario Acquista, Elka Altbach, Ron Altbach, Lewis Black, Daniel Boulud, Bill Bratton, Brian Burry, Susan Bulkeley Butler, Ilene Cavagnola, Howard Childs, John Curtin, Julia D'Amico, Blake Davis, Julia Davis, Susan Davis, Laura Day, Samson Day, Loraine Despres, Susan Dey, Terri Dial, Deborah Domanski, Carlton Eastlake, Jill Eikenberry, Elizabeth Eulberg, Georgette Farkas, Victor Garber (for 6/28/11), Ashley Garrett, Michael Gelb, Gael Greene, Jana Irglová, Marek Irglová, Markéta Irglová (whose CDs with Glen Hansard "Once" and "Strict Joy" were the soundtrack for much of our writing), Tim Iseler, Alan Jones, Thomas Keller (for Thanksgiving-morning Champagne), Rikki Klieman, Barbara Lazaroff, Brendan Milburn, Walter Moora, Jody Oberfelder, Steve Olsen, Heidi Olson, Kelley Olson, Cynthia Penney, Jeff Penney, Deborah Pines, Steven Richter, Juergen Riehm, Stuart Rockefeller, Marla Schaffel, Tony Schwartz, Kim Brown Seely, Katherine Sieh, Bernard Sofronski, Michael Sofronski, Sue Torres, Michael Tucker, Valerie Vigoda, and Steve Wilson. Many thanks to Rikki & Bill, Terri & Brian, Loraine & Carl, Robert Zimmerman, and others for so generously opening their homes to us during our travel and research (or recovery!). Thanks, too, to the entire Irglová family for introducing us to so many Czech wines that won a place in our hearts. Special thanks to all our previously named friends and colleagues who provided comments on the manuscript, and especially Yannick Benjamin of Le Dû's Wines, Chris Cottrell of Crush, Italian wine authority Aurora Endrici, Knut Wöhncke of Windsor Wine Shop, and wine enthusiast Valerie Vigoda.

We thank everyone who supported our two most recent books, including the "Visionaries" who were early supporters of *The Flavor Bible*, including Bill Bratton, Susan Bulkeley Butler, Barbara Cohan-Saavedra & Adam Saavedra, Gary Collins, Laura Day, Loraine Despres, Mark and

Meredith Dornenburg, Heather Evans, Fahrusha, Alan Federman, Ashley Garrett, Charlene Garrison, Heather Gere, June Guterman, Eugene Haslam, June Jacobs, Lane Jantzen, Alan Jones, Rikki Klieman, Anne LeClair, Susan and Dave Mabe, Lauren Martey, Daisy Martinez, Jan & Bob Meyer, Brendan Milburn & Valerie Vigoda, Judy Paul, Cynthia & Jeff Penney, Kimberley Slobodian, and Frances Spangler.

While it's been cited as one of the world's best spas by *Forbes* and *Travel + Leisure*, The Lodge at Woodloch in Hawley, Pennsylvania (just a couple of hours outside Manhattan), is our kind of place because, unlike spas that ban alcohol, The Lodge embraces the health-giving properties of wine. For all the times we've enjoyed taking (and teaching) its afternoon wine-tasting classes and exploring its wine list at dinnertime, very special thanks to The Lodge's GM, Paul Fitzpatrick, and to Renee Gamboni. Although circumstances were such that we were unable to take a vacation over the last three years we spent completing this book, we had the good fortune to visit some other extraordinary properties for a night or two here and there that magically restored us as much mentally and physically as if we'd spent an entire week away! Heartfelt thanks to the teams at The Inn at Little Washington (especially Patrick O'Connell and Rachel Hayden), Blantyre (especially Christopher Brooks plus Christelle & Arnaud Cotar), Glenmere Mansion (especially Alan Stenberg and Daniel DeSimone), Hotel Fauchere (especially Christopher Bates, Isabel Bogadtke, Robyn Mack, and Sean Strub), The Inn at Barley Sheaf Farm (especially Eva Silvernail), Windham Hill Inn (especially Katja Matthews and Dan Pisarczyk), and Winvian (especially the Smith family).

Last but not least, we offer our thanks to our talented photographer, Tom Kirkman, for contributing his keen eye and gorgeous photos to this book. We join Tom in extending thanks to Jason Friedman, and to all the restaurants (as well as their staffs) who opened their dining rooms and kitchens to us, including Aldea (Heather Laiskonis, George Mendes), Bellavitae (Jon Mudder), Le Bernardin (Mandy Oser, Eric Ripert, Aldo Sohm), BottleRocket Wine and Spirit (Tom Geniesse), Chanterelle (Roger Dagorn, Karen & David Waltuck), Eleven Madison Park, Jean Georges (Jean-Georges Vongerichten), Le Dû's Wines (Jean-Luc Le Dû, Yannick Benjamin), The Modern (Gabriel Kreuther), Bar Breton (Cyril Renaud), Oak and Steel, Porter House New York (Michael Lomonaco), Sherry-Lehmann (Matt Wong), Solera (Ron Miller), West Bank Cafe (Steve Olsen, Joe Marcus), and Wild Edibles (Paul Jambor).

During our final week working on this book, the Grammy-winning band Train sent us samples of its new wine club's impressive "Drops of Jupiter" Petite Sirah, which for $9.99 has the potential to open up a whole new music-loving audience to the pleasures of wine (especially when accompanied by barbecued or braised lamb). We thank the band along with everyone else who clearly shares our mission of bringing the pleasures of wine to even more food lovers!

KAREN PAGE AND ANDREW DORNENBURG

Jason Friedman, for his incredible energy, Photoshop magic, and studio expertise; Cliff Hausner (and Profoto), for his support and world-class lighting equipment; David Nicholas, for his generosity, support, and studio space; Hector Carminero, for his friendship and support on this project; Melissa Love, for her great advice; and my mother, for a lifetime of great food and for my genetic predisposition for appreciating it.

TOM KIRKMAN